Dark Dreams 2.0

ALSO BY CHARLES DERRY

The Suspense Thriller:
Films in the Shadow of Alfred Hitchcock
(McFarland, 1988; paperback 2001)

Dark Dreams 2.0

*A Psychological History of the
Modern Horror Film from the
1950s to the 21st Century*

CHARLES DERRY

Foreword by JOHN RUSSELL TAYLOR

McFarland & Company, Inc., Publishers
Jefferson, North Carolina, and London

LIBRARY OF CONGRESS CATALOGUING-IN-PUBLICATION DATA

Derry, Charles, 1951–
Dark dreams 2.0 : a psychological history of the modern horror
film from the 1950s to the 21st century / Charles Derry ;
foreword by John Russell Taylor.
p.   cm.
Includes bibliographical references and index.

ISBN 978-0-7864-3397-1
illustrated case binding : 50# alkaline paper ∞

1. Horror films — History and criticism.   2. Motion pictures —
Psychological aspects.   I. Title.
PN1995.9.H6D38   2009   791.43' 6164 — dc22   2009025183

British Library cataloguing data are available

On the cover: Ralph Fiennes in a scene from the 2002 film *Spider*.
Front cover design by Chase Whiteside

Manufactured in the United States of America

McFarland & Company, Inc., Publishers
Box 611, Jefferson, North Carolina 28640
www.mcfarlandpub.com

To Thomas G. Kohn
and again to the memory of
Charles Homer Derry, my father,
who loved a good story

Contents

Acknowledgments

I would like to acknowledge those who have been instrumental in preparing *Dark Dreams 2.0*: research associates Kyle Forquer, Scott Bowers, and Michael Collins, whose contributions over many years were invaluable and central, with special kudos to Kyle for his extraordinary work helping compile frame grabs; my current students Michael Ward, Chase Whiteside, Matt Mulcahey, Andrew Grigiss, Erick Stoll, and Joe Lurie, who located errors and offered suggestions, with particular gratitude to Chase for providing the striking cover design; my colleagues Mark Lyons, who helped amass the perfect collection of horror DVDs, Russ Johnson, a horror enthusiast who devised a great system for capturing high-quality frame grabs, and Julia Reichert, whose work influenced and inspired me; Victoria Oleen, who lent her problem-solving skills and support; the estimable organization the Ohio Arts Council, along with Wright State University administrators Stuart McDowell and Mary Ellen Mazey, who provided financial support; my friend Ben Putman, who offered film titles, graphic design ideas, and notable insights; my friend Ben Grossberg, who volunteered his discerning editor's eye; my film school colleague from long ago, Susan Pisoni Tavernetti, an extraordinary critic, teacher, and friend who was never far from my mind as I wrote; all those at McFarland Publishing, who were both encouraging and patient; and above all, my friend Bob Pardi, who knows more about horror film than anyone I know and who has provided me thirty years of cinematic companionship despite our always living hundreds, if not thousands of miles apart.

And of course, as I did when the earlier version of *Dark Dreams* was published, I would like to thank the prodigiously talented Stuart Kaminsky for his encouragement, friendship, and service as my mentor; the Northwestern University film faculty of the early seventies, including Jack Ellis and Paddy Whannel, for their part in instilling in the author an approach to film study; the gracious and generous John Russell Taylor for his Foreword and his lifelong commitment to the highest standards of criticism; the late Frederick S. Clarke, the visionary founding editor of *Cinefantastique,* for access to his personal archives; and Dan R. Scapperotti, Dale Winogura, Tony Scott, and Bill Crouch for the interview material on William Castle, Curtis Harrington, George A. Romero, and William Friedkin respectively.

Finally, I thank and acknowledge my life partner and not-yet-legal husband of twenty-nine years plus, Thomas G. Kohn, who provided research assistance as well as more understanding and support than this obsessive writer could have ever hoped for.

Introduction to
Dark Dreams 2.0

Is it odd to begin *Dark Dreams 2.0* by admitting that I don't like horror films as much as I used to? I know I once so loved the genre that I would stay up till 4 A.M. to catch a local TV broadcast of a low-budget horror film like Joseph Cates' *Who Killed Teddy Bear?* Unfortunately, today's suburban multiplex filled with teens flocking to see Paris Hilton (!) in a remake of *House of Wax* does not seem similarly compelling. Yet I feel nostalgia still for the time I dragged my friend Bob Pardi to downtown Los Angeles to see *What's the Matter with Helen?* The seedy, 24-hour theatre ran triple features, which meant it did double duty as a flophouse for the homeless and the addicted; the environment was at times scarier than the movie. Of course one might argue that personalities like Sal Mineo and Elaine Stritch (the stars of *Who Killed Teddy Bear?*) or Debbie Reynolds and Shelley Winters (the stars of *What's the Matter with Helen?*) are inherently more complex and intriguing than a PR-hyped personality like Paris Hilton, who is more famous for being famous than for having talent. Perhaps another reason for my diminished interest is that the horror film — a genre never accused of subtlety — has always particularly appealed to adolescents and young adults peering for the first time into the forbidden components of the id: sex and violence. Today, over thirty years after *Dark Dreams*' original publication, I am even further from adolescence. If the sensational aspects of horror interest me less and less, what horror films *mean* and what horror films are trying to tell us about ourselves and our fears, fascinate me even more.

I am grateful for the opportunity to publish this new, revised, and greatly enlarged edition of *Dark Dreams*, virtually four times the length of the original, which until now has been out-of-print for thirty years. Yet as I was preparing the reissue, it became evident that the last thirty years — not only in terms of horror film, but in terms of cultural history — required its very own companion volume. Americans have experienced the Reagan Revolution, the rise of the religious right, AIDS, the culture wars over abortion and gay rights, 9/11, the "War on Terror," the wars in Iraq and Afghanistan, and George W. Bush instituting torture in the name of democracy. Indeed, consideration of these tumultuous decades prompted not only some reconsideration of my original text, but wide-ranging examination of a great number of films. The ideas I put forward in the 1977 volume, which feels written by some distant version of myself, have held up well: my basic premise that the horror film underwent a radical transformation in the sixties, developing three subgenres (the horror of personality, of Armageddon, and the demonic), seems from today's perspective to be fairly obvious. It is worth remembering that my initial ideas broke some new ground — primarily because the horror films like *Psycho* and *The Birds* that I discussed with such enthusiasm were very different from the classic Universal films like *Frankenstein* and *Dracula* which were so commonly understood as the very definition of horror. Indeed, it is hard to believe there was ever a time when *Psycho* was considered neither a horror film, nor a universally-acclaimed work of art.

The most glaring error in my original edition was its prediction that the future horror genre might include "an occasional reworking of *Psycho*."

In *Psycho*, Hitchcock takes us on a new horror journey; and as Marion Crane, played by Janet Leigh, discovers, danger can be anywhere.

What an understatement! There have been three *Psycho* sequels, an unusually interesting frame-by-frame remake, and literally dozens of films inspired directly which include quotation or *hommage*. On the scholarly front, the Hitchcock industry (which I, too, have contributed to with my book *The Suspense Thriller: Films in the Shadow of Alfred Hitchcock*) has been so busy for the last three decades, that now, one rather wishes for a moratorium! Of the seminal films I wrote about in *Dark Dreams*' original edition, *Psycho, The Birds, Rosemary's Baby*, and *Night of the Living Dead* seem increasingly secure in any pantheon of American film classics. The irony is that in their own time, these films were largely condescended to as shallow sensation (if not disdained), but in comparison to the violent special-effects excesses of today, they appear to be virtually philosophical. Even *What Ever Happened to Baby Jane?*— often characterized as camp or dismissed as voyeuristic sadomasochism — now seems to be a prime example of the finest Hollywood artistry just before the collapse of the classic studio system. The most glaring omission in the original *Dark Dreams*— written in the days not only before DVDs, but before VCRs — is the absence of a detailed discussion of Michael Powell's 1960 *Peeping Tom*, which was simply unavailable to me for screening. Now, with Powell's film widely available, it is absolutely evident that

Stark contrasts between dark and light, evil and good, in *Peeping Tom*. Although Mrs. Stevens (played by Maxine Audley) offers comfort, the killer (Carl Boehm) is himself revolted by his murderous obsessions.

Peeping Tom was visionary in how it connected the violence of serial killing to the voyeurism of the camera, implicitly indicting the cinema audience for its troubling appreciation of the spectacle. And indeed, this spectacle has grown more powerful and pervasive since, with today's profit-driven media obsessed with exploiting images of violence for the voyeuristic pleasure of massive audiences.

I have purposely *not* reconceived or rewritten the text of my original 1977 volume, except to add some material originally excluded, to correct the occasional error, and to clarify some of the writing. More importantly, *Dark Dreams* is now followed by "Millennial Nightmares," a section much longer than my original book and which offers insights and close readings of the most notable horror films of the last thirty years; as a result, *Dark Dreams 2.0* provides a comprehensive analysis of the fifty-year history of the modern horror film, extending through to the very scary present of the post–9/11 world. Notable, too, is that with the help of new graphic technologies, *Dark Dreams 2.0* almost exclusively uses frame grabs from the films discussed rather than staged publicity photos (which are more typical in film books). This choice allows for a sustained, demonstrable explication and criticism of the unique visual components of these horror films — thus providing an ongoing, parallel argument to *Dark Dreams 2.0*'s main text.

As well, I am including the Foreword to the original edition, written by John Russell Taylor, former film critic for the *London Times*, internationally-known film festival jurist, and one of the most widely-published film and art scholars. Written in an era in which often impenetrable structuralist jargon was sweeping the academy and making film criticism markedly less humanist and accessible, Taylor's Foreword was subtextually arguing for a genre criticism which promoted understanding of the movie itself. Taylor's opposition to the then increasingly self-reverential and arcane nature of film theory seems today an important and historic corrective.

My original volume emphasized the ways in which films reflect our society's values, and horror films reflect additionally our society's fears. Were I originating *Dark Dreams* today, I would include significant material on how film also has the capacity to influence society — and not always for the better. But writing as I was in the early seventies, when American society was rapidly changing and the American cinema was in a remarkable renaissance, positioning itself in opposition to the status quo, these horror films — with their unbridled sexuality, violence, and personal visions — impressed as progressive and passionate works of art. And so I emphasized what these films meant and what truths they revealed, as opposed to how these films may have impacted us. As part of the sixties generation embracing new and inspiring films like *The Graduate, Bonnie and Clyde,* and *2001: A Space Odyssey* ("cinema" rather than "movies"), I saw these new horror films as emerging from the same *Zeitgeist*. In recognizing the similarities among the sixties films I called "horror of personality," for instance, I felt not unlike the French *auteurists* who had looked at certain American films of the forties and fifties to discover the *film noir*. Discovering my new horror (sub)genres hiding in plain sight, I was more interested in describing what I had found than in projecting the eventual impact of those discoveries. The original *Dark Dreams* had an inherent optimism, too, a naive enthusiasm for the cinematic medium.

But who could have known then that in 1977 *Star Wars* would shepherd in an end to the American renaissance and inaugurate the longest, most fallow cycle in American film, one dependent on special effects and distraction? As well, just as *Dark Dreams* was initially published, these new currents of horror (particularly *The Exorcist*–inspired, demonic films) were themselves becoming fossilized, their lulling conventions and special-effects violence distracting audiences from growing reactionary elements in American society. With the Reagan Revolution, the impeachment of Bill Clinton, and George W. Bush's War in Iraq supported by a plethora of Americans, particularly red-state fundamentalists, it is clear that the popular films on our movie screens were not exactly moving audiences toward political action or even a progressive sensibility. And yet, it had seemed — or had it been only an illusion? — that the American audiences long ago who had been passionate about *Night of the Living Dead* had been equally passionate about politically-engaged films like Costa-Gavras' *Z*, which was about fascism in then-contemporary Greece. Today's horror audiences, on the other hand, are unlikely to be able to locate Greece on the map, let alone express much interest in the aggressive political leanings of their own country or in the ideology of the film blockbusters they accept mindlessly.

Certainly in the original *Dark Dreams*, I never discussed the possibility that films, and specifically horror films, could be bad for society. The fact that I didn't surprises me now, since my original subtitle — *A Psychological History of the Modern Horror Film* — was paraphrased from the subtitle of *From Caligari to Hitler*, the influential, classic history of German cinema by Siegfried Kracauer, who disapproved of so many of the films he discussed, seeing them as harbingers of the German acquiescence to the approaching Nazi state. Kracauer's argument was that a society embracing formalism over realism is a sign that the society is ignoring its own political and social realities. The shadows painted on the floors and walls of the sets of *The Cabinet of Dr. Caligari* (produced in 1919) — an attempt by its filmmakers to subvert even the (realist) physical properties of light itself — were seen by Kracauer as an ominous sign of the German people's retreat from reality. And so Kracauer felt there was a clear connection from *Caligari* to Hitler. Kracauer's argument is instructive, since it is easy to see similarities to the American cinema since *Star Wars* — in which horror, fantasy, and science-fiction films so overwhelmingly emphasize the formalist special effects that lure audiences into a mindless good time.

Our American cinema has largely become a cinema of *distraction*: so when we Americans awoke on 9/11/2001 from our long dream of avoidance to witness the destruction of the World Trade Center towers, we were stunned to discover that there were so many people in the world who hated us. And yet why should we have been surprised, when for decades we had been paying so little attention?

Nevertheless, despite this vision of genuine apocalypse, we barely turned away from our formalist preoccupations. Why start paying attention now when we could be distracted by American TV shows: home remodeling, plastic surgery make-overs, entertainment news on celebrities, and so-called "reality" shows in which reality is completely manipulated? Four years later, again in September, in the aftermath of Hurricane Katrina, Americans discovered poverty and suffering in Louisiana so pervasive and our government so inept that America looked like a third-world country. Who had allowed this to happen? Or for that matter, who had allowed the War in Iraq to be waged, despite the absence of weapons of mass destruction (these weapons the supposed key reason for the invasion)? Once again, the truth, like Poe's "Purloined Letter," had been hiding in plain sight. *We* had. And as a result, our political life was turning into its own horror film, scarily apocalyptic.

In *The Cabinet of Dr. Caligari*, painted shadows and unnatural angles work to subvert reality.

The mindless good time that is the meat-and-potatoes of much contemporary American cinema is increasingly associated with violent effects. While I still have my childhood memory of the audience screaming at *Psycho*, contemporary audiences are as likely to greet violence in new horror films not with screams, but with excited laughter or delighted applause. With formalism so dominating contemporary popular culture, we risk creating a generation of spectators who are empathy-deprived, unable to respond to real-life suffering or violence with anything approaching appropriate levels of compassion. And once horror films start consistently eradicating compassion, they have effectively become political propaganda for reactionary forces.

When Hitchcock released *Psycho*, the film was much criticized for its violence; detractors took the film to task, as well as other films that followed, for their potential to cause violence. Hitchcock often joked about one serial killer who had supposedly committed murder after seeing *Psycho;* doubtful that there had been a cause-and-effect relationship, Hitchcock wondered what the killer had watched before killing his other victims. Could it have been *Romper Room* or something equally pacific? When I was writing *Dark Dreams*, these issues seemed not that interesting to me; today, I am no longer sanguine about their irrelevance.

Yet I resist seeing film's effects on society simplistically, as those who argue for censorship tend to do when they divide popular culture into the clear-cut categories of the good and the bad. Although films influence our behavior, they do so in inordinately complicated ways. For instance, no one who has seen the great French film *Irréversible* can cheer its two horrendous acts of violence. The murderous assault at the beginning and the dreadful rape near the middle are so visceral, that it is impossible to cheer on the acts of violence as "cool." Yet many contemporary audiences do exactly that in response to the violence in films such as *A Nightmare on Elm Street VI: The Final Nightmare*. Violence should not entertain us, but revolt us and make us feel that humanity itself is being profaned. The argument that acts of violence in film are not created equal is a subtle one. But there is violence, and there is violence; and it is imperative that we characterize the differences. For example, I defend on both moral and artistic grounds the violence Hitchcock perpetrates on Marian Crane in *Psycho*, in part because he constructs the first third of his film in such a way that virtually every image promotes compassion for his troubled heroine, despite her moral failings. Hitchcock's strategy contrasts with many films today, where the victims are mere props, cardboard creations dispatched without a second thought.

Once, in the early seventies, I was helping a friend make a film on the streets of Chicago. (Ironically, the film was an elaborate *hommage* to Hitchcock and his violence.) I was to operate the camera, which I had already set up on its tripod, and we were waiting for our actors to arrive. Suddenly, we heard gunshots, and then right on the sidewalk where our camera was pointed and focused, a horrible scene erupted: two men, bleeding, ran out of a jewelry store they had just tried to rob. Almost immediately, a third man ran out and stumbled directly in front of our camera, chased by the enraged store owner, who proceeded to strike him with a crowbar again and again, until this thief, now collapsed, completely stopped moving. Had I the wherewithal to turn on the camera and expose our film, I would have captured documentary footage of a man violently killed — especially untypical in a pre-camcorder age. The footage would have probably run on the network news. But the real-life violence had been so horrifying that neither my friend nor I had been able even to *think* of filming it. Yet I can't help wonder: if the same thing were to happen today, all these decades later, would I now be able to photograph the violence without hesitation, capable of distancing myself from the human toll of what I was seeing? So while I'm not especially alarmed about a specific film's effect on a particular individual, I *am* concerned about the harder-to-quantify, long-term effect of popular culture on our capacity to be compassionate and to retain connection to reality. Certainly, much contemporary culture is coarsening us, making us less human rather than more. And when raucous audiences cheer for more mayhem, it is hard to argue that our filmic appetite for violence doesn't bleed over into the real, into the social sphere — whether in solidifying suburban obliviousness to American poverty, or in promoting unthinking acceptance of a War in Iraq that begins with the cinematic spectacle of "Shock and Awe."

If the theories of semiology and structuralism have taught us anything, it is that films and television programs must be analyzed not only in terms of what they contain, but of what they lack: often, these *constituent lacks* reveal the hidden functions of the works themselves. For instance, the lack of African-American faces in American television shows of the fifties like *Father Knows Best* and *Leave It to Beaver* probably helped postpone the civil rights movement and solidify white suburbia. Similarly, the lack of gay men and lesbians in most American culture of the fifties and sixties reinforced the closet and contributed to the homophobia that has led to so much horrific and casual violence against gays (including Matthew Shepard, the University of Wyoming student who was beaten to death and left virtually crucified on a fence).

Unfortunately, too many of the contemporary horror films of the last twenty years seem to be dominated by their *constituent lacks*. Foremost is the lack of consequences. Horror-film violence too often has a make-believe quality; when someone dies, although there may be surprise and screaming, there is not particularly grief. Nor is there suffering that lasts beyond the momentary, nor survivors emotionally wrecked for life, nor hospital vigils, nor doctor bills, nor economic deprivations, nor lifelong disabilities. And though these films promote voyeurism, they too often lack, even discourage, compassion. And though action and extroversion (supreme American values) are constant, reflection and introversion (virtually anti–American) are lacking. A society which can neither grieve, reflect, feel compassion, nor understand consequences, is not a society likely to act with caution and humility to make appropriately humane political choices.

When I began writing about horror film in the early seventies, my work was in part an apologia, because the horror genre was not particularly respected. In fact, it was probably *Rosemary's Baby* in 1968 — by the Polish art-house director Roman Polanski (though in concert with William Castle as producer, an American with the likeably vulgar sensibility of a sideshow barker) — that was one of the first modern horror films to receive notable, contemporary recognition. But not until William Friedkin's *The Exorcist* in 1973 was horror recognized as a genre consistently able to make loads of money *and* garner critical acclaim. In the fifties and sixties, studios had left Hitchcock and horror directors relatively alone, because their work wasn't considered significant enough to much meddle with. (Indeed, it took the French to alert the American critical establishment that *Invasion of the Body Snatchers* wasn't schlock, but potent political allegory.) Even Hitchcock's admirers are often surprised that Hitchcock never won a competitive Academy award, despite the international acclaim that now accrues to his work. For the most part, the horror films in the fifties and sixties which were especially interesting were by Hollywood directors like Hitchcock, Robert Aldrich, or Don Siegel, who had considerable studio autonomy, or by independent directors outside Hollywood like Pittsburgh's George A. Romero, director of the groundbreaking *Night of the Living Dead*.

Today, the horror genre is no longer so disregarded. Because studios recognize that horror films can be cash cows, these projects are subject to rigorous scrutiny and audience-testing; and truly challenging or personal material largely fails to survive the production process. Horror films — like most Hollywood movies — are more than ever being reduced to the least common denominator; politically neutered, they are losing many of the subversive qualities so often associated with the genre. Incidentally, the most insightful

Mia Farrow in Roman Polanski's *Rosemary's Baby*: horror can invade our homes and quotidian lives.

writing on subversiveness in seventies horror film undoubtedly comes from Robin Wood, who in his essay "The American Nightmare" discusses how the violence in these largely incoherent texts results from the Puritan repression of sexuality and the inherent limitations of the traditional American family that our culture is otherwise unable to acknowledge. Wood is convincing; although to me, the most popular eighties and nineties horror films seem markedly less subversive. For example, the blockbuster *Scream*, directed in 1996, was certainly Wes Craven's most technically proficient film to date. Yet few would claim it superior to his 1977 *The Hills Have Eyes*, which is profoundly upsetting, as well as more original and personal. *Scream*, on the other hand, is not so much a film about contemporary horror, but a film about other contemporary horror films. As a result, it is largely a formal exercise at least one level abstracted from the real horror of the everyday.

Because film audiences are significantly dominated by adolescents and young adults, virtually every Hollywood horror film must attract the teenage boy. According to genre theory, popular films inherently reflect society, but I'm afraid that today, the genre of American horror too often reflects only the society of the teenage boy — which is why so many horror films are filled with sex, women's breasts in tight T-shirts, special-effects violence, a lack of subtext or subtlety, and structures easily apprehensible without any intellectual effort. Even more alarming is the often total absence in these films of any challenge to either the world of the teenagers or the world of their baby-boomer parents which these teens are expecting to inherit. Around 1999, in part as a response to the success of *The Sixth Sense*, studios discovered the surprising truth that young *women* actually made up a significant percentage of the horror audience. As a result, many films became less gory and more atmospheric. Still they were skewed towards adolescents, if now to both sexes.

As a result of this teen audience, horror film is impacted in several unfortunate ways. The most debilitating impact is that horror films are now seen almost exclusively as consumer items, rather than personal works of art. This is particularly true for certain films, such as *A Nightmare on Elm Street* (itself an interesting film), which have come to be regarded, like McDonald's, as a fast-food franchise — profitable and filling, if not particularly nutritious or tasty. *A Nightmare on Elm Street* has been followed (as of this writing) by seven sequels; *Friday the 13th* by ten sequels, *Halloween* by seven, *Hellraiser* by seven, *The Exorcist* by four, and so forth. Several of these sequels contain some inspired scenes to be sure, but without a personal vision, these sequels are largely brazen attempts to make money by imitating the original as closely as possible while offering a modicum of new spin to help motivate the trip to the theatre. Diminishing returns (both critically and financially) are typical in the sequel game. It is especially disappointing that the films in these franchises emerge, increasingly, as so impersonal and insincere. For instance, the eight *Nightmare on Elm Street* films have been directed by seven different directors (Wes Craven, Jack Sholder, Chuck Russell, Renny Harlin, Stephen Hopkins, Rachel Talalay, Wes Craven again, and Ronny Yu) in a relatively consistent style which has become a virtual corporate brand. These franchise films may offer slightly different flavors, but ultimately, they're all Campbell's soup. It is relevant to point out that Alfred Hitchcock *never* made, contemplated, or authorized a sequel to *Psycho*, one of his biggest hits. Nor did a true artist like Roman Polanski milk the commercial success of *Rosemary's Baby* by making a sequel. (Incidentally, a history of these commercial horror franchises — which is what many might expect in a horror history of the last twenty-five years — will not be the approach of this new edition. Also ignored here will be the hundreds of direct-to-DVD horror films — gruesome, pandering, and exploitative — whose primary aim is to generate a quick and modest profit.)

Another negative impact from this targeting of the teenage market is that Hollywood, all atwitter over how to expand its audience demographics, is now in full retreat into postmodernism. Terrified of putting millions of dollars into new, authentic material which is personal and progressive, producers have scavenged the Hollywood archives to find "safe" material: the pre-owned and previously made. The result of producers attempting to make everything old new again is a postmodern smorgasbord. For instance, in the summer of 2005, I went to the Regal Hollywood 20, a movie theatre in Dayton, Ohio. On those twenty screens only nine films were playing: *War of the Worlds*, *Bewitched*, *The Longest Yard*, *Dark Water*, *Herbie Fully Loaded*, *Batman Begins*, *Star Wars Episode III — Revenge of the Sith*, *The Fantastic 4*, and *Mr. & Mrs. Smith*. Of these films, five were remakes, two were sequels, and one (*The Fantastic 4*) — though "original" — was a clear attempt to imitate the recent successes of "comic book" movies. Of the nine titles, the only truly original idea was *Mr. & Mrs. Smith*, which nevertheless borrowed its title (including its ampersand) from a 1941 Hitchcock film, as if to offer something at least vaguely familiar to American audiences. The incidental byproduct of so many remakes and sequels is a built-in anachronism that inherently carries a reactionary, backwards-looking sensibility. When Hitchcock made *The Birds* in 1963, no one had created special effects on quite that level before. Despite the commercial success of *The Birds*, Hitchcock *never* attempted to cash in by making another film which depended upon special effects. On the other hand, after *Star Wars* in 1977, George Lucas (once the promising director of *THX 1138* and *American Graffiti*) spent the next thirty years prostituting his talent by producing five sequels of self-plagiarism, some using directors-for-hire. The spectacular success of Lucas' sequels propelled the entire industry — including the horror genre — into an unusually naked obsession with reworking past success for contemporary profit. For instance, despite almost universally negative reviews, the largely impersonal 2008 remake of *The Day the Earth Stood Still* nevertheless managed to make more than $250 million in worldwide theatrical release (with a potential doubling of that after its DVD release) based on the efficient machinery of special effects alone.

All directors must shoulder a moral responsibility, if not to the society about them, at least to the honest and authentic impulses within themselves. As the horror film has embraced this postmodern impulse, the horror subgenres I originally described have become less distinct, and contemporary horror films steal from each other with increasing profligacy. (For instance, at least a hundred recent horror films have stolen the "surprise" ending from the demonic *Carrie*; the "dead villain suddenly lunging up, apparently still alive" is now so ubiquitous that only horror films *without* it particularly surprise.)

There is a great irony that much of the most striking horror imagery in recent film comes not from horror films *per se*, but from films situated within other genres. For instance, *Beloved*, a sociological drama directed in 1998 by Jonathan Demme based on Toni Morrison's novel, is not only an incisive, historical portrait of the African-American soul, set after the Civil War, but a film filled with atmospheric elements borrowed from the demonic horror film — particularly the mysterious haunting of an ex-slave by her murdered child. *Magnolia*, a brilliantly creative film by Paul Thomas Anderson in 1999 which presents interweaving, fateful stories in the San Fernando Valley, stuns its audience with a climactic sequence of Armageddon horror in which suddenly, millions of frogs rain down upon its characters. It's as if Robert Altman's *Nashville* has turned into Alfred Hitchcock's *The Birds*. Another notable film, Christopher Nolan's 2000 thriller *Memento* (released in the United States in 2001), has overtones of the horror of personality in the way its mystery ultimately turns on the revelation of a purposive psychological madness; and its narrative skillfully confounds the easy apprehension of the audience by moving backwards in time, scene by scene, in the process becoming a meditation on memory and time itself. (How very French for an English language film!) *Syriana*, written and directed in 2005 by Stephen Gaghan, depicts a climactic assassination by the American military which is horrifying largely because it's accomplished with clinical precision from an extraordinary distance. *Sweeney Todd*, a Broadway musical that took almost thirty years to become a Hollywood movie in 2007, shocked audiences and critics alike with how over-the-top bloody were its serial murders set to Stephen Sondheim's slashing, soaring melodies. And even an apparently conservative 2008 film like Clint Eastwood's *Changeling*, ostensibly a period piece emphasizing historical reconstruction, ultimately reveals itself as a quasi-horror film about a serial killer.

For many years now, cutting-edge directors have known that the simple narrative and traditional three-act Hollywood structure — so fossilized by screenwriting guru Syd Field — have been largely exhausted. A low-budget, independent horror film like 1999's *The Blair Witch Project*, though overrated, recognizes — in part through its sensibility of improvisation — that there is little vitality left in Hollywood's preoccupation with special effects. So it is not surprising that Alejandro González Iñárritu, the brilliant Mexican director of those

These typical images from *Sweeney Todd* (showing actors Helena Bonham Carter and Johnny Depp) hardly suggest a Hollywood musical, but *grand guignol* horror.

interwoven tales *Amores Perros*—one of the most arresting films of the last twenty-five years—should have gone on to make arguably the single most horrific, creative film about the terrorist attack on the World Trade Center towers. González Iñárritu's segment of the multi-part *11'09"01, September 11*, in which 11 international directors in 2002 were given free rein to make a relevant short in any genre or style, is an experimental work only 11 minutes, 9 seconds, and 1 frame long. And yet González Iñárritu's short is more horrifying than a typical horror feature, even though most of his film—almost totally lacking narrative—is comprised of an empty black screen which allows us mentally to project the nightmarish images which haunt us. Even a fictional documentary reconstruction with virtually no character development and no narrative contrivance, Paul Greengrass' *United 93*, about the hijacked flight that crashed in Pennsylvania on 9/11, is more creative and more *horrifying* than contemporary Hollywood horror film.

In the immediate days after 9/11, Fran Lebowitz predicted, rather convincingly, that the whole culture was going to change: that soon movies would look different, magazines would look different, in fact, every accouterment of the popular culture would transform in response to the new global realities. Yet Lebowitz underestimated the *inertia* of postmodernism, its amorphous ability—like *The Blob* (yes, the 1958 Steve McQueen horror film)—to accommodate and overtake everything in its path. Or at least to overtake everything for a significant while. So although very little in the Hollywood horror film of the last twenty years is especially new, I suspect that we are just now seeing glimmerings of new horror themes about to emerge: of aliens among us, of our fears of cultural and sexual otherness, of our lack of compassion, of our moral failings and profound obliviousness, and of our complicit rationalizings of the even greater political repressions that many of us fear may yet come.

Also, I should note that when *Dark Dreams* first came out, there was still a raging battle between popular culture and high culture; and it seemed important to claim for popular culture its rightful place at the table. But my interest was in securing that place, not in overturning the table. Film, television, and the internet—democratic arts of the moving image—have irrevocably triumphed, even though these media tolerate intellectual variety much less well than one might suspect. Now, at the beginning of the twenty-first century, high culture is struggling just to remain in the room and, quite frankly, is not doing a very good job at demonstrating its relevance. Classical music as an important force is largely dead; funerary orchestras play the safe music of the dead and too often eschew the contemporary. Few people actively read new poetry. Serious theatre has been largely banished from Broadway, which has been turned over to Disneyfied musicals and revivals for tourists. Except in a handful of

Claude Lelouch's segment of *11'09"01, September 11* incorporates cataclysmic horror within the casual of the everyday.

American cities which can support a progressive vision, opera companies offer retreads of *La Bohème* and *Carmen* year after year. Even dance companies increasingly turn to inevitable *Nutcrackers* and holiday pageants to remain afloat financially. In most American cities, high culture does not present challenging or profound artistic experiences, but events — vaguely obligatory — which require you to dress up in nice clothes to be seen by other nicely-dressed people who all want to consider themselves cultured. (And what does it say that a supposedly serious art museum like the Dayton Art Institute, located in my own city, should have a major 2006 "art exhibit" of Princess Diana clothes and memorabilia and a 2007 exhibit dedicated to Marilyn Monroe hagiography?) Only literature seems not yet overwhelmed by the popular culture — aided perhaps by Amazon.com, by the mega-bookstore as meeting place, and by Oprah Winfrey's book club. Nevertheless, the fact that every year, young people spend less and less of their leisure time reading does not augur well for literature's future.

Decades ago, when I first started writing about film, there were still thriving art-house theatres and film societies in all major cities. Today, the art-house theatre is long dead; even major films by directors as notable as Bergman, Fellini, and Chabrol failed to make it to American shores, so xenophobic has been the American sensibility. Once I had hoped that critics would recognize that popular horror films could be art. Now I hope that audiences can recognize that highbrow "art" films can be horrific. Once upon a time the most culturally-central discussion of film came from *Film Comment*, *Cahiers du Cinéma*, and *Screen*, all of which were actually interested in analysis and meaning, and from notable national critics like Andrew Sarris and Pauline Kael, whose writing engendered discussion precisely because it *mattered*. Today, the most culturally-central discussion of film comes from *Entertainment Weekly*, television shows like *Entertainment Tonight*, and a host of internet sites, all of which are focused on box-office revenues, consumer reviews, celebrity gossip, behind-the-scenes pap, and press-agentry. And no national critics seem to matter much at all, trotted out primarily to offer predictions at Academy award time or to deliver succinct sound bites on transitory trends for airport readers of *USA Today*.

And so my newest writing on contemporary horror film, "Millennial Nightmares," found as the second half of *Dark Dreams 2.0*, serves as a kind of reaction (if not remedy) to the intellectual poverty of the fanzine mentality. In these recent writings I emphasize the more personal work of independent American directors who bring vitality to the horror genre, and of intellectual foreign directors who bring a high-culture, challenging, art-house sensibility. Certainly it seems more important to praise those directors actively trying to comment critically upon Western culture through the horror genre (and perhaps to change that culture), than to criticize those directors devoid of ideas who are primarily trying to make money off the genre. So if this new edition is not written by someone who unambiguously still loves horror film, it *is* written by someone who still loves the idea of horror film and feels great nostalgia for what the genre has lost.

PART ONE

DARK DREAMS
(1977)

Foreword to the
Original Edition

by John Russell Taylor

Now that the *auteur* theory has faded somewhat from intellectual fashion, taking with it a passion, briefly evident among critics, for dividing filmmakers into the Elect, who could do no wrong, and the rest, mere capable craftsmen who could do precious little right, it has been replaced by a new orthodoxy: genre criticism. The point of this, of course, is that certain stars, certain props, certain situations, have an immediately recognizable significance in certain cinematic contexts. If you cast John Wayne in a Western or Gloria Grahame in a *film noir*, you are using a sort of shorthand which any seasoned moviegoer can instantly read: their mere presence tells us what sort of a character they are supposed to be and more or less what can be expected of them. But the context of genre is vital: John Wayne in a drawing-room comedy or Gloria Grahame in a musical would be an unknown quantity. In other words, much of genre criticism is concerned with the examination and re-evaluation of cliché: we tend to forget that truisms are, after all, as a rule true.

The problem of genre criticism is generally one of definition. Some genres define themselves by obvious externals: the Western or the musical, for example. But others require a much more relative judgment. Fantasy in particular is a stumbling block. Is fantasy a genre on its own, or does it include a number of genres, such as the horror film, the fairy tale, science fiction, allegory, the musical? For that matter, are any of these possible sub-genres necessarily fantastic? Is fantasy defined by its subject matter, or its treatment, or a bit of both? Can one man's fantasy be another's hard reality? Is a film such as *The Exorcist* a fantasy or not? Its treatment is firmly realistic, but its supernatural subject matter will place it at once in the realm of fantasy for most people. And yet almost anyone subscribing to Christian belief in one form or another is required to accept the possibility of demonic possession as an objective reality; if one does so believe, then surely there is nothing at all fantastic about the film. Similarly, fantasy may be closely connected with one's place in time. *Destination Moon* may have seemed an out-and-out fantasy in 1950, whereas now, with hindsight, its depiction of man's first steps on the moon looks like the soberest documentary.

The argument can go on forever. The structuralist critic Tzvetan Todorov, for example, goes so far as to define two categories: the uncanny (that which seems to be supernatural, but finally proves susceptible of explanation according to known natural laws) and the marvelous (that which is governed by laws unknown to us and requires some modification of our ideas of the world around us); the fantastic, he says, is the duration of our uncertainty between these two choices. By this standard, I suppose, *The Turn of the Screw* would be an ideal example of the sustained fantastic, since we can never certainly decide whether the governess' experiences are uncanny (she is having delusions) or marvelous (the ghosts really exist), but either way we have to bend language somewhat to redefine two words just in order to define a third in relation to them.

Wisely, it seems to me, Charles Derry elects to sidestep this rather fruitless area of controversy. The area he is dealing with, the horror film, is ambiguously related to fantasy. According to Todorov's formulation, it may contain the uncanny, the marvelous, and the fantastic; it may also contain none of them. It also has a considerable area of overlap with science fiction, though stalwart attempts have been made to insist on the separateness of the two genres. What has been sorely needed in studies of the horror film genre is some sort of pattern which would enable us to fit everything we vaguely feel to belong to the genre into a sensible definition without either straining the definition or distorting the individual examples. This Charles Derry provides through a detailed study of the horror film in the 1960s and 1970s, examined mainly in terms of how they direct their audiences' responses, what the prime sources of horror in them are.

These sources Derry categorizes into three broad types: horror of personality, horror of Armageddon, and horror of the demonic. Without compromising too much his complex and subtle arguments, one may point out that the first category comfortably contains a lot of psychological thrillers and dark dramas (as well as some black comedies) in which there is no question of possible supernatural participation, but in which the chills come from the uncharted depths of the human psyche (the menace is within us). The second category is mainly occupied by the more frightening (though not necessarily the more fantastic) areas of science fiction, in which the horror derives from some outside threat to humanity and the world as we know it. And the third, the only one which directly involves the supernatural, gathers up all those films which concern themselves with the workings of some malign non-human force aiming at a revolution of evil through a radical reshaping of human personality, individually or collectively.

What all of these have in common is that they present varied facets of the same malevolent universe. Man is threatened from within and without. He cannot fathom his own nature, he cannot be sure the birds and beasts will not turn on him, the earth split open or burst into flames, or creatures from another planet come and deprive him of his birthright; he may doubt, but how can he ever know for certain, that the dark gods are dead; that a personal devil may impregnate his wife or transform his child into a monster. Horror is insecurity, horror is uncertainty; and horror is also the dawning conviction that our worst fears cannot hold a candle to the enormity of the reality they half reveal, half conceal from us. Horror films are distinguished as a genre by the stratagems they use on us to make us explore our own fears, to force us to consider the possibility that bad as we think things are, they are probably in actuality a lot worse.

Given this emphasis in Derry's definition of the horror genre on the ways an audience's responses can be manipulated, it is hardly surprising that Hitchcock should occupy such an obviously key position in his argument. For of Hitchcock above all other film-makers it has been said that he directs the audience much more than he directs the film. I once ran into some argument over my inclusion of Hitchcock in a book subtitled "Some Key Film-Makers of the Sixties." But the seminal role played by *Psycho* in the development of "horror of personality" and by *The Birds* in "horror of Armageddon," both of them important sub-genres belonging specifically to the 1960s, would seem to bear out the contention. It is curious, though, that Hitchcock, a devout Catholic from childhood, should not have touched the third type, "horror of the demonic," and has had virtually no truck with the supernatural at all in his career. Does it perhaps come too close to home for a true believer? Who knows?

But the fact remains that Hitchcock, an unarguable *auteur* if there ever was one, here plays a vital role in the definition of a genre. One wonders, when Hitchcock these days speaks of doing a chase in a certain way just because it is always done another way, just how clearly he realizes that it is always done that way largely because he himself set the convention. Whether he does realize this or not, he clearly lives at the point where *auteur* criticism and genre criticism join hands, since the great individual creates or re-creates the genre, and then is influenced by it in his subsequent practice just as much as anyone else, as though the conventions have become a fact of life. This is just one of the fascinating lines of thought *Dark Dreams* leads us to. Maybe in a later book Charles Derry will be moved to pursue them further himself, building on his own original insights which are so plentifully in evidence here.

Introduction

Like every critic who has written about movies, I have some very vivid memories of my earliest filmgoing experiences. *Snow White and the Seven Dwarfs* (at the downtown Cleveland theatre, the Hippodrome, with its plush velvet curtains!), *The 7th Voyage of Sinbad*, and even *A Hole in the Head* provide a few of those memories. But no memory is stronger than of a particular Saturday afternoon in 1960—when I was nine years old—that I insisted my reluctant parents take me to see Alfred Hitchcock's *Psycho*, a very adult movie that I was much too young to really understand. Although my parents rarely went to the movies and had never before gone to a horror film, they also, oddly enough, wanted to see *Psycho*, although they were afraid that the movie would horrify me. I tried to reassure them that *that* was the whole point of going—and besides, I had it on the very good authority of the seven-year-old girl across the street that *Psycho* had only two or three really scary parts anyway. The film was shown at the Southgate Cinema in Maple Heights, Ohio, one of the first suburban movie theatres to be located within a huge shopping center. Unlike the old theatres, the seats of the Southgate had an upright and a reclining position; how scary the movie was could be judged by how often the pressure of your feet against the floor pushed the seatback to its uncomfortable, upright position. Throughout *Psycho*, the noise of the seats—at that time still a novelty—was often louder than Bernard Herrmann's strings, so memorable throughout the film. I remember being enthralled when during the brutal shower murder the entire audience screamed in unison. (Actually, the audience screamed for the first time at Hitchcock's daring image of a toilet. In 1960, if a director was willing to show that, there was no telling *what else* he might show!) Why did the audience scream? And how was it that a film that was supposed to horrify could at the same time be so entertaining—or were all of us masochists? Indeed, what was the nature of the relationship between this horror film and its audience? And why in 1960 were we all trooping off to see *Psycho* and not a sequel to *Frankenstein*? The purpose of this study is to explore these questions, and while doing so to provide a history of the three new subgenres of horror film which emerged during the sixties.

1— The Horror of Personality

"We all go a little mad sometimes. Haven't you?"
— Anthony Perkins as Norman Bates in *Psycho*

"Well you met someone who set you back on your heels, Goody, Goody!
So you met someone and now you know how it feels, Goody, Goody!...
Hooray and Hallelujah, you had it comin' to ya..."
— Played on the piano by Shelley Winters as the demented
Helen Hill in *What's the Matter with Helen?*

"This long disease, my life..."
— Mary Astor as Jewel Mayhew in *Hush...Hush, Sweet Charlotte*

Why are horror films so popular?

Certainly horror films connect with our profound and subconscious need to deal with the things that frighten us. In the way they work upon us, films are much like dreams, and horror films are like nightmares. Some horror films deal with our fears more directly than others, but in general, horror films speak to our subconscious and — as do our dreams — deal with issues that are often painful for us to deal with consciously and directly. In a sense, the B-film accouterments so long associated with the horror film — low budgets, few stars, primitive production values, less than literate dialogue, and exploitative advertising — serve to displace and disguise what might be termed the genre's rather profoundly affecting psychoanalytic discourse. Many reason-oriented adults, so sensitive to the lack of sophisticated surface, often take a defensive and negative attitude toward this culturally devalued genre, dismissing the films as distastefully unpleasant or unimportant and silly. Other adults, more sensitive and less oblivious, may be rather hostile to the psychoanalytic discourse itself, which is regarded, so to speak, as an uninvited intruder upon the viewer's own carefully guarded psyche. Children, on the other hand, less connected to the value judgments of a culture, often take an attitude of joyful anticipation and enthusiasm toward horror film, even though the films sometimes traumatize them. As well, children have not yet learned to civilize and repress their fears: they know that there are monsters in the closet who will kill them if the nightlight goes out.

Children's response to the psychoanalytic discourse in the Friday night "Creature Features" programmed by local television stations across the country is as direct as to the underlying discourse in the nightmares they will tell over the Saturday morning breakfast table. Among the most common of all dreams, particularly among children, is the dream in which one is chased by a large dog or monster and, as if drugged or in slow motion, one can't seem to lift one's feet to run — an archetypal scene replicated in films such as *Night of the Living*

Dead (1968) and *The Omen* (1976). And for teenagers, a major audience for horror films, these films represent not only a rebellious rejection of adult values, but also a titillating glimpse into the forbidden contents of the id, especially the sexual and violent impulses that so dominate the contemporary genre. If dreams are personal, then films — offering a shared rather than solitary experience — are social, produced for a large audience and screened in a public place where one can be aware of the responses of others. Horror films speak, therefore, to shared fears, to a culture's anxieties. The atomic bomb, the Holocaust, the social cataclysms brought about by World War II, and the accelerated pace of scientific developments and social change have irrevocably altered the horror film. By the sixties, the classic horror film — as represented by *Frankenstein* (1931), *Dracula* (1931), and *King Kong* (1933) — had been by and large supplanted by the new horror film.

So did the horror film die in the fifties and early sixties? Although a good case could be made for the answer *yes*, it is probably more accurate to suggest that the classic horror film had been supplanted in the fifties by some rather horrific science-fiction, which was a logical outgrowth of the end-of-the-war, atomic-bomb anxieties. When the horror film returned in the sixties without the science-fiction paraphernalia of spaceships and inter-planetary monsters, the traditional horror genre had been transformed largely into one of three new subgenres — the first and most important of which I call the "horror of personality." In order to understand exactly what the horror of personality entailed and why it managed to become the dominant force in box-office horror in the early sixties, one must first understand the horror traditions from which this subgenre began to break.

One of the most important aspects of the classic horror film is the physical form of the horror itself. Usually the form (in other words, the monster) is something abstracted from man: a horror that keeps its distance from man both aesthetically and metaphysically. For instance, Dracula is physically unlike the average man in his dress, his fangs, and his behavior; although any man may become a vampire, the world can quite visibly be divided into vampires and nonvampires. King Kong is also quite physically unlike man: he is gigantic and an ape. Quite obviously these monsters are horrible because they present alternatives to the tenuous human equilibrium; that is, a vampire is too close to man for comfort; even on a simplistic level it is obvious that King Kong represents an aspect of man that man has managed to suppress. As presented in the classic horror story, the horror itself is both distanced from man and, what is more important, highly symbolic. The horror may be a metaphorical manifestation of man's animal instincts (*King Kong*), his evil desires (witches,

Anthony Perkins in *Psycho*: in the horror-of-personality film, even the most common-place can be rendered ominous.

Horror films promote fear; and as William Castle suggests in this iconic image from the stylized credit sequence of uncredited extras in *The Tingler*, screaming can actually provide a healthy catharsis.

In classic horror films such as *King Kong* and *Frankenstein*, the horror does not look human.

Satanism), or his fear of being dead yet not at rest (*The Mummy*, zombies); but the horror is certainly not man itself. This separation usually enables man in the horror films to confront directly his evil enemy as surely as one could confront one's reflection in a distorted mirror. Almost always the horror is vanquished.

An interesting variation of this pattern, and one that by contrast makes the symbolic schizophrenia in the usual classic horror film even more clear, was the *Doctor Jekyll and Mr. Hyde* series, in which the normal man and the horror actually coexist in the same body. This lessening of the aesthetic and metaphysical distances between the horror and man makes the Jekyll-Hyde series an interesting precursor to the horror-of-personality film; for in the Robert Louis Stevenson–inspired films, the horror is already less symbolic and, indeed, quite literal: a struggle between man's rational and animal instincts. The horror-of-personality films in the sixties, such as *Psycho*, *Strait-Jacket*, and *What Ever Happened to Baby Jane?*, decreased the distance of the horror even further. The horror became not at all symbolic, but quite specific.

Aside from studying the nature of the horror, it is equally important to study the explanation of the horror within the context of the story. In the classic horror story, there are two basic methods of explaining things away — either supernaturally or pseudoscientifically. Into the supernatural group one could fit all the monsters and horrors that are somehow involved with religions and ritual. This would include all the witchcraft movies (with their obvious Christian basis) and other horrors, such as *The Mummy* (Egyptology and reincarnation), *Dracula* (Christianity, again), zombie movies (with their stress on voodoo), and perhaps even *The Golem* (with its magic book and magic star). Into the other, the pseudoscientific group, one could fit all the monsters and horrors that result from a scientist character who goes too far. This group would include all the *Frankenstein* variations, *The Invisible Man*, and many of the "animal" men, such as the Hyde incarnation of *Dr. Jekyll and Mr. Hyde*. An interesting variation of the mad-scientist explanation is used in *King Kong*, where the mad scientist is represented by the "mad" movie director who quite literally goes too far; that is, back to a prehistoric island.

Historically, the pseudoscientific basis proved to be more fruitful during the fifties. It was during this period that the science-fiction genre became important, helping both to blur the distinctions between the two genres and seemingly to end temporarily the popularity of the supernatural basis — at least until the very personal Roger Corman cycle in the early sixties and the striking reemergence of the witchcraft cycle in the late sixties. It is impor-

Sixties horror films were strongly influenced by the stairways and shadows in *film noir*: note the striking visuals of Rhonda Fleming in Robert Siodmak's *The Spiral Staircase* and Teresa Wright in Alfred Hitchcock's *Shadow of a Doubt.*

tant to notice that in movies such as *Psycho*; *What Ever Happened to Baby Jane?*; *Hush... Hush, Sweet Charlotte*; *Lady in a Cage*; and *Peeping Tom* the extreme specificity of the horror, and the horror's manifestation as insanity, made both of the classic bases for explanation unnecessary. Can *Psycho* be explained away either supernaturally or pseudoscientifically? Quite clearly, the terms seem not only unnecessary, but not relevant. It was in the early sixties, during the John F. Kennedy years, that the country began to be racked by violence. Crime went up greatly, and suddenly there were riots in the streets, which many people just could not understand. And perhaps even more importantly, senseless serial killers or mass murderers (Richard Speck, the Boston Strangler, Charles Whitman, et al.) were constantly in the headlines. (Indeed, it is interesting to note that the highest numerical concentration of these films was in 1964 and 1965, directly after President Kennedy's assassination.) Thus, in this period, one can see why neither pseudoscientific horror nor supernatural horror was really the concern of the day. What *was* horrible, however, was man. It was a horror that was specific, nonabstract, and one that did not need a metaphor. Since the symbolic schizophrenia of the classic horror film had now become a literal insanity, it was necessary for a whole new basis of explanation to be applied. What seems to have been adopted in the early

Precursor to the psychopathological horror film: Joseph Cotten as crazy Uncle Charlie in *Shadow of a Doubt.*

sixties in these horror films (however sometimes skeptically) was the psychological explanation. Violence and horror were not explained in terms of science or religion, but in terms of psychology. This is made obvious by the very Freudian Oedipal complex in *Psycho*, the recurring Electra complexes in the Aldrich films, and the obsession with sex in all the films from *Psycho* to *Maniac* to *Strait-Jacket* to *Berserk* to *Orgasmo*. In a way, the psychological explanation enables us to distance ourselves from the horror: "It's all right, it was something in his mind that made the killer sick." It's really amazing to notice how often in these films the Freudian explanation seems to make almost no sense, yet the viewers, willing to grasp

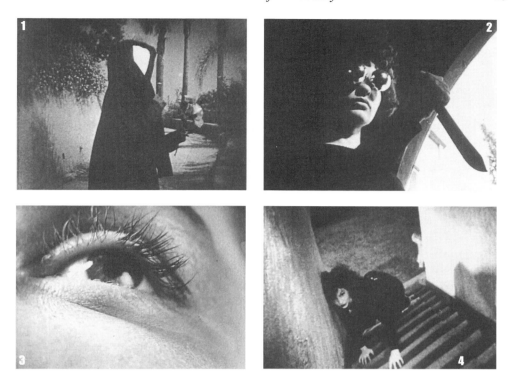

Meshes of the Afternoon (with its director Maya Deren) pioneered the iconography that would come to dominate the horror-of-personality films: (1) the mirror as an identity symbol, (2) the knife, (3) the singly-photographed eye, and (4) the stairway.

onto anything in order to alleviate their own fears, will quickly accept it. How many people have come out of *Psycho* reassured, saying: "It was about a crazy man who thought he was his mother," rather than: "It was about a man who seemed to be just about as normal as you or me, but really wasn't." It was not until the end of the sixties that the psychological basis also began to be rejected overtly. *The Devil's Own* in 1966 and especially *Rosemary's Baby* in 1968 marked the reemergence of the supernatural as a major force in explaining away evil; and *Targets* and *Pretty Poison* in 1968 both exhibit a strange kind of matter-of-factness to their violence, which suggests that — and this perhaps is the most horrible of all — there is no explanation: some people just kill.[1]

Certainly the one group of films that had a tremendous developmental influence on the horror-of-personality films were the *films noirs* of the forties: Robert Siodmak films like *Phantom Lady* (1944), *Uncle Harry* (1946), *The Dark Mirror* (1946), and *The Spiral Staircase* (1946); Fritz Lang films like *The Woman in the Window* (1944), *Scarlet Street* (1945), and *Secret Beyond the Door* (1948); the John Brahm film *Hangover Square* (1945); and the Charles Laughton film *Night of the Hunter* (1955). These *films noirs*, with their atmospheric lighting, their strong relation to German expressionism, and their preoccupation with disintegration, madness, and decay, come very close to the horror of personality. Oddly enough, so do several of the films by the American West coast avant-garde working outside the established Hollywood system. Maya Deren's celebrated 1943 short *Meshes of the Afternoon*, with its preoccupation with mirrors, disintegration, and the schizophrenia of multiple identity, is quite suggestive of later psychopathological horror. Deren's colleague Curtis Harrington, who would go on to a Hollywood career in horror film, began as the director of the 1946 short *Fragment of Seeking*, with its unambiguous, if surreal, exploration of homosexuality and gender identity within a society which would consider such exploration aberrant and criminal. Even clearer as precursors to the horror of personality are many of the Hitchcock thrillers of the forties dealing with psychopathology, such as *Suspicion* (1941), *Shadow of a Doubt* (1943), *Spellbound* (1945), and especially *Strangers on a Train* (1951). If some of these Hitchcock films are a bit too cheerful in their development and sunny in their denouement to come across with the sensibility of the horror genre, they augur nevertheless the two films I consider seminal to the genre: *Diabolique* and *Psycho*.

Diabolique [*Les Diaboliques*] was made in 1955, and its inclusion as a seminal film may seem initially surprising. First of all, the film did not come out of the horror tradition as much as out of the tightly constructed, suspense-melodrama *oeuvre* of its director, Henri-Georges Clouzot. And, secondly, the film predated the cycle of the true horror-of-personality films by at least five years. Nevertheless, the film was responsible for delineating many of the horror elements that would later become so dominant in the genre. The plot, based on the novel by Pierre Boileau and Thomas Narcejac (the same team that wrote the novel on which Hitchcock's 1958 *Vertigo* was based, his pre–*Psycho* exercise in psychopathology), is very complex; at its center is the rather strange and almost perverse relationship between two women played by Simone Signoret and Vera Clouzot, two women who are inextricably entangled in a monstrous crime: the murder of the one woman's husband. At the end of the film it is discovered that the plot is even more complicated than originally thought, and that the unmarried woman had plotted with the husband all along (who was really not killed), and was trying rather to drive the other woman crazy. Of course the plot idea of trying to drive someone crazy is not completely new; Charles Boyer tried to do it to Ingrid Bergman in *Gaslight* in 1944, but in that film (and those of that type) the emphasis was on the mysterious elements belonging more to the Gothic romance of a Daphne du Maurier or Mary Stewart. In *Diabolique*, the emphasis is on the rather everyday, matter-of-fact, sordid horror, and on the tense psychological relationships between the characters. The subject matter of *Diabolique*, that of two women in a psychological, horrific situation, can be seen in many of the notable horror-of-personality films of the sixties and early seventies — specifically *What Ever Happened to Baby Jane?*; *Nightmare*; *Hush...Hush, Sweet Charlotte*; *Picture Mommy Dead*; *Games*; *The Mad Room*; *What Ever Happened to Aunt Alice?*; and *What's the Matter with Helen?* Of course the Clouzot film does not quite have the same poetically pessimistic quality of some of the later films, in that its action is surprisingly void of sad, poignant time jumps; as well, the relative youth of its women deprives the film of a particular pathos. The film also lacks the very strong emphasis on insanity itself, which was, with *Psycho* in 1960, to become perhaps the strongest of the genre's traits. The film does, however, contain strong elements of the ambiguity that later was to become such an important part: the unanglicized title of the film is *Les Diaboliques* [*The Fiends*]. While

A lesbian subtext in *Diabolique*: two women (Vera Clouzot and Simone Signoret) psychologically bound.

watching the film, one assumes that the fiends are Simone Signoret and Vera Clouzot; at its end one presumes the true fiends are Simone Signoret and Paul Meurisse. The question to be asked is: "Who, then, are the true *Diaboliques*? Or are we all fiends?" In the sixties, with *Psycho* and *Hush...Hush, Sweet Charlotte*, we ask a similar question, but with a different object: "Who, then, are the true crazy people? Or are we all?"

Except perhaps for *Screaming Mimi* (a film made in 1958 that contains many of the same ideas as *Psycho* but in a less-integrated form), *Psycho* marked the true beginning of the horror-of-personality genre. It is a seminal film not only because of its emphasis on the ambiguity and horror of insanity, but also because it was tremendously successful in terms of its box-office. It was evidently dealing with issues to which the audiences were responding, and it, almost single-handedly, managed to spawn the genre. I will not deal with the film in terms of Hitchcock as *auteur* (as has been done quite admirably by critics such as Robin Wood and V.F. Perkins), but instead will deal with it in terms of the genre it was breaking away from, a manner in which *Psycho* has rarely been discussed. As stated earlier, the classic pseudoscientific horror film evolved in the fifties into the dominant science-fiction film, or the science-fiction horror. The supernatural horror film seemed to become relatively recessive during the fifties, although the supernatural tradition was carried on rather strangely by a series of haunted-house movies in the late fifties. In fact, during the period between *Diabolique* in 1955 and *Psycho* in 1960, these haunted-house movies were the dominant element (in terms of number of films released) in the supernatural horror; although of course these films were, by and large, continuations of the grade-B haunted-house films that were such a staple in the forties. Some of the titles of these fifties films include *Macabre* (1958), *The Screaming Skull* (1958), *Terror in the Haunted House* (1958), *I Bury the Living* (1958), *House on Haunted Hill* (1959), *Horrors of the Black Museum* (1959), *The Bat* (1959), *The Tingler* (1959), *The Hypnotic Eye* (1960), and *13 Ghosts* (1960). Many of these films were William Castle Productions or for American International. Even more of them featured some special gimmick, such as the thousand-dollar life-insurance policy from Lloyds of London that the theatre patrons of *Macabre* would receive in case any of them should die of fright; or the free burial services offered to expired patrons of *The Screaming Skull*; or "PsychoRama," the gimmick used in *Terror in the Haunted House*, in which subliminal pictures were used to psychologically affect the audience; or "Emergo" in *House on Haunted Hill*, where a wired skeleton would "float" over the heads of the audience; or "Percepto," in *The Tingler*, where vibrating motors were attached to the underside of selected theatre seats, which at the proper moments inflicted tingling sensations to a delicate portion of the theatergoer's anatomy; or "Hypnomagic," in *The Hypnotic Eye*, in which one of the onscreen actors tries to hypnotize the audience; or "Illusion-O," in *13 Ghosts*, in which special glasses allow the ghosts to become visible to the audience; or the "Fright Break" in *Homicidal*, where the narrative stopped for 45 seconds near the end and allowed any terrified moviegoers to get their money back if they would humiliate themselves by walking in a yellow light to the yellow "Coward's Corner" that had been set aside in the theatre. Not all of these movies took place in haunted houses (*I Bury the Living* took place in a graveyard); nevertheless, the idea of horror in these films was very clearly associated with a dark environment. And in almost all of these movies the horror was experienced by the audience as supernatural and mystical: in *House on Haunted Hill*, there are scary apparitions; in *I Bury the Living*, people who own funeral plots begin dying as a psychic result of the cemetery owner's error of mixing up the plots on his map. Yet ironically enough, although the shocks in these films are largely experienced by the spectator as belonging to the horror genre, the endings reveal that the films really belong to the mystery genre and have only been masquerading as horror. For instance, in *House on Haunted Hill* we discover that all the apparitions have only been carefully sustained illusions carried out by Vincent Price; and in *I Bury the Living* we discover that the people have really been killed by a gravedig-

The Screaming Skull took advantage of its own unique gimmick, one of many used by fifties horror films.

ger who, being phased out of his job, wanted revenge. Thus in both of these films, the horror of the supernatural, in terms of the plot itself, never really existed in the first place. Perhaps this tradition can be traced back to that famous theatre and film staple, *Seven Keys to Baldpate*, and also (though less directly) to those mystery novels that proliferated in the twenties and thirties in which, one by one, people in a haunted house/island/ski lodge/etc. are killed; except that in the haunted-house films, the horror-mystical elements are played up and the rational explain-it-all denouements are played down. *Psycho*, quite apart from any *auteur* considerations, can be seen to relate quite clearly to this spate of haunted-house

Low-budget exploitation in *13 Ghosts*: producer William Castle demonstrates the "ghostviewer" spectacles to be used for watching his film.

Dark shadows and geometric patterns dominate the haunted house films of the fifties: Carolyn Craig in *House on Haunted Hill*, and Gavin Gordon as *The Bat*.

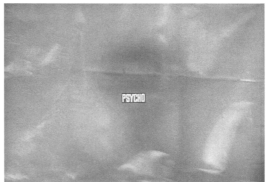

Unlike William Castle, Hitchcock did not use as much gimmickry to sell his films, but he was not above appearing in his own trailers. In the *Psycho* trailer, Hitchcock gives a tour of the film's locations, then pulls back the shower curtain. Note that the woman revealed is not Janet Leigh (who gets murdered), but Vera Miles (who does not). Notably, virtually every patron of *Psycho* would know, before entering the theatre, that a murder will take place in the bathroom. Hitchcock is purposely diminishing the surprise to heighten the anticipation and the suspense.

movies — most obviously, since the main house in *Psycho* is absolutely typical with its stairways, dark corners, and hidden basement. Yet the most amazing thing about *Psycho* is that from the beginning to the end it very consciously goes against all the established conventions, and in doing so manages to redefine exactly what horror is by relating it to the modern sixties sensibilities. For instance, although the major horror in the haunted-house movies

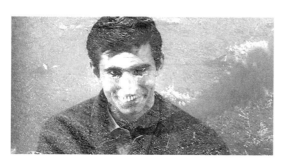 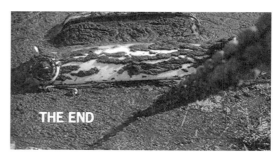

The final sequence of the seminal *Psycho* with star Anthony Perkins: stasis which leads to disintegration, both psychological and physical. Note how the skull's superimposition on Norman's face underscores the narrative movement toward death.

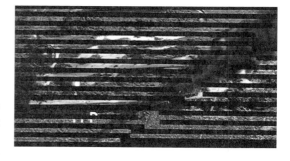

takes place in the dark of the house, *Psycho*'s major horror takes place in the bright whiteness of a shower stall. Hitchcock uses the very generic house in his film to foil the audience's expectations of having the most horrific act happen there. And when Hitchcock finally does use the house as the environment of horror (when Arbogast is killed), the horror does not proceed from the house itself; rather, it proceeds from the character of the killer for which the house is only a metaphor. Whereas many of the haunted-house films are really mystery films masquerading as horror, *Psycho*, with its inquiring detective, is really a horror film masquerading as a mystery. (After all, director Hitchcock even murdered the detective.) Although in many of the haunted-house movies the explanation at the end alleviates, or actually repudiates, the earlier horror, the explanation and denouement at the end of *Psycho* tend to crystallize the horror even further. In regard to the classic horror genre, *Psycho* also breaks away, in that the fear in *Psycho* is not particularly of death or symbolic evil; the fear is instead of living in a crazy world, a world in which one can be mutilated physically in close-up. As such, *Psycho* takes what had been a minor theme from the mad-scientist films — insanity — and augments that horror by using it completely unrelated to any mystic-scientific superpositions, such as a Frankenstein monster or a Wolf Man. Thus, Hitchcock broke away from the two standard realms of horror — the pseudoscientific and the supernatural — and substituted instead the psychological. Indeed, in its redefinition of horror as the psychological, a step that seemed in 1960 (five years after *Diabolique*) particularly suited to the times, in its concern with the anxiety of living and the nearness of mutilation, and most especially in its emphasis on the ambiguity of insanity ("We all go a little mad sometimes," says Anthony Perkins as Norman Bates), *Psycho* can be viewed as the fountainhead from which all the horror-of-personality films were to flow.

Right after *Psycho* began breaking box-office records, the Louis Malle film, *L'Ascenseur pour L'Échafaud*, was released in the United States with the changed title *Frantic*, probably to try to cash in a bit on *Psycho*'s success. *Frantic* was followed by the William Castle production of *Homicidal* (1961). *Homicidal* is about Miriam Webster's relationship with her half-brother Warren and his strange wife Emily. At the end of the film, after some killings

(a knife again being the horrible and phallic weapon), it is discovered that Warren and Emily are one and the same person. Although I have never been able to make complete sense of the explanation at the end (although it appears that Warren/Emily was at birth a biological girl), it is clear that transvestism, an unconventional sexuality, and perhaps even an operation in Denmark were involved in his/her horrific identity. The confusion is further compounded by a literal double curtain call at the film's end

In *Homicidal*, parallel shots of the newlyweds "Warren" and "Emily," with their contrasting shadows, suggest sexual schizophrenia; what does it mean to be male, female, "normal?" Note how the film's odd curtain call obscures the gender of performer Jean Arless, who played two manifestations of a single psyche.

Most post–*Psycho* horror films were largely exploitative, as revealed by their gaudy, imaginative, title graphics.

in which the star's name is revealed as Jean (Gene?) Arless, without much clue as to whether he/she was in real life a man or a woman. The effect is really quite unsettling. It may be possible that Jean Arless' nonappearance in film thereafter may be related to the ambiguity of her gender. Ironically, before the surprise ending of the film, both Warren and Emily appeared to be relatively physically attractive; after the surprise is revealed, they are both perceived by the audience as looking bizarre, as if in drag. *Homicidal* is especially important for its re–association of insanity with sexuality, a relationship that is reaffirmed in many of these horror films — especially those of the early sixties, such as *Peeping Tom*; *The Psychopath*; *The Collector*; *Hush...Hush, Sweet Charlotte*; *Die! Die! My Darling!*; and *Twisted Nerve*. Indeed, the element of sexual "perversion," or at least of a sexuality off-kilter or indeterminate (as in *What Ever Happened to Baby Jane?*), is present in many of the films even when it is not related directly to the possible insanity of the protagonists. The influence of *Psycho* is also obviously apparent in many of the titles released in the sixties — titles that include *Mania, Trauma, Maniac, The Sadist, Anatomy of a Psycho, Dementia 13, Strait-Jacket, Pyro, Shock Treatment, The Psychopath, Psycho-Circus, Berserk, Twisted Nerve, The Mad Room, Fanatic* (the alternate title of *Die! Die! My Darling!*), and even *Paranoia* (an Italian sexploitation film originally called *Orgasmo*, but partially an *hommage* to Robert Aldrich's two horror films).

The next really important film in the horror-of-personality genre was *What Ever Happened to Baby Jane?*, made in 1962. This film, like its subsequent companion piece,

Hush...Hush, Sweet Charlotte, was directed by Robert Aldrich. The reviews of *Baby Jane* were on the whole much better than those of *Sweet Charlotte*, but even in the laudatory reviews, there was a general tendency to dismiss these films as only horror films — as *grand guignol*— as if a horror film could not be worth serious consideration. Actually, the contribution of Robert Aldrich to the horror-of-personality films cannot be overestimated. There arises here the question of *auteur* vs. genre: It seems to me that while Aldrich is most

definitely an *auteur*, it is equally obvious that he is an *auteur* working within and against certain genre conventions (just as Curtis Harrington was to do later in *Games* and *What's the Matter with Helen?*). It does not seem that these two approaches —*auteur* and genre — need to be necessarily antagonistic. The reason Aldrich was so important to the development of the genre is because it was he and his scriptwriter, Lukas Heller (and of course the novelist Henry Farrell), who realized the relevance of *Diabolique* and, in *What Ever Happened to Baby Jane?*, joined the major idea of *Diabolique* to the major idea of *Psycho*. What emerged then was a psychological study of two women whose relationship was based on some past crime, yet a study that dealt very overtly

Aging movie stars Bette Davis and Joan Crawford as sisters Baby Jane and Blanche Hudson: imprisoned within their home by a secret in *What Ever Happened to Baby Jane?*

with the ambiguity of insanity. After combining these two basic premises, Aldrich went on to invent more or less his own conventions — conventions that he would follow very carefully in his next film, and conventions that would be followed just as carefully in some of the Curtis Harrington films years later. (Why is it that when Greek tragedy follows conventions and repeats itself it is intellectual, but when a horror film follows conventions it is too often regarded as clichéd repetition?) The first major element that Aldrich added is the casting of aging movie stars who trigger complex associations for the audience. The sight of a bizarre Bette Davis making her comeback by torturing Joan Crawford, whom Davis had always disliked, adds an extra dimension to *Baby Jane* that fits right in with its tone: a poignancy, mixed with voyeurism and revulsion. In *Hush...Hush, Sweet Charlotte*, Aldrich went even further: he used four aging movie star actresses — Olivia de Havilland, Bette Davis, Agnes Moorehead, and Mary Astor, and one aging movie star actor — Joseph Cotten. Particularly effective is Mary Astor: although the audience may remember her as the beautiful young female lead in *The Maltese Falcon*, all the audience sees is a bloated, wrinkled, pale woman who is half dead when she first appears. Surely this cannot be the Mary Astor we once knew so well. But, of course, time stops for no one, and everyone must get old and, so it seems, ugly. In each film Aldrich also cast Victor Buono — a rather bizarre actor. In the first film he plays a grotesque mama's boy, and in the second, father to the grotesque "papa's girl." Perhaps the most important difference between *Diabolique* and the Aldrich films is the distance Aldrich puts between the main crime and his story. In *Diabolique* the narrative was structurally simpler: a crime was committed (supposedly), and the story proceeded immediately from there. In both *Baby Jane* and *Sweet Charlotte*, a crime is committed, and then the narrative jumps ahead about thirty years to continue the story.

And this jump is not merely a structural maneuver, but also a thematic one; while the tragedy of *Diabolique* is a specific tragedy of a specific time, the tragedy of the Aldrich films is more expansive and shows the horror of many completely wasted lives. Although *Baby Jane* and *Sweet Charlotte* work within Aldrich's very tight framework much like a musical theme and variation, each film is a remarkably integrated work unto itself.

The first thing we hear in *What Ever Happened to Baby Jane?* is a girl crying and a voice saying: "Want to see it again little girl? It shouldn't frighten you." The sound of tears, the immediate suggestion that *Baby Jane* will be a tragedy, is particularly apt. We are then introduced to the two sisters, Blanche and Jane. From the very beginning, the little girl Jane (the Bette Davis character) is flamboyant, while Blanche (the Joan Crawford character) is sullen. The highlight of the 1917 episode is a close-up of the young Blanche as her mother tells her: "You're the lucky one, Blanche. Someday you'll be the famous one ... and you can treat your sister kinder than she's been treating you." And then from Blanche, very coldly: "I won't forget." We skip to the year 1935. The roles have been reversed, and Blanche is the famous actress, Baby Jane the untalented sister and has-been. Yet it appears that Blanche is treating her sister very kindly and exerting her influence to get Jane some parts. However, Aldrich inserts touches that in retrospect suggest the true nature of Blanche. When a studio executive walks past Blanche's big car, he asks, "What do they make monsters like this for?" And the answer is: "For Blanche Hudson." And not: "For Baby Jane." Thus, Joan Crawford's Blanche is very clearly equated with a monster. The climax of the pre-credit sequence is the very confusing presentation of the accident. We see close-ups of feet, of a light dress against a fence, of a hand shifting gears, then a crash. Later we are to take it for granted that Baby Jane ran over Blanche, thus causing her paralysis. Yet what image does Aldrich provide us with as a metaphor for the accident?—a Baby Jane doll with its head crushed. And indeed, it is Baby Jane (who always dresses in light colors) who is the victim. In retrospect it is amazing how many clues Aldrich provides us with that we go right ahead and ignore. Finally we get to the credits, and then the bulk of the story starts with the title "Yesterday." We are prepared for the introduction of the aged Joan Crawford and Bette Davis by first watching the neighbors discuss Blanche and Baby Jane while watching an old Blanche Hudson movie (Joan Crawford in *Sadie McKee*, 1934). Although *Baby Jane* is unlike both *Psycho* and *Diabolique* in that the crime does not seem to have been sexually related, there is a remarkable emphasis on either an off-balance sexuality or an asexuality. The neighbors, played by Anna Lee and B. D. Hyman (Bette Davis' real-life daughter), are never shown with men; neither is Blanche. The only suggestion of a romantic relationship is between Baby Jane and the effeminate, overweight Edwin Flagg, played by Victor Buono, but this relationship is presented as a gross parody, a grotesquery. (Note that in *Hush... Hush, Sweet Charlotte* that "romantic" element is provided by the genteel actor Cecil Kellaway, and it becomes, unlike in *Baby Jane*, affirming.) And indeed, our first view of Edwin Flagg standing with his tiny possessive mother suggests the disturbing Diane Arbus

A Baby Jane doll is a poignant symbol for psychological damage in *What Ever Happened to Baby Jane?*

photographs of the seventies. Certainly the relationship between this mother and son is not normal. Notice too the *hommage* to the seminal film *Psycho*, in that the name of the neighbor is the same as Norman's mysterious mother: Mrs. Bates.

Although the basic situation of the story seems to be that Baby Jane is the crazy and evil sister, and Blanche the suffering, good, and sane sister, Aldrich constantly includes details that foreshadow the ending and suggest otherwise. Our first view of the aged Joan Crawford's Blanche is that of her kindly sweet face suddenly becoming harsh as she criticizes an old movie director. Suggestively, it is Baby Jane who wears light colors, and Blanche who wears black. For someone who is supposed to be crazy and evil, Baby Jane shows remarkable intelligence. She realizes that Blanche called the business manager and accuses her rightly of lying to her: "You're just a liar. You always were." The revelation that Baby Jane's whole life was wasted because of Blanche's lying adds particular irony to her accurate accusation. Not only is Baby Jane intelligent, but she has a sense of humor that truly draws us toward her. "It's not me that needs a doctor, Blanche..." says Baby Jane; or after particularly frightening her sister: "You're just a neurotic." And there is the whole business of the surprise dinner with the dead rat, which, although horrible, shows amazing creativity. The innuendo, "By the way, Blanche, there's rats in the cellar," is hilarious. Funny too is her baby-talk explanation: "I didn't forget your breakfast.... I didn't bring your breakfast ... because you didn't eat your din-din." Blanche, on the other hand, seems amazingly devoid of either wit or a sense of humor. But after all, she is the dark sister — despite her name. The basic crisis in *Baby Jane* (just as in *Sweet Charlotte*) is the question of the house. Since it was built for Baby Jane by her father, she doesn't want to leave it. (And in *Sweet Charlotte*, the house is again identified with the father figure.) In the Aldrich films, the house is used very differently from the way it is used in the conventional haunted-house films, which often show a young woman tormented by nightmares and memories that she cannot exorcize until she returns to the house. In both *Baby Jane* and *Sweet Charlotte*, it is quite clear that the Bette Davis title character in each cannot exorcize her demons until she gets away from the house. Perversely, in both films the Bette Davis character wants to stay. Another important element that recurs in most of the films from *Diabolique* to *Psycho* to *Sweet Charlotte* to *Pretty Poison* is the disposal-of-the-body sequence, although in *Baby Jane* there is a nice initial ambiguity as to whether Baby Jane is disposing of a body or her black-shrouded

Bette Davis in *What Ever Happened to Baby Jane?* Weighed down by guilt, she looks old and trapped, surrounded by the interior darkness, a monster in low-key lighting. With guilt lifted, she looks younger and free, surrounded by the exterior glow, a heroine in high-key lighting.

Bette Davis and Olivia de Havilland as cousins Charlotte and Miriam in *Hush...Hush, Sweet Charlotte*: a complex psychological relationship as a result of a murder committed long ago.

sister. It is not until the end of the film and away from the house in the light of a sunny beach that Blanche finally tells Baby Jane the truth: Blanche's paralysis resulted when Blanche tried to cripple Baby Jane. After a life of self–torture and unnecessary guilt, Bette Davis' Baby Jane answers with a compassion that is horrifying: "You mean, all this time we could have been friends?" She goes off to try to rekindle the friendship by buying ice-cream cones (and it was an ice-cream cone she wanted in the pre–credit 1917 sequence). Almost magically, the grotesque makeup and wrinkles disappear from her face. She becomes truly beautiful; and with the guilt no longer heavy on her shoulders, her movements are light. Ironically, in her salvation she reverts to her childhood. Yet, as Baby Jane sheds guilt and years, Blanche takes them on. The movie ends with Bette Davis's Baby Jane doing a dance of liberation as she approaches that black, corpselike figure which is Joan Crawford's Blanche. Despite the relatively "happy ending," it is too late for the revelation to really matter. If only it had come decades sooner! The two sisters' lives have already been wasted; there is really no time left to make of them anything meaningful or worthwhile.

Hush...Hush, Sweet Charlotte was made by Aldrich in 1964 and written by the same group of writers as *Baby Jane*— Lukas Heller and Henry Farrell; and were it not for Joan Crawford's illness (potentially psychosomatic or feigned), Bette Davis would have again played opposite her. As it turned out, Olivia de Havilland stepped in and took Crawford's part. *Sweet Charlotte*, like *Baby Jane*, starts in the past. The year is 1927, and almost immediately we get the strong father figure, "Big Sam" Hollis, played by Victor Buono. Even the father's portrait towers over John Mayhew, the married man that Charlotte loves. In this remarkably integrated film, one of the first icons we notice is a painting of Charlotte, her father, and her cousin Miriam — except that Charlotte and her father are painted in bright shades that attract the eye, while Miriam is in dark shades that recede into the background. Thus the two girls' relationship should be discernible quite early. The crime, this time very overtly related to sexuality, is again handled in confusing and horrifying close-ups. John Mayhew's decapitation and the severing of his hand are clearly suggestive of castration. Immediately after the killing, Aldrich cuts to the bandleader who yells out, "One more time," a juxtaposition which may at first seem only terribly heavy-handed black comedy, but is actually quite a foreshadowing device; before Charlotte can be "cured" she will have to re-experience the violence at least one more time. In many respects this suggests a clear relationship between these two Aldrich films and Hitchcock's *Marnie*. In *Marnie*, the heroine was similarly forced to reenact the crime (through the symbolic shooting of her horse Forio); only then could she leave the house of her mother with no guilt. The same thing holds true in Aldrich's films. In *Baby Jane*, Baby Jane cannot leave the house until she really has "tortured" her sister, as she supposedly had in the past. The parallel is even stronger in *Sweet Charlotte* (in fact, the John Mayhew character whose murder causes Charlotte's madness is played by Bruce Dern, the actor who played the sailor who caused the heroine's madness in *Marnie*). Before Charlotte can leave the house of her father, she must go through the experience of reenacting the crime in the dream sequence and "shooting" Dr. Drew Bayliss, played by Joseph Cotten. Yet the difference in attitude between *Marnie* and the Aldrich films shows why *Marnie* is not a horror film: Marnie is really guilty of the past crime and is cured while she is relatively young. Baby Jane and Charlotte are not guilty, and they are not cured of their madness until their whole lives have been wasted and it is too late. After the crime (the killing of Mayhew), the story jumps to 1964. Immediately, the problem of moving out of the house is made clear: Charlotte pushes a gigantic flower pot off the second-floor balcony in an attempt to stop the bulldozers from razing her house. (At the end of the film, she will, quite symmetrically, push the second and final flower pot off the porch in order to execute her cousin Miriam and Dr. Bayliss.) The house is again bizarrely stopped in time; the Southern gentility of 1927 now appears faded, run-down, but unchanged. When cousin Miriam, played by Olivia de Havilland, first arrives she says: "It's just as I left it." And that was thirty-seven years ago. Ironically, Bette Davis had always wanted to play the archetypal Southern belle, Scarlett O'Hara. Now, in 1964, she manages to do just that — but decades too late; her Charlotte-Scarlett is a pathetic creature to behold. Out of place, out of time, she wears clothes from 1927, and even treats her best friend, Velma, the maid, with a particularly Southern *noblesse oblige*. The contrast between the two cousins is obvious, for Miriam has changed with the times and is stylish and modern. It is obvious that Charlotte is at least a little insane, but in the horror-of-personality films, the supposedly insane often exhibit a remarkable insight. When Velma, played by Agnes Moorehead, doubts that Miriam will come, Charlotte claims assuredly that she'll arrive the next day. And she does. When Miriam refuses — apparently graciously — to help Charlotte keep the house, Charlotte accuses her of coming only to try to get the Hollis fortune — a fact that, again, turns out to be true. And when Charlotte talks about Jewel Mayhew, played by the great Mary Astor, and claims "she deserves to die," that too turns out to be accurate, for it was Jewel who had killed John Mayhew (that is, Charlotte's lover and Jewel's husband) in 1927. Indeed, Aldrich again gives us much information that suggests that Charlotte is not the treacherous, crazy one. When Miriam hires some women to help pack, one admits that Charlotte "sure acts crazy sometime, but I wouldn't bet on it." And when Charlotte throws her hate mail on the bed (all of it secretly from Miriam), one letter falls to the floor. The maid, Velma, picks it up and gives it to its sender, Miriam: It says "Murderess." The moment is absolutely electrifying in its truthfulness; and, before long, Miriam does murder Velma. The film is filled with many striking visual moments. When Miriam talks about her old romance with Dr. Bayliss, the outline of light on the pillar she is leaning against looks exactly like a wedding veil (an effect which originally appeared in Hitchcock's 1943 *Shadow of a Doubt*, also starring Joseph Cotten). Miriam and Dr. Bayliss acknowledge that the romance had never worked out, and she moves into a more natural, nonsuggestive light. Or later, when she is plotting with Bayliss, Miriam very casually turns off the light on Big Sam's portrait. There are the billowing curtains, the close-up of footsteps, and then the corpse that comes alive that all seem to be direct *hommages* to the film that started it all: *Diabolique*. One of the most interesting visual ideas in *Sweet Charlotte* is Aldrich's photographing Miriam through windows. The icon of the window seems a complex one; photographing some-

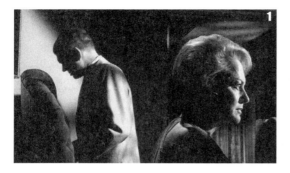

Although Olivia de Havilland's Miriam is introduced as a potential savior for Charlotte in *Hush... Hush, Sweet Charlotte*, director Aldrich visually presents darker truths. Miriam is shown to be (1) emotionally distant from Joseph Cotten's Dr. Bayliss, although involved with him in dark intrigue; (2) guilty of criminal behavior which should put her behind bars; (3) evil, as shown by the ominous and expressively unreal shadow she casts; (4) yearning for her evanescent innocence, as suggested by the wedding veil of light; and (5) ultimately inscrutable, as she parts masking curtains to peek stealthily through a window.

one through a window (especially with curtains) suggests that the person's true nature is inscrutable, hidden, and ultimately evil. I think immediately of the final window image of Bette Davis in William Wyler's *The Little Foxes*, or of the little boy in Robert Mulligan's *The Other*. De Havilland's Miriam (and never Davis's Charlotte) is photographed three times looking through a window: once when Miriam arrives, a second time after she kills Velma, and a third time before she stages the elaborate masquerade with Dr. Bayliss. Ultimately, Miriam does not survive. When Charlotte leaves the house triumphantly after discovering the truth and killing her tormentors, she is dressed in modern clothes and leaves her music box, the symbol of her past, behind. Nevertheless, the attitude of the film can well be represented by a line Mary Astor delivers as Jewel Mayhew: "Ruined finery," she says to the actor Cecil Kellaway, "that's all I have left." And that is true; for, in this genre, any finery must be ruined. It is not death so much that is horrible, but life. If it is already too late for Charlotte and Jewel and Velma and Miriam and for all of us, Jewel's poignantly expressed line taken from Alexander Pope, "This long disease, my life," works both as a voluntary metaphor and a reminder of the truly horrible sense of life embodied by this genre.

Especially after *What Ever Happened to Baby Jane?*, Aldrich's first venture into the genre, and certainly after *Hush...Hush, Sweet Charlotte*, his second, films in this genre became associated very directly with the old movie stars who were increasingly picking them as vehicles for their comebacks. For instance, *Strait-Jacket* (1964), written by *Psycho*'s Robert Bloch and directed by William Castle, gave Joan Crawford the opportunity to be a suspected ax murderess. The film roughly fol-

A sick relationship between a daughter and mother whose dresses match the wallpaper. This striking image in *Strait-Jacket* of Joan Crawford apparently fighting herself (but actually Diane Baker) is a metaphor for the character's internal struggle.

lows the same pattern as the Aldrich films: a crime in the past, the bulk of the story in the present, an emphasis on the relationship between two women (in this case, Diane Baker and Joan Crawford playing daughter and mother), and the revelation that madness and guilt are much more complex than they had seemed. And *Die! Die! My Darling!*, written by Richard Matheson and directed by Silvio Narizzano in 1965 — equally *grand guignol*— provided a comeback role for an over-the-top Tallulah Bankhead, who got to torture the young ingénue Stefanie Powers. *Lady in a Cage*, directed by Walter Grauman in 1964 and starring Olivia de Havilland, was in some ways a departure from the genre. Although de Havilland is presented as a smothering mother who is a lady of leisure, she is never considered either guilty or mad; rather, she undergoes a terrible torture when her house is invaded by an insane young gang led by James Caan and including a rotund Ann Sothern. What happens in the film is truly horrible, and no one — not even passing motorists or pedestrians — will stop to help her. *Lady in a Cage* is important for at least two reasons: first, it has a clear and notable visual style unlike the heavy Gothic expressionism of the previous films; and, second, it suggests the direction toward which the genre may be heading — that is, the horror is very specific, unambiguous, and not particularly metaphorical for any more profound general fear. This may be because *Lady in a Cage* is based on a true incident; the film's horror — a lady's home is invaded senselessly, and no one will help her — can be taken on a

Olivia de Havilland, the *Lady in a Cage* trapped in her home's elevator, is attacked by James Caan. After escaping, she beseeches apathetic passersby for help; unfortunately, in the modern world we are alone even when surrounded by others.

purely literal level as a representation of what in the sixties seemed to be an increasing fear. As such, the film predates *The Incident* (1967), *In Cold Blood* (1967), *The Boston Strangler* (1968), *Targets* (1968), *The Honeymoon Killers* (1970), and *10 Rillington Place* (1971).

These six films of the Nixon era were all essentially real-life crime stories, most of them shot with a gritty realism. Both *The Boston Strangler* and *10 Rillington Place* were directed by Richard Fleischer, dealing with the American serial killer Albert De Salvo and the British serial killer John Christie, respectively. *In Cold Blood*, dealing with the murder of the Kansas Clutter family by Perry Smith and Dick Hickock, came with the most impressive credentials: source material by Truman Capote, cinematography by Conrad Hall, direction by Richard Brooks, four Academy award nominations, and a social thesis in opposition to capital punishment. The performance by Robert Blake as the sexually conflicted Smith is as powerful as the blindingly crisp black-and-white cinematography which precisely situates these murders in rural Kansas, an epitome of supposedly safe Americana. Yet ultimately, it is the low-budget *The Honeymoon Killers*, a black-and-white independent American film clearly ahead of its time which shocks the most. Starring the unlikely pairing of stolid Shirley Stoler and Tony Lo Bianco as the real-life "Lonely Hearts Killers" Martha Beck and Ray Fernandez, whose murder spree is propelled by an *amour fou* that both Luis Buñuel and François Truffaut would be proud of, *The Honeymoon Killers*, written and directed by Leonard Kastle, impresses with its casual depiction of the sordid everyday.

Targets, directed by Peter Bogdanovich and the most critically important of these subsequent films, was based on the Charles Whitman killings at the University of Texas. Bogdanovich, a student of film history certainly, used Boris Karloff as a representative of what the horror film used to be. Within the film, Karloff plays a gentle actor (Byron Orlok) who is a little out of his time. The main thrust of the story, however, is carried by the Bobby Thompson character who (and could there be a more basic American-sounding name?) for no reason at all kills his wife, mother, and a delivery boy, and then snipes from atop a gas tank, and then from a drive-in theatre, getting confused and stopping only when confronted by Boris Karloff—both in the flesh and on the screen. The idea of one set of horror values (being embodied by Boris Karloff) confronting another set of horror values (that is, the horror-of-personality values embodied in the Bobby Thompson character) is particularly strong. Although Bobby Thompson is then apprehended, *Targets* can be looked at as a kind of wistful elegy for the kind of supernatural classic horror that is no longer as meaningful as it once was. Most clearly for Bogdanovich, the horror of 1968 rests in the mystery and incomprehensibility of Bobby Thompson, who, as he is being taken away says only: "I

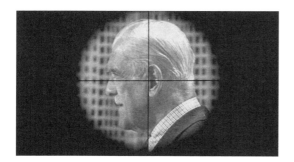

In a horror-of-personality film like *Targets*, anyone can be a victim of violence, whether the horror icon Boris Karloff or a suburban mom with a nice dining-room set.

hardly ever missed, did I?" Bogdanovich does not try to explain Bobby Thompson; he even shuns any psychological conjecture. It was this one reticence that particularly bothered the critics. As Howard Thompson asked obsessively in the *New York Times*:

> Why? This invariable question of today's headlines about the random sniper-murder of innocent people is never answered in *Targets*. This is the only flaw, and a serious one, in this original and brilliant melodrama. This one count simply can't be ignored.... Why? How come?

Once again it seems a critic has missed the obvious point: were an explanation given, we could rest easy with the insanity carefully catalogued. It is the very absence of any reason, the very refusal on Bogdanovich's part to give us the slightest grounds for reassurance, that makes *Targets* so disturbing. And it is the germ of *Targets* that can be seen in *Lady in a Cage*.

Another important film during the post–Kennedy assassination period when the genre flourished was *The Nanny* (1965), directed by Seth Holt, and starring Bette Davis. In this film, the question is again one of sanity and of a past crime. Though instead of using two women, Holt uses Bette Davis and the little boy she watches over. The climax (with its generic revelation) is simultaneously poignant and repulsive. A similar switch in the formula was made in the 1968 *Pretty Poison*, in which the two protagonists were not two old women, but a young man and a girl in love. Beneath the film's obvious individuality, one can see that *Pretty Poison* really works nicely within the framework of the horror-of-personality film. Anthony Perkins plays Dennis Pitt, the supposedly insane character (and after all, haven't we learned from *Psycho* that the all-American boy is really crazy?), and Tuesday Weld plays Sue Ann Stepanek, the typical, luscious, all-American girl who is a sweet cheerleader with mother problems. Dennis has a crime in his past (having set his house and par-

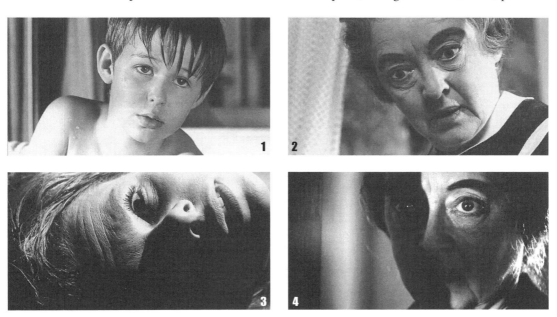

In *The Nanny*, **either (1) master Joey (William Dix) or (2) his erstwhile nanny (Bette Davis) is crazy and murderous. Have we lost faith in the innocence of children or in that occupational paragon of dependability? (3) Joey's mother (Wendy Craig), remarkably unstable herself, is at one point photographed similarly to (4) the nanny — with only one eye visible, suggesting inscrutability and imbalance within women in general.**

Pretty Poison shows a variety of all-American images of Tuesday Weld as Sue Ann Stepanek: (1) as a drum majorette, (2) as a teenager who chats on her Princess telephone while dreaming about ballet, and (3) as a cold-blooded killer.

ents on fire), and has been in an institution. Only after years have passed does Dennis come out of the institution, and the movie essentially begins there. (Unlike *Baby Jane* and *Sweet Charlotte,* which have pre-credit sequences which show the initial crime, *Pretty Poison,* like *Strait-Jacket,* instead telescopes that information into traditional exposition.) As *Pretty Poison* goes on, we discover the horrible truth: Dennis, despite being quite decidedly weird, is not the crazy one; rather, it is sweet, nubile Sue Ann who is crazy. The revelation comes shockingly when Sue Ann very nonchalantly coldcocks a guard with a pipe wrench and then sits on his head in shallow water in order to drown him. Are these the new sensibilities of American youth? The film is made all the more horrifying because, like *Targets,* the actions of Tuesday Weld's Sue Ann, a very *Pretty Poison* indeed, are not even explained psychologically — they are merely taken for granted. The irony is that after experiencing the horror and violence of a supposedly sane person, Perkins' Dennis is quite content to go back to the institution, which he considers safe. And if it's safer to live in an insane asylum, what does that say for the basic quality of human nature?

Another important development was Curtis Harrington's realization that he could work in the horror genre with great distinction. *Games,* made in 1967, stars Simone Signoret in virtually the same role she played in *Diabolique* and within an only slightly altered plot. The power of *Games* is basically derived from the density of the visual images — especially the bizarre set decorations. Although *Games* deals in no major way with the ambiguity of insanity, the film does emphasize the relationship between two women, and the revelation that one (Signoret, of course) is trying to drive the other one crazy. There is, however, one important difference between this film and *Diabolique*: In *Diabolique,* the character played by Signoret was sincerely in love with the husband of the woman she was driving crazy. In *Games,* there is an added twist when Signoret kills the husband here, played by James Caan; and Harrington's vision is revealed as, if not more sordid, certainly more stylishly bleak than Clouzot's. Harrington's ideas are continued in *How Awful About Allan* (a 1970 variation in which Anthony Perkins is pitted against Julie Harris), and particularly in *What's the Matter with Helen?* In this 1971 film, sprightly Debbie Reynolds, playing Adelle Brackner, is pitted against Shelley Winters, playing the mad Helen Hill. And Agnes Moorehead, sup-

Silhouettes in horror film can have different meanings. (1) The more traditional, stark silhouette of Anthony Perkins in *How Awful About Allan* is ominous, whereas (2) the midtoned silhouette of Susannah York in *Images* is more subtle and elusive.

porting player in *Hush...Hush, Sweet Charlotte*, also supports here, as Sister Alma, a faith healer character inspired by Aimee Semple McPherson. *What's the Matter with Helen?*, like *Games*, is remarkably dense in its images: bizarre midgets, slaughtered rabbits, a little girl impersonating Mae West, a room full of girls tap-dancing in front of their rather disgusting mothers, etc. Like Aldrich's *Baby Jane*, *What's the Matter with Helen?* is concerned with Hollywood — and the portrait of Hollywood that emerges is grotesque and pathetic. For one of her few straight dramatic roles, Harrington lets Debbie Reynolds play a mother who runs away with Winters' Helen Hill from the notoriety of a crime committed by their sons. Together, the two women then start a dance school that suggests the Mount Hollywood Art School in *Singin' in the Rain*,

The typical woman in the horror-of-personality film is eventually in open-mouthed fear, whether she is (1) an innocent bystander (in *The Tingler*); (2) a psychopath (Jessica Walter in *Play Misty for Me*); (3) a raped professional about to be strangled (Barbara Leigh-Hunt in *Frenzy*); or (4) a still-fearful corpse (Anna Massey in *Frenzy*). It's hard to argue that the horror film is not more misogynist than other popular genres.

in which Reynolds long ago played a now-iconic role. In fact, the street and exterior of Debbie Reynolds' apartment in *Helen* remarkably echo her street and apartment in *Singin' in the Rain*. It seems that Harrington's intent is to show the underside of that film's Hollywood view; and, indeed, *Helen* does contain at least twenty minutes of singing and dancing. Unlike Aldrich's films, Harrington's do not even have a nominally happy ending; and *Helen* ends with the dead Adelle propped up on stage as if to perform, and the dollying camera taking us (although we don't want to go) into a close-up of the now completely deranged Helen. And it is a horror that not even Adelle's attempted relationship with the ineffective male hero, played by Dennis Weaver, can attenuate.

Other later films of the genre include *Twisted Nerve*, made in 1968, which attempted to explain insanity by equating it with bad chromosomes; *What Ever Happened to Aunt Alice?* in 1969, which pitted the older Geraldine Page against the even older trooper Ruth Gordon, with the trooper getting killed; *Who Slew Auntie Roo?* in 1971 with Shelley Winters again as a madwoman; and *Play Misty for Me* in 1971 with Clint Eastwood as the normal one and Jessica Walter as the incomprehensible psychopath who (almost) kills a maid and tries to kill Eastwood. Five horror-of-personality films of the early seventies have also been among the most notable: *See No Evil* (1971), starring Mia Farrow as a blind girl terrorized by a madman; *Frenzy* (1972), a film directed by Alfred Hitchcock about a sex murderer, which was the surprising recipient of near-unanimous raves; *Images* (1972), a film exquisitely photographed by Vilmos Zsigmond and directed by Robert Altman about a young woman's descent into madness; *The Killing Kind* (1973), a reworking of the *Psycho* theme, directed by Curtis Harrington; and *The Legend of Lizzie Borden* (1975), a TV movie directed by Paul Wendkos and starring Elizabeth Montgomery in an amazingly precise and convincing reconstruction of the most famous American murders.

Perhaps the most self-conscious of the horror-of-personality films was Brian De Palma's *Sisters*, made in 1973. Dealing in part with the separation of Siamese twins, *Sisters* represents De Palma's attempt to pay *hommage* to Hitchcock by carefully recreating and reinterpreting the many elements of *Psycho*. The film opens with a scene of Phillip (played by Lisle Wilson) watching a supposedly blind Danielle (played by Margot Kidder) undress, a scene that immediately suggests Hitchcock's fascination with voyeurism. That this scene is ultimately revealed not as reality, but as a set-up television consequence in a clever parody of *Candid Camera* called *Peeping Toms* (with Danielle as an actress playing "jokes" on unsuspecting subjects) suggests the whole fictional and voyeuristic aspect of the cinema itself.

 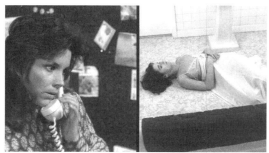

With Siamese twins as his subject in *Sisters*, director Brian De Palma chooses split-screen technique as an apposite style. Margot Kidder plays the twins, and Jennifer Salt plays a snoopy neighbor with similar facial features.

From their meeting on the television show, a romance of sorts develops between Phillip and Danielle. While making love with Danielle, Phillip discovers a huge scar on her side, which is later revealed as the result of her separation from her Siamese twin Dominique. When Phillip returns to Danielle's apartment after buying her a birthday cake, the sleeping form of a woman on the bed suddenly grabs the knife on the cake plate and stabs him repeatedly in the groin and the mouth. Up to this point, Phillip has been treated as the film's protagonist; his sudden murder—apparently by Danielle's psychotic sister, Dominique—strongly resembles the sudden murder of Janet Leigh's Marion in *Psycho*. Indeed, the resemblance is further highlighted by the score's similar orchestration—written, as was the score of *Psycho* twelve years earlier, by Bernard Herrmann. Phillip's death is emotionally harrowing because it is slow and his agony is prolonged; the music shudders and shrieks as Phillip drags himself across the room, leaving a wide trail of blood on the white floor. He does not die until he has managed to write "help" in his own blood on the window—a message that is seen by an investigative reporter, Grace Collier (who is played by Jennifer Salt). Just as in *Psycho* the murderer does not turn out to be Norman Bates' mother, but Norman Bates himself, in *Sisters*, the murderer does not turn out to be Danielle's sister, but Danielle herself. Danielle is revealed as a split personality who at times takes on the identity of her sister, who, it is revealed, was killed during the operation that separated them. Thus, the *Diabolique*-style relationship between two women (that De Palma borrows from Clouzot) turns out to be the relationship between the two opposite aspects of one split personality. Like Hitchcock, whom he is emulating, De Palma is careful to break up his *mise-en-scène* into montage, which takes much advantage of point-of-view shots. De Palma's reworking of *Psycho* is also in part a sexual inversion, with Lisle Wilson's Phillip corresponding to Janet Leigh's Marion; thus, just as Hitchcock opposes Anthony Perkins' psychotic with the physically similar actor, John Gavin, De Palma opposes Margot Kidder's psychotic with the physically similar actress, Jennifer Salt. Indeed, Jennifer Salt's function in the film as the psychotic's alter ego and unraveler of the mystery parallels the function of *Psycho*'s John Gavin. In this regard, De Palma, like Hitchcock, emphasizes the constant duality of his story, even down to the red designer stripe on the wall of Grace's apartment, paralleling the stripe of blood on the floor of Danielle's apartment. Perhaps the most striking duality is De Palma's use of split screen: Danielle and her former husband rushing to clean up her apartment and hide Phillip's body on the left image, while Grace and the detective make their way up to Danielle's apartment on the right image. Thus De Palma counterposes the two separate images in the one widescreen frame—a technique that functionally creates suspense and metaphorically suggests the schizophrenic state of Danielle. By the end of the film, the identification between Danielle and her alter ego, Grace, is so complete that in the final hallucinatory flashback, when in the operating room the horrible butcher knife is raised to separate Danielle and Dominique, it is the surrogate image of Grace that we see actually attached to Danielle. When Danielle's schizophrenia is finally unraveled for the audience through Grace's efforts, and when Danielle is taken away by the police, Grace—under hypnotic suggestion from Danielle's former husband—is unable to explain the bizarre events to the baffled police. Instead, a bit crazy now herself, she is compelled to repeat over and over the clearly erroneous statement: "There was no body and there was no murder!" What is madness and what is sanity? As usual, this horror-of-personality film offers no easy answer.

Iconographically, the films of the genre display an amazing consistency. The icons can be divided roughly into three groups: weaponry, locations, and identity symbols. First of

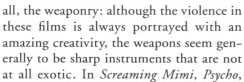

Weapons in the horror-of-personality film: (1) the knife Jean Arless uses to threaten Eugenie Leontovich in *Homicidal*; (2) the ax Diane Baker wields when in disguise as Joan Crawford in *Strait-Jacket*; (3) the knife — in expressive shadow — Margot Kidder swings in *Sisters*; (4) the meat cleaver Shelley Winters brandishes in *Who Slew Auntie Roo?*

all, the weaponry: although the violence in these films is always portrayed with an amazing creativity, the weapons seem generally to be sharp instruments that are not at all exotic. In *Screaming Mimi*, *Psycho*, *Homicidal*, and *What's the Matter with Helen?*, Anita Ekberg, Anthony Perkins, Jean Arless, and Shelley Winters respectively play characters who dispatch their victims with a knife. In *Dementia 13*; *Strait-Jacket*; *Twisted Nerve*; *Hush...Hush, Sweet Charlotte*; and, of course, *The Legend of Lizzie Borden*, the weapon is an ax. Other variations include the pointed elevator part in *Lady in a Cage*, the sharp blade of a threshing machine in *What's the Matter with Helen?*, and the saber in *The Mad Room*. The weapon that takes second place is certainly the blunt instrument: the weapon used in *What Ever Happened to Baby Jane?*;

Fire is a weapon in *Pretty Poison* and *How Awful About Allan*, both starring Anthony Perkins.

The house is an iconic location for violence, whether its architectural style is (1) American Gothic in *Psycho*, (2) Southern plantation in *Hush...Hush, Sweet Charlotte*, (3) California eclectic in *Lady in a Cage*, or (4) Kansas contemporary in *In Cold Blood*. The message is clear: violence is coming soon to your house, too.

Hush...Hush, Sweet Charlotte; and others. Other recurring weapons include fire (in *Pyro*, *What Ever Happened to Aunt Alice?*, *Pretty Poison*, and *Who Slew Auntie Roo?*), and, of course, the occasional gun. However, it is interesting to note that the gun is most important in films like *Targets*, which directly and very specifically reflect the fear of unexpected and matter-of-fact violence.

The second group of icons are the locations, and it is obvious that the locations in these films often work as metaphors. The most dominant location is, of course, the house. The house is always something frightening, something that is descended from the haunted-house film, but whose terrors are always specifically real rather than mystical. It is the house that contains the dead Mrs. Bates in *Psycho*, the memorabilia in *What Ever Happened to Baby Jane?*, and the suggestion of a once-thriving South in *Hush...Hush, Sweet Charlotte*. It is the house in films from *Games* to *The Mad Room* to *Who Slew Auntie Roo?* that reflects the insanity so central to the story. Usually the house is a dead thing, containing memories, corpses, or reminders of an old way of life; the horror usually arises because, while the times change, the house and its occupants do not—such as in *Baby Jane*, *Sweet Charlotte*, *Auntie Roo*, and *Psycho*. There seem to be three particular locations within the house that take on individual importance: the stairway, the bathroom, and the basement. First of all, the images in these films of stairways cannot be overemphasized. In *Psycho*, the detective is killed on the stairway. In *Baby Jane*, two of the most important scenes take place there: Blanche trying to get to the telephone, and Baby Jane killing the maid. In *The Psychopath*, the villainess falls down the stairs and is killed. In *Sweet Charlotte*, Agnes Moorehead's Velma is killed by cousin Miriam and falls down a snakelike staircase; later, as Charlotte

In the horror-of-personality film, stairways are expressive, ominous, and fraught with danger: (1) one of the earliest stairways, from 1919's *The Cabinet of Dr. Caligari*; (2) the spiral staircase in *Hush...Hush, Sweet Charlotte*, which unwinds like a snake; (3) the exterior stairs that Olivia de Havilland crawls down in *Lady in a Cage*; and (4) the zigzag stairway that creates a no-man's land between the separate realms of Julie Harris and Anthony Perkins in *How Awful About Allan*.

tries to get to her room, she is finally driven crazy as she crawls down the stairway backwards (giving Bette Davis the opportunity to chew the scenery in spectacular, melodramatic form). And in *What's the Matter with Helen?*, the outside rickety stairway works as a focal point of the horror. There is a sense in which the stairway functions as a gateway between two separate domains. In *Baby Jane*, it takes us from the crazy domain of Bette Davis' Baby Jane to what seems the more reasonable domain of Joan Crawford's Blanche. In *What's the Matter with Helen?* it works the same way. In fact, there is a particularly horrifying scene in *Helen* in which the sane Debbie Reynolds, as Adelle, comes down the stairway into the domain of the mad Shelley Winters, as Helen, and discovers the butchered rabbits. In this film, the stairway separates the domains: mad from sane. In some of the other films, especially *Sweet Charlotte*, the use of the stairway is more complicated; for instance, although it would seem that the mad domain would be the upstairs room of Charlotte, all the crazy goings-on take place on the first floor: the supposedly sane domain. The end of *Sweet Charlotte*, with the revelation that cousin Miriam is really a villainess and that Charlotte is, for all her problems, remarkably sane, makes it clear why the "mad portion" of the film never took place in Charlotte's upstairs domain, but rather in Miriam's — with the climaxes taking place on the stairway. Although complicated, the stairway remains a tenuous gateway, a gateway that when crossed over is always terrifying and, for someone, usually fatal.

The stairway is a dangerous location where people die: (1) Martin Balsam as Arbogast in *Psycho*; (2) Agnes Moorehead as Velma in *Hush...Hush, Sweet Charlotte*; (3) and (4) Beverly Garland as the mother in *Pretty Poison*— shown shot, and then fallen in a heap; and (5) Allen Pinson as the mysterious caller in *What's the Matter with Helen?*

The two other locations in the house that are particularly important are the bathroom and the basement. The bathroom's importance is easy to understand: it is the room that is the most personal, that is used to cleanse the body, to make it pure. Hence, whenever violence takes place in this room, it is particularly obscene and upsetting. There is the bathtub scene in *Diabolique*; the famous shower murder in *Psycho*; the orgy in *Lady in a Cage*; the image of a vulnerable Glynis Johns in a bathtub in the 1962 remake of *The Cabinet of Caligari*; Samantha Eggar as the kidnapping victim being tied in the bathtub in *The Collector*; and the horrible "drowning in a bathtub" scene in *The Nanny*. The recurring cellar image is probably related to the womb and/or darkness. Thus we have the irony of Norman Bates putting his mother in the womb of the house in *Psycho*, or of the Tallulah Bankhead character tending to her little underground dungeon in *Die! Die! My Darling!* Perhaps the best example, one that clearly unites the idea of the cellar with a perverse sexuality, is that of *The Collector,* in which Terence Stamp plays a sexually off-kilter kidnapper who imprisons a young woman in a little underground apartment. Aside from the house, the other main location that continually appears is the mental institution — a location whose literalness needs no explanation. Institutions appear in *Maniac, Strait-Jacket, The Nanny, Shock Treatment, Screaming Mimi, The Cabinet of Caligari, Nightmare,* and *Pretty Poison.*

The last group of icons that appears with regularity are the identity symbols. These are the many objects that reflect on the characters' identity and (in)sanity. For instance,

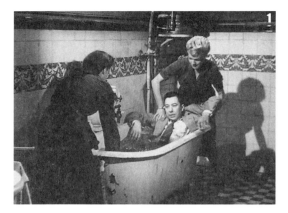

The bathtub, where we are naked and vulnerable, is also a violent location: (1) Vera Clouzot and Simone Signoret drowning Paul Meurisse in *Diabolique*; (2) Samantha Eggar tied hostage in *The Collector*; (3) the bludgeoned John Fraser being submerged by the psychotic Catherine Deneuve in *Repulsion*; and (4) Angharad Aubrey about to be drowned in *The Nanny*.

there are the dolls and/or puppets that are in *Baby Jane*, *Bunny Lake Is Missing*, and *The Psychopath*. There are the photographs and paintings in *Baby Jane*, *Sweet Charlotte*, *Repulsion*, *What's the Matter with Helen?* and *Die! Die! My Darling!*; the movie screen and the camera in *Baby Jane*, *Sweet Charlotte*, *What's the Matter with Helen?*, and *Peeping Tom*; the recurring windows in all the films; the statues in *Screaming Mimi* and *Games*; and the birds in *Psycho*, the parakeet and rat in *Baby Jane*, and the rabbits in *Helen*. The question

Voyeurism in the horror film: (1) The killer Carl Boehm literally and symbolically rails against the movie screen which symbolizes his murderous compulsions in *Peeping Tom*; yet, as voyeurs to the spectacle of *his* murders, are we similarly disturbed by *our* relationship to the screen? (2) We are more like the voyeuristic photographers in *Hush...Hush, Sweet Charlotte*, only too happy to ambush Bette Davis who recoils in horror at the exploitation of her image.

Ubiquitous identity symbols populate the horror-of-personality film. (1) In *Psycho*, Anthony Perkins' Norman Bates is juxtaposed with the image of a bird, just after he kills Marion Crane, whose name is a kind of bird. (2) In *Homicidal*, a little boy (or is it a little girl dressed like a boy?) is juxtaposed with a doll. (3) In *What Ever Happened to Baby Jane?*, the young Baby Jane is juxtaposed with a creepy Baby Jane doll. (4) In *Strait-Jacket*, the old Joan Crawford must come face-to-face with the violent legacy of her past, as represented by a statue of the young Crawford, and (5) by a Crawford mask that looks like a severed head. And (6) in *What's the Matter with Helen?*, a troubled Debbie Reynolds is juxtaposed with a cutout that looks permanently cheerful, untouched by trouble.

of identity and sanity is presented especially succinctly in *Sweet Charlotte*: When Charlotte opens the door in the dark and the photographer rudely takes her picture, she recoils, not only because of the shock, but because of the realization of what her identity really is. At the end of the film, a photographer again asks for her picture, but this time she smiles, quite able to accept her identity now that her sanity is almost intact and the guilt has been lifted from her shoulders. In *Baby Jane*, the crushed doll head works as a marvelous symbol for Baby Jane's sanity. And in the same film, the scream that Baby Jane/Bette Davis

Identity symbols generally comment obliquely: (1) in *The Boston Strangler*, naked mannequins are metaphor for women as interchangeable and dispensable; (2) in *The Collector*, butterflies are metaphor for women as pretty creatures to be trapped by men; (3) in *Repulsion*, old potatoes on the counter are metaphor for sex organs and their dark mystery.

gives out after seeing herself in the mirror is truly heartrending. The discrepancy between self-concept and image, or ideal and reality, is further illustrated by the shot in *Baby Jane* when the painting of a young Blanche is juxtaposed over the Blanche/Joan Crawford that looks like a corpse. Another striking category of identity symbols are the mirrors which are ubiquitous in these films, from *Psycho* and *Sweet Charlotte* to *Repulsion* and *The Boston Strangler*— mirrors which often offer multiple reflections which suggest fractures in personality. And finally, among the weirdest iconography in all of film genre are the recurring close-ups in these horror-of-personality films of a single eye, images which inherently suggest both extraordinary intimacy

and lack of balance. Can there be any other group of movies in which identity symbols recur so consistently? This concern with identity nicely reflects the often-heard sixties' question: "Who am I?" It is this genre's answer to this question that is particularly disturbing.

Multiple mirror reflections suggest the inherent schizophrenic nature of personality: (1) Vera Miles in *Psycho*, (2) Debbie Reynolds and Shelley Winters in *What's the Matter with Helen?*, and (3) Susannah York in *Images*.

Mirror images in horror films can serve a variety of aesthetic effects: (1) create a dazzling depth (*The Cabinet of Caligari*, a remake); (2) suggest duality and schizophrenia (*The Boston Strangler*); (3) show imbalance and dislocation (*The Boston Strangler*); (4) imply a narcissistic homoeroticism (*In Cold Blood*); (5) predict a future: "Your day ends..." (*In Cold Blood*); and (6) express a distorted reality (*Repulsion*).

Ironically, just as the various concerns of the fifties and sixties seemed to end the classic horror film, the spreading concern with and fear of the possible innate insanity and violence in man appeared to be headed toward eradicating the clear distinctions between the horror-of-personality films like *Targets* and what would seem to be nonhorror "prestige" films like *The Boston Strangler, 10 Rillington Place, In Cold Blood, Deliverance, The Wild Bunch, Straw Dogs, A Clockwork Orange,* and *Dirty Harry.* Horror films have always reflected our deepest anxieties about ourselves. In a time where life, or at least our awareness of it, seems to be increasingly horrible, it is most understandable that elements from the horror-of-personality films (violence, insanity) are now being fed into the mainstream. No longer are horror films (if ever they really were) escapist fare for children. Although films such as *Psycho, What Ever Happened to Baby Jane?, Play Misty for Me, What's the Matter with Helen?,* and *Hush...Hush, Sweet Charlotte* have been previously dismissed or ridiculed as shocking, gory, silly, excessive, and violent, one hopes that critics will realize that the "strict"

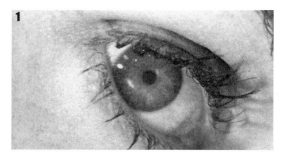

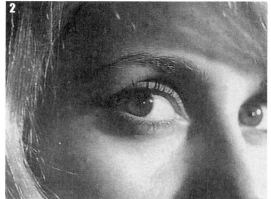

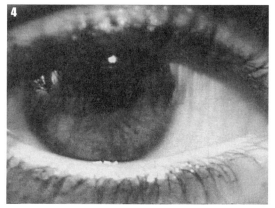

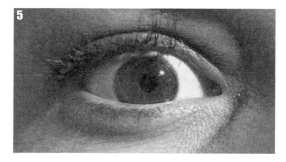

One of the strangest recurring icons of the horror-of-personality film is the close-up of a single eye — voyeuristic, disturbed, murderous — sometimes accompanied by a probing camera movement. Here are the eyes of (1) Janet Leigh in *Psycho*, (2) Catherine Deneuve in *Repulsion*, 3) Carl Boehm in *Peeping Tom*, (4) Deneuve again in *Repulsion*, (5) Jennifer Salt in *Sisters*, and (6) Anthony Perkins in *How Awful About Allan*.

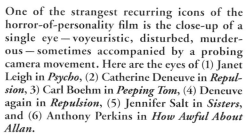

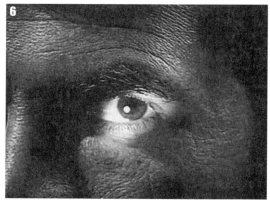

horror-of-personality films can, through considerations of genre, show as much about our society and be as artistic a statement on man's nature as films like *Straw Dogs* and *A Clockwork Orange*— works that largely because of their *auteur* considerations have already been accepted as worthy of study.

2 — The Horror of Armageddon

"Watch the skies..."
— The warning in the Howard Hawks/Christian Nyby
horror film, *The Thing from Another World*

"Mitch, this isn't usual, is it?"
— Tippi Hedren as Melanie Daniels in *The Birds*
asking about the murderous bird attacks

"I will not capitulate!"
— Bérenger's last words in Eugène Ionesco's play *Rhinoceros*

"Lady, it's the end of the world!"
— Bum in *The Birds*

If the horror-of-personality films are both a clear reflection of the fears of the sixties and yet a departure from the linear development of the horror film in the fifties, the second new subgenre of horror film, which I call the horror of Armageddon, continues the linear development of the horror film from the science-fiction horror of the fifties into a

This little girl in *Them!*, from 1954, was one of the first cinematic characters to be horrified by visions of Armageddon.

55

more pure horror film which deals, nevertheless, with most of the same issues and ideas as its precursors. The archetypal horror-of-Armageddon film is Alfred Hitchcock's *The Birds*; in this subgenre, the world is constantly being threatened with extinction, usually by non-human, unindividualized creatures such as birds, bats, bees, frogs, snakes, rabbits, ants, or plants. Although the nucleus of the horror-of-Armageddon subgenre is distinct, the outer reaches of the subgenre are downright fuzzy; indeed, the horror of Armageddon includes in its periphery films as disparate as *Yog—Monster from Space* (Japan, 1970), *The War Game* (Great Britain, 1965), and *They Shoot Horses, Don't They?* (USA, 1969). Before going into a detailed discussion of the horror-of-Armageddon films, it is first important to understand exactly what these films drew upon and from where they descended.

The monsters of the thirties and forties horror film gave way in the fifties to a horror that was almost united with science fiction. Perhaps the two archetypal horror films of the fifties were *The Thing from Another World*, directed by Christian Nyby in 1951 (with some of the direction often credited to Howard Hawks), and *Five*, directed by Arch Oboler in the same year. Each film dealt specifically with a major horror science-fiction theme: *The Thing* with the idea that there exists life on other planets that could threaten life on earth; and *Five* with the idea that the earth could be virtually destroyed by the atomic bomb and subsequent radiation. Thus, both horror films dealt with the unearthly: *The Thing* with its creature from outer space, and *Five* with its re-creation of an earth stripped of those things such as flora, fauna, and civilization, which normally make up the operative iconography of "earthliness." In *The Thing*, the outer-space creature was something to be feared: a monster in the best horror tradition. Note how in *The Day the Earth Stood Still*, directed by Robert Wise in the same year, the civilized amiability of the superiority of Michael Rennie's outer-space creature turns that film into strict unhorrific science fiction. Like so many of the fifties horror films, *The Thing* ended with the admonition that we should watch the skies; and, although I'm sure Christian Nyby didn't mean for us to watch the skies for birds, when *The Birds* came in 1963, the emotional effect was similar. In a malevolent universe, one is not allowed to be complacent; one of the strongest images in *The Birds*, largely derived from the same fear as in *The Thing* and other fifties films, is that of the little girls looking tearfully up to the skies after the birds have mysteriously attacked them and then disappeared. *The Thing*, like *The Birds* and rats and rabbits to come, is something mysterious

Although the title credit font suggests exploitative sensation, ***The Thing from Another World*** was a remarkably sober Howard Hawks–produced drama of military scientists confronting an alien (James Arness), who makes his sudden, first appearance in this foreboding silhouette.

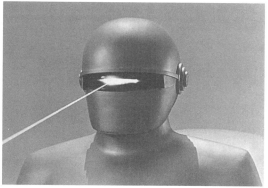

In the fifties, the television replaced the fireplace as the center of the American home, but in addition to bringing us warmth and comforting entertainment, it brought bad news and new fears. With TV came technologies of destruction, as demonstrated by the ray-gun eyes of the robot in *The Day the Earth Stood Still*. Will the American suburban family survive?

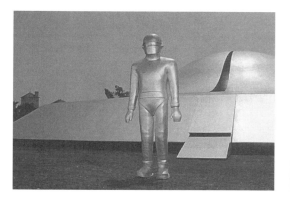

In *The Day the Earth Stood Still*, parallel frames show the outer space robot exhibiting the same unnatural calm as the alien played by Michael Rennie, who is shown in an expressive silhouette as he visits a suburban home to decide whether the earth should be destroyed.

and inexplicable. *The Thing* does not violate our civilization's rules of conduct or the universe's natural order; it merely conducts itself independently of these things — and therein lies the horror.

The mythic patterns of *Five* are by now very familiar to us: with the world destroyed by the atomic bomb and its radiation, it is now up to a nucleus of individuals to somehow continue civilization even if (and this is the overfamiliar part) there is only one truly desirable female — which, of course, the fifties morality would not allow the men to share. The desirable female is often the daughter of the scientist figure, who, in the aftermath of the atomic fallout, may rightly and skeptically be viewed as a defeated, rumpled figure. Inevitably, the scientist's authority is gradually eroded by the villain's quest for power. The villain's secondary quest is generally the seduction of the "innocent," desirable female. The hero figure is usually young, attractive, thoughtful, very physical, and eager to protect the heroine. The archetypal atomic-survival film often ends with only the hero and heroine alive: as Adam and Eve figures ejected from the Garden of Civilization and having to cope not with the guilt of the Original Sin, but with the guilt of the Ultimate Sin: the destruc-

The Day the Earth Stood Still presents archetypes of fifties science-fiction horror: the scientist, the desirable female, and the alien — played by (1) Sam Jaffe, (2) Patricia Neal, and (3) Michael Rennie.

tion of virtually all human life on the earth; their only expiation is in trying to repopulate and renew the civilization on their own. Note that, in an important sense, the horror science-fiction movie is very close to the Frankenstein story, with the atomic bomb representing the monster. Are there some things into which man must not delve? In *Five* and the other atomic-survival films —

The World, the Flesh, and the Devil (1959), *Panic in Year Zero!* (1962), and *The Last Man on Earth* (1964)— the atomic Frankenstein has created its havoc, destroying itself, often its creators, and all civilization. The mad scientist is shown to be, in a quite complex sense, sociologically and humanistically mad. But now that there is nothing left, what next? These movies start where the Frankenstein movies leave off. And even survival in this post-atomic netherworld is no easy task, because the survivors' safe little area is often surrounded by hostile mutants anxious to attack and kill for no reason other than that their existential purpose is to attack and kill. Thus in this pattern of nonhuman, unindividualized creatures attacking, we already have a major element of the horror of Armageddon.

The word "Armageddon" comes, of course, from the Bible, and is the name of the place where the last battle between the forces of good and evil is to take place. I use the term not because of its connotations of good and evil (for in this genre what is good is often intermingled with what is evil), but because these films always deal with a struggle that is obviously ultimate, mythical, and soul rending. The final bird attack in *The Birds* transcends itself; these birds are not merely birds, they are a metaphor for existential struggle and horror. If every bird in the last frame of that film were to disappear, the horror would remain; it is the knowledge that the birds are "out there" that is horrifying. The term Armageddon also seems relevant because there seems to be a strong relationship between these films and many of the stories in the Bible — for instance, the many plagues sent out to express the wrath of God; or even more dramatically, the most archetypal destruction story in the Bible: the flood. Take God away from the flood, and you have a true horror-of-Armageddon

In its haunting opening, the 1964 horror film *The Last Man on Earth*, starring Vincent Price, evokes Michelangelo Antonioni's 1962 masterpiece *L'eclisse*. In both, the same modernist building, shaped like an atomic cloud, looms ominously over widescreen landscapes which suggest alienation and loneliness. Only the last image here (at left) is from *L'eclisse*, starring Monica Vitti.

movie: Suddenly, out of the sky, it begins to rain. What was previously considered a normal aspect of nature turns abnormal when the rain starts acting unlike rain and refuses to stop. The rain attacks and kills everyone; only Noah and his family manage to survive the existential test by working hard to hold tightly onto their floating house. Ultimately, a rainbow appears as congratulations and in promise that the existential horror has come to an end. The pattern is similar to that in *The Birds*, only Hitchcock refuses us the satisfaction of the horror-releasing rainbow. The use of the word Armageddon also has a modern relevance: while ancient peoples could imagine an Armageddon caused by God, modern man can all too easily imagine an Armageddon caused not by God, but by man. Armageddon is the "war to end all wars," the ultimate confrontation: in short, the atomic bomb. If Hiroshima and Nagasaki marked the beginning of Armageddon, then *On the Beach* (1959) and *Dr. Strangelove* (1964)—which both essentially destroy the world—marked the fictional Armageddon's final paroxysm.

The three great themes of the horror of Armageddon are (1) proliferation, (2) besiegement, and (3) death. What makes

Frankie Avalon, Jean Hagen, Ray Milland, and Mary Mitchel try to escape from the *Panic in Year Zero!* Will the atomic bomb turn us into nomads who look to American cars and Eisenhower highways for deliverance?

In *On the Beach*, Stanley Kramer asked whether mankind could yet save itself from atomic destruction. Fred Astaire's lined face bears the weight of the cynical answer: no. All that will be left will be deserted monuments to our egos.

the formal enumeration of these themes interesting is that they are precisely the same great themes of the French-Rumanian playwright, Eugène Ionesco. Ionesco's "theatre of the absurd" has been widely acclaimed; the obvious similarity between Ionesco's *oeuvre* and the horror of Armageddon is testament to the relevance of both. Accepted by the intellectuals, Ionesco's plays, although they spring from an individual man with a specific background, deal nevertheless with the same fears and concerns that seem to spring unconsciously from the mass of minds of the thousands of collaborators who have worked on the horror of Armageddon. If Ionesco is an individual genius, it may be because he consciously was able to work out these themes years before they emerged as mass-media, popular-culture concerns. Ionesco:

> To discover the fundamental problem common to all mankind, I must ask myself what my fundamental problem is, what my ineradicable fear is. I am certain then to find the problems and fears of literally everyone. That is the true road into my own darkness, our darkness, which I try to bring to the light of day.[1]

Ionesco's three plays that most clearly correspond to the horror of Armageddon are *The New Tenant* [*Le Nouveau Locataire*] written in 1953, *Rhinoceros* in 1958, and *Killing Game* [*Jeux de Massacre*] in 1970, the latter of which bears an astounding resemblance to that horror-of-Armageddon masterpiece *Night of the Living Dead*.

Ionesco's one-act play *The New Tenant* may be his most successfully realized creation. It opens typically both for Ionesco and for the genre with a scene of overriding banality. A talkative *concierge* is preparing an absolutely empty room for her new tenant; she quite busily talks out the window, expending all sorts of energy while doing absolutely nothing. When the new tenant finally arrives, he is a dapper, quiet, thoughtful, introspective Everyman. He tells the *concierge* he will take the room, but refuses her help. As she leaves a bit irritated, the moving men start moving in the tenant's furniture; and the moving of the furniture makes up the bulk of the play. At first, the furniture comes in quite nicely, the new tenant giving the men directions and arranging the furniture according to his predetermined plan. Gradually the men begin moving the furniture in faster and faster until there is no space left in the room. The new tenant insists that all the furniture will fit, for he claims that he has carefully measured the room. Suddenly, the furniture starts moving in by itself without the aid of the movers — in short, behaving quite unlike furniture usually behaves! Furniture comes in from both sides, from the ceiling, through the windows. We hear reports

In the famous concluding sequence of *Dr. Strangelove*, the epitome of Armageddon horror, American generals annihilate the planet in a slow-motion ballet of surreal beauty. When director Stanley Kubrick announces "The End," he really means it.

In this sequence from *The Birds* in which Melanie Daniels (Tippi Hedren) is initially oblivious to the birds, Hitchcock employs Eugène Ionesco's themes of proliferation and besiegement.

The Birds starts with banality, moves gradually to the extraordinary, and inexorably to the horrific.

that the furniture is causing traffic jams outside as well; indeed, it has damned up the Seine River, besieging Paris as well as the little room. The play ends as the stage is completely filled, and the new tenant is literally buried in the furniture. As the moving men leave, the new tenant calmly asks them to turn off the light.

The similarity between *The New Tenant* and *The Birds* is obvious. Structurally they are the same: starting from banality, moving gradually to the extraordinary, and inexorably to the horrific. In both works the emphasis is on the besiegement of one area (the room, the house across Bodega Bay), although we hear reports that other areas are under similar attack. In both, the inexplicability of the proliferation creates the horror. The main differ-

In *Invasion of the Body Snatchers*, Becky Driscoll and "everyman" Miles Bennell (Dana Wynter and Kevin McCarthy) are besieged by pod people imposing robotized conformity; when Becky becomes a pod, Miles, horrified, is determined not to lose his identity.

ence between the two works, of course, is in that which is chosen as the metaphorical symbol of the existential forces (although it must be pointed out that both birds and furniture, which are generally considered homely and benign, are bizarre and original choices for monster-horror figures). Perhaps the most interesting thing about the horror of Armageddon is in the way the choice of the metaphorical, proliferating horror sharply affects the overall meaning and thrust of the work. "The world is too much with us," the furniture in *The New Tenant* seems to be saying; there is no escaping from civilization — wherever you go, it will follow you to torment and horrify you.

Ionesco's next horror-of-Armageddon, theatre-of-the-absurd play — and the one for which he is primarily known — is *Rhinoceros*. Like *The New Tenant*, *Rhinoceros* starts with a scene of banality: the Everyman figure Bérenger (the recurring character in Ionesco's work) is sitting outside a French café talking to a friend, while at the next table a logician babbles on endlessly, fracturing logic. Suddenly, a rhinoceros charges past them. There is some argument as to whether the rhinoceros had one horn or two, and discussion as to where it came from. Before long it becomes clear that rather than fight the stampeding rhinoceroses, everyone is instead gradually turning into rhinoceroses. As "rhinoceritis" reaches its frenzied peak, and Bérenger sees first his best friend turn into a rhinoceros before his eyes and then his girlfriend Daisy too (compare *Rhinoceros* in 1958 with Don Siegel's *Invasion of the Body Snatchers*, also in 1958, especially the parallels between Bérenger and Daisy to the characters played by Kevin McCarthy and Dana Wynter), Bérenger decides, albeit reluctantly, that "Je ne capitule pas!" ["I will not capitulate!"] Again the structural and thematic relationship between an intellectual play and the cinematic horror of Armageddon is clear. What is most interesting about *Rhinoceros* is its metaphorical component. Rhinoceroses, unlike birds and furniture, are already frightening. Although much has been written suggesting that the rhinoceroses are a metaphor for Nazis, this is really a limited reading — a reading so widely accepted that the play has come to be widely rejected as overrated and simplistic. (It didn't help that the 1973 film version, which badly Americanized the play into an anti–Nixon tract, was very cheaply produced and artistically misguided on almost every level.) The critics should instead discard their rather shortsighted evaluation. The play is not merely anti–Nazi, but anti–Communist; the symbol of the rhinoceros works not only as an image of any totalitarian state where free speech, human dignity, and individualism are prohibited, but also of social conformity of any kind. As such, rather than being a political and Brechtian *pièce à thèse*, *Rhinoceros* is a profoundly prohumanist work. Its emphasis is not on the evil of totalitarian thought as much as on the influence of this evil on

Bérenger, our Everyman. At the end of the play, the rhinoceroses have Bérenger in an almost schizophrenic state of longing to be beautifully green with horns, yet adamant about retaining his identity as an individual. The rhinoceroses are truly living dead, for in their conformity they have no identity; that last act of *Rhinoceros*, in which Bérenger watches helplessly as all his values — friendship, loyalty, and romantic love — are stripped away as everyone turns into dreaded rhinoceroses, is truly his *Night of the Living Dead*, a night as dark as that in any horror film. The image of the rhinoceros herd is a faceless unindividualized one; the mass of rhinoceroses instantly relates to the columns of faceless Nazis united behind Hitler, or, even more strongly, the masses of Chinese in Maoist China, united in their work suits, faceless in their sameness. There is something about this robotic sameness that relates to the mathematical precision of atomic technology. The end of the twentieth century's cataclysmic fifth decade marked (1) the defeat of Hitler and his Nazi masses; (2) the extending of the Communist Soviet empire into the masses of Western Europe; (3) the revolution of Mao and his masses, all reading the same Little Red Book; and (4) the scientific breakthrough in the atomic bombings of the masses at Hiroshima and Nagasaki. There is even a link between this unindividualized proliferation of totalitarian masses in the forties with the proliferation of a population explosion and eventual ecological concerns

in the sixties. Indeed, the remarkable capacity of the proliferated symbol to work as a metaphor for so many different concerns, which all relate nevertheless to the end of World War II, is one of the hallmarks of the horror of Armageddon.

Sandy Descher plays a catatonic girl traumatized by the horror she has seen. All she can utter, over and over, is the single word: "*Them!*"

While Ionesco created *The New Tenant* in 1953 and *Rhinoceros* in 1958, it took the movies a little longer before coming up with much the same formulas. Perhaps the first horror film that came close to the horror of Armageddon is *Them!* in 1954 with James Arness. A little girl is found almost out of her mind on the highway, muttering over and over the one word: "Them…"

Played by Peter Graves and Peggie Castle respectively, Dr. Wainwright is stunned and Audrey Aimes revolted by the giant grasshoppers in *Beginning of the End*. Adding to the film's charm are the cheesiest special effects, the monsters clearly normal grasshoppers moving across a photograph of a skyscraper.

Gradually, we discover that "them" refers to giant ant mutations that proceed to wreak havoc in Los Angeles. *Them!* is really a transitional film; largely science fiction, it uses the idea of atomic mutation to explain away the giant ants. Furthermore, the use of giant, rather than normal-sized ants, suggests a more specifically fantastic (and thus less existential) kind of horror. Nevertheless, the giant ants clearly relate more to *The Birds* than to the traditional King Kong type of monster. While King Kong, the animal monsters in *Dinosaurus!*, and even the giant spider in *The Lost World* clearly represent man's animalistic nature and his past, the ants in *Them!* are the beginning of a new tradition because they represent the most complex scientific leanings of man and his future. The irony is that after millions of years of advancement, man is now pursuing dangerous scientific ambitions which are bringing him back to the same point of horror from which he had been working those millions of years to escape. Out of the frying pan of King Kong we go into the fire of mutant grasshoppers, unable to hold onto that tentative balance between inhumane savagery and inhumane overcivilization.

Beginning of the End, in 1957, featuring James Arness' brother Peter Graves, covered much the same ground as *Them!*, only this time the metaphorical object of proliferation was gigantic grasshoppers. An extremely low-budget film entitled *The Killer Shrews* followed in 1959; although *The Killer Shrews* is one of those occasionally laughable horror films, it is most interesting to study. In this film, we again get the archetypal fifties pattern of characters: there is the logical scientist, the desirable girl, the coward who wants power, and the hero. The scientist has been experimenting with the genetic acceleration of little rats; to his amazement and ultimate stupefaction, what resulted were not superintelligent rats, but horrible killer shrews. The low-budget special effects are ludicrously inferior to the effects of later films like *The Birds*. The shrews appear to be rather docile dogs covered with tar and straw; an occasional insert of a stuffed, fanged head is edited in for good measure. Nevertheless, these creatures take on a rather adult, existential meaning. Almost the entire film takes place inside the house of the scientist as it is constantly besieged at night by the killer shrews. And this is only right, for it is in the night that we are the most susceptible to our fears. There are some very powerful scenes of people running crazily to get back into the house while the fanged shrews frenziedly chase them. Some of the scenes work powerfully despite their amateurish execution because they tie into a kind of universal childhood fear: the recurring primal dream of so many children of being chased by something scary. Invariably in these dreams, your feet are like lead, the house door is locked, you fumble with the key, you trip over the stoop, etc. For some reason, some of the very "worst" and most amateurish horror films constantly surprise us by tying into these fears so effortlessly. *The Killer Shrews* also contains one of the classic archetypal moments: the superlogical scientist who very calmly records his own responses to his imminent death so as to leave an official, properly scientific record. The unlikely climax of *The Killer Shrews* takes place when, after a final horrible night of besiegement by the shrews, the hero, heroine, and her father make their escape from the house by duckwalking in upside-down cans to the beach, where they are able to survive the night by immersing themselves in the water, which luckily stops the shrews, who do not swim. Even in such a crude film, the water works symbolically as a kind of river of life that simultaneously rebaptizes the characters in a more natural faith and repudiates the modern faithless science that created the shrews.

And next, in 1963, came the seminal film of the genre: Alfred Hitchcock's *The Birds*. Like Ionesco's plays, *The Birds* starts with a scene of banality: Melanie Daniels (played by Tippi Hedren) trying to play a rather pointless joke on Mitch Brenner (played by Rod Tay-

The Birds is often remembered as a "special-effects" film, which does this masterpiece a disservice. Emulating a silent-film pictorial style, Hitchcock is especially skillful at presenting expressive close-ups of his characters (played by Doreen Lang, Tippi Hedren, an uncredited extra, and Jessica Tandy) at moments of great vulnerability.

lor) by pretending to be an employee at a bird store. People who see the film only once remember in retrospect only the bird attacks; in actuality, most of the film is a rather clever comedy of manners, the bird attacks providing the *frissons* and the focus, but certainly not the film's nucleus. Just as the rhinoceroses in *Rhinoceros* may tend to obscure the fact that the play is about the character of Bérenger, the birds obscure the fact that *The Birds* is about its human characters and the importance of their relationships in existential terms. And the bird attacks are in some bizarre way comic: there are terrifying yet absurd images of an out-door children's party in which the children run from ... birds; an old woman suddenly hysterical because her farmhouse is being filled with sparrows; birds watching while a group of people are being kept virtually caged in a roadside inn. The relationship between comedy and horror in Hitchcock's films, as well as in Ionesco's plays, is often that of synthesis. (One thinks as far back as Hitchcock's *Sabotage*, where a soon-to-be-committed stabbing is juxtaposed with the animated cartoon "Who Killed Cock Robin?") There is something about Hitchcock's and Ionesco's type of comedy that is, if not more tragic than tragedy, certainly more pessimistic; for if classical tragedy deals overtly with the problems and pains of existence, comedy, although dealing with the same problems, tends to disguise these essentially disturbing, thematic concerns by emphasizing instead its invitation to laughter or amusement.

Hitchcock may have regarded *The Birds* as one elaborate joke constructed from the comic premise of reversing the traditional relationship between bird and man, but the joke is a dark one: can there be human dignity when a society woman, a farmer, and even innocent children can be attacked by birds at any moment? J. L. Styan's description of Ionesco's style works very well to describe Hitchcock's own style in *The Birds*:

He has a talent for presenting his characters ... as immobile puppets in a world that is alive and constantly threatening.... It is knock-about charade ... where *Grand Guignol* violence surrounds the unconscious victims, and the walls rock ironically round their doomed heads.... It is the method of classical comedy grown cruel and cold, and its satire grown hysterical.[2]

In *The Birds*, Hitchcock presents "a world that is alive and constantly threatening ... [a] knock-about charade...." So said critic J.L. Styan about Eugène Ionesco.

Although *The Birds* is visually a very bright film with the horror taking place in broad daylight, it is as thematically dark as *Psycho*, its possibly fruitless suggestion to "only connect" in order to make this malevolent universe bearable, disguised under layers of special-effects set pieces. There has been much discussion as to what, if anything, the attacks of the birds are supposed to represent; excellent and persuasive analysis has been provided by Robin Wood in his book *Hitchcock's Films*.

Certainly Hitchcock has gone a step beyond *Them!* and *The Killer Shrews*; the birds are not explained away through the device of a scientist whose genetic injections simply went out of control. The key to the puzzle lies in the café scene (compare with the café scene in *Rhinoceros* which serves the same purpose) in which Hitchcock has various characters volunteer their own explanations. The birds are a punishment from God; they mean the end of the world; they suggest that nature is getting even; they have come to criticize the attitudes of Melanie Daniels — all these explanations are suggested only to be rejected. Descended from the atomic-bomb age of anxiety, *The Birds* no longer represents the atomic bomb, but simply that existential anxiety; the birds themselves are the horror — the sickness, the death, the violence, the cruelty, the absurdity, the random trouble — that is at any moment capable of coming seemingly out of nowhere, whether created by man or sent by the malevolent universe as part of the very inexplicable nature of things. In short, *The Birds* works as a metaphor for the human condition. The brilliant ambiguous ending allows the viewers, through the substitution of their own view of life, to decide what will happen (just as they must in the final moments of *Rhinoceros*). Completely surrounded by birds, will Mitch's family and Melanie escape this death, or will they discover at the end of the road more birds which will peck them to pieces even more ferociously? When one considers that most horror films end happily (that is, Frankenstein and Dracula are, albeit temporarily, destroyed, or the giant grasshoppers are repelled), *The Birds*, along with *Psycho*, is one of the few horror films up to this time to which the question — "Does it have a happy ending?" — is unanswerable. Indeed, the final image of *The Birds* is among the film's most suspenseful even as the image clearly approaches total stasis. In this final moment, the birds hardly move (just as in *Psycho*'s final moments, Norman Bates refuses to "even bat

Total existential ambiguity in the surreal final tableau of *The Birds*: Is our impulse to "only connect" enough to save us and give life meaning?

Portrait of a woman who must be reminded of her identity: Suzanne Pleshette as the lonely school-teacher Annie Hayworth, who does not survive *The Birds*, her white picket fence — redolent with American values — offering no protection.

that fly"). It is this stasis that is so horrifyingly bleak. One again thinks of Ionesco's plays: the final scene in *The New Tenant* when the gentleman is completely buried in furniture and cannot move; the ambiguity in *Rhinoceros* of Bérenger's final "Je ne capitule pas!" when we truly do not know if he is going to survive as a human being; the final horrible tableau in *The Chairs* [*Les Chaises*] when the stage is completely covered with chairs and invisible people; or the last act of *The Killer* [*Tueur Sans Gages*] in which after two acts of madcap movement, the Everyman, Bérenger, finds the Killer and delivers a fifteen-page monologue on why the Killer should not kill, only to have the Killer chuckle, raise his knife, and step closer to Bérenger who lowers his head and asks, "My God ... what can we do ... what can we do..." as the curtain swiftly descends — preventing the audience from seeing the ulti-mate murderous outcome. In *The Birds*, we can try to love one another and to establish relationships, but whether our efforts will accomplish anything is unclear. Though "the bridge is love, the only survival, and the only meaning" — to quote Thornton Wilder's *The Bridge Over San Luis Rey* — will that bridge nevertheless break and precipitate its travelers into the gulf below?

If there is a gulf below, exactly what is it that is above? In *The Birds*, the object of pro-liferation is only slightly more important than the object of besiegement; that is, the farm-house. In *The Killer Shrews*, the house that was besieged was strangely devoid of any meaning: at one point a character tried ineffectually to escape the shrews by going into the cellar (the womb), but the house had no distinctive definition apart from "the world of sci-ence." In *The Birds*, the house is much more important. The first inclination of the char-acters is not to escape from the house, but to cling to it; the home is quite clearly a place of comfort and safety. The school is not safe (for it has big windows); the town of Bodega Bay — and hence civilization — is not safe (for the birds absolutely control it); the character of the schoolteacher (played by Suzanne Pleshette) is killed when she goes outside the house; and Mitch's little sister is saved because the schoolteacher is successful in pushing her inside the house. Although the widower neighbor is killed in his house, he is attacked while asleep, and there is the clear sense of the house being raped. In the horror-of-personality films, the house was inevitably a dark, dead place of memories, a place of corruption, secrets, and unhealthy twists. The house in much of the horror of Armageddon, when it appears, works

Opposite: Those who are alone are especially vulnerable to *The Birds*: the montage sequence in which broken coffee cups lead the lonely Lydia (Jessica Tandy) to the dead body of her widowed neighbor is one of Hitchcock's most expressive achievements.

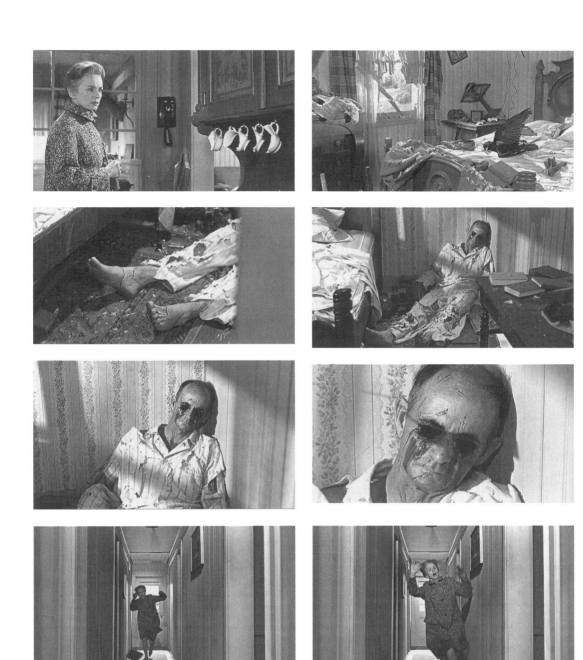

differently: it is a symbol of family life, a symbol of the materialism that allows us to organize our lives (Mitch's mother, movingly played by Jessica Tandy, patiently fooling with her coffee cups), even a symbol of self-expression or of folk culture (Melanie Daniels playing the piano amidst the house's distinctive furnishings). The house is never so safe as when the fireplace is lit, creating a mythic Hestia-warmth within the house and prohibiting the birds from attacking down the chimney. Although as a symbol, the house is something to hold onto, it is eventually only a symbol: it be given up when the birds threaten to destroy it. Family culture and family must inevitably be carried out and continued, not by the house, but by the characters who truly feel for each other and can carry those feelings with them wherever they go, building on the past only as a foundation for some future they hope will be fulfilled.

Contemporary to *The Birds* in 1963, the horror-of-Armageddon film *The Day of the Triffids* was an ingenious film based on the novel by John Wyndham. In this film, a meteor shower causes the proliferation of triffids, which are voracious, self-locomoted, man-eating plants. Ultimately there is a happy ending as the triffids are killed by seawater. (The pattern here harkens back to *The War of the Worlds*, where the Martians are killed not by the men who are fighting them, but by the "natural" bacteria of the earth.) Yet even in *The Day of the Triffids*, the big scene is when an army of triffids besieges a farmlike house. Other films of this period include *The Deadly Bees* in 1967, which used bees as the object of proliferation, and *Eye of the Cat* in 1969, which used cats. In addition to starring Eleanor Parker in her second wheelchair (the first was in *The Man with the Golden Arm*), *Eye of the Cat* featured the deservedly classic (though certainly erroneous) observation that "French directors have gone from *Marienbad* to worse."

Meanwhile, in 1970, Jacques Demy was working on a musical remake of that rat extravaganza, *The Pied Piper*, starring Donovan as the piper. Demy was sending his rushes back to the Hollywood studio, but the executives kept sending them back to him with the comment: "Yes, very nice, but do you have to show all those rats? They're really nasty, distasteful, little things. Perhaps you can leave them out of the story somehow." Demy reportedly was still continuing his work, putting aside the constant memos to cut down on the rats, when he suddenly started getting memos saying: "More rats. We like the rats. Give us more close-ups of the rats."

The sudden turnabout of the sponsoring studio was of course the result of the film that proved rats were big box-office, the film that reactivated the genre in 1971 with a vengeance: *Willard*. An all-time moneymaker, *Willard* is the story of a lonely young man (played by Bruce Davison) who makes friends with a pack of rats. When Willard's mother dies and the villain of the piece (played by Ernest Borgnine) threatens to foreclose on the mortgage, Willard sends his rats into action: they kill the villain. Interestingly, the house in *Willard* is used more like the house in *Psycho*—as a kind of sick repository, a tomb to the past. Although it is clear that the villain's motives in wanting the house are entirely self-serving, it is just as clear that Willard alone cannot manage the house on his limited finances, and would be truly better off both financially and mentally were he to get rid of the house. But Willard is unlike the typical horror-of-Armageddon protagonist; like Norman Bates in *Psycho*, he is mentally disturbed. Eventually Willard tries to make some sort of human contact with the beautiful heroine (played by Sondra Locke), but the rats get in the way. Making her leave the house, Willard realizes that he has created a monster and must get rid of his rats. At this point the irony becomes clear: Willard is no longer master of his rats; rather, Ben, the biggest rat, has somehow managed to acquire both a superior intelligence and complete control of the other rats. Before Willard is able to complete his extermination plan, the rats attack and kill him, while their leader Ben watches. The ending is surprisingly bleak, allowing Ben and the rats to survive so they can appear in their own sequel *Ben*, the following year. The fear of rats, notoriously the scavengers and garbage pickers of the animal world, seems to be almost universal. If *Willard* and *Ben* are not the overwhelmingly disturbing works that *The Birds* and *The New Tenant* seem to be, it may be because we are more delighted and aesthetically moved by the awesome, ironic creation of a horrific world composed of traditionally harmless birds or furniture than by the less-awesome creation of a horrific world composed of traditionally frightening rats.

As the box office went wild over rats, the genre flourished. The next notable film in the genre was *Night of the Lepus* (in 1972), in which huge rabbits ravage a countryside. *Night of the Lepus* tried to take advantage of many of the same elements as *The Birds*, in that the rabbit is essentially a loveable creature, although the *Lepus* creators made the rabbits fifteen feet tall (and the mouth of a gigantic rabbit is peculiarly unnerving). Just as in *The Birds*, where birds in cages are ironically juxtaposed later with birds attacking people in their own "cages," *Night of the Lepus* opens with documentary scenes of men killing rabbits, then builds gradually to a climax where giant rabbits kill men. If there is throughout the film the feeling nevertheless that a bunny bounding in slow motion is silly rather than horrifying, it must be because of the rather poor special effects. The most interesting thing about *Night of the Lepus*, however, is the way the object of proliferation is used to tie into a new fear: an unbalanced ecology. Much is made of the fact that ecological balance is a very fragile thing. The movie tells us that when the Australian farmers tried to get rid of their excess rabbits by using poison, the poison killed birds as well as the rabbits, and the killing of the birds in turn caused a plague of grasshoppers, which was just as destructive as the rabbits. Janet Leigh and Stuart Whitman play the scientists who are trying to get rid of the rabbits safely, but even these scientists are not able to do the job without upsetting the ecological balance. The crazily disruptive rabbits, obviously a symbol of fertility, also seem to work as a metaphor for our potential for overpopulation, or for our ever-expanding consumption of ecological resources. Thus, *Night of the Lepus* depicts another view of the end of the world — an end not by atomic bombs, but by ecological madness and environmental irresponsibility.

Much the same is suggested by 1972's *Frogs*, starring Ray Milland as the ultimate victim. In this film, the cast members are gradually killed by a variety of animals in this mutated ecological niche: there is asphyxiation by smart lizards, bites from poisonous rattlesnakes, attacks from crocodiles and alligators, electric shocks from eels, a successful snapping by a hungry sea turtle, and a heart attack induced by frogs who subsequently eat their victim. Again the structure is similar to that of *The Birds*, with all the action taking place around one main house. When, at the climax, the hero, heroine, and children escape the house and find safety, they are picked up by a passing motorist whose son just happens to have a pet frog. The reference is clearly to the lovebirds in *The Birds* that accompany the Brenner family's escape from Bodega Bay. The movie ends rather incongruously, in the best tradition of American International, with a cartoon frog hopping across the screen and gulping down a human hand. (Apparently, Ray Milland is difficult to digest.)

Perhaps the most remarkable film in this series was the documentary, *The Hellstrom Chronicle*, produced by David Wolper in 1971. The documentary opens with an explosion and beautiful images: water droplets, cell formations, the creation of life. The narrator then tells us that insects, the first to be created, will be the last to survive. Nils Hellstrom, the fictional scientist in this film (played by actor Lawrence Pressman), is constantly undercutting the dignity of mankind by placing our species at the mercy of the insects. One shot pans from bugs in the grass to two human lovers as Hellstrom tells us not to confuse size with importance. Insects, we are later told, can survive the atomic bomb and live in complete harmony with the environment. Only two kinds of creatures are increasing their numbers — man and insects — and in the battle between the two it is obvious who shall "inherit the earth." There is one beautiful, almost Peckinpah-like scene of black hamster ants fighting red ants. Another scene shows caterpillars rapidly eating a plant while on the soundtrack we hear the most horrible, augmented chewing sounds. Although it is true that insects have no intelligence, we are reminded that they also have no stupidity; purely instinctual, able to carry on doing only that which has been programmed into them, the insects are compared to a perfectly constructed computer. One of the film's ultimate images is that of a mile-long column of driver ants in Kenya. Discussed in military terms, the ants remind one of Nazis, or at least an insect perversion of *Triumph of the Will*. Truly a horror-of-Armageddon film, *The Hellstrom Chronicle* is one of the genre's best. The film has a fascinating documentary form: images of unspeakable beauty that are nevertheless truly horrible; the same generic interest in proliferation, besiegement, science, and uniformity; and a strong sense of an ultimate struggle which will climax with the overthrow of man.

Certainly the bleakest horror-of-Armageddon film, among the two or three masterworks of the sixties, is that low-budget horror film released in 1968, *Night of the Living Dead*. As a film it has been much maligned: ignored by many critics, crucified by others — particularly when it was first released. *Variety*'s review of the film was fairly typical of *Night of the Living Dead*'s initial reception. Almost hysterically, the usually even-handed *Variety* claimed:

> In a mere 90 minutes, this horror film (pun intended) casts serious aspersions on the integrity and social responsibility of its Pittsburgh-based makers, distributor Walter Reade, the film industry as a whole, and exhibitors who book the picture, as well as raising doubts about the future of the regional cinema movement and about the moral health of filmgoers who cheerfully opt for this unrelieved orgy of sadism.... Russo's screenplay is a model of verbal banality and suggests a total antipathy for his characters ... if not for all humanity.

The casual opening images of *Night of the Living Dead* hardly suggest the huge impact this low-budget, black-and-white film would have on American horror. Yet George A. Romero must have known his political allegory would be attacked for being obscene and un–American — hence his tongue-in-cheek juxtaposition of his own credit with the flag.

The film originally got in trouble when it was attacked by the *Reader's Digest* for scaring children. In actuality, the attack saved the movie from oblivion and obscurity by elevating it to a position of some notoriety. Nevertheless, although the film has become a cult masterpiece, there still remains the inclination that somehow it is not quite right for it to be so lavishly honored; it is, after all, just a horror film, and a rather cheaply made, often amateurish, and exploitative one at that. It is useful here to discuss Ionesco's 1970 play *Jeux de Massacre*, translated alternately as *Killing Game* or *Here Comes a Chopper*, not only because Ionesco himself and the theatre of the absurd seem so instrumentally relevant to this genre, but because *Killing Game* specifically bears resemblances to *Night of the Living Dead*, and these resemblances help to illuminate its horror film companion as well as promote *Night of the Living Dead*'s "acceptability."

Alongside Ionesco's great themes of proliferation and besiegement is the theme of death. For the first time for Ionesco, the themes intermingle directly: *Killing Game* is about the proliferation of death. To quote the play itself:

> The scene is the town square. Neither a modern nor an ancient town. This town should have no particular character.... There are plenty of people about. They look neither gay nor sad. They have either been or are just going shopping.

This town of no character is suddenly hit by the plague. What follows is a series of scenes with unrelated characters who come on stage, say their lines, and then die of the plague. A housewife says: "My husband told me most of these people have no particular morals. That's why they die. They live incoherent lives." But the good also die. Another man says: "The whole world has become a distant planet, impenetrable, made of steel, remote. Something completely strange and hostile. No communication. Cut off." The plague gets worse. In the middle of the play a character comes out, announces the intermission, and falls down dead; the stage is almost hilariously cluttered with bodies. The dignitary announces:

> Fellow citizens and strangers. An unknown scourge has been spreading through the town for some time now.... Suddenly, with no apparent cause, with no previous sign of illness, people have started dying in their houses, in the churches, at street corners, and in public places. They have started dying, can you imagine that?... Death is advancing by geometrical progression!

Night of the Living Dead effortlessly draws upon deep-seated fears of the bogeyman: the two powerful and aesthetic images here show the monster approaching inexorably.

Initially lauded as a goremaster, George A. Romero must be recognized as a master of composition. Note the artistry of his horror portraits: the hapless victim, passive and doomed (Judith O'Dea); and the monstrous ghoul, as unstoppable as death (Bill Heinzman).

The town is completely enclosed, besieged by Death, who appears metaphorically as a black-robed monk who, occasionally, silently walks across the stage. People lock themselves in their houses, trying to stave off death, but nothing does any good; the evil, the good, the young, the old, friends, enemies, lovers — everyone — dies. Suddenly and inexplicably, the plague stops. The people tentatively come out of their houses and begin to applaud and cheer their own victory over death, when just as suddenly the whole town catches on fire, and the survivors of the plague begin an ordeal even more terrible and hopeless than the one before.

Philosophically, *Night of the Living Dead* is just as nihilistic. Structurally, it works the same, although what proliferates in this film is not the principle of death, but the living dead: dead who arise to kill the living. Starting slowly, the living dead gradually increase their numbers by geometric progression, and when they are quite suddenly vanquished and the hero emerges from his besieged house, the horror of the living dead is replaced by another horror: the inhumanity of the living; the hero is killed anyway.

The film starts deceptively and almost comically. A car speeds down a road toward a corroded cemetery entrance sign. It is autumn, and the leaves are all dead upon the ground. We meet Johnny and Barbra who are visiting their father's grave — for their mother's sake. Barbra wishes that the flowers on the grave didn't have to die. There is distant thunder as Johnny makes fun of the church and then starts joking about Barbra's childhood "bogey-man" fears: "They're coming to get you ... Barbra ... they're coming to get you..." The more she tries to get him to stop the teasing, the more he continues, pointing at a very large man who appears to be slowly walking toward them. Instantaneously, the comic tone changes to spellbinding horror as the walking man reaches out and for no reason kills Johnny, and then starts inexorably chasing Barbra, her childhood fears suddenly confronting her in reality. She runs to the car and slams the door, but can't get the car started, while the man picks up a rock and begins smashing the car window to get in. The whole sequence is amazingly frightening, but Barbra does eventually manage to escape to a little farmhouse. (In these films, it's always a farmhouse.) She runs in hysterically to look for help and climbs a *Psycho*-like stairway only to find a horribly mutilated dead woman, which sends her into a catatonia she retains for the remainder of the film.

Inside the house she meets the hero of the film, Ben, a young black man. While the house is gradually surrounded by more and more of the creatures, Ben tells Barbra almost ritualistically of his encounters with the creatures. Barbra's account to Ben of her own experience is disjointed and inaccurate; she refuses to believe the truth that her brother is dead. After Ben puts a few of the creatures out of commission, the two of them begin boarding up the house, but Barbra brings only useless pieces of wood. When she takes the tablecloth, she folds it carefully, cradling it as if its homey materialism will give her strength — much like Mitch's mother and her coffee cups in *The Birds*. The radio announces that mysterious mass murder is taking place in the eastern third of the nation; we dolly in to a close-up of Barbra as the announcer says the killers appear to be eating the flesh of their victims.

Gradually, more people are discovered in the house, the most important of which is a rather mean, balding, "villain" named Harry, who has been hiding with his wife and injured daughter in the cellar. In the discussion of what to do, Harry is absolutely convinced that they should all lock themselves in the cellar and not come out; he gives a list of perfectly rational reasons to justify his position. For some reason, Ben disagrees, feeling that it is important for all the survivors in the house to work as a group and to stick together upstairs. Perhaps because Ben is so obviously the hero, we in the audience find ourselves taking his side, judging Harry to be a close-minded and selfish coward. The sentiment — "We'd all be a lot better off if we could do it together" — is persuasive, and there is a strong sense here of something allegorical in the black man urging cooperation: a kind of faith that liberalism will get us through. Yet all the personal confrontations are punctuated by images of the creatures sticking their fingers in through holes in the windows, always trying, like *The Birds*, to get in and kill. In the central scene of the film, we watch a news report on television which says that the mysterious creatures that have arisen to eat the living are actually dead. There is the fuzzy suggestion that the phenomenon may have something to do with an earthly satellite sent to Venus that was destroyed, but this is only suggested as one possible explanation that is not particularly persuasive. One of the newscasters interviews a posse to get more information; and consonant to our remarkable need to reduce everything to logical terms we can understand — terms that in this instance take the guise of crudely funny slogans — we discover that "Kill the brain and you kill the ghoul," and "Beat 'em or burn 'em, they go up pretty easy." The interviewer asks, "Are they slow moving?" "Yeah," is the answer, "They're dead." Although the sniveling Harry refuses to cooperate, the group under the leadership of Ben finally agrees that the thing to do is to try to get some gas for the truck so they can make their escape from the house. A young couple, Tom and Judy (who represent, perhaps a bit too obviously, "idealistic love"), volunteer to try to make it to the farm pump. Because of the living dead, however, the gas spills over the truck and is suddenly ignited as Tom and Judy are both killed in a scene that strongly resembles the scene in *The Birds* where the birds set the town on fire with a gas pump. Back in the house there is another confrontation between Ben — the black hero — and Harry — the white villain. While Ben is outside with the dead, Harry locks the door on him, claiming: "Two people are dead already on account of that guy" — a statement which is actually true, because it was Ben who instigated the escape attempt. Ben forces his way inside, however, and in a rage shoots Harry dead, taking Harry's body downstairs to the cellar with his little girl. Upstairs, Harry's wife is being strangled by a living dead, but she manages to escape. The film suddenly accelerates to an almost unbearable pace. Harry's wife runs downstairs and reacts in horror as she sees that her little girl has died, has come back to life as a living dead, and is now eating Harry, her father! The little girl suddenly turns, picks up a trowel, then repeatedly stabs her mother until she's dead. Upstairs, there is the sound of screams: the living dead are now

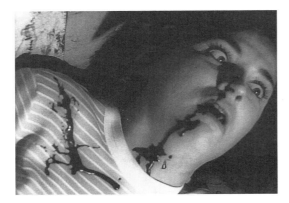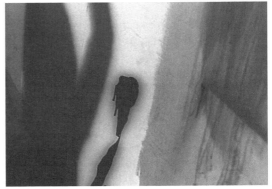

In *The Night of the Living Dead*'s final *Walpurgisnacht*, obscene violence is not only photographed graphically, but abstractly, like a modern-art painting.

beginning to overrun the house. Barbra's brother Johnny suddenly appears as a living dead and grabs his sister in order to kill and eat her: more incestuous cannibalism. The little girl then tries to kill the hero, Ben, who runs into the cellar, locks the door, and listens as upstairs the living dead have managed to take over the whole house. Downstairs, Harry comes to life as a living dead and is killed again by Ben. Harry's wife suddenly opens her eyes, and Ben shoots her. Unfortunately, no description of this scene can even begin to express its horror. The loud screams of the adult audience and the moral revulsion at the thought of a little girl eating her father and killing her mother are overwhelming. The climax is filled with morally unnerving violence, suggesting that there is no dignity to human life, that there are no values — only violence, death, and more horror. Even our expectations of traditional heroism are disturbed, for our hero is able to escape the living dead only by holing himself up in the cellar, the solution that Ben (at the cost of all the others' lives) and even we, as the audience, overtly rejected. In other words, Ben is able to survive the night only because the selfish pettiness of Harry has in some strange way been justified, and any faith in liberalism, communication, or human connection, has been refuted.

From this *Walpurgisnacht* we dissolve to a helicopter shot of the meadow area the next day. At first, what we see appears to be more of the living dead making their way across the countryside. A closer look reveals that they are the police "posse," the liberators slowly and methodically safeguarding the area by shooting in the head any of the living dead that remain. Yet for some reason, the appearance of the liberators is not as anxiety-relieving as we would like. Their crude humor ("Somebody had a cookout here, Vince...") is mildly disturbing, and they carry out their mission with such a plodding rhythm that they seem like zombies themselves. And indeed they are, for when our hero Ben hears them coming and runs jubilantly outside to rejoin a world that is once again back to normal, the men mistake him for a living dead and shoot him dead. The end credits are superimposed over still photos of Ben's dead body being taken away, thrown on a pile of corpses, and burned. Thus even without this one special night of the living dead, the world is nevertheless populated with its own living dead. The nihilism of *Night of the Living Dead*'s director George Romero is as pervasive as Ionesco's: nothing survives or is worthwhile — liberalism, brotherhood, family, love, integrity, faith, not even heroism. Certainly the bleakest horror film, devoid of even an iota of hope, *Night of the Living Dead* reflects the underlying hopelessness that marked the social upheavals, assassinations, and senseless violence of the sixties. And for Romero, this absolute hopelessness is the only and ultimate truth.

Perhaps the most distinctive and idiosyncratic variety of the horror of Armageddon was the Japanese cycle of horror films that started in the mid-fifties and continued through the sixties, almost all of them directed by the prolific Inoshirô [Ishirô] Honda. At first, this cycle of films may seem to be related more to the *King Kong* formula, with giant monsters wreaking havoc, but careful study reveals their relationship to the horror of Armageddon. First of all, the proliferation of creatures is not within a single film, but rather in serial proliferation. The series started with the monster *Godzilla* in 1956, added *Rodan*

In the original *Godzilla*, the destruction wreaked by the monster clearly evokes the firestorms following the atomic bombings of Hiroshima and Nagasaki.

later that same year (though released in the United States in 1957), *Mothra* in 1961, *Ghidrah* in 1964, and so on. The end-result of this fantastic series was the creation of a comprehensive popular-culture mythology. The use of the monster in these films is most telling; in the very early films the monsters were fear-inspiring creatures, and Godzilla would come out of the water in a rage, destroying Tokyo. Indeed, Tokyo is partially destroyed in almost every one of these films; and rightfully so, because this destruction is a ritualistic reenactment of the atomic bombings at Hiroshima and Nagasaki. Yet what is important to note is exactly *how* the atomic bomb is reenacted. Godzilla redefines the bomb in terms of overt animalistic, natural instincts, rather than in terms of some intellectual "humanity." It is one thing to have thousands of people killed because it has been very coolly decided by men that this mass destruction would ultimately be best for humanity; it is another thing to have thousands of people killed by a natural phenomenon like Godzilla. Thus Godzilla represents the atomic bomb in terms understandable and comforting to the masses. (Indeed, it is interesting to note that the 1956 *Godzilla, King of the Monsters!* is a virtual remake of

In *Rodan*, traditional images of Japan (such as a woman in a kimono) exist side-by-side with frightening modern images (the atomic bomb).

the 1953 Eugène Lourié film *The Beast from 20,000 Fathoms*, in which the blame for the monster is explicitly put on an atomic explosion.)

One of the most fanciful of the Japanese films was *Mothra*, made in 1961, but released in the United States in 1962. After H-bombing Infant Island, members of a Japanese expedition find a pair of foot-high twins (the Ito Sisters) and an egg. The twins are kidnapped to be exploited. As one character asks: "We live in the atomic age; are miracles of nature obsolete?" Eventually the egg on the island hatches, and a gigantic larva emerges. The larva then comes to Japan and spins a cocoon against the Tokyo power station. The city tries to get rid of the cocoon by using atomic heat rays, which instead hatch it. Then, from within the cocoon, there emerges the all-powerful Mothra — a beautiful but bizarre, gigantic butterfly. Mothra then proceeds to destroy the city while the charming Ito Sisters, the ever-patient captives with their sing-song, simultaneous speech, use their telepathy to direct Mothra. Eventually the government decides to give the twins up and, like some airplane of nature, Mothra takes the Ito Sisters back to Infant Island, and peace is restored. One can see how the mass destruction of the city is related, not to some mathematical, pseudohumanistic intelligence, but to the natural instincts of some superanimal reclaiming its spiritual children. There is, incidentally, also the theme of beauties and the beast: the beast larva turning quite spectacularly into the princely butterfly Mothra.

Monster Zero in 1965 developed many of these ideas even more clearly, especially the idea of mechanization versus natural instincts. In this film, the monster Ghidrah (who also appeared in the 1964 *Ghidrah, the Three-Headed Monster*), begins terrorizing Japan. Ghidrah is a winged, three-headed dragon, each head with two horns. We then learn that Ghidrah is actually magnetically controlled by the leaders of Planet X; thus he is a kind of atomic bomb in the disguise of a monster. Furthermore, the people from Planet X represent the usual kind of unindividualized mass horror associated with this genre: with their expressionless faces and goggles, they all look exactly alike. *Monster Zero* deals with the question of what happens when men start acting like machines. One character pleas for compassion and for acting natural: "Man must not live as machines!" Using the same magnetic rays, the people from Planet X also manage to activate Godzilla (the original Tyrannosaurus Rex–like monster) and Rodan (who is a cross between an eagle and a pterodactyl). Eventually, Japan realizes that the magnetic rays controlling the monsters can be stopped by sound waves. Once the Planet X people no longer have control, there is a spectacular fight scene in which the nuclear holocaust is again symbolically reenacted when Godzilla and Rodan battle against Ghidrah. Ghidrah finally flies back to Planet X, and Godzilla and Rodan go back to their homes in the sea, more than willing to remain dormant and natural. (*Warning from Space*, an earlier film not from Toho Studio, which made almost all of these monster films, but from the rival Daiei Studio, presents much the same plot: a friendly planet warning Japan about the danger of the atomic bomb and then helping Japan repulse an attack from another planet.)

Perhaps the most interesting of all the Japanese horror films was *Frankenstein Conquers the World* (in 1965, released in the United States in 1966), because this film took the Frankenstein monster, but absolutely nothing else from the archetypal Frankenstein movie. The Japanese Frankenstein is not a created monster, but a wild boy who has been exposed to atomic radiation. (In addition to its metaphorical presence, the atomic bomb is specifically referred to in almost all of the Japanese horror films.) Running wild in the streets, the mutant boy gradually grows until he is as gigantic as Godzilla. One of the charming aspects of this film is the instant, almost childlike acceptance by the adults in the film that the

In *Destroy All Monsters*, the original, primal monster Godzilla is horrifying; yet by the time of *Godzilla's Revenge*, Godzilla's son can be presented as a cuddly monster who makes friends with a cute Japanese boy. Who says atomic technology has to be scary?

monster really lives; one of the characters reminds another that he should remember that although they may have thought Frankenstein had been previously destroyed, it is well known that his heart is indestructible and that he could therefore come to life again at any time. The fear of Frankenstein is thus the fear of an always-present atomic bomb, though the ideas of a real Frankenstein with a heart and an atomically radiated boy in the city ruins are never reconciled — at least in the English-dubbed version. Both explanations are presented as somehow (though mysteriously) not mutually exclusive. Most of the movie is made up of the gigantic Frankenstein falling in love with a girl reporter, and, King Kong–like, destroying the city and looking into skyscraper windows. The climax of the film is once again a ritualistic re-creation of the nuclear holocaust as Frankenstein fights the earthquake monster in the midst of fire, earthquake, falling buildings, and massive death.

The 1967 film *King Kong Escapes* (released in the United States in 1968) develops the idea of natural instincts versus scientific programming even further. In this reenactment, King Kong is pitted against Mechni-Kong, a robot who is activated through the use of Element X — an atomic-bomb element. The struggle ends on top of the Tokyo Tower, with the instinctual King Kong victorious over Mechni-Kong, although of course the city is once again in ruins. In many of these later films, with their emphasis on the unindividualized alien masses from other planets, there seems to be a subtextual fear of the Chinese Communists or North Koreans.

Destroy All Monsters in 1968 is one of the series' most epic films. At the end of the twentieth century, all the monsters have been placed on Ogasawara Island (symbolizing nuclear disarmament). Suddenly, the monsters escape and begin massive destruction all over the world: Godzilla in Paris, Mothra in Peking, Manda in London, and Rodan in Moscow. Again, it is people from another planet — this time the planet Kilaak, which obviously represents science — that are controlling the monsters through the use of tiny transistors. Once the Kilaaks' control is broken, there is a final battle between the earth monsters and the Kilaaks' reserve monster. Godzilla, of course, is triumphant, and, as he destroys the Kilaaks' base, Baby Godzilla jumps up and down and claps his claws in proud jubilation. Still, nuclear disarmament cannot be trusted.

Another charming aspect of the Japanese series is that once the monsters' rampages are completely understood as the result of natural instincts as opposed to scientific (in)humanity, the monsters become friendly heroes who, positioned around Japan, are even willing to protect the island against attack. Thus in the 1969 fantasy, *Godzilla's Revenge*, the funniest of all the films, a little boy meets Godzilla's son in his nightly dreams and learns to fight by watching the instinctual Godzilla.

By the end of the sixties, the Japanese mythology was overwhelming: their army of atomic forces included Godzilla, Manda, Mothra, Rodan, King Kong, Frankenstein, Baby Godzilla, Ghidrah, Yog (the octopus monster), and Hedorah (the smog monster). The use of mythology has always been to explain away the unexplainable. The use of this cinematic mythology to explain the atomic holocaust and to build from those fears a creative world with its own rules and moral order is an achievement not to be dismissed as cheap, popular *kitsch*, but to be studied as a source of a Japanese creative consciousness and conscience.

There is also a relationship between this Japanese variety of the horror of Armageddon and the American *Planet of the Apes* series (1968–1973) with its vision of destruction. Unlike most sequels, the *Ape* sequels (*Beneath the Planet of the Apes, Escape from the Planet of the Apes, Conquest of the Planet of the Apes,* and *Battle for the Planet of the Apes*) are not greatly inferior to the first. Of course the quality is variable, but all five can be taken together as an intertwined mythology. While the *Apes* films contain many of the elements of the horror of Armageddon — an object of proliferation (the apes) and, most notably, an overriding concern with the ultimate atomic destruction of the world — their focus is clearly not on the horror, but on the inherent intellectual criticism of man through the apes parody; thus, whether the *Apes* series should be included in the horror of Armageddon or in a separate science-fiction category is debatable. Nevertheless, the series — which presents a world in which talking apes, at the top of the evolutionary ladder, control men — is filled with horror elements; indeed, the shock at the climax of *Planet of the Apes* when Charlton Heston sees the ruins of the Statue of Liberty and realizes that all along, he and his fellow astronauts have actually been on earth, whose human civilization has been destroyed by atomic warfare, is clearly one of the most horrific moments of the cinema.

Other films on the periphery of the genre include several British films, including Peter Watkins' *The War Game* (1965), a "documentary" about the atomic warfare in World War III, a movie which was called by Bosley Crowther "a powerful, isolated horror film." Many of the images in *The War Game* are very powerful, especially because of their *cinéma vérité* quality: burning eyeballs, people in pain, gigantic explosions, etc. Also from Great Britain is *Lord of the Flies* (1963), based on the novel by William Golding and directed by Peter Brook, which begins when a group of children crashes onto a deserted island while being evacuated to safety during World War III. On the island, the children gradually revert to savagery, reenacting in microcosm the same petty power struggles and dark natures that

As action-adventure satire, ***Planet of the Apes*** emphasizes the ironies of a topsy-turvy world: Kim Hunter plays Zira, the most compassionate ruling-class ape who shares a kiss with Charlton Heston's George Taylor, even though he's "so damned ugly." Only at the ending does the film reveal its surprise: Taylor is not on another planet, but on earth, post-apocalypse.

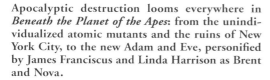

Apocalyptic destruction looms everywhere in *Beneath the Planet of the Apes*: from the unindividualized atomic mutants and the ruins of New York City, to the new Adam and Eve, personified by James Franciscus and Linda Harrison as Brent and Nova.

brought the outside world to nuclear confrontation. Both *Village of the Damned* (1960) and *Children of the Damned* (1964), as well as Joseph Losey's rarely seen *The Damned* [*These Are the Damned*] (1963), all British, use children as a bizarre intimation of some atomic destruction yet to come. At least three notable French films deal with similar issues. The shocking *Hiroshima, Mon Amour* (1959, released in the United States in 1960) is in part a

horrific examination of the trauma of the atomic bombing of Hiroshima. In the anthology film *The 7 Capital Sins* (1961), Ionesco's "Anger" ["La Colère"], in collaboration with director Sylvain Dhomme, is a clever panorama of a world whose incessant squabbling climaxes with nuclear destruction. And Chris Marker's exquisitely beautiful *La Jetée* (1962), one of the most influential short films ever made (comprised of hundreds of still photographs but only one moving image), is a metaphysical, existential examination of time and mortality in the context of post–World War

In Peter Brook's powerful *Lord of the Flies*, the marooned schoolboys retain civility for only a while before regressing to a primal state, increasingly dark and violent.

In *Village of the Damned* in 1960, blonde children are the harbingers of apocalypse. In the sequel *Children of the Damned* in 1963, as more countries were acquiring nuclear weapons, the children are more international in appearance.

III apocalypse. In the United States, the daring *They Shoot Horses, Don't They?* (1969) uses the dance marathon as a metaphor for the human condition and finds apocalypse on the personal level. However, as the Armageddon subgenre progresses, American films are definitely positioning themselves in the mainstream, including Saul Bass' *Phase IV* (1974), which deals with invading ants; and *Bug* (1975), perhaps the most repugnant of all, which deals with foot-long cockroaches.

If the horror of Armageddon seems in any way to be a limited or transient subgenre without much lasting energy, the remarkable success of *Jaws* should disprove this idea. Released in the summer of 1975, *Jaws* managed to become the all-time box-office champ, besting in less than four months such other contenders as *The Sound of Music*, *Gone with the Wind*, *The Godfather*, and *The Exorcist*. Working with certain generic conventions and against others, *Jaws* provided the new twist to keep the genre going for many more years. Based on the best-seller by Peter Benchley, *Jaws* was directed by Steven Spielberg, a Hollywood newcomer (if not for long!), whose previous work included the Goldie Hawn adventure *The Sugarland Express* (which garnered excellent reviews and disappointing box office) and the 1971 TV movie *Duel*.[3] The latter, a close relative to the Armageddon genre, if not a member of the family, deals with the psychological duel between a motorist (played by Dennis Weaver) and a ten-ton truck that tries to run him down on an interstate highway. Because the face of the trucker is not revealed, the truck is readily turned into a metaphor for existential horror. *Jaws* deals with violent shark attacks in a New England resort city, and, as in *Duel*, Spielberg turns his shark monster into a metaphor for existential horror by not actually showing the shark until almost two-thirds into the movie. When the shark does finally appear (in the form, incidentally, of a persuasive mechanical model expertly constructed for the production), the audience has such overwhelming expectation and has already invested the monster with such dread that its appearance is invariably greeted with wild screams. Not since *Psycho* in 1960 or *The Birds* in 1963 had an audience so enjoyed being manipulated from *frissons* of fear to heights of horror.

The opening scene of *Jaws* shows a group of people around a fire, instantly suggesting the primitive, tribal origins of man. A young man then chases a young girl down the beach in a timeless sexual rite. With this emphasis on man's basic urges and primordial needs, the audience is clearly prepared for the horror that is to come; that is, the most primordial fear of all: the fear of being eaten. When the girl is attacked by the shark, the screams intermingle and become ambiguous: love screams, childish screams, screams of fear. Spielberg shifts from this night scene to the beach community the next day: modern, clean, invari-

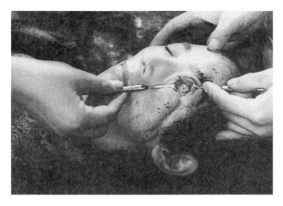

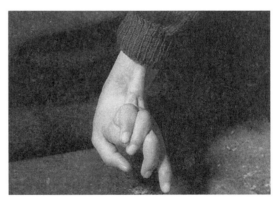

Although the bombs America dropped on Hiroshima and Nagasaki triggered cataclysm, most Americans have seen no images showing that destruction, and no American horror film has ever dramatized those events. However, in 1959, essential documentary and reconstructed images were shown by the French director Alain Resnais in his horrifying art film *Hiroshima, Mon Amour.*

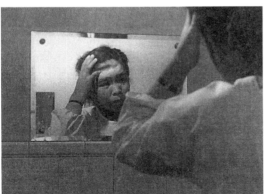

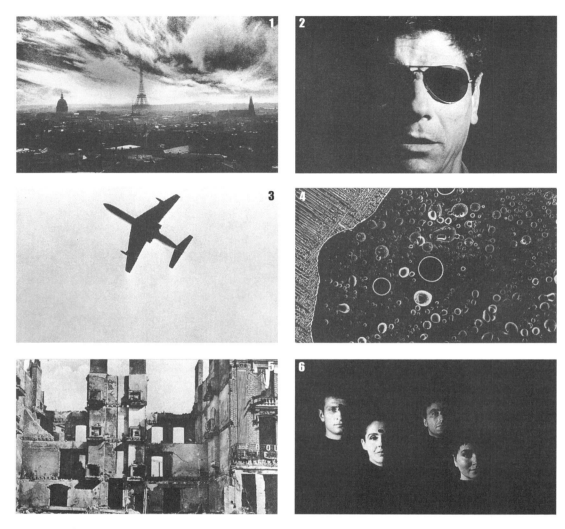

One of the most influential shorts of all time, *La Jetée* presents its poetic, apocalyptic vision through hundreds of still images which are supremely ambiguous, including (1) a firestorm over Paris, (2) a time traveler, (3) "a screaming comes across the sky," (4) a new Paris, (5) a Paris in ruins, and (6) an underground where inhabitants from the future live.

ably bright, and photographed in pleasing pastels. Certainly this cannot be a horror story: the name of the town is Amity, and it is the fourth of July weekend — a time for independence and celebration, not fear. Yet the shark attacks continue. When a young boy is attacked by a shark and the town is plunged anew into terror, Spielberg ferociously tracks in and zooms out on his protagonist Chief Brody, played by Roy Scheider. This visual effect (a favorite device used by Hitchcock both in *Vertigo* and *Marnie*) seems to thrust Brody into the water, literally changing the perspective, forcing him to get involved, even foreshadowing the film's ultimate scene when Brody, who has always hated the water, will be miles out to sea in conflict with the monstrous shark and up to his neck in water in a virtual baptism. Brody is like Melanie Daniels in *The Birds*, who was forced to admit the horror of life and to shed her complacency. Early in *Jaws*, Brody admits that he came to Amity as a

The suspenseful *Jaws* was also noteworthy for its witty compositions. Here, on guard for a shark attack, Chief Brody (Roy Scheider) struggles to see past a portly resident of Amity.

refuge from the horror of New York City with its astronomical crime rate; thus, it is not until he experiences and admits the universally precarious equilibrium of the human condition that he will be free from his fears. Indeed, the final shot of the film (after a fellow shark-hunter is devoured by the shark, seemingly in two separate bites) finds Brody swimming almost happily to the shore with a newfound respect for the world, mankind, and the water: "I used to hate the water," he says, "I can't imagine why..."

Not surprisingly, the generic resemblances to *The Birds* are extensive. Both films deal with a tranquil and picturesque beach community thrust suddenly into the meaningless horror of animal attack. Just as birds could never peck their way through inches of wood, neither could a shark swallow people whole. The besiegement in *The Birds* of Bodega Bay in general and of the Brenner house in particular is paralleled in *Jaws* by the besiegement of Amity in general and of the ship *Orca* in particular. In fact, almost half the film takes place at sea aboard the claustrophobic *Orca*, with the shark in relentless attack. The only convention not followed by *Jaws* is the proliferation of the horror; *Jaws* uses only one shark instead of an army of sharks. This single focus may have something to do with the film's ultimate sensibilities, which seem related as much to the Hawksian adventure film (with the emphasis on men doing their jobs) as to the Hitchcockian suspense film. Yet the horror is inevitably the most striking factor.

Quint, the master shark killer (played by Robert Shaw), is introduced with one of those clever flourishes heretofore called Hitchcockian, but perhaps just as properly called Spielbergesque: the horrible sound of fingernails scratching against a blackboard — certainly one of the most horrendous sounds, almost universal in its ability to provoke involuntary grimaces and shudders. Quint's crude drawing on the blackboard of a shark eating a man foreshadows his own demise. Even more telling is the story he relates on board the *Orca* about his wartime experiences.[4] During the summer of 1945, Quint was on board the U.S.S. *Indianapolis* when from San Francisco it delivered the atomic bomb to Tinian island in the

Only at the climax of *Jaws* do we finally see the shark clearly: when master hunter Quint (Robert Shaw) is devoured and his boat sunk.

Images in *Earthquake* offer a powerful metaphor: a world which is literally out of balance and lead-ing to apocalypse.

Pacific. Several days later, having completed its mission and now on its way to the Philip-pines, the *Indianapolis* was suddenly torpedoed several times by the Japanese submarine *I-58,* sinking the ship. The 1196 men, many dead and wounded, all ended up in the water, but the blood attracted schools of sharks. After many suspenseful days of watching their screaming colleagues disappear under the water's surface, Quint and the remaining men were rescued. Perhaps 300 died from the Japanese attack, and another 500 or so were eaten by the attacking sharks. This seemingly gratuitous reference to the atomic bombings at Hiroshima and Nagasaki should come as no surprise to those familiar with the genre. What-ever the horror may be — birds, grasshoppers, a shark, or Rodan — the horror seems always to relate somehow to the atomic bomb. There is a sense that here, as in the Japanese hor-ror films, the shark in *Jaws* is Godzilla-like in his instincts. As soon as we hear Quint's story, we know that Quint must die. The shark is inevitably returning to finish the job left undone that day in 1945 in the Pacific; only after Quint is punished and destroyed (for his role in delivering the bomb?) can the shark be vanquished. Yet Frankenstein was never really destroyed; he lived to horrify again in many a sequel. And certainly this is not the end for *Jaws*, either, the biggest box-office monster as of its release in the history of the cinema. How could those jaws *not* inexplicably return to Amity to wreak more havoc?

Apart from the phenomenon of *Jaws*, it must also be pointed out that the horror of Armageddon has influenced another genre which made a startling comeback in the seven-ties: the disaster film. *Airport* (1970), *The Poseidon Adventure* (1972), *Airport 75* (1974), *The Towering Inferno* (1974), *Earthquake* (1974), *Juggernaut* (1974), and even *Tidal Wave* (a 1975 American alteration of the 1973 Japanese film *Nippon Chinbotsu [Japan Sinks]*) — all these films deal with many of the same patterns of endless struggle. The major plot difference, of course, is that in the disaster film the unindividualized horror is not a proliferated one, but one that is whole — such as fire, water, earthquake, etc. A major tonal difference results because in many of these disaster films the resemblance is more to the soap-operatic qualities of a *Grand Hotel* than to the relentlessness of pecking birds. The most important difference, however, is a philosophic one: if, as in *The Poseidon Adventure*, the emphasis is on a similar, horrific *Birds*-like struggle, these films embody a sense of life which generally allows them to emphasize the means of salvation. Their outcomes do not revel in the existential horror, but affirm an abiding faith in a basic human ascendancy. Thus, the disaster films become the heroic reflection of the horror of Armageddon. The one outstanding exception, of course, is *Earthquake*. Its surprisingly bleak ending has Los Angeles smoldering in ruins, while the archetypal American hero, Charlton Heston, and American beauty, Ava Gardner, are swept down a sewer to meet their horrific destinies. With *Earthquake*, the disaster film copies the horror of Armageddon.

And, indeed, in its essentially existential vision, the too-long-ignored subgenre of the horror of Armageddon illustrates a *Weltanschauung* as consistent and as challenging as that expressed by any *auteur*. From their relationship to the rather elitist and avant-garde theatre of the absurd to their successful box-office status, the horror-of-Armageddon films exhibit a particularly perceptive understanding of that modern cataclysmic corner of our everyday fears.

3 — The Horror of the Demonic

"You're telling me I should send my child to a witch doctor?"
— Ellen Burstyn as the mother of the possessed girl in *The Exorcist*

"Holland, where is the baby?"
— Chris Udvarnoky as Niles in *The Other*,
to his brother who no longer exists

"All of them witches..."
— The anagrammed truth that terrifies Mia Farrow in *Rosemary's Baby*

"Get thee behind me, Satan."
— The Bible, Mark 8:33

Why is the world so horrible? Each of the horror subgenres of the sixties tried to answer that question in a different way. *Psycho* and the horror-of-personality films suggested that the world was horrible because it was insane and therefore perversely violent. *Night of the Living Dead* and the horror-of-Armageddon films suggested that the world was horrible either because man was becoming over-scientific and antihumanist, or simply because the malevolent universe by definition compelled the world and human condition to be naturally and existentially horrible. The third great horror subgenre of the sixties, the horror of the demonic, suggested that the world was horrible because literal, evil forces were con-

Max von Sydow in *The Exorcist*: the high-contrast lighting suggests the clear distinction between good and evil that is so common in demonic horror.

Carl Dreyer's *Day of Wrath* includes one of cinema's most moving nude scenes: actress Anna Svierkier playing Herlof's Marte in the passion of her religious inquisition. The second image shows Marte being burned as a witch.

stantly undermining the quality of existence. The evil forces could remain mere spiritual presences, as in *"Don't Look Now,"* or they could take the guise of witches, demons, or devils. Although the high concentration of these demonic films came in the mid-sixties and continued through the seventies, films about witchcraft and ghosts have always been with us. Indeed, the idea of an evil incarnate has a long American tradition. The Puritanism of eastern America, with its emphasis on damnation and antichrists, had as its climax the burning of several witches in seventeenth-century Salem, Massachusetts. The themes of repression and evil forces have long been a staple of American literature, from Nathaniel Hawthorne's *The House of Seven Gables* and Washington Irving's "The Legend of Sleepy Hollow" to Edgar Allan Poe's "The Raven" and Henry James' *The Turn of the Screw*. Of course the tradition of mystic evil extends to other cultures as well: voodoo in Haiti, witches in eastern Europe, and so forth.

Perhaps two of the most important and serious forerunners of this genre are *Day of Wrath* and *The Devil's Wanton*, both of which emerged from the spare countryside of Scan-

In *Day of Wrath*, although Anne (Lisbeth Movin) slowly comes to realize she is a witch, her attractive image promotes our empathy and is erotically appealing; in opposition, although Meret (Sigrid Neiiendam) represents conventional morality, her monolithic, dark image suggests forces which are repressive, alienating, bigoted, and unstoppable.

dinavia. *Day of Wrath* was directed by the Danish Carl Dreyer in 1943. Permeated by a carefully sustained tone of persecution, *Day of Wrath* deals with a young girl's gradual acceptance that she may be a witch because she cannot stop herself from thinking evil thoughts. Eventually and inexorably, events lead to her being burned at the stake, and the bigotry of her persecutors does not mitigate the girl's disturbing acceptance of her own evil inclinations. This subtle film of persecution, witchcraft, and fear is made even more disquieting by the painstaking photography, which skillfully resembles Flemish painting. *The Devil's Wanton* (although not a horror film), made by the Swedish Ingmar Bergman in 1948, deals with the idea of evil in even less fantastic terms than Dreyer. Very much a philosophical film, *The Devil's Wanton* suggests that the earth is hell and ruled by the devil. This proposition is then illustrated by the rather soap-operatic machinations of the plot.

The most important American forerunners of the demonic subgenre are the subtly atmospheric horror films produced by Val Lewton in the forties, particularly those directed by Jacques Tourneur and Mark Robson. *I Walked with a Zombie*, directed by Tourneur in 1943, deals with voodoo as a powerful, mystical cult in opposition to Christianity. Even more relevant is *The Seventh Victim*, directed by Robson in 1943 as a powerfully evocative tale of devil-worship in Manhattan that pre-dates *Rosemary's Baby*. The Lewton films, already widely studied, have been praised for their visual aesthetic, clever use of sound, and poetic ambiguities.

The two different demonic figures from *Day of Wrath* and *The Devil's Wanton*, the witch and the devil, returned in the sixties with a vengeance (pun intended), accompanied by the evocation of ritual evil from the Val Lewton films. It is not surprising that the rebirth of the devil should come in the sixties; in this period of social strife, any easy explanation for the chaos was most welcome. Further, the election of John Kennedy to the U.S. presidency in 1960 signaled a new awareness and acceptance of Catholicism the world round. The early sixties were also the period of the very popular Pope John XXIII; and when Pope John died in 1964 and the Vatican sought a new pope, the Catholic Church again attracted worldwide attention. Pope Paul VI's visit to the United States in 1965 to plead for world peace before the United Nations General Assembly marked the first time a pope had visited the United States. At the same time this Catholic awareness reached an all-time high, the percentage of Americans who faithfully went to church reached an all-time low, and *Time* magazine (on April 8, 1966) asked provocatively in a cover story "Is God Dead?" Thus, it is not unusual that Roman Catholicism, the religion with perhaps the most elaborate mythic and ritualistic ceremonies and structures, should discover — while undergoing its tests of leadership changes, liberal dissent from young priests, and identity crises — that so many of its followers were leaving the flock and so many others were expressing interest in witchcraft: the inversion of Catholic ritual. In part because of this Catholic decline, devils and witches made a comeback in the horror films of the mid- and, especially, late sixties.[1]

The movies in this diabolic genre run the gamut from the most stylized and fantastic like *The Mephisto Waltz* to the more everyday and realistic *Rosemary's Baby*. Yet the films throughout the genre exhibit a remarkable consistency and tend to share at least four main themes, the first of which is the idea of vengeance. Inevitably, the witches or devils do their work in order to get revenge on people who did them harm in the past. The idea of a vengeance that is compelling, inevitable, and can span centuries recurs in films like *The Haunted Palace* and *Horror Hotel*. In *The Exorcist*, the possession of the little girl is carried out not because the devil has any particular designs on Regan, but first, because the devil wants to conquer Father Merrin who the devil knows will be called in to perform the exor-

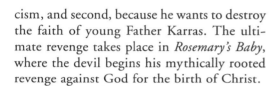

Since a key theme of the demonic is the corruption of innocence, children consistently appear as major characters; examples include (1) Miles in *The Innocents* (Martin Stephens), (2) Regan in *The Exorcist* (Linda Blair), and (3) Niles in *The Other* (the Udvarnoky twins).

cism, and second, because he wants to destroy the faith of young Father Karras. The ultimate revenge takes place in *Rosemary's Baby*, where the devil begins his mythically rooted revenge against God for the birth of Christ.

The second main theme is the corruption of innocence. Inevitably, one target of the demon or the witch is a young person, who, if he or she cannot be corrupted, will be killed. Thus we have the possibly corrupted Miles in *The Innocents*, the ambiguously corrupted Niles in *The Other*, the certainly corrupted baby in *Rosemary's Baby*, and the demonically corrupted Regan in *The Exorcist*— as well as the children that are killed in *The Devil's Own*, "*Don't Look Now*," and *The Mephisto Waltz*. Thus, in the demonic universe, nothing innocent can survive: it must be blotted out or perverted. Although the idea of innocence perverted is not revolutionary (one thinks of *The Bad Seed* or Agatha Christie's *Crooked House*), the idea does contain particular relevance to the period of the sixties; for if young people are out on the street demonstrating against war and espousing political causes, how can they still be innocent?

The third theme is that of mystic phenomena, especially possession. In the world of the demonic, anything is possible: animals can have human heads (*The Mephisto Waltz*); stone eagles can come to life (*Burn, Witch, Burn*); locks can be mysteriously broken (*The Other*); and matters of life and death can be effortlessly controlled (*Rosemary's Baby*). Accompanying these mystic tricks is the very primary demonic tool of possession; that is, the demon's ability to influence or completely control another individual and to use that influence or control for the promotion of evil. Thus we have *The Possession of Joel Delaney*, as well as the possessions of Tansy Taylor in *Burn, Witch, Burn*; of Miles in *The Innocents*; and of course Regan in *The Exorcist*.

The fourth theme in these films is the emphasis on Christian symbology. Demons and witches can generally be repelled by a crucifix (as in *Horror Hotel*), and some aspect of the church appears in almost every film: the appearance of the Pope and the Madonna-blue that Rosemary wears in *Rosemary's Baby*; the stained-glass window representing an angel in *The Other*; the church scaffold in "*Don't Look Now*"; and the ritual exorcism in *The Exorcist*. The most consistently recurring Christian image in these movies is fire, with its suggestion of hell and ultimate damnation. Note, however, that although the fire usually kills the demons and damns them with quite proper Christian justice (as in *Burn, Witch, Burn*;

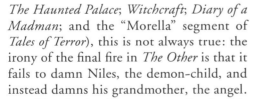

The Haunted Palace; *Witchcraft*; *Diary of a Madman*; and the "Morella" segment of *Tales of Terror*), this is not always true: the irony of the final fire in *The Other* is that it fails to damn Niles, the demon-child, and instead damns his grandmother, the angel.

Religious iconography dominates demonic film; examples include (1) a crucifix showing the suffering Christ in *Day of Wrath*; (2) the Assyro-Babylonian demon Pazuzu, appropriated as an anti–Christian image in *The Exorcist*; (3) a statue of the Virgin Mary, also from *The Exorcist*; and (4) a cemetery cross which spontaneously generates hellfire in *Horror Hotel*.

Two foreign films compete for the title of first demonic film of the sixties, both released in their respective countries within weeks of each other in late summer of 1960: *Black Sunday* in Italy, and *Horror Hotel* in the United Kingdom. By far the more enduring of the two is *Black Sunday*, originally entitled *La Maschera del Demonio* [*The Mask of the Demon*]. Adapted from the pedigreed short story by Nikolai Gogol, Mario Bava both directed and did the cinematography, which is unusually dark and atmospheric, exuding the cold bitterness of its evil antagonist. Actress Barbara Steele became a cult figure in her double role as Princess Asa — a seventeenth-century witch, and as Princess Katia — a twentieth-century heroine and potential victim of her look-alike nemesis. Many of the violent effects of *Black Sunday* were gruesome for their time, such as Barbara Steele having a spiked mask driven into her face, or getting horrifically burned at the stake. *Black Sunday* made its audiences believe that genuine evil *could* return from the dead and inhabit the darkness. Indeed, when *Black Sunday* was released in the United States in February of 1961, it was immediately a success, going on to become one of the most commonly programmed horror films on local television stations across America in the sixties (typically screening on Friday and Saturday nights to adolescent boys not yet able to drive but without a weekend bedtime).

Horror Hotel, made in 1960 under the British title *The City of the Dead*, was not released widely in the United States until 1963; like *Black Sunday*, it quickly became a staple for

In *Horror Hotel*, Patricia Jessel plays a witch who is burned in Puritan Massachusetts; resurrected, she leads a contemporary coven. Note the emotional resemblance between the witch's passion at the stake to Christ's on the cross.

local television, as did so many other low-budget foreign horror films that followed. A surprisingly good film, *Horror Hotel* stars Patricia Jessel, Betta St. John, and Christopher Lee. The movie starts at the beginning of the eighteenth century when Elizabeth Selwyn is burned as a witch. Jumping ahead 250 years, we discover that because of a pact she made with the devil, Elizabeth has been reincarnated as Mrs. Newless. Our main character, however, seems to be Nan Barlow, a fresh and innocent student interested in the occult who stumbles across Mrs. Newless' coven of witches. When Nan is suddenly killed by the witches, the effect is not unlike the sudden killing of Janet Leigh's Marion Crane in *Psycho*. Instantly we become aware that the demonic world is a violent and dangerous one; it is not a world that will respect that popular code whereby the heroine escapes all danger to be united with the hero in time for the denouement. Eventually two of Nan's friends go to the scene to investigate (again, much like Lila and Sam in *Psycho*) and manage after a series of scares and close calls to destroy the witches at the last instant by throwing the shadow of a crucifix over them.

The Innocents, made in 1961 and based on the novella *The Turn of the Screw* by Henry James, boasted a remarkably sensitive screenplay by Truman Capote. In this story, a governess fears that the two children under her charge may be coming under the possession of the dead gardener Quint and previous governess Miss Jessel (who shared some shocking but unspecified sexual relationship). Deborah Kerr, who plays the present governess, Miss Giddens, hits just the right balance between rational concern and neurotic fantasy. The focus of the film is clearly on the boy Miles and whether he is truly an innocent or a child-demon. Expelled from school for supposedly corrupting the other children by "telling stories," Miles exhibits the most child-like, wide-eyed beauty. Unlike most children of his age, he claims he doesn't want to grow up. Yet at the same time, he seems almost perversely mature. Insightful beyond his years, he retorts at one point: "Miss Giddens was just being polite"; his too-long sustained kiss of Miss Giddens is simultaneously childlike yet perverse. The soundtrack of this movie is amazingly dense, creating in the audience a kind of awe and wonder: we hear the singing of

In *The Innocents*, Deborah Kerr plays Miss Giddens, the sexually-repressed governess of two potentially possessed children, Flora and Miles, played by Pamela Franklin and Martin Stephens.

The sensuous images in *The Innocents*, photographed by Freddie Francis, lend a tactile dimension to the horror.

In *The Innocents*, Miss Giddens (Deborah Kerr) is often photographed at great distance from the other characters, promoting our mistrust of her perceptions, which may be just as distant from reality. In these two images, Deborah Kerr is shown with Pamela Franklin's Flora and Megs Jenkins' Mrs. Grose, respectively.

The dream images in *The Innocents*, hypnotically beautiful and ambiguous, strongly suggest the narrative to be unreliable, reflecting the neuroticism of the repressed governess.

birds, the chirping of crickets, the buzzing of bees, the rustling of curtains, etc. The heart-rending beauty of nature in this film is sensuous, yet somehow evil: we see a beetle crawling in the mouth of a statue, and the first apparition of Miss Jessel is at the lake surrounded by the trees and the water and the children. Later when Miss Jessel appears sobbing in the schoolroom, the moisture of her ghostly tears presents itself to us as a physical reality that bespeaks an unbearable suffering. When, at the climax of the film, the now-hysterical governess forces Miles to say the name of Peter Quint in confession of Miles' own possession, we see the hand of Quint as Miles either faints or dies. As Miss Giddens kisses him on the lips, the night birds begin almost magically chirping. Like most horror films, *The Innocents* works on at least two levels. The ambiguity created by the viewer's constant perception of the two simultaneous levels creates both tension and texture: it is never certain whether the children are being possessed by Quint and Miss Jessel, or whether Miss Giddens is neurotically creating the demons from her own sexually repressed psyche.

The density and ambiguity of this film contrast strongly with the 1972 Michael Winner film, *The Nightcomers*, which is based on the same material, but which graphically shows the relationship between Quint, Miss Jessel, and the two children, before the adults' deaths and the arrival of Miss Giddens. Although the Winner film deals with the same characters and ideas, the horror is of a different nature: by replacing the understatement of *The Inno-cents* with the overstatement of *The Nightcomers*, the horror of such beauty and fragility is transformed into a more direct stomach-churning horror.

Another notable demonic film was the British thriller *Burn, Witch, Burn* (1962), star-ring Janet Blair. One of those rare horror films that actually received quite a few very good reviews, *Burn, Witch, Burn* (originally entitled *Night of the Eagle* in the UK) derives much of its scare power from its slow and realistic buildup. In this film, Janet Blair plays Tansy Taylor, who discovers that she has been able to help her husband's career through the use of charms and magic ingredients. When her skeptical husband destroys her magic tools, his luck begins to worsen. (It seems witches always try to advance the careers of men: note the piano career in *The Mephisto Waltz* and the acting career in *Rosemary's Baby*.) After the destruction of the charms, the twists then come faster: Tansy disappears, and when she is found, tries to kill her husband. It turns out that she is now possessed by Flora Carr (played by Margaret Johnston), who is a full-fledged witch. Eventually the house catches on fire, and a stone eagle attacks the husband. The husband manages to escape, but then the masonry supporting the eagle collapses, and his wife Tansy is killed. The husband breathes a sigh of relief, unaware that Tansy is still holding tightly onto one of her charms. Thus, like many of the demonic films, *Burn, Witch, Burn* ends with a twist that suggests, despite the "happy" ending, that the evil has not yet been conquered.

In "Morella," the first story in the Roger Corman 1962 *Tales of Terror* anthology, Morella is possessed by her mother's spirit when she finds the corpse that her father had been sav-ing for twenty-six years. At the climax, the father (played by Vincent Price) drops a can-dle, and all three die in a hell-vision fire. In 1964's *The Haunted Palace*—again directed by Roger Corman and starring Vincent Price — Joseph Curwin, a practitioner of black magic, is burned in his mansion in 1765. One hundred ten years later, his spirit possesses the new owner of the mansion. The horror in this film comes to an end only when the mansion is set on fire and Curwin's portrait is destroyed. In *Diary of a Madman* in 1963, Vincent Price kills a condemned murderer and then inherits the evil spirit — or Horla — that had possessed the murderer. Various nasty things follow, including the decapitation of a young woman. Eventually, the reflection of a crucifix awakens Price from his trance; determined to end the horror, he sets the Horla on fire, and he and the Horla both perish. In the 1964 *Witchcraft*, which uses many of the same patterns, the Whitlock family of witches tries to get even with the Laniers for taking their land away three hundred years previously. The most important witch, Vanessa Whitlock, is able to rise from the dead when the Laniers bulldoze the Whit-lock cemetery. Included in this tale is a variation on the Romeo and Juliet theme: one of the girl Whitlocks (who is not yet a witch) falls in love with one of the Lanier men. The finale is fairly catastrophic; as Amy Whitlock sacrifices herself to save her Lanier love, all the Whitlocks are killed in a gigantic fire, their vengeance foiled. *The Devil's Own*, made in 1966 under the original title *The Witches* and starring Joan Fontaine, is somewhat of a departure from the rest of the florid films in this period. A British production for Ham-mer, *The Devil's Own* is a much more realistic film, which finds its horror through every-day observations. The leader of the witches is Granny, a seemingly typical, cantankerous small-town grandmother. Again an important aspect of the film is the sacrifice of an inno-cent (here, a teenage girl to the witches).

Protagonist and antagonist in *Rosemary's Baby*: the innocent Rosemary Woodhouse, played by Mia Farrow, chosen to be the mother of the Antichrist and contemplating a Tanas root charm (an anagram of "Satan"), and the evil Minnie Castavet, the nosy neighbor (played by Ruth Gordon), an unlikely, if terrifying, witch. Note that the charm is the same shape as the view of Minnie.

In retrospect, all these films seem to be mere overture to the truly demonic, for the seminal film of the genre did not come until 1968 with Roman Polanski's *Rosemary's Baby*. Polanski, whose previous films showed a very strong influence of the theatre of the absurd, collaborated very faithfully with American novelist Ira Levin, on whose best-seller the film was based. The collaboration proved fruitful: Ira Levin provided the painstaking plotting and careful structure; Roman Polanski provided the visual style and emotional menace. *Rosemary's Baby* is the story of one woman's anxiety-fraught pregnancy and her gradually increasing fears that the people around her are witches who intend to take that baby away from her. Although the ambiguity is not completely dispelled, the implication clearly is that Rosemary has been raped by the devil and is going to give birth to the Antichrist. This compelling plot is worked out with the most fascinating inversions: Rosemary's husband becomes a demonic St. Joseph; like Mary finding no room at the inn, Rosemary cannot find a place to have her baby; when the baby is finally born exactly six months after Christmas, the gift-bearing visitors to the shrouded crib suggest a dark version of the traditional nativity. In the novel, the witches chant: "Hail, Rosemary Mother of [the Devil]..." As Rosemary, Mia Farrow captures just the right tone of poignancy, appearing at times in the film to be so convincingly weak and pale that the audience almost fears for the actress. Perhaps the most intriguing scene of the film is the dream Rosemary has while she is being raped: like a surrealist painting, the dream includes the ocean, the Pope, Jackie Kennedy, a bizarre creature with claws (Satan), etc. The film derives much of its strength from its portrayal of witches, for the witches are not bizarrely mystical creatures, but the kind of slightly strange people that we all encounter in our everyday lives and think: "I wonder what's wrong with them?" Polanski's witches are fussy and friendly; it is precisely this ingratiating quality that makes them so horrific. Polanski's sense of the absurd remains very strong: one of the film's most horrifying, yet hilarious, moments is when we see the witches through the partially opened door, tiptoeing past, almost in parody of traditional stealth.

The denouement of the film, which is very quiet in relation to the frenzied scene of Rosemary running from the witches and giving birth (which comes immediately before), has Mia Farrow's Rosemary tremulously approaching the black-curtained cradle to see her baby; the question as to whether her maternal instincts will turn out to be stronger than her moral precepts is left unanswered. The suggestion, however, is that Rosemary will willingly take on the role of mother to the Antichrist. Polanski's film is filled with the most remarkably sustained tension. Building slowly but inexorably (like *The Innocents*), the ten-

In *Rosemary's Baby*, the striking dream sequence covertly shows Rosemary raped by the devil; comprised of ambiguous images, this sequence reflects director Roman Polanski's interest in art-house surrealism.

sion arises as a result of the audience's knowledge that something demonic must be going on beneath the surface, even if there have been no dramatically mystic happenings; the horror derives from the subtleties of a glance, the tone of a voice, an unnecessary smile. Thus, from its Biblically mythic foundation to its depiction of a New York in decay, Polanski and Levin managed to create a truly demonic universe.

The amazing box office and critical success of *Rosemary's Baby* (which included an Academy award for then seventy-two-year-old Ruth Gordon as a Manhattan witch) spawned a series of films dealing with witchcraft, demons, or the occult, many of them with some artistic pretensions like *The Other* and *The Exorcist*. Some of the films were simply blatant reworkings of *Rosemary's Baby*—such as *The Devil's Daughter* (1973), a TV movie with Shelley Winters as the head witch; *The Stranger Within* (1974), a TV movie with Barbara Eden as the impregnated mother; and *It's Alive!* (1974), a theatrical feature which worked as a kind of sequel to Polanski's film.

"Never Bet the Devil Your Head, or Tony Dammit," a 1968 short by Federico Fellini presented within the multi-part *Spirits of the Dead*, is notable not only because it further expressed Fellini's distinctive vision, but because it dealt peripherally with a devil that takes the form of a little girl who innocently bounces a ball and eventually walks away with Terence Stamp's head. *The Devil's Bride* (also known as *The Devil Rides Out*), released in the United States in late 1968, dealt with devil worship and initiation rites and brought back Gwen Ffrangcon Davies—the same actress who portrayed the grandmother witch in *The Devil's Own*—as the demonic Countess d'Urfe. Other films of the period included *Night of Dark Shadows* (1971), which was based on *Dark Shadows*, the first daytime–TV horror soap opera, which ran from 1966 to 1971. In fact, *Dark Shadows* during its prime attracted millions of viewers who tuned in to the mysterious adventures of Quentin, Angelique, and vampire Barnabas Collins in order to discover the secret of the seven-room dream curse. At one point the series even jumped back in time for a two-month sequence in Puritan New England. *The Blood on Satan's Claw*, released in 1970, began with a farmer discovering the remains of Satan in the form of a one-eyed skull and a claw, and progressed to a satanists' orgy and the rape of the hero's innocent sweetheart. The independently made *Equinox*, also 1970, used surprisingly convincing special effects of a gigantic blue ogre, as well as a slightly

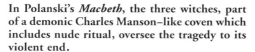

In Polanski's *Macbeth*, the three witches, part
of a demonic Charles Manson–like coven which
includes nude ritual, oversee the tragedy to its
violent end.

different demonic manifestation called
Asmodeus. *The Brotherhood of Satan* (1971)
dealt with a devil cult that was quite arche-
typally stealing away a town's children in
order to initiate them into lives of evil. And *Mark of the Devil*, a German film made in 1970
but not released in the United States until 1972, strongly resembled the film *Witchfinder
General*. Originally rather colorfully entitled *Hexen bis aufs Blut gequält* [*Witches Tortured
Till They Bleed*], *Mark of the Devil* emphasized the sadism of the witchhunter, graphically
presenting the burning of witches, the amputation of limbs, and various impalements and
decapitations. Polanski's own *Macbeth*, in late 1971, with its strong emphasis on the witches'
understanding of fate compelling the tragedy of Macbeth, was equally filled with blood-
letting and violence. The obvious relationship between *Macbeth* and the real-life tragedy
of Sharon Tate, Polanski's wife, who was killed by the hippie-mystic/Rasputin Charles
Manson and his family of followers, has been pointed out by critics as often as it has been
denied by Polanski. Yet because this *Macbeth* is pervaded with a mystically existential fate
and almost ritualistic violence, the film clearly seems to be Polanski's own exorcism — if not
of his personal demons, certainly of the demons of the violent sixties.

The Mephisto Waltz, directed in 1971 by Paul Wendkos, dealt with many of the same
elements as *Rosemary's Baby*, but in an extremely fantastic manner. When the famous pianist,
Duncan Ely, dies, his soul seems to be transferred into Myles Clarkson's body. Myles acquires
Duncan Ely's piano-playing ability as well as Duncan's increased sexual desire. In fact, we
discover that Myles had been carefully chosen as the body to house Duncan's spirit so that
Duncan could (through Myles) carry on his incestuous relationship with his daughter Roxanne, who, we are told, had at one time literally given birth to a monster by Duncan. Filled
with potions, magic books, and satanic circles, the story is told from the viewpoint of Myles'
wife, Paula, who is dismayed by the changes her husband is undergoing. After Paula's child
is killed by the witches (innocence can never survive), Paula is so determined not to lose
her husband to Roxanne that she learns as much as she can about witchcraft; at the film's
climax, surprisingly, she kills herself in the bathtub. The next day when Myles rushes passionately to the arms of his Roxanne, there is the suggestion that Paula's soul has now taken
over Roxanne's body. Although the film leaves many questions unanswered (such as: "Where
did the soul of Myles go?"), the story is told with such energy and style that the audience
doesn't mind. The camera is forever swirling and swooping to the extremely romantic music
of Jerry Goldsmith and Liszt; the witches' celebration of sexual performance and passion
is compellingly attractive; and the physical colors and textures of the production are always

gaudily sensuous. Starting from the same idea as *Rosemary's Baby* (that is, a wife gradually driven to hysteria over her husband's relationship with people she believes are witches who want to harm her child), *The Mephisto Waltz* proceeds with an exuberant style that is the complete antithesis of the style in *Rosemary's Baby*. The consistently downbeat reviews of *The Mephisto Waltz* may not be especially surprising, since so many critics insisted on downgrading it for not being *Rosemary's Baby*, rather than praising it for its own unique style.

Two demonic films of the early seventies — *Simon, King of the Witches* in 1971, and *The Possession of Joel Delaney* in 1972 — might be called the first social-problem demonic films. In *Simon, King of the Witches*, the world of Satanism is intermingled with the world of drug addiction. Andrew Prine plays Simon, who discovers he has demonic powers, aspires to be a god, and takes revenge on the world by murdering narcotics agents. In one scene he meets up with no other than Andy Warhol's Ultra Violet, who, as a leader of Satanists, does little more than strip off her clothes orgiastically. When Simon's girlfriend dies from an overdose of drugs, and Simon is framed by corrupt police, he uses his curses to plunge the city into chaos. Ultimately, Simon is stabbed to death by drug addicts. One can clearly see in this film the innate parallels between the mysticism of witchcraft and the mysticism of the modern drug culture; it is most telling that as Simon is beaten by the "crummyness of the world" and the "system," this almost hippie anti-hero becomes a cult satanic martyr: a kind of horrific Mick Jagger or Charles Manson to which the dissatisfied young could relate.

The Possession of Joel Delaney has even more pretensions. In this film, the rich Joel Delaney, who has taken to living in the slums so as to alleviate his class guilt, is possessed by a Puerto Rican demon who is filled with rage over the social conditions under which Puerto Ricans have been forced to live. In turn, the demon forces Joel Delaney to commit the most antisocial behaviors, such as decapitating his girlfriend and forcing a well-to-do little boy to eat dog food (to make the boy come to terms with his role as a member of the exploiting class). Shirley MacLaine plays the sister of Joel Delaney, and when an attempted exorcism of her brother fails, it is suggested that it may have failed because MacLaine was not a believer (similarly, in *The Exorcist* in 1974, the atheism of Regan's mother is nicely contrasted with the seeming mumbo-jumbo of the exorcism ritual). If *The Possession of Joel Delaney* seems at times pretentious, it is because it is initially off-putting for many to find in a horror film such overtly applied liberal social protest. According to the film, the demon is not to be blamed, because he was but a product of his environment; the only way he can get back at the white master class that has suppressed him is through demonism, suggesting (albeit in acceptable, disguised form) that the crime and violence of the lower classes directed at the upper classes is acceptable as revenge or as consciousness-raising. Even further, it is right and only-to-be-expected for a Puerto Rican to have possessed the soul of Joel Delaney, because the system has for too long possessed and crushed the souls of a multitude of poor Puerto Ricans. Even if *The Possession of Joel Delaney* grinds its ax rather obviously, the film works well as both a horror film and an allegory of modern class conflict. When, at the end of the film, the policemen kill Joel Delaney, there is one of those fadeout twists that so often manifests itself in these films. Shirley MacLaine cradles her dead brother in her arms, closes his unseeing eyes, and then suddenly snaps open a switchblade herself as the Puerto Rican demon jumps into *her* body in order to continue his revenge against the white upper classes.

The next truly important demonic film is *The Other* (1972), directed by Robert Mulligan and based on the novel by former actor Thomas Tryon. *The Other*, like *The Innocents*, is hard to describe: its power and magic residing in its gestures, its glances, its perform-

In *The Other*, omens of evil, such as this black crow, confront innocent-looking Miles (played by the Udvarnoky twins) everywhere; ironically, Miles must be forced to acknowledge that the real evil lives inside himself.

ances, the specific nature of its visual evocation, the rhythm of its editing, the psychological connotations of its moving camera. Like all Mulligan films (from *To Kill a Mockingbird* and *Up the Down Staircase* to *Inside Daisy Clover* and *Summer of '42*), *The Other* chronicles the end of innocence — in this case, not as a result of maturing, but as a result of perversion. Beautifully photographed in a rural America in the era when boys played with frogs, climbed trees, and jumped in the hay, the film introduces us to a pair of twins: Niles and Holland. As it is so often with twins in literature, the twins are essentially opposites: Niles seems to be the good little boy, while Holland seems to be the dark brother, the mischief maker. Respecting the integrity of his visual technique, Mulligan keeps each of the boys in separate shots until the revelation that Holland has been dead for years and now exists only in the imagination of his brother Niles, who has taken on demonic qualities.

The revelation scene is remarkably reminiscent of the climax of *The Innocents*, when Miss Giddens was positive that the young boy Miles (note how similar is the name of the boy in *The Other*) would be free of Quint's spirit if only Miles said his name. In *The Other*, Uta Hagen, as the grandmother, dramatically forces Niles to look at the name of his brother on a stone marker in the cemetery. This idea of release seems related to the

In the climax of *The Other*, director Robert Mulligan shows a visual parallel between the angel on a stained-glass window and Miles' loving grandmother (played by famous acting teacher Uta Hagen), who becomes an angel of death as she tries to end Miles' evil by setting the two of them on fire.

The producers of the 1956 movie version of *The Bad Seed* (Warner Brothers and Mervyn LeRoy) thought the idea of a child being congenitally evil so disturbing that they tacked on a curtain call so actress Nancy Kelly could give actress Patty McCormack her "deserved" spanking and prove that the film was just in good fun. By the early seventies, no such codas were necessary: we could accept evil anywhere.

Rumpelstiltskin story, where the knowledge of the demon's identity becomes the magical means to the demon's eternal banishment. But in *The Other*, Niles refuses to give up the existence of Holland. In one of the film's most compelling scenes, when Niles is talking to Holland, the camera pans from Niles to the place where Holland is supposed to be; the attempt, for the first time in the film, to unite them both in the same frame is shattering; and what we see, surprisingly, is not Holland, but the empty space where poor Niles imagines his brother Holland to be. As innocent-looking Niles finds himself doing more and more mischief, the effect is quite disturbing. Niles' query, "Holland, where is the baby?" is exclaimed on a wonderfully archetypal night of thunder and lightning above and about the Gothic farmhouse and precedes the discovery of the dead baby. It is Niles, of course, who is guilty; especially as we understand how he is transferring his own guilt and responsibility to his dead brother, the innocence of Niles' sweet, blonde, wide-eyed features becomes fraught with an ambiguous and horrific beauty. When, ultimately, the grandmother decides that she must bring an end to Niles' evil once and for all, her actions strongly resemble the mother's actions in *The Bad Seed*. But trying to destroy that which she helped create did not work for Rhoda's mother either: although the poison killed the mother (in the original book and play, if not in the film version), the demonic bad seed escaped. "Isn't it a comfort," said one of the neighbors to the husband, as the audience realized that the neighbor was going to be the little girl's next victim, "that you still have Rhoda." At the end of *The Other*, although the grandmother sets herself, Niles, and the barn on fire, she is killed and Niles mysteriously escapes; the three successive shots of the cut lock (derived, incidentally, from the three shots of Janet Leigh's face at the beginning of the shower sequence in *Psycho*) are mysterious yet inevitable, for the evil behind that innocent face is fathomless and indestructible. Our last shot of Niles looking out the window from behind the curtains defines implicitly the veiled nature of his evil. Filled throughout with wonderful little shocks (such as the macrocephalic fetus in a jar and the sudden appearance of a sideshow entertainer suffering from Proteus Syndrome), *The Other* is noteworthy for its tone of innocence and horror, its evocation of Niles' youthful exuberance, and its dark vision of the nature of the demonic soul.

"Beyond the fragile geometry of space": In *"Don't Look Now,"* Nicolas Roeg makes visual connections through tonal montage, particularly the sequence showing the drowning of the Baxters' daughter. Each image relates visually to the next in some way, especially in the original color, featuring a bright red. For instance, note the position in their frames of the ball and of the drowned girl's head.

Other films of this period include the TV movie *Crowhaven Farm* (1970), in which Hope Lange tries to protect herself and her baby from a coven of witches; *Child's Play* (the 1972 Sidney Lumet film based on the play by Robert Marasco) in which evil goings-on disrupt a boys' school; and *The Pyx* (1973), starring Karen Black as a prostitute who gets involved in witchcraft. In 1973, two of the most noteworthy horror films of all time appeared: *"Don't Look Now"* and *The Exorcist*, two films that, although not universally praised, were at least treated by the critics as films well worth responding to on an intellectual and artistic level.

"Don't Look Now," directed by noted cinematographer Nicolas Roeg, displays an almost mathematical sensibility to horror. An examination of second sight and extrasensory perception, every event and image in the film seems to be inter-related directly and geometrically. The protagonists, John and Laura Baxter, are played by Donald Sutherland and Julie Christie. As the film starts, the early image of John and Laura's little girl reflected in the water suggests a world turned upside down. When their little boy cuts himself, the blood is distinctly red — as are the raincoat and the ball of their daughter. When, inside the house, John notices some red fluid effusing from a red figure on one of the slides on which he is working, it is instantly clear that his daughter outside is dead. The connection between the two events, although "beyond the fragile geometry of space," is compelling nevertheless. When John and Laura go to Venice to recover from the death of their daughter, it is clear to the well-read viewer that one of the two will surely die, for Venice is, after all, from Ruskin to Thomas Mann to Henry James, the city of death, the beautiful city of water and light, slowly sinking to its own destruction. Throughout their stay in Venice, John and Laura keep running across a child robed in red like their dead daughter. Simultaneous to their attempts to get over their grief, a mad killer is terrorizing all of Venice. The film structurally resembles Ionesco's 1958 play *The Killer* [*Tueur Sans Gages*]. In *The Killer*, the beautiful Radiant City is gradually turning ugly and disgusting as a similar mad killer terrorizes it. After losing his love, Bérenger is finally brought face to face with this killer who turns out to be a misshapen dwarf, and who, as the play ends, raises his knife to kill Bérenger. In *"Don't Look Now,"* John Baxter is inexorably brought face to face with his own fate in the same way. After his wife disappears and he sees her mysteriously mourning with two women on a passing boat, he again sees the little girl in the red robe. He chases the girl, and when he gets her cornered so as to see her face, she removes her hood: she is not their daughter at all, nor even a little girl, but a misshapen dwarf who is the unknown Venetian killer; as the killer (played by Adelina Poerio) stabs John to death, the blood oozing from his body resembles the oozing slide in the opening scene of the movie. The ugly dwarf as metaphor for the nature of the demonic forces in Roeg's universe is truly fascinating. The cycle is fully completed when in the normal progression of time Laura Baxter mourns her husband's death, comforted by the two women on the Venetian boat, those premonitory moments that John had previously seen. *"Don't Look Now"* may not contain physical demons, but its exploration of dark and mystic forces is horrifying nevertheless. Unfortunately, *"Don't Look Now"* was widely overshadowed by its brother horror film and *cause célèbre, The Exorcist.*

At the moment Laura Baxter (Julie Christie) in *"Don't Look Now"* makes contact with "the other side" regarding her dead daughter, director Nicolas Roeg photographs Christie with her own reflection — in essence to show Laura suddenly seeing the world from two different perspectives.

Why *The Exorcist*? If the beginning of the sixties marked a heightened world consciousness of Catholicism, the end of the sixties and the early seventies marked a fascination with all kinds of devil worship. The much-publicized Church of Satan started in the mid-sixties in San Francisco and acquired branches in many cities with followers estimated to number two hundred thousand. The church's satanic bible, which advocates indulgence in the classic seven deadly sins of greed, pride, envy, lust, gluttony, anger, and sloth, sold well over a quarter-million copies. Other related fields of study enjoying a wave of interest in this period included fortune-telling, séances, magic, and Wicca. It was estimated that there

Max von Sydow plays *The Exorcist*; his arrival in dark silhouette suggests the horror that will follow.

were more than six hundred witches' covens operating in the United States, with more than one hundred thousand avowed witches — and at least half these witches seemed to be making appearances on contemporary TV talk shows like *Merv Griffin* and *Tomorrow* and on the various "freak spot" segments on radio talk shows all across the country. At the same time, the rock musical *Hair* emphasized free love and the "Age of Aquarius." Astrology and horoscopes were in; "What's your sign?" was the most common party question. Jeanne Dixon, internationally known psychic, wrote a horoscope column and made widely read predictions. Everyone wanted to know about reincarnation, as past lives and future reincarnations were analyzed in national best-sellers. Bizarre violence in San Francisco and Los Angeles spread all across the country, with messages written in blood and Charles Manson proclaimed a messiah by his followers. At the same time, a subset of the drug cult that had been fascinated by various bizarre ritual rites, gave birth to a new movement, the Jesus Freaks, resulting in some parents finding it necessary to kidnap their children away from these Jesus communes of brainwashed youth. According to many theologians, these manifestations were stemming from a widespread conviction that the balance between good and evil had been upset.

    The Exorcist, which deals overtly with this balance between good and evil, managed to reflect perfectly the fears and concerns of its audience members: by scaring the devil into them, it reaffirmed some absolute, religious, moral order and provided a hopeful alternative to the scientific community's "God is dead" cynicism. The consistent reports of vomiting and fainting in the theatres where *The Exorcist* was playing (perhaps planted at first by the Warner publicity department?) prob-

The most famous special effect in *The Exorcist* was the head rotation of the possessed girl, played by Linda Blair.

ably attracted those so predisposed to vomiting and fainting that they needed no more than the film title to set them off in fine Pavlovian style. Yet, in some strange way, the possibility that a viewer might faint or vomit was an attractive one; seeing *The Exorcist* was a rite of passage, and only those who fainted or vomited were the winners. In an era when acts of violence — in the form of killings in Vietnam, live riots, and assassinations — were watched daily over long periods on the evening news, and our responses to death had become complacent and anaesthetized, going to *The Exorcist* and throwing up reaffirmed our ability to be revolted, our ability to feel; thus, the vomit of the spectators became a valid aesthetic response to the world around them.

Since almost everyone in the country seemed to have been *Exorcist*-ed to death by the contemporary media, the artistic value of Friedkin's film seems almost a moot point. Indeed, I think one could easily argue that simply because it dealt with an implicit moral order, *The Exorcist* fulfilled such an overwhelming audience need that it worked like a Rorschach test to which each viewer responded by seeing exactly what he or she wanted to see; thus, how much of the result was due the film and how much due the psyche of the viewer may be impossible to ascertain. In fact, when I first saw *The Exorcist*, at least a third of the viewers — presumably neutral viewers who were not emotionally predisposed and/or did not feel a spiritual need — found the most "horrific" parts of the film absolutely unscary in every way; and this response came even as other members of the audience were fainting — a response which, even a few years later (considering how tame and unconvincing many of the effects seem in retrospect) strikes one as rather quaint and unbelievable. Whether terrifying or not, much of the film is pictorially inspired: the Iraq sequence when the priest sees the *malocchio*; the dogs fighting at the demon's statue; the billowing white of the nuns; the flickering light on the bum's face; and especially the image of the wind blowing the curtains out from the window, as if the source of the wind came from the demon Regan herself. Yet at the same time, for a ten-million-dollar film, *The Exorcist* shows surprisingly many technical faults: scenes out of focus, reflections of film lights, out-of-sync dialogue, etc. But after all the potential flaws are tabulated, trumping all is the once innocent twelve-year-old Regan (played by Linda Blair), enthroned in her bed, cursing, vomiting, wiggling her tongue, propelling herself up and down, moving the furniture, masturbating with a crucifix, talking in strange tongues, and killing people; in short, doing all sorts of things a well-behaved child should never do — so, of course, she must be possessed by the devil. *The Exorcist*, as everyone alive during the film's first six months of release was well aware, is about a mother's attempts to cure her troubled daughter. A mother's love does not work, nor does the highly technical and advanced godlike science of the curiously soulless doctors, who perform a spinal tap. So what to do? "You're telling me I should send my child to a witch doctor?" asks Regan's atheist mother (played by Ellen Burstyn). At the film's climax, after a horrible night of spit, screams, green vomit, and taunts (with the help of Mercedes McCambridge's voice as the devil in Miss Blair), the devil finally gets its revenge on Father Merrin, the exorcist, who dies of a heart attack induced by the demonic struggle. The devil is now free to pursue exclusively his true victim, young Father Karras, whom he has already tormented by an accusation of homosexuality. Guilty, too, over his mother's death, Karras has had his faith severely shaken by the whole experience with Regan. Yet the devil underestimates Karras' inner strength; for when Karras realizes that Merrin has sacrificed his life to the service of God, Karras' resolve is strengthened. Livid, Karras challenges the devil to come out of Regan and directly possess him instead. When the devil accepts the challenge, there is a struggle, and the devil and Karras plummet through the window. The ending of the film is surprisingly upbeat in implication: Karras' banishing the demon through the Christian sacrifice of his own death reassures the audience that if there is a devil, then there must be a God, and the imbalance in our time between good and evil will eventually be corrected. This is the legacy of *The Exorcist*.

Whether the artistic legitimacy of the horror genre brought about by *The Exorcist* and *Jaws* will be only transient is not completely clear, but the overriding question suggested

The traditional horror monster leaves a trail of blood. In the witty *It's Alive*, the monster is a newborn baby who leaves a trail of milk. When even newborns are sources of horror, it's clear that our belief in any kind of contemporary innocence has alarmingly evaporated.

by the extraordinary box-office success of these seventies horror films is quite simply: where do we go from here? Before *Psycho* came out in 1960, who would have guessed that a whole new horror subgenre was about to be born? The horror of personality began the decade of the sixties and thrived alongside the horror of Armageddon. Until *Jaws* rejuvenated the horror of Armageddon, the horror of the demonic seemed to overtake them both. We can certainly expect *The Exorcist* to be followed by a succession of demonic films anxious to cash in on *The Exorcist*'s popularity (*Abby, It's Alive, Trilogy of Terror, Beyond the Door, The Devil's Rain, The Reincarnation of Peter Proud, The Omen*, etc.), just as we can expect more horror-of-Armageddon films trying to outdo *Jaws*, and an occasional reworking of *Psycho*. Nevertheless, as we now move through the seventies on our way to the eighties, these three horror subgenres are sure to evolve and reveal new formulas, new fears, and new films.

What horror will be next?

PART TWO

MILLENNIAL NIGHTMARES (2009)

4 — A Context; and Why What's *Not* Happening in American Horror Isn't

The approach of a new century has often been a harbinger of great cultural anxiety. At the end of the 1990s, as one millennium was ending and another was about to begin, one would have expected the horror genre — reflecting the extraordinary social tensions competing for our attention — to come into a renaissance. (Certainly, the theatre produced at least one millennial masterwork, Tony Kushner's *Angels in America*, a seven-hour play which took on the era's most contentious themes and issues.) The end of the twentieth century forced the world to deal with the AIDS pandemic, genocide in Europe and Africa, the fall of the Soviet Union and virtual end to the conflict between capitalism and Communism, the rise of Muslim fundamentalism, and the transformation of the world through computer technology and the internet. With the last twenty-five years ushering in a rate of

In the TV series *Mary Hartman, Mary Hartman*, Mary responds to the slaughter of the Lombardi family by worrying about the waxy yellow buildup on her kitchen floor — a perfect indication of our postmodern culture's inability to attribute appropriate value. Mary (played by Louise Lasser, with mop, on the right) and her sister (Debralee Scott) become a new American Gothic.

anxious change so exponential that it became impossible to keep up, it is surprising that the horror film did not exploit that *Zeitgeist* with wild abandon. On the contrary, the horror genre — particularly in its Hollywood variety — was represented by largely unnotable films pitched to the least common denominator of the teen market.

As of yet, there has been no new *Frankenstein*, no new cultural horror touchstone. *Psycho* (1960), *The Birds* (1963), *Rosemary's Baby* (1968), *Night of the Living Dead* (1968), and *The Exorcist* (1973) seem clearly to have been archetypes of horror that perfectly reflected their times in new and disturbing ways. But since? There have been horror films that have made lots of money, yes, and films that have attracted critical attention, but in the last two decades, no film has become a definitive testament to the end of this American century. *The Silence of the Lambs* (in 1991) was successful and unforgettable, yet as much as I admire that film, it didn't break new ground, for the most part simply following — if cleverly — in the footsteps of *Psycho*. *The Sixth Sense* (directed by M. Night Shyamalan in 1999) is worth consideration — not just because it was a critical hit that made lots of money, but because its agonizingly slow pace seemed out of sync with other contemporary horror and suggestive of something new. Certainly *The Sixth Sense*'s theme of (American) obliviousness seems relevant to a pre–9/11 era, even if the film's clear debt is to a film like *The Innocents* (1961) and to standard demonic horror. And it is possible that the extraordinary Mexican film *Pan's Labyrinth*, directed by Guillermo Del Toro in 2006, may yet turn out to be a generic fountainhead, but as of this writing, it is too early for such a pronouncement, which would be more hopeful than certain.

If forced to pick one American horror film for enshrinement in the canon, I would choose that masterpiece of subtlety *Elephant*, directed by Gus Van Sant in 2003. Although *Elephant* won the top prize at the Cannes film festival and was recognized around the world as a great work anatomizing America with unusual, understated perception and the coolest of empathy, the film's truth was of little interest to Americans. Surely, a dramatization of the real-life killings of students by other students at Columbine High School should have been a popular subject for Americans, who are unnaturally fearful of crime and unusually fascinated with guns. Although the news from Columbine was followed avidly throughout America, *Elephant*— despite its awards — didn't even secure a release in most of America, its truths too subtle and challenging for the tabloid attentions of the typical American.

Unfortunately, the horror genre has been largely reduced, by considerations of the American market, to the commercial sensibilities of teenagers, an audience notably undereducated and not known for empathy. Perhaps as the culture moves to absorb the shocks of 9/11, the horror genre will be able to take stock and eventually respond. But for the most part, our lives have become so fraught with real anxieties and horrific fears that the Hollywood horror film has become unnecessary.

Americans live in a postmodern world. We no longer receive our information from the daily newspaper and one of three television networks. Today, hundreds of cable channels provide for every interest or prejudice; and internet sites compete with digital radio, television, billboards, junk mail, specialty magazines, faxes, e-mail spam, cellphone text messages, and advertisements on shopping carts and even supermarket floors. In essence, what Gertrude Stein once quipped about Oakland seems now to be true about the culture: "There's no *there* there." As a result, it becomes increasingly difficult for any work of art to capture the country's total attention. It even becomes difficult for factual information to filter through. When George W. Bush won election to a second presidential term in 2004, more than half the American people still believed Saddam Hussein was responsible for 9/11.

In the context of how difficult it is for *anything* to become part of the cultural consensus, it is not surprising that to date, no horror film has particularly emerged to reflect the complex *Zeitgeist* of the day. It is hard to distinguish what is important from what is trivial, because everything arrives with equal loading, as was communicated so clearly in an episode of that prescient, 1976 TV series *Mary Hartman, Mary Hartman*, in which Mary is sent word that a mad killer has killed the entire Lombardi family and their two goats and eight chickens. Mary's response — "What kind of a madman would shoot two goats and eight chickens ... and the people ... the people, of course..." — is followed by the return of her attention to the waxy yellow buildup on her kitchen floor. When everything is democratically equal, even the trivial, what *are* we to value? To a great degree, this moral disarray is an unfortunate byproduct of our postmodern age. When the "Runaway Bride" or the Michael Jackson trial is presented as equally important as the War in Iraq, which part of the American culture is any particular film to reflect? And so it becomes disconcerting, if not surprising, that Steven Spielberg — as schizophrenic as the culture — should have followed his horrific and moving 1993 concentration camp film *Schindler's List* with 1997's *The Lost World* — a *Jurassic Park* horror sequel which makes money on violence offered up as almost pornographic entertainment. One can't help wonder: were *Schindler's List* and *The Lost World* made with equal sincerity? Would it be more disturbing to discover that they were or that they weren't?

With postmodernism, too, time conflates — as reruns of *The Munsters*, Universal horror films of the thirties, the original *Psycho*, and contemporary horror films become available on TV simultaneously, with only a click of the remote control necessary to access whichever works you desire. And you can also find a postmodern smorgasbord of film and television at your local video/DVD store, by mail through Netflix, downloadable through the internet, on pay-per-view cable, or delivered electronically to your video iPod or cellphone. If, as a culture, we spend much of our time responding to old works of art that reflect the *Zeitgeister* of previous eras — works significantly unmediated by any re-thinking or re-interpretation for our own moment — we can't help but feel disconnected from the *real* of today. For this reason, I fear that the postmodern impulse becomes inherently reactionary. And for a genre like the horror film, which has always explicitly challenged the status quo and been inherently subversive, this postmodern impulse cannot be seen as a particularly good thing.

In the context of the skyrocketing costs of making a movie — $40 million and higher for the typical *low-budget* Hollywood film, and at least a matching sum going to advertising and distribution — moviemaking has become a business run largely by risk-averse accountants. Since young men under twenty-five are the only audience that can be counted on, it is not surprising that most horror films would be pitched to that demographic. Nor is it surprising that most American horror films — and indeed most American films of any genre — should for the most part imitate the successes of the past. The result is not only that the horror subgenres of the sixties and seventies — the horror of personality, of Armageddon, and of the demonic — are slavishly imitated and remade, but that the commercial horror juggernaut is dominated by a number of film franchises. The *Halloween* and *Friday the 13th* films, the *Hellraiser* films, the *Nightmare on Elm Street* films, ad nauseam continue their unthinking onslaught. And even the mildly-successful horror film begets sequel after sequel as well as hundreds of direct-to-DVD imitations, until neither vitality nor authenticity remains, if indeed those qualities were ever really there to begin with.

5 — The Horror of Personality, Revisited

Of the three subgenres I originally discussed in *Dark Dreams*, the horror-of-personality film seems by far to have since been the most vital. *Psycho* is more influential now than in the sixties or seventies, as influential in its own way as *Citizen Kane*, and certainly more seminal, because it anticipated the social catastrophes and upheavals that subsequent horror films so thoroughly reflected. And Hitchcock has truly become the most undisputed *auteur* to have worked within the horror genre. Amazon.com lists over 900 book entries for "Alfred Hitchcock." In addition to the many full-length biographies and studies of Hitchcock's *oeuvre*, you can find entire books on Hitchcock's relationship with his wife Alma, with producer David O. Selznick, with screenwriter John Michael Hayes; books about Hitchcock as filtered through philosophy, through Jacques Lacan, through feminism, through homophobia; books on Hitchcock's London, on his America, his San Francisco, his France, his last days, his owned art, his TV show, his style, his reputation, his irony, his music, his motifs, his posters, his architecture; and books containing Hitchcock interviews with François Truffaut, with Hitchcock scholars, and with Hitchcock himself. Virtually every one of these volumes includes material on *Psycho*. And if that's not enough, there are at least six books completely devoted to *Psycho*: Robert Kolker's *Psycho: A Casebook*, Janet Leigh's *Psycho: Behind the Screen of the Classic Thriller*, Stephen Rebello's *Alfred Hitchcock and the*

In terms of its influence, Hitchcock's *Psycho* has dominated the horror film for almost fifty years. In the 1998 remake, Vince Vaughn played Norman Bates, voyeur and serial killer. Compare with the Anthony Perkins picture on page 30.

Technically proficient, **Halloween** defined the "franchise" horror film and introduced the scary Michael Myers; here is a portrait of the monster as a young man ... and as a young boy.

Making of Psycho, Amanda Sheahan Wells' *Psycho*, Phil J. Skerry's *The Shower Scene in Hitchcock's Psycho*, and Raymond Durgnat's compelling *A Long Hard Look at Psycho*. For even more material, you can go to the internet, where a Google search on "Alfred Hitchcock" produces, staggeringly, over 7 million hits, and a search on "Alfred Hitchcock" and "Psycho" produces almost a million hits. In short, *Psycho* is big.

The last two decades especially have produced hundreds of films inspired by *Psycho*, many imitating scenes from the original in explicit *hommage*. And yet it must be noted that it is the violence in *Psycho* that has been most emulated (and exceeded), not the film's psychological complexity nor its extraordinary empathy for its characters. Because post–*Psycho* films are preoccupied with sensational mutilations, it does take remembering that fewer than two minutes of *Psycho* show violence and that Hitchcock devotes much greater screen time to the aftermath of his film's violence. Particularly less notable are the *Psycho*-inspired franchises: If the ongoing *Friday the 13th* (1980–) and *Halloween* series of films (1978–) seem to be less artful and more exploitative than their predecessors, they seem also, as many commentators have pointed out, to be much more sex-obsessed. These films' (reactionary) presentation of punishment for teenage promiscuity seems relevant to a society that has gone beyond the early exhilaration of the sexual revolution to the anxiety associated with record outbreaks of sexually transmitted diseases, including HIV/AIDS. Many horror-of-personality films subsequent to *Psycho* seem to reflect as well a disturbing hostility toward women, which seems a direct response to the feminist movement and male uneasiness with feminism; consequently it is hard to respond to some very well-made horror films enthusiastically without also feeling and expressing reservations.

Oddly enough, although Brian De Palma's *Dressed to Kill* (1980) was among the most virulently attacked as sexist, this film is arguably the most successful and stylish *hommage* to *Psycho*, as well as less misogynist than many of the other films exploring similar territory. Robin Wood has suggested that the violence in many of the horror films of this period can be seen as a reflection of America's increased dissatisfaction with traditional sexual roles and the nuclear family.[1] In this context, the violence in certain films can be revealed not as reactionary, but as a release of social tensions, perhaps even a necessary first step toward a more liberated society with more responsive social and familial structures. De Palma's Kate, the protagonist in *Dressed to Kill* (played by Angie Dickinson), is a tragic figure because she is unable to understand the source of her problems. She retains a naive and stupid faith in the American family, despite the fact that her marriage seems not particularly happy and her husband not especially equipped to fulfill her sexually. Kate is reduced to fantasizing and prowling museums in search of some man to provide fulfillment. Kate's error, of course, is in looking outward, toward a man for her happiness; indeed, her encounter with the museum pick-up proves ultimately no more satisfactory than her dealings with her hus-

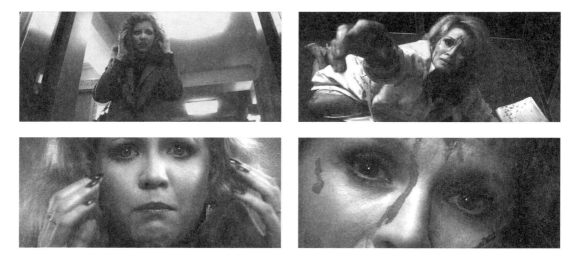

In the beautifully conceived montage of *Dressed to Kill*'s elevator scene, one woman reaches out at the moment of her death to another woman, and director Brian De Palma transfers the narrative from Angie Dickinson's Kate to Nancy Allen's Liz.

band. Her discovery that she has probably contracted a venereal disease works as a concrete example of the new morality which innocent, naive Kate is quite incompetent to deal with. To view her murder (and it is not a rape-murder, as many have falsely claimed)[2] as a sign of violence against women is to misunderstand the structure of the film: Kate is a representation not of Everywoman, but of woman as victim, woman as helpless creature without a strong man to protect her. It is interesting to note that it is only at the moment of her own murder that Kate reaches out for help toward another woman, who successfully (if too late) removes the murder weapon from the clutches of the killer.

What many have failed to note about *Dressed to Kill* is that De Palma clearly provides an alternative to Kate in the character of Liz (played by Nancy Allen). Like Kate, Liz is a woman stalked by the killer; unlike Kate, Liz is able to survive. If Kate's reactionary identity is symbolized by her status as bored housewife, Liz's liberated identity is symbolized by her status as enterprising and highly paid call-girl. Although one can argue that the hooker option for women — long a Hollywood staple — is itself sexist and limiting, Liz's hooker is nevertheless by no means a passive victim. Indeed, the cursing, tough Liz, the antithesis of Kate, is the independent, active protagonist of *Dressed to Kill*. The explicit trans-

Consonant with the horror-of-personality's emphasis on doubles and schizophrenia, *Dressed to Kill* uses multiple images to great effect, such as this expressive frame of Angie Dickinson's Kate, and this split screen of Michael Caine's psychiatrist and Nancy Allen's prostitute both watching the same TV show about transsexualism.

Dressed to Kill skillfully employs sixties horror-of-personality iconography when it shows Nancy Allen (1) in a maze of stairways and (2) in a bathtub, naked.

ference of the narrative from Kate to Liz is marked by the extraordinary close-up of Liz in the elevator sequence: her horrified eyes responding to the unbearable suffering of Kate. It is the courageous and direct Liz, the least vulnerable of would-be victims, who provides the film with its hard-edged moral force and dominates the narrative's second half. And although Kate and Liz, while in showers, are both associated with imagined acts of violence, only Kate's shower scene represents a personal fantasy. For Liz, violence is a nightmare that is not yearned for in the slightest. Liz — in contrast to Kate — rejects the male idea that women wish to be victims; in fact, Liz attempts to take a razor and return the violence in kind upon her male attacker. Too, it must be pointed out that although Liz does not elude the killer completely on her own, it is, at the final moment, another *woman* who saves Liz and brings an end to the tyranny of man's violence. And yet to call "man's violence" the subject of *Dressed to Kill* may itself be misleading. Although the killer is a man, the killer's transvestitism implies a split sexual identity which indicates that gender-role confusion — and the subsequent anxiety associated with changes in sexual mores and sex roles — may more precisely be the film's subject.

The horror film and the suspense thriller have a long, if unfortunate, tradition of using women as victims: in 1944's *Gaslight*, for instance, Ingrid Bergman was the hysterical victim of her husband's plot to drive her crazy; in 1960's *Midnight Lace*, Doris Day was similarly traumatized. In the traditional thriller, woman is seen as victim because of at least two factors: her physical inferiority to man in terms of simple strength, and, more insidiously, her "archetypal innocence." Because it was necessary in the past for the good woman to be seen as virgin, woman's lack of sexual sophistication often resulted in a view of women as helpless and naive. (And it is not coincidental that De Palma's Kate, cut from this cloth, is dressed completely in white, whereas Liz, at least in her first appearance, is dressed in grays and black.) Ingrid Bergman, Doris Day, and Angie Dickinson in *Gaslight*, *Midnight Lace*, and *Dressed to Kill* respectively, are significantly dumb, slow to realize what is actually going on, requiring the help of a strong, smart man to rescue them. The error of the heroines in *Gaslight* and *Midnight Lace* is not that they put their faith in a man, but that they put their faith in the wrong man. The three adult men that *Dressed to Kill*'s Kate is connected to — husband, pick-up, psychiatrist — all offer silence and betrayal in varying degrees. It is unfortunate that Kate should insist on putting her faith in any man, let alone the one whose appearance of strength and support should ultimately be revealed as only cosmetic; when this man turns against Kate so violently, it becomes clear that in our contemporary society, traditional sexual roles can no longer be counted on — for in *Dressed to Kill*, to expect masculine protection is to damn oneself to cosmic vulnerability. The only unambiguously positive male role model in *Dressed to Kill* is Kate's teenage son, a would-

The centerpiece of *Dressed to Kill*, a deliciously purple patch of cinema, is the extraordinary museum montage, where the ambiguous images invite great empathy for Angie Dickinson's Kate and the camera prowls sensuously, suggesting her sexual longing. Here are a few of the sequence's 110 images.

be protector who is neither controlling nor patronizing to women, but accepting of female strength. As a result, he becomes an embodiment of a new, more acceptable masculinity. What might actually be found most objectionable in *Dressed to Kill* is not that Kate comes to a violent end, but that the expressive, hyper-aesthetic style of the museum sequence, which promotes such empathy with Kate, itself contradicts the deep structure of the film by reflecting an almost nostalgic attitude toward female vulnerability.

Oddly, *Dressed to Kill* is, if more violent, less sexist than Hitchcock's *Psycho* (1960) — upon whose narrative De Palma ingeniously rings variations. It is also less sexist than Hitchcock's own late horror-of-personality film, *Frenzy* (1972), which casually presents the female body as analogous to discarded food and depicts a horrifying rape-murder with a disturbingly clinical detachment. Ultimately, De Palma's film is most notable for its style. The museum sequence with Kate, virtually without dialogue, is sensuously beautiful; the exuberance with which its 110 separate shots are edited together to form a unified whole (which later finds its parallel/opposition in the subway sequence with Liz) is incredibly fetching. Noteworthy, too, is the formal perfection of the film, with its constant parallelism and doubling of scenes, and the way De Palma uses color and camera movement. With so many

In *The Hills Have Eyes*, one "monster" is played by actor Michael Berryman, whose hypohidrotic ectodermal dysplasia guaranteed him many roles, particularly in horror films. And yet the conventional-looking actors in *The Hills Have Eyes* are ultimately more violent.

characters spying on each other and constantly framed through windows or doorways, *Dressed to Kill* reveals its organizing concept of voyeurism, which De Palma relates not only to his bravura use of the point-of-view shot, but also to his rather reflexive use of the film within the film, which inherently comments on the voyeurism of the movie audience as well as of the De Palma characters.

The secondary strain of early horror-of-personality films — Robert Aldrich's *What Ever Happened to Baby Jane?* and William Castle's *Strait-Jacket*, for instance — have had a less striking legacy. Because the classic studio system has been dead for well over thirty years, the sixties gambit of casting aging Hollywood divas like Bette Davis and Joan Crawford is no longer as tenable a convention, which is why the female movie-star–driven horror film has generally become less prevalent. (A remake of *What Ever Happened to Baby Jane?* starring sisters Vanessa and Lynne Redgrave in 1991 and *Notes on a Scandal* starring Judi Dench and Cate Blanchett are the two most notable exceptions.) As a result, the women in recent horror-of-personality films seem less important.

And so, in a later horror-of-personality film like *The Hills Have Eyes*, directed by Wes Craven in 1977, we don't see two larger-than-life female Hollywood stars in a battle royal, but unknown actors playing two competing families. Specifically, the representative American family traveling across the desert in their recreational vehicle — father, mother, grown children, infant grandchild, and dog — comes into conflict with a nether-family of monstrous cretins who revel in violence and cannibalism. (One of these monsters was played by Michael Berryman, a talented actor with hypohidrotic ectodermal dysplasia, a deforming condition which contributed to the audience's sense of horror.) Once when I showed this film in a seminar on horror film, one woman retreated after the screening to the corner of the room, where she began sobbing quietly. "I don't understand these things," she said to me later, "I'm only a housewife." By the end of the quarter, however, she had written that *The Hills Have Eyes* was indeed her favorite film of those I had shown, because once she had examined her emotional response, she was put in touch — perhaps for the first time so directly — with her deepest-rooted feelings and fears. Upon reflection, she realized that the values of the American family in the film (and, by extension, the values of her own family) were inordinately disturbing: the father was a racist, clear and simple; the mother, a simpering housewife with virtually no personality whose death is mourned by her family much less emotionally and extensively than their dog's. In fact, the mother is so disrespected that her dead body is set afire by her son as a weapon against an attacker. And the most horrifying acts in the film are not committed by the "monsters," but by the members of the American family, who give themselves over to violence with an enthusiasm that is frightening. A film like *The Hills Have Eyes* shows how contemporary horror films can almost effortlessly reflect the tensions within the American family. And for this older student, the film represented a full-scale attack on the conservative/reactionary values that she had heretofore been only slowly coming to reject, a rejection implicit in her decision to begin pursuing her own college degree long after her children had already received their degrees.[3]

But the truth is that the contemporary horror-of-personality film has changed its emphasis, particularly in the United States, where there has been an obsessive interest in the serial killer. This emphasis is not particularly surprising, considering the attention serial killers have received in the last two decades from an American media now covering crime and celebrities rather than politics. The single most influential serial killer (in cinematic terms — inspiring *Psycho*, *The Texas Chainsaw Massacre*, and *The Silence of the Lambs*, among other films) was Ed Gein, from Plainfield, Wisconsin, who killed and mutilated his victims from 1947 to 1957, turning their body parts into utilitarian objects such as bowls and belts. The most infamous of the recent serial killers was Jeffrey Dahmer, who first killed in 1978, but dispatched most of his victims between 1990 and 1991. Dahmer, who was homosexual, worked at a chocolate factory and lured over a dozen young, nonwhite men to his apartment, where he killed them and had sex with their corpses. After dismembering his victims, he often saved or ate selected body parts to insure that these men he loved would never leave him. Other recent killers attracting attention were (arguably) Jack Kevorkian, the doctor who openly arranged for the mercy killings of as many as 130 of his patients, all wishing to die; Donald Harvey, the nurse who killed at least thirty of his patients, possibly twice that number; John Wayne Gacy, the Chicago contractor who often wore a clown costume and strangled over thirty boys he subsequently buried under his house in a crawl space; Leonard Lake, the motel manager who killed and tortured women, claiming inspiration from *The Collector*; Joel Rifkin, the New Yorker who killed at least seventeen prostitutes; Richard Ramirez, the Los Angeles transient known as the "Night Stalker," who killed women after breaking into their homes; William Bonin, the "Freeway Killer," who raped and murdered male hitchhikers; Gary Ridgway, the "Green River Killer" who killed over forty women, primarily prostitutes and runaways in the Seattle area; Dennis Rader, the devout Lutheran churchgoer and alarm systems salesman from Kansas who was known as the "BTK killer" because of his propensity to "bind, torture, and kill" his victims; Kenneth Bianchi and Angelo Buono, the killing cousins who raped and murdered Los Angeles women; Aileen Wuornos, the lesbian prostitute (and rare *female* serial killer) who murdered her johns in apparent revenge for the prostitutes killed by so many other serial killers; David Berkowitz, the "Son of Sam," who terrorized New York City for two consecutive summers; and Theodore Bundy, the most handsome and charming of all the serial killers, who tended to bite, rape, and bludgeon beautiful coeds on college campuses. Most of these serial killers operated out of a sexual pathology; and the killers with a homosexual orientation especially galvanized the attention of a homophobic American society struggling with the issue of sexual orientation. In fact, perhaps the most notorious and avidly-covered moment in the cultural history of American serial killers was when gay *arriviste* Andrew Cunanan capped his killing spree of gay victims by shooting the famous fashion designer Gianni Versace on the steps of Versace's Miami beach home. Not surprisingly, many of the recent horror-of-personality films take details from these real-life stories. Although most of these killers have a low-budget horror film dedicated to their psyche and their crimes — among them *Ed Gein* (2001), *Ted Bundy* (2002), *Dahmer* (2002), *Gacy* (2003), *The BTK Killer* (2005), and *The*

Green River Killer (2006) — these biographical horror films (perhaps with the exception of *Dahmer*) are significantly less artful and interesting than the fictional horror films which borrow liberally from these realities but eschew fidelity. The fact that there is so much of a popular culture built around serial killers is disturbing enough. But the prevalence of serial killers in America suggests that there are deep fissures built into capitalism not easily overcome; otherwise, why would there be so much crime, sexual dysfunction, pathology, and violence in a country successful by so many other measures? In fact, violence is now so common and expected as to routinely go unreported by the media unless a specific violent act incorporates a mind-boggling, grisly variation theretofore unheard of, or some spectacularly high body count, in which case the media exploits the violence in *Guinness Book of World Records* style.

In fact, the American interest in the pathological now extends beyond serial killing to celebrity voyeurism. In 1994, when O. J. Simpson was charged with the brutal murder of his ex-wife at her Brentwood home, almost every American watched at least part of the televised trial, which was shown daily for months. Was it possible to glimpse pathology in Simpson's eyes? So great was the interest, 142 million people tuned in to radio or television as the "not guilty" verdict was delivered, with white America overwhelmingly believing that this good-looking athlete, affable and rich, was guilty. In 2001, Robert Blake (who in 1967 had played the real-life killer Perry Smith in *In Cold Blood*), was indicted for the murder of his wife Bonny Lee Bakley. Although widely considered guilty, Blake was also found "not guilty." (Simpson and Blake were both found guilty in subsequent civil trials awarding financial compensation to the families of the respective victims.) In 2005, Michael Jackson, international pop star, was finally put on trial for child molestation, a behavior he had long been accused of. Although the trial resulted in a "not guilty" verdict, the American public was largely not buying it. In 2006, the eccentric superstar — his bleached face disfigured by plastic surgery — was hiding out in the Muslim country of Bahrain, wearing a woman's *abaya*, which covered him from head to toe like the monstrous elephant man Jackson so empathized with. Even noncelebrities were becoming celebrities as a result of their infamy. Was Scott Peterson — handsome and charming — the cold-blooded killer of his pregnant wife, Laci, at Christmastime in 2002? Apparently so. And how could Andrea Yates in 2001 — her clinical depression notwithstanding — have drowned her five children in the family bathtub? Pathology, it seemed, could be found everywhere. And in an America increasingly segmented — red state, blue state, straight, gay, MTV–watchers, *700 Club* fans, NASCAR dads, soccer moms, Howard Stern listeners, Limbaugh dittoheads, religious conservatives, secular humanists, and so on and so forth — the primary place for Americans to come together was in the voyeuristic apprehension of the murder in our midst.

The tabloid sensibility of the American media was perfectly in sync with Americans growing increasingly fearful of everything. Local TV news seemed especially designed to frighten. ("Your Foods Can Cause Cancer! Details at 11." "What's Really Going on in Your Kids' Schools!" "Does the Gay Agenda Want Your Children?" "This just in: Terrorist Cells Are Already Here!") Americans, retreating into their churches and fundamentalism, were believing more strongly now than in the sixties that it was impossible to trust anyone, and that they would not remain safe, even when holed up in their suburban (or exurban) refuges. *Be afraid*, the media seemed to tell us every day, *be very afraid...* And yet the focus on killers dispatching *multiple* victims meant, too, that as the body count went up, less screen time was spent on each victim, thus diminishing our ability to empathize with each or to consider fully the true meaning of suffering or loss of life.

Here is an image from Van Sant's *Psycho* along with the same image from Hitchcock's *Psycho*: the only real difference between them is that Van Sant's was shot in color.

And so *Psycho*— the subgenre's seminal film and single most notable horror film of the last fifty years — not only dominated the still rich subgenre of horror-of-personality, but was itself resurrected as a franchise. *Psycho II* (in 1983) brought Norman Bates out of the mental institution to continue his killing spree, the role again played by Anthony Perkins, twenty-three years after the original. In 1986, Perkins agreed to play Norman in *Psycho III*, but only as long as he could direct — which he did, quite competently. *Psycho IV*, again starring Perkins, appeared as a made-for-TV movie in 1990. Perhaps the franchise could have continued indefinitely had Perkins not died, an AIDS-related death which finally revealed the actor's homosexuality and titillated audiences with the sense that Perkins truly understood the nature of a secret life, further conflating actor with role for all time. Aside from these franchise films, at least 72 other films released since Hitchcock's original include "Psycho" in their title, certainly a sign of the *Psycho* cachet.

More interesting than the *Psycho* sequels, which were designed primarily to make money, was Gus Van Sant's controversial idea to remake *Psycho* in 1998 as a virtual shot-by-shot, word-for-word copy of Hitchcock's original. That Van Sant had previously filmed the short parody *Psycho Shampoo* for a Los Angeles comedy troop in 1979 demonstrated his interest in Hitchcock; nevertheless, his new version of *Psycho* was in no degree a parody. Many critics, like Joseph Andrew Casper, missed the point and felt Van Sant's *Psycho* was misguided and debasing, shameless postmodernism run amuck. But the visual art tradition from which Van Sant emerges — whereby young artists often go with their paints into galleries to copy a masterpiece in order to learn and acquire the master's techniques — is hardly postmodern; and Van Sant felt he was inherently honoring Hitchcock's original film in a reverent experiment by purposely *not* changing it. And isn't, for instance, Shakespeare's *Hamlet* continuously reproduced, so actors can be given the opportunity to play famous, challenging roles? What is weird and fascinating about the "new" *Psycho* is that we in effect watch two films: Van Sant's version, which plays on the screen, and Hitchcock's original, which plays in our head. As a result, we cannot help but be turned into deconstructionists, into active critics rather than passive consumers. Van Sant's important choice to remake Hitchcock's classic in color adds an expressive element missing from the black-and-white original. Many of the colors are vivid and garish; of course, the expected red in the bloody shower scene is visually shocking, but what does it mean that Van Sant has chosen a particularly bright green as the background field for Saul Bass' famous credit sequence? Although our knowledge of the original guarantees we watch the film as an act of criticism, that aesthetic distance works *against* the suspense. Still, notwithstanding the excellence of the new

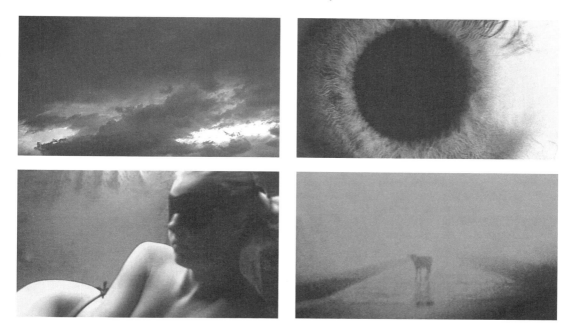

A shot-by-shot remake, Gus Van Sant's *Psycho* includes only a handful of images completely new: in these four, which Van Sant presents as subliminal flashes, the tendency is toward the abstract and surreal.

Psycho's design, direction, and performances, and despite the film's virtually exact replication of the original, what results is merely a good film, not a masterpiece — which suggests that there is something profoundly mysterious about great art, which is *not* reducible to the sum of its parts.

Vince Vaughn gives a credible, giggling performance; his Norman Bates masturbates while spying on Marion Crane, also played credibly by Anne Heche. Alfred Hitchcock, through the magic of special effects, still makes his cameo appearance on the street, but in this version, while talking to Van Sant, who cleverly makes an appearance in tandem. One notable difference in the shower scene (aside from the obvious red blood) are two new images: a rather ambiguous image of storm clouds and an extreme close-up cut-in of Marion's eye dilating at the moment of her death. As well, the camera movement out from Marion's eye is more elaborate and dizzying, a full 540-degree spiral. Another change is that Arbogast's murder rather mysteriously includes shock cuts of a naked woman and a black calf— surreal memory fragments from his life flashing before his eyes? And this version of Norman keeps not only his dead mother in the cellar, but also an aviary of birds — a reference to Hitchcock's other horror masterpiece, *The Birds*. And Hitchcock's much criticized final scene with the psychiatrist here includes rewritten dialogue, which makes it considerably less naive psychoanalytically. The fact that *Psycho*— by Gus Van Sant — works so well today is a sign that the horror-of-personality material is still relevant and seminal.

Indeed, *Psycho* is so seminal, that its influence can be found in the most unlikely places. For instance, *Mommie Dearest*, a biographical film about Joan Crawford (made in 1981), seems as much a horror film as biography or melodrama. The face of Joan Crawford, who is played by Faye Dunaway, is initially kept concealed from the audience in an extended, almost terrifying credit sequence which suggests that Crawford is as frightening as any hor-

These images reveal that *Mommie Dearest* is more horror than biography, because it presents the monster Joan Crawford (played by Faye Dunaway) as (1) an obscure silhouette, (2) a schizophrenic in mirror reflections, (3) a Kabuki demon, (4) an embodiment of emotionless evil, and (5) a sociopathic ax murderer.

ror-film monster, including Norman Bates. And when we do finally see that face, mask-like with its thick eyebrows and overly made up features, it seems already schizophrenic, belonging both to Crawford and Dunaway in an uneasy partnership. And *Mommie Dearest* constructs itself so paradoxically, with scenes of such *grand guignol* pitting mother against daughter, that Joan Crawford seems perilously close to clinical insanity. Her ominous, middle-of-the-night exclamation "Christina, bring me the ax!" is not only a classic horror-of-personality moment, but an *hommage* to Joan Crawford's own foray into horror-of-personality filmmaking, *Strait-Jacket*, which presented the Hollywood icon as a potential ax-murderer. From scene to scene, we wait for an explanation for Crawford's egregious abuse of her children, but none is forthcoming (not even one as obligatory and unconvincing as at the end of *Psycho*); in fact, Crawford's single happiest moment — winning her Academy award — is purposely juxtaposed with Crawford's most terrifying violence: beating her daughter, Christina, with a coat-hanger while Crawford's face is covered in cold cream. This horrifying scene climaxes (as in *Psycho*) in a bright bathroom and with the dutiful child having to clean up the mess created by the mother's violence. Also like *Psycho*, *Mommie Dearest* ends with the quiet stillness of a close-up — though here, it is not of the monster, but of the victim, Crawford's daughter Christina, who is quietly plotting her revenge.

Another unlikely film influenced by *Psycho* and the horror-of-personality films of the sixties is the Academy Award–winning documentary *The Times of Harvey Milk* (1984), which presented the intersecting stories of two men forced to work together in an uneasy relationship: Harvey Milk, the first publicly elected, openly gay politician in the country, who served on the San Francisco Board of Supervisors; and Dan White, an ex–police officer and ex-firefighter, who won election to the same board. Mainstream America would have considered Milk the one with the pathology, yet it was Dan White, the handsome "boy next door," who cracked under pressure and assassinated both Milk and San Francisco Mayor George Moscone. Filmmaker Robert Epstein interviews White's friends, who look

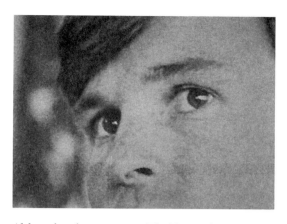

Although a documentary, *The Times of Harvey Milk* includes a typical horror image: a slow zoom into an unnerving close-up of the eyes of the murderer of Harvey Milk — the homophobic politician/fireman Dan White.

at the camera quizzically: how could this devout Christian family man have committed murder? Most terrifying is the whining, sociopathic confession of White (who tearfully sees *himself* as the victim) as the camera slowly zooms into a tight close-up of his eyes, a scene as powerful and disturbing as anything in *Psycho*. In those eyes, we search for signs of White's pathology, which certainly must be secreted there. But Dan White is a horror-of-personality crazy because he embodies the homophobia embedded within American Christian fundamentalism, from which such violence and hatred flow. Dan White's wife, equally out of touch with reality, imagines a future where she and her husband can return to the lives they shared before the murders. In a surprise to many, the pathology extends to the San Francisco courts, which give White a shockingly light sentence, revealing its own institutional homophobia. History reveals that not too many months after Dan White's release, he turned his violence inward by committing suicide, rendering his wife's dream unattainable.[4]

Perhaps the key horror-of-personality film of the period is the extraordinary *Henry: Portrait of a Serial Killer*, made for only $100,000 in 1985 and 1986, but not released until 1990. *Henry*, set in Chicago, and based on the exploits of real serial killer Henry Lee Lucas, was directed by John McNaughton, a filmmaker associated with Columbia College. Originally rated X by the Motion Picture Association of America, *Henry* was well-received by mainstream critics — untypical for a horror film — and even appeared on many "Top Ten" lists for the year. The film's inclusion of a subtitle suggests a documentary sensibility to the horrific subject. The film's measured opening shot, an outward spiral from the face of one of Henry's nude victims, immediately references the outward spiral from the murdered Marion Crane in the shower scene in *Psycho*. The gruesome color images of Henry's victims, all artfully arranged and color-coordinated within perfect frames, evoke the art film. Other imagery, more quotidian, is almost documentary. Henry's work as an exterminator is consonant with his serious vocation: serial killing. One scene, set in a kitchen in which Henry (played persuasively by Michael Rooker) and his would-be girlfriend Becky talk about their troubled lives, recalls the parlor conversation between Marion Crane and Norman Bates in *Psycho*. Becky, an incest victim, learns that Henry's prostitute mother had made the young

Henry: Portrait of a Serial Killer takes its kitchen sink realism literally. Here is the killer's kitchen sink, followed by a portrait at home with his friends, and a cityscape of his neighborhood.

Henry dress in girls' clothing and watch her have sex. At first, we see only the aftermath of Henry's murders — gruesome, aesthetic images of the dead, while the soundtrack lets us hear the final moments of the victims' lives. As the film progresses, we see the actual murders as they are committed by Henry with his friend Otis, who is also sexually conflicted. Not only does Otis rape his sister Becky, he makes passes at a male high school athlete. When Otis and Henry acquire a camcorder, they videotape their murders, producing documentary footage which is unusually compelling. Henry and Otis are neither criminal masterminds nor romantic "raving things" (to quote Norman Bates). Rather, they are barely-literate, sociopathic thugs who drive a jalopy. *Henry*'s successful depiction of class issues is especially notable, bringing a kitchen-sink realism to its familiar horror

Henry: Portrait of a Serial Killer includes numerous images of the aftermath of violence as pornographic, yet aesthetic *tableaux*.

subject. Because Henry and Otis are so unfeeling, their violence is brutal: one victim is stabbed with a soldering iron, smashed over the head with a TV, then electrocuted. Especially horrifying is the murder of a suburban family and Otis' necrophilic abuse of the mother's corpse — all shown in one continuous *vérité* shot. In another horrific scene, Henry kills Otis while straddling him and shuddering in orgasm. By the film's end, it is clear that the romance between Henry and Becky is problematic, to say the least. "I love you Henry," says Becky, but the most Henry can muster in response is "I guess I love you, too." Not surprisingly,

Henry later kills her in a rented room, one of the few murders this film presents elliptically. Notable too, referencing *Psycho*, is our discovery that Henry killed his mother and her boyfriend, though the film suggests three different versions as to how (with a baseball bat, knife, or gun). Unlike the often-criticized final scene in *Psycho*, *Henry* doesn't attempt to offer a psychological explanation for its protagonist and is quite content to offer an accumulation of evidence which posits Henry as a sociological case study. Nor does Henry get caught or suffer consequences for his acts. Yet *Henry: Portrait of a Serial Killer* does pose a very serious question: if so many killers like Henry can be hatched from the economic and psychological deprivations found in America, what does that say about America and its values?

The Stepfather, compellingly directed by Joseph Ruben in 1987, is an unacknowledged re-conceiving of Alfred Hitchcock's masterpiece *Shadow of a Doubt*. Noted mystery writer Donald E. Westlake wrote the ingenious script with its underlying feminist message. Jerry, *The Stepfather*'s psychotic killer played chillingly by Terry O'Quinn, is no lower-class thug, but an Everyman gone mad over his obsession with possessing the perfectly conventional wife and family. His *modus operandi* is simple: when a family he marries into fails his expectations, he butchers them and establishes a new family elsewhere. A clever subplot shows a young, macho male positioned to be the traditional, sympathetic hero who will save the heroine in the nick of time. Yet just when this male is cued at the climax to save the day, he's killed off *so* quickly without even a narrative flourish, foiling our expectations, that it is clear that women must themselves take responsibility for ending the cycles of violence against them. And so it is the mother and daughter, working together, who destroy the unhealthy patriarchy. At the end of *The Stepfather* when Jerry is killed, a totemic, wooden birdhouse — a sly symbol of the conventional nuclear family — is purposely torn down, not only because such traditional definitions of the family are outmoded, but because these definitions are driving men to violence and making everyone unhappy. *The Stepfather* strongly argues that a patriarchal family in which wife and children are expected to dedicate themselves to the husband's needs is *not* a worthwhile ideal, and that men are not worthy of that kind of total sacrifice. If less documentary than *Henry*, *The Stepfather* offers similar incisive criticism of America, particularly the conventional social roles that create such familial tension and violence.

Two exceedingly interesting foreign films of this period used the horror genre to deal with themes of even greater and laudable pretension. The Spanish *In a Glass Cage* (also known as *Tras el Cristál*), has sequences as horrifying as any film ever made. Directed in 1987 by Agustín Villaronga in post–Franco Spain, *In a Glass Cage* is about Klaus, a Nazi ex-*kapo* and child molester, who, years later, is living in Spain, but confined to an iron lung, unable to move. The movie's ponderous pace creates anxiety and anticipation; and the disturbing sound of the iron lung, almost constant throughout the film, creates a claustrophobic tension. "Horror, like sin, can become fascinating," is what Klaus has long ago written in his diary. In flashback, we see powerfully disturbing scenes of pedophilia and the murder of chil-

In a Glass Cage announces its serious intentions with its visual quotation of historical concentration camp photography.

In a Glass Cage presents two unpleasant characters: a former torturer of children (played by Günter Meisner), barely visible in an iron lung, and one of his victims (David Sust), who now wants to torture children himself.

dren. But the greatest horror begins when Angelo, one of Klaus' victims and a witness to murder, now grown into a young man no more than twenty, returns for revenge. But Angelo's revenge is not simple. Yes, Angelo disconnects the iron lung for long moments, threatening to smother Klaus, but more disturbing is that Angelo masturbates onto the face of his former tormentor. *Most* disturbing is that Angelo has returned to show Klaus exactly what the sexual abuse has created: a new monster, Angelo himself. We see this monster when Angelo befriends an innocent little boy, only to abuse and kill him in front of Klaus by injecting poison directly into the boy's heart. By the end of *In a Glass Cage*, Angelo has effectively become the sadistic, evil killer that Klaus had been; only then does Klaus ironically come to understand how insanely evil he *himself* had been. The scenes of violence and perversion in *In a Glass Cage* are all shocking: we watch, in flashback, as Klaus forces the young Angelo to service him sexually; we watch, in the film's present, as Angelo forces another little boy to sing sweetly to Klaus until Angelo slashes the boy's throat. In fact, *In a Glass Cage* may be the only film with an end-credits disclaimer attesting that no children were harmed during the making of the film — which seems hard to believe, considering how viscerally we respond to the children's scenes, no matter how Villaronga's child actors may have been protected psychologically by technical cinematic trickery. As the visuals become increasingly surreal, with a smoky blue obscurity settling over everything, Angelo has killed both Klaus and Klaus' wife. By the film's end, Angelo, now ministered to by Klaus' "wifely" young daughter, himself goes into the iron lung to take Klaus' place. Who would have guessed that this horror genre could have been used so skillfully to examine the relation-

The simple gesture of stroking a child's cheek becomes a horrific sign of pedophilia in *In a Glass Cage*. Ricardo Carcelero plays the young Angelo to Günter Meisner's Klaus.

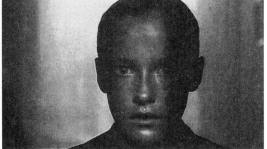

At the climax of *In a Glass Cage*, the pedophile's innocent daughter (Gisèla Echevarría) becomes a worldly vampire who chooses a life of perversions and violence. Note the reference to the famous image of Max Schreck in *Nosferatu*, reflected even in how the daughter's face in close-up seems elongated by purposive shadows.

ship between fascism and pedophilia? And *In a Glass Cage* seems also a complex political parable about how German fascism informed Spanish fascism — one of the rare contemporary Spanish films in which Franco's legacy is unambiguously, if horrifically, represented.

A second compelling foreign film from the very next year is *The Vanishing*, in 1988, written by its director, George Sluizer, with Tim Krabbé. This Dutch film has gone by several other titles — *Spoorloos* [*Without a Trace*], and *L'Homme qui voulait savoir* [*The Man Who Wanted to Know*]. The French title best suggests the existential subtext of this film, which — unlike the American horror films discussed in this subgenre — does not exactly deal with a serial killer, except by the implicit theological indictment of its godhead antagonist. The film's first image — that predatory insect, the praying mantis — immediately associates prayer with murder, God with death. Rex Hofman is *The Vanishing*'s Everyman; and he runs out of gas in the middle of a dark tunnel which already seems a metaphor for death. In that tunnel, his companion Saskia has told about her dream of floating in space, forever trapped in a golden egg, another metaphor for death. But does the egg provide a protected transition to rebirth? Or is it only Saskia's poetic way of conceptualizing an eternity of non-existence? (Later, Hofman will also dream of being "imprisoned in a golden egg," but in reunion with Saskia.) When Hofman returns with the gas, Saskia has disappeared from the waiting car. Is this the "vanishing?" Not quite yet, because he sees her again as he drives through the black tunnel toward the light — a voyage which signifies the surrender to death. The metaphor is intellectually precise, because when Saskia vanishes a second time, Hofman must die in order to rejoin her. Saskia's kidnapper, Raymond Lemorne, has a striking, old-fashioned beard, which suggests a stern, Old Testament aura. Although evil and an admitted sociopath, he is — essentially — God: brilliant, a perfectionist, and the holder of knowledge and secrets. And like God, who is the quintessential serial killer, Lemorne kills.

The spiritual symbolism in *The Vanishing* is actually quite specific, if generally arcane to contemporary audiences. Lemorne is presented as a professor of chemistry, a detail by no means arbitrary. As a child, he is shown reading the *Mutus Liber*, a seventeenth-century

The Vanishing shows many images of Saskia (Johanna ter Steege) which suggest death as transcendence, including (1) Saskia at the end of a tunnel in a metaphorical, glowing egg; and (2) Saskia in a purposely overexposed frame indicating her movement to the light.

book of fifteen plates dedicated to alchemy, a predecessor to modern-day chemistry. Although today alchemy is widely considered crackpot science dedicated to the transmutation of common metals into gold, historical alchemy had a spiritual, philosophical impulse. If popular alchemy focused on gold, it was because gold was considered God's element: the metal that could not corrode or become corrupted. Alchemy was interested in transformation in general, in the creation of higher things from lower things, in Creation itself, in the practices of God. The holy grail of alchemy — the key to unlocking its processes — is the mythical "Philosopher's Stone," a magic element potentially revealed in the symbolic pictures in the *Mutus Liber* that we see Lemorne studying. For Lemorne (and alchemists), science becomes the road to God, who is best described as the Master Chemist, the proprietor of all transformations. More important than incorruptible gold, which is ultimately just a metaphor, is God's ability to transform mortal man into an immortal entity with an afterlife. (Alchemical concepts remain in religious rituals today, as evidenced by the Transubstantiation in the Catholic Mass, whereby wine and bread ostensibly transform into Christ's blood and body.) *The Vanishing* thus presents Lemorne as the alchemical godhead, the chemist with the book. As such, he can turn an egg into gold, and he doesn't hesitate to kill mortal man at will to facilitate alchemical transformation.

The chronology of *The Vanishing* is unusual, because the narrative jumps to a flashback which is only gradually revealed as such when it culminates with Saskia as she is just about to be abducted by Lemorne. And then, shortly, there is another jump — this time, three years into the future, although we still haven't been shown what happened to Saskia and so are increasingly curious and anxious. Finally, Hofman and Lemorne meet. When at the end of the film, Lemorne admits that Saskia is dead, but won't reveal exactly what happened to her unless Hofman allows himself to be drugged, the suspense is excruciating. Of course Hofman wants to know what happened, but what price will he pay to *know*? How strong is the human thirst for knowl-

In *The Vanishing*, Lemorne (Gene Bervoets) is presented as a godhead — here, visually as a head floating in the cosmos, a bearded and stern God-the-father.

Hofman (Bernard-Pierre Donnadieu) is on a theological journey in *The Vanishing*, as evidenced by the architectural crosses he confronts at a gas station. Hofman's nemesis and guide is Lemorne, who as child and adult is associated with the Crucifixion pose. Sadly, if Lemorne is God, he is a cruel god.

edge? And how much would *we* pay, in the same circumstance? We watch in suspense as Hofman struggles to decide whether to take the drugged drink, until finally, he just gives in to the killer's will, to God's will, to his existential fate. Isn't it true that the only way to know God's plan is to accept death and to hope that there will be a hereafter which includes both consciousness and understanding? So Hofman takes the drink, because like all of us, he wants to partake in the forbidden fruit; he is "*L'Homme qui voulait savoir.*" Indeed, perhaps the drink is the magical Philosopher's Stone which facilitates transformation and mystical understanding. When Hofman wakes from his drugged state, he discovers that he has met the same fate as his Saskia: been buried alive. And this is the film's inevitable conclusion, not only because our fate is predestined, but because the Fall of Man in the Garden of Eden — linked to our appetite for knowledge — must result in suffering and death for each one of us. Twice we have seen an image of Saskia as she falls outside the gas station, and we recognize now that her fall — highly symbolic — is a metaphor for *the Fall*; at that moment, her fate is sealed. God, as represented by Lemorne, kills us for our *hubris*. At the film's end, Lemorne is presented as a solitary floating head, weirdly abstracted from his body — an unforgiving God-the-father who speaks from the dark chasms of the universe. Equally theological is Hofman's juxtaposition against the multiple architectural crosses of a gas station as he is about to embrace his own symbolic crucifixion, arranged by God-the-father Lemorne. Even the advertising tag line for *The Vanishing* captured the universality of the film's theology: "What if the man who wanted to know ... is you?"

Whether *The Vanishing* is a horror film or a thriller[5] is not clear-cut, because in *The Vanishing*, the most horrific element — the almost demonic presentation of the nature of God — is only implicit and requires interpretation. But many of the horror-of-personality films live at the intersection of the horror and thriller genres, tipping one way or another based on subtle issues of style and sensibility. It's been said — only partially facetiously — that a horror film that makes a lot of money and gets good reviews is a thriller. Because of its success, *The Vanishing* was much noted by Hollywood, which has historically "purchased" and imported foreign talent, even when subsequently forcing that talent to repudiate their integrity and indigenous originality — precisely those qualities which were so compelling to audiences in the first place. So it was only a little bit odd that Hollywood, inherently understanding that the average xenophobic American would not have gone to a foreign film with subtitles, should have hired director George Sluizer to make an Americanized version of his masterpiece, which was seen as a lucrative property yet to be fully exploited. What is alarming about the 1993 American version, also called *The Vanishing*, is its bowdlerization. The hero does not die, the villain is vanquished, and the film has a romantic, happy ending. That Sluizer was willing to destroy his reputation by bastardizing his own work and shooting these changes, even though they contradict the theological and philosophical meaning of his existential original is a sign of how powerful are Hollywood's inertial forces (and how much money Sluizer must have been paid). Whereas the original was a genre film *informed* by the personal fears of its director about the nature of God — fears which struck an international chord — the sequel was a genre film *deformed* by its projected market and dumbed-down to safeguard the film as feel-good entertainment: a date-movie for teenage boys and their girlfriends.

   Misery reinvigorated Hollywood's love affair with the horror film in a major way. Directed in 1990 by that *metteur en scène* Rob Reiner from a script by the notable William Goldman, *Misery* was based, like so many post–*Carrie* horror films, on a novel by Stephen King. James Caan plays Paul Sheldon, an injured writer held prisoner by his "number one fan," Annie Wilkes, played by Kathy Bates, then a film newcomer. Our first view of Annie is from a menacingly low angle, already suggesting she is dangerously unbalanced. Ultimately, *Misery* is a fairly conventional cat-and-mouse horror film, though with Kathy Bates giving a witty, gutsy, over-the-top, star-making performance, veering from homey charm to cold-blooded calculation or wild lunacy. Like other Reiner films, *Misery* seems a skillful imitation of other directors' more original films. With the emasculated James Caan immobile or in a wheelchair, he is like Joan Crawford as Blanche Hudson in *What Ever Happened to Baby Jane?* When he sneakily hides his pills, he is like Mia Farrow as the victimized heroine in *Rosemary's Baby*. Like *Psycho*, *Misery* contains a basement in which things are hidden. Also like *Psycho*, an investigator meets his death while on a stairway. By the end of *Misery*, Annie is revealed as a serial killer, having killed not only her father, but others under her nursing care. And *Misery* ends, like *Carrie*, with the now expected back-from-the-dead attack. Still, *Misery* does contain one truly original, horrifying scene: when Annie hobbles her hostage by breaking each of his feet with a sledge hammer and then immediately afterwards tells him with shocking incongruity, "God, I love you." Entertaining enough, *Mis-*

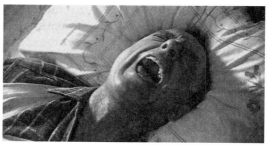

In *Misery*, Hollywood's conventional camera angles are reversed. The woman (Kathy Bates as Annie) is shown from a low angle to look powerful, whereas the man (James Caan as Paul) is shown from a high angle to look weak.

ery succeeds largely on the strengths of its two performances, which catapulted the film to great financial success and allowed Kathy Bates to win the Academy Award for Best Actress by playing, essentially, a horror film monster. Even more importantly, *Misery* showed that it was once again possible for a horror film to be written and directed by A-level Hollywood talent.

Misery paved the way for *The Silence of the Lambs* the next year, which became one of the most successful films in Hollywood history. Who could have predicted even a few years before that a film about a serial killer who is caught with the help of a modern-day cannibal would emerge as the *prestige* picture of 1991? Horror films, even when successful, have rarely won respect or awards at the time of their original release. For instance, *Psycho*, arguably one of the greatest, most influential films of the American cinema, won *not a single* Academy Award in 1960. *Rosemary's Baby* won just one Academy Award in 1968 for the supporting performance of Ruth Gordon. *The Exorcist*, despite many nominations in 1973, won two Academy Awards—one in a technical category and one for best adapted screenplay. And *Jaws* managed to win three Academy Awards in 1975, but all in technical categories. Jonathan Demme's *The Silence of the Lambs*, on the other hand, won a whopping five Academy Awards—and in each of the five major categories: best film, best director, best actor in a leading role, best actress in a leading role, and best adapted screenplay—a feat accomplished only twice before in Academy history—for *It Happened One Night* in 1938 and *One Flew Over the Cuckoo's Nest* in 1975. To say that *The Silence of the Lambs* created a sensation would be an understatement.

The Silence of the Lambs combines the horror genre with the police procedural—Jodie Foster playing Clarice Starling, an FBI agent assigned to capture Buffalo Bill, a vicious serial killer. Not only is it notable that the protagonist is a woman, but she is a woman given no traditional love interest. Certainly her untraditional interest is the serial killer and cannibal Hannibal Lecter, the brilliant elderly prisoner who gives her clues to catching Buffalo Bill. And yet it is her cannibal contact who seems more dangerous. Clarice is warned to "Tell him nothing personal. You don't want Hannibal Lecter inside your head." (And there is irony here, because in the film's sequel—*Hannibal*, in 2001—Hannibal literally gets into a living adversary's head in order to serve human brains as a culinary delicacy.) Certainly we understand that Hannibal is so powerful psychologically that even a conversation with him could be dangerous. The build-up to his first appearance is enormously suspenseful and foreboding, as Clarice must walk through labyrinthine corridors and locking passageways, as cell doors close behind her. At the end of her pilgrimage is Hannibal Lecter,

The Silence of the Lambs is indelibly sparked by the first scene between Clarice Starling and Hannibal Lecter, played with a searing emotional intensity by Jodie Foster and Anthony Hopkins which is intensified by the director's tight close-ups.

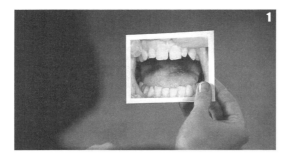

Although ostensibly a police procedural, *The Silence of the Lambs* includes lots of imagery that conforms to the iconography of the horror film — such as (1) the photograph of a mouth, apparently screaming, and (2) a horror-of-personality derived stairway.

standing at attention in the middle of his glass cell, waiting like an expectant groom for his bride. Anthony Hopkins, as Hannibal, gives an understated performance of such great stillness and power, that the American Film Institute in 2003 picked Hannibal Lecter as the single greatest villain in the entirety of the American cinema, followed — not surprisingly — by Norman Bates from *Psycho*. And Jodie Foster, as Clarice, projects strength, intelligence, and vulnerability in a performance so resolute and poignant that the American Film Institute chose Clarice the 6th greatest hero of the American cinema, greater than the heroes of *Rocky, Shane, Butch Cassidy and the Sundance Kid*, as well as scores of others. Very powerfully, every exchange between Clarice and Hannibal crackles with tension and emotional connection. (In fact, their first meeting, arguably the film's most riveting scene, serves a similar function as does the parlor scene between Marion Crane and Norman Bates in *Psycho*.) Hannibal is especially terrifying as he explains that "A census worker once tried to test me. I ate his liver with some fava beans and a nice Chianti," one of the most memorable lines in American popular culture. Scathingly, Hannibal notices that with her good handbag and cheap shoes, Clarice looks "like a well-scrubbed, hustling rube." And he intuits amazing details about her past — including that she is from West Virginia and one generation away from poor white trash. As Clarice leaves the prison corridor containing the most dangerous criminals of the country, she is pelted with ejaculate — which primes the shocked audience for more horror to come.

Buffalo Bill, the antagonist of the film, has been killing and skinning women, trying to patch together a new female skin for himself because he wrongly believes he is a transsexual.[6] Like Norman Bates in *Psycho*, Buffalo Bill sometimes dresses in women's clothes, though the clothes are not enough to satisfy his perverse needs. (Of course, both of these iconic characters — Buffalo Bill and Norman — were inspired by the real-life fifties serial killer Ed Gein.) Later, one of the first things Clarice finds while searching a storage facility used by Buffalo Bill is a stuffed owl, which references the taxidermy in *Psycho*. Also typical to the horror-of-personality film with its emphasis on mutilation and amputation, Clarice finds the almost-obligatory severed head. Yet in the throat of his victims, Buffalo Bill has been carefully placing a Death's Head moth, a symbol of transformation relating to his own sexual (mis)identity.

The rest of *The Silence of the Lambs* sets its strong, three-dimensional characters into suspenseful set pieces of amazing technical facility. One set piece involving a caged cell, an elevator, and Hannibal's attempt to escape is so diabolically clever that it takes our breath away; and we can't help but admire this monster! Yet it is the final set piece, a confrontation between Clarice and Buffalo Bill, which is the most memorable, because a key narrative trope, via editing, purposely misdirects the viewers. The words "Calumet City, Illinois" are superimposed over an image of an urban house far from Clarice, who is in Belvedere, Ohio. When the director cuts between the Calumet exterior, about to be charged by FBI agents, to an interior with Buffalo Bill, we presume that the interior "belongs" to the Calumet exterior. But when the FBI agents are finally shown storming inside and Buffalo Bill is *not* there, we realize that the interior with Buffalo Bill is actually from the house in Belvedere, Ohio, that Clarice is just about to enter, unawares. The effect is stunning, because like Clarice, we feel suddenly thrust into totally unanticipated danger. Again like *Psycho,* still its model, *The Silence of the Lambs* culminates in the basement of the killer's home with a set piece of extraordinary power; although Clarice is victorious, the battle with Buffalo Bill is harrowing. And yet the film ends with a kind of lugubrious *quid pro quo,* for if one killer — Buffalo Bill — has been caught, an even more terrifying killer — Hannibal Lecter — is now on the loose. He calls Clarice to congratulate her, then adds, "I do wish we could chat longer, but I'm having an old friend for dinner." It's a grisly *double entendre,* because he is stalking an old enemy he plans to eat. Yet because Hannibal, although a killer, has come to love Clarice, we find ourselves rather liking him, which is disturbing.

Taking note of this success, other American films in the next several years also told notable stories about serial killers — *Kalifornia* (in 1993) and *Seven* (or as graphically written, *Se7en,* in 1995). *Kalifornia,* directed by Dominic Sena, has a far-fetched plot: a graduate student and his girlfriend, who are taking a cross-country trip to explore the sites of serial killers' crimes, unknowingly ride-share with a lowlife serial killer and his girlfriend. Although Brian Kessler (played by David Duchovny) is a scholar of a certain class, and Early Grayce (played by Brad Pitt) is "poor white trash," the film suggests that all of us have the capacity to commit violence; what distinguishes serial killers is that unlike most of us, *they* don't feel guilt and remorse afterwards. The "K" in *Kalifornia* suggests that the film is a political attack on those fascist qualities within AmeriKa that breed such violence; and yet, as a destination, California is that place characterized within the film as "if it wasn't OK there, it wasn't going to be OK anywhere."

Kalifornia is successful in poetically capturing the American roadside in one beautiful widescreen composition after another. Certainly, the film's iconographic legacy comes from *Psycho*: the motels, the bathrooms, the highways. Even the *Psycho* rainstorm is re-created in *Kalifornia.* And true to *Psycho* and the horror-of-personality film, there are doubles and reflections, not the least of which is the way the antagonist, Early, is presented as the distorted image of the protagonist, Brian. With Early's help, Brian connects not to his inner child, but to his inner serial killer. One expressive widescreen image in a hotel room reveals impressive double reflections; yet it is difficult to tell the good from the bad, the innocent from the guilty, particularly when the "good" female — Carrie, the girlfriend of the protagonist — takes sexually compromising pictures and is therefore hardly innocent. Yet Carrie is self-aware enough to be disturbed by the inherent voyeurism in what she and Brian are doing: taking photos of places where people died violently. Notably, when Early starts his own rampage, he documents his crimes with his girlfriend Adele's pink camera. So the two couples may not actually be all that different.

Brad Pitt, as Early, gives a witty performance which is an accretion of low-life tics: he scratches, spits, swears, burps. No mastermind, Early is just a dumb, if sly, guy who cannot control his impulses. His serial killer recalls the protagonist of *Henry: Portrait of a Serial Killer* and not at all Norman Bates in *Psycho.* And no one plays dumb more heartbreakingly

Cinematographer Bojan Bazelli's exquisite widescreen compositions of the American roadside in *Kalifornia* provide a poetic visual counterpoint to the film's violence.

Kalifornia is filled with doubling images which suggest parallels between the couples. (1) The serial killer Early Grayce (Brad Pitt) puts "devil horns" on the hapless Brian (David Duchovny), which suggests that Brian also has the capacity for violence. And although Brian's girlfriend (Michelle Forbes) is a photographer, it is Early's girlfriend (Juliette Lewis) who takes the photograph. (2) The two girlfriends, further doubled by their mirror reflections, contemplate their resemblance. And (3) Early forces Brian into a parallel, violent stance.

than Juliette Lewis, as Adele, who makes every thought visible. We can't help but empathize as she waxes eloquent about a cactus without realizing she is talking about herself: "You know what makes cactuses so strong? You can just leave 'em and forget about them forever and they'd still live." As typical to the horror genre, the murders are *Kalifornia*'s highlights.

Kalifornia's images are always striking, whether (1) the serial killer in the rain (Brad Pitt) or (2) the innocent academic in the throes of realization (David Duchovny). And yet each man is often photographed on one side of an empty frame, suggesting that they need each other to be complete.

One brutal stabbing takes place in a dingy gas station bathroom, the floor awash in blood and urine. It is sociologically notable that the film's culminating violence takes place at the Dreamland Range nuclear test site on the California/Nevada border. (And through the use of this location, the film implies that the atomic bombings of Hiroshima and Nagasaki should be considered government-sanctioned serial killing on a massive scale.) Old nuclear test dummies provide this film's identity symbols, so typical to the horror-of-personality subgenre. And there is irony that after the murderous climax at the test site — an image of Armageddon — that the final scene (referencing the film *On the Beach?*) takes place on the beach in California, which seems — at least visually — far from the violence which has dominated the film.

In contrast to the unshaven, greasy-haired, low-life killer Brad Pitt plays in *Kalifornia*, in *Seven* Pitt plays David Mills, a well-groomed, smart but naive police detective who is tracking down a serial killer. *Seven*, like *The Silence of the Lambs*, is half police procedural and half horror. From the police procedural, we get the rich relationship between the rookie police officer and the veteran detective; from horror, we get the gruesome violence, amputations, escalating suspense, foreboding menace, and obligatory references to *Psycho*. Just as *Psycho* first presents Marion Crane reclining in bed as a foreshadowing of her death, *Seven* first presents Tracy (the protagonist's wife, played by Gwyneth Paltrow) similarly reclining. So it shouldn't be surprising that Tracy comes to a similarly grisly end.

Seven— directed expertly by David Fincher — reveals its technical facility from the opening credits, which are graphically amazing and disquieting, the equal of anything created by Saul Bass for Alfred Hitchcock or Otto Preminger, and looking much like an avant-garde film, with what appears to be direct scratching onto the film stock itself. The subsequent cinematography of *Seven* is amazingly composed, in essence turning New York City into Dante's *Inferno*, with sin at every level; and it's a dreary hell, too, almost always dark and raining, recalling the storm that brought Marian Crane to the Bates Motel in *Psycho*.

Yet the serial killer in *Seven* is not drawn in the bleak naturalism of *Henry*, but in the larger-than-life fabulism of *The Silence of the Lambs*. "John Doe" (played by Kevin Spacey) is a mastermind whose killings — inspired by the seven deadly sins — are both his work and his art. For gluttony, he forces a man to overeat to the point of internal explosion; for greed, John Doe bleeds a victim to death; for pride, he cuts off a woman's nose to spite her beautiful face; and so on. William Somerset, the cultured veteran detective (played by Morgan Freeman) tracks the intellectual references embedded in the crimes by researching works of Milton, Chaucer, Shakespeare, and Aquinas. One of the first appearances of the monstrous serial killer is an almost abstract shot of his reflection in a puddle while rain pours down.

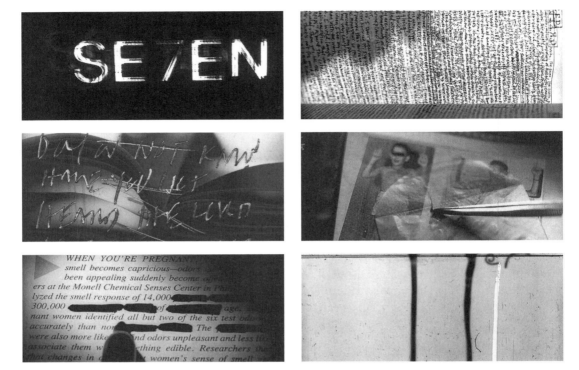

The abstract, avant-garde credit sequence for *Seven* [aka *Se7en*] employs signifiers with unknown signifieds that set us up to be anxious for the rest of the film. In congruence to the atypical credits is the atypical ending, which shows the success of the villain and the abysmal failure of the hero.

Typical to the voyeurism common to the horror of personality, both the police *and* the killer photograph the victims; later, we learn that the killer had posed as a newspaper photographer to stalk David Mills, the young detective trying to stalk the killer. If *Seven* begins like a police procedural, it ends like a horror film. Certainly the dismemberments become increasingly horrifying: a hand, a nose, and then finally a head. And the imagery is increasingly sadistic — for instance, a man forced at gunpoint to wear a horrifically huge strap-on dildo to disembowel a prostitute while having violent intercourse with her (*this* as the mastermind's punishment of lust). Yet no matter how gruesome is the killer's violence, Somerset insists that these killings are no demonic enterprise: "He's not the devil, he's just a man." Somerset, whose name evokes the end of a happy season and the Fall of Man itself,

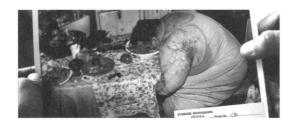

As these two images show, the horrific naturalism of the crimes in *Seven* is so grisly and unnerving that we fear what else the filmmakers might show us. And indeed, *Seven*'s ending shocks us well beyond our capacity to anticipate it.

The widescreen portraits in *Seven* of its three principals are unusually serious: Morgan Freeman as William Somerset, Gwyneth Paltrow as Tracy, and Brad Pitt as David.

seems to know the darkest secrets of the human condition. He predicts — matter-of-factly, not ominously — "You know, this isn't going to have a happy ending."

Seven's key narrative surprise is when the killer turns himself in *before* the cycle of seven killings is finished. Similar to the end of *Psycho*, we see the killer in custody, totally still and apparently insane. Yet the fact that the killer calls himself John Doe suggests that he is as much Everyman as lunatic. *Seven* implies, like many of these horror films, that any of us — given the right fated circumstances — could turn into such a killer. John Doe claims that none of his victims were innocents, but sinners deserving punishment; he makes a good case that he is on a godly mission. The ending, which includes several shocking twists, turns on the horrific revelation that David's wife Tracy has been killed already, and her severed head put in a package which John Doe arranges for David to open. John Doe has killed Tracy because of his own envy of the couple's happy life, but John Doe knows that the shock of seeing Tracy's head will manipulate David to feel the last deadly sin — wrath — and kill John Doe, shockingly concluding the murders that John Doe has been masterminding. The final words of this extraordinarily bleak film belong to Somerset, who says: "Ernest Hemingway once wrote, 'The world is a fine place and worth fighting for.'" After a pause, Somerset adds: "I agree with the second part."

What helps make the expensively produced *Seven* so stunning, in the true sense of the word, is that by the mid-nineties, the big-budget film had been given over almost completely to feel-good entertainment, and the unhappy ending — not unusual in Hollywood's golden age (think *Camille, Now Voyager, The Maltese Falcon, Gone with the Wind*, and so on) — had become an endangered species. With the exception of the occasional film like *Seven*, it is not surprising that the most downbeat, disturbing horror films should start coming from outside Hollywood. Two significant sources for this subgenre were the independent film and the art-house, Francophone cinema.

A good example of an early independent horror film from this period is *Clean, Shaven*, the 1993 debut film from Lodge Kerrigan. *Clean, Shaven* is largely a character study of Peter Winter (played by Peter Greene), a schizophrenic who is searching for his daughter and who may have been responsible for killing several little girls. Kerrigan shows us Peter's bizarre traits, which go beyond the quirky: his habit of drinking three cups of coffee, all lined up in a row; his need to cover his car mirrors and windows with old newspapers dominated by lurid headlines; and his occasional attempts to cut off pieces of his own scalp. The most horrifying scene of the film shows Peter using a knife to cut off one of his finger-

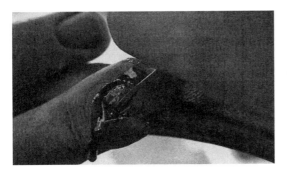

This tight close-up of a mutilated fingernail in *Clean, Shaven* is extreme even for a horror-of-personality film. Of course, the close-up of the protagonist's solitary eye is a well-established iconographic convention.

nails in a misguided attempt to alleviate pressure from the voices he hears in his head. In this scene, which reportedly caused spectators at the Sundance Film Festival to faint, Kerrigan alternates a close-up of the finger as the nail is being removed with a close-up of one of Peter's eyes. (Yet oddly, after his self-mutilation, Peter's voices do recede.) Perhaps the most notable component of *Clean, Shaven* is that Kerrigan works hard to create a stunningly complex and subjective soundtrack which forces us to hear the world the way Peter does: the voices in his head are like a buzzing radio transmission which comes in irregularly and unclearly. Especially powerful is the brilliant score by Hahn Rowe, which eclectically uses sound effects, electronic distortions, and snippets of traditional music to create

In *Clean, Shaven*, director Lodge Kerrigan skillfully photographs his protagonist in compositions which suggest psychosis: Peter (played by Peter Greene) is shown (1) cut off by the frame, (2) without an apparent head, (3) without a body, and (4) in the fetal position.

a kind of *musique concrète* perfect for communicating mental illness. Peter's perspective, if always off, can sometimes seem only subtly off. For instance, what are we to make of the fact that his mother's dress seems often to match the paint or wallpaper pattern of whatever room she is in? Is this oddity real or a subtle manifestation of Peter's illness? By the end of *Clean, Shaven*, it becomes clear that the narrative may be even more unreliable than we had thought, and that Peter could be totally innocent of the child murders, even though we apparently heard one of the murders taking place. After Peter is killed by Detective McNally (the only real dramatic event in the film), the director's subjective sound technique seems to transfer onto the detective, which suggests that *his* mental problems may also be significant, if more subtle than Peter's. By the end of *Clean, Shaven*, with its beautifully photographed abstractions, meaning seems hard to grasp, and ambiguity rules, truths which make this film seem more like a foreign art film than an American horror film.

Although France certainly has a horror tradition (from filmmakers Georges Méliès, Louis Feuillade, and Georges Franju), it is nevertheless remarkable to discover so much brilliant contemporary horror coming from French, Belgian, and Austrian filmmakers working in the French language. In fact, one could easily argue that foreign films like *Man Bites Dog* are putting American studio horror to shame.

Man Bites Dog was made in 1992 by Belgian film students Rémy Belvaux, André Bonzel, and Benoît Poelvoorde. Its original title — *C'est arrivé près de chez vous* [*It Happened in Your Neighborhood*] — inherently suggests the film's quotidian, ordinary world. Essentially a *faux cinéma vérité* documentary (or mockumentary) about a serial killer, *Man Bites Dog* commands attention from its opening scene showing the film's killer, Benoît, strangling a woman and then discussing the physics of underwater body disposal. Since the filmmakers within the film lose objectivity and bond with their subject, *Man Bites Dog* becomes a sly satire on contemporary voyeurism and exploitation. Is it the filmmakers' self-centered ambition which is responsible for their moral failure to intercede on behalf of Benoît's victims? Or is it something more universal in their human nature? In any case, the filmmakers just keep recording the violent footage.

Sequence after sequence is downright creepy, such as when footage of the killer playing toy guns with two children is juxtaposed with a montage of the killer's murders. In another sequence, Benoît discusses Gandhi and then kills a little old lady after getting into her home under the pretext of his taking a survey on loneliness among the elderly. Despite being a serial killer and inveterate racist, Benoît has loving family and friends; and

In *Man Bites Dog*, Benoît (played by Benoît Poelvoorde) is just your average guy holding forth at a café, in turn charming and arrogant. Of course, he is also a serial killer and a demanding exhibitionist who very quickly becomes media-savvy.

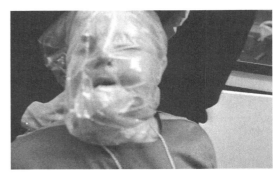

At its best, the *cinéma-vérité* style of the serial killings in *Man Bites Dog* recalls the raw, immediate sensibility of *The Battle of Algiers*.

the juxtapositions between Benoît's violent acts and his ordinary life make for riveting cinema.

"Doomsday is near," claims Benoît shortly before one of the filmmakers — the sound man — is killed. Although the filmmakers cry over their colleague's death, they remain oblivious as to how they are themselves contributing to the violence. Their obliviousness is a metaphor for the ways in which many films — particularly horror film, which emphasizes sensation — inure us to violence and thus promote more violence. *Man Bites Dog* shows us — to quote Hannah Arendt — "the banality of evil." The film's key moment, its turning point, is when the serial killer chokes a child and one filmmaker holds the child down, definitively becoming complicit. Later, Rémy, the documentary "director," aggressively participates in killing a video crew that crosses paths with his own production. Most horribly, the filmmakers participate in a loathsome gang rape before bloodily butchering a woman and her husband. The filmmakers, now as evil as their subject, still don't recognize their complicity. At another point, when Benoît kills a petty gangster, we discover the gangster was being followed by his *own* camera crew — suggesting that Western media and culture are thoroughly fixated on the violent and sensational.

Amidst all the violence, the film still has time to show Benoît's birthday party — where the filmmakers give him a holster. Even though Benoît kills his brother-in-law at the party, covering his family with sprays of blood, the ritual of gift-giving continues. When Benoît again and again looks at footage of one of his murders in slow motion, the scene recalls the documentary *Gimme Shelter* (by the Maysles Brothers), in which footage of a murder at the Rolling Stones' Altamont concert is played over and over. Near the end of *Man Bites Dog*, the documentary filmmakers spontaneously sing in praise of cinema — an ironic indication that the real *Man Bites Dog* filmmakers consider their beloved art form responsible for our increasingly depraved, oblivious culture.

If there is a weakness to the satire of *Man Bites Dog,* it is that the film feels like a single idea, spun to redundant length, though perhaps this redundancy is part of the film's strategy; by the time the film ends, has the redundancy inured us to the violence? The end credits identifying the cast are essentially a necrology to those who "sont morts a l'écran" [died onscreen]; as a final de-humanizing joke, characters are identified by the essential violence perpetrated against them: "une balle dans l'oeil" [a bullet in the eye], "en pleine poitrine" [squarely to the chest], "la nuque brisée" [the neck broken], and so forth. It is notable, too, that the serial killer and the documentary filmmakers within the film are played by the actual filmmakers of *Man Bites Dog,* which suggests that Belvaux, Bonzel, and Poelvoorde do not exempt themselves from their own film's criticism.

I Can't Sleep [*J'ai pas sommeil*] was directed by the French filmmaker Claire Denis in 1994. Set in the immigrant Paris of the 18th and 19th arrondissements, *I Can't Sleep* is an Altmanesque tale in which the lives of a number of characters collide. Because the mix of competing cultures seems so odd, the ordinary is made strange, with scene after scene offputting. For instance, the film starts with a vintage recording of Dean Martin singing Sammy Cahn's "Relax Ay Voo"—ersatz Francophilia. On one level an art film, on another an ethnographic document, *I Can't Sleep* reveals its characters through scenes which powerfully accumulate to form a structural complexity. The film is so devoid of obvious, conventional horror structures and traditional suspense music that not until an hour into the film are we allowed to understand that two characters we've been watching are serial killers. This revelation is stunning, because we have been privy to many of their private actions, and they have not seemed extraordinary in any way. Yet one of the killers, Camille—in the generic tradition of psychopaths in *Psycho, Dressed to Kill,* and *The Silence of the Lambs*—is a man who dresses as a woman. (In fact, Camille is based on the real-life Thierry Paulin, nicknamed "*le monstre,*" an HIV+ black man who in the eighties killed at least nineteen elderly women.) Camille involves himself in Mapplethorpe-like photography, borderline pornographic, which raises the voyeurism theme so typical to the genre. Certainly Denis' point in making her horror film so ordinary is to show that violence has become a normative constant in our society, rather than an aberration. And so her killers have neither more nor fewer problems than any other characters, who are all presented with equal psychological depth. The most horrific parts of *I Can't Sleep* are elliptical. For instance, at one point, a character carrying a heavy satchel comes down a stairway with one of his eyes bleeding. There is no loud, insistent music to remind us to be scared (just as there would be none in real life); although we can imagine what (or who) has been put inside the satchel, the narrative never reveals what's there. The horror of the satchel and bleeding eye relates in some ambiguous way to the cultural tensions of contemporary Paris; thus *I Can't Sleep* becomes a prescient film—seven years before 9/11 and eleven years before the riots in the

Although *I Can't Sleep* eschews most of the stylistic accouterments of the horror film (such as scary music), it still uses some horror conventions, such as associating the killer with a stairway.

banlieue of Paris. Because *I Can't Sleep* seems so anthropological and understated, we hardly notice its recurring generic elements, such as the conventional horror scene (if without suspenseful music) of the heroine searching the killer's home for clues while the killer is away. Camille, a self-professed easygoing guy, knows that no one wants to suffer. But everyone does suffer; and the film — echoing Norman Bates' line from *Psycho:* "We all go a little mad sometimes. Haven't you?" — puts forward the thesis that "The world's gone crazy." Claire Denis offers no solution to problematic assimilation and its attendant urban violence; perhaps all we can do is accept defeat and go with the flow, to "Relax Ay Voo," as we were counseled at *I Can't Sleep*'s opening, before we understood the extent of the social violence being examined.

La Cérémonie, directed by Claude Chabrol in 1995, may be more thriller than horror film, yet it too deals with the revelation that serial killers are living in our midst — and within striking distance of even the best neighborhoods. We learn that two women in town with no prior connection have each committed murder, though they seem now to be living ordinary lives. The ominous friendship they strike up re-ignites the violent, vengeful components of their personalities which had been long kept in check. *La Cérémonie* is based on the novel *A Judgment in Stone* by Ruth Rendell, which begins with that notable opening

In *La Cérémonie*, Sandrine Bonnaire and Isabelle Huppert play murderous women who are hiding their pasts.

sentence: "Eunice Parchman killed the Coverdale family because she could not read or write." Sandrine Bonnaire plays the illiterate Sophie (in the novel, Eunice), who is hired to be the maid for the Lelièvre family (in the novel, the Coverdale family); Isabelle Huppert plays Jeanne, the postmistress whose job is to see that the mail — filled with words, so mysterious to Sophie — gets delivered. When the illiterate and superliterate come together, these kindred women complete each other and create an estimable force for violence. By the film's end, it feels strangely inevitable that these two working women trash the affluent Lelièvre home and violently kill the entire Lelièvre family, one by one, without mercy. In French, "la cérémonie" is also the term associated with the ritual of the guillotine during the French revolution; and Chabrol has described his film, made after the fall of the Soviet Union, as "the last Marxist film." Its upsetting horror also creates an ambivalence within us, because the three-dimensional Lelièvres, though empathetic and nice, are also subtly condescending and wear their privilege for all to see. Although we are horrified when Sophie and Jeanne massacre the family (like so many rabbits, which is what the word "lièvres" means), we can nevertheless recognize the women's murderous impulses as quite human.

As wonderful as Isabelle Huppert is in *La Cérémonie*, she is nothing short of revelatory in *The Piano Teacher* [*La Pianiste*], giving one of the great performances of the cinema. In this 2001 masterpiece, an art-house horror film written and directed by Michael Haneke (born in Germany, raised in Austria, but making his recent films in French), Huppert plays Professor Erika Kohut, a pianist who teaches at a conservatory and lives with her mother, played by the venerable Annie Girardot. The two women share a bed; and their dysfunctional relationship makes sexual the inherent sadomasochism in a film like *What Ever Happened to Baby Jane?*, which also emphasized family pathology. Directors have often

The Piano Teacher first shows Isabelle Huppert's Erika in formally balanced compositions which are the epitome of musical harmony. Yet Erika's psyche is immeasurably darker than these images suggest.

used Huppert to play cool characters; here, we cannot help but see in her Erika some legacy from her extraordinary early success in Claude Chabrol's *Violette Nozière* (1978), where she played a calculating teenager who poisons her parents. *The Piano Teacher* concerns itself not with a serial killer, but with the psyche of Erika—a woman poised on the knife edge between sanity and insanity. As we wait for her to tip one way or another, the suspense becomes excruciating, and we feel like voyeurs given insights into the shocking, secret life hidden behind her perfectly tailored exterior. One of Erika's favorite composers is Robert Schumann; she characterizes his *Fantasia in C Major* as "Not Schumann bereft of reason, but just before. He knows he's losing his mind. It torments him, but he clings on, one last time. It's being aware of what it means to lose oneself before being completely abandoned."

This speech is one of our first major clues that *The Piano Teacher* is a horror film in the guise of a film about classical music. Erika's father died in an asylum, and we understand that Erika is afraid of the same fate, though we don't immediately understand why.

But then in one very upsetting early scene, the apparently proper Erika—to the soundtrack of classical music—goes into a porn shop booth, where she watches pornog-

In a brief, telling sequence in *The Piano Teacher*, Isabelle Huppert's Erika runs onto an ice skating rink to escape her sexual obsessions. When straightaway she loses her balance, she reveals herself as a fragile, overwhelmed woman.

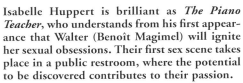

Isabelle Huppert is brilliant as *The Piano Teacher*, who understands from his first appearance that Walter (Benoît Magimel) will ignite her sexual obsessions. Their first sex scene takes place in a public restroom, where the potential to be discovered contributes to their passion.

raphy while smelling the ejaculate she's found on a discarded tissue. The truth that there may be people who look as "normal" as Erika and yet do these kinds of things is disturbing. (Or must we revise our understanding of "normal?") Later, in her bathtub, Erika takes a razor to her vagina, and clearly derives sexual pleasure as she bleeds herself. And at a drive-in, excited by a couple who is copulating, she urinates on the pavement outside their car while watching them. There is a horrifying contrast between her personal behaviors and the cool, accomplished professional life she leads, so dominated by her rigorous classical music. Yet her madness (if that is what we should call it), like Schumann's, is escalating, and starts to spill over into her professional life, particularly when others start playing the piano as well as she does. One creepy sequence shows Erika humiliating Anna, a young student with no self-confidence, but then when Anna performs well at a concert, Erika fills Anna's coat pocket with broken glass, a sadistic act which results in a major hand injury and emotional breakdown for Anna.

Erika grudgingly allows herself to become involved with Walter, a young student (well played by Benoît Magimel) who pursues her. Although Walter is talented, handsome, and sensitive, Erika, retaining control, refuses to allow him to orchestrate a traditional romance and insists that their sexual expression be limited to activities he finds troubling. In a public washroom, Erika fellates and then masturbates Walter, all the while insisting the door remain open, so they can potentially be caught. She also tries to require Walter to indulge her fantasies: that she be tied up, debased, beaten, and locked in her room while her mother, helpless, hears everything from outside the door. Erika wants to experience sexual powerlessness, but why? Is it because in her professional life, she has always had considerable control? No answer is provided. Although we know that Erika has a love/hate relationship with her mother, we are nevertheless surprised when Erika jumps on top of her mother in bed and kisses her passionately — an incestuous impulse that makes us (and her mother) recoil. *The Piano Teacher* is horrifying not because we fear a madman will come out of the dark to kill or scare us, but because Erika's pathology is so disquieting and inexplicable that we are shaken from our moorings. If this well-put-together, accomplished woman can behave so self-destructively and disintegrate, then perhaps anyone can, even ourselves.

The final sequence of *The Piano Teacher* is genuinely unnerving. Not only do we see Erika experience the most subtle but devastating humiliation, we see her utter self-loathing as she stabs herself in the heart. Afterwards, though just for a moment, she looks again in control as she demurely covers her wound.

At the end of the film, Erika hides a knife in her purse on the way to a concert in which she is to perform. Is Erika about to turn into a raving Norman Bates? Will she use the knife? And if so, when? And whom will she target? Walter? Although her mother, her colleagues, and her students are all there, Walter is not. Only when the concert hall is full and Erika stands waiting in the lobby alone, needing to go onstage, does Walter — at the last suspenseful moment — arrive. We fear he may get too near Erika and be stabbed (although of course there is no traditional scary music to warn us); foiling our expectations, Walter walks past Erika quickly, offering encouraging words, but not many, and then is beyond her, inside the concert hall: Erika again alone. Unmistakably, Walter has finally washed his hands of Erika and their problematic affair. In one of the most disquieting endings in the entirety of cinema, Erika takes out her knife and stabs herself in the heart, forcefully dragging the knife across her chest before pulling it out and letting it drop. The supremely expressive face of Isabelle Huppert so powerfully registers Erika's repugnance with herself and with life itself, that this moment is both heartbreaking and profoundly alienating. As blood starts to seep out, Erika covers the wound chastely with one hand; and just for a moment, she looks like a normal person, rather than a lunatic. Somehow able to stand, though moments from death, she exits the concert hall and stumbles down the street and out of frame, as the traffic goes by, oblivious to the horrifying melodrama. As the credits roll, we hear neither classical music coming from the concert hall, nor extra-diegetic soundtrack music. Although devoid of horror clichés, *The Piano Teacher* nevertheless functions as a horror film. While so many horror films of the last twenty years successfully startle their spectators with riffs of loud music or sudden movements onscreen, most of these films totally evaporate from memory. The first time I saw *The Piano Teacher* — one of those rare

In Michael Haneke's *Funny Games*, intense close-ups contribute to a claustrophobic sensibility. The father (played by Ulrich Mühe), the mother (Susanne Lothar), and the child (Stefan Clapczynski) comprise Haneke's Everyfamily. The villains (Frank Giering and Arno Frisch) are not monstrous physically, but when one looks directly at the camera to make eye contact with the viewers, we feel indicted for the violence we are watching.

films that stays with you forever — was at a matinee in San Francisco; when the film ended, the sophisticated spectators were so stunned they felt compelled to stay seated for many minutes to recover enough composure to leave.

Michael Haneke's directorial brilliance can also be found in his earlier *Funny Games*, made in 1997 in German, from his own script. Like many of these art-house entertainments, *Funny Games* is a disguised horror film. It begins with Georg and Anna Schober with their little boy and dog, photographed in beautiful, aerial long shots of their car zooming along the highway to their summer house. The selection from Handel played in their car gives the scene a calm, pastoral feeling. Suddenly, director Haneke replaces the Handel with the extra-diegetic music of John Zorn: screaming, disjointed, anguished, screeching tracks played at such volume that the pastoral feeling immediately transforms to one of extraordinary tension, despite the same kinds of images as before. The substitution is Haneke's reflexive comment on how easy it is to use music to manipulate an audience's emotions. Haneke brings the unbearable Zorn to an abrupt end, then refuses for the rest of his film to use any extra-diegetic music to tell the audience what emotions to feel or when to feel them. As a result, because we are forced to interpret situations which seem often inscrutable, *Funny Games* is disquietingly ambiguous.

Although Georg and Anna have relatives who summer around the same lake, the

In *Funny Games*, because both mother and child (Susanne Lothar and Stefan Clapczynski) wear clothes which blend in to the design of their cushy summer home, they lose psychological weight and seem weak and ineffective. It is not surprising that neither survives.

Schobers' casual reunion with these relatives—who have guests who call themselves Paul and Peter, young men who both wear white gloves—seems oddly formal. The typical spectator puts aside any reservations and does not quite register the subtle anomalies—at least until the odd scene when Peter, dressed in country-club white, visits Anna to borrow eggs. At first, the scene appears charming, if pointless. When Peter drops and breaks the eggs, then asks for more, Anna gives them willingly, though less graciously. But then, in the process, comes something even more awkward: Peter tips Anna's cellphone into the sink. The scene becomes stranger when Peter is joined by Paul, also in white, who wants to try out Georg's golf clubs. And then the Schobers' dog jumps up on Peter, and the second batch of eggs gets broken. Might the visitors be given a third? Eventually, it becomes clear what's going on: Peter and Paul are playing some "funny" games which lead to a full-fledged terrorizing of this family. For the most part, the sadistic games are played with cold civility; Peter and Paul resemble charming Nazi brownshirts, using polite logic as they carry out their violence. The first horrific act is when Paul, looking like a privileged tennis pro, kills the Schobers' dog with a swung golf club—an act of violence which the scrupulous Haneke keeps offscreen, with only the sounds of the blow and the dog's yelp to alert us. Later, Paul attacks Georg with the same club. In the typical horror or action-adventure film, characters recover easily from multiple blows to fight for their lives. Director Haneke is disinclined to embrace that cliché: after Georg is attacked, he remains effectively unable to walk for the rest of the film. These are not "Hollywood" attacks, but "real" ones, where injuries have *consequences*. The villains commit a variety of atrocities: in a game they call "Kitten in the Bag," they ominously cover Anna's son's head with a pillowcase; they humiliate Anna by making her strip; they tie her up. Their evil seems totally casual, indeed, banal; Paul seems never to break a sweat or lose a beat, no matter what horror he perpetrates. Virtually every act of violence in *Funny Games*—which is essentially an art-house version of *The Hills Have Eyes*, in which one family is attacked by another kind of family, even to the details of killing a dog and a child—takes place offscreen, another attempt by the director to avoid the most overused horror clichés. For instance, while we watch Paul make a sandwich, we hear a shot and huge commotion from the next room. Haneke refuses to immediately cut to the action. When he finally does cut to the living room, all we see at first are horrific blood splatters on the TV. A subsequent long shot shows partial glimpses of mother, father, son—none of them moving; and we watch for a long time, unclear as to who has been killed. Finally, we discover that the victim is the little boy; and in contrast to the typical horror film, we see real grief. In fact, the parents' grief is so protracted we cannot escape

Left: In a shocking demonstration of Brecht's *Verfremdungseffect*, the key villain (Arno Frisch) accuses us directly of wanting to see more violence. If we reject his accusation, shouldn't we walk out of the theatre or turn off our DVD player? *Right:* The most unsettling image in *Funny Games* is this close-up of the child forced to wear a pillowcase as part of a sadistic, violent game. From today's perspective, it is hard to look at this 1997 image without thinking of similar images created by American torturers in Abu Ghraib prison during the War in Iraq.

into the typical complaisance to violence that most recent horror films engender in their audiences.

But why are these young men engaging in such sadism? Peter offers a suggestion to explain his own behavior, claiming it's because he comes from the expected background of parental abuse, alcoholism, and drugs. But Paul demurs: "Do you really think [Peter] comes from a deprived background? He's a spoilt little shit-face, tormented by *ennui* and world-weariness, weighed down by the void of existence." It's unclear what we're to think, but both explanations seem inadequate. Perhaps the truest explanation is the most horrifying: *there is no explanation.* Yet independent of *why* is a more important question: *How* are the defenseless to respond when confronted with implacable evil? Are they supposed to give in? Are we? The sad history of the world is a cavalcade of the defenseless millions slaughtered by the politically powerful.

Haneke is an intellectual, aware of Bertolt Brecht's ideas — particularly *Verfremdungseffect*, the "alienation effect" which breaks our suspension of disbelief to force our awareness that we are watching a work of art. At one point, the lead villain Paul looks directly at the camera and winks at the spectator, implicating *us* and suggesting that we're enjoying these sadistic games as spectacle, which on some level is undeniably true, whether we are watching Haneke's film in a movie theatre or at home using a DVD player. At another point — which is even more surprising — Paul turns to us and asks: "What do you think? Do you think they have a chance of winning? You are on their side, aren't you?" Paul (and Haneke) are now indicting us directly. A bit later, the husband, Georg, asks the young villains to stop the games and just kill him and his wife, to end it all quickly. Paul's response is so reflexive that it stuns us. "We're not up to feature film length yet," he says; and then again looking directly at the camera, asks us: "Is that enough? But you want a real ending, with plausible plot development, don't you?" Haneke is saying that the violence, a rule of the genre, cannot yet end, because the requirements of the commercial cinema — largely set by the market — *demand* that Georg and Anna be further tortured. This Brechtian revelation is breathtaking. In another game, Paul tries to force Anna to pick the order in which she and her husband will be killed, and whether with a knife or gun. And Paul requires Anna to pray to God, but insists she recite the prayer in reverse. Instead, she unexpectedly reaches for the rifle and bloodily shoots Peter. At this point the narrative goes through such a Brechtian rupture that the spectator can barely believe what is happening. Paul starts crazily shouting for the remote control, and when he finds it on the coffee table, starts pressing buttons. For a moment, the screen "freezes," and then the narrative reverses in fast motion — responding to Paul's operation of the remote — until *Funny Games* returns to the moment just *before* Anna's successful act of defiance. When the narrative resumes in forward motion, this time Paul *anticipates* Anna's lunge for the rifle and foils her. As a result, Peter is not shot, and Georg is killed instead. "When Kelvin overcomes gravitation, it turns out that one universe is real, but the other is just a fiction," Paul explains.

The very insistence of this image of the knife in *Funny Games* implies its critical importance to the film's resolution. So we wait and wait and wait ... and it isn't. Haneke's gambit is his intriguing, funny game on the audience.

The villains Paul and Peter, hardly "apostalic" in their plans to kill Anna in the middle of the lake, take her out to the boat. The alert spectator has known all along that the drama would end there, because earlier, a knife had been left in the boat by Georg and his son. To make certain even the dullest spectator would remember that moment, director Haneke had pointedly cut to a medium shot of that knife falling into a crevice of the boat. And so we *know* that that knife will be the element to Anna's escape.

Except that it isn't. Although Anna finds the knife and starts to cut through her ties, Paul, in an elegant, spare movement, tips her backwards into the water, drowning her in an instant: Anna alive, Anna dead. The knife is pointless, because there is *no* successful way to respond to such implacable evil. (Didn't the Nazi concentration camps demonstrate that?) One can imagine Michael Haneke's glee in breaking the often-quoted rule of dramaturgy (long attributed to Chekhov) not to show a rifle over the fireplace in the first act, unless you're going to shoot that rifle in a subsequent act. But the genuine horror of real life does not proceed with the archaic logic of traditional dramaturgy. We finally realize, if we haven't already, that the Schobers' relatives we earlier saw acting so stiffly were themselves being held hostage by the young villains and have doubtless long ago been killed. And we understand belatedly that the white gloves on Paul and Peter that we barely registered earlier were to prevent traceable fingerprints. The film ends in a circular fashion, as the villains proceed to borrow eggs from another privileged family with a lake house. Only now does the anguished extra-diegetic music of John Zorn come back in — almost as if director Haneke is bragging about his ability to have put us through an emotional maelstrom without resorting to a single musical cliché anywhere in this most brilliant film.

Haneke's reputation has had an interesting arc in the United States. Few of his films achieved theatrical release in an America increasingly disinterested in intellectual or foreign films since the release of *Star Wars*. If one wanted to see *The Piano Teacher* theatrically, one needed access to an international film festival or had to live in a city like New York or San Francisco. And several of Haneke's films didn't play theatrically even in those cities. But Haneke has become one of those international directors whose work has been discovered in America largely on the strength of the DVD release, which is increasingly how American cinephiles discover foreign film: creating personal international film festivals in their living rooms. For Haneke, a limited Fox Lorber 1999 DVD release went out of print fairly quickly and was reissued only in 2006 by Kino Video. Still, these DVD releases allowed *Funny Games* to gradually become a surprising cult success in the United States — but not until almost a *decade* after the film's European release. Even more impressively, the 2006 DVD success of *Funny Games* prompted the 2007 DVD release of Haneke's first three theatrical features, previously unavailable to American audiences. *The Seventh Continent* (1989), *Benny's Video* (1992), and *71 Fragments of a Chronology of Chance* (1994) — all brilliant films — compose what Haneke has called his "glaciation trilogy." All deal with the alienation of human beings from their emotional, human selves. At the same time, these films come so close to the horror genre, an argument could be made that they are essentially art-house horror films.

Haneke is overwhelmingly interested in the phenomenon of violence, and his characters move mysteriously toward some transgressive act, often committed casually. Unlike other horror-of-personality directors, Haneke tends purposely to diminish the psychological, believing it provides little explanation of any individual's violence. Instead, Haneke explores the sociological, and even the political. In other words, we may not understand why X kills, but we can watch how X lives: what he eats for breakfast, how he moves, what are the important objects in his life, and certainly what television shows he watches. And we can note the political realities around him (ethnic cleansing, war, revolution, technological advance) which affect him without his awareness. But why *X* commits the violence, rather than Y, or commits it precisely at point of time A rather than B, is not definitively knowable. Unlike the chattering journalists of our time, Haneke is under no illusion that either therapy or jail is the answer; the causes of violence are not so much personal as anthropological. If we are to reduce violence, we must, like Archimedes, find a way to move the world itself, to halt and reverse its inertial pull.

Although Haneke worked as a director for Austrian television from 1973 on, *The Seventh Continent* in 1989 must nevertheless be considered one of the more impressive theatrical feature debuts. Based on an event reported in the Austrian news, this film presents the deterioration of a "typical" Austrian family defined largely by their consumerism. The details of their lives are anthropologically

In *The Seventh Continent*, director Michael Haneke comments on the capitalist consumer culture by composing frames that require careful scanning to see the characters, who are dominated by their objects.

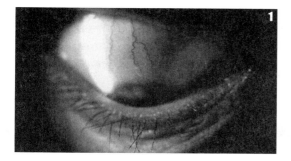

Alongside the social commentary in *The Seventh Continent* is traditional horror iconography: (1) Haneke's unusually unpleasant "single eye" image; (2) this bathtub image, which suggests a detachment that prefigures the film's horrific climax; and (3) this surreal and ambiguous landscape, especially beautiful because it is devoid of consumers or signs of consumerism.

specific: we see the products they enjoy, the brand names they prefer. These are people who do not so much live, as perform tasks. They work, they eat, they shop, they rest, they travel, they get their car washed, they consume. But Haneke wonders: isn't that true for most of us in the West? Might we not secretly yearn for some better place, some seventh continent where living seems more elemental, more vital? Especially striking images show the family's elaborately set breakfast table, more laden with meaning than are the faces of Haneke's characters. In fact, Haneke consistently shows us the family in shots which exclude their faces, which makes them less particular and more universal to the West. Because we see the accouterments of their lives, Haneke suggests that these characters define themselves by their things and habits, not by their minds and souls. In other words, they don't have lives, they have lifestyles. Haneke presents their actions without comment. We see a typical encounter with an incompetent boss at work, an accident on the freeway, isolation while going through a car wash, clients overheard complaining at an eyewear shop, and an elementary school visit to deal with the daughter's unexplained feigning of blindness. Other Western families exhibit lifestyles (if including some different particulars) which are essentially the same.

In Godardian style, Haneke uses solid colors and loud sound effects. Ubiquitous, too, are the TV and radio filled with depressing news (about "the Palestinians" or the "European Union") which seems like so much dissonant ambience: semiotic static. And segments of Haneke's film are divided by seconds of black leader which force us to think about what we've just seen and to anticipate what we might yet see. As we become voyeurs, the family parents, Georg and Anna, gradually descend into a casual madness which results in their destroying virtually every object in their home. They tear up their pictures, they smash their furniture, they rip up their clothes and drapes, they break their phonograph records. Yet their demolition is totally methodical and carried out without emotion or catharsis. The primary object they don't destroy is their TV set—perhaps a significant cause of their glaciated state? As climax to their inexplicable behavior, they kill their daughter Eva and commit suicide.

The violence in *The Seventh Continent* expresses the horror of personality through a contrarian, Marxist impulse. The pick-axe, appropriate for murder in any contemporary horror film, is here used to destroy a well-designed home, including its aquarium. The toilet (a horror staple since Hitchcock's *Psycho*) is used not to flush body parts or blood, but cash and coins — suggesting that Western consumer capitalism is what needs to be murdered.

Certainly Haneke's images are shocking: at one point, with the camera focused on the toilet bowl in a heightened horror-of-personality tradition, Georg and Anna flush down their possessions one after another. The moment they flush their paper money is absolutely electrifying. The association of *cash* with a receptacle for feces and urine creates the most startling transgressive image, a rejection of the supreme value of the Western world. Indeed, the fact that their cash-flushing feels *more* horrifying than the murder of their daughter shows how materialistic our consumer society has become. Incidentally, Haneke has reported that in festival screenings, the cash-flushing always prompted gasps as well as outraged audience exits. This is not surprising, considering that from *Medea* on, infanticide has been used as a common artistic theme. Uncommonly horrifying is the destruction of money, a repudiation we can barely process. The cash-flushing is followed by an equally surreal shot of a pile of coins being flushed down the toilet. And horrifying, too, is when the father takes an ax to a huge aquarium in their home, which is immediately flooded; we watch for a long while, stunned, as a flopping goldfish dies.

What makes *The Seventh Continent* particularly surprising within the horror-of-personality conventions is that Haneke rejects the possibility for any psychological explanation. We have *no idea* why this family breaks down; indeed, from scene to scene, we have little idea why any of them do the things they do. And things we can't decipher are scarier than things we can. For Haneke, people break down *not* because of personal psychology, but because of the accumulation of troubling anthropological details inherent in contemporary Western civilization. We are the passive products of TV, the internet, technology, and a capitalist consumer structure which have stripped away our humanity. Because soci-

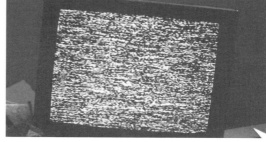

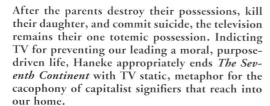

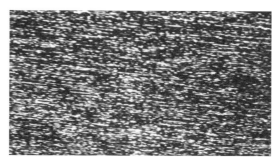

After the parents destroy their possessions, kill their daughter, and commit suicide, the television remains their one totemic possession. Indicting TV for preventing our leading a moral, purpose-driven life, Haneke appropriately ends *The Seventh Continent* with TV static, metaphor for the cacophony of capitalist signifiers that reach into our home.

ety seems monolithically unmovable, no solutions to the problems of alienation and violence seem even remotely possible — and so Haneke's films become especially horrifying. *The Seventh Continent*, elegant and thought-provoking, is a shocking masterpiece of austerity and integrity.

Three years later, Haneke produced another great film, *Benny's Video*, which explored many of the same themes as *The Seventh Continent*. *Benny's Video* begins with a *cinéma-vérité* video of a pig killed by a farmer with a stun gun.[7] The video was taken by Haneke's protagonist, the fourteen-year-old Benny, who is obsessed with video technology and watches the killing of the pig over and over (evoking a similar scene in the documentary *Gimme Shelter*, in which Mick Jagger repeatedly watches the killing of someone attending a Rolling Stones concert). On another monitor, Benny watches his own video surveillance of the street outside his bedroom rather than looking out the window to see the street directly. And tellingly (or maybe not?), he watches low-budget horror and action-adventure films with lots of violence. In the film's key scene — which at several points appears to be moving toward an awkward expression of affection between Benny and the young girl he brings to his bedroom — Benny is asked whether he's ever seen a dead person, and Benny talks about the special effects violence of the cinema, where "it's all ketchup and plastic." The scene, with its occasional undercurrents of tension, turns nightmarish when Benny shows her the pig video, produces the stun gun, impulsively dares her to shoot him, and then — with absolutely no emotion — shoots her. The girl moves out of frame, but does not die instantly, requiring Benny to shoot two more times. Her dying takes a long time, and Haneke mainly keeps the violence offscreen, though some of it can be glimpsed on Benny's video monitor, since Benny had also been "shooting" the girl on videotape. In essence, with no apparent premeditation, Benny has created his own snuff film. Borrowing aural techniques from director Robert Bresson, Haneke uses the sounds of the girl dying to make this scene unusually visceral. Yet Benny is unconcerned, alienated from the moral meaning of his actions. Having killed the girl as coldly as the farmer killed the pig, Benny can afterwards calmly eat a yogurt. (And later, Benny will clean up some spilled milk with the same nonchalance he cleans up the girl's spilled blood.) Benny's parents, named Georg and Anna

In *Benny's Video*, Benny (Arno Frisch) is shown as (1) the nerdy kid, surrounded by video technology; (2) a killer whose acts can be watched obliquely on his video monitor; and (3) as a traditional monster in silhouette whose motivation remains obscure and complex, whether in close-up or (4) in extreme long shot, as a barely apprehensible entity.

(like the couple in *The Seventh Continent*), are oblivious. ("Georg and Anna" are Haneke's recurring representation of the typical, educated couple of Western capitalist democracy.) When Georg sees that Benny has shaved his head, Georg asks him, "Don't you think there are better ways to rebel?" The oblivious question is hilariously off the mark, considering the murder his son has just committed. Or is it a murder, exactly? Does murder require emotion, or at least motive? And was it even a rebellion, or something virtually normal that society has come to expect? Later, when the parents find out what Benny has done, they become complicit in his crime; in a nod to Hitchcock, Benny's guilt is transferred onto them. To help their son avoid ruining his life (or creating scandal for them), the mother takes Benny to Egypt on vacation, to lay low. There, life is very different; Anna and Benny see poverty, not just privilege; and if there is killing, it is for a reason. When asked why he killed the girl, Benny can only answer, "I wanted to see what it's like, probably." But to the question, "And what's it like?" Benny can give no answer: either he is not articulate enough to respond or is no longer appropriately human to have an answer.

As in *The Seventh Continent*, Haneke refuses to offer a psychological explanation for his film's central act of violence. But Haneke also stunningly refuses to show even a moment of the most egregious, extended violence in *Benny's Video*: the violence committed by Benny's father. For while Anna and Benny are out of the country, Georg is cutting up the corpse of the girl his son murdered and carefully flushing it down the toilet in the tiniest of smashed pieces, an enterprise which requires forethought and planning, days of grisly effort, and meticulous dedication. Evidently, violence in the Western world can be accomplished either with premeditation or without. So who is the greater monster, Benny or his complicit parents? Haneke seems not to indict Benny as much as he indicts the consumerist society of

Michael Haneke's close-ups make his *Benny's Video* characters specific, rather than generic. In portraits which are intense yet casual are Benny (Arno Frisch), his mother (Angela Winkler), his father (Ulrich Mühe), and a schoolmate (Ingrid Stassner).

the Western world, particularly its newest technologies. With the scandal of Benny's act of violence apparently averted, the parents attend a school concert where Benny and his classmates sing a beautiful Bach cantata whose words take on a cruelly ironic meaning: "Despite the gaping jaws of death, despite the constant fear, let the world rage and toss, I stand here, and I sing ... in perfect calm." At the end of the film, with his own perfect calm,

Michael Haneke composes cinematic still life to communicate the anthropological roots of the horror within Western capitalism: (1) fine china and money, (2) fast food and consumer advertisements, and (3) the bourgeois "good taste" of well-designed furniture and of culture that fits on your wall.

Benny gives up his parents and himself by providing the police a videotape of Georg and Anna discussing their plans for the murdered girl. Why does Benny betray them? Again, Haneke offers no answer, not even the psychological clues that are *de rigueur* for this kind of film. Benny can only offer the incoherent explanation: "Because." But we do find out that "the peace plan for Bosnia has failed..." and that "seven people have been killed in a train disaster in Sweden." In other words, because violence is pandemic in our contemporary world, it is ludicrous to search for psychological explanations. Ultimately, we are left with the ubiquity of video technology, which makes all of us emotionally detached voyeurs. In fact, the closed-circuit surveillance video at the police station is not unlike the video system in Benny's bedroom. Haneke's key idea is that we no longer live in reality, but live vicariously through video images that increasingly dominate our lives. The girl's murder seemed unreal to Benny precisely *because* it took place in reality in front of him; the slaughter of the pig *was* real, because the mediation of the video camera gave it an *imprimatur* of importance. On some level, events become real only when we capture them via a technological, consumable product. It is not enough for us to have the memory of visiting the Eiffel Tower or the Red Sea, we must have a photograph of ourselves in front of the Tower or the Sea.

The irony, of course, is that video images are inherently false, even when "true"—for among other things, they lack smell and a third dimension. More importantly, they even lack the immediacy of real experience, the real-time generation of feeling—which may be why we find video images so fetching. As historical events (which we see on video) and our own lives (which we do not) become separate, we conceptualize ourselves as outside history, and outside responsibility too. Haneke fears that we may increasingly feel that we become "real" only by committing acts which propel us onto the video screen. (YouTube, anyone?) Only the "newsworthy" or the consumable will seem valuable. Sadly, our lives and the lives of others will not.

Arno Frisch, who here plays the young Benny, would return to Haneke's cinema five years later to play the primary killer in *Funny Games*. It is thematically meaningful that actor Ulrich Mühe, who plays the father to Frisch's character in *Benny's Video*, would play the husband who is the victim of Frisch's character in *Funny Games*. Does Mühe die in the latter because he was responsible for fathering Frisch in the former? Although Benny is one of the most inscrutable horror-of-personality monsters, I think Haneke believes we should be more scared of Benny's parents. Members of the educated elite who have access to a certain power and money, the Schobers are the regretful, if cold enablers of the arrogant hubris of the Western world; it is the Schobers and the legion like them who help propel political disasters of international proportions.

The final film of Haneke's trilogy, *71 Fragments of a Chronology of Chance*, with its ambiguous long takes (that is, shots of unusually extended duration) revealing the influence of American experimental filmmaker James Benning, is the most complex of the three films. Comprised of elliptical, overlapping stories told in segments, *71 Fragments* makes us struggle to make sense of its narrative. Eschewing the fast cutting typical in the Hollywood film, Haneke uses a preponderance of long shots and unusually long takes, with narrative segments divided by a caesura of black leader to slow the pace. As *71 Fragments* begins, a title card discloses that "On 12-23-93, Maximilian B., a 19 year old student, shot three people in a Viennese bank and killed himself with a shot in the head shortly afterwards." Haneke is alerting us that although experimental, his film will present a typical horror-of-personality plot. The film then shows the activities of a variety of characters, including several young men about nineteen years old. But which man (if any) is Maximilian is never

Although *71 Fragments of a Chronology of Chance* starts with a title card that indicates how the film will end, this declaration enables director Haneke, like a magician working in plain sight, to create even greater ambiguity and mystery.

revealed until the very end, so we watch with a certain confusion, a desired response that Haneke has purposely worked to create. We also follow the narrative movement of a gun that is stolen, then passed from the thief to another, and to another, and so forth, until it reaches ... Maximilian? At one of those key chance encounters that this film documents so perfectly, two male college students play "Mikado," the game that Americans have always called "pick-up sticks"; if the second student wins, he will win the first student's gun. Slyly, Haneke cuts away before we find out who has won; though without knowing definitively who Max is, we couldn't in any case have assigned or interpreted the proper ironies. Only later, after one of the two goes on the shooting rampage, do we realize that not only was the first student Max, but that Max must have won the game of pick-up sticks and retained the gun. Does murder always depend on some chance event so disturbingly trivial? The pick-up sticks game works as an expressive metaphor for the chaos of the world: the way we collide seemingly randomly, our lives intersecting here, receding there, on top, underneath, all the while creating patterns that will determine our fates. And it is difficult to move or remove even one stick without affecting the positions of the other sticks. This symbolism suggests the need to understand the interconnectedness of all people, critical if we are to live in a world not dominated by violence and strife. Another image Haneke uses metaphorically is a set of geometric puzzle pieces which can be put together in different ways to create various, recognizable shapes—a potent symbol of the ways the fateful narrative segments might come together to create various outcomes. Indeed, we must put together Haneke's fragments to make sense of his film and see it whole, just as his charac-

Dominating *71 Fragments of a Chronology of Chance*, the visual metaphors of pick-up sticks and a geometric puzzle suggest the variety of ways fate can bring people together.

ters try to put together the puzzle pieces into a whole. In the Western world, we pretend it is possible to know everything, but Haneke contends that we know things only in fragments, and thus truth remains illusory.

Typical for Haneke, the characters whose stories we watch are three-dimensional, and the plot fragments raise interesting questions. For instance, when an armored-truck driver transfers money to the bank, the process is shown in great technological detail. Ironically, it is more exacting than the process by which an orphan girl is transferred to a young couple who ultimately decide to return her. There is irony, too, in that a middle-aged bank teller finds it easier to be friendly and open to her customers than to her aging father, who is alienated and lonely. (Why must Western culture so little value the elderly?) And continuing the video theme Haneke incisively explored in *Benny's Video*, a refugee boy who smuggles himself into Austria and is largely invisible to all as he lives on the streets, becomes worthy of attention (and adoption) only once his story becomes an item on the evening news: a consumable video.

Although the opening title card of *71 Fragments* seems to indicate the film will be about psychological disintegration, almost immediately the film cuts to several minutes of political reporting on a television newscast, a segment which breaks off abruptly in the middle of a story on a political crisis in Haiti. Thus, Haneke is insisting that we see his characters in the context of history and politics, even though the crises of his characters may seem personal. Haneke is disallowing us a strictly psychological interpretation. Although the arbitrary bank killings we will eventually see are announced immediately, Haneke is asking us to consider the significance of such killings in the context of worldwide political violence — such as the genocide of the Bosnians by the Serbs, just one of the news stories that surfaces within *71 Fragments*. By the film's end, with Maximilian at a gas station, a variety of fateful circumstances contribute to his sudden, violent rampage: the gas station attendant doesn't have change and is rude to Max, the bank's automatic teller machine is not working properly, the line inside the bank to get money is long, and an obstreperous bank patron accosts and humiliates Max. Had even one circumstance been different, might Max's violent impulses have remained unexpressed? (On an even more subtle level, *71 Fragments* hints at the possibility of an entirely different scenario: that Max might have acquired the gun not on a lark and not for committing suicide, but for killing his college ping-pong coach. This reading suggests that the unplanned bank violence might have actually saved his coach's life, an ironic serendipity, albeit technically unknowable.)

Haneke skillfully manipulates his narrative so that at the climax of the film, at least four characters we have been following end up at the bank at the precise moment that Max starts shooting with such a stunning suddenness. Whereas the typical director might have emphasized the sensation of bullets ripping flesh, Haneke does not. Instead, he holds on images emphasizing Max's shooting arm, Haneke refusing to revel in the violence or make these killings consumable, when they should remain reprehensible. Only later do we see a close up of a fallen man's arm in a blue jacket; in an unusually long take, we are forced to watch blood slowly but inexorably collecting into a huge puddle. Haneke's most brilliant choice in *71 Fragments* is his refusal to reveal conclusively which three people have been killed (although he does offer some narrative clues that are open to interpretation). Is Godless chance the only driving force in the universe? Do the victims include characters we have been following, or have "our" characters managed to escape? At the moment of Max's humiliation in the bank, a woman we had not seen before offered a simple act of kindness when she asked Max, "Can I help you?" Did her compassionate question result later in her

Haneke presents vivid portraits of his lost souls brought together by fate in *71 Fragments of a Chronology of Chance*. But who is destined to die? Tomek (Otto Grunmandl)? Hans (Branco Samarovski)? Max (Lukas Miko)? Maria (Claudia Martini)? Anni (Corina Eder)?

own murder or did it contribute to fewer people being killed by having diminished the magnitude of Max's humiliation? And what does it mean that we would prefer to believe that those killed are bank patrons whose stories we have not followed? Are we all guilty of a tribal thinking, whereby the lives of our own friends and family are by definition worth more than the lives of others? And if we *are* guilty, as the psychological mechanism incited by Haneke's narrative seems to indicate, what does that say about the chances for success in the greater political realm — in Bosnia, in Haiti, in the Middle East, and so forth?

At the end of *71 Fragments*, we leave the intersecting personal dramas and return to the TV news, where the film ends ironically with the most trivial: detailed news about Michael Jackson's resolve to "start a worldwide comeback" after his trial for sex with a child. This is actually the second time we have seen Michael Jackson news — news which seemed already irrelevant the first time. Now it is clear that Haneke, with the accuracy of a visionary, is predicting that twenty-first century phenomenon by which "news" would come to be dominated by celebrity gossip and the trivial: news not as journalism, but as consumer commodity to attract ratings and profit. Certainly we should be more concerned about "a worldwide comeback" for peace, prosperity, and international human rights than one for Michael Jackson. Consistent with its conceptual structure, Haneke's film cuts off in the middle of this final Jackson news story.[8] Impressively using the same horror subgenre as *The Texas Chainsaw Massacre*, Haneke demonstrates the artistry of a cold clinician in his *71*

Fragments of a Chronology of Chance, a bleak work of art that is political, philosophical, and profound.

As Haneke's reputation grew — particularly with his nonhorror film *Caché* (2005) garnering over twenty prestigious international awards, including best director at Cannes and the European Film Awards; and best foreign film from the London, Los Angeles, Chicago, and San Francisco Film Critics — news came that Michael Haneke was slated to direct an English-language remake of his masterpiece *Funny Games,* to star Naomi Watts for an American release in 2008. This news was met with understandable alarm: could Haneke resist his integrity being co-opted by the Hollywood money machine? The fear that the *Funny Games* remake would follow in the dubious footsteps of *The Vanishing* remake was groundless, since Haneke's remake, unlike George Sluizer's, emerged scrupulously faithful to the original conception, indeed, as a shot-by-shot reproduction, even down to details of set and costume design. Sadly, Haneke's fidelity resulted in the remake not attracting a huge audience. Americans inherently understood (was the poster too stylish?) that *Funny Games* was not the sort of horror film you could mindlessly whoop and holler at. Whereas the original *Funny Games* felt like an art film which alarmingly turned into a horror film, the remake felt like a horror film which peculiarly turned into an intellectual art-house film. So although the original and remake are virtual twins, their audiences came at them from diametrically different perspectives — which helps explain why the remake did disappointing box office.

If there is a subtle difference between the original and the remake, it is that there is great sexual tension coming from Naomi Watts' performance and a stronger feeling that Ann's husband has betrayed her by not immediately responding to her alarm and not forcefully taking the masculine role of protector. "Please forgive me," he says, as Ann goes to the window to escape, essentially abandoning him. As well, the remake makes even more clear the "false" choices presented by the narrative — i.e., when Ann escapes and seeks out help, should she flag down this car or that? *Of course* she stops the wrong car — the one belonging to Peter and Paul — and is recaptured; but even had she stopped the other car, *it* would have been the wrong car, as the later remote-control scene makes evident. It is not Peter and Paul who will not allow her to escape, but the narrative itself, acting on the behalf of director Michael Haneke, who is himself acting on behalf of the audience's darkest, subconscious desires. Later, Ann offers a prayer to try to keep safe: "I love you God with all my might, please keep me safe through all the night." But even God — if he exists — does not keep her or us safe, does not have the ability to change our base human natures.

Unfortunately, the 2008 *Funny Games* also received a preponderance of mixed and negative reviews from critics who were sarcastic and hostile. I suspect there are several reasons why. First may be the *Bonnie and Clyde* syndrome: that is, the inability of many critics to actually recognize a film as essentially different when they are so used to seeing films which are almost interchangeably the same. (In fact, few American critics even noted that Haneke, breaking one of the most constant conventions of the horror film, used no music in his film proper.) But second: Foreign directors are rarely acclaimed when they make an English-language film which inherently attacks America or Americans, as Antonioni's *Zabriskie Point*, Bruno Dumont's *Twentynine Palms*, and Lars von Trier's *Dogville* attest. And Haneke has suggested in many interviews that he was particularly interested in remaking his original film in English *because* he wanted to more directly attack the American component of Western culture responsible for the popular celebration of violence as a commodity of entertainment. A third more subtle reason for the vitriol is the inherent anti-intellectualism of so many American critics, who think of *themselves* as intellectuals, but pooh-pooh the intellectual pretensions of others, particularly those directors who are more thoughtful and well-read. Yet these same (male) critics will invariably rave about popular culture blockbusters that connect to their inner teenage boy. So it is not that surprising — to pick just one typical dismissal of the *Funny Games* remake — that in the prestigious journal *Film Comment* (March/April 2008), a contributing editor should claim "the remake's major innovation is to put [Naomi Watts] in panties during the central traumatic setpiece. A stupid movie has now become slightly less stupid.... Oooh, shades of Abu Ghraib in that black hood over Watts' head!" Of course, the pillowcase over the head in the original, pre–Iraq War *Funny Games* itself suggests Abu Ghraib to a contemporary audience. Was Haneke to omit such details in order to avoid being charged with condescending to the American audience? Of course, this was the audience that — as of 2008 — still largely believed that Saddam Hussein was responsible for 9/11. Critics understood that Haneke's attack was not only on the American audience, but on critics who had allowed American film culture to become so debased. And so they dismissed Haneke's film in order to stand up for themselves. Indeed, the same *Film Comment* writer that panned *Funny Games* claimed the Rob Zombie 2007 *Halloween* remake to be "an independent feat of imagination ... [the] most original and morally complex of the current remake cycle." And although the *Film Comment* writer dismissed a *New York Times* 2007 profile of Haneke as "breathless," at least he included the truly perceptive *Times* contention that watching (the original) *Funny Games* "is not unlike watching snuff-porn clips late at night in your bedroom, only to have your mother or Jacques Lacan switch the light on periodically without the slightest warning."

In some ways even more disturbing than these violent Haneke films is *Irréversible*, a horror masterpiece directed by Gaspar Noé in 2002 that became notorious because it prompted more walk-outs than any acclaimed film in recent memory, certainly a sign of its profound subversiveness. *Irréversible* starts with the "end" credits moving *down* the screen, rather than up, which immediately indicates a lack of conventionality. In fact, the entire film moves backwards chronologically scene by scene, in the process becoming a meditation on time. Like the narrative, the style is also unconventional: the bravura camera — never stopping — swoops, tilts, and rotates, creating a choreographic counterpoint to the characters, who are as often concealed as revealed. The camera thus becomes a metaphor for time: inexorable in its movement,

Irréversible's title sequence — which scrolls "backwards" and tilts recklessly — puts us off-balance immediately, as does the first sequence, also at a tilt, of a masturbating convict (Philippe Nahan). The style supports the film's proposition that "Time Destroys Everything."

Irréversible is based on ironic oppositions. The brutal rape of Alex (Monica Bellucci) by the Tenia (Jo Presti) contrasts with the intimate lovemaking of Alex and Marcus (Vincent Cassel). Similarly, the sordid sex club Rectum, where the Tenia avidly watches violence and sex, contrasts with the affirmation and tenderness inherent in the pregnant belly of Alex.

and showing humans as relatively unimportant in the overall scheme of things. *Irréversible* purposely avoids conventional editing or the fast cutting of montage by using a series of extremely long takes — even for its violent passages. Also untypical for horror, the film's dialogue seems largely improvised by its talented actors — particularly its trio of stars: Monica Bellucci, Vincent Cassel, and Albert Dupontel.

The first words spoken in *Irréversible* — by one of two men who are idly masturbating while incarcerated just across from a gay S/M bar called "Rectum" — feels like a postulate about to be proven: "You know what? Time destroys everything." ["Le temps détruit tout."] As audience members (and voyeurs), we recognize that a crime has been committed in Rectum, but what the crime *is* we don't know. When the narrative takes us to the film's first flashback, we are propelled into the gay bar, where we see muscled and semi-naked leathermen masturbating and having anal sex as Marcus rages in, looking manically for a man called "the Tenia" ("ténia" being the French word for the parasitic tapeworm). The sex we see is explicit and aggressive; and the low-frequency soundtrack rumblings, almost inaudible, make the scene physically disquieting. In one of the most disturbing scenes ever filmed, Marcus (played by Vincent Cassel) attacks a man he believes is the Tenia, but is quickly overpowered. As the man audibly breaks Marcus' arm and starts to rape Marcus, the onlookers masturbate (including the film's director Gaspar Noé, playing one of the sex-club voyeurs). But then Marcus' friend Pierre (played by Albert Dupontel) intercedes and strikes the attacker twenty-three times directly in the face with a metal fire extinguisher. Within an apparently single shot, we see the blow-by-blow damage until no face is left and the man's head is hollowed away. (But is it actually the Tenia? Only later, as we go back much further in time, do we discover definitively that the "wrong" man has been killed.) Because the shot showing Pierre attacking *appears* to be devoid of special effects, making what we are watching feel "real," this violence is as emotionally wrenching as any act of violence ever set to film. (Unlike typical horror films, which revel in their special effects, *Irréversible* works hard to disguise its effects, which we tend not to recognize, including the seamless digital/compositing effects which hide edits and create the illusion of continuous camera movement through space and time.)

As *Irréversible* continues its reverse chronology, hints abound as to why Marcus and Pierre had been in such rage: someone earlier had been raped (but who?), Alex is in the hospital (but who exactly is Alex?), and a transvestite prostitute may know something important (but what?). *Irréversible* asks whether "Vengeance is a human right," as claimed by a neighborhood godfather. Because of the violence committed by Marcus and Pierre, we have already found it difficult to empathize with them; we recoil from Marcus even further when he racially

Even in the only comedic sequence of *Irréversible*— with Alex, Marcus, and Pierre (Monica Bellucci, Vincent Cassel, and Albert Dupontel) — there is a subtext of male menace: note how Marcus' caress of Alex can be read as a physical threat.

harasses a Chinese cab driver. And yet it seems Marcus and Pierre are the film's protagonists. Finally, *Irréversible* arrives at its most fateful moment in the past — Marcus' girlfriend Alex (fearlessly played by Monica Bellucci, the real-life wife of Vincent Cassel) is trying to cross a Parisian street so busy with traffic that a passerby urges her to take the tunnel underpass instead: "It's safer." But it's really not. Because it is there, in that reddish tunnel, that we see the extraordinary rape of Alex by the Tenia — filmed in one shot, but, for the first time in the film, with the dizzying camera coming virtually to a stop. After the horrifying rape, the Tenia attacks Alex further with almost the same numbers of blows that will later kill the man mistaken for him: he kicks her and punches her in the face, which he smashes into the concrete. The physical and psychological horror of this scene creates a Proustian moment which makes us reconsider the horrendous murder that opened the film; only now do we understand why Marcus would come to such a rage. As the flashbacks go ever deeper into the past, we apprehend the irony that the more sensitive of the two men is actually Pierre, who disapproves of Marcus' lack of control and is still in love with Alex, who had earlier been Pierre's lover. Clearly, *Irréversible* suggests that even the most sensitive among us has the capacity for horrific violence, given the right circumstances. And in no way is Pierre someone we would have considered capable of such a murderous act.

As the film progresses, the two acts of violence recede. In a charming subway scene that plays like an Eric Rohmer or Woody Allen film, Marcus, Pierre, and Alex banter. The intellectual Pierre talks with a light nostalgia about how Alex once hit her head on a side table during sex — blood going everywhere. "The closest we got to orgasm was a bruise," he quips. His story, of course, immediately recalls the rape (yet to take place, but already shown), with Alex's head bloody from her beating. Significant too is what Alex offers: "I'm reading a book. It says the future is already written ... and the proof lies in premonitory dreams." Although this film goes backwards, its chronology is ironic, since time, for the characters, is clearly irreversible; and none of us in life get the chance to replay even a moment. Later when we see Marcus and Alex in bed (even earlier in the chronology), there are premonitory details. Alex says, "I had a dream. I was in a tunnel." And Marcus says, "I can't feel my arm." Each detail is charged with significance: the former to her rape, the latter to his broken arm. In another key scene, we see Alex naked in the shower, then sitting on the toilet, urinating for a home pregnancy test. The revelation that she is pregnant is another Proustian moment, forcing us to re-evaluate the meaning of the rape/murder, now

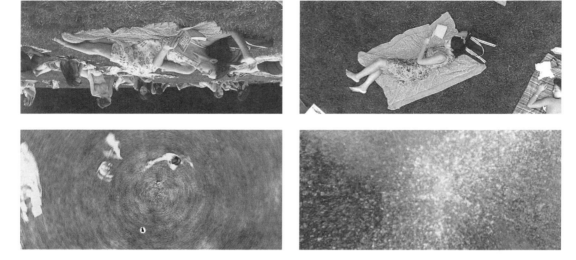

In *Irréversible*'s stunning final sequence, an upside-down image of Alex (Monica Bellucci) evolves into a spinning image which time-travels to the creation of the universe ... and to oblivion.

revealed as violence also against her unborn child. Later, with the second movement Allegretto of Beethoven's Seventh Symphony on the soundtrack, the camera pans down from the space fetus on a poster from *2001: A Space Odyssey* to Alex's pregnant belly, and then to the sky. (This second movement has often been considered a funeral march, though more inexorable than lugubrious, and with inherent mystery and a resignation to suffering.) Then, while focused on an idealized green lawn as Alex reads the book she has already referenced (entitled *An Appointment with Time*), the camera spins dizzyingly. At one point, Alex appears to be floating, and the grass appears suspended above the sky; and then — to a thunderous cacophony and stroboscopic light — it is the universe itself which is spinning in its very creation, until finally everything stops: the universe returned to nothingness. The postulate with which the film began, appears, Godard-like, on the screen: "Le temps détruit tout." As the film ends and the cacophony cuts off, we hear just the faintest sound of seconds ticking away. Typical to the French cinema which has so often been preoccupied with time and fatalism, *Irréversible* is not only unforgettable, but more powerful — both viscerally and philosophically — than any American horror film of the same period.

In My Skin [*Dans ma peau*], released the same year, was written and directed by Marina de Van, who also stars as the film's protagonist, Esther. De Van, a colleague of François Ozon, had previously directed *Psy-Show* (a pun on *Psycho* and *si-chaud* [so hot]), a black comedy short about a sadistic, crazy psychoanalyst who coldly tries to unbalance his patients, who are ultimately saner than he. (Still, one patient offers, "I'm afraid my anus will crack and make star-shaped excrement. It's part of my fear of America.") It's clear that de Van is interested in the Western obsession with body image and the influence of American culture. *In My Skin* most strongly references Roman Polanski's classic horror-of-personality film *Repulsion*. Like *Repulsion*, de Van's film is a beautifully-shot study of one woman's gradual descent into madness — particularly her alienation from her own body. The film begins with positive and negative still images side by side, immediately suggesting the duality of alienation. The film's inciting incident — Esther's accidental slicing open of her leg — leads to her surprising discovery that the cut gives her an inscrutable pleasure. As a result, Esther

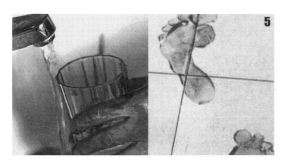

In My Skin communicates its themes of duality by dividing its frame into right and left halves, sometimes with a literal split screen, as in these examples: (1) a split screen emphasizing the stairway iconography of the horror of personality; (2) an image of the protagonist (Marina de Van) with the right-side background cluttered and the left-side background empty; (3) an establishing shot, perfectly divided by the edge of a building; (4) a two-shot of lovers, yet with a clear demarcation between left and right sides; and (5) a split screen with imagery specifically evoking Brian De Palma's *Sisters*, also about female madness.

starts purposely disfiguring herself, wanting her body to bleed. (Here, her film seems to reference the work of David Cronenberg, particularly *Crash*.) Not an obvious candidate for such pathology, Esther is an educated woman with professional goals and a stable relationship with her boyfriend. But she is a perfectionist at work and obsessive/compulsive. In one horrifying and affecting scene, Esther is at a business dinner with colleagues when her left arm starts acting independently, eventually appearing to sever itself from her body entirely. Surreptitiously, Esther reattaches her arm, then starts cutting into it to taste her blood. Later in the film, she eats flesh from her body and forces her leg to bleed onto her face so she can drink the blood: a self-vampirization. As in many of these European films, the effects are especially horrifying because they seem so casual — unaccompanied by the bombastic film music American films use to manipulate audiences into a targeted response. Without clichéd music, horror sequences become more surreal and expressive. But what does Esther's descent into pathology mean? When her boyfriend (played by Laurent Lucas) is repelled by what is happening to her and confused, Esther chastises him with "You always look for meanings!"—indicating the futility of such an enterprise.

After some scary hallucinations in a shopping mall, the narrative ruptures into split-screen images of more self-mutilation. The split screen clearly references Brian De Palma's

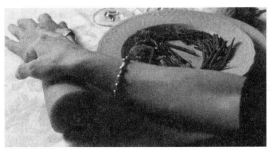

In My Skin's surreal restaurant scene shows Esther (Marina de Van) trying to cover for the fact that her arm has apparently severed itself from her body—the amputated limb a common icon of the horror-of-personality film.

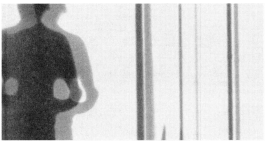

In My Skin's vampire subtext is made explicit by this image of Esther (Marina de Van) and her boyfriend (Laurent Lucas).

Using images of visual sophistication and beauty, *In My Skin* shows Esther's hallucinatory visions.

Drawing upon the bathroom iconography of the horror of personality, *In My Skin* shows Esther (Marina de Van) in both the bathtub and the shower. Ironically, she need fear no external monster, just herself.

Sisters, also about pathology. Esther is now irretrievably over the edge, cowering and contorting herself as she flirts with mutilating her face, then cutting off a large patch of skin for tanning into leather. *In My Skin* ends with a series of images in which the camera spirals out from a close-up — the movement recalling the final image of *Psycho*'s Marion Crane dead in the bathroom; Esther, similarly prostrate, is presumably dead from an auto-cannibalism that has neither meaning nor explanation. Has Esther withdrawn from the world because she's unable to relate to anything except what's inside her own skin? Certainly, the power of *In My Skin* derives not only from its ambiguity, but from its suggestion that any of us

Bruno Dumont's image of David and Katia (David Wissak and Yekaterina Golubeva) making love in *Twentynine Palms* evokes a similar image in *Zabriskie Point*, which also used the Southern California desert to evoke the casual violence and ennui of contemporary life. Evoking Antonioni, too, is this widescreen image of the empty space between the lovers in their hotel room.

could suffer a pathological fate as strange as Esther's, given the right trigger. And the horror that comes from within is scarier than what comes from without because you can't physically escape it. One final notable point: it is impossible to imagine any American actress directing, writing, and starring in such a troubling film that requires her abused body to be presented so nakedly, let alone using her "stardom" in the service of such an unflattering profile. Marina de Van demonstrates as much raw talent as did Polanski in *Repulsion*, and one hopes for an equally spectacular career.

Twentynine Palms, also made in 2002, though largely ignored or reviled by American critics, is essentially a disguised horror film that the French director Bruno Dumont shot in the United States. The film's protagonists — David and his girlfriend Katia — drive through the Southern California desert to the town of Twentynine Palms, desultorily scouting movie locations. For an hour and a half of the film, virtually nothing dramatic happens: David and Katia visit Joshua Tree National Park, argue, make up, watch an art film on TV, order Chinese food, go swimming, visit windmills, go shopping, almost run over a dog, and eat ice cream. And too, they have sex in widescreen locations, their couplings revealing both passion and conflict in their relationship. It is notable that their sex looks actual, rather than simulated, which contributes to the sense that David and Katia are real people, rather than movie characters. And we can hardly imagine a film more prosaic and less dramatic, until suddenly, in the middle of a desolate desert landscape, a Ford pickup truck rams David and Katia's car to a stop. Three young American men emerge from the vehicle and proceed to use their fists and a baseball bat to beat up David and Katia. More horrifically, they then rape David, sadistically forcing Katia to watch. Although the couple survives, David is in shock. Katia unsuccessfully tries to comfort him, but David refuses to call the police. Later, in a cheap motel, comes the most horrific surprise of all: David, with a badly shaved head, emerges from the bathroom with a knife held aloft and viciously stabs Katia sixteen times. (Earlier, Katia had joked that if David ever cut his hair, she would leave him.) The shock of this totally unexpected attack is overwhelming: David has turned into a psychological and physical monster. The last image — elliptically returning to the desert — shows David's corpse (a suicide?), as a police officer wanders about it, any melodrama eclipsed by the extreme long shot of the landscape and the petty bureaucracy of police politics, which we understand from the officer's walkie-talkie conversation with an uncooperative dispatcher. In essence, *Twentynine Palms* has shown us, minute-by-minute, the events that push an ordinary man to the breaking point. Ironically, of the two primary characters, it was actually Katia who had seemed the most neurotic and mentally capricious.

Throughout this third film by Bruno Dumont — the acclaimed director of *La Vie de*

Director Bruno Dumont uses extreme long shots even for *Twentynine Palms*' dramatic moments: (1) the sex between David and Katia; (2) the aftermath of David's rape and Katia's assault; and (3) the police discovery of David's corpse. Invariably, the spectator must search the frame to find the subjects. Even when Dumont shows a character more closely, the face is not always visible, impeding our empathy, as in (4) this image of a nude David straddling Katia after murdering her.

Jésus [*The Life of Jesus*] and *L'Humanité*— Dumont again uses very long takes and presents the action from such a great distance that characters look lost and insignificant. Indeed, we must often search the frame in order to find them. Images throughout are ominous and show characters as predatory, such as the shot of David in a swimming pool looking like a crocodile gliding toward its prey, Katia. A director of art films, Dumont is clearly self-conscious regarding the horror conventions his film draws upon. According to Dumont's DVD commentary, "Here, it's not so much the subject that matters as the air itself, the atmosphere, its hue. In this way, *Twentynine Palms* is a horror film — an extreme horror, built up innocently, dependent on a delicate plot." About his direction: "Ostensibly, nothing should be apparent. The force isn't visible, it isn't audible.... The time and these spaces will form the strong mass of the direction in which the protagonists of the imperious culture return for a few days to nature (nudity, wild sex, idleness, rape) and die." Regarding his implacable long shots, Dumont says: "Long shots are the means of showing consideration for the audience and its peace of mind: draw power from this." How the film ends, as the director attests, is by coincidence and chance. But what exactly does the film mean? *Twentynine Palms*

When David swims toward Katia in *Twentynine Palms*, he is already a monstrous crocodile approaching his prey. By the film's end, David turns into a full-fledged, horror-of-personality psycho as a result of the monster in the next image, who screams in orgasm while raping David.

Unusually sophisticated, Todd Haynes' *Poison* imitates a variety of styles, including fifties science-fiction horror with its cheesy special effects and its flat lighting and dated styles.

is a meditation on American violence and on the valuelessness increasingly seeping into Western culture, particularly American culture. And the film's horrific culminating acts of violence suggest that all of us are equally unsafe, because a Godless destiny can doom us all.

Another group of films important to horror came directly out of the gay/lesbian independent film movement, so centrally established and championed by the remarkable Christine Vachon. Studying one of the most erudite fields of all, semiology, before going on to an unusually distinguished career, Vachon produced a number of films which — if not quite horror — used horror conventions more creatively than most horror films. For instance, *Poison*, directed in 1991 by Todd Haynes and produced by Vachon, presents three related stories which skillfully employ the theme of "the other" in order to dramatize important truths about societal fear of homosexuality, with one story explicitly satirizing fifties science-fiction horror. Another Vachon production, *Swoon*, directed by Tom Kalin in 1992, revisits the real-life story of Leopold and Loeb, the homo-sexuals who murdered a boy for the pleasur-able experience of committing such a transgression. Richard Fleischer's *Compulsion* and Alfred Hitchcock's *Rope* had dealt with

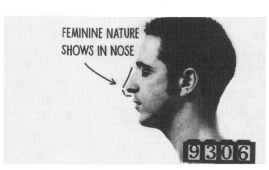

FEMININE NATURE
SHOWS IN NOSE

9306

Tom Kalin's experimental *Swoon* reclaimed mur-derers Leopold and Loeb (Craig Chester and Daniel Schlachet) for the gay movement. Kalin's images, like Haynes' in *Poison*, are aesthetic and self-consciously intellectual.

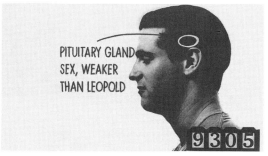

PITUITARY GLAND
SEX, WEAKER
THAN LEOPOLD

9305

the same story, but with the homosexual element sub-textual. *Swoon* is skillful in the way it unabashedly presents these men as killers, without promoting a homophobic view of gay men; in fact, *Swoon* suggests that if society holds gayness to be intrinsically evil or morally disordered, it is only logical that gay men should profoundly feel themselves outsiders to that society and thus have few reservations about committing additional transgressions. *Swoon* implies that society's insistence that the homosexual orientation is shameful and must be kept secret is what turned these men into monsters. (Fifteen years later, director Kalin and producer Vachon would return to another historical subject in *Savage Grace*, a Julianne Moore period film which most reviewers didn't even recognize as a disguised horror film. Beneath the exotic locales and cunning art design, *Savage Grace* focuses on the heterosexual/homosexual/incestual dynamics within the moneyed nuclear family heir to the Bakelite plastics fortune. This subtle horror film — culminating with an inevitable, if surprising murder after a variety of transgressive sexual acts — signals its generic identity most strongly by several iconic close-ups of a single eye.) Even Todd Haynes' *Safe* in 1995, also produced by Vachon, was influenced by horror conventions — here, the conventions of Armageddon — in its apocalyptic story of a woman being poisoned by the escalating toxicity in everyday life. These Vachon films laid the groundwork for a decade of notable gay-themed horror-of-personality films, including *Frisk* (directed by Todd Verow in 1995), *American Psycho* (by Mary Harron in 2000), and *Elephant* (by Gus Van Sant in 2003).

Frisk, like *In a Glass Cage*, continues the association of eros with violence. A kind of *Notes from the Underground* adapted from the novel by Dennis Cooper, *Frisk* presents the confessions of "Dennis" — the protagonist's name borrowed from the novel's author. Obsessed with sadomasochism, Dennis has had lifelong desires to cut open his sex partners and take in their internal fluids in order to achieve the highest level of intimacy. Certainly *Frisk* has resonance with the Jeffrey Dahmer murders, though Cooper had been writing similar material well before Dahmer's crimes became public. If gay orientation is not learned, but genetic, is the inclination toward sadomasochism also genetic? In perhaps the film's most horrific moment, the sadist says to one of his sexual partners: "It's like this: I usually fantasize about killing people, but something usually stops me. Whatever it is, it's not there with you." At one notable point, the protagonist asks a lover to spit into his mouth (recalling a scene in

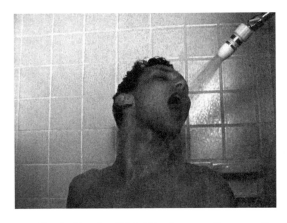 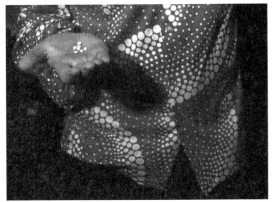

Symbolism in *Frisk*: The horror-of-personality shower iconography is renewed by this homoerotic image with a distinctly phallic shower head. Similarly, drug use within gay culture is emphasized by the clever design choice of a "pill"-covered garment.

Poison) and then becomes aroused by licking blood. *Frisk's* extreme sexual scenes extend even to necrophilia. The protagonist gravitates toward other sexual sadists (including the stylish Parker Posey), who together enjoy committing torture and sexual murder as an act of community. As in *Henry: Portrait of a Serial Killer*, these killers enjoy watching films they've made of their own transgressions. Unlike Henry, these killers are well-educated and sophisticated. By the end of *Frisk*, it is not clear whether what we have seen throughout has "really" happened, or is the fantasy projection of its protagonist—which gives the spectator a kind of psychological out and allows for the levying of a less harsh judgment on the film's gay characters. But this narrative ambiguity didn't placate many leaders within the gay community, who found *Frisk* no better than *Cruising* in its conflation of gay sexuality with violence. Even if Dennis does *not* really commit the murders we see, is *Frisk* nevertheless suggesting that these fantasies are typical to gay men? (And yet, why should one generalize? Would anyone consider *Kalifornia* an exposé of the typical heterosexual male?)

American Psycho, directed by Mary Harron, is another horror film connected to the emerging independent gay cinema. (Harron's first notable film, the 1996 *I Shot Andy Warhol*, had been produced by Christine Vachon and based on the real-life story of Valerie Solanis, the lesbian who attempted to assassinate Andy Warhol.) Written by Harron with lesbian icon Guinevere Turner, *American Psycho* seems quite clearly a thoughtful, horror masterpiece informed by a surprising, intellectual feminism. Based on the much-attacked novel by Bret Easton Ellis, virtually every critic felt the film version was superior, because it more sharply and clearly criticized American cultural values and put the novel's violence in a more ironic context. *American Psycho* begins with a brilliantly designed title sequence in which perfect drops of red blood against a white field give way to other abstract images eventually revealed to be an extraordinary lunch for which young New York City financial executives are spending $570. It is food as pornography—a sensuous, purchasable commodity. Thus, *American Psycho* immediately makes the connection between the violence in American society and the empathy deficit provoked by consumerism.

The film's protagonist, composed of contradictions, lives in a perfectly designed, modernist, luxury high-rise. His name—Patrick Bateman—explicitly evokes *Psycho's* Norman Bates; one of our earliest views shows him uri-nating, then showering in a stark, Antonioni-inspired version of *Psycho's* bathroom. Unlike Norman Bates, Bateman has a huge ego as well as a great body, which the film shows off throughout. Bateman is obsessed with his perfect skin and worships skin-care products: his "water-activated gel cleanser," his "honey-

A "trail of blood" is revealed as food pornography in *American Psycho*, which correlates high-end consumerism with violence.

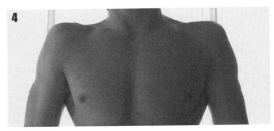

The homoerotic subtext of the horror-of-personality film is more explicit in *American Psycho*, which exploits Patrick Bateman's narcissism by emphasizing the nudity of actor Christian Bale. We see Bateman (1) as a high-end furnishing in his condo, (2) in the archetypal horror location the shower, albeit a luxury version, (3) as reflection in mirrors, symbols of identity and madness, and (4) as an abstract body part devoid of humanity.

almond body scrub," his "herb mint facial mask." His reflections in the multiple mirrors are a sign of his madness; and his self-obsessed voice-over announces: "There is an idea of a Patrick Bateman, some kind of abstraction, but there is no real me.... I simply am not there." In other words, when *American Psycho* starts, Bateman is already the vacant Norman Bates at the end of *Psycho*, bereft of humanity. Bateman's humanity has been stolen by America's consumer culture and obsession with material possessions; and Bateman's violence is an extension of his cold sexism. Unlike Norman Bates, Bateman is not an outcast, but the most "in" of the "in." Indeed, his ultimate goal is to become the archetype of recognized success. Not surprisingly, Bateman's talk is dominated by brand names, name-dropping, and other signifiers of status ("Valentino," "sea urchin ceviche," "Donald Trump"), although should a social situation require it, Bateman is also capable of talking about apartheid or equal rights for women (albeit in meaningless political slogans which function like sound bites). Bateman is a product of the Reagan/Bush years, when only the lives and lifestyles of the rich and famous were valorized. To quote Oliver Stone's *Wall Street*: "Greed is good."

Like all his Wall Street friends, Bateman is a vice president. And yet these young vice presidents are all so similar and interchangeable, that even they cannot remember who is who. One hilariously satirical scene shows them jockeying for position by comparing the subtlety of their off-white business cards. (Bone? Eggshell?) One card so impressively upstages the others that contemplating it virtually gives Bateman an orgasm. Status *is* sex. Because what Bateman fears most is being without job, prospects, or status, the first person we see him kill is a homeless man. The act of violence is shocking, because the film's satirical tone has heretofore been so amusing. But the tone darkens, and director Harron succeeds in balancing her film on the knife edge between horror and comedy. "I like to dissect girls. Did you know I'm utterly insane?" says Bateman, apparently joking, but just before taking seven ax-blows to a business rival in a violent scene which is unnervingly disturb-

Horrific images in *American Psycho*: (1) a severed head stored next to brand-name ice cream; (2) a naked killer brandishing a chainsaw over a stairway recalling Hitchcock's *Psycho* and *Vertigo*; and (3) President Ronald Reagan, whom the filmmakers indict for a compassionless era of greed and apathy.

ing *because* of the satirical subtext. In so many horror films, violence makes us excited; here, the violence makes us uneasy, promoting some internal shame for our being concurrently amused by the ironies.

Everyone around Bateman is oblivious to his violence. Even when friends see him disposing of a body he has chopped up into an overnight bag, they're interested *not* in what's in the bag, presumably still bleeding, but in the bag's designer label (Jean-Paul Gaultier!). And although at one point we glimpse a severed head in Bateman's freezer, we see it only because it sits next to something important to Bateman: his brand-name sorbet. It is ironic that the name of Bateman's firm is Pierce & Pierce — which suggests that just as Bateman pierces and destroys women, his firm may be piercing and destroying American decency and compassion. The filmmakers clearly contend that as Americans, we are deep within an era in which obliviousness to social reality is our dominant trait. In truth, we would rather *not* know, so long as we're not held responsible for the consequences. Status and sensation are all that matters.

One of Bateman's few moments of panic occurs not when he feels remorse (which, in fact, he never does), but when he feels jealousy upon learning the colleague he so coolly dispatched had a better apartment. To acquire status or sensation, Bateman embraces shortcuts: cocaine for the quick high, steroids for quick muscles, hookers for quick sex. Bateman's encounter with two hookers is dominated by his own pretentious, absurd monologue on the intellectual significance of Phil Collins' pop music. An absolute narcissist, Bateman barely looks at the women during their three-way, but videotapes the sex so he can flex for the camera and admire and become aroused by his own body. Although Bateman peppers his conversation with popular culture references, this, too, is a way of claiming status and demonstrating the superiority of his own taste. Like his colleagues, Bateman is sexist and glib. Bateman asks, "Do you know what Ed Gein said about women?" A buddy responds, "Ed Gein? *Maitre d'* at Canal Bar?" Bateman — knowledgeable regarding his *Psycho* influences — clarifies: "No. Serial killer, Wisconsin, fifties." Infamy, a form of celebrity, imposes status, so Bateman also drops the name of serial killer Ted Bundy into small talk. Like the heroine of *Mary Hartman, Mary Hartman*, the pioneering satirical soap opera, Bateman cannot always distinguish what is real from what is fictional, and so he talks about Cliff Huxtable, Bill Cosby's sitcom character, as if Huxtable were a real person.

A scene in which Bateman and the secretary who cares for him are unknowingly talking about different things is especially witty and disturbing. When Bateman says, "I think if you stay, I might hurt you," she thinks he's being sensitive and not wanting to lead her on; in actuality, he's talking about the nail gun he's planning to use to shoot nails into her skull. In a terrifying scene which seems like an over-the-top parody of a horror film, a naked Bateman chases a woman while brandishing a chainsaw — dispatching her on a dizzying staircase. The strings of the music track, similar to Bernard Herrmann's in *Psycho*, go wild when *American Psycho* references classic horror situations. The violence becomes increasingly incongruous and surreal, as when Bateman stuffs a stray kitten into an ATM machine, or shoots an older woman and four police officers in a gun-battle on the street. Finally, in a monologue resembling an aria from an opera's climactic mad scene, Bateman, in total meltdown, confesses, "I ate some of their brains. And I tried to cook a little." It's as if Bateman aspires to the "psychotic killer" status of Hannibal Lecter. Bateman confesses his transgressions to his lawyer again and again, but in keeping with the Reagan ethos, the lawyer refuses to believe him — for that would require acknowledging that we don't live in the best of all possible worlds, that it is *not* eternally "morning in America." In fact, Bateman's lawyer is so oblivious to social reality that he doesn't even recognize that Bateman is Bateman.

American Psycho's widescreen images of architectural interiors recall Antonioni's *L'eclisse*. Here, Patrick Bateman (Christian Bale) stands between a life-size photo of a model and a real woman (Chloë Sevigny). Alienated from human feeling, Bateman would prefer the objectified photograph, a manageable consumer object.

By the end of *American Psycho*, the subtextual criticism of Reaganism becomes explicit as director Mary Harron includes a CNN report showing a Reagan press briefing. "Foreign policy can't be run by committee," says Reagan. "We can accomplish more by cooperating. And in the end, this may be the eventual blessing in disguise to come out of the Iran/Contra mess." As Reagan tries to spin the Iran/Contra scandal, an interchangeable executive watching the report attacks Reagan: "He presents himself as this harmless old codger, but *inside*..." In voice-over, Bateman says: "But the inside doesn't matter." Ironically, the young executives — so self-oblivious — can see a coldness in Reagan that they cannot see in themselves. A colleague admonishes: "Come on, Bateman, what do you think?" Bateman's response is the perfect rejoinder for a politically detached generation, a horrifying punch line to the entire film: "Whatever." And then, just as at the end of *Psycho*, we go deeply into the killer's mind as we hear what Bateman is thinking, and it's frightening:

> There are no more barriers to cross. All I have in common with the uncontrollable and the insane, the vicious and the evil, all the mayhem I have caused and my utter indifference toward it, I have now surpassed.... I do not hope for a better world for anyone. My pain is constant and sharp, and in fact, I want my pain to be inflicted on others. I want no one to escape. My punishment continues to elude me. But even after admitting this, there is no catharsis, and I gain no deeper knowledge of myself. No new knowledge can be extracted from my telling. This confession has meant ... *nothing*.

The final image of Bateman parallels the final image of Norman Bates in *Psycho*. Like Norman, Bateman is completely detached, his detachment the embodiment of evil. Unlike Norman, Bateman is a sophisticated, affluent, Wall Street type that the country looks to as a

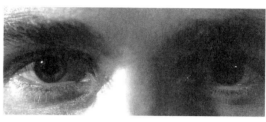

Like many other horror-of-personality films that end with the camera on a crazy, unfeeling protagonist, *American Psycho* brings us horrifically ever closer to its madman's eyes. Might we recognize ourselves there?

role model. That damning fact makes *American Psycho* even more powerful, not only as horror, but as social criticism.

By the end of *American Psycho*, many visual details suggest we have been watching an unreliable narrative. Ultimately, it is not clear whether Patrick Bateman's violent acts are real or the visual manifestations of the violence-filled doodles that reflect his subconscious impulses. (His secretary discovers these doodles in her final scene.) And truly, many of the scenes make more sense as fantastical emulations of the movie genres through which Bateman envisions his life: horror, pornography, action-adventure. So maybe Bateman really *is* the "boring, spineless lightweight" others accuse him of being, the indistinguishable cog powering the Reagan revolution, indispensable to the prevailing social order, yet secretly filled with rage. Bateman represents what Tony Kushner—in his groundbreaking *Angels in America: A Gay Fantasia on National Themes*—called "Children of the new morning, criminal minds. Selfish and greedy and loveless and blind. *Reagan's children...*" In *American Psycho*'s final scene, Bateman is dressed in virtually the same clothes and colors as in his first scene. Whereas his colleagues had previously dressed similarly to each other, *now* they are virtually indistinguishable—all in red ties and *couture* suits—which suggests that the culture has moved even further toward mindless conformity. Because several of the filmmakers central to *American Psycho* are gay, the attack on Reaganism becomes even more personal in this complex, challenging film that attacks consumer capitalism, exposes yuppie culture, and predicts a horrifying political future for America. Sadly, within only a few years, America would be so obsessed with valorizing status (who's in, who's out, what's hot, what's not) and so preoccupied with the mindless worship of celebrity (Britney Spears, Brad Pitt, Jennifer Lopez, Angelina Jolie, Paris Hilton, et al.), that an apathetic press and oblivious public could allow George W. Bush and Dick Cheney—claiming Reagan's mantel—to invade Iraq, scale back American liberties, and demonize gay people. *American Psycho*, ever prescient, anatomized more than the fictional Patrick Bateman.

More subtle, but equally perceptive in its American portrait is *Elephant*, directed by Gus Van Sant in 2003. Van Sant began his feature career with the very personal *Mala Noche*, a gay film-festival favorite about a gay man's love for a disenfranchised teen migrant worker. Van Sant's subsequent *Drugstore Cowboy* and *My Own Private Idaho* also explored—with empathy and clarity—the troubled lives of American young men. *Elephant* does much the same, but this time within a suburban setting. Winning the top prize at Cannes, but only a limited American release, *Elephant* is a brilliant horror film which fictionalizes the

Columbine High School killings, a subject fraught with the potential for artistic failure.[9] Yet Van Sant produced an ambiguous film that avoids every cliché: neither a facile made-for-TV *pièce à thèse* nor a craven exploitation of violence. Almost anthropologically, *Elephant* coolly shows us so many possible reasons for the violent eruption, that by the film's end, our understanding is comprehensive, yet totally inadequate. And so *Elephant* emerges as an expressive, surreal masterpiece.

Elephant positions itself outside conventional Hollywood style by using extended-duration long shots, often with a tracking camera. Van Sant's style here (like Michael Haneke's in *71 Fragments of a Chronology of Chance*) suggests the experimental films of James Benning, which similarly present American landscapes in exquisite long takes and cannily attack Hollywood fiction. (In fact, Benning's 1986 *Landscape Suicide*— an experimental horror film which juxtaposes the grisly crimes of Wisconsin's Ed Gein with a stabbing by the California teen Bernadette Prott — may have been Van Sant's model.) In *Elephant*, the style of the camera work forces us to look for meaning, for explanation of the violence we know will come. Although the characters interrelate in their daily routines, they are largely oblivious to each other. For instance, one beautifully mysterious shot shows boys playing football while Michelle, a geeky girl, stops in the foreground to watch something in the sky. Similar to how Michelle doesn't see what we see happening in the football game behind her, we don't see what Michelle is looking at. (Forty-five minutes later in the film, which is not chronologically linear, Van Sant shows us a potential omen of the coming carnage: a plane's jet stream in a threatening sky. Might this be what Michelle had been looking at?)

In *Elephant*, Gus Van Sant presents poetic, mysterious portraits of high school students: (1) Michelle, the outsider (Kristen Hicks), who stops to look at something never definitively shown to us; (2) Eric (Eric Deulen), in a silhouette which is painterly and homoerotic, before stepping into the shower with Alex; (3) John (John Robinson), center-frame, face not visible, but with the killers visible at a distance; and (4) the dream couple, Nathan and Carrie (Nathan Tyson and Carrie Finklea), looking oddly disconnected because the lighting treats their faces differently.

In *Elephant*, Gus Van Sant presents his high school students with an increasing opacity. Although John (John Robinson) is comforted by Acadia (Alicia Miles), both faces move toward obscurity.

Van Sant is smart enough *not* to try to get into his characters' minds; he understands the impossibility of such an enterprise. Like Michael Haneke, Van Sant rejects psychology as the grand skeleton key. The only thing truly comprehensible about the characters is their names, which we are given in intertitles on screen; the fact that the students are mostly played by nonprofessional actors who lend their first names to their characters adds verisimilitude. Yet *Elephant* is also poetic, with some images going unexpectedly into a laconic slow motion. Other images — shot with an extreme telephoto lens — show the backgrounds so out of focus that characters seem utterly alienated from their surroundings.

Elephant is one of the few films which really gets right the *feel* of high school. Although the students have problems, these problems are never hyped to seem fictional or melodramatic. And Van Sant paints vivid portraits of high school archetypes: John, the sensitive loner; Elias, the artist; Nathan and Carrie, the athlete and the prom queen; Michelle, the dreamy misfit; and Brittany, Jordan, and Nicole, the gossipy popular girls. Where do Eric and Alex fit in, the ordinary students who become killers? The details of these lives are presented with insight and empathy: the latch-key kid Alex letting himself in and drinking milk directly out of the bottle; the shy Michelle, after gym class, discreetly changing back to school clothes without showering, to avoid showing her body; the bulimic Brittany, Jordan, and Nicole purging together as casually as they shop together; the sweet John, older than his years, taking away the car keys from his drunken dad; the artistic Elias wearing a bent fork as his bracelet to indicate, wordlessly, that he marches to his own drummer. And what does it mean that Alex, one of the homicidal students, plays the piano, and though his "Für Elise" is sweet enough, his "Moonlight Sonata" is graceless and angry?

At the Gay/Straight Alliance meeting when students discuss whether you can tell who is gay, the camera pans from one face to the next, inviting the viewers to make their own

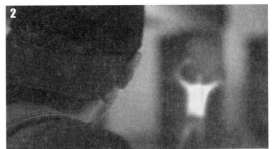

Before their rampage, (1) the killers (Eric Deulen and Alex Frost) are photographed from a power-ful low angle that ironically evokes the all–American football huddle. Once the rampage starts, the images become increasingly ambiguous and aesthetic, with (2) victims so out of focus as to be barely apprehensible.

determinations. Yet Van Sant refuses in this scene to reveal who is gay, adding to the film's inscrutability. Also adding inscrutability is how often the camera follows characters in track-ing shots from behind, not allowing us to see faces. When the sensitive John needs to cry, he goes to an empty classroom to be alone, although even there he covers his face, prevent-ing our ability to get close. Even the title is inscrutable, the only elephant a pencil draw-ing by Alex, barely perceptible on the wall. Does "elephant" refer to that obvious thing in the room that everyone avoids mentioning? But if so, what is it? American homophobia? The pervasive gun culture? Suburban alienation? The acceptance of bullying? Our inabil-ity to confront the limitations of American culture? Or does "elephant" refer to the story of the blind men unable to understand what an elephant is, because the animal is too large for any of them to touch but a portion of it? Is Van Sant suggesting that American violence can never be understood, because the problem is too large and Americans are so blind?

Even when the narrative seems chronological, it often isn't. When Eric and Alex enter dressed in camouflage and carrying heavy bags, we expect to see their violence, but we don't. Instead, the narrative moves on to other things and even backtracks to repeat earlier scenes, but with the camera following different characters to give us alternate perspectives. (In fact, some scenes are shown as many as three times, but still without leading us to any definitive understanding.) Certainly we see lots of scenes with the two teens who will commit the killings: We see Alex studiously practicing classical piano, but we also see him "killing" when he plays violent video games with Eric. Yes, Alex and Eric are victims of teasing at school, but they are also fascinated with Nazis and guns, although they are a little fuzzy as to what Hitler looked like. In the film's most shocking moment — because it seems so casual — Eric joins Alex in the family's small shower and says quietly: "I guess this is it. We're gonna die today.... I've never even kissed anybody. Have you?" And then Eric and Alex kiss tenderly. Are they gay? It is unclear; the sexual revelation here *adds* a level of mystery, rather than subtracts. No soundtrack music announces this as a portentous moment; in fact, the utter ordinariness of the scene suggests that neither Alex and Eric's mutual sexual desire nor the homophobia they must doubtless experience at school is the "Rosebud" which explains away the mystery of their violence. Just before they embark on their attack, Alex instructs Eric: "Most importantly, have fun, man!" As the violence begins, Eli, the student photog-rapher, takes the killers' pictures, but Michelle — the least deserving of attack — is the first to die. Is her murder random, or does she represent the outcast status the killers are trying to kill in themselves? Nate, a student from the Gay-Straight Alliance is also killed. The rampage is horrifying, because its haphazard nature allows us to imagine ourselves as victims. When Eric traps the principal, Eric's monologue terrifies with its flat rhythms suggesting a teen's version of action-adventure film dialogue:

> Fuck. Anyway, Mr. Luce. Whatever. You know there's others like us out there too. And they will kill you if you fuck with them like you did me and Jared... Get out of here before I change my mind. Go! Bitch.

But Eric does change his mind, immediately, and kills Mr. Luce anyway.

Inspired by Columbine, *Elephant* is by no means a docudrama *about* Columbine. (In fact, *Elephant* includes dialogue that refers to the Columbine killings.) Nor is *Elephant* an exploitative potboiler intended to make quick money, which is made obvious by *Elephant*'s notable soundtrack, which is devoid of the popular rock music so typical for Hollywood movies about young people and so lucrative for film producers wanting a financial cut of soundtrack CD sales. Instead, *Elephant*'s scenes tend to be unaccompanied or set to classical music. This unexpected, spare soundtrack prevents us from a facile emotional response; in this regard, *Elephant* recalls Pier Paolo Pasolini's 1961 *Accatone*, where classical music also gave a nobility to its young people and their world. An American horror classic at once complex and unexpected, *Elephant* expertly shows our profound obliviousness to each other. Even more distressing is the film's portrait of an America with no unifying sense of community or of shared responsibility. If one looks to Van Sant's film for a simple explanation for Columbine, there is none to be found; like Alain Resnais' *Last Year at Marienbad*, another film with cool surfaces and exquisite tracking shots, *Elephant* is a modernist masterpiece — a puzzle without a solution, yet seemingly without missing pieces.

In addition to *Elephant*, the twenty-first century brought us a series of low-budget, horror-of-personality films that were essentially powerful character studies. The notable *Chasing Sleep*, directed by Michael Walker in 2000, attained minor cult status, if not widespread success. In a *tour de force* performance, Jeff Daniels plays Ed Saxon, an insomniac who takes the sleeping pill "Dreamatol." Unusually claustrophobic, *Chasing Sleep* is largely limited to the interior of Ed's home. And when we finally do leave the claustrophobic interior, it is via hallucination and so not especially liberating. As we wait for his wife, Eve, to return, scenes become subtly surreal and we wonder whether Ed might have killed his wife, then chopped her into pieces and flushed them into his water pipes. Is Ed hallucinating, perhaps because of the Dreamatol? Or is he actually becoming a homicidal maniac? Like the classic horror-of-personality film, a significant portion of *Chasing Sleep*

In the subtle *Chasing Sleep*, this surreal gigantic baby becomes the clearest sign that the narrative is unreliable and includes hallucination.

takes place in the bathroom, where we see recurring images of the shower and the toilet and where one of Ed's students is bloodied. And is that a blood stain in his sink? When a severed finger refuses to be flushed and instead crawls down the hallway like a worm, it is clear that not everything we're seeing is really happening. What helps make these potential hallucinations so disturbing is the lack of music to tell us what to feel or when to be scared. Instead, we only hear odd and inscrutable ambiences. With these spare aural tracks, *Chas-*

Expressive images of Jeff Daniels' Ed in *Chasing Sleep* tend to emphasize claustrophobia. (1) He is dwarfed by the cloud ceiling, even though photographed from a low angle; (2) he is trapped by his own hands; and (3) he seems imprisoned by the film's frame itself when he answers a shadowed door.

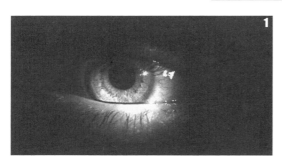 

 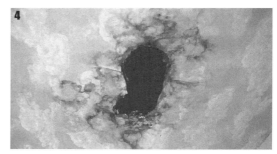

Chasing Sleep is filled with dozens of references to the circular images in *Psycho*'s shower sequence, including (1) Ed's eye, (2) the garbage-disposal drain, (3) the toilet bowl, (4) the hole in the ceiling, and (5) bathtub blood.

ing Sleep positions itself outside the Hollywood popular tradition and allies itself with the more subtle art-house cinema of a film like Michael Haneke's *Funny Games.*

Perhaps the best way to look at *Chasing Sleep* is as a male variation of *Repulsion.* Ed's masculinity seems besieged; and the claustrophobic house, with its plumbing issues and sense of imminent disintegration, works as a symbol of Ed, or perhaps of his marriage. With great integrity, the narrative is scrupulously associated with Ed's point of view—which means, for instance, that in at least a dozen of Ed's phone calls, we never see the faces of those he talks to. Nor are we given referents external to Ed to aid our perception as to what is real and what is not. Because the acting is naturalistic and low-key, and the film's execution so unmelodramatic, *Chasing Sleep* becomes memorable in its creepiness and ambiguity. The narrative's unreliability becomes evident slowly, after we are drawn in.

What does Ed's insomnia signify? Is it "merely a symptom of a greater unwholesomeness?" Or is it a sign he needs a "prescription for his conscience?" One distinctive image juxtaposes Ed with a ceiling wallpapered with images of clouds—a cosmic metaphor which suggests we should look at Ed, literally, within a symbolic context. But of what is Ed a symbol? Of contemporary man's inability to distinguish what is real? Of the tensions and sense of failure brought on by our being overstimulated by the everyday? *Chasing Sleep* never quite consummates its central metaphor of sleeplessness, which only adds to the film's ambiguity. At the end, Ed's wife is suddenly just there, alive; and we accompany the camera, as it dollies into the dark hole in the blue room with the cloud ceiling—a black hole in the universe, terrifying and close.

Also released in 2000 is the extraordinarily disquieting *Requiem for a Dream,* directed by Darren Aronofsky from the novel by Hubert Selby, Jr. A horror film about addiction—to food, to drugs, to television, to hope itself—*Requiem for a Dream* follows four interre-lated characters: Harry, his mother Sara Goldfarb, his girlfriend, and his best friend (played by Jared Leito, Ellen Burstyn, Jennifer Connelly, and Marlon Wayans respectively). The film takes place in the Coney Island area of Brooklyn, which adds immeasurably to its texture. The imagery of *Requiem for a Dream* is consistently surreal; indeed, Aronofsky presents such a bravura, visual display that his film evokes comparison to the similarly pyrotech-

In ***Requiem for a Dream***, the main characters are all victims who are often photographed as monsters, particularly Ellyn Burstyn as Sara, shown (1) through a distorting fish-eye lens, (2) in a tight close-up, and (3) within a surreal superimposition.

Among the most relentlessly downbeat American movies ever, *Requiem for a Dream* contains one uplifting sequence: a vision in overexposed blues when Harry (Jared Leto) imagines his girlfriend (Jennifer Connelly) on the Coney Island boardwalk.

nical *Citizen Kane*. Aronofsky uses fast motion, slow motion, special kinds of camera mounts, spectacular montage, complicated camera movements, split screen, subliminal imagery, fish-eye lenses, and more. Whereas in the classic horror-of-personality film, there are two interconnected characters struggling with psychological health, here there are four; and their various addictions take each to the edge of psychosis.

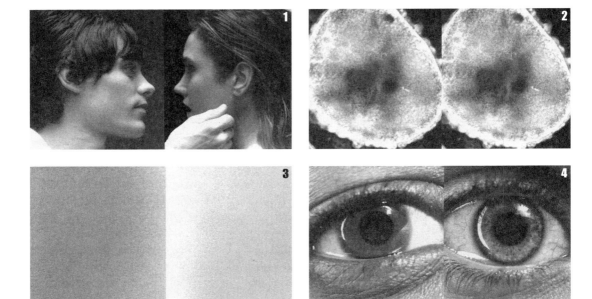

Even in *Requiem for a Dream*'s love scene between Harry and his girlfriend (Jared Leto and Jennifer Connelly), (1) a split screen suggests the lovers are alienated despite their proximity. Director Darren Aronofsky uses (2) a parallel split screen — part of an abstract montage indicating drug use — to suggest love is no more than addiction; and (3) a split screen of contentless space to suggest physical release. Finally, (4) the "doubled" single eye updates a conventional horror-of-personality image.

Requiem for a Dream is also one of the most despairing films to come out of the American cinema in the last thirty years: none of the four characters comes to a happy end, nor for that matter, to much understanding of their abject failures. The most moving psychological portrait is of Sara Goldfarb, who becomes addicted to food and to diet pills. Sara's refrigerator becomes a monster, at one point literally opening like a fanged creature to eat *her*. Still, she fantasizes about doughnuts and cupcakes floating from the ceiling. Burstyn's superb, full-frontal assault on this material is gutsy and riveting (and resulted in an Academy Award nomination as well as many critics' prizes): in one scene she allows herself to look like a demented Baby Jane, in another like a bag lady terrified of being stalked by pedestrians on the street. *Requiem for a Dream*'s view of drug addiction is — along with Danny Boyle's *Trainspotting* and Otto Preminger's *The Man with the Golden Arm*— one of the most unglamorous ever, with many scenes that are physically difficult to watch. Unlike so many drug films that use contemporary rock or rap music, *Requiem for a Dream* uses expressive contemporary classical music (performed by the Kronos Quartet), which provides this sordid material with at least the ennobling patina of tragedy. From beginning to end, *Requiem for a Dream* is emotionally over the top, with an intensity so overwhelming that watching it becomes a draining experience. By the film's end — with the audience feeling a claustrophobic need to flee the theatre — we have witnessed the degradation and fall of all four characters. Indeed, each of them ends bleakly, in a similar fetal position. Prostitution, anal penetration with a dildo in front of an audience, incarceration, the amputation of an arm, and electro-shock therapy are just a few of the consequences of addiction that Aronofsky presents in his film's final minutes. And commenting ironically on these tragedies is the ever-present television infomercial star "Tappy Tibbons" with his message of hope in JUICE ("Join Us in Creating Energy"), if only you would buy his series of inspirational videos.

Suspenseful and disquieting, *One Hour Photo*, released in 2002, distinguishes itself by being a horror film without a single act of violence. Because of its production (by 20th Century Fox) in association with Christine Vachon's Killer Films, *One Hour Photo* is connected to the gay independent cinema movement. The film stars A-list actor Robin Williams as Sy Parrish, an aging photo processor at a SavMart drugstore who becomes obsessed with the photos of a family — mother, father, son — whose lives seem perfect. In many ways, and partially because it is about a man's search for the perfect family, *One Hour Photo* recalls *The Stepfather*. One understands Vachon's interest in such material, given how the political right has used "family values" as a club to exclude gays and lesbians from the human family; *One Hour Photo* inherently argues not only for the re-integration of the family, but for its expansion to include the disenfranchised.

Sy understands that "No one ever takes a photograph of something they want to forget." When he tells Nina Yorkin, "You have a wonderful family," Sy doesn't realize that her family is not especially happy or that her husband is an emotionally neglectful father. But Sy does realize that for all families, their photos represent "their little stands against the flow of time." These photos say: "I was here. I existed. I was young. I was happy. And

As in the typical horror-of-personality film, the psycho in *One Hour Photo* (played by Robin Williams) is shown in reflection, here with an ironic comment on the mirror.

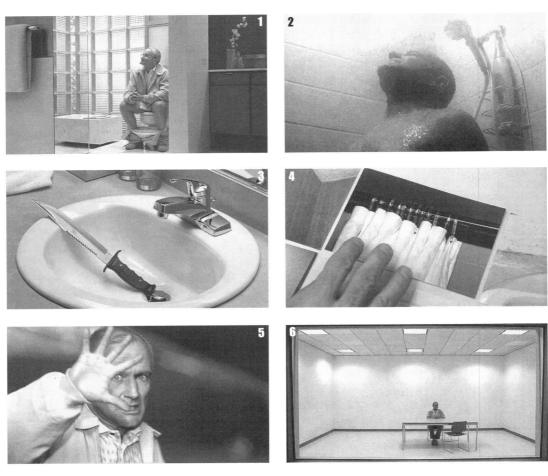

Although virtually without violence, *One Hour Photo* nevertheless disquiets, in part because of specific references to *Psycho*: (1) a casual, yet shocking image of a toilet; (2) a protagonist in a shower; (3) a knife as a potential weapon; (4) a shower curtain, seen in a photograph; (5) the gestural mannerism of *Psycho*'s most famous Anthony Perkins publicity photo; and (6) a largely empty room where the psycho, alone, is photographed against a white wall.

The photos Sy collects of the family he idealizes in *One Hour Photo* contrast starkly to the photo representing his own family: a photo of nothing.

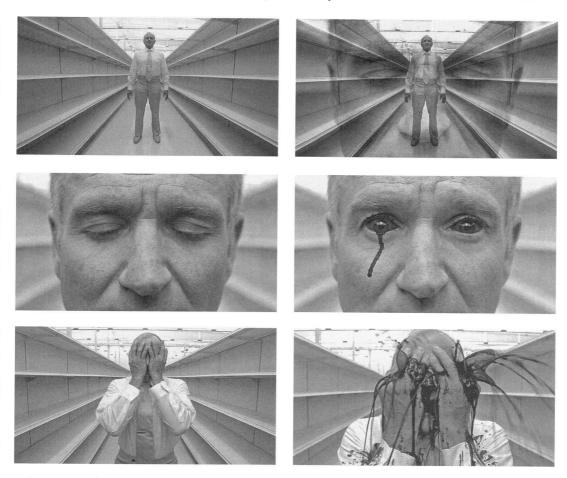

An expressively surreal sequence in *One Hour Photo* shows Robin Williams' Sy standing in a drug-store aisle with empty shelves which look like wings. The edited montage suggests hovering and meditation — at least until a bloody eruption.

someone cared enough about me in this world to take my picture." Robin Williams' performance is understated and poignant; he is the lonely man so cut off from family that no one ever takes his picture. The irony is that Sy's job is to develop the photos of those who, unlike himself, have made family connections. So when Sy uses Nina's camera to take his *own* picture, the moment is heartbreaking. (At one point, we see Sy holding a totally blank photograph, the blankness a metaphor for his life.) After Sy examines photographs for another of his customers and realizes that Nina's husband, Will, is having an affair, Sy arranges for Nina to receive the incriminating pictures. When Sy steals a knife and stalks Will and his mistress, *One Hour Photo* threatens to become a slasher film. Yet surprisingly, Sy is too impotent to kill them; instead, he takes their photographs in forced pornographic poses. Certainly this scene is disquieting, but it is sad, too, especially because in the final scene, we learn that Sy was sexually abused by a father who exposed and exploited Sy's image in horrendous child pornography. *One Hour Photo* ends, pityingly, with a series of photographs Sy has taken of his empty hotel room — yet more symbols of Sy's loneliness and profound inability to connect.

The technical components of *One Hour Photo*, written and directed by Mark Romanek, are flawless. Unlike so many Hollywood films which throw money into expensive special effects, *One Hour Photo* succeeds on the merits of its controlled and impressive production design by Tom Foden, art direction by Michael Manson, and cinematography by Jeff Cronenweth. Photographed in monochromatic images in which green, yellow, or especially blue dominate, the SavMart shines in a cold, hyper-realist light. A wide-angle lens keeps images in sharp focus as the camera tracks formally up and down the aisles. These compositions are all so precisely composed that Sy's world seems sterile and unfulfilling. Only when Sy is outside the store is a telephoto lens used, and only at the Yorkin home are there warmer colors. Like most recent horror films, there are nods to *Psycho*: Sy's hand extended toward the camera, like Marion Crane's or Norman Bates' in key *Psycho* scenes; Sy photographed against a blank wall in the police station, like *Psycho*'s final images of Norman; a shower curtain and curtain rings, like those in *Psycho*'s first murder sequence. And when Sy enters the Yorkin home, it is especially creepy that one of the first things he does (at least in his imagination) is to use the family's toilet — a toilet being the taboo icon that Hitchcock in *Psycho* introduced so shockingly to sixties audiences.

Dahmer (2002) and *Monster* (2003) both dealt with historical serial killers — the notorious cannibal Jeffrey Dahmer and the lesbian prostitute Aileen Wuornos, respectively. Of the two films, *Dahmer* was ignored, despite some excellent reviews, because too many audiences and critics presumed it impossible to make a film on such a tawdry subject without resorting to exploitation. Yet *Dahmer* is surprisingly affecting and not particularly exploitative. *Monster*, on the other hand, inherently appealed to male viewers, who presumed (correctly) they would see titillating lesbian sex in addition to violence. As well, A-list actress and former model Charlize Theron gained weight and de-glamorized herself to play Wuornos; cannily, the film's publicity campaign — geared to the stunt casting of the beautiful model playing the unattractive killer — attracted audiences oblivious to the reality that they were watching a horror film. Sold as a prestige picture, *Monster* became a sociological document like *Boys Don't Cry*, and as a result, Theron won the Academy award for best actress as well as a variety of critics' awards. *Dahmer*, which was unable to disguise its genre, lacked major stars, although its performances by Jeremy Renner as Jeffrey and Bruce Davison (the long-ago star of *Willard*) as Jeffrey's father Lionel, are impressive. Written and directed by David Jacobson, *Dahmer* opens with dripping chocolate within the candy factory Jeffrey works at; because of the associations we immediately bring to the film's subject, the chocolate looks like human viscera. When Jeffrey offers to buy one of his future victims a pair of shoes, and the young Asian asks whether Jeffrey is some kind of nut, Jef-

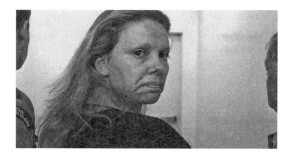

The grimy naturalism of *Monster* relentlessly emphasized the stunt casting which transformed glamorous Charlize Theron into unattractive Aileen Wuornos.

The visual choices in *Dahmer* reveal different sides of the serial killer played by Jeremy Renner: (1) in close-up as sensitive, but troubled young man; (2) in extreme low angle as powerful, ominous monster; and (3) in superimposition as libidinous, unstoppable force.

frey responds, "That's sad. That we've gotten to a point where doing nice things for people is considered insane." Of course there is irony here — since although Jeffrey makes a reasonable point, he is, nevertheless, violently insane. One of *Dahmer*'s strengths is its sociological insight — particularly the horrifying truth that one of Jeffrey's first victims would have escaped but for the racism of the police who refused to take seriously the African-American witnesses to what Jeffrey was doing.

In a key flashback, Lionel invades his son's privacy, demanding to see a mannequin that Jeffrey has stolen and dressed. Jeffrey is humiliated when his father discovers the mannequin is male. Lionel insists Jeffrey open up a locked box, which we presume is being used to stash gay pornography. Because we fear another humiliation, we feel empathy for Jeffrey and are relieved when he manages to avoid opening the box. Only after Lionel has left and we discover that what's inside the box is a human head do we realize how wrong we were to feel any empathy at all. The whole scene is exquisitely Hitchcockian, because it creates both suspense and audience guilt. Ironically, all Jeffrey's subsequent offenses could have been prevented had Lionel not relented.

Jeffrey is homosexual, certainly, but self-hating, which contributes to his pathology as a necrophiliac aroused by raping the dead or the unconscious. As his murders continue, ironies accumulate. For instance, just as we feel compassion for one would-be victim, that victim steals cash from Jeffrey's wallet. And Jeffrey kills using a knife that he had bought from the victim. Another flashback in which Jeffrey tries to seduce a hunky, naive high school wrestler, is fascinating. Jeffrey tells him:

> You're a rebel.... You're against the establishment.... So why don't you see that having sex with only girls is following the most fascist social law of them all? Don't you see how you're being programmed? Don't you see what's going to happen? It's all there. You're going to get married, and then you're going to get a boring job. And before you know it you're going to have

a pot belly. And you're going to start hating your wife and she's going to start hating you. At which point, you're going to become completely depressed. Then you're not going to want to have sex with anybody. Not even yourself.

Jeffrey is cleverly manipulative, yes, but his speech nevertheless carries more than a little bit of accuracy. Indeed, we almost see — though it is a horrifying insight — that by killing the wrestler, Jeffrey is saving him from this other fate. Because of Jacobson's skill as a film-maker, in the scene showing a policeman stopping Jeffrey as he is driving with bags filled with the wrestler's body parts, we so empathize with Jeffrey that we *want* him to elude capture. Of course we feel even guiltier than before. What makes *Dahmer* so disturbing is that not only does it make us feel compassion for Jeffrey, although we abhor everything he does, but it truly allows us to understand his motives. (As director Jean Renoir famously said, "Everyone has their reasons.") And the more we understand Jeffrey, the harder it becomes to hate him simply, without ambivalence.

Dahmer is laden with irony: Jeffrey dances with a visitor who is oblivious that the skeleton he skirts is not only real, but a harbinger of his own future as a Dahmer victim.

Yet Jeffrey knows exactly what he is. "I'm a pervert. I'm an exhibitionist. I'm a masturbator. And a killer." The various social milieus of the film are presented perfectly: the bad Milwaukee neighborhood of the older Jeffrey — populated by disenfranchised minorities no one especially cares for; the good suburban neighborhood of the young Jeffrey — populated by no one with enough imagination to conceive that genuine horror can dwell there. Indeed, Jeffrey's suburban house is not unlike the one in *Leave It to Beaver*, and when Lionel calls out to his son that he's home from work, Lionel's cluelessness is both hilarious and terrifying. *Dahmer* ends as Jeffrey cuts open the stomach of a lobotomized victim and enters him with his fist and arm. The victim is in effect turned into a mannequin, which recalls the earlier flashback. Then, in a rather ambiguous, final flashback, Jeffrey jumps a concrete wall and disappears into the woods — deeper into his perversions?

It is odd to think a film about Jeffrey Dahmer could be subtle, but in *Dahmer* we see only two murders, one near-miss, and not a single act of cannibalism. The director's focus is on Dahmer as a killer-in-training, on the psychology that leads Jeffrey to his future. What emerges is a persuasive psychological drama which — unlike the typical horror film — contains no jangling musical riffs to make us jump or tell us we should be scared. Although Dahmer was convicted of 15 murders, sentenced to 937 years, and killed in prison, the writing and direction in *Dahmer* is so skillful that we see Jeffrey as a human being — however horrifying and unforgivable.

The German film *The Child I Never Was* [*Ein Leben lang kurze Hosen tragen*], which was written and directed by Kai S. Pieck in 2002, shows surprising similarities to *Dahmer*, made the same year. Pieck's film is also based on an infamous historical figure: Jürgen Bartsch, the youngest serial killer in German history, who at the age of seventeen tortured and murdered a number of young boys and had sex with their dead bodies. What makes this case-history film unique is that it is narrated by the killer himself, based on his private

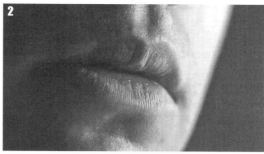

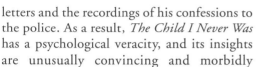

The Child I Never Was utilizes various narrative strategies that emphasize the film's first-person, documentary sensibility, including (1) testimony given directly to the camera, (2) expressive composition in the service of non-fiction re-creation, and (3) handwritten words superimposed onto the image.

letters and the recordings of his confessions to the police. As a result, *The Child I Never Was* has a psychological veracity, and its insights are unusually convincing and morbidly intriguing. In an affecting confession to a priest who hardly looks older than Bartsch, Bartsch talks for the first time about the irresistible sexual compulsions which led to his committing murder. Although the film will later show us an older priest molesting Bartsch, neither Pieck nor Bartsch imply that this was responsible for Bartsch's crimes in any way. Nor does the film indict the coldness of Bartsch's mother or the occupation of Bartsch's father (a butcher). And Bartsch takes great pains in his confession to distinguish homosexuality from his own obsession with murdering children for sexual gratification. About the former, Bartsch says only somewhat flippantly, "If you want to breed homosexuals, I would recommend ... [a Catholic school]." About his tendency toward pederasty, Bartsch movingly remembers the horror he felt when his father gave him his first razor and Bartsch realized that he could not prevent himself from growing up and turning into something that he would not find sexually desirable. Pieck's narrative comprises dramatized scenes of Bartsch's childhood, similar scenes of his murders, and extended documentary-style scenes showing Bartsch as a young adult confessing to as much as he can remember. The most striking visual technique in the film, however, is how Pieck beautifully superimposes the handwritten words of Bartsch's confessions directly onto the film images of Bartsch's past. These stunning images powerfully belie the film's gruesome subject. *The Child I Never Was* concludes by telling us that after serving years in prison, Bartsch, as an adult, was actually released and got married. Ironically, he died shortly thereafter from the ensuing complications as a result of a surgical castration that Bartsch himself requested.

Identity, directed by James Mangold in 2003, is another underrated film. Filled with mirrors and reflections, the identity symbols so common in horror-of-personality films, *Identity* starts ominously with the nursery rhyme: "As I was going up the stair, I met a man who wasn't there. He wasn't there again today. I wish, I wish he'd go away." (By the end of the film, a variety of characters who aren't really there *will* go away.) The narrative in *Identity* develops along two alternating tracks without apparent connection. On one track: a psychiatric patient we do not clearly see, convicted of serial killings and sentenced to death, is interviewed by a psychiatrist while a thunderstorm rages in the classic horror tradition. On the other track: a variety of travelers are stranded at the same motel by a storm — an actress, a prostitute, a chauffeur, suburban parents with their son, a young couple, and a police officer with his prisoner. Someone has apparently run over the suburban mom, and we tend to presume (incorrectly) that the prostitute was responsible; we also presume (incor-

Identity's clearest reference to *Psycho* is the ubiquitous motel used as refuge on a dark and stormy night.

rectly) that the prisoner may be the psychiatric patient from the other narrative. The relationship between the two narratives is ambiguous: are they chronologically simultaneous, or is one a flashback? The book the chauffeur is reading — Sartre's *Being and Nothingness* — is a clue that director Mangold is up to something more metaphysical than usual for a horror film. The motel narrative, conventional and old-fashioned, references *Psycho*'s archetypal Bates Motel, but in the context of the Agatha Christie book (and film) *And Then There Were None*, in which one victim after another dies, slowly reducing the number of stranded victims. And indeed, all but one of the motel visitors in *Identity* die in grisly ways. But what seems like a classic mystery we were asked to solve rationally becomes increasingly irrational and incapable of solution. The clever climax reveals that what is most crucial, as the title suggests, is *identity* — because in actuality, *none* of the people, nor the motel itself, ever really existed. Rather, the motel was a representation of the mind of the serial killer, and the "people" we saw there were the multiple personalities created by the killer's dissociative identity disorder. And these personalities are dying off as each is successfully integrated by the psychiatrist into one unified personality. So which personality will remain? *Identity*'s climax genuinely astonishes when the motel narrative ruptures and is subsumed by the initial narrative, as the sole living motel character is suddenly transported into the psychiatrist's office and revealed as the dominant, remaining personality of the serial killer. (However, a fadeout twist suggests that the most diabolical personality might actually be "Timmy," who is like the killer child in a demonic horror film.)

It is worth noting that *Identity* is much like *The Sixth Sense* (1999) and *The Others* (2001) — films of the period which also climaxed with revelations that the characters we were empathizing with were not really alive. How odd that so many horror films with "surprise" endings should end with the same surprise! In its indirect way, *Identity* seems a post–9/11 horror film — focused on obliviousness and indirectly on Americans' insistence on trying to remain disconnected from reality and alienated from the meanings of their own behaviors.

The Machinist, an atmospheric independent film directed by Brad Anderson in 2004, is one of the most disquieting recent horror films. Unusually lugubrious, it begins with its protagonist, Trevor Reznik, disposing of a body in a manner suggesting the parallel scene in *Psycho*. The blue-suffused images, which make *The Machinist* virtually monochromatic, are especially appropriate to its despairing view of the monotonous routine of blue-collar factory life. When Trevor is asked "Are you OK?" he retorts, "Do I look OK?" The response: "If you were any thinner, you wouldn't exist." This exchange underscores the film's most disturbing component: the handsome actor Christian Bale, who played the narcissistic muscular lead in *American Psycho*, as well as — years before — the little boy protagonist in *Empire*

The Machinist draws on two horror traditions: (1) the modern horror of *Psycho*, by showing Trevor Reznik (Christian Bale) in a contemporary bathroom with shower and toilet; and (2) the silent-film horror of the German expressionist *The Cabinet of Dr. Caligari*, by showing Trevor within a frame of severe angles, artificial shadows, and asymmetrical windows.

of the Sun, lost 63 pounds to play this psychologically tortured factory worker. We see Bale shirtless more than once, and he is so thin that his bones visibly protrude, and so gaunt of face that the actor himself looks critically ill. As a result, we watch with greater unease than usual: if a real person like Bale can physically deteriorate so drastically, then so can we. Many critics and viewers, feeling like voyeurs, wondered whether an actor would have to be somewhat deranged to threaten his health by committing so completely to what was dismissed as just a horror role. (In fact, one suspects *The Machinist* would have been more successful had the film's previews highlighting Bale's weight loss been less distressing.) Nevertheless, as a portrait of mental illness, Bale gives a magnificent, heroic performance.

As *The Machinist* proceeds, film references abound, particularly to Martin Scorsese's *Taxi Driver*. A close-up of Trevor at a diner staring into his cup, shown in close-up, recalls Robert De Niro's Travis Bickle staring at his fizzing Alka-Seltzer — an image portending a cataclysmic conclusion. And "Trevor Reznik" sounds similar to "Travis Bickle." Like Travis, Trevor is associated with both a prostitute and a woman who is the embodiment of his dreams. Making explicit another parallel between the films, the prostitute asks Trevor to rescue her from her life. And *The Machinist*'s soundtrack — including strings, low horns, and even a Theremin — evokes the style of *Taxi Driver*'s composer Bernard Herrmann (who also composed the *Psycho* soundtrack). Notable, too, is the presence of actress Anna Massey — who played key roles so memorably in Michael Powell's *Peeping Tom* (in 1960) and Alfred Hitchcock's *Frenzy* (in 1972) — whose praiseworthy performance as Trevor's landlady works as *hommage* to her own iconic relationship to the horror-of-personality subgenre for over forty years.

Like Catherine Deneuve's protagonist in *Repulsion*, Trevor is descending into madness, a journey which is compelling and hypnotic. He reads Dostoyevsky's *The Idiot*, about an epileptic outsider destroyed by the evil around him; and later, a little boy that Trevor tries to help, suffers an epileptic seizure. Early in *The Machinist*, Trevor is asked if he has sustained a recent head injury. Later we discover that his car was totaled a year before, potentially explaining his hallucinatory adventures. In fact, the narrative is increasingly revealed as unreliable, but which scenes are the figments of his imagination? Like Marion Crane in *Psycho*, Trevor drives at night and imagines conversations. And as in the sixties horror-of-personality films, mutilation seems a constant danger. A mysterious and reappearing game of Hangman suggests decapitation. Trevor's co-worker, Miller, loses virtually his whole arm, which we see severed and spinning on a mill. Another character, Ivan — ultimately revealed as coming from Trevor's guilty imagination — is missing fingers and has two toes grafted onto his hand to create an exceedingly strange deformity. Trevor's own hands are

The Machinist consistently references other films. Note the similarity between (1) Trevor Reznik in the *Machinist* and (2) the title vampire of *Nosferatu* (made in 1922). Note the similarity between the images 3 and 4 from *The Machinist* and the images 5 and 6 from *Taxi Driver* (made in 1976), each film using atypical close-ups of a beverage to indicate the inner state of their protagonist (Christian Bale and Robert DeNiro, respectively).

vulnerable and skeletal, and his constant washing of them seems a sign of suppressed guilt. As Trevor loses more weight (and Bale too?), he looks increasingly ill; and when Trevor sustains facial injuries, he looks like he's in the late stages of HIV/AIDS, with Kaposi's sarcoma lesions. Typical to the horror-of-personality film, there are lots of mirror images which seem to ask, as does a Post-it note that haunts Trevor: "Who are you?" Like *Psycho*, several scenes take place in the bathroom, including a stabbing where blood flows and a shower curtain is pulled back dramatically. Particularly at the end of *The Machinist*, Bale looks much like Anthony Perkins — even ending up, as did Norman Bates, in a white room lock-up.

Ultimately, we learn that a repressed *idée fixe* is responsible for Trevor's madness, an *idée* which tries to surface at every opportunity, manifest in the film's skillful art design, where the surreal upside-down pyramid of a water tower is mimicked by other objects around Trevor which take on the same foreboding shape. *The Machinist*'s revelation is that Trevor's madness has been caused by what he's been repressing: that he killed a young boy in a hit-and-run accident near that tower. Trevor is a tragic, contemporary character out

Many of the surreal images in *The Machinist* resist easy interpretation: (1) three sets of abstracted legs that look almost like they're floating; (2) a post-it note asking a profound question; and (3) a woman juxtaposed against an oddly-shaped water tower.

of Dostoyevsky: like the Holy Fool in *The Idiot* who retreats into epilepsy, Trevor tries retreating into his delusions. Fortunately, like Raskolnikov in *Crime and Punishment*, Trevor *can* take responsibility for his crime. Of course, he must first accept the truth if he is to find forgiveness from others, let alone from himself.

In contrast to the laudable ambition of *The Machinist*, with its carefully contrived narrative and subtle atmospherics, two other films around the same time were artlessly exploitative: *High Tension* in 2003, and *Hostel* in 2005. Surprisingly, *High Tension* (originally titled *Haute Tension*) is a French film which achieved wide release in the United States. When, in its opening minutes, a man fellates himself with a woman's severed head, you know that this film — nonsubtle, unambiguous, anti-intellectual, and straining to appeal to the American teen market — is only technically French. Like American horror, *High Tension* is dominated by its ominous music, heavy with indication. With its emphasis on decapitations, amputations, stairways, and bathrooms, *High Tension* qualifies as a horror-of-personality film. Unfortunately, it is more mercenary pandering than work of art and almost totally without interest — except for its sad demonstration that American film hegemony has made inroads into French cinema and culture. As devoid of characterization, theme, or ideas as a horror film can be, and counting on titillating imagery to carry it (such as two blood-covered women kissing), *High Tension* culminates with a surprise ending that feels arbitrary and obligatory.

And yet *High Tension*, which made almost $4 million in the United States, far beyond its low budget (and much more than it made in France) has inspired its compatriot filmmakers to eschew their French sensibility and "go gore." A recent typical example is *Inside* [*À l'intérieur*], whose major innovation is to replace the male loony brandishing a knife with a female loony brandishing a knife. The most interesting component of *Inside*, at least potentially, is its barely confronted social context of immigrant riots in the *banlieue* of Paris. Unfortunately, the riots are taking place *outside*, while the filmmakers are concentrating on the psychotic sadism taking place *inside*. *Inside* chronicles an evil woman in black (identified metaphorically only as *la femme* and played by Béatrice Dalle) who breaks into a pregnant woman's home in order to violently cut out the fetus from her belly. From its credits viscous with blood, the entire film is preposterously contrived solely to create the maximum amount of spurting. Again and again our basest instincts are appealed to, as the villain single-handedly commits one act of violence after another, each more unspeakable than the last. In fact, strangling the cat is so minor as to hardly merit mention. (We are probably supposed to laugh.) By the film's end, bloody pools and other human splatters are everywhere: on the floors, on the walls, on the eight corpses, mutilated and still bleeding in the claustrophobic space. Throughout the violence, directors Alexandre Bustillo and Julien Maury periodically cut to shots of the unborn baby reacting to each blow; and the film's final indignity is seeing the pregnant woman literally flayed in front of us, and her baby stolen. The unregenerate glee with which the film presents this sadism is more upsetting than the sadism itself, which ultimately seems juvenile, since one can imagine the filmmakers chortling over the manufactured cynicism of their vision. Notably, the American distributors of *Inside*'s DVD quote a favorite review on their DVD box cover. There was a time when the most sought-after blurb might be something highbrow from a *Cahiers du Cinéma* writer, or perhaps something from Andrew Sarris in *The Village Voice* or Pauline Kael in *The New Yorker*. The fact that *Inside* quotes the website bloody-disgusting.com ("One of the scariest movies I have ever seen in my life...") provides everything else one needs to know about a certain contemporary tendency of the French cinema.

 Hostel, in 2005, attracted a considerable cult audience and attention in part because it was officially "presented" by Quentin Tarantino (whose affection for the exploitation film had been demonstrated by his collaboration with Robert Rodriguez on *Grindhouse*). Directed by Eli Roth, *Hostel* panders to its young audience by immediately showing its male twentysomething protagonists getting stoned and having sex in Amsterdam while demonstrating that they are the ugliest of Americans. Yet their boorishness, sexism, and homophobia are presented as amusements for *Hostel*'s audience; later, when the protagonists fall victim to violence, there is no sense that they are getting their rightful punishment, just horror that their idyllic, shallow libertinism has come to an end. *Hostel*'s horror is in part an excuse to show bare-breasted women; and for our amusement, human beings are attacked, drilled, chainsawed, mutilated, sliced, operated on, and given amputations. At one point our American "hero" shows his mettle by cutting off someone's popped eyeball. *Hostel* is a little like Pasolini's *Salò*, but without the slightest intellectual or political framework. The premise of *Hostel*'s story is that somewhere in Slovakia, a business allows customers to pay for the privilege of killing procured victims in the controlled setting of an abandoned factory filled with torture chambers. It costs $5,000 to kill a Russian, $10,000 to kill a European, and $25,000 to kill an American — a price structure which suggests that the capitalist marketplace puts a premium on American lives, a detail which both strokes the American ego and allows Americans to nurture their status as international victims who should thus be allowed to do whatever they damn well please. Japanese director Takashi Miike makes a guest appearance as a customer who emerges from the killing factory with a warning to other customers to "Be careful. You can spend all your money in there!" In other words, killing is fun.[10] Just as disturbing was the marketing campaign for *Hostel*'s DVD release, which came with a (temporary) tattoo for the buyer to put on to indicate that he (or less likely, she) was a member of *Hostel*'s elite killing club. (What's next: *Kapo* insignia so consumers can pretend they helped engineer the Holocaust and gassed Jews?) Although this casual description of the film's violence might suggest *Hostel* is similar to a gory film like George A. Romero's *Night of the Living Dead*, the comparison would be misguided, since Eli Roth's film is without moral impulse, and its violence works powerfully to coarsen our decreasingly-human temperament.

 As 2006 came to a close, three major new works made clear it had been a banner year for the horror of personality: a big-budget foreign film in English from a German director—*Perfume*; an Academy Award–nominated British film with a high-class pedigree—*Notes on a Scandal*; and, most surprisingly, an acclaimed TV series with a serial killer as its hero—*Dexter*. Could there be any more persuasive proof that obsession with violence and the psychopathological were central to the Western *Zeitgeist*?

Perfume, subtitled *The Story of a Murderer*, tells the eighteenth-century tale of Jean-Baptiste Grenouille, a French *parfumeur* who kills in order to find the perfect human scent to mix into his perfume. Directed by Tom Tykwer (who made the striking *Run, Lola, Run*), *Perfume* is an obsessively beautiful horror film in the guise of historical drama, even down to a pedantic narrator (voiced by John Hurt). Sensuously expressive, *Perfume* presents an era not unlike our own, with venality and casual violence everywhere. Particularly effective are the early scenes which present Grenouille's birth, time in an orphanage, and development of his olfactory genius. Tykwer's ambitiousness in making a film so totally devoted to smell, a sense which cannot yet be communicated directly in the cinema, is laudable. Especially helpful to *Perfume*'s impulse for synesthesia is its extraordinary cinematography by Frank Griebe, whose rich style gives the film a dreamy inexorability, a swoony obsessiveness. How the film presents a connection between scent and fetish is both hyper-romantic and extraordinarily creepy. Although Grenouille's first murder is accidental, his subsequent murders are not. (As well, with a fated mysticism, almost all major characters associated with Grenouille die after he exits from their lives.) Grenouille seems to understand that his olfactory prowess stems from the quirk that he possesses no scent himself. He realizes, too, that the *amour fou* of his morbid pursuits may lead to his oblivion; still, he must follow his bliss. *Perfume* becomes a surreal, anarchic, amoral document that evokes Buñuel, even down to the film's rejection of church sanctimony and hypocrisy. For Grenouille, his pursuit of scent transcends the immorality of his violence, because his perfume aspires to the highest level of art. Indeed, in *Perfume*'s amazing climax, Grenouille, about to be executed, releases a perfume into the air that is so extraordinary it creates rap-

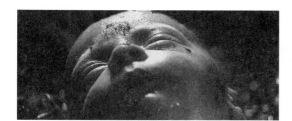 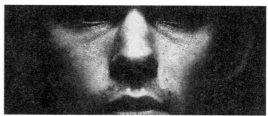

The protagonist in *Perfume*, whether as newborn or adult (played by Ben Wishaw), is shown in images which emphasize his olfactory prowess.

By the end of *Perfume*, Grenouille (Ben Wishaw) has powers so horrific (or marvelous?) that he can unleash unstoppable sexual desire; for organized religion, this is horror of apocalyptic proportion.

ture, inciting a public orgy that allows thousands to find physical ecstasy and spiritual transcendence. The mysticism of this surprising ending suggests that Grenouille is as much angel as devil, "a power stronger than the power of money or love or death." And perhaps sometimes, a serial killer may have valid aesthetic reasons — as was suggested as far back as 1827 by writer Thomas de Quincey in his essay "On Murder Considered as One of the Fine Arts."[11]

As notable as *Perfume*, though for different reasons, is *Notes on a Scandal*, one of the rare films of the last several decades to evoke the sixties horror-of-personality films like *What Ever Happened to Baby Jane?* and *Strait-Jacket*, films that reveled in pitting two extraordinary actresses against each other, at least one of them aging, and then watching the sparks fly while we tried to figure out which of the two was more psychopathic. In *Notes on a Scandal*, the actresses are the redoubtable Judi Dench and her potential successor in the Commonwealth acting firmament, Cate Blanchett. Dench plays Barbara Covett, and Blanchett plays Sheba Hart, both of them teachers in a British high school. Barbara, bitter and wry, heads the history department and is dismissive of academic bureaucracy as well as of her students; Sheba, sincere and dangerously open, teaches art and wants to get close to her students — in fact, too close, leading to an affair with an underage boy. The teacher's names are significant: Sheba has "heart," which Barbara doesn't; and Barbara "covets" Sheba sexually, although Barbara cannot quite admit to her lesbianism, a repression responsible for many of her psychological problems. In the film's unique plot development, Barbara uses her knowledge of the affair to blackmail Sheba into a friendship ... or will it be a love affair? And thus the cat-and-mouse between the two women is on, each disturbed in her own way. Because Barbara is the smarter of the two, perceptive about everyone if not always about

herself, the expert screenplay by Patrick Marber wisely allows Barbara to narrate the film; her commentary is witty and devastating. She knows that knowledge is power and that "People have always trusted me with their secrets." Early on, Barbara notes that it is "Hard to read the wispy novice. Is she a sphinx or simply stupid?" Although Barbara tries to befriend Sheba (despite the obstacle of Sheba's husband), Barbara cannot resist the dismis-

Much that is dramatic passes between Barbara and Sheba (Judi Dench and Cate Blanchett) in *Notes on a Scandal*, but nothing as portentous as the single hair, from Sheba's head, that the completely smitten Barbara fetishizes. Although the women are often photographed within the same shot, the limited depth of field creates a selective focus that emphasizes their disconnection.

Notes on a Scandal renovates horror-of-personality conventions within a women-centered drama. The mirror identity symbol is represented by an elongated reflection of Cate Blanchett's Sheba in a frame which pointedly excludes her actual self, thus avoiding the suggestion of schizophrenic fragmentation. And the traditional bathroom scene — so often with a young, beautiful woman — is represented by a scene with Judi Dench's aging Barbara, neither conventionally attractive nor erotic.

sive insight, with its subtextual accusation of hypocrisy: "They do things differently in bourgeois Bohemia." Barbara's erotic designs on Sheba seem creepy, not because of the lesbianism, nor quite because of the differences in age and in level of attractiveness, but because Barbara seems to deny her lesbianism, even as — in a horrifying moment — she caresses an errant blonde hair from Sheba that falls upon Barbara's lap. Later, when Barbara starts stroking Sheba's arm, the advance is so unwanted that we squirm in our seats. After learning that a past relationship of Barbara's ended tragically, we begin to understand that Barbara can be genuinely dangerous, that people who get involved with her can end up dead. Suspense and the sense of impending disaster increase. Barbara is horrifying, delusional, a monster, obsessive (and her obsessiveness is matched by the expressive, appropriate score by Philip Glass); nevertheless, Barbara evokes our empathy, in part because she can admit that "I have such a dread of ending my days alone." As she realizes she will not win Sheba, Barbara feels betrayed and becomes even more demented. Yet her bitterness is witty as she notes that "Judas had the grace to hang himself, but only according to Matthew, the most sentimental of the apostles." Judi Dench gives a performance which is largely one-note, but of such magnificence that it dazzles, amuses, and terrifies all at once. Matching her performance, if less showily, is Cate Blanchett, whose Sheba finally attacks Barbara with a violent outburst: "You're a fucking vampire!" By the end of the film, Sheba — betrayed by Barbara — prepares to enter prison for a ten-month sentence; and Barbara serendipitously meets a new young woman (and victim) to focus on. Like Paul and Peter in *Funny Games* asking a new family for eggs, or like Sue Ann Stepanek in *Pretty Poison* chatting up a new young man at the soda fountain, Barbara is destined to play out the same plot over and over. The sociological irony of *Notes on a Scandal* is that in 2006, Barbara's sexual repression is needlessly archaic. If only she could allow herself to enter a gay club or embrace her lesbian identity, if she could access even half of the emotional abandon or courage exhibited by Sheba, Barbara would not be destined for the tragic end we can all too clearly anticipate.

Finally, in a kind of apotheosis for the horror-of-personality film came the extraordinary 2006 TV series *Dexter* (for HBO) starring Michael C. Hall in a devastating and sly performance as a serial killer who works in police forensics. *Dexter* combines the horror genre with the police procedural, in the process creating a serial killer who is a hero. Created by James Manos, Jr., from the novel *Darkly Dreaming Dexter* by Jeff Lindsay, Dexter

Telling close-ups of *Dexter*, played by Michael C. Hall: (1) the obligatory single-eyed portrait, common to the horror of personality; (2) Dexter's hands, but about to floss or about to strangle?; and (3) the insect on the skin that Dexter, unlike *Psycho*'s Norman Bates, is quite willing to kill.

is a sociopathic personality whose violent proclivities were recognized by his foster father when Dexter was an adolescent. Although Dexter cannot control these impulses which he knows are wrong, he has been taught by his father to channel them toward killing *other* killers, thus saving the innocent lives of others and saving society the cost of trials and imprisonments. Dexter is a memorable character in the same mode as *Taxi Driver*'s Travis Bickle, but with the New York City underbelly traveled by Bickle replaced by a seedy Florida that Dexter describes as "another beautiful Miami day: mutilated corpses with the chance of afternoon showers." As Dexter anticipates a horrific murder he is about to commit, he says to himself, "Tonight's the night.... And it's going to happen again and again. It has to happen." One serial killer that Dexter tracks down beseeches Dexter for mercy: "I couldn't help myself. You don't understand." But of course Dexter does understand, because Dexter can't stop himself either. Although Dexter has a deep psychological bond with these other killers, he must fake all his other human connections. When looking at an empty donut box, Dexter says that it's "Just like me. Empty inside." Is it Dexter's fault that he is only sexually aroused by amputations and mutilations? Yet Dexter can say, with only a little self-conscious irony as he

Dexter's madness is often photographed subtly: he can look relaxed and erotic, or he can confront the viewer with that slightly cross-eyed look that signifies *crazy*. Compare this second pose with the final shot of Norman Bates in *Psycho*, as shown in the fourth image on page 30.

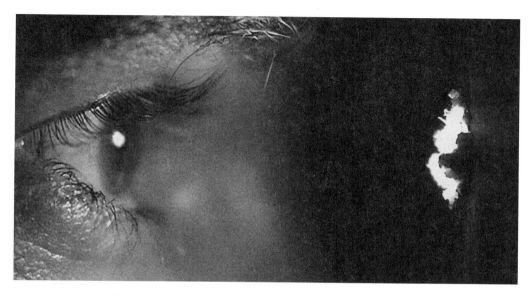

Almost fifty years after Anthony Perkins as Norman Bates (shown here) spied on Marion Crane in ***Psycho, Dexter*** **also reveled in our human impulse for voyeurism. When we watch these horror-of-personality tales, we harbor secret desires just as do the depraved protagonists we empathize with.**

watches people smashing crab legs on their plates with little hammers, "Normal people are so hostile." *Dexter*'s pilot rather expertly sets up the show's brilliant premise; and the subsequent episode opens with Dexter swatting a mosquito—a reference to Norman Bates at the end of *Psycho* and an *hommage* to Hitchcock, who effectively created this horror subgenre. (Although of course Norman Bates *wouldn't* swat that fly, and Dexter clearly would and does.) Fetching, too, is the series' opening credit sequence, a witty montage of Dexter performing his morning rituals: shaving, tying his shoes, making breakfast, and so forth, but with these actions photographed to look like aesthetic violence, visual *double entendres* which help us see the world the way Dexter does. This extraordinary series not only creeps us out, but makes us feel the genuine tragedy of Dexter, too, who is victimized by these feelings and impulses he cannot control. Regarding the people around him, including his murder victims, Dexter attests: "I see their pain. I can understand their pain. I just can't feel their pain." And as our new millennium approaches the end of its first decade, is there any psychological condition more worthy of consideration than the empathy deficit that has contributed to such horrific violence in our contemporary world?

6 — Sequels and Insincerity

Because genre is a dynamic critical concept, genres evolve to reflect new cultural energies. Yet there are several signs that a genre is losing its vitality. The first is when sequels churn out endlessly, each revealing less creativity and variation than the one before. A second is when sincerity gives way to self-parody, and genre conventions turn toward satirical reflexivity. For instance, Mel Brooks' *Young Frankenstein*, in 1974, was a tacit acknowledgment that the classic black-and-white Universal Studio monsters no longer held much terror for us. Similarly, *Scream*, written by Kevin Williamson and directed by Wes Craven in 1996, suggests that the horror-of-personality film is no longer as vital — at least in its American "slasher" incarnation.

In *Scream*, a killer versed in horror films tortures and kills according to the conventions (or clichés) of the genre. Like an expert film-school project, *Scream* is filled with references — not only to *Psycho*, but to less distinguished franchise films aimed at teen audiences such as (so far) the nine *Halloween* films and the eleven *Friday the 13th* films. The characters in *Scream* explicitly enumerate the horror film conventions that are killing them. The fact that the characters — like the audience — can easily perform what are essentially acts of criticism indicates that the conventions have become dangerously fossilized and transparent. What are these conventions? *The killer never comes through the door you think he's going to. The heroine is always attacked whenever she goes to investigate. Only the virgin can outsmart the killer in the big chase at the end.* And the rules if you want to survive a (teen-targeted) horror film are simple: *You can't have sex. You can never drink or do drugs. And you should never say, "I'll be right back."* In keeping with the referential sensibility, *Scream*'s catch phrase is what the killer asks his potential victims: "Do you like scary movies?" But scary movies are derided by one of the female characters: "They're all the same. Some stu-

Scream and *Scary Movie* (shown here) use the same killer, whose abstracted mask reflects the increasingly formulaic face of the American horror film.

200

pid killer stalking some big-breasted girl who can't act, who's always running up the stairs when she should be going out the front door. It's insulting!" Should the audience of *Scream* be insulted? Later, when the killer attacks, the big-breasted actress playing this character *also* runs up the stairs when she could have run out the front door. These reflexive juxtapositions are clever, if also essentially *uninteresting*. *Scream*, though pleasurable, feels largely like an attempt to milk the teen horror genre for more (multi)millions by congratulating the audience for having the little intelligence necessary to recognize — after dozens of routine sequels and rip-offs — the generic patterns. At one point, a reporter in the film watching "real" violence on closed circuit TV thinks she's watching a televised horror movie and offers her assessment: "Boring." Here, *Scream* is more or less attacking itself; but if it attacks, shouldn't we? Perhaps the filmmakers are claiming a secret sensibility superior to that of their audience. Certainly, *Scream* is positioning itself (to use Pauline Kael's terminology) as "trash"—flashy trash, but trash nevertheless. The reflexive joke about the closed circuit TV spins further as the heroine protests, "That is life, this isn't a movie." Unlike Michael Haneke in *Funny Games*, these filmmakers never cross into the Brechtian territory that requires the audience to think. Why? Because as a character attests: "If [a horror film] gets too complicated, you lose your target audience." So *Scream*'s cinematography is perfectly conventional, including reflections in bathroom mirrors and a killer photographed at a Dutch angle; and one teen even quotes Anthony Perkins' famous *Psycho* line, "We all go a little mad sometimes," before revealing himself as a killer. (At least *Scream* offers the trivial pleasure of a cameo appearance by the middle-aged Linda Blair, who played the little girl in *The Exorcist*.) Although not quite an all-out parody, because it asks its audience to take its plot seriously, *Scream* depicts violence as entertaining fun, but doesn't acknowledge in any way the moral ambiguities raised by such a depiction. If we are invited to laugh at violence, will we ignore real violence? Will we accept even "shock and awe," no matter how flimsy the justification, because we are oblivious to violence's moral meaning?

That *Scream* (in 1996) received a number of rave reviews, but that *Funny Games* (in 1997) didn't even get an American release, is a sign of how the debased critical establishment has become more attuned to PR–generated buzz and consumerism than to genuine art. So far, *Scream* has been followed by two sequels. And *Scary Movie* (2000), directed by Keenen Ivory Wayans, is an explicit, almost scene-by-scene parody of *Scream*, which is odd, because *Scream* was almost a parody already, which makes *Scary Movie* a comic horror film about a horror film about other horror films. Whereas horror films used to be about the culture, now they are as likely to be primarily about each other, thus reflecting America's

From its first scene showing its heroine (Drew Barrymore) cowering next to a VCR, television, and horror videotapes, *Scream* makes clear it will not be about real horror, but about other horror films. By the time of *Scary Movie*— a year before 9/11 would lead to wars in Afghanistan and Iraq — the monster lives in a world without consequences, and his decapitation of a young woman is nothing but a comic punch line, intended as fun.

increasing disinterest in examining itself. *Scary Movie* was a huge hit because its jokes about sex, drugs, and violence were perfect for its suburban teen audience. This film, with its comic monsters, exclusively positioned itself as a consumer product that additionally provided opportunities for product placement. Brand names abound in the many in-film commercials: for instance, the monster eating Doritos and drinking Miller beer and Pepsi. *Scary Movie*'s visual wit includes the "hilarious" image of a killer holding a talking, severed head in a girl's locker room. Tellingly, several years later, after the American invasion of Iraq and subsequent decapitation of many by Islamic militants, a severed head would take on quite a different meaning.

Followed by three sequels, *Scary Movie* has gradually morphed into a sketch-comedy franchise making fun of a wide variety of contemporary movies and TV. And for many genre theorists, sequels, in general, remain a problematic concern. On one hand, purists find it difficult to criticize any genre works that maintain an allegiance to convention and type. On the other hand, even the most critically indolent must recognize a distinction between a sequel like *Friday the 13th Part VIII: Jason Takes Manhattan* and *The Godfather, Part II*.[1] Thankfully, the horror-of-personality subgenre has not been that exploited through endless franchises and sequels. The same, unfortunately, cannot be said of the demonic horror film.

7 — The Horror of
the Demonic, Revisited

Of the three horror subgenres enumerated in *Dark Dreams*, the demonic subgenre has by far been the one most dominated throughout the last thirty years by franchise films of diminishing interest. As of this writing, *The Exorcist* franchise (begun in 1973) has been followed by four sequels[1]; *The Omen* franchise (begun in 1976) by three sequels and a remake; *Halloween* (in 1978) by seven sequels and a remake; *The Amityville Horror* (in 1979) by seven sequels and a remake; *Friday the 13th* (in 1980) by ten sequels and a remake; *A Nightmare on Elm Street* (in 1984) by seven sequels; *Children of the Corn* (in 1984) by seven sequels; *Hellraiser* (in 1987) by seven sequels; and *Child's Play* (in 1988) by four sequels. Although these films were immeasurably aided by new technologies and sophisticated special effects for a cinema in the midst of a digital transformation, one must nevertheless wonder: Has there ever been such an extensive collection of sequels so strikingly devoid of notable variation or artistic elaboration?

It isn't surprising that these demonic films, increasingly gruesome, should dominate American horror in a period coinciding with the ascendance of the religious right in the United States, with its Biblical perspective on so many contemporary political and cultural

John Nance as an *Eraserhead* confronting the world's surreal, malevolent forces.

issues. Beginning in the Reagan years with stealth candidates who kept their religious affiliations largely private, the movement has long since abandoned indirection or discretion. This religious right responded (and continues to respond) to what it regards as the secularization of America with a far-reaching agenda to obliterate the boundary between religion and government and to imbue every component of American life with a fundamentalist morality. The first eruption of major demonic films (*Rosemary's Baby*, *The Exorcist*) was

By emphasizing physical monstrosity, horror films like *Hellraiser* and *Eraserhead* owe a debt to Todd Browning's controversial 1932 *Freaks*, which cast real-life sideshow attractions. (1) Here is Schlitze, one of the "pinheads" (someone born with microcephaly) in *Freaks*. (2) *Hellraiser*'s demonic pinhead offers a more literal interpretation. And (3) David Lynch's *Eraserhead* disturbingly reimagines pinheadedness.

largely an inspired response to the chaos of the sixties — the Vietnam War, Watergate, the sexual revolution — a period which seemed to eschew traditional Christian values. Subsequent waves of demonic films seem an inspired response to the religious right, particularly its rhetoric of damnation. The 1991 fall of the Soviet Union allowed the religious right to abandon "Godless Communism" as its number one enemy and to target the secular humanists in the United States, particularly gays and feminists whose moral values and "lifestyle choices" would doubtless (in the view of the right) result in divine retribution. Objectives of the religious right included the rolling back of gay civil rights, the definitive restoration of a view of homosexuality as morally disordered, a repudiation of feminism, a rejection of *Roe v. Wade* in order to outlaw all abortion, the insertion of God in public discourse, the imposition of the Ten Commandments in schools and public buildings, the censorship of pornography or works of art with sexually explicit or political themes, the prevention of stem-cell research and certain other scientific advances, the adoption of a constitutional amendment barring marriage between two men or two women, and the teaching of "creationism" in science curriculums. When Osama bin Laden's terrorists, largely from Saudi Arabia (where homosexuality is outlawed and women have almost no rights) destroyed the World Trade Center towers, evangelists and media moguls Pat Robertson and Jerry Falwell blamed American homosexuals and feminists for bringing punishment onto America. Religious rhetoric was dominating American culture, with organizations like The Moral Majority, Focus on the Family, Eagle Forum, the Family Research Council, and networks like CBN and Trinity all demonizing feminists, gays, artists, academics, scientists, and progressive thinkers. Within this new social sphere, people with whom one disagrees were no longer considered uninformed, illogical, or just plain wrong, they were considered *evil*. It is therefore not surprising that demonic horror should be among the most continuously popular genres of the last twenty-five years, if not the most critically acclaimed. Nor is it surprising that the more recent demonic films would be more graphic in their presentation of America's sexual "fall" and more apocalyptic in their imagery, sharing themes with the horror-of-Armageddon sub-genre. *Rosemary's Baby*, in 1968, showed no real imagery of hell (except for the briefest dream glimpses, barely apprehensible), yet the contemporary demonic films are dominated by images of damnation, torture, and dire consequences. Of course this does not mean that these demonic films would automatically be pleasing to the fundamentalists, because even as these demonic films punish those characters who are the most independent or sexually adventuresome, these horror films are also profane and erotic. Films that are wildly successful are often able to embody contradictions effortlessly; and so these demonic films (with their ambiguous meanings) are open to a variety of ideological readings.[2]

One could easily argue that many of the demonic films made since the American film renaissance of the late sixties/early seventies lack the electric cultural energy and sincerity of their forebears. The existence of *Look What's Happened to Rosemary's Baby* (1976) or *The Final Conflict* (1981) or *Amityville 3-D* (1983) seems less to reflect a social need as to reveal Hollywood's characteristic insistence on exploiting financially successful trends as long as possible. And yet, many of the high-profile demonic films of the early eighties — *Ghost Story* (1981), *Cat People* (1982), and *Something Wicked This Way Comes* (1983) — were not especially successful financially. With the notable exception of *Carrie* (1976), even many of the films based on the novels of Stephen King — *Cujo* (1983), *Christine* (1983), *The Dead Zone* (1983), and *Firestarter* (1984) — have not been hugely successful. Perhaps the Stephen King–based 1980 film *The Shining*, directed by Stanley Kubrick, should be seen in a class by itself: a hugely expensive horror film from one of the world's most accomplished directors, years in the making and eagerly anticipated. An attempt to synthesize the popular generic elements of horror with the director's cool, ironic, art-house sensibility, *The Shining*'s almost maniacal technical proficiency dominates the film itself, which is ultimately less thought-provoking or conceptually challenging than either the best horror films or the best Kubrick. One would not be wrong to ascribe the relative commercial disappointments of many of these films — despite some sophisticated special effects for the time and often interesting narratives — to the transition from the more hedonistic, subversive sixties to the more repressive, reactionary eighties. In the era of Ronald Reagan, the Moral Majority, the advocacy of school prayer, the attack on abortion rights, and an anti–Communist Polish pope (John Paul II) upholding conservative sexual values, it would be difficult to contend that "evil" (if unfairly conflated with liberal humanism) was as metaphorically ascendant as in the sixties. In fact, one can argue that if the Nixon culture of America was dominated by the pessimistic, mystic mode of horror, the Reagan culture of America was dominated by the optimistic, mythic mode of fantasy, as reflected by successful blockbusters such as *E. T.—The Extra-Terrestrial* (1982), and *Star Wars* (1977) and its many sequels.

It is noteworthy, then, that the most popular demonic horror film of this period was the remarkably benign *Poltergeist* (1982), a considerably reactionary film that views suburban American life as predominantly good and demonic spirits as anomalous and vanquishable. In *Poltergeist*, parents are loving and nurturing; conventional consumerism is valorized rather than criticized; and violence is unambiguously derived from outside the political structures of the family. The upbeat ending of *Poltergeist* contrasts strongly, for instance, with the downbeat endings of *Rosemary's Baby* (1968), *The Other* (1972), and *The Omen* (1976), all of which suggest that "good" is irrevocably imperiled and that evil will have an even greater victory down the line. In a similar vein was Joe Dante's *Gremlins* (1984; produced, as was *Poltergeist*, by Steven Spielberg), which often views its title spirits as comical and cute. The violence in *Gremlins*, in direct opposition to the graphic violence of, say, *The Omen*, reflects a comic-

Children, television, suburbia: sources of horror for many contemporary films, including *Poltergeist*.

book sensibility; the protagonists we empathize with are not killed or seriously injured, and the most flamboyant death is reserved for the female villain (a cross between the villainous capitalist in Frank Capra's *It's a Wonderful Life* and the Wicked Witch in *The Wizard of Oz*) for whom we have little empathy. Films like *Poltergeist* and *Gremlins* certainly seemed to indicate that the cultural tensions that initially spawned these demonic films had been somewhat transformed ideologically.

For instance, compare the fundamental conservative ethos of *Poltergeist* and *Goonies* with *Carrie*, directed by Brian De Palma in 1976, one of the most creative horror films, coming at the end of the cycle ushered in by *Rosemary's Baby*. Subject to much discussion since its initial release, *Carrie* needs little description here. Still, it is worth noting that the subversive *Carrie* clearly attacks the religious zealotry of Carrie's mother and revels in the eros of its teenage girl, though positing the menstrual cycle as something horrifying. The extravagance of Brian De Palma's expressive vision — with buckets of blood and psychokinetic energy wreaking destruction in split-screen overload — excites the audience and promotes empathy for Carrie, its superpowered misfit. Unlike the demonic films that followed (such as the *Friday the 13th* films), *Carrie* is part of the progressive American renaissance of the late sixties — films like *Bonnie and Clyde* and *The Graduate*, which clearly attack Amer-

In *Poltergeist*, affectionate images of suburbia alternate with images of an American family in abject terror, including Heather O'Rourke as the screaming daughter and JoBeth Williams as the screaming mother.

ican values and conformity. (Indeed, what could be more disquieting than a high school prom turned into a bloodbath, with the top of the pecking order — the future Rotary Club members and their wives — dispatched violently?)

Visually spectacular like *Carrie*, but in a more explicitly German expressionist tradition, was the Italian film *Suspiria* (1977), directed by Dario Argento. Rarely has a horror film been so aurally dense, including

Zelda Rubinstein, who looks like an eccentric Tupperware-party hostess, plays the exorcist in *Poltergeist* with dignity and gravitas.

almost constant use of wind, rain, thunder, quirky sound effects, and a music track by the Goblins augmented by odd breathings, sighs, and screams used as tympanic musical punctuation. Set in the German Black Forest, *Suspiria* is a kind of high concept *Mädchen in Uniform* meets *The Cabinet of Dr. Caligari*, but with an eccentric multinational cast led by Jessica Harper, Alida Valli, Udo Kier, and the Hollywood beauty Joan Bennett — at the twilight of her career — playing the Black Queen, a witch at the center of a contemporary coven. Few horror films have made such a bravura use of colored light (bright blues, oranges, greens) or of such deliriously geometric set design that itself suggests madness and promotes sensory overload. The extended murder scenes play out like cinematic arias, even though ultimately, *Suspiria* offers nothing new or inspiring except for its style.

A more thought-provoking foreign horror film of the period — one which clearly bucks the rightward trend in America — is *The Fourth Man*, an inventive 1983 Dutch film released in the United States in 1984. Directed by Paul Verhoeven with a contemporary sensibility that took its protagonist's sexual orientation as a premise rather than a problem, and based on a novel by Gerard Reve, *The Fourth Man* has been described by the astute filmmaker/commentator Paul Bartel as "the first gay, Catholic, horror film"[3] — which is, indeed, precisely what it is. Verhoeven's witch is a contemporary seductress, a siren who leads men

(1) *Carrie* (played by Sissy Spacek) can create apocalyptic hellfire, yet retain our sympathy. When (2) her mother (Piper Laurie) is crucified by Carrie's telekinetic powers, the pose resembles (3) a crucifix shown in the film. What does it suggest about director De Palma's view of Christianity that Carrie's mother is a religious maniac who deserves her crucifixion?

The demonic imagery in *The Fourth Man* is erotic, surreal, and ambiguous. Renée Soutendijk and Jeroen Krabbé play the seductress and her potential victim, a gay writer. Yet the writer prefers her boyfriend, played by Thom Hoffman. Could the key to escaping the *femme fatale* be homosexual lust?

to their doom, including, perhaps, the protagonist, who is a bisexual man clearly more interested in the *femme fatale*'s boyfriend than in the *femme fatale* herself, whose demonic identity is only gradually revealed. What makes *The Fourth Man* especially interesting — despite its misogyny (typical for horror) that turns women into symbols, updating the archetypes of the whore and virgin into the super-archetypes of the she-devil and Virgin Mary — is that the homosexuality of the protagonist is presented as a positive moral alternative to the heterosexuality of the *femme fatale*. Indeed, one almost delirious fantasy scene (in a dense film packed with provocative surreal images) shows the protagonist kissing and embracing the near-naked boyfriend who is hanging Christ-like from a crucifix in the church. That this scene works not only to provide an erotic thrill but to foreshadow the surprising ending in which the identity of the fourth man is revealed testifies to this film's formal and skillfully organized structure.

Two other films released in the same period, *Eraserhead* in 1977 and *A Nightmare on Elm Street* in 1984, are both key horror films, although the former is a late example of the American renaissance, and the latter is an early harbinger of the religious right's focus on images of damnation and apocalypse. Both films, as surreal documents, seem intent on probing the connection between film and dream and reaching deep into the Freudian world

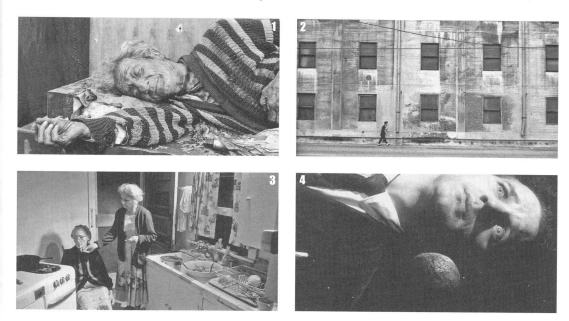

Surrealist David Lynch shows the eclectic influences of a great number of artists: (1) Walker Evans, who photographed depression-era America; (2) Michelangelo Antonioni, who filmed alienation within the contemporary urban landscape; (3) Diane Arbus, who photographed American misfits in their home environments; and (4) Stanley Kubrick, whose *2001: A Space Odyssey* ushered in a creative cinematic age perfect for Lynch.

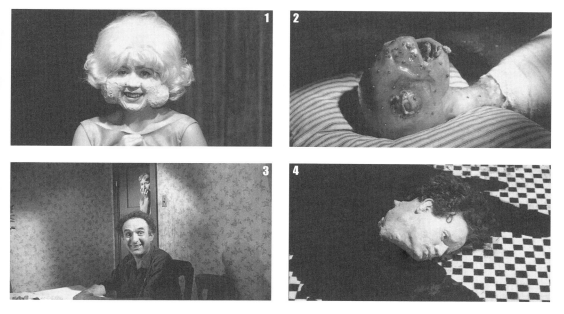

David Lynch's *Eraserhead* portraits are horrific and disturbing: (1) the Lady in the Radiator (Laurel Near); (2) the "baby"—who exhibits, ironically, the most recognizably human suffering; (3) Mr. X and Mary X (Allen Joseph and Charlotte Stewart), whose expressions resemble silent-film clichés; and (4) Henry Spencer (John Nance), after his head has been severed from his body.

of the subconscious. Although watching movies is isomorphic to experiencing dreams, few horror films have taken advantage of these isomorphisms so directly: in both *Eraserhead* and *A Nightmare on Elm Street*, there are constant signifiers with unclear signifieds, a nearness of sex and violence, an ominous lack of clarity, and a peculiarly illogical narrative which refuses to heed traditional dramatic form. *Eraserhead* is certainly the more spectacular film, one of the few one can discuss alongside Luis Buñuel's surrealist masterpiece *Un chien andalou* and Maya Deren's seminal *Meshes of the Afternoon*. (Not surprisingly, David Lynch's education was largely in painting, with a strong interest in more contemporary surrealist painters like Francis Bacon.) From its first frame to its last, *Eraserhead* plays like a long, irrational, disturbing dream. Impossible to explain, *Eraserhead* is a unique film (perhaps owing some debt to Todd Browning's *Freaks*) that needs to be experienced, an unforgettable *ne plus ultra* even for the iconoclastic David Lynch, who was then only beginning his illustrious career — and with a film as startling, in its own way, as *Citizen Kane*. As well, the sound design of *Eraserhead*, created by Alan Splet, is totally disquieting and evokes unearthly beauty. And hardly an image in the film is not both expressive and dreadful — whether the odd hairdo of the protagonist, which looks like the eraser on a pencil, or the oddly demonic baby, which looks like nothing ever seen before, except in a forgotten nightmare. The baby's constant crying, bleating, inability to be comforted, and monstrous illness compose one of the most horrifyingly memorable sequences in the history of horror. (And exactly how the demonic baby effects were created is still a mystery thirty years later,

since Lynch, wisely, refuses to say.) Ultimately, what makes *Eraserhead* such an unparalleled masterpiece is its resistance to logical interpretation.[4]

Although not in the same league, *A Nightmare on Elm Street* — at least in its first incarnation, before its success spawned so many sequels — was truly scary, if in a more traditional way. Like the classic horror film, *A Nightmare on Elm Street* puts a monster at its center: Freddy, a surrealistic ringmaster noted for his bladed fingers and unlimited power to alter your dreams and inflict real physical damage — but only when

A Nightmare on Elm Street, like most demonic films, includes many religious symbols like the crucifix in the upper left of the frame, apparently protecting actress Amanda Wyss.

When menaced by a night terror like Freddy (Robert Englund), you must wake with the classic waking-from-a-dream movie posture: bolt instantly upright and open your mouth wide in horror. This mouth belongs to actor Mark Patton in *A Nightmare on Elm Street, Part 2: Freddy's Revenge*.

you're asleep. But when exactly *is* that? Can we always recognize when we are dreaming and when we are awake? The film plays mightily with the often tenuous distinctions between different states of consciousness. Is a daydream a dream, and can we dream within a dream? In a mainstream way, *A Nightmare on Elm Street* recalls the surrealism of Luis Buñuel's late, 1972 masterpiece *The Discreet Charm of the Bourgeoisie,* with its construction by set piece and elaboration of dreams. Notably, *A Nightmare on Elm Street* was made in 1984, almost a decade after *Star Wars,* at that juncture in the American cinema when special effects were not only dominating the industry, but developing new levels of sophistication via ever-evolving technologies. As a result, the complex visions of the unbridled, hellish, nightmare worlds could be captured with less artistic compromise. In at least the first *Nightmare* films, the special effects — which by today's standards look primitive — seem an integral component rather than the whole point. By the time Freddy had become more camp than frightening, and in the process become one of the most popular Halloween masks ever and a favorite character even for children, it was clear that the *Nightmare* vision, turned into a consumer product, had lost the surrealist, philosophical edge which had inspired it. As proof: in order to spark interest in a new DVD release twenty-two years after its original release, for two days on September 20 and 21, 2006, *A Nightmare on Elm Street* was re-released in theatres, along with a compilation short advertised as *Freddy's Best Kills.* Note the wording: *not* Most Horrifying Kills, or Most Morally Reprehensible Kills, but *Best* Kills. In those two decades since the original release, American society had become almost totally disconnected from the moral meaning of violence and now was just unabashedly cheering the most gruesome mutilations on, like spectators in the Roman Coliseum.

Nightmare ushered in a great number of horror films totally dominated by special effects, including many which presented literal trips between life on earth and life in the hereafter. Perhaps the films at the poles of contrasting sensibility are *What Dreams May Come* in 1998 and *Constantine* in 2005. Unusually beautiful in a pictorial sense, both films use computer graphics to create credible, breathtaking visions of heaven and/or hell. In *What Dreams May Come,* which owes much to the myth of Orpheus and Eurydice, Robin Williams plays a man who dies in an accident and ends up in heaven; but when his grief-stricken wife commits suicide, he must journey to hell in order to rescue her. This film not only reinforces some fundamentalist teachings of the afterlife (punishing suicide with hell, for instance), but also dismantles the most unforgiving fundamentalist teachings (allowing hell to have a kind of "escape clause," whereby Robin Williams is able to free the damned soul of his wife, so he and she can be reunited for eternity). Although *What Dreams May Come* traffics with demons and other accouterments of horror, the film ultimately feels like a love story — which suggests that although we should live moral lives, one can alter God's universal plan if one truly loves enough. The actors, including Robin Williams, are largely props walking through impressive special effects; but on the large screen of the movie theatre, the environmental tableaux (like computer game graphics brought to grander life) are stunningly beautiful and painterly.

In opposition to *What Dreams May Come,* the film *Constantine* is pessimistic. Keanu Reeves plays a professional exorcist and demon-hunter who works for the angel Gabriel. Revived after his suicide took him briefly to hell (in the contemporary world of the religious right, it seems everyone is a hell-bound sinner), our protagonist struggles to redeem himself. Totally dominated by special effects of unusual repugnance, *Constantine* credits hundreds of special effects artists. As in *What Dreams May Come,* the effects dwarf any human story; and the sound — in the style of action-adventure — is so loud and overmixed with ambience, echo, sound effects, and music, that dialogue is often unintelligible, which probably matters little to the filmmakers or the audience. The point of *Constantine*, simply, is to amaze with effects: human flesh that literally cracks, a monstrous mouth that emerges from someone's neck, a possessed woman who crawls on the ceiling, a demon which is physically trapped in a mirror, a legion of demons who fly through the sky in horrific attack, a fly that crawls out of an eye, a demon composed of protoplasmic cockroaches, millions of souls burning in hell, and finally, most impressive of all, a woman in a high-rise who is sucked backwards through one wall after another until she crashes through a window and falls to potential doom far below. With so many special effects collaborators toiling to meet deadlines, it becomes impossible for much of a personal vision (or even control?) to come from the director. We do learn at least one amusing fact about hell: that you can visit it by putting your feet in a bucket of water while looking deeply into a cat's eyes.

Other demonic films of the last twenty years presented their own visual representations of the devil or his world. For instance, in *Angel Heart*, in 1987, the devil is Louis Cyphre (a homonym for Lucifer), played by a foppish Robert De Niro; in *End of Days*, in 1998, an Arnold Schwarzenegger vehicle (whose failure helped propel the actor into politics), the devil is an urbane New York investment banker played by Gabriel Byrne; and in *The Ninth Gate*, directed by Roman Polanski in 1999, the devil is never shown to us, although we learn a lot about him, including that he's a fine artist. Polanski's cerebral film is about an attempt to determine the authenticity of a rare book with Lucifer's disturbing engravings — which have the potential to open the ninth gate and summon Lucifer himself. (There is irony in Polanski presenting the devil as an artist, since the artist Polanski has certainly been demonized in America over his decades-old charge of statutory rape.) Although Polanski tries for a horror film which is subtle and indirect, what results is simply slack, with the director unable to create too much excitement with this intellectual exercise. And yet *The Ninth Gate* feels ahead of its time, with its bookishness, religious history, and analysis of visual symbols suggesting the sensibility of *The Da Vinci Code*, which would become a mammoth best-seller only a few years later and huge financial success as a 2006 film, enraging the religious right who believed that their faith was being maligned.

Another *Da Vinci Code* precursor, *Stigmata*, in 1999, also stars Gabriel Byrne, but this time not as the devil, but as a priest who is led by the stigmata on an atheist hairdresser to discover a previously unknown gospel containing revelations that threaten the supremacy of the Vatican and traditional views of Christianity. What makes *Stigmata* interesting — particularly on the eve of an election year that brought the born-again George W. Bush to power as the American president — is the way *Stigmata*'s premise implies that fundamentalism was now exerting such a powerful force in America that its reactionary influence could be weakened or undone only by a new gospel.

Certainly, fundamentalists in particular had been dismayed by the behavior of President Bill Clinton regarding the Monica Lewinsky scandal. Not only had they fueled — through their churches and spokesmen like the reverends Jerry Falwell and Pat Robertson — the successful effort to impeach Clinton, they continued to amass enough political influence to bring a born-again George W. Bush to the White House in the 2000 election. This religious tide helped fuel the creation of a group of demonic horror films that were specifically targeted to the fundamentalist audience. Based on the hugely successful books by Reverend Tim LaHaye and Jerry B. Jenkins (sixteen so far, many of which have topped the American bestseller lists), *Left Behind: The Movie* was released in 2000, based on the first *Left Behind* novel, subtitled *A Novel of the Earth's Last Days*. Both book and movie dramatize the Rapture foretold in the Book of Revelation (that moment when millions of people vanish off the earth, taken up to be with Christ, while those remaining must endure seven years of chaos). Subsequent works confront the Rapture's aftermath, the second coming of Christ, the appearance of the Antichrist, and the final battle between Good and Evil. This LaHaye/Jenkins series was telling the fundamentalist community to spread the good word and get ready. So far, three major *Left Behind* movies — like the books, intended half as entertainment, half as proselytism — have been released, continuing with *Left Behind II: Tribulation Force* in 2002 and *Left Behind: World at War* in 2005. Although the films included elements one could find in other demonic movies, their particular evangelical perspective was new. In fact, most notable about the series was the unconventional releasing strategy that developed. The first film was released on DVD and video *before* its theatrical screening, doing better with the former than with the latter. As a result, the second film was released only on DVD and video, so it could more efficiently reach the fundamentalist audience — which apparently was not as comfortable in movie theatres and not as put-off by low-budget production values, more readily apparent when pointed out by national reviewers. The third film, even more ingeniously, was released directly to churches around the country to show to their members, and only afterwards released on DVD and video.

These fundamentalist forces would come to the fore in one of the most successful horror films of all time, *The Passion of the Christ*, produced, directed, and co-written by Mel Gibson in 2004. Although Gibson claimed his version of the Passion was the first to stick closely to the Gospels and thus was an objective re-telling, when criticized he simultaneously claimed the right to make a personal film corresponding to his own vision of conservative Catholicism. A supporter of Opus Dei (the Catholic organization exposed in *The Da Vinci Code*), Gibson produced one of the most controversial films on Christ's crucifixion. Attacked for its sadistic violence and anti–Semitism, *The Passion of the Christ* became the cinematic event of the new century, inciting strongly held feeling (both pro and con) and drawing huge audiences to the cinema, many from the same churches that had mobilized in support of George W. Bush. Notably, the church members buying tickets included many who had long before stopped going to the movies. So contentious was *The Passion of the Christ* that even culturally and politically conservative columnists attacked the film, such as Charles Krauthammer, who wrote in *The Washington Post* that the film was

> ... a singular act of interreligious aggression, ... [which] using every possible technique of cinematic exaggeration, gives us the pre–Vatican II story of the villainous Jews. And Gibson's personal interpretation is spectacularly vicious. Three of the Gospels have but a one-line reference to Jesus' scourging. The fourth has no reference at all. In Gibson's movie this becomes 10 minutes of the most unremitting sadism in the history of film.... The most subtle, and most revolting, of these [deviations from the Gospels] has to my knowledge not been commented upon. In Gibson's movie Satan appears four times. Not one of these appearances occurs in the four Gospels. They are pure invention. Twice, this sinister, hooded, androgynous embodiment of evil is found ... where? Moving among the crowd of Jews. Gibson's camera follows close up, documentary style, as Satan glides among them, his face popping up among theirs — merging with, indeed, defining the murderous Jewish crowd. After all, a perfect match: Satan's own people.[5]

Certainly Gibson's film is anti–Semitic, despite his claim to the contrary.[6] But what Krauthammer missed is that Gibson's film is as homophobic as anti–Semitic. Herod, with eyeliner and wig, is presented as an effeminate partygiver attended by a homosexual hairdresser and male courtiers wearing makeup. And the devil (played by Rosalinda Celentano) that Krauthammer notes as androgynous seems a symbol of today's blurred sexual bound-

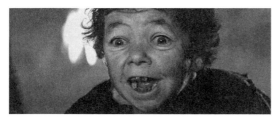

Although director Mel Gibson claims fidelity to the Gospels, *The Passion of the Christ* has greater fidelity to the demons and grotesques in modern horror film. Gibson's innovation is to introduce demonic images of gender ambiguity, suggesting a connection between demons, homosexuals, and Jews — groups his film holds responsible for the Crucifixion.

aries and the gradual acceptance of homosexuality that Gibson and the contemporary Catholic Church so abhor. This demon in *The Passion of the Christ* celebrates Christ's death; when his/her black cowl flies magically up into space, the image suggests a drag queen losing a wig. The homophobic elements seamlessly woven into the film and ignored by so many critics are inspired by the writings of the widely-revered Pope John Paul II, which labeled homosexuals "morally disordered" and "intrinsically evil." (These words, incidentally, were crafted by then Cardinal Ratzinger, John Paul's papal successor.) *The Passion of the Christ* thus became a major event in the culture wars, supporting a theological return to the most reactionary positions of the Catholic Church before Vatican II began liberalizing the church in the sixties. Liberalism is presented by Gibson as the epitome of evil: indeed, as the evil that killed Jesus.

    The Passion of the Christ is slow like an art-house film, a sensibility reinforced by being presented in Aramaic with English subtitles. The film begins with a verse from Isaiah ("He was wounded for our transgressions, crushed for our iniquities; by His wounds we are healed.") and a beautiful image of the moon accompanied by a heavenly chorus of voices. The inspired cinematography is often monochromatic, suffused with amber or azure, and the film becomes darker as it proceeds, not only in subject, but in its quality of light. *The Passion of the Christ* looks often like the horror film it secretly is. One scene shows monstrous children — inhabited by demons — who actually bite the flesh of Judas like living dead, cannibals for Satan. When a crow pecks out the eye of one of the thieves crucified with Jesus, Gibson's film evokes the horror of *The Birds*. And the connection between Christian ritual and the vampire film is reinforced by the line, "If we don't eat his flesh and drink his blood, we won't inherit eternal life." But what is front and center in Gibson's interpretation is the constant violence against Christ, who is battered and bruised by his tormen-

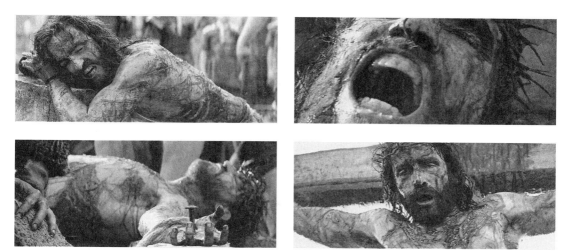

These progressive, violent images from Mel Gibson's *The Passion of the Christ* show Christ (James Caviezel) lacerated and covered with blood; he is virtually dead even *before* he is crucified.

tors even before being given the forty lashes. The soldiers laugh almost orgasmically while beating Christ with a knife-bladed cat-o'-nine-tails, the camera seeming to so rejoice with each blow that what we see becomes a sadomasochistic, almost pornographic scene, with close-ups of flesh ripped away for the religious impact on the moviegoers. The casting of Monica Bellucci as Mary Magdalene adds an (unintended?) irony to the film — particularly as Bellucci is shown trying to sop up puddles of Christ's blood to cleanse the violence: Is this Bellucci's penance for having appeared basically naked in *Irréversible*, not only in a tender bedroom scene, but as the subject of perhaps the most graphically depicted rape ever? (One wonders what the churchgoing audiences would have thought had they been aware of Bellucci's career history. For example, in 2006, a Christian production company was surprised that its historical, spiritual feature *End of the Spear* was boycotted by many Christians and fundamentalist leaders because its central character, an evangelical missionary martyred in the Ecuadorian jungle, was played by openly gay actor Chad Allen.) The sadism directed against Christ before the Crucifixion is so extreme that the Crucifixion seems almost dramatically unnecessary. Yet the violence continues just as viscerally, and Christ's right arm is pulled out of its socket before being nailed to the cross. Mel Gibson's Christ is no girlie-man, but a man's man who can endure pain. Is the horror of brute violence the only meaning of the Crucifixion? It would seem so, since largely missing from *The Passion of the Christ* is the spiritual dimension usually associated with a religious subject: the sense of transcendence. Instead, what emerges is pure horror. (In defense of Gibson, note that *The Passion of the Christ* was released during the War in Iraq, in an era in which atrocities — hangings, beheadings, and torture — were available on the internet and the nightly TV news; so Gibson's film violence is at least of a piece with the times.) Notably, film critic Bob Pardi, one of the few who accurately saw Gibson's work as a horror film, characterized *The Passion of the Christ* as

> ... *Night of the Living Jews.* It was as close to a snuff movie as I would like to get: all these slow-motion shots of Jesus taking it to the jaw like *Rocky*. There's no dignity to His suffering, only details — lots of them. The last film that made me want to take a bath afterward was *Dawn of the Dead.* All this hoopla — just like *The Exorcist*; only instead of mass hysteria

Although images of horror and violence emotionally dominate *The Passion of the Christ*, Gibson also includes conventional, reverential images that emulate Catholic calendar art such as Christ in Gethsemane and Christ arisen.

telling you that you are going to be scared to death, this time the message is: you'll accept Jesus ... *or else*.[7]

Another enormously perceptive commentary comes from Garry Wills, Professor Emeritus of History at Northwestern University and the author of *Why I Am a Catholic*. In "God in the Hands of Angry Sinners," Wills wrote:

> If you relish the sight of a healthy male body being systematically demolished beyond the farthest reach of plausible endurance, *The Passion of the Christ* is your movie. It is not simply the scourging scene that is at issue, though that deals out an unspecified number of stripes — more than sixty and still counting, half of them inflicted by whips that have been made into multiple-hook tearing instruments. Even earlier, at the arrest of Jesus, he is chained, beaten over and over, thrown off a bridge to crash below. He arrives at his first legal hearing already mauled and with one eye closed behind swollen bruises. From then on, he is never moved or stopped without spontaneous blows and kicks and shoves from all kinds of bystanders wanting to get in on the fun. On the way to execution, he is whipped while fainting under the cross. A soldier says to lay off or he'll never make it. But the crowd just keeps whipping and beating him all the rest of the way.
>   My wife and I had to stop glancing furtively at each other for fear we would burst out laughing. It had gone beyond sadism into the comic surreal, like an apocalyptic version of [Richard] Swinburne's *The Whipping Papers*....[8]

Wills is especially insightful in his analysis of the almost paranoid, ego-inflated, defensive reaction of Gibson to criticism and of the cultural impact of the film — particularly the religious mania it incited in its supporters:

> In Gibson's film the union of the divine and human in Jesus is not explored or explicated. He is just a sponge for punishment. Which makes one wonder why so many call their viewing of the film a conversion experience. From what, or to what, are they being converted? From Christianity to philoflagellationism? Some fear that the real conversion will be to anti–Semitism....
>   Gibson has characterized resistance to his movie as resistance to Christ himself, to his suffering church: "I didn't realize it would be so vicious.... The acts against this film started early. As soon as I announced I was doing it, it was 'This is a dangerous thing.' There is vehement anti–Christian sentiment out there, and they don't want it. It's vicious.... There's a huge war raging, and it's over us!"
>   That mood is reflected in the large number of people who have praised the movie by attacking its critics. This may be at the root of the "religious" experience so many receive from the film. These people feel persecuted, like Gibson, victimized by a secular world or by unfaithful fellow Christians.... Some see the cooperation of evangelical Christians, Catholics, and some conservative Jews in praising *The Passion of the Christ* an ecumenical aspect to the film.... But the bond between these groups is not ecumenical. The bond is religious extremism. What

Two interesting images in *The Passion of the Christ*: a close-up of a crow that pecks out the crucifieds' eyes, a Gibsonian invention taken from Hitchcock's horror film *The Birds*; and perhaps the film's strongest image, an extreme long shot of Judas which tempers the violence of his suicide with a pictorial distance that adds irony and prompts audience reflection.

> its admirers like is precisely the unflinching nature of the film, reflecting their own sense that a true church must make extreme demands. That other people do not accept the film just confirms their own sense that the world is against them.

No one has captured the film's political meaning more astutely than Wills, who understands that Gibson identifies less with the sinners (despite his reportedly providing the hand that we see pounding the first nail of the Crucifixion), than with Christ himself. For Gibson, *The Passion of the Christ* is about how Christians are being persecuted today; like Christ, religious conservatives must take whatever abuse the (liberal) society dishes out, because ultimately, God the Father is on their side, the side of the righteous. The only thing Wills doesn't capture is the extent to which Gibson's film is a horror film — demonic, scary, and filled with more blood than *Night of the Living Dead*. Although one of the top money-makers of all time (over $370 million in the United States, $611 million worldwide), thanks to clergy who encouraged their congregations to see it and even arranged field trips, *The Passion of the Christ* was finally overtaken in the weekly domestic box-office revenues by the *Dawn of the Dead* remake — an irony which revealed the essential horror-film sensibility of Gibson's film, which doesn't exactly uplift its audience, but scares it into faith, much in the style of a fire-and-brimstone preacher.

That the success of *The Passion of the Christ* surprised Hollywood (which thought the film a huge gamble for Mel Gibson) was a sign of how woefully disconnected Hollywood was from the religious sensibilities of much of the country. The election by a narrow margin of George W. Bush to a second presidential term was aided by conservative Christians who came to the polls in pivotal states to vote their church's position on state constitutional amendments forbidding marriage rights for gays and lesbians. As even Democratic politicians began talking about faith, Hollywood finally recognized a key demographic was being under-served and began pitching films (and products) to evangelicals. Lest one think *The Passion of the Christ* followed a spiritual high road in relation to the profits available from consumer licensing, the film did not. Although there was no McDonald's McPassion sandwich, the film licensed a variety of products for purchase by the faithful: an Aramaic witness card-pack (25 cards for $5.99); a nail pendant, so you could wear a crucifixion nail as a necklace (two sizes, for $12.99 and $16.99); and a pewter crucifixion bracelet ($12.99). Of course there were also T-shirts and book tie-ins.

The Exorcism of Emily Rose, released in 2005, was specifically sold with an ad campaign exploiting its "strong spiritual message." Based loosely on the real story of Annaliese Michel, a German woman who died during an exorcism, *The Exorcism of Emily Rose* is half demonic horror and half courtroom drama — a cross between *The Exorcist* and *Inherit the*

Wind. On trial for the homicide of the possibly possessed young woman, a priest is defended by an agnostic lawyer. The trial becomes a modern-day Scopes trial — with the real battle between science, which denies the possession, and religion, which asserts limits as to what science can explain. By the film's end, the agnostic lawyer (played by Laura Linney) has found some faith. Science is posited as dogmatic, and religion as enlightened and open-minded. Despite a mixed reception, *The Exorcism of Emily Rose* was a hit precisely because it attracted Christian audiences excited by its message.

Revelations, a 2005 made-for-TV miniseries in the demonic subgenre, was produced and written by horror veteran David Seltzer, the writer of *The Omen* and *The Hellstrom Chronicle*. Only loosely Biblical, *Revelations* pitched itself as Biblical horror for the new Christian audience, as "faith-based programming." Notable elements include a baby incongruously found as the only survivor at sea (is he the returning Christ, or the Antichrist?), and a young girl struck by lightning and brain-dead, but so possessed by the Holy Spirit that she quotes scripture in Latin (in translation: "The time is short, the world will pass away"). Each major sequence is introduced by a Biblical verse, giving *Revelations* the patina of adequately religious veracity. The character of Dr. Massey, a cynical professor who offers scientific explanations for Bible stories, speaks for the secular audience, but the character of Sister Josepha Montafiore, a devout nun who converts Massey to a more Biblical orthodoxy, speaks for the Christian audience which believes that Armageddon and the End of Days are near. The inherent problem with *Revelations* was that NBC wanted it to evolve into an ongoing series. As a result, the End of Days could not be allowed to arrive, which made the miniseries feel terminally pre-climactic.

Other demonic horror films made around the same time as *The Passion of the Christ* were more conventional in presenting the traditional possessed child. Three typical examples — of varying quality and interest — were *Birth* (in 2004) and the Robert De Niro vehicles *Godsend* (in 2004) and *Hide and Seek* (in 2005). *Birth*, with a proper art-house pedigree, was the edgiest of the three, written in part by Luis Buñuel's longtime surrealist screenwriter, Jean-Claude Carrière, and starring Nicole Kidman as Anna. *Birth* begins with a beautiful tracking shot of a hooded black figure running through the snow. His collapse (and death) in a bridge underpass which is photographed much like a womb, is juxtaposed with an almost surreal image of a baby being born, apparently under water — thus presenting almost immediately this film's conundrum with utmost expressiveness: has this dead man, Anna's husband, been reincarnated as this baby? Ten years later, when that little boy (played by Cameron Bright), sullen and creepy, arrives on Anna's doorstep and announces he is her

Birth contrasts a "life" image of a jogger surrounded by bright light with a "death" image of the same jogger surrounded by darkness. Yet the death image, with its womb-like characteristics, also suggests rebirth.

Clear sexual tensions between adult and child (Nicole Kidman and Cameron Bright) make the eroticism in *Birth* surreally unsettling.

husband, *Birth* becomes a contemporary, drawing-room version of *The Turn of the Screw.* Despite the witty, energetic presence of Lauren Bacall, *Birth* is surprisingly slow-moving and obsessive. In its most unnerving scene, the little boy removes his clothes and joins Anna in the bathtub, as she is bathing. Is he her husband? Or just a little boy? And how should Anna act toward him? As wife, mother, or stranger? The bathtub scenes (and there are two of them) are erotic and pedophilic — which makes the viewer very uneasy, but certainly riveted.

Less notable is the over-produced, if visually adept, *Godsend*, which is narratively predictable and conventional. (Two examples: right after the husband disagrees with his wife's desire to leave the city, their son is killed in city traffic; at the cemetery, with its vertical headstones perfectly snow-covered, a crow caws to conventionally communicate mournfulness.) Especially literal and simplistic is the music track, which never fails to indicate when we should be scared and when we should be sad. The music removes every bit of emotional ambiguity, ultimately working *against* the anxiety the film hopes to engender. The story is interesting enough in how it combines demonic elements with a scientific spin: the mother allows a "mad scientist" (played by De Niro) to implant her with a "cloned" cell from her dead son in an attempt to give birth to him again. Of course, nothing in a horror film could be quite so easy, because the cloned cell turns out to have had a biological connection to the scientist; in essence, this mother, like Rosemary in *Rosemary's Baby*, has been raped by a devil, this scientist. The cloned child grows up possessed by a prior life — but whose life is it? Cameron Bright, from *Birth*, again plays a possessed child, and very well. The filmmakers liberally borrow the central theme from *The Bad Seed*, as well as that film's drowning.

Mad scientists exist even in the 21st century: no longer in personal laBORatories in Transylvania, they work in respectable medical environments and look like Robert DeNiro in *Godsend*. And science is visible even in this overhead shot of a stairway, which resembles a DNA helix, key to *Godsend*'s horror.

Godsend uses traditional silhouetting to communicate horror, as in this image of the creepy clone played by Cameron Bright. The second silhouette shows the separation of fingers, conventional horror iconography relating to the claws of animal monsters like the Wolf Man as well as to the third image shown here: the outstretched fingers of Marion Crane as she dies in *Psycho*.

And for no intrinsic reason, there are several obligatory *Psycho* references, including one via a shower curtain.[9]

    Hide and Seek, if not especially important, is the more ingenious film. Its opening credits are accompanied by John Ottman music which cleverly evokes the *Rosemary's Baby* soundtrack, immediately putting us in the world of demonic horror. Robert De Niro plays David, a psychologist whose daughter Emily is unable to come to terms with her mother's suicide. Played by the talented Dakota Fanning, Emily is often photographed looking through windows like an appropriately haunted child. After Emily creates an imaginary friend, Charlie, truly horrible things start happening, and Charlie is implicated. Is Emily literally being demonically possessed or is Charlie merely a manifestation of Emily's psychic pain? Only at the end of *Hide and Seek* do we discover that neither alternative is accurate; what is really going on was hiding in plain sight, lurking in the film's iconography, which had not really

seemed all that consonant to demonic horror. For instance, the mother's death, scary enough, was in the bathtub, as was also the cat's drowning, even scarier. And then there was that murderous attack on the stairway. Bathrooms and stairways derive from *Psycho*,

The blank stare, often shot with a telephoto lens, is the most telling expression for any potentially possessed child: Cameron Bright in *Godsend*, Dakota Fanning in *Hide and Seek*, and Haley Joel Osment in *The Sixth Sense* are virtually interchangeable.

not *The Exorcist*; and even the identity symbols represented by *Hide and Seek*'s dolls come from horror-of-personality films like Freddie Francis' *The Psychopath*. In the surprising but satisfying ending, we discover that De Niro's David, like Norman Bates in *Psycho*, is a psychopath not totally aware of his actions; he is unhinged not because his wife killed herself, but because *he* killed her. So it is not coincidental that he is the one who has been discovering each new horror, often after waking in the middle of the night — after a narrative ellipsis. Wielding a bloody knife, the lunatic David searches for his terrified daughter to kill her in one final game of hide and seek. And so what seemed a demonic film is revealed to be something different, a film about a psychopath, the surprise abetted by a skillful, contrived script by Ari Schlossberg. Although David is dispatched, the film ends — in a kind of contemporary horror mannerism, or tic — with a scene that suggests that as a result of her ordeal, Emily may now have actually developed a personality disorder of her own.

All these potentially possessed children and surprise endings derive from what is the most accomplished demonic horror of the last twenty years: *The Sixth Sense*, a breakthrough film which catapulted its director, M. Night Shyamalan (but for how long?), into the front ranks of American genre stylists. Made in 1999, *The Sixth Sense* showed — more skillfully than its imitators — that a successful horror film could eschew the conventional style of contemporary horror in favor of a more idiosyncratic, personal style. Unlike the typical American film, *The Sixth Sense* moves at a slow, even ponderous pace — more like the art-house film of classic Antonioni. As well, *The Sixth Sense* is unusually quiet, not deafening; austerely produced, not over-produced; and composed of long takes, not fast-paced montage assaulting our senses and sensibility. And on an emotional level, *The Sixth Sense* moves toward transcendence and epiphany, refusing to wallow in violence. It is strange for a scary film from Hollywood not to be the slightest bit cynical. *The Sixth Sense* is that rarest of breeds: a horror film that is humanist and emotionally moving, and not at all dominated by special effects. In the context of so many impersonal horror films assaulting our screens, it is impressive that Shyamalan's film, refusing to play safe, feels so very personal, at least in terms of its *mise-en-scène*.

The first image is an extremely slow fade-up to a hanging lightbulb. The pace of the fade is an immediate sign that Shyamalan is refusing to be rushed. Bruce Willis plays Dr. Malcolm Crowe, a child psychologist we see reflected in a framed citation. We can see right away that Dr. Crowe loves his wife. Precipitating the film's first plot point, a strung-out drug addict emerges nearly naked from the bathroom (we wonder how he got there) and asks an existential question (relevant to horror film, certainly): "Do you know why you're afraid when you're alone?" Then, with shocking suddenness, the addict shoots Dr. Crowe. The moment is unforgettable, because the film, though just getting started, seems already at its climax, since we recognize that Bruce Willis is the star. Is he being killed off prematurely as was Janet Leigh in *Psycho*? Was that the clue that the opening image of the hanging lightbulb (taken from *Psycho*?) was offering us? There is a caesura associated with a fade; and then, when the narrative starts up again, it is the next fall. We see Dr. Crowe, apparently healed, about to treat a nine year old boy, Cole, for a possible mood disorder. We *should* be wondering what happened during the ellipsis, but for the most part we don't, because the narrative flow to this new story about Cole distracts us. Yet the secret of the film is hidden in this ellipsis, because from this point on, the narrative works on two simultaneous levels: the story we think is going on, and the story that is really going on. What made *The Sixth Sense* such a sleeper — achieving critical raves and huge box office despite its slow pace — was that almost no one in the audience tended to "get" the film until the

Actor Haley Joel Osment emotionally dominates every scene he is in, although often dwarfed in the frame: (1) by the church pew and his oversize glasses, (2) by the door knob that reflects him, and (3) by the empty space of a long shot.

clever surprise ending, when Shyamalan reveals all — not the least of which is his skill as a screenwriter. And we don't feel cheated, but elated over how psychologically profound and right the surprise feels. With *The Sixth Sense*, Shyamalan instantly cemented "the surprise ending" as a hallmark of his personal signature, as well as a new convention for other contemporary horror films to imitate.

Although we don't know it until the film's end, the reason we never see Dr. Crowe recovering from his gunshot wound is because he *didn't* recover. Bruce Willis is playing a ghost — a dead man refusing to go to the afterlife — though he, like us, doesn't realize it. Cole, played brilliantly by Haley Joel Osment, is a moody, spooky kid so filled with empathy for others that his empathy seems psychologically dangerous to himself. When Cole plays with his toy soldiers, Dr. Crowe writes down the English translation of the Latin the soldiers apparently speak: "Out of the depth, I cry to you, oh Lord." We think of the line as an indicator of Cole's inner state, but it's actually Cole's intuition regarding Dr. Crowe's subconscious plea. Later, Dr. Crowe sits down at a restaurant opposite his wife. Only on second viewing do we realize that this is not a real-life scene as it appears; rather, the ghost is speaking a monologue, and because he is not there alive, his wife neither sees him nor offers clear response.

Cole seems quasi-demonic: he connects psychically to horrors from the past, such as the humiliation of criminals being spat upon as they were about to be hung in the building now used as his school. And when Cole's schoolteacher is about to criticize him, Cole, disconcerting everyone, starts screaming about the teacher's past humiliations as a stutterer. How did Cole know? And can Cole ever fit in? When Dr. Crowe tells Cole a bedtime story, Cole tells him "You have to add some twists and stuff"— Shyamalan's sly, reflexive comment on his own methodology in *The Sixth Sense*. When Cole presses: "Tell me a story about why you're sad," his request, at least on first viewing, seems merely a sign of Cole's extensive reservoir of empathy. In actuality, Cole is serving as psychoanalyst for Dr. Crowe, not the other way around, wanting Dr. Crowe to face the truth and speak it. Cole shows Dr. Crowe how, when in an emotionally expressive confession, Cole admits his own secret truth: "*I see dead people.*" On first viewing, we think of this moment as a revelation about Cole; on second viewing, we realize it is also a revelation to the audience about Dr. Crowe, since Cole is looking directly at him when Cole offers it. Yet Dr. Crowe refuses to accept the truth (just as most of the spectators do not yet recognize the real narrative). He is in denial because he is still in love, because "I want to be able to talk to my wife again — the way we used to talk to each other." Only in retrospect do we understand the impossibility of that ever happening.

Although Dr. Crowe does not realize he's dead, he subconsciously understands that the dead who are visiting Cole psychically don't want to hurt Cole, but want his help with unfinished business so they can be released to the world that follows. Haley Joel Osment's performance is so adroit and fully adult that we are not afraid of Cole, but moved by how beset he is by burdens no child should have to shoulder. Two riveting scenes turn on Cole using his psychic gifts productively: first, when he reveals the Munchausen by Proxy Syndrome that led to a little girl's murder by her mother; second, when he reveals his gifts to his own mother (played by Toni Collette) — offering as proof a communication from his grandmother that reduces his troubled mom to tears. Thus does *The Sixth Sense* move toward the most moving epiphanies between parent and child. Only at the end of the film does the final revelation come: Dr. Crowe's own epiphany as he realizes he has been dead all along — and the narrative jumps back to the initial ellipsis to make clear to us what has been really happening. We see snippets of scenes we saw already, but only now do we see them clearly and realize that in the entire film, we had never seen Dr. Crowe in conversation with anyone except the psychic Cole.

Although the surprise of *The Sixth Sense* feels shocking, in truth it shouldn't. It's almost the same surprise as in the 1990 demonic horror film *Jacob's Ladder* (directed by Adrian Lyne from a screenplay by Bruce Joel Rubin). In *Jacob's Ladder*, Tim Robbins plays an American soldier who is killed in Vietnam, but doesn't know he's dead; the whole film is revealed as his elaborate dying hallucination. This surprise — probably inspiring Shyamalan — was itself taken from that staple of American high school literature classes, "An Occurrence at Owl Creek Bridge," a short story by Ambrose Bierce about a Confederate soldier who appears narrowly to escape execution by the Union army and struggles to return home to his wife, only to be snapped back to the gallows at the narrative's end. This story was most notably made into a 1961 short film by the French director Robert Enrico, which was then purchased in 1964 by Rod Serling for presentation as the final new episode for his famed TV series *The Twilight Zone*. The same Bierce story had been earlier adapted into a 1959 episode of the TV series *Alfred Hitchcock Presents*.

The success of the surprise ending in *The Sixth Sense* ignited Hollywood interest in surprise endings in general. In 2001, another slow-moving horror film, *The Others*, written and directed by the Spanish director (born in Chile) Alejandro Amenábar, attracted similar critical attention — even winning an Academy Award nomination for its star Nicole Kidman. Typical to the industry, the surprise ending in *The Others* was the same as the one in *The Sixth Sense*: a protagonist who is dead, but doesn't know it until the end of the film. Still, *The Others* was skillfully written and expressively directed, a subtle and atmospheric film almost devoid of special effects. The idea of telling a ghost story from the point of view of the confused, tormented ghosts is genuinely clever. *The Others* starts with a retelling of Genesis, revealing immediately its spiritual interests. Although set on Britain's Jersey coast after World War II, the film seems of an even older period, and there are purposive design anachronisms we either accept without question or fail to register. The first image of *The Others* is of Nicole Kidman, as Grace, screaming as she awakens. Psychologically tormented, she is religious, lives in a mysterious dark mansion, and has two children whose allergy to light requires all curtains to be closed — all useful ingredients for creating an appropriately frightening atmosphere for horror. Afraid that there is "something diabolic" in the house which is "not at rest," Grace teaches her children about the afterlife. Are there ghosts lurking? Or are the servants hatching a plot? Kidman's Grace — so proper and controlled, almost neurotic in her religiosity — recalls Deborah Kerr's governess in *The Innocents* (based on Henry James' *The Turn of the Screw*), both women on the verge of madness. One scary scene shows the curtains suddenly missing and light streaming in as Grace's children scream uncontrollably. And there is a stunning revelation in that moment when Grace discovers that the servants are indeed ghosts, having died in 1891. But that revelation is only part of the surprise, for in the extraordinary climax, we see intruders suddenly in the house; and these intruders, dressed in clothes more contemporary than what we've seen so far, are holding a séance. They are the new owners of the mansion; and the shock is our realization that these intruders are not the ghosts, but that Grace and her children are. Grace screams "We're not dead! We're not dead!" And as she maniacally bangs the table and sets papers flying, we suddenly see things as they really look: without Grace and her children visible, and with frightening telekinetic objects flying by themselves into the air. Clearly, Grace and her children are not the ones being haunted, but the ones unknowingly doing the haunting. Another

Especially stylish, *The Others* uses a number of expressive visual ideas: (1) misty, low-contrast cinematography, (2) odd angles in the style of German expressionism, (3) visually scary images, such as this blind psychic (Renée Asherson), (4) atmospheric silhouettes of ghosts at the window (Fionnula Flanagan, Eric Sykes, and Elaine Cassidy), and (5) the measured gesture, here by a child (James Bentley) who does not know he is dead.

When French directors make scary films, they make stylistic choices with mathematical precision. These formally composed over-the-shoulder shots from three different scenes of *Lemming* emphasize different permutations of "the couple" using actors Laurent Lucas, Charlotte Gainsbourg, and the luminous Charlotte Rampling. These choices indicate subtextually that *Lemming* is about the survival of the couple as social institution.

revelation, even more depressing, is that so very long ago in a profound depression, Grace had smothered her children and then shot herself. Unhappy ghosts, they have been unable to accept their horrific fate and move on. As the new owners fearfully leave the house, the ghost servant Mrs. Mills (played by Fionnula Flanagan) tries to reassure Grace: "The intruders are leaving, but others will come. Sometimes we'll sense them, other times we won't. But that's the way it's always been." The film ends as we watch the real ghosts looking out the window; although Grace now realizes she's dead, she is less sure of her religious beliefs — since the Bible does not really explain the lugubrious state she now finds herself in.

Just as *The Others* profits from its European sensibility, so too does the excellent *Lemming*, one of the few French horror films in the demonic subgenre. Directed in 2005 by Dominik Moll (the director of *With a Friend Like Harry*), this Gallic vision — emerging from the secular French culture — eschews symbolism of Christianity and damnation. Instead, *Lemming* focuses on the psychological component inherent in possession. Unlike

In a key *Lemming* sequence, Alain (Laurent Lucas) watches helplessly as his wife Bénédicte (Charlotte Gainsbourg) is physically replaced by Mrs. Pollock (Charlotte Rampling), possessing the younger woman's body.

the increasingly heavy-handed, American demonic films, *Lemming* teases its audience with a great ambiguity — at times presenting an apocalyptic vision, too. Married to the beautiful Bénédicte (played by Charlotte Gainsbourg), Alain Getty (played by Laurent Lucas) is a home construction expert who can devise computer programs to control complex plumbing systems, but who can't fix his own blocked sink. The sink, as it turns out, is clogged with a dead lemming. Lemmings are famous for their self-destructive behavior: overpopulation triggers a mass migration which causes untold lemmings to die while attempting to swim to somewhere new. "They drown from exhaustion." So did the lemming purposely jump into the drain to kill itself? What propels the dramatic conflict in *Lemming* is a key scene in which Alain and Bénédicte Getty meet the Pollocks, an older couple played by André Dussollier and the incomparable Charlotte Rampling. The exhausted Pollock marriage is clearly what the Getty marriage might be in thirty years: bitter, recriminatory, and filled with funny games. Mrs. Pollock acts always strangely inappropriately, whether publicly throwing wine in her husband's face, or privately trying to seduce Alain. Most weirdly, she later returns to the Getty house to ask if she might take a nap, then slightly thereafter kills herself, a ghastly, unguestly thing to do. It is noted, perhaps ominously, that the lemming in the sink was female — like Mrs. Pollock: did the suicidal impulse transfer to Mrs. Pollock from the lemming? And perhaps the lemming, one of thousands, is a symbol of every unhappy woman in a suburban marriage. Certainly Mrs. Pollock is somewhat crazy (a sign that *Lemming* also embraces elements of the horror-of-personality film). Notably, when she dies, there is an absolutely electric moment between her and Bénédicte: an ambiguous mental transference. After Mrs. Pollock's death, Bénédicte starts acting oddly.

Lemming is especially creepy because its horror is subtle. There are no obvious monsters or special effects; instead, the odd interrelationships among the characters disquiet us:

Psycho references show up even in French films. Hitchcock's gambit of three consecutive shots from the same angle, successively more closely composed — which Hitchcock used to show the murder of Marion Crane (Janet Leigh) — is imitated in *Lemming* to show the suicide of Mrs. Pollock (Charlotte Rampling).

the subtextual angers, the inappropriate questions, the unexpected behaviors. On one horrifying night which draws upon horror-of-Armageddon conventions, the Getty house is overrun by thousands of lemmings. The context is ambiguous: is this onslaught a nightmare, a sign that Alain is losing his mind? Or is it real? As *Lemming* progresses, it becomes clear that Bénédicte has been possessed by the spirit of Mrs. Pollock. The film's most chilling effect is when the actress Charlotte Gainsbourg is replaced, momentarily, by the actress Charlotte Rampling, who, as the late Mrs. Pollock, requests that her husband be killed and produces the key to her house. Will the Gettys be drawn into a murderous plot against their conscious will? Although its characters may be unbalanced, *Lemming* is not a horror-of-personality film, and although lemmings may be destroying themselves, *Lemming* is not a horror-of-Armageddon film; most centrally, *Lemming* is a demonic horror film — with Mrs. Pollock a witch of sorts, inhabiting the body of another to gain revenge.

But Mrs. Pollock's revenge is not part of an ancient curse or an anti–Christian plot. It is simply a response to her sad, defeated life of marital discord and of psychological, spousal abuse—certainly not uncommon in many unhappy marriages. (Though in truth, Mr. Pollock seems as abused by his wife as abuser of his wife.) Demonstrating its art-house pedigree, *Lemming* begins as a horror version of *Who's Afraid of Virginia Woolf?* (anatomizing the respective marriages of an older couple and younger couple), but turns into a horror version of *Persona* (presenting the process by which two women come to share a soul). As well, *Lemming* contains significant social commentary, particularly in regard to the issues of surveillance and lack of privacy in our contemporary world. (For instance, as the film's major subplot, Alain has created a mobile camera that functions like a remote-controlled toy helicopter.) And is the lemming migration a symbol for the human migration to the suburbs and exurbs, with their shallow satisfactions and concomitant sexual games to help make the lethargy bearable? Or do the lemmings symbolize women as the victims of traditional marriage, willing to kill themselves rather than remain trapped? At the end of *Lemming*, when Bénédicte is "returned" to her body, she asks her husband, "Will you still love me when I'm old?" It is clear that despite their resolve to love each other, the young Gettys will not easily escape the Pollocks' destiny. *Lemming* ends with a tangential image which is ambiguously disturbing and oblique: a neighbor boy kicking a ball against a wall repeatedly and pointlessly, a solitary activity that seems not particularly to be providing enjoyment. An unfulfilling ritual of play, its position as the final image of *Lemming* elevates the ritual into a Sisyphean metaphor for a manicured suburbia.

As endnote to this discussion of demonic horror is the less subtle, but fascinating American independent film *The Blair Witch Project*, from 1999. This film purports to be the found footage of three student filmmakers who disappeared while shooting an investigative documentary in the woods of Burkittsville, Maryland, on the subject of local leg-

ends of hauntings and violence. The film's mockumentary concept is strong, if shallow, certainly showing the influence of the far more complex *Man Bites Dog*. *The Blair Witch Project* was immensely popular precisely because it was low budget, low-tech,

The Blair Witch Project, which starts as a traditional *faux* documentary, (1) reflexively shows its filmmakers with their equipment (actor Joshua Leonard); with (2) and (3), and virtually no visual horror, the film becomes increasingly abstract and experimental.

and devoid of special effects. With most Hollywood horror films heightening spectacle, the *Blair Witch* filmmakers (Daniel Myrick and Eduardo Sanchez) understood that heightening fear is what is key to horror. And to do that, you don't need a big budget. As the film begins, we are introduced to the filmmaker protagonists: Heather, Joshua, and Michael; the fact that the character names correspond to the purposely unknown actors chosen to play the parts (Heather Donahue, Joshua Leonard, and Michael Williams) adds to the film's sense of reality. When the protagonists conduct interviews about the legends, these scenes amuse, since the eccentric locals tell horrible, grisly stories with an offhand gusto. Throughout *The Blair Witch Project*, the style is of a fetching improvisation which feels real. Since the protagonists are college students, their banter is appropriately juvenile: they drink beer, make fart jokes, sing the *Gilligan's Island* theme song, and say "fuck" a lot. It is the casual naturalism in these scenes of *temps morts*, where nothing really happens, which sets us up for the fear we feel later. Some of *The Blair Witch Project* seems experimental, with the filmmakers' conversations evoking the improvisatory quality of Andy Warhol's work in the sixties. Some of the supposed *vérité* footage evokes the short films of Stan Brakhage, too, in that there are extended scenes when the screen is out-of-focus, virtually black, or visually ambiguous. One of the characters, Joshua, says reflexively to his colleague: "I can see why you like this video camera so much. It's not quite reality." Not quite, but close enough.

It takes over thirty minutes of *The Blair Witch Project* before anything really happens: the discovery of rocks found mysteriously piled outside the filmmakers' camp site, hardly a high-tech horror! And yet the homely rocks work quite adequately to scare, tying in to the fear of the unknown as well as to the archetypal childhood fear of going "into the woods." (It's not for nothing that so many fairy tales like "Hansel and Gretel" begin with characters going into the woods, only to discover some horrific fate awaiting them.) As the film proceeds, its footage is increasingly hand-held, point-of-view shots: characters often in the dark and walking, running, breathing heavily, screaming, and more. These dark images force us to listen carefully and use our imagination; in fact, *The Blair Witch Project* often feels less like a film than a radio drama. The lack of a musical score requires us to interpret the images and sounds on our own, without guidance. When the film was originally released on the huge screens of the suburban multiplexes, the frantic moving-camera images, often out-of-focus and using zooms, made some spectators literally sick, inducing

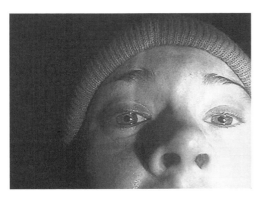

The Blair Witch Project's strategy of showing a filmmaker photographing her own hysteria in an off-center composition has become one of the most iconic images in all horror film.

vertigo and nausea. When the film's violent climax comes so abruptly, it's as if all hell has broken loose; and yet the ending is ambiguous. Perhaps one character is dead, another is in process of being killed, and the third is waiting his turn, but only perhaps... Who is committing the violence and why, remains unclear. Although no one could accuse *The Blair Witch Project* of being profound, nor, for that matter, of expressing even a single notable idea, perhaps never in horror history has so much been made out of so little. *The Blair Witch Project* proves that a smart, canny style can take filmmakers a long way.

However, what makes *The Blair Witch Project* so important is that it became one of the most financially successful horror films ever. The film's production budget was reported at a meager $30,000 (though some sources suggest twice that amount), and the film went on to make $248 million worldwide — an 8266:1 profit ratio which puts even the most successful Hollywood blockbuster to shame. Oddly, this film turned out to be a horror dead-end for almost a decade, with Hollywood not certain how a multi-billion dollar industry might profit from the film's low-budget lessons. (Perhaps the highly-acclaimed TV series *Lost* displays at least one influence: that of never underestimating the emotional power of showing frightened people running through the woods in scene after scene!) But finally, in 2008, two other films followed in *The Blair Witch Project*'s aesthetic footsteps with the same conceit: *Cloverfield* (a high-concept cross between *Godzilla* and *Blair Witch*), purporting to be found camcorder footage of a monster destroying Manhattan; and George A. Romero's *Diary of the Dead*, purporting to be found camcorder footage of an eruption of zombies. *Cloverfield* captured the public imagination — for at least a short while — and took in $170 million worldwide, though it needed a production budget of $25 million to do so, over 800 times the budget of *Blair Witch*. Romero's effort, on the other hand, made less than a million dollars domestically, a popular failure for Romero suggesting that whatever cultural energy was attached to *The Blair Witch Project*'s aesthetic strategy may have already been spent.

8 — The Horror of Armageddon, Revisited

In the seventies and eighties, the horror-of-Armageddon subgenre also continued to proliferate, though with much greater variety and much less adherence to the narrative structures codified by *The Birds*. George A. Romero's 1968 cult horror film, *Night of the Living Dead*, for instance, was followed by his 1979 *Dawn of the Dead*, in which the violence became almost comically hyperbolic, and the black-and-white horror of the original was replaced by gaudy, color, social satire in which apocalypse played out against the excess of a suburban shopping mall. The notable blockbuster *Alien* in 1979 suggested apocalypse could come from outer space, and its taut artistry turned it into a horror adventure fable for its time. (Surprisingly, the high-budget, effects-driven *Alien* was largely inspired by the low-budget, low-tech 1958 film *It! The Terror from Beyond Space*, whose wonderful last line — "Another name for Mars is death" — had been a great warning regarding apocalyptic danger from scientific progress.)

Perhaps the most notable director to work within this apocalyptic genre in the seventies and eighties was Australian Peter Weir. *The Last Wave* (1977) is especially evocative, taking as its subject the dreamworld of the Australian Aborigines and their conflict with Western civilization — a conflict that augurs the "Last Wave," that is, a cataclysmic tidal surge that would end all civilization. What proliferates in *The Last Wave* are not creatures, but different manifestations of the natural element of water: from the opening scene, in which hailstones fall from an absolutely clear sky, to a scene in which overflowing bathtub

In Andrei Tarkovsky's ***The Sacrifice***, actors Allan Edwall and Erland Josephson wait, with dread, for the apocalypse.

231

In *The Last Wave*, Richard Chamberlain plays a white lawyer defending Aborigines; by extending his hand to their culture, he becomes a prophet to the coming apocalypse.

An exceedingly odd cloud formation in *The Last Wave* resembles a sacred Aboriginal artifact that predicts the end of the world.

The Aboriginal actor Gulpilil plays Chris, who guards the secrets of apocalypse in *The Last Wave*. Director Peter Weir photographs Gulpilil with a mistily dark, soft-focus expressiveness.

water pours down the stairs to find the protagonist David (played by Richard Chamberlain); from a prophetic vision in which David drives his submerged car as drowned people and other vehicles float by around him, to the terrifying final image of an approaching tidal wave. In *The Last Wave,* the conventions and visual effects of the horror film are wedded to an essentially Jungian world view to create a riveting fable about a society punished for losing touch with its collective unconscious, with its soul. Like *The Last Wave*, Weir's *Picnic at Hanging Rock* (1975) has an apocalyptic vision as well: portending, as it does, the end of the Victorian era. Sexual liberation, lesbianism, psychic violence, and authoritarian repression come to a confluence so shrouded in mystery and ambiguity that apocalypse

becomes all but inevitable. People die or disappear mysteriously; the girls' school must close; and above it all, like the sword of Damocles or Hitchcock's birds, rests Hanging Rock — a symbol for the unknowable mysteries of nothingness and existence. Not surprisingly, Weir's nonhorror films share the same kind of apocalyptic vision: *Gallipoli* (1981), which, in its horrifying climax, shows large numbers of men senselessly massacred during World War I because of the misplaced imperialist pride of the villainous British; *The Year of Living Dangerously* (1983), which shows the apocalyptic end of the Sukarno regime in

In *Picnic at Hanging Rock*, Peter Weir photographs Miranda (Anne Lambert) in an oval mirror which evokes a Victorian cameo.

Indonesia, overseen by the metaphorical little person, Billy Kwan (played spectacularly by Linda Hunt), as well as by the mythic characters of Indonesian puppet theatre; and the virtual horror film *The Mosquito Coast* (1986), which shows a protagonist so anxious to leave a chaotic civilization he feels is on the road to Armageddon that he escapes to a jungle idyll

only to bring with him his own inevitable apocalypse. Weir's sensibility was somewhat shared by his Australian countryman, George Miller, whose *The Road Warrior* (1981) and *Mad Max* (1980), its predecessor, were hugely successful in presenting a

The Atomic Café traces the cultural history of the atomic bomb. (1) In the forties, Americans celebrated its use; (2) in the fifties, established the suburbs as their safe haven; and (3) in the sixties learned, ludicrously, that they might survive attack if they would "duck and cover" under their Formica dinettes.

In *The Day After*, Kansas residents watch with a surreal casualness as nuclear warheads are launched from their backyards; with a stunning immediacy, they become victims of enemy warheads launched back at them.

semipunk vision of an apocalyptic, post-atomic future in which all values have disintegrated, gasoline is routinely killed for, and leather-garbed musclemen roam the land to loot and plunder.

With the Reagan era, too, came the end of détente and the renewal of atomic bomb

anxieties, which were expressed in a variety of films on a fairly literal level: *The Atomic Café* (1982), a satirical documentary about the early atomic education of the American public by its government; *Testament* (1983), which harrowingly shows a family dying in the aftermath of nuclear war; *WarGames* (1983), a compelling albeit juvenile thriller about the potential for computer-activated apocalypse; *Special Bulletin* (1983), a made-for-television

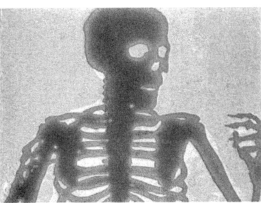

American audiences of the time were genuinely shocked by the atomic violence *The Day After* depicted, particularly the human bodies disintegrating at ground zero.

movie (in the this-is-really-happening style of Orson Welles' original "The War of the Worlds" radio broadcast) that not only explores the possibility of terrorists detonating an atomic bomb, but also examines the probable media coverage of such an event; *The Day After* (1983), a highly hyped television movie that attempts to show the reality (through fairly conventional tricks of makeup and special effects) of a nuclear bomb dropped on Kansas City; and *Countdown to Looking Glass* (1984), a fictional HBO film-for-television that shows newscasters broadcasting late-breaking news on a Persian Gulf crisis that leads the world to the brink of thermonuclear destruction. Some of these films, like *Testament*, recall science fiction-inspired horror films of the fifties, like *Five* (1951) and *On the Beach* (1959); all these films play upon the audience's fears — the exploitation of everyday anxiety, in all its guises, being perhaps the hallmark of the contemporary horror film.

After the collapse of the Soviet Union and the end of the Cold War during George H. W. Bush's presidency, the fear of the atomic bomb diminished significantly. With the American right-wing deprived of its decades-old Communist enemy, its sights were set on a new enemy: gays, lesbians, feminists, secular humanists, and supporters of abortion rights — those, in the view of the right, who were leading America to a cultural apocalypse. Until the 9/11, 2001, terrorist attack on America by al-Qaeda reinvigorated the subgenre, apocalyptic horror was being dominated not by atomic bomb films but a variety of low-budget B-films, not especially notable, which presented images of the end of the world as a result of animal attack. By far, the cleverest of these films is *Tremors* (1990), which stars Kevin Bacon and Fred Ward as good ol' boys in Perfection, Nevada, fighting giant underground worms who surface to attack. With surreal creatures inspired by the sandworms from *Dune*, *Tremors* is the perfect Saturday matinee movie: frightening without taking itself too seriously, and funny without lapsing into parody. The film's set pieces are extraordinarily well-done, and its convincing monster effects and professional look belie its low budget. Spiders, frightening in any size, could be found in *Arachnophobia* (1990), *Spiders* (2000), *Spiders 2: Breeding Ground* (2001), *Arachnid* (2001), *Eight Legged Freaks* (2002), and *Arachnia* (2003). Snakes attacked in *Anaconda* (1997, with A-listers Jon Voight and Jennifer Lopez), *King Cobra* (1999), and the cult hit *Snakes on a Plane* (2006), which was promoted by a grassroots online community. Giant cockroaches invaded the New York subway system in *Mimic* (1997) and came back, in morphed forms, in *Mimic*'s straight-to-video sequels. And a flesh-eating virus tore apart a group of friends in *Cabin Fever* (2002). In tacit acknowledgment that the danger of future apocalypse can derive from imbalance in the natural world, many of these films — unlike the seminal *The Birds*, set in a civilized California — are set in primeval places like the Amazonian rain forest, forcing characters to return to a pre-industrial past. Even the TV series *Survivor*, a sensation in the United States since its premiere in 2000, brought contestants to a deserted wilderness with only the clothes on their backs and then let them descend into *Lord of the Flies*-like chaos as they forage for food, build shelter, avoid animal attack, and plot against each other. Who would have anticipated that one of the most popular incarnations of the horror of Armageddon would essentially be a capitalist quiz show in which reality-TV stars, "killed off" one by one, compete for a million dollars? (And oddly, this subgenre was also reflected in the popular TV series, *Fear Factor*, where contestants won cash by competing in stunts requiring them to eat a large number of disgusting insects or brave swim-tanks filled with a repellant breed of animal.)

On some level, all these works reveal our subconscious desire to return to a time when our concerns were more elemental — without cellphones, video games, e-mails. The most high profile Armageddon horror of the era was Steven Spielberg's special-effects blockbuster

Jurassic Park, a return all the way to the Jurassic period through the efforts of a scientist (played by Richard Attenborough) who has propagated dinosaurs and plans to make money with a dinosaur island theme park for ecotourists. A cinefantastique wonder showing dinosaurs wreaking havoc, *Jurassic Park* is a roller-coaster ride which became, in 1993, the most commercially successful film internationally of all time (until *Titanic* bypassed its record several years later). Although the special effects were mostly marvelous and definitely the reason for the film's appeal (who can forget the startlingly graceful images of Brachiosaurus grazing in the forest?), there remains a certain desultoriness in the construction of the narrative, with loose ends and scenes which seem not to pay off. *The Lost World*, a *Jurassic Park* sequel in 1997, seemed unnecessary for any motive except craven profit. Psychologically vacuous (unlike the best of these films), *The Lost World* shows men with gadgets who say things like "*Lindstrade* air rifle. Fires a sub-sonic impact delivery dart." The exposition is obligatory, the villains are cardboard, a Disneyfied African-American child functions as an improbable attempt to expand the film's demographics, and characters behave stupidly so that dinosaurs can attack them. When at one point we see a man ripped in half by dinosaurs competing for the same dinner, we understand that the humanism Spielberg displayed in *Schindler's List* has been replaced by the expediency of efficient, crowd-pleasing violence: the scene feels pornographic. The few pleasures in *The Lost World* come from its irony — Jeff Goldblum, for instance, responding to a

Although Richard Attenborough essentially plays the mad scientist who created the *Jurassic Park* of dinosaurs, he is grandfatherly, casual, in hero's white, and untypically affable.

"Watching the skies" pervaded horror-of-Armageddon film in the fifties and sixties and pervades this subgenre still. Here, Laura Dern and Sam Neill watch the *Jurassic Park* skies for dinosaurs.

colleague's awe at the dinosaurs: "Yeah, 'ooh, ahhh,' that's how it always starts. But then later there's running and then screaming." A few scenes invoke Hitchcock's *The Birds*, generally to *The Lost World*'s disadvantage. Only the climactic scenes showing a Tyrannosaurus Rex drinking from a swimming pool in suburban San Diego evoke, through their surreal wit, any lasting sense of awe.

In contrast to a film like *The Lost World*, packed with effects, stands the more interesting and personal *Open Water*, written and directed by Chris Kentis and released in 2004 "based on true events," as the film immediately tells us. Because it is shot on high-end video, *Open Water* feels somewhat documentary and has that low-budget patina that works so well for horror. The story of a young married couple accidentally abandoned in open water while on an ecotourism diving expedition, *Open Water* is a kind of anti–*Jaws*, and ultimately more existential in its meaning. Contributing to its documentary sensibility is its lack of traditional horror music. Many images — of a shark circling, a school of jellyfish

Some *Open Water* images have a postcard prettiness, while others have an ambiguous abstraction, neither aesthetic especially typical to the horror film.

Here is one of the few clear images in *Open Water* of a prowling shark. Overwhelmingly the camera focuses on the human heads bobbing in the expanse of ocean as unseen sharks attack from below.

The moment of death in *Open Water*: (1) humans, without qualm, kill a mosquito which is hardly apprehensible (note the extreme wide-angle lens); (2) sharks, without qualm, kill humans, hardly apprehensible, and these deaths, in the natural scheme of things, look just as inconsequential.

stinging, the open water itself— become very abstract; the low-angle shots from water level are unusually claustrophobic. The wife (played by Blanchard Ryan) offers, "I don't know what's worse ... seeing them or not seeing them." Though she's talking about sharks, her question metaphysically refers to more: to all horror, to danger, to that unexpected thing just around the corner which threatens the complacency of our lives. Although the husband (played by Daniel Travis) quickly retorts "Seeing them," the film suggests the opposite in a horrific scene in which the husband, stranded for hours, suddenly starts screaming for no apparent reason. His screams are as unsettling as the later shark attacks. When the husband and wife engage in a marital fight, bitter and incongruous in the endless sea, each ascribing blame to the other for being stranded, the wife's final line —"I wanted to go skiing!"—

The husband and wife in *Open Water* (Daniel Travis and Blanchard Ryan) do not act like horror film characters, but ordinary people on vacation. They (1) brush their teeth, (2) feel sexual desire, (3) take vacation photographs, and (4) clown around (in this case, adopting a sadly prophetic jokey pose).

works as a veritable punchline. Although they make up, their mutual declaration of love is followed by the shark attack. So *Open Water* also asks the question that Hitchcock left purposely unanswered in *The Birds*: Can love and trust truly stave off the existential horror?

Resoundingly, this film answers: *No*. After night has fallen, a subsequent shark attack during a storm takes place within a largely black screen: we can hear the attack, but cannot see it. Clearly, the husband was very wrong. It is much scarier *not* to see the sharks. Especially moving is when the wife releases the dead body of her husband the next morning; and then the sharks, virtually unseen, silently eat from below until his body disappears. Only after the husband disappears do we briefly see a whole school of sharks; and then, we watch from a distance as she, too, is silently pulled underneath the surface. Or does she willingly release herself into the water, bowing to the inevitable? In any case, without a scream (and without strident horror music), she disappears into the void of oblivion in this very existential fable.

There are a few shots of the expedition leaders instigating a search after realizing their mistake of having abandoned the couple, but the film makes no attempt to create suspense from their efforts and instead just notes, rather unemotionally, the simultaneity of their attempts with the demise of our protagonists. Thus the film's ultimate note is irony; and a shot showing what the vast ocean looks like from a helicopter trying to find the couple makes clear the overwhelming unlikeliness of even sighting the couple, let alone saving them. The end-credits sequence shows an offending shark sometime later, caught, with its stomach being cut open to reveal, undigested, the couple's camera. We can't help but wonder what those final photographs might be. Might the last image resemble the joke photo taken before the expedition's start, of the husband putting his head into the open jaws of a mounted shark?

What makes *Open Water* so notable is its integrity and its unwillingness to imitate other American horror films with their unrelenting exploitation of violence and celebration of special effects. Our reaction to violence does not become further inured by *Open Water*. Although we may not scream out in fear, the violent end of these two somewhat likeable people seems horrifying enough, but also relatively inconsequential, because their end is set philosophically within a universe of similar inconsequence. Earlier in the film, in their hotel room, we saw the husband stalk and kill a mosquito that invaded the couple's "territory." Haven't the sharks killed the couple for the same reason? And so are we not hypocrites to feel sympathy for our protagonists when we felt none for the mosquito?

The subgenre of apocalyptic horror was largely creatively dormant throughout the eighties and nineties, but that was to change after September 11, 2001, when young men working for the Saudi terrorist Osama bin Laden hijacked four commercial jets. Two of them crashed into the World Trade Center towers, which collapsed; one crashed into the Pentagon; and a fourth was brought down by passengers in a Pennsylvania field before it could crash into its probable target, the Capitol Building. Thousands were killed, thousands narrowly escaped, and the world watched it all on TV in real time, avidly and helplessly: the most harrowing and traumatizing images of destruction irrevocably seared into our consciousness. 9/11 was the most shocking and successful attack on the United States to date, arguably surpassing Pearl Harbor in 1941. But 9/11 also provided—particularly to those who had previously felt immune—a view into future apocalypse. A previous apocalyptic vision, provided by the 1945 bombings of Hiroshima and Nagasaki and revelations of the Holocaust, was for most Americans a vision that was intellectually, emotionally, and physically removed. 9/11, on the other hand, was not only in our backyards, but in our living rooms and bedrooms: on the TV screen. Since *Star Wars* in 1977 and Ronald Reagan's election in 1980 (or in other words, since "A long time ago in a galaxy far, far away…" and "It's morning in America…") a cultural period was inaugurated in which Americans looked largely to fantasy and escapist sensation, turning their backs on a variety of real-world problems: homelessness, AIDS, world poverty, the growing gap between rich and poor, the growth of worldwide religious fundamentalism, the abuse of human rights, global warming. In other words, Americans *checked out* of the here and now. This culture of escape has been relentless: with fewer foreign films released in the United States each year, and native-born Americans learning fewer languages than ever before. On September 11, 2001, we awakened with the most brutal start from our long dream of avoidance and asked ourselves, for the first time in more than a generation: "Why do so many people around the world hate us?" Yet why should we have been surprised, when for so long we had been paying so little attention?

And so 9/11 was one of the most perspective-shifting "before-and-after" events in the history of the United States. The attack on Pearl Harbor had brought into dramatic focus the need to defeat the Fascists; 9/11 had terrifyingly signaled the need to defeat fanatic, Muslim terrorism. President George W. Bush, who on the day of the attack had seemed fearful and slow to respond, eventually jumped into aggressive attack mode. Before long, the United States, with a coalition of countries, went to war with Afghanistan to rout the Taliban government, which had been harboring bin Laden and his al-Qaeda terrorist training camps. In March of 2003, more controversially, the United States went to war with Iraq as part of the ubiquitous "War on Terror"—even though the weapons of mass destruction asserted there had long been destroyed, and Saddam Hussein had played no part in the 9/11 attacks, despite the administration's continual assertions that he had. What resulted was one of the

"Watch the skies" is the horror-of-Armageddon mantra. On 9/11/2001, New Yorkers watched as a terrorist attack took place, as shown in images (1 and 2) from the documentary *Fahrenheit 9/11*. Although the images are similar to (3) the fictional image of a woman watching the skies in *Independence Day*, the differences in emotional power are visually manifest: real fear, which comprehends consequence, is unlike a blockbuster's fictional fear, which ignores consequence and celebrates the expressiveness of narcissistic posing.

most polarizing wars in American history, brought about by an administration which scaled back civil liberties; instituted wire-taps; invaded the privacy of Americans' phone, bank, and computer records; endorsed the torture of prisoners; created secret prisons in foreign countries; refused to abide by the Geneva Convention; created a bitterly divided electorate; linked virtually every political issue to the "War on Terror"; and impugned the patriotism of detractors. Not surprisingly, Americans were very, *very* afraid: some by the specter of terrorists plotting other apocalyptic attacks, some by the movement away from civil liberties toward repression, and many by both. As one might expect, films in the Armageddon subgenre immediately reflected these new political realities in ways both explicit and implicit.

Michael Haneke's *Time of the Wolf* [*Le Temps du Loup*], made in 2002, stars Isabelle Huppert as Anne Laurent, who wanders a desolate landscape with her children, Ben and Eva, after some unspecified apocalypse. Haneke's title derives from Ingmar Bergman's *Hour of the Wolf*, whose title refers to that folkloric, momentous hour before sunrise when there are more deaths and births than at any other hour. Haneke's film also references an apocalyptic film by a Bergman disciple: Andrei Tarkovsky's *The Sacrifice* (with cinematography

by Bergman regular Sven Nykvist). Made in 1986, *The Sacrifice* deals with the emotional anxiety of global atomic war; and the film's key images of house, fire, and bicycle find their way into Haneke's film, too. Whereas most Armageddon horror films revel in the special effects of destruction, *Time of the Wolf* begins *after* the apocalypse, but before any spiritual dawn. Haneke emphasizes the emotional toll on the survivors and the dehumanizing effect of a cataclysmic event. The cinematography, often

For director Michael Haneke, one tragedy of apocalypse is how it casually teaches children helplessness and despair, which is why *Time of the Wolf* focuses on Ben (Lucas Biscombe).

In *Time of the Wolf*, elemental images are disturbing: air relates not to breath and clarity, but fallout and obscurity; fire not to warmth, but immolation; blood not to life, but violent death.

overexposed and gray with desaturated colors, suggests some post-atomic landscape where the air is filled with ash. Still, neither the cause nor nature of the apocalypse is ever revealed; and the disturbing apocalyptic images — such as a mound of horses set on fire — are symbolically ambiguous. Like the daughter in *The Birds* who was given lovebirds, the son Ben also has a bird. But whereas the lovebirds thrived, inherently expressing the hope that Hitchcock's characters might be delivered from the apocalypse, Ben's bird dies, because in *Time of the Wolf* deliverance is already impossible. Traditional, masculine heroism cannot help: Anne's husband is killed almost immediately by squatters who want his supplies. Later, in an elemental image, Ben throws branches onto a fire and then adds all his clothes to it as well, standing naked in front of the flames like the boys in *Lord of the Flies* after their civilization has broken down. Emotionally naked, too, Ben is about to throw himself into the fire when a man who is watching intercedes and offers comfort. For Haneke, although we can't prevent apocalypse, we can recognize the community to be found in others and be open to the occasional kindness. And in the aftermath of apocalypse, class distinctions are stripped away, which is good. But is that enough? Oddly, Ben is comforted by the thought that "maybe the dead will come back to life." (Would zombies be more of a comfort than this chaotic nothingness? Or does Ben just want his father?) The last image of *Time of the Wolf*, ambiguous like the final image of *The Birds*, is a shot of unusually extended duration which shows the landscape from a moving train. Looking green and verdant, the landscape suggests hope; is this the train that will arrive to save this family of melancholy pilgrims?

One of the first American films reflecting 9/11 fears was M. Night Shyamalan's *Signs* in 2002. Ever since Steven Spielberg's *E.T.* and *Close Encounters of the Third Kind*, extra-

In Michael Haneke's apocalyptic vision, the earth seems filled with hope only when shown without human beings, which is why *Time of the Wolf* begins and ends with a landscape.

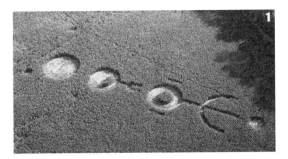
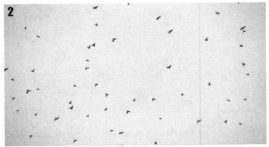

Many images in *Signs* have an abstract quality appropriate to the semiological concerns indicated by the film's title. (1) The mysterious crop circles are a sign of aliens. (2) But do the birds signify something equally ominous, or are they just a reference to Hitchcock's seminal 1963 horror film *The Birds*?

(1) The wide-angle lens used to photograph Graham (Mel Gibson) at the moment he finally sees the alien in *Signs* contributes to a sense of dislocation and danger. (2) The normal lens and backlight used to photograph the alien, on the other hand, makes it look more casually real, if obscure.

terrestrials had been generally presented not only as more evolutionarily advanced than human beings, but as more humanist in their values. *Signs*, a major Hollywood film starring Mel Gibson, totally rejects this benign view and harkens back to the low-budget, science-fiction horror of the fifties, which tended to present extraterrestrials as dangerous and powerful aliens.[1] Set on a Pennsylvania farm, *Signs* starts with manifestations of that folk phenomenon: the crop circle. By *Signs'* end, we learn that the crop circles have been created by horrifying aliens — unseen till the final reel — who are trying to invade and take over the earth. These alien monsters, in our midst and trying to destroy us and the civilization and culture we've created, represent one of the earliest, implicit representations of the 9/11 terrorists: stealthy aliens with language, symbology, and values antithetical to our own.

By the summer of 2004, just months before the American presidential election, it seemed that every film released was either explicitly or implicitly about 9/11 or the politics inspired by 9/11. In short, it was the summer of George W. Bush cinema. For many Americans (and certainly most Democrats), the most horrifying scene in any movie that summer came not from a traditional horror film, but from Michael Moore's documentary exposé of George W. Bush's presidency, *Fahrenheit 9/11*: the scene that shows Bush failing to act for seven long minutes after being told a plane has just hit the south tower of the World Trade Center and that "America is under attack." Weirdly, surreally, the "War President" does not spring into decisive action, but sits listening to an elementary-school class read "The Pet

Independence Day, made in 1996, delineated iconic landmarks as targets — the Statue of Liberty, the World Trade Center towers — and then showed those targets in ruins, destroyed by alien invaders. Did Osama bin Laden get the inspiration for his 9/11 attack from American movies?

Goat," from *Reading Mastery: Level 2 Storybook*. One can't help but wonder: wasn't there something more important a President could have been doing? Although Bush supporters dismissed Moore's film as propaganda (generally without refuting its individual charges), watching this scene is genuinely disquieting. No matter what one's politics or what one thinks of Moore, this display of inaction is really beyond spin: for seven terrifying min-

A horror sequence in the political documentary *Fahrenheit 9/11*: Beginning (1) from cheerful obliviousness, (2) President George W. Bush hears the news about the attack on America and then (3) transitions through grim realization to (4) paralyzed indecision. Now what?

utes, the leader of the Free World was scared and didn't know what to do, and we can see all this clearly in his eyes. It is only a bit hyperbolic to suggest that the *frisson* of George Bush reading "The Pet Goat" in *Fahrenheit 9/11* now joins Linda Blair's Regan twirling her head 360 degrees in *The Exorcist* and Anthony Perkins' character Norman Bates flinging open the shower curtain in *Psycho* as one of the most memorable scenes of American horror.

Fahrenheit 9/11, the highest-grossing documentary in cinema history to date, was not the only Bush-inspired documentary to attract legions of viewers. Also successful were *Control Room*—about the Al-Jazeera network, *Outfoxed: Rupert Murdoch's War on Journalism*—about the Republican neoconservative bias of the Fox News Network, and *Bush's Brain* (which certainly sounds like a horror title)—about presidential advisor Karl Rove. Although remarkable, these documentaries were by no means the only films about Bush dominating that 2004 summer. Indeed, not a week went by with-

The *Night of the Living Dead* films all functioned as political/social allegory. Note the resemblance between images from (1) Zack Snyder's *Dawn of the Dead*, and (2) Spike Lee's *When the Levees Broke*. The first is fictional horror, the second a documentary on the destruction of New Orleans by Hurricane Katrina and government inaction.

out the release of yet another narrative *fiction* film in which Bush and his policies were central—even if these political considerations were often coded. In films like *Dawn of the Dead* and *The Village*, just two of the many Hollywood films intended for mass consumption the summer of 2004, these subtextual political meanings drove their content. Indeed, the president and his policies were so mightily on our minds that even our attempts to escape into fantasy became transformed by our preoccupations with him.

For instance, in *Dawn of the Dead* (a remake by Zack Snyder of George A. Romero's 1978 original), the zombies (read: terrorists) return to attack mainstream America and foment fear. The film's opening credits actually juxtapose an image of hundreds of praying Muslims with an image of the chaos caused by the living dead, inherently suggesting *Dawn of the Dead*'s political subtext. In fact, the Secretary of Defense who talks about the apocalypse on TV physically resembles Vice President Dick Cheney. With apocalypse near, how do Americans try to escape the horror? By declaring, "We're going to the Mall!"—an ineffective strategy suggestive of Bush's advice that Americans fight the economic terrorism of 9/11 by being good consumers and buying durable goods. Notably, at the center of the mall in *Dawn of the Dead* is a coffee shop with the ironic name "Hallowed Grounds"—the designation so often used to refer to the Ground Zero site where the World Trade Center towers once stood. Because in *Dawn of the Dead* you can anticipate which people will turn into zombies (again read: terrorists), the film raises the moral question: Do you kill adversaries now, while they are still technically innocent, for something they are likely to do later? This moral issue is relevant not only to the American foray into Iraq, attempting to prevent anticipated actions by Saddam Hussein, but to a number of provisions in the Patriot Act, too,

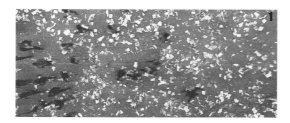

Many images from the **Dawn of the Dead** remake evoke current events; for instance, (1) an overhead shot of a street littered with destruction by the dead evokes the Twin Towers detritus strewn about the post–9/11 Manhattan streets and is just as abstract as (2) a striking shot of a survivor about to shoot a zombie, which is more traditionally horrific.

curtailing certain civil liberties of the innocent. And the fact that much of the most horrific violence in *Dawn of the Dead* is perpetrated by the "good guys" suggests the horror of Iraqi civilian casualties and the torture carried out by Americans at Abu Ghraib prison and at Guantanamo. Certainly the emphasis on the incineration and mutilation of bodies in *Dawn of the Dead* suggests the violent indignities of the 9/11 attack, just as the film's images of debris-filled streets strongly evoke the aftermath of the World Trade Center towers' collapse. Although *Dawn of the Dead* appears to end "happily" with protagonists surviving the dead, the film's final credits are chaotically intercut with surprising images which effectively undo the "happy ending" by killing off everyone who had been left alive. This is an interesting device, considering that most viewers leave the movie theatre before the credits are done and thus would not see the "second" ending. As a result, *Dawn of the Dead* effectively provides two contrasting experiences and meanings: one suggesting a "War on Terror" we will win, the other suggesting a war we will lose.

Another notable film of the 2004 summer was *The Stepford Wives,* ostensibly a horror remake of the 1975 original, but actually a sly satire spoofing the rightward trends in Bush's America. Centered on a conspiracy to bring back a fifties sensibility, women are reprogrammed through their being implanted with computer chips, along with "sugar, spice, and everything nice." (Or perhaps the women are literally replaced with robot counterparts — the exact *Stepford Wives* process being not especially coherent narratively.) In this film about cabals with enormous power (Cheney, Rove, Rumsfeld), the clear visual highlight is a pastel vision of women with shopping carts filled with Alpha-Bits, Purex, and Mazola Oil — an orgy of consumerism to hearten any Fortune 500 executive. The fifties ambience of the film suggests parallels between the blacklist era (dominated by Joseph McCarthy and the anti–Communists) and the "Patriot Act" era (dominated by George W. Bush and the neoconservatives). Visually, *The Stepford Wives* is gorgeous: the robot women, in witty fifties emulation, all in floral-print dresses. At one point, the women objectify themselves when, in their aerobic exercise, they pretend to be washing machines. And just like televisions, the wives can be operated by remote control. Not only do they dispense sex, but they dispense cash, too, like an ATM machine: truly the American dream. Perhaps not surprisingly, the plotters include ex-executives from Microsoft, NASA, Walt Disney, and AOL. When the men are asked if they really want their wives to do nothing but serve them twenty-four hours a day, they all chime in "yes" without any hesitation. To a certain degree, *The Stepford Wives* was a relative to popular American television shows like *Extreme Makeover* and *The Swan*, which generally transformed "unattractive" women (and occasionally men) into conventional beauties, often through extreme plastic surgery. In a progres-

In *The Stepford Wives* remake, beautiful women can (1) dispense smiles (Glenn Close), (2) dispense cash (Lorri Bagley), (3) prop up American consumerism (Nicole Kidman), and (4) reveal they are programmed robots, shells without souls or selves.

sive update to this concept, the flamboyant half of the gay male couple in this version of *Stepford* is made over into a Log Cabin Republican who is a born-again Christian in a Brooks Brothers suit. The ultimate joke is that the real creator of the Stepford wives is a woman, a scientist (played by Glenn Close) who has been driven mad by her attempt to have it all in a post-feminist world. In her defense, she says that women were already turning themselves into robots through their careers, so why not turn them into robots literally? It's as if feminism — in the post–9/11 era — has become equivalent to weapons of mass destruction. When the robot women regain their souls and free will, this scientist shouts out, "There's something unspeakable going on in the ballroom. It's an apocalypse!" The film most relevant to *The Stepford Wives* is *Invasion of the Body Snatchers* (from 1956); as surely as Don Siegel's *Body Snatchers* is a parable about the political witch-hunts and the fifties pressures to conform, *The Stepford Wives* is a parable about the rightward trend in the United States and the post–9/11 pressures to identify as lockstep patriots. *The Stepford Wives* got mixed reviews not only because of its explicit politics, which were off-putting to many, but because many reviewers were not expecting social satire, but science-fiction horror. Indeed, the film's sensibility is so unfailingly satirical that *The Stepford Wives* hardly seems horrific, except for how it embodies many of the genre's recurrent concerns: the zombie, the loss of free will, the sense of conspiracy, the threat that emerges from within familiar surroundings.

In *The Day After Tomorrow*, a 2004 cautionary ecological tale that shows global warming leading to cataclysm and a new Ice Age, the primary villain is an American vice president who is a Dick Cheney look-alike, and the president is an affable incompetent who asks his vice president what to do. Although much was made of the film's attack on Republican skepticism about global warming, largely missed was how subtly the film presents an indirect, metaphorical attack on Bush's position on al-Qaeda — that is, largely dismissing and ignoring the threat until a catastrophe (i.e., 9/11) shocked him into action. (This inaction by Bush to the al-Qaeda threat is well documented in — among many other sources — the 2004 best-seller *Against All Enemies: Inside America's War on Terror* by Richard A. Clarke, the former NSC National Coordinator for Security and Counterterrorism.) Certainly the movie's images of massive crowds running from a wall of water coursing through Manhattan streets strongly evokes the

The vice president in ***The Day After Tomorrow***—who resembles Bush's vice president, Dick Cheney — is certainly fictionalized, because *he* admits error: having caused apocalypse by ignoring global warming.

horrifying images of real New Yorkers racing from the approaching debris cloud of the collapsing World Trade Center towers. In many ways, *The Day After Tomorrow* is a generic synthesis: of horror, of political thriller, of disaster film. The film's striking surreal images include thousands of birds fleeing New York City; multiple simultaneous tornados attacking the southern California landscape; huge floods in New York City, particularly a tidal wave that engulfs the iconic Statue of Liberty; the New York City Public Library filled with snow; and an abandoned Russian ship floating through the flooded Manhattan streets. The frozen Statue of Liberty, as the film's heroes walk past it in snow shoes, is as archetypal an image of apocalypse as found in the seminal *Planet of the Apes*. Yet the statue works also as a symbol of the civil liberties being frozen in George W. Bush's post–9/11 America. The actor Jake Gyllenhaal functions as did Gene Hackman in *The Poseidon Adventure*, offering contrary though accurate advice on how best to survive. Mitigating the film's sensibility of horror is that few characters die, although the most notable exception is the Bush-patterned president, which reveals the political motives of the filmmakers. By the end of *The Day After Tomorrow*, as a sign of the filmmakers' wishful thinking, the vice president has an

epiphany regarding the need for American humility, particularly in regard to the environment. This change of heart may be what most upset the film's right-wing detractors; of course the film contains scientific inaccuracies (as do all fables intending to entertain for two hours rather than to lecture), but *The Day After Tomorrow* had the audacity to show its

Apocalypse has a surreal beauty in ***The Day After Tomorrow***: (1) the polar ice cap cracks, (2) Manhattan floods, and (3) the Statue of Liberty freezes — a symbol of the American rights and values the film contends were being lost in the George W. Bush era.

In *The Village*, M. Night Shyamalan borrows imagery from the American west, such as (1) sheep dutifully following their leader, here a metaphor for patriotic Americans' duty post 9/11. Oddly for a horror film, there are also several references to John Ford's western *The Searchers*: (2) the insistent low-angle shots which make characters look heroic, even if women relegated to cleaning; and (3) the icon of the rocking chair, which romanticizes conventional family values of home and hearth as natural for all, no matter the human or moral cost.

fictionalized Dick Cheney admitting pigheaded error. The last line in the film — uttered by an astronaut who watches the cataclysm from afar — is "Have you ever seen the air so clean?" From space there is no chaos, but a beautiful, glowing, new earth, largely covered with ice.

The summer entertainments of 2004 which considered the Bush presidency most transparently were released within a week of each other: M. Night Shyamalan's *The Village* and Jonathan Demme's remake of *The Manchurian Candidate*. In *The Village*, a millionaire's son (read: George W. Bush), responding to terrorism and violence in the world, decides with his village elders (Bush's cabinet) to lie about the existence of monsters (weapons of mass destruction in Iraq and the supposed connections between Saddam Hussein and al-Qaeda) in an attempt to keep his people in a permanent state of fear so they will revert to the conservative values of an idealized, previous century. In *The Manchurian Candidate*, a millionaire's son (read: George W. Bush), enters politics as a result of a pathological relationship with his successful political parent (George H. W. Bush) and is groomed to be the tool of the special interests in the powerful circle of his family, particularly the conglomerate Manchurian Global (read: Halliburton and big oil). When a character opines, "This isn't an election, this is a coup," it's hard not to recall the Florida debacle in the 2000 presidential election, when the outcome was decided by vote of the Supreme Court. When Eleanor Shaw, played by Meryl Streep, talks ferociously about her "vision of what this country can be ... which is better and better ... safer, braver, stronger, a beacon of freedom in a world troubled by shadows..." it is clear that her neocon sentiments of patriotism are being attacked by the filmmakers as little more than hypocritical rhetoric; she is out for herself and her rich friends. Although these two films are similar in theme, they have radically different endings and sensibilities — *The Village* ending with the Bush stand-in secure as the respected, affable, noble leader of his neo–Pilgrims, even though his lies have been revealed; *The Manchurian Candidate* ending with the Bush stand-in assassinated violently, rejected for high office by an avenging *nemesis*. All of these Bush-inspired films are certainly a response to polarization in the United States as a result of the War in Iraq, but these films

In *The Manchurian Candidate* remake, (1) the hype and heroic posturing of a typical politician (Liev Schreiber) is entirely media spin. In actuality, (2) politics is inadequately transparent and a distortion of truth and democracy. (3) Because politics is dominated by shadowy, unseen interests, even a hero out to change things (Denzel Washington) will find himself besieged.

also show a level of political interest and obsession unseen in a generation. The fact that *The Village*, which is *sympathet*ic to its leader who purposely bases his political choices on a fiction, made almost $50 million more in the United States than the better-reviewed *The Manchurian Candidate*— which is unsympathetic to its leader, was an indication of the strength of the Bush constituency and of how much fear 9/11 had instilled in Americans.

After the 2004 election returned Bush to office, fear increased as a different kind of apocalypse entered the American consciousness: On December 26, 2004, a 9.1 magnitude earthquake shook the Indian Ocean floor and caused a massive tsunami that devastated parts of Indonesia, Thailand, Malaysia, Bangladesh, India, and Sri Lanka. There were 230,000 people killed, including Americans on vacation in Indian Ocean resorts; and television was there, showing the most grisly, apocalyptic images imaginable — images that made *The Day After Tomorrow* look not so very fictional. Then in August of 2005, in a summer of hurricanes, Hurricane Katrina brought catastrophic destruction to Alabama, Mississippi, and Louisiana. Most alarmingly, 80 percent of New Orleans was destroyed and under water; and over 1800 people were killed. Americans watched the most devastating footage on

When the Levees Broke uses symbolic images to show humanity imperiled and Christian precepts dismantled by a willfully indifferent, incompetent government.

An unidentified survivor in *When the Levees Broke* tries to escape early stage flooding; after the apocalypse, the majority of the city is in ruins.

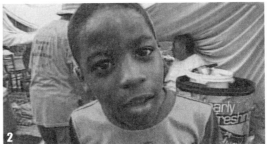

When the Levees Broke juxtaposes (1) President George W. Bush, amidst American flags, dispensing bromides, with (2) an African-American boy, amidst grim reality, offering profound and urgent insights. Ironically, (3) a dispossessed victim uses an American flag towel to keep warm and dry.

national TV, saw its own citizens — largely African-American — abandoned and sacrificed to government incompetence on every level: local, state, and national. Americans saw thousands of people suffering in the streets, surrounded by dead bodies, or waiting on rooftops for rescuers that often failed to arrive in time. Long after the New Orleans levees had failed and flooded the city, at the same time that over 20,000 flood survivors were being shown live on TV at the Ernest N. Morial Convention Center literally begging for rescue, Head of Homeland Security Michael Chertoff was surreally claiming in a live NPR interview that the federal response was "really exceptional" and that he had "not heard a report of thousands of people in the convention center [needing help]." Was there no television set or radio anywhere in Washington? It was profoundly sobering to discover that America could be one disaster away from transformation, at least temporarily, into a third-world country with neither a functioning infrastructure nor an adequate social safety net. The horror of Katrina, particularly in regard to the government's incompetence in dealing with it, has been covered extensively by the American TV networks, but especially notably by Spike Lee in his Emmy Award–winning, four-hour documentary *When the Levees Broke: A Requiem in Four Acts*, whose images are startling, horrifying, amazing, and moving.

One result of all this weather-based apocalypse was the dramatic return of the disas-

> Scientists warn that due to the increase in global warming, existing weather patterns are becoming steadily more severe; creating...

Ten years before *An Inconvenient Truth*, *Tornado!* explicitly warned that global warming could destroy even the most poetic and sylvan American way of life, as represented by this vulnerable farmhouse.

ter film, which like horror, presented images of Armageddon. There had already been *Twister* and *Tornado!*, both in 1996, which presented tornados in the Midwest (most startling was *Twister*'s image of an airborne cow); *Volcano* in 1997, which presented a newly-discovered volcano under Wilshire Boulevard erupting and transforming the Los Angeles landscape (just as the eruption of Mount St. Helens had transformed the Washington state landscape in 1980); *Dante's Peak* in 1997, also about a volcano erupting in Washington, this time near a perfect, all–American town; and *The Perfect Storm* in 2000, based on the Sebastian Junger nonfiction account of a meteorological crisis at sea off the Massachusetts coast. Although *Poseidon*, in 2006, a remake of *The Poseidon Adventure*, failed at the box office, works which presented new stories of apocalypse, particularly low-budget TV movies, did quite well.

One of the earliest of these was *10.5*, a made-for-TV miniseries presented on CBS in May of 2004, which opens with a 7.9 magnitude earthquake that destroys Seattle's iconic Space Needle. By the end of the film, after a 10.5 earthquake, huge portions of the American west coast have literally sunk into the sea. *10.5* is by no means distinguished, conforming not so much to convention as to cliché. For instance, Kim Delaney plays the female protagonist given a male first name ("Sam") obligatory for the spunky heroine that inhabits this kind of film. Perfunctory, too, are the scenes where the brilliant scientist must convince others of her theories regarding the upcoming quake. Most surreally presented is a California earthquake fissuring the exact route of railroad tracks, almost demonically chasing a moving train. And there are some startling images of being buried alive and of the collapse of the Golden Gate Bridge. Although much of *10.5* is dramatically ludicrous, its primary function was to present images of destruction in an attempt to help Americans subconsciously work out their terrors regarding the very public destruction of 9/11. In this regard, *10.5* (and other works like it) suggest the Japanese mythological horror films *Godzilla* and *Mothra*, which helped the Japanese deal with the atomic bombings of Hiroshima and Nagasaki. However, *10.5* also represents a kind of fantasy wish-fulfillment for many Americans in these polarized times, showing the "liberal left coast" literally disappearing forever and the continent reconfigured. (Yet, oddly, not a single major character dies.) Later that same year, also on CBS, came *Category 6: Day of Destruction*, another four-hour miniseries, this time about the (fictional) worst storm in American history — demolishing much of the country, particularly Las Vegas and Chicago.

By the time the Indian Ocean tsunami and Hurricane Katrina had joined 9/11 as nightmares in the American consciousness, American television was overrun with works that tried to deal with such fears. The year 2005 brought *Supervolcano*, about a fictional eruption underneath Yellowstone National Park. And 2006 brought five major weather-related works. The TV movie *10.5: Apocalypse* (a sequel to *10.5*) showed more earthquakes literally cutting the United States in two, a perfect metaphor for the polarization in contemporary America between blue-state liberals and red-state conservatives. (The most notable apocalyptic images include the collapse of the Hoover Dam, the destruction of Las Vegas, and the flooding of John Ford's beloved Monument Valley.) *Magma: Volcanic Disaster* showed increased volcanic activity around the world about to cause Armageddon if its protagonist cannot convince the world of his theories in time. *Disaster Zone: Volcano in New York* showed New York City again in the cross-hairs, as on 9/11, this time for a wildly unexpected, volcanic disaster. *The Great San Francisco Earthquake*, disaster horror about the real 1906 calamity, implicitly attempted to calm audiences by showing how even a century ago in a simpler time, America — which is still here and strong — had to deal with disaster. And the far most impressive of the lot, *Tsunami: The Aftermath*, was a docudrama miniseries shown on HBO which dealt with the apocalyptic Indian Ocean 2004 tsunami. Boasting a distinguished international cast and excellent production values more typical to a theatrical feature, *Tsunami* followed a variety of personal stories, dramatizing the massive destruction, dislocation, and death while still remaining true to its log line: "The Story of Those Who Survived."

Other TV movies, in a cheesier vein, returned to more traditional Armageddon themes. Perhaps the most representative example is *Locusts* in 2005, which also clearly shows the influence of 9/11 and offers implicit criticism of the War in Iraq as a faulty response to terrorist danger, with invading locusts standing in for the terrorists. In *Locusts*, the Department of Homeland Security must exterminate the invaders before the American population is decimated. True to contemporary, paranoid politics, the locusts are shown to have been genetically developed in an American lab (as were Iraq's weapons developed with the help of the United States when Iraq was courted as the political counter to Ayatollah Khomeini's Iran). In order to kill the locusts, the government and military are quite willing to use VX poison gas, even though this weapon of mass destruction will exert "collateral damage" and kill an ungodly number of human beings. In *Locusts*, the female characters consistently come up with better ideas; their ultimate solution requires the cooperation of all Americans *not* to use energy so that the saved electricity can be diverted to create a kind of electric fence to zap the locusts. Thus, *Locusts* criticizes the Bush energy policies as well as the administration's aggressive, go-it-alone, war strategy. *Locusts* suggests that using less energy can lead us to salvation — from the locusts, as perhaps also from Arab terrorists dependent on Middle East oil income? Finally, in 2006 came *Fatal Contact: Bird Flu in America*, which added more to paranoid Americans' storehouse of fears: the potential for viruses to mutate into virulent forms. With the new realities of the global village in the twenty-first century, not even America's two oceans would save us.

By the summer of 2006, these works about ecological disaster had reached critical mass. The country — politically hostile to environmental issues for at least a decade — was ready to give the pro-environmental argument a serious hearing. Taking a leaf from the book of the religious right, former vice president Al Gore, playing the congenial preacher calmly showing us how apocalypse will come if we don't change our ways, released *An Inconvenient Truth*, an extraordinary documentary about global warming. Based on a slide-show that Gore had been giving for well over a decade, *An Inconvenient Truth* (like the earlier *The Hellstrom Chronicle*), tries to scare us — if not to death, to political action. Based on

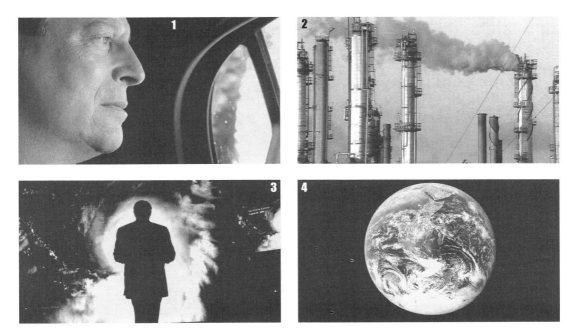

An Inconvenient Truth presents Al Gore in reverential terms: (1) as a serious, otherworldly messenger who flies over the earth (2) to point out the evils of pollution; and (3) as a moral messiah who walks toward the light and invites us to contemplate (4) an *unpolluted* earth, hurtling toward its destiny.

scientific argument and presenting clear visual proof, Gore's film is academically rigorous, yet emotionally affecting, which is probably more important. Images of the polar ice caps and the snows of Kilimanjaro melting, projections showing American land which will eventually be under water, and news footage showing recent meteorological catastrophes caused by global warming are all frighteningly persuasive. *An Inconvenient Truth* is also inherently partisan, at least subtextually revealing the environmental indifference and failures of George W. Bush and implying, wistfully, that a different 2000 election outcome could have prevented the ecological disaster that now seems almost certain to come. As of this writing, it appears that *An Inconvenient Truth* has succeeded at being one of those rare films that actually does have a direct political impact—since (at least temporarily) the controversy as to whether the science of global warming is real seems to have dissipated, with pundits and politicians now disagreeing less as to the existence of the phenomenon as to whether there are politically and economically viable ways of dealing with it. Al Gore's film worked to provide the much-needed tipping point. As some consolation to the election disaster of 2000, on the American cultural level Al Gore was rewarded when Hollywood gave *An Inconvenient Truth* the 2007 Academy Award for best documentary film of the year; even more impressively, on the international level, Al Gore was honored as the recipient of the 2007 Nobel Peace Prize for his work to end global warming.

With the specter of 9/11 hanging over the subgenre of Armageddon horror, it was only a matter of time before films took 9/11 as their explicit subject. Of course in the days after 9/11, much television was pre-empted with ongoing news coverage, not only on the destruction, but on the heartbreaking, often ironic human stories connected to the horror (such as the two best friends on their way to meet up for a vacation reunion, each friend on a dif-

In *9/11*, images of destruction become increasingly abstract, resembling experimental films of the sixties in which the film stock was directly manipulated. It's as if meaning itself has collapsed into nothingness.

ferent plane, and each plane crashing into a different World Trade Center tower, the friends reunited in their deaths). Before long, some extraordinary documentaries were released, such as the riveting *9/11* (in 2002), directed by the French brothers, Jules and Gédéon Naudet, with James Hanlon, who had been in New York City making a film about a firehouse and its crew. When the World Trade Center towers were hit and the firefighters they were covering roared into action, the film's "firehouse" subject — in one of the most extreme examples of documentary fortuity — was itself hijacked; the finished film became one of the most affecting documentaries ever.

The portraits in the documentary *9/11* are unforgettable. Even within a *vérité* context, the low angle with which the fireman is photographed lends a heroic (if tragic) dimension to his face.

The destruction of the World Trade Center towers (shown here in the film *9/11*) first required the modern technology enabling their construction. In the Iranian segment of *11'09"01, September 11*, there is so much poverty and so little technology that students must be taught about the 9/11 events using a local smokestack as a visual aid.

Siegfried Kracauer, the champion of film realism, might have been pleased, because *9/11* realizes his ideals: taking advantage of the fortuitous, the unstaged, and the indeterminate (which requires us to work to arrive at meaning); and celebrating the flow of life (and death!), with the film's subjects going on heroically despite the chaos all about.

A different kind of film, *11'09"01, September 11* (released in the United States as *September 11*), was an international co-production in which directors from 11 countries were asked to make a film about 9/11— the only requirement that each film be 11 minutes, 9 seconds, and 1 frame long. (The countries represented were Iran, France, Egypt, Bosnia, Burkina Faso, Great Britain, Mexico, Israel, India, the United States, and Japan.) With only one film from the United States (a sentimental narrative by Sean Penn), it is not surprising that

the overall sensibility of *11'09"01* is not wholly sympathetic to the United States. Although *11'09"01* was too intellectual and critical for Americans, the film is intriguing and instructive—because the shorts encompass the modes of narrative fiction, documentary, and experimental film and reflect unique personal styles. The memorable short from Claude Lelouch is a fiction film about a troubled rela-

هل نور الله يهدينا أم يعمينا؟

Does God's light guide us or blind us?

"Does God's light guide us or blind us?" The Mexican segment of *11'09"01, September 11* is a study in blacks and whites, evil and good, with an experimental black screen dominating the film. The prominent "blemish" in the abstract second image is one of the many persons who jumped from the burning World Trade Center.

tionship between a man and a deaf woman living in New York City; because the film is presented mostly from her point of view, the soundtrack is often totally silent. When the couple communicates using sign language, the fact that most of us don't know what they're saying works as a metaphor for our inability to understand the world of fundamentalist Muslims and Middle East politics. Later, after the man has gone to the World Trade Center, she composes a letter on her computer; not facing her television, she cannot see the World Trade Center destruction that is being televised as she types. Because we see these now familiar images without sound or commentary, they seem new again and acquire a grave, surreal power. The silence makes us feel as if at a wake or in church, the silence a sign of the solemn importance of the images and of our respect for the victims. The silence also allows us to be attentive to our own thoughts, forcing us to confront our feelings about 9/11. Lelouch's film ends with the man alive, returning to the apartment — shell-shocked and covered with the detritus of the towers' fall, his earlier argument with his partner now trivial.

The most powerful of the shorts is the experimental offering by Mexico's Alejandro González Iñárritu. Whereas Lelouch's film is almost entirely silent, with dense imagery, González Iñárritu's film is almost entirely a black, image-less screen, with dense sound. As the film starts, we hear faint Muslim chanting that builds in intensity. Gradually mixed in are 9/11 broadcasts, frantic phone calls, people crying and screaming, a plane crashing... Particularly in a movie theatre, this film builds to a deafening crescendo. The black screen allows us to provide our own images — to pull from our imagination the most traumatic images we remember, those that still play in our nightmares. Occasionally on the black screen we see the briefest image — flashes initially impossible to register. These images reappear, each time a bit longer, until we realize we are seeing people plummeting to their deaths after having thrown themselves from one of the towers. At the film's end, there is finally a longer image: a tower engulfed in smoke, filling the screen as it collapses. González Iñárritu's film is an invitation to nightmare — reminding us we will never forget what we saw and heard on that day. Yet González Iñárritu's film is not from a simplistic American perspective. The Arabic words we hear (and the ones we see, at the end), though inscrutable to most of us (without translation), are presented respectfully; and in the complex sound mix, we hear an appalling, if understandable, American call to avenge the attack by murdering the enemies' mothers and children. Because the film is experimental, it engages our subconscious unusually forcefully. To use Peter Wollen's "Counter-Cinema" term, González Iñárritu's film not only refuses us pleasure, but purposely causes us *unpleasure*, encapsulating the 9/11 experience in a complex, sensuous film only 11 minutes long that is utterly unforgettable.

By 2006, American audiences were arguably ready to deal with 9/11 in their mall multiplexes. Although *25th Hour* (released in 2002, directed by the socially-conscious Spike Lee, and largely ignored by the public) was at least subtextually about 9/11 and included a major scene at the Twin Towers cleanup site, *United 93* was the first theatrically-released narrative feature which took 9/11 as its story: specifically, the airliner on target to Washington, D.C., that instead crashed in a Pennsylvania field when its passengers stormed the cockpit. *United 93* is the filmic equivalent of Truman Capote's book *In Cold Blood*. Just as *In Cold Blood* made history for how it straddles the genres of novel and journalistic nonfiction, *United 93* made cinematic history for how it straddles the modes of documentary and narrative fiction. A scrupulous reconstruction of the day's events leading up to the crash, *United 93* adds little that could not be explicitly documented, although it does suggest that the

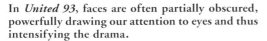

In *United 93*, faces are often partially obscured, powerfully drawing our attention to eyes and thus intensifying the drama.

Capitol building was the terrorists' Washington target, and not the White House. Half the film deals with the passengers and hijackers, the other half with ground control officials who struggle to understand what is going on and to take what meager steps they can to limit the horror. In *United 93*, we never see these characters in their lives external to the event on this fateful day. As a result, *United 93* totally lacks that made-for-TV (or disaster movie) sensibility by which characters are given the "perfect" flashback or contrived scene to economically reveal their usually simplistic psychological profile: "idealistic hero," "cold-blooded villain," "young woman with a dream," "spunky grandmother," and so on. Greengrass' characters are just people, three-dimensional in their specificity, yet without elaboration. Especially creative conceptually is that Greengrass cast dozens of real people who were part of the events of that day to play themselves, lending great authenticity to his film. Because there is not an iota of false drama, and because we know what happens but are helpless to prevent the action from playing out, *United 93* is unusually horrifying. Half documentary, half horror film, *United 93* is a rigorous, unsentimental achievement. Yet when it was released, the cable-show talking heads, newspaper columnists, and even those chatting at work around the water cooler, all asked the same question obsessively: is it too soon for this movie? Or as the perceptive syndicated columnist Leonard Pitts, Jr., wrote:

> Is it too soon for *United 93*? Is it too soon for a stark, solemn and sobering depiction of how passengers on the fourth hijacked jet of that awful morning overpowered their captors, driving their plane into the ground and sparing us what might have been the most emotionally crippling blow of all: the destruction of the U.S. Capitol.
>
> Is it too soon for that? The question vexes me.
>
> We're not talking about taste here, after all. No one has said *United 93* is a bad or exploitative movie. So the issue of whether it is "too soon" for this film clearly springs from a less high-minded concern: that it will hurt too much; that it will be too visceral a reminder of too painful a day. As director Paul Greengrass [has said], the question "is just code for 'I don't want to talk about it.' But we have to talk about it."
>
> I could not agree more.
>
> And I wonder: When did we become like this, a people too dainty for emotional heavy lifting? Where, in our lives of therapy, acquisition and entitlement, did we evolve the notion that we have a constitutional right to never feel bad? How did we become such wimps?[2]

All excellent points, I agree. But I would add another question: What does it mean that a film that deals honestly and directly with real, contemporary issues in our lives — issues which are historical, political, and emotional — should be considered worthy of comment prima-

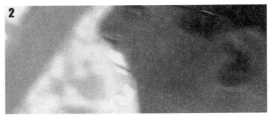

Paul Greengrass uses a variety of techniques to simulate the haphazardness of documentary in his fiction feature *United 93*. For instance, in the following images: (1) Exposure seems unprofessional, with the left side underexposed and the right side overexposed. (2) Movement so blurs the subject as to render it almost unreadable. (3) The frame is so crowded with information we must work to discern what is the significant subject.

rily as some kind of freak event we don't know how to deal with? What it means is that for too long, American films and filmmakers have abrogated their responsibilities. It means that most American filmmakers and audiences no longer understand the most basic function of art. And it means that amusement and distraction have so pervaded American culture that Americans have become incapable of serious reflection. And this last truth, in particular, is as tragic in its own way as the events of 9/11, because it suggests that we are incapable of the thoughtful attention required to pursue solutions.

Incidentally, the first film on the same subject as *United 93* was *Flight 93*, a made-for-TV movie which was broadcast three months earlier on the A&E cable network. Although effective, *Flight 93* is definitely less edgy thematically and more conventional. For instance, instead of beginning its narrative with the terrorists, it begins with the United pilot getting ready for his day, which is a more secure strategy for drawing in the mainstream TV audience and ensuring the channel not be changed. As written by Nevin Schreiner and directed by Peter Markle, *Flight 93* is more powerful than one would expect from a (low-budget) TV movie, impressing with its expressive impulses, such as the dissolve from the crash site horror to that same site several years later, where the contrasting tranquility creates a melancholy irony. Perhaps most surprising is how similar *Flight 93* is to *United 93* in its *faux* documentary style.

Later in 2006, after the publicity generated by Paul Greengrass' *United 93*, Oliver Stone released *World Trade Center*. Known for hard-hitting social dramas imbued with leftist criticism of American institutions, Stone produced a film devoid of political perspectives. Although inspired by the experiences of Port Authority officers John McLoughlin and Will Jimeno, *World Trade Center* was Stone's most benign film, and as a result, a strangely irrelevant one. Although some images are powerful, particularly a plane's huge shadow moving across a building (which recalls the cover illustration of Parker Tyler's famous book of film theory *The Shadow of an Airplane Climbs the Empire State Building*), *World Trade Center* emerges as a surprisingly sentimental film, expensively produced, but with the sensibility of a TV movie. At one point, referencing the 9/11 horror, a Stone character opines, "It looks like God made a curtain with the smoke, shielding us from what we're not ready to see." The political Stone would have forced us to see that truth, not sided with God for shielding us. *World Trade Center*—which even includes a miraculous vision of Jesus that

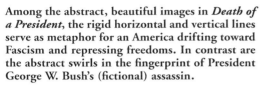

Among the abstract, beautiful images in *Death of a President*, the rigid horizontal and vertical lines serve as metaphor for an America drifting toward Fascism and repressing freedoms. In contrast are the abstract swirls in the fingerprint of President George W. Bush's (fictional) assassin.

comforts a trapped policeman — employs a Copland-esque score that celebrates America and emphasizes faith, hope, and patriotism. By so emphasizing the physical procedures of the rescue, Stone's film becomes tedious, and the complex moral meanings of 9/11 totally recede: the rescue dramatized in *World Trade Center* could have just as easily been for a mine disaster, so apolitical is Stone's effort, so generic to the action-adventure film. It is ironic that the other 9/11 films created that year by "lesser" directors were more vital, political, controversial, and creative than Stone's film.

For instance, *The Path to 9/11*, a TV miniseries based in part on the 9/11 Commission report, was a dense docudrama as fast-moving as a Costa-Gavras film, clearly one of its models. More political thriller than horror, but with elements of the horror of Armageddon, *The Path to 9/11* reveals the disturbing behind-the-scenes realities leading up to the 2001 terrorist attack on America. The pseudo-documentary style of the miniseries, not dissimilar to *United 93*, uses hand-held camera, selective focus, and rapid editing and storytelling. Although its publicity campaign emphasized its documentary nature, *The Path to 9/11* is filled with many more fictionalized imaginings than *United 93*, such as a scene showing a policeman about to apprehend a terrorist on the street, but to our surprise going after a homeless man sleeping *behind* the terrorist. Directed by David L. Cunningham and produced by the politically conservative Iranian expatriate Cyrus Nowrasteh, *The Path to 9/11* had its own political agenda: to counter the constant criticism of Bush's Republican administration within the media and popular culture by ascribing significant blame for 9/11 to Clinton's Democratic administration, particularly Secretary of State Madeleine Albright.

In opposition to the right-wing slant of *The Path to 9/11* came the left-wing slant of the British *Death of a President*, which drew upon the style of Peter Watkins' *The War Game* to offer a *faux* documentary on political events which have not taken place — in this case, the assassination of George W. Bush as a result of international political fallout relating to 9/11 and the War in Iraq. Directed by Gabriel Range, *Death of a President* was understandably controversial and attacked by the political right. Although the film is thoughtful, politically savvy, more even-handed toward Bush than one might expect, and surprising in its forecast regarding the assassination's aftermath, it is undeniable that this film drew progres-

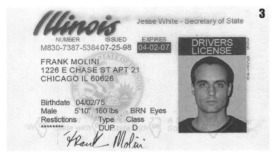

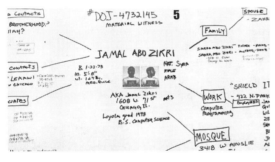

The *faux* documentary *Death of a President* blurs the lines between what is real and what is not. (1) Is the anti–Bush political demonstration real? Fictional? Computer-enhanced? Note (2) the familiar network news desk, with its anchors looking appropriately sober, (3) the persuasively real driver's license of the suspect, (4) the assassination moment captured in a *vérité*, Pulitzer Prize style, (5) the hand-drawn flow chart regarding the suspect, (6) the glare of lights on the real Dick Cheney, looking scary as he fictionally becomes president. And especially notable: image 7. Another demonstration advertises a website — www.worldcantwait. org — which long after the film's release connected viewers to a political action group agitating for the end of the Bush presidency and the Iraq War.

sive audiences who were appalled by Bush, the Patriot Act, and the War in Iraq, and pleased to be offered the wish-fulfilling fantasy of the premature end of the Bush presidency by whatever means necessary. Indeed, before Bush left office, his unpopularity reached an all-time low for modern American presidents, a circumstance that *Death of a President* inherently anticipated. In the fictional extrapolations of this film, George W. Bush's assassination took place on October 19, 2007, and as a result, the "US Patriot Act III" was passed and made permanent, a law which "granted investigators unprecedented powers of detention and surveillance, and further expanded the powers of the executive branch." Incidentally, at least two national theatre chains — Regal and Cinemark — refused to play the film, ostensibly fearing it might provoke an assassination attempt, but more likely fearing it might provoke offended audiences to initiate long-term boycotts of the chains' theatres. As well, a variety of outlets, including the CNN cable network, refused to run commercials for the film.

Other recent films in the Armageddon subgenre, if not dealing directly with the events of 9/11, have been nevertheless influenced by the geo-political aftermath of these events. In fact, the conflation of 9/11 issues with the War in Iraq resulted in an interest in all things apocalyptic. One unusual example is the release on DVD (in 2006, 2007, and 2008) of several different editions of *Nazi Concentration Camps: Official Allied Forces Film Record of Nazi Death Camps*, a compilation of footage originally taken in 1945 by soldiers who were liberating the camps. Edited originally by filmmaker George Stevens, this film record was subsequently used in the Nuremberg Trials. Its gruesome and horrific images — including torture chambers, severed body parts, and thousands of emaciated bodies exhumed from mass graves — once again, in a post–9/11 culture, seemed relevant. Another example is the 2007 release of the powerful documentary *White Light, Black Rain: The Destruction of Hiroshima and Nagasaki*, which begins with a title card announcing: "The American government suppressed photographs and film footage depicting the aftermath of the bombings for twenty-five years." Although this documentary is riveting *vis-à-vis* its subject, the way the title card questions the American government's secrecy draws attention to the now

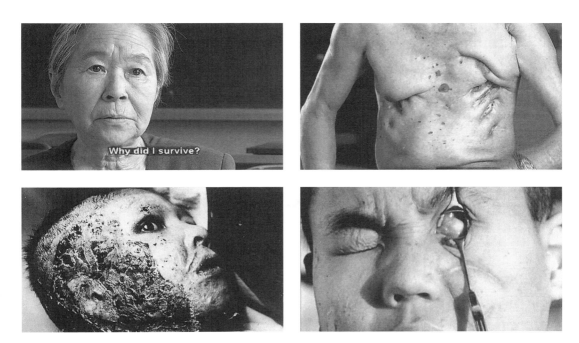

"Why did I survive?" asks an actual atomic bomb survivor. Although *White Light/Black Rain* presents documentary evidence from Hiroshima/Nagasaki, many of its images look straight out of a David Cronenberg horror film.

well-documented suppression of material by George W. Bush's administration in order to build support for the War in Iraq and discourage any belief that Bush incompetence contributed to 9/11. Director Steven Okazaki suggested as much in an August 1, 2007, internet interview at twitchfilm.net where he said that "Had we made the film and released it earlier, we perhaps would have had more of the reaction of people just reflecting back. Certainly with the war we're in now and the insecurity of potential nuclear weapons in the hands of North Korea or Mideast terrorists and with 9/11, people will look at the film very differently and connect it to the future. 9/11 certainly gives the film a different read and unfortunately, yeah, while we were making the film there seemed to be a story every other week in the paper connecting to some aspect of it." In other words, 9/11 made old apocalypse new again.

Other films influenced by the geo-political aftermath of 9/11 were decidedly fictional, particularly those films which show death and the dead proliferating as the world is attacked by zombies (*28 Days Later...*, *Shaun of the Dead*, and *Land of the Dead*) or by aliens from other planets (*The Forgotten* and *War of the Worlds*). *28 Days Later...*, directed by *Trainspotting*'s Danny Boyle and released in the United States in 2003, starts with news footage of war and atrocities being broadcast on monitors in front of a shackled, laboratory ape. Other apes undergoing their own ordeals are in cages. When animal rights activists break into the facility, they ignore the implications of freeing the animals, which have been infected with a virus called "Rage" that is now deadly for humans as well. With a shocking suddenness, the released chimps attack; immediately, there is pandemonium, blood everywhere, ape-to-human transmission of virus, and human beings who are now monsters, out of control and infected with "Rage." Before we have the chance to take stock of everything that's happening, a title card reveals that it is "28 days later..."—and we are thrust into an apocalyptic

world where almost all human beings have already died horribly. Of course it is ironic that the progressive, radical politics of the activists should be responsible for bringing *Homo sapiens* to near extinction. Incidentally, the "Rage" virus clearly seems an (even more virulent) evocation of the AIDS virus (HIV), which had its own probable roots in simian virus that mutated efficiently to attack its millions of human targets.

Images of apocalypse in *28 Days Later*: (1) a discarded newspaper announcing disaster; (2) silhouetted figures in the darkness (refugees? looters? survivors? mutants?); and (3) distorted reflections of catastrophe, surreally suggesting confusion and dislocation.

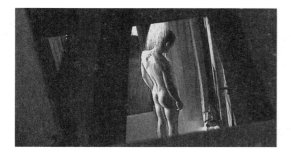

The major characters in *28 Days Later* are archetypal: Jim (Cillian Murphy), who is several times shown naked to identify him as a new Adam; Selena (Naomie Harris), who becomes his Eve; and the Major (Christopher Eccleston), a military man who believes he is heading off apocalypse, but is actually a devil who is one with nature only with the masquerade of his khakis.

After the title card, we meet our protagonist Jim, a bicycle courier shown naked and medically attached to a hospital bed (an image which recalls the shackled ape earlier). Awakening from a month-long coma and unaware of what has happened, Jim exits the deserted hospital to discover the London streets are deserted, too, though with signs of social cataclysm everywhere. On an errant newspaper, we see the words "Evacuation" and "Global Chaos"; on a large, external wall, we see the publicly posted messages so common to many social dislocations. Sadly, it seems that those who have posted the messages are now as dead as those who had been looked for. It is wryly ironic that the first infected person we see is a priest: violent, diseased, dying, filled with rage, wanting to infect others, a monster. Another notable *frisson* is provided by thousands of rats, themselves terrified, running from the attacking infected. After meeting Selena and Mark, two fellow survivors, Jim is shocked when Mark, bitten by an infected, is immediately killed by Selena to prevent him from attacking. Clearly, *28 Days Later...* is suggesting that in an apocalypse (whether caused by virus, ecological disaster, terrorism, or war), loyalty will be a luxury difficult to retain.

Throughout *28 Days Later...*, we see horrifying images of the monstrous infected, who move, with the help of special effects, in a jerky, fast-motion, stroboscopic style. We also see mounds of corpses littering the deserted urban landscapes. *28 Days Later...* recalls 1959's *The World, the Flesh, and the Devil*, since both gain considerable power from the surreal beauty of their desolate cities. At the center of *28 Days Later...* is the developing interracial love story between Jim, who is white, and Selena, who is black. (*The World, the Flesh, and the Devil* also contained interracial romance — though there, the woman was white, played by Inger Stevens, and the man was black, played by Harry Belafonte.) Central to *28 Days Later...*, too, is the need to make human connections and to work together, particularly since there is always more danger when people separate physically. The film's most horrifying moment may be when the rather lovable Frank, a fellow survivor traveling with his daughter Hannah, wanders off on his own, and we watch the inevitable flight of one drop of blood that falls from high above him to enter his eye and infect him. As much as any recent horror-of-Armageddon film, in regard to this need for communion and coop-

Water and wind in ***28 Days Later***: (1) The hundreds of mismatched containers to catch rain water suggest social chaos. (2) Post-apocalypse, curves and angles on a windy road suggest a world that has become contorted, unbalanced.

eration as part of the human condition, *28 Days Later...* emulates *The Birds* and *Night of the Living Dead*. In fact, just as the protagonist Melanie Daniels in *The Birds* turns to fellow survivor Lydia to be her substitute mother, the protagonist Jim in *28 Days Later...* turns to fellow survivor Frank to be his substitute father. This is most clear in a moving scene where Jim unconsciously calls Frank "Dad" when Frank comforts him during a nightmare.

With London deserted, Manchester on fire, and worldwide civilization imperiled, it is not clear where our protagonists should go. They end up at a small military compound (devoid of women), where there are opposing views as to what "normal" means in the context of apocalyptic chaos. The Sergeant contends that since for most of the history of earth, human beings were not on it, it is more normal for the earth to exist *without* people than *with* them. The Major's position is no more optimistic; he contends that since the Rage infection, normal has meant "people killing people," but he also notes that this was true before the Rage infection. These viewpoints, offered by opposing characters, are both profoundly cynical and suggest that since killing is normal for human beings, we deserve to be banished from the earth. The British military men enjoy killing the infected a little too avidly; in their sexism, violence, and attempts to rape Selena, these men — totally crazed, if not technically crazy — emerge as greater threats to our protagonists than are the infected. Key to the pragmatic values of the film is the scene in which Jim frees a shackled infected to help fight against the sociopathic military. In the final *Walpurgisnacht* of horror, the besieged outpost is attacked by the proliferating infected, a climax which conforms to the conventions established by the final besiegements in *The Birds* and *Night of the Living Dead* (and thus revealing the centrality of those masterpieces to the Armageddon subgenre). Our protagonist Jim becomes such a savage killing machine that he is virtually indistinguishable from the infected; if that isn't disturbing enough, he is almost mistakenly killed as an infected by Selena.

Just as *28 Days Later...* used an ellipsis at the beginning, it uses an ellipsis at the end, again with a title card indicating the narrative has jumped "28 days later..." Now we see Jim and Selena (a new Adam and Eve?), with the young Hannah who has become a kind of adopted daughter, the three of them reconstituted as a nontraditional family in an oddly verdant valley. But this family is interracial, includes a nonbiological child, and is not cemented by marriage. (How could they be married? The priest we saw was a monster, not a sanctifier.) This new landscape seems more benign than the earlier landscapes. Surprisingly for contemporary horror film, *28 Days Later...* ends (if ambiguously) with the hopeful possibility that there is thriving life elsewhere and that this new family is about to be rescued. A plane streaks across the sky and gives a sign which suggests its pilot has recognized in the landscape Jim and Selena's huge message, stitched together from sheets. Notably, the last letter added to the message transforms the word "HELL" into the greeting "HELLO," which suggests the surprising displacement of the bleak nihilism of *28 Days Later...* by something more hopeful.

Shaun of the Dead, also a British film and with a similar subject, was released the very next year, in 2004. Directed by Edgar Wright, *Shaun of the Dead* is a satirical remake of *Night of the Living Dead*, but pitched so perfectly that its mordant comedy never interferes with its genuine pathos. The film is filled with quirky little shocks, including sudden close-ups and insistent musical punctuation. At the beginning of the film, the characters we see dressed similarly to each other in their boring jobs and their regular lives resemble the dead: they move in robotic unison. Are they only metaphorically dead, or are they literally *already* zombie monsters? One disturbing, funny conceit is that the protagonist, Shaun, is surrounded by living dead long before he realizes it — for instance, when he mistakes a zombie attacking a victim for a necking couple, or when he slips on blood from a zombie attack without realizing that it's blood. The satirical point is that we have become distanced from the reality of our own lives. We have stopped paying attention, as had much of the Western world before the 9/11 attacks. One character professes anger at a roommate: "The next time I see him, he's dead." Of course, that roommate is destined to become a living dead. We discover that removing the head (shades of decapitation by Iraqi insurgents and terrorists?) or destroying the brain can kill the zombies. In one horrifying scene, also comic, two roommates beat two zombies to death, smashing their heads with gardening tools until the roommates are covered in blood. So is it the dead or is it us, the film asks, who are actually more bloodthirsty?

Shaun of the Dead was clearly made for cinephiles and intellectuals, with many smart references. It even quotes Bertrand Russell: "The only thing that can redeem mankind is cooperation." Cinematically interesting is a scene clearly referring to the German film *Run, Lola, Run*, that shows three potential realities. And a clever image of Shaun taken through

Shaun of the Dead effectively works in two genres. The casting, costumes, and relatively flat, even lighting of these first two images suggest a slacker comedy, whereas the atmospheric lighting and dramatic shadows of the last two images suggest a traditional horror film.

a large circular hole in a zombie's body oddly refers to a similar shot in the Meryl Streep/ Goldie Hawn comedy *Death Becomes Her*. In one witty sequence, five characters going one direction to escape zombies pass by five escaping characters going the opposite direction; parallel compositions and editing emphasize the man from each group who is obsessed with his cellphone, despite the "coming apocalypse." Yet *Shaun of the Dead* is also surprisingly insightful and depicts relationships with great emotional resonance. And the film has empathy for the zombies: "Look at the face — vacant, with a hint of sadness." Not incidentally, that description would also apply to the British working class that Lindsay Anderson photographed at an amusement park in his influential social documentary *O Dreamland*. Making somewhat the same point more explicitly is the plot device whereby the protagonists escape the zombies by pretending to be zombies. At another point, Shaun gets hundreds of dead to leave his friends alone by standing above the zombies and appealing to them to follow him. It is easy to recognize the scene as a political metaphor: Tony Blair or George W. Bush leading their countries of unthinking zombies in the "War on Terror." To the film's misguided "living" characters, perhaps the most telling sign of the apocalypse is that every TV station goes off the air, including Bravo and MTV. There is an emotional climax after Shaun's mom is bitten by a zombie and says, with traditional British understatement as she dies, "It's been a funny sort of day, hasn't it?" Although the line is comic, it is so casual as to be very moving, too. When she comes back to life as a zombie, Shaun won't let his friend David kill her, despite the danger she now poses. David tells Shaun, "For a hero, you're quite a hypocrite." But then Shaun himself kills his zombie mother, an emotionally difficult act.

The climactic siege takes place at night at the pub, where David is torn apart by the dead, and the rest of the protagonists use David's detached legs as weapons. Shaun's leadership choice — to have taken his friends to the pub for safety — is as terrible as the protagonist's leadership choice in the original *Night of the Living Dead*. When Shaun, driven to his emotional limit by the amoral actions he's had to take, says, "I don't think I have it within me to shoot my flat-mate, my mom, and my girlfriend all in the same evening," his girlfriend quibbles semantically: why does he presume that she still considers herself to be his girlfriend? Like Mary in *Mary Hartman, Mary Hartman*, the characters here are hilariously out of touch with the most immediate, important realities in their lives. Ironically, six months later, the zombies have been more-or-less contained and life goes on, as everyone adjusts to a new reality. There is the charity Zomb-Aid, TV shows with zombies, and talk shows with people who are married to zombies. The zombie apocalypse — like the ongoing "War on Terror" — becomes, essentially, just one more channel of information that we must learn to live with in the twenty-first century.

Land of the Dead, in 2005, represents director George A. Romero's fourth installment of his zombie mythology, an even more explicit allegory than the previous installments. The dead — the enemies of the civilized world — have overtaken most of humanity. What is left of society largely lives within a walled city — with the rich in affluent splendor in Fiddler's Green, a luxury skyscraper complex that can accommodate every whim, and the poor left to scrape by in the street, in shantytowns. The name "Fiddler's Green" recalls the emperor Nero, who fiddled while Rome burned and was oblivious to the suffering of others. In *Land of the Dead*, as in the United States, society is polarized economically, with the gap between the rich and the poor having ever more severe political implications. The film is clearly suggesting that George W. Bush's America is on a path to similar disaster: exacerbating class problems are the Bush tax cuts for the richest Americans, the criminal failure of Enron and hence corporate America, the lack of health insurance and equal access to quality health care, and so forth. And the gaps between the rich and poor in America mirror the gaps between the Western, industrialized world, with its materialist values, and the rest of the world. The cautionary power of this allegory is how destructively the society of the living divides itself into classes who fight among each other, rather than pull together to fight the real enemy: the dead. And the dead (like al-Qaeda?) are evolving as they amass more power. The real villain of the film is Mr. Kaufman, the capitalist businessman who leads the affluent humans and expects his rich constituency to be served. He sees the world in unambiguous terms: the zombies are a kind of Axis of Evil, and yet an Axis that can be exploited, just as the poor can be exploited to work as mercenaries, expected to go outside the walled city to forage for supplies for Kaufman — supplies representing Mideast oil? Kaufman is intransigent regarding the social structure of this society. "We don't negotiate with terrorists," he declares, and he will allow neither the poor nor the dead into Fiddler's Green, even though he expects the poor to sacrifice their lives (just as soldiers in the War in Iraq are sacrificing), so the rich can live well and have access to their profits. Not only are the poor about to revolt against the rich, but the dead are evolving, growing a greater consciousness and the ability to plan. Whereas an African American was the leader of the survivors in Romero's first *Night of the Living Dead*, here an African American is the leader of the dead — a kind of zombie Che Guevara about to understand his potential. Romero's zombies seem increasingly human, just as his rich humans, with their sense of entitlement and smug superiority, seem increasingly inhuman. And so Romero is clearly suggesting that the United States, unless it changes its policies, will face its own destruction from revolution by the poor or from an apocalypse brought about by terrorists.

The Forgotten, directed by Joseph Ruben and released in October of 2004, right before the presidential contest between George W. Bush and John Kerry, is less overtly a political allegory than *Land of the Dead*. In *The Forgotten*, Julianne Moore plays Telly, a woman unable to stop mourning for her young son Sam, killed in a plane crash. But before long, all signs of Sam's existence are disappearing: newspaper accounts of his death, photographs, mementos. Even those who should remember him no longer do. Almost immediately the question becomes: Is Telly a psychotic, delusional woman, or is there a

In *The Forgotten*, Telly (Julianne Moore) is photographed in soft-focus images using telephoto lenses, an artistic choice which suggests that she (like her son, like all of us) will eventually become a hazy memory and then: forgotten.

diabolical plot against her? Did her child actually exist or not? For the longest time, we see no independent corroboration which allows us to know, definitively, whether we can trust her; and *The Forgotten* is filled with beautiful images of the melancholy Julianne Moore which are photographed with telephoto lenses that blur the backgrounds as her world becomes stranger and stranger; accordingly, our own uncertainty, our haziness, grows. Especially strong are the many expressive images of Moore in her neighborhood playground, sitting on the swings. Significantly, the playground contains several geodesic jungle gyms, particularly suggestive of the otherworldly plot that is revealed at the film's end.

Joseph Ruben is a director well-versed in both the horror and thriller genres. Like his

The Stepfather, which was a reworking of Hitchcock's *Shadow of a Doubt*, *The Forgotten* is a partial reworking of *Rosemary's Baby*, with Telly much like Rosemary struggling to protect her child against a vast conspiracy she cannot understand. Telly's husband is played by the so-trustable Anthony Edwards — so how could he be part of the conspiracy? And her therapist, played by Gary Sinise, who readily reminds us of the kindly young doctor in *Rose-*

A striking special effect in *The Forgotten* works as a narrative turning point and a beautiful metaphor for forgetting. The effect is powerful precisely because it is one of the film's few effects and in no way dramatically gratuitous.

mary's Baby played by Charles Grodin, turns out to be just as untrustworthy. Yet because Telly, like the governess in *The Innocents*, may be suffering a kind of hysteria, perhaps we really shouldn't automatically accept her version of reality. Tellingly, *The Forgotten* also references a 1955 TV episode of *Alfred Hitchcock Presents* in which the protagonist (played by Patricia Hitchcock, Hitchcock's daughter), loses her sister while they are both traveling to Paris and is unable to prove that she really existed in the first place. In Hitchcock's TV episode, the conspiracy is government-created to prevent economic disaster for the Paris World Exposition by suppressing the news that plague has claimed the sister.

As *The Forgotten* develops, its political subtext becomes more explicit. Telly says to a fellow parent who she believes has also lost a child: "Our children have been forgotten!" Her plaint becomes a political metaphor, particularly when Telly, warmly compassionate, is juxtaposed with the government officials, cold and unfeeling, that she has been appealing to. Yet the film's surprise ending creates monsters even colder: outer space creatures who have been visiting earth for centuries and performing experiments. Their current experiment is to test the strength of the mother/child bond by attempting to destroy it. The outer space creature — a well-dressed man in a suit — screams at Telly: "There are worse things than forgetting! You need to forget!" In other words, this creature, working with the NSA (the National Security Agency of the U.S. government's Department of Defense) wants us to learn not to care, wants us to lose our compassion. Although the government is powerless to stop the experiments, it is also unwilling to try; and so the film becomes a metaphor for unfeeling bureaucracy. Cutting welfare? Defunding schools? Working against universal health insurance for children? Cutting after-school programs to fund tax-cuts? "Our children have been forgotten!" And as an added bonus: if people learn not to care, government can become even stronger and do whatever it wants with absolute impunity. Although Telly wins back her son — who is not dead after all, neither she nor we have any confidence that the soulless cabal who runs the world — with the secret support of the United States government — can be overcome. And because the aliens have mastered the ability to make us believe whatever they program us to believe, we will soon have no objective understanding of reality at all — and certainly not of the political realities of our own time.

The Forgotten includes some especially startling scenes, such as an extraordinary collision where a car we see through the side window of Telly's car seems to slam directly into her, and by extension, into us — all in one shocking, continuous shot. Another scene starts with Telly exploring a deserted house in Long Island on a beautiful afternoon filled with the sound of seagulls. Suddenly, she senses a disquiet as the wind rises and a curtain flutters, and we sense, too: "They're in the house with us." Although at that moment we see nothing more, we experience a *frisson* of foreboding. The startling event associated with Telly's intuition takes place shortly thereafter, when with shocking suddenness, the kind policewoman who believes Telly's story is suddenly catapulted up into the sky and away into the oblivion of the cosmos — all in an instant, gone. The moment is horrifying, certainly, but strangely transcendent as well, because we realize, definitively, that Telly is not crazy and that there are powerful, fantastical forces all around her (and us?), secretly controlling things.

Another Armageddon film worthy of discussion is *War of the Worlds*, remade by Steven Spielberg in 2005. When H. G. Wells wrote the original 1898 novel *The War of the Worlds*, set in London, he was inherently attacking the concept of empire, with the British discovering a power — the Martians — greater than their own. Orson Welles' 1938 radio broadcast of *The War of the Worlds* effortlessly played upon Americans' brewing fears, on the eve of World War II, of Fascist attack. The 1953 movie version, produced by George Pal and directed by

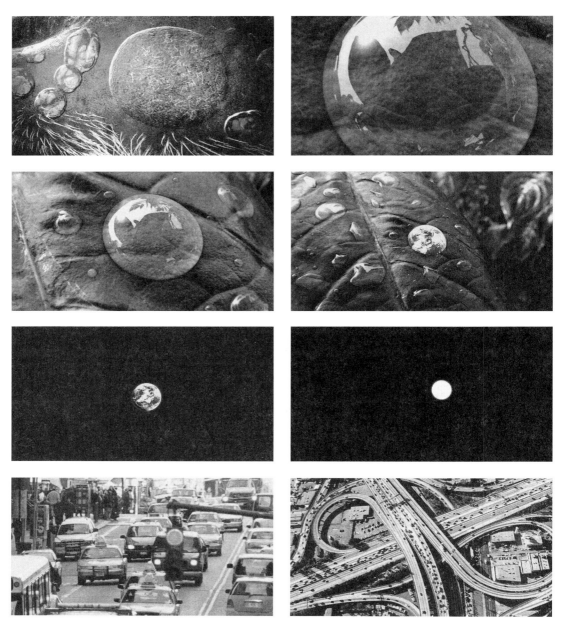

Spielberg's technical proficiency, often taken for granted, is present in the opening sequence of *War of the Worlds*, where camera movement and editing based on tonal montage emphasizes the circle: cellular bacteria, a drop of water, the earth from the moon, the moon from the earth, the red light of a traffic signal at rush hour, and finally, a freeway cloverleaf exchange symbolizing all of civilization.

Byron Haskin, emerged out of atomic bomb fears, showing the United States — which had exploded these bombs on Japan — what it felt like to be on the receiving end of awesome power. Spielberg's *War of the Worlds*, released in the summer of 2005, must be seen in the context of the "War on Terror" and its conflation with the War in Iraq. *War of the Worlds* begins with microscopic cells, and then the camera pulls back to show a drop of water, and then even further back to show our planet, as a sober narrator announces that the earth has

War of the Worlds is filled with visual references to 9/11, including (1) an information board dedicated to the missing and the dead, (2) a crashed plane, and (3) city residents fleeing from catastrophe.

been studied for attack. It is hard for a contemporary audience not to think immediately of the 9/11 attacks, planned by Osama bin Laden after careful study. The attack by Martians comes quickly in the film; a church, tellingly, is one of the first things they destroy. Spielberg's scenes of destruction are enormously persuasive and scary, and the images of crowds who alternately watch in awe and run terrified through the streets evoke the parallel actions of real New Yorkers on 9/11. The connection is made explicit when Rachel (played by Dakota Fanning), asks her father Ray (played by Tom Cruise): "Is it the terrorists?" When Ray tells her "No, it came from someplace else," she responds: "You mean, like Europe?" On one level, her response is endearing; on another, it reveals that Americans, even precocious children, know little about the rest of the world.

The attack of the Martian "tripods"—spider-like adversaries hundreds of feet tall, with eerie, eel-like appendages—is devastating. The tripods uproot streets, buildings, and bridges, which all collapse. Terrifyingly, the tripods "disintegrate" people, tearing limbs into odd pieces that explode and dissolve into the air. One expertly-realized scene shows the aftermath of a jumbo jet crash and its acres of debris, a clear parallel to the 9/11 crash of United flight 93. As after 9/11, the survivors here create walls of photographs showing their missing relatives. The images of violence and destruction are among the most beautiful of Spielberg's career; especially surreal is an image of hundreds of bodies reflecting glints of sun as they float down a river. Almost immediately, the alien attack provokes conflict among the terrified survivors, who often turn on each other, creating a culture of polarization. Eventually we understand that the tripods are not actually the aliens, but their weaponized vehicles, which had been hidden underground. The aliens, who look like reptilian spiders, have waited patiently, like terrorist sleeper cells, till the best moment to attack. And because the aliens drink blood and then spray it back out, the landscapes are bathed in blood. The recording we hear of Tony Bennett singing "If I Ruled the World" is definitely ironic, for any idea of American interests ruling the world is undermined by the Martians (or by inference, by Muslim terrorists).

Like Hitchcock's *The Birds*, *War of the Worlds* is a series of action set pieces alternating with scenes of interpersonal discord that raise questions about the family. If *The Birds*

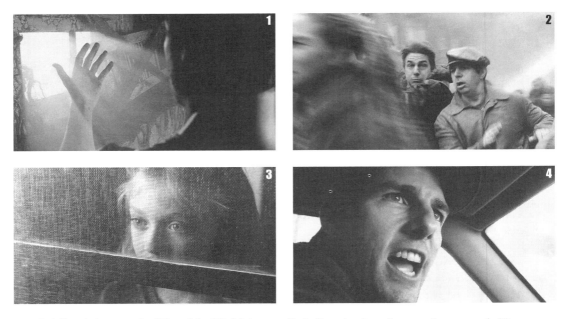

Spielberg's imagery in *War of the Worlds* is as stylistically eclectic and expressive as usual: (1) a person poetically informed by strong backlight, (2) a blurry image evoking *cinéma vérité*, purposely haphazard and unbalanced, (3) a nuanced, textured portrait (Dakota Fanning behind a screen door), and (4) a conventional, unadorned low-angle shot of a strong-jawed hero (Tom Cruise).

explores the need to connect, *War of the Worlds* explores the need to let go, as Ray must his son, who feels the need to fight in the new militia and establish his own identity. The most disturbing scene is one that Spielberg doesn't let us see directly — when Ray, our hero, kills an innocent man to ensure that Ray's daughter will remain safe. Ray's ethically suspect action raises questions regarding post–9/11 America. Should the United States take ethically suspect actions — commit murder, torture prisoners, bomb innocent civilians — to indirectly safeguard Americans? Does the end ever justify the means? Are the lives of "our" people more valuable than the lives of "their" people? And if we answer *yes*, are we guilty of the worst kind of racist thinking? The man Ray kills (played by actor Tim Robbins, famed Hollywood activist) knows that the aliens' attempt to occupy the earth will fail, because "Occupations always fail." That line, combined with the earlier detail of Ray's son writing a term paper on the French occupation of Algeria, are clear, critical comments about the American occupation of Iraq.

    Throughout the film, the family's goal is to reach Boston — a city which has always been a potent symbol of American culture and education. *War of the Worlds* ends with the reunion of all family members safe and sound — including even Gene Barry and Ann Robinson, the lead actors in the 1953 *The War of the Worlds,* who make last-minute, welcome cameos as the family grandparents. Full circle, *War of the Worlds* ends with a return to the universe within a drop of water — including an image of the bacteria which ultimately kills the Martians. Although *War of the Worlds* is emotionally effective, particularly in how it connects to the emotional trauma suffered on 9/11, Spielberg directs the tripods and special effects more persuasively than some of his actors. The father/son conflict seems obligatory, rather than authentically integral; and the "happy" ending for the family is less persuasive as drama than as strategy designed to attract box office — toadying to the teen audience which gets to enjoy the rash rebellion of Ray's heartthrob son, without either the son or the audience suffering any consequence. The film may start as an emulation of 9/11, but it moves toward an emulation of the military conflict in Iraq, but with no one we really care about being critically injured or killed. Most alarmingly, *War of the Worlds* ignores the moral consequences of the murder that Ray commits. Instead, by film's end, Ray is relatively happy and safe, his conscience untroubled, his actions justified by the fact that everything he did was for his family — "the family" increasingly the justification in America for virtually every political position, particularly by the political right. Sadly, Spielberg may have his finger on the American pulse, since from September 11, 2001, until, arguably, the 2006 congressional elections — which seemed to indicate, finally, some political reservations — the majority of Americans have hardly been troubled by the actions taken by their government, from Abu Ghraib to Guantanamo. And that is certainly a kind of horror, too.

By the end of 2006 — with the War in Iraq increasingly perceived as an all-out disaster; with the number of American soldiers killed and maimed escalating dramatically; with Iraq involved in what even conservative American news broadcasters were finally calling a civil war; with thousands of Iraqi casualties inflicted by a panoply of al-Qaeda, Shiites, Sunnis, and miscellaneous factions and insurgents; with North Korea conducting nuclear tests and rattling its sabers; with soldiers in the Sudan committing genocide in Darfur; with enmity in the Middle East having created a second Israeli-Lebanon War; with Iran pushing forward in its development of a nuclear bomb; with George W. Bush's popularity sinking lower and lower; with more of Bush's men (including Secretary of Defense Donald Rumsfeld) forced to quit under clouds of scandal or incompetence, undermining confidence in democracy itself; and with freakishly murderous storms and weather patterns appearing to support the most extreme predictions of ecological disaster from global warming — *Children of Men*, a masterwork of Armageddon horror which seems to reflect all these things and more, was released to international acclaim. The film's production design and cinematography are nothing short of brilliant; and although on some level we are aware that special effects are involved, *Children of Men* does not seem to be a special effects film *per se*, because the film's moral and human sensibilities are so powerfully disturbing and connect to our contemporary fears.

Directed by the Mexican director of *Y Tu Mamá También*, Alfonso Cuarón, *Children of Men* was based on the 1992 novel by P. D. James, but updated to a 2006 sensibility. The film, set in 2027 but credibly postulating the logical consequences of today's political events, establishes the horrifying milieu of its world immediately. We see a news report on British Homeland Security, which is in continual crisis mode as "only Britain soldiers on" in a world whose economy has collapsed. When a terrorist bomb goes off in the London streets, it is a commonplace. Because virtually every other major city in the world has been significantly destroyed, the London streets are filled with illegal immigrants, many being rounded up and shipped off to camps, like livestock. A great number are from Africa, whose continent has been devastated by nuclear fallout. Especially unsettling and unique to this film: after eighteen years of mysterious, worldwide infertility, the last child born, in 2009, has died, setting off an international panic. Strange cults are flourishing, including the "renouncers" and the "repeters"; and fundamentalist protestors carry placards reading "Infertility is God's punishment." In a darkly witty detail emblematic of this film's insightful creativity, a top-selling consumer item in this anxious world is "Quietus," a slickly-packaged suicide potion. At one point, refugees are given masked hoods which recall the hoods that Americans put on Iraqis in Abu Ghraib before torturing them. Certainly, both terror-

Children of Men quotes artistic and religious imagery: (1) Picasso's *Guernica*, as a symbol of apocalyptic war, juxtaposed with Theo (Clive Owen); (2) Michelangelo's damaged *David* as a symbol of the death of Renaissance reason and hope; (3) a contemporary *Pietà*, recreated spontaneously on the street; and (4) a new Virgin Mary, about to give birth to a messiah in a humble barn.

ism and ecological disaster have led to precipitous catastrophe; in *Children of Men*, just as in *28 Days Later...*, the survival of *Homo sapiens* is in grave danger. And if no one is left to inherit culture or civilization, what is the point of going on? And why should we *not* behave badly?

A disturbing image of a damaged Michelangelo's *David*—the Renaissance sculpture symbolic of the triumph of reason over brute strength and chaos—becomes the perfect metaphor for contemporary decline. Relevant, too, is the violence depicted in Picasso's *Guernica*, which is displayed prominently in another key scene. Although we discover that Michelangelo's *Pietà* was destroyed (a destruction relevant for an infertile world where there are no more new mothers), we later see a real Pietà: a mother cradling her dead adult son on the street. One especially terrific scene shows the protagonist Theo as a passenger in a car with his ex-wife and her colleagues as they drive along a wooded highway. The scene starts out as light comedy banter between Theo and his ex, and then, with great suddenness, their car is attacked by a roving gang which swarms out of the woods. The mood switches instantly to adrenalin-pumped excitement, then to fear, then to frantic horror, and then to disbelief and desperation, as their car is set on fire, guns are drawn, and shocking violence changes these characters

In the horror-of-Armageddon fifties film, the most consistent message was "Watch the skies." In 2006's *Children of Men*, the message is "Watch the TV"—which becomes a communal experience.

Children of Men contains beautiful, but melancholy images. (1) What is the point of a swing set, if no children will be born to enjoy it? (2) And what is the point of nature itself if no humans will be left alive to be part of it?

forever — and all of this in an astonishing long take lasting well over four minutes, as the camera executes its choreography, re-framing and re-focusing with absolute precision from a perspective inside the maneuvering car. Cuarón makes us feel as if we're in Iraq, and we viscerally understand what it means to live in a war zone. When Theo's ex-wife, played by Julianne Moore, the biggest star in *Children of Men*, dies in this attack, she is precipitously removed from the narrative as strikingly as was Janet Leigh's character in *Psycho*.

The key plot point in *Children of Men* is the revelation that a young black immigrant has mysteriously become pregnant. "Jesus Christ," says Theo, genuinely moved; we almost wonder whether the baby might be a new Christ. With a great Christian resonance, the immigrant reveals her pregnant nakedness in a barn, surrounded by straw. It is notable, too, that she reveals herself to Theo, whose names signifies "God." Is it Theo's job in this new world to "play" God and secure a future for mankind? Certainly *Children of Men*'s allegory becomes increasingly religious. Will the baby be born or not? Because the birth will confer political power, many people want the child dead or want access to the pregnant mother for their own purposes. As a result, the child seems to be a messiah, a savior whose birth will signify the end of human infertility and another chance for mankind. Indeed, the sight of the newborn actually compels an army to put down its weapons, a moving scene in part because it was such a hopeful fantasy for 2006, when violence in Iraq and the Mideast and Darfur seemed unstoppable. The *deus ex machina* of the film's ending — which shows that there is a "Human Project" working for the future (their members arrive on a rescue boat named "Tomorrow") — is similar to the *deus ex machina* of the earlier dystopian fantasy *Fahrenheit 451* (written by Ray Bradbury and directed by François Truffaut). Its somewhat hopeful ending notwithstanding, *Children of Men* most impresses with its expressive and uncompromising chaos and lugubriousness: the future is terrifying, yes, but even worse, it is depressing. *Children of Men* asks if life is random or if there is a plan. But which would be worse: to learn that there can be no children of God, because there *is* no God in this random universe, or to learn that God was willing to largely abandon us to apocalyptic horror?

Also released in December of 2006 was *Apocalypto*, a strange film directed and produced by Mel Gibson. Just as Gibson's subtitled *The Passion of the Christ*, with dialogue spoken in an archaic language (Aramaic), was essentially a horror film in the demonic subgenre, his subtitled *Apocalypto*, also with dialogue in an archaic language (Maya), was a horror film in the Armageddon subgenre. Evoking Peter Weir's *The Last Wave*, *Apocalypto* also presents an apocalypse emerging from an aboriginal culture: in this case, the Mayan culture which ended in the sixteenth century. *Apocalypto* begins with a title card quotation from Will Durant: "A great civilization is not conquered from without until it has destroyed itself from within." This epigraph indicates that the film's vision of Mayan civilization is intended as a metaphor for our own civilization, but Gibson's metaphor is not easily congruent, but speculative and evocative. Like the American TV series *Lost*, most of *Apocalypto* shows people running through the jungle. And like the TV reality series *Survivor*, *Apocalypto* emphasizes the struggle to survive and the eating of odd foods. The Mayan civilization, like ours, likes scatological humor; much screen time is devoted to a sequence in which a character is essentially tricked into eating raw, bloody, tapir testicles. Like contemporary Western man, Mayans will do much to increase sexual potency: do tapir testicles or *soanza* leaves best represent Mayan Viagra? And like many countries in the Western world, Mayans must deal with the problem of immigrants and refugees whose own lands offer inadequate opportunity. In *Apocalypto*, these "illegals" bring incertitude and fear to the young protagonist, who later must watch his father's neck slashed in a Mayan culture more violent with every new day. A little girl with "the sickness" (a metaphor for AIDS?) offers prophecies, and we are told that "The sacred time is near" and "Day will be like night." (Was day like night on 9/11 when the detritus of the collapsing towers enveloped

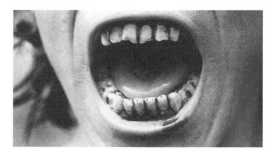

Drawing inspiration from Hitchcock's *Psycho*, made forty-six years before, Mel Gibson quickly cuts three, successively closer shots to show the strange horror of *Apocalypto*. Compare with the frame grabs on page 227.

lower Manhattan with a thick, ominous, carcinogenic cloud?) The girl's prophecies parallel Biblical prophecies held by the religious right in America (including Mel Gibson), that suggest apocalypse is near, along with the second coming of Christ. Is Gibson suggesting that the attack on the World Trade Center towers marked the beginning of our own "sacred time?" The Mayans commit human sacrifice to their Mayan god, whose return they await. Again, there are parallels, if not precise ones: is Gibson suggesting that Americans are committing human sacrifice when they allow legal abortions? Or are Americans committing human sacrifice when they allow American soldiers to die in Iraq, a war based either on faulty intelligence or the deceptions of the U.S.A. leaders? Or perhaps the human sacrifice in *Apocalypto* is more a metaphor for Muslim terrorism: particularly when leaders like Osama bin Laden sacrifice young believers to a supposedly greater cause, reversing, through decapitations and suicide bombings, civilization's progress? Certainly, Gibson revels in the Mayan violence: decapitated heads are everywhere, many of them rolled down the huge temple

In the powerful final sequence of *Apocalypto*, the solar eclipse announces a Mayan apocalypse: the coming of the Spanish Christians. Is director Gibson suggesting that Christianity may be about to face its own apocalypse in the twenty-first century?

pyramid that dominates his film. *Apocalypto*'s most horrifying image is an expansive field filled with thousands of decapitated bodies, not only suggesting the Holocaust (an event which Gibson's anti–Semitic father has denied), but recent genocides, too, such as the killings (and amputations) in Rwanda, Sierra Leone, Darfur, etc.

At its best, *Apocalypto* emulates *Fellini Satyricon*, thought-provoking and visually dazzling, strongly imprinting its surreal imagery. More often, *Apocalypto* feels prosaic, like *The Naked Prey*, an exciting 1966 action-adventure film in which a semi-naked Cornel Wilde is chased through the jungle with no profundities in sight. At its worst, *Apocalypto* is a cheesy Italian Maciste film which sacrifices Christians in the Coliseum. At its dramatic climax when its protagonist narrowly escapes beheading, *Apocalypto* suggests contemporary al-Qaeda atrocities. Because the Mayans unwisely violate their god's rules by killing a jaguar (the "son" of their god), they fulfill revelation and justly bring about their own apocalypse. There are parallel, contemporary implications for Gibson, who is associated with Opus Dei and is a radically conservative Catholic who firmly believes much of contemporary culture violates God's rules: legalized abortion, gay rights, birth control, women's liberation, and so forth. (And many apocalyptic Christians believe that the end times will be marked by beheadings; is that why *Apocalypto* emphasizes these images?) For Gibson, Western culture has too long blasphemed its core values; unless it can marshal the resolve to reclaim those values and force them upon the secular culture, even many Christians may deserve damnation after the coming apocalypse.

The most shocking image in *Apocalypto* is its *deus ex machina* when the surreal culture we have been watching for over two hours comes face-to-face with the unstoppable: the three huge, Spanish, sailing ships, just arrived to the continent with its sailors about to disembark ... and bring with them the diseases and new technologies of violence which will destroy the Mayans. In part, the image is so powerful because it remains unexplored and is thus ambiguous. Is Gibson simply pointing out ironies: indicating that just as the Mayan civilization, already decaying from within, was brought to its end by Christian civilization, that today's Christian civilization, similarly decaying, will be brought to its own ignominious end? Or is Gibson indicating that Christian civilization should — with violence, if necessary — bring an end to the secularism dominating contemporary Western civilization? Or is today's contemporary Christian task to confront and defeat the growing militarism of the Muslim world? What is weird about *Apocalypto* is that it seems simultaneously incoherent and expressively ambiguous — that is, both artless and artful. And why not? Perhaps incoherence and ambiguity, as paradox, are themselves the perfect metaphors for the hurtling, violent cacophonies of the nascent twenty-first century.

As the century's first decade was approaching its end — with the George W. Bush presidency limping through its final, lame-duck days — the United States was in a recession that had become global, the American stock market had crashed more precipitously than at any time since the 1929 crash which had instigated the Great Depression, millions of foreclosures had caused the housing market bubble to deflate critically, unemployment and inflation were up alarmingly, the War in Iraq was continuing, the War in Afghanistan was again spiraling out of control, and a higher percentage of Americans believed the country was on the wrong track than ever previously measured (89 percent according to an October 2008 CBS/*New York Times* poll). Not surprisingly, as Americans were counting the days until Bush was replaced by someone else, whether Republican or Democrat, apocalyptic themes were streaming onto American screens. *Right at Your Door*, an apocalyptic film that made a sensation at the 2006 Sundance Film Festival was one of the most notable. Equally apocalyptic was the American TV series *Jericho*, which premiered in 2006, beginning with a group of characters in Jericho, Kansas, shocked by a mushroom cloud they see at the horizon. But there was also *The Mist, The Invasion*, George A. Romero's *Diary of the Dead*, and particularly the blockbuster *I Am Legend* in 2007; and *Cloverfield* and *The Happening* early in 2008. The fact that *Blindness*—a "prestige film" directed by Fernando Meirelles starring Julianne Moore, and based on the novel by Nobel Prize winner José Saramago — was the opening film at the 2008 Cannes Film Festival, showed how important visions of apocalypse were in world cinema as well. *Blindness* is an allegorical tale of an epidemic of "white blindness" that spreads in an unnamed city, resulting in the government quarantining the blind; as in *Lord of the Flies*, what is left of the social compact quickly disintegrates until mankind's most venal attributes create an apocalyptic chaos worse than the affliction of blindness. Even the monumentally successful 2008 Pixar animated film *Wall•E*— as far away in tone from *Blindness* as one can possibly imagine — was basically an apocalyptic warning that as citizens of the earth we must change direction before it is irrevocably too late.

Right at Your Door begins with a radio announcer saying that it is a typical day in Los Angeles, but it isn't typical for long. From inside an L.A. home with the film's protagonist Brad, we experience the news of multiple explosions: downtown, in Beverly Hills, at the airport. Because *Right at Your Door* is low-budget (with virtually no special effects), rapid editing, hand-held camera, and sound effects communicate the tension of erupting chaos. As during 9/11, cellphones provide the conduit for some of the most moving communication. The terrorist bombs are "dirty bombs" emitting toxic clouds, and Angelenos are told: "Please do not tend to the medical needs of anyone contaminated." When the disaster strikes, the husband and wife at the center of the film — Brad and Lexi (played by Rory Cochrane and Mary McCormack) — are not together. Although Brad is safely inside the house, Lexi is near one of the bomb sites. Brad frantically tries to find his wife to save her, but before too long is forced to retreat to his home, where he seals up the windows and doors, as instructed, to protect from the toxicity. When a shell-shocked Lexi manages to return, Brad — though emotionally torn — will not let her in. *Right at Your Door* shows how apocalypse can alienate us from even those we most love. In this regard, the dirty bombs' toxicity suggests parallels to the HIV/AIDS virus: segregating society into those who have been exposed and those who have not. *Right at Your Door* asks whether we should *choose* to be infected if infection would bring us closer to those we love. (Another character in the film, a handyman, ultimately chooses to do just that: potentially die with his wife, rather than live alone.) *Right at Your Door* also shows that apocalypse will inevitably require government to make decisions as to whose circumstances merit their being saved and whose merit their being abandoned: when resources are overwhelmed, some lives will be considered more valuable than others, no matter that democracy's ideals suggest otherwise. *Right at Your Door* asks us to consider, in real terms, how we might behave during apocalypse. The film's surprise ending is a stunning revelation: the government instructions for survival were erroneous. By sealing himself inside, Brad actually created a toxic breeding ground. Had he ignored instructions and altruistically opened up his house to reunite with his wife, potentially sacrificing himself, he would have *not* become so infected and toxic to others. Because of the danger he now poses, the military men — whose job is now revealed as focused killing, not focused saving — put Brad down for society's greater good. The film ends, as it began, with an equally ironic announcement from the media: "Plans to honor these specialized rescue teams are underway in Washington."

The Mist, written and directed by Frank Darabont from a Stephen King novel, shows a variety of characters trapped in a grocery store that is surrounded by a growing mist. As apocalypse edges nearer, we discover the mist is inhabited by giant insects, birds, spiders, and tentacled monsters. What makes *The Mist* so intense is how it focuses on the emotional tensions among the besieged struggling to survive physically and trying to understand what is happening to them metaphysically. Mrs. Carmody (memorably played by Marcia Gay Harden), whose original type appears in the diner scene in *The Birds*, is a religious fundamentalist who explicitly believes the horrifying creatures have been sent by God to punish us for the wickedness of abortion and stem-cell research. As the horror augments, Mrs. Carmody's convictions become increasingly persuasive; like the characters in Shirley Jackson's short story *The Lottery*, the survivors embrace human sacrifice as a credible strategy. Yet the horrors of the mist have actually been caused by the American military. By engaging in a project to connect to other worlds, the military released unanticipated horror. Once again, it is hard not to see this explanation as a metaphor for Iraq: American entry into an alien world without any realistic understanding of the forces we would be unleashing. With the War in Iraq still going when this film was written, produced, and released, it is not surprising that *The Mist* ends bleakly, especially for the protagonist and his son at the center of this allegorical horror.

Diary of the Dead, directed by George A. Romero, and *Cloverfield*, directed by Matt Reeves (and produced by *Lost*'s J.J. Abrams) both use a *Blair Witch* documentary shooting strategy to communicate their respective horrors: the return of the dead, and a new gargantuan monster, respectively. Whereas the former was not successful, the latter was very much so. Perhaps Romero' s film of yet more zombies was a bit too familiar, or perhaps its nihilism and political implications were too severe for the general public. The camcorder operator Jason, who films the dead, intones that "All that's left ... is to record what's happening for whoever remains when it's over"— which presumes utter and total failure. In Jason's speech, Romero, long political, is offering relevant commentary on the myriad of books published and interviews granted, finally, on the real stories behind the political failures of 9/11, the War in Iraq, and Hurricane Katrina. Another character, Debra — echoing ideas put forth by director Michael Haneke in *Benny's Video* and *71 Fragments*— asks "If it's not on camera, it's like it never happened, right?" Yet Romero knows that just as the early war footage from reporters embedded with military units in Iraq was fundamentally misleading, so too can any footage, obviously including this *faux* documentary of the dead.

Cloverfield, on the other hand, is much more explicitly a symbolic reenactment in Manhattan of 9/11, though with the terrorist planes replaced by a newly-invented rampaging monster, which on some level is easier to accept. Monsters should be expected to kill; humans ... not so much. In other words, the *Cloverfield* monster is our Godzilla. Scene after scene evokes familiar documentary images from the early 9/11 television coverage. Particularly striking are scenes of people running through smoke-filling streets to escape the horror. The most memorable single image, referencing the apocalypse of *Planet of the Apes*, is the huge head of the Statue of Liberty, severed from its monument by the monster and thrown into the Manhattan streets, landing right in front of our protagonists. In the context of potential apocalypse, is that the fate for Lady Liberty in the United States?

Both *The Invasion* (a remake of the 1956 *The Invasion of the Body Snatchers*) and *The Happening* (directed by M. Night Shyamalan) seem significantly less successful than they could have been. Of all the horror films that have been remade, the original *Invasion of the Body Snatchers* has provided the most fertile material, adaptable to fit the political circumstances of just about any time. (The 1978 version by Philip Kaufman is by far the best of the three remakes, indeed, one of the best horror remakes ever, extraordinarily interesting thematically and stylistically.) At least *The Invasion* clearly invokes the politics of today with a promising script by Dave Kajganich: there are references to New Orleans and Katrina, references to the War in Iraq, criticism of the American media for not covering news events truthfully, images of people jumping off a building to their deaths, as happened on 9/11, and so forth. Cleverly, the end of the original film is reenacted twenty minutes into the remake, as a hysterical woman wanders amidst traffic shouting "They're coming! They're coming!" Notable, too, is that Jack Bennell, the male protagonist from the original (played by Kevin McCarthy) is gender-switched to Carol Bennell (now played by Nicole Kidman). In *hommage* to Veronica Cartwright's appearance in the 1978 *Invasion of the Body Snatchers* (which was itself an *hommage* to her appearance, as a little girl, in the seminal *The Birds*), Cartwright is cast here in a fascinating role as the psychiatric patient who may not be crazy after all. The irony in this remake is that, as more people around the world become infected and transform into unemotional people, the world starts to lose its appetite for conflict. Via TV reports we glimpse in the backgrounds, we discover that since the beginning of the invasion, peace has been declared in Kabul, President George W. Bush and Hillary Clinton have announced universal health care for all Americans, there has been a Darfur ceasefire, the United States occupation of Iraq has ended, and President Bush and Venezuela's Marxist Hugo Chavez have reached accord. This version of *Invasion of the Body Snatchers* dares to ask if it would really be that bad for humans to become more conformist, more agreeable. The inherent problem with *Invasion* is that the box office impulse to include huge action-adventure chase sequences contradicts the emotionless, violence-eschewing impulses of the post-humans. And quite weirdly, in a way that suggests extensive studio tinkering with a film in which at least one director was replaced by another, the climactic scenes seem disjointed, truncated, and badly edited. Even worse, the film ends with a totally inexplicable *deus ex machina* which puts the world back as it was. If ever a horror film needed to end nihilistically, it is an *Invasion of the Body Snatchers* released when the vast majority of Americans believed that the country had been hijacked onto the wrong track. With snatchers (of our minds? of our values?) in our actual midst, how can the fictional bacterial invaders turn out to have been less powerful?

M. Night Shyamalan's *The Happening* is a film that begins from a great conceptual premise, but which gets virtually every component of its execution wrong. The premise is that one day, for reasons unknown, people start casually committing suicide. It's a terrifying idea that we can be at the mercy of subconscious impulses that remain totally unanticipated until the moment those impulses manifest themselves. The film's opening image — ominous clouds rolling in the sky — is more memorable than most of what follows and harkens back to the classic Armageddon warning to "Watch the skies." Despite the opening shot, we learn that the skies have nothing to do with what is happening; and unlike Hitchcock, who wisely refused in *The Birds* to provide the definitive reason for the bird attacks, Shyamalan makes everything clear: the trees and plants in our environment have spontaneously developed the capacity to emit toxins which induce suicide (particularly if we stick together and gather in large groups), because of our depletion of the world's natural resources and our lousy record on environmental protection. This specificity strips away ambiguity and turns *The Happening* into a *film à thèse*, a pedestrian cautionary tale. A billboard we see advertising a tract of new homes ironically announces our culpability: "You Deserve This!" The suicides we see are varied: construction workers jump off skyscrapers (more echoes of 9/11), Central Park visitors hang themselves from trees, a police officer shoots himself, and so forth. One character comments in awe: "Just when you thought there couldn't be any more evil invented!" Yet in the more interesting Japanese film from 2002, *Suicide Club*, which begins with somewhat the same premise, the suicides are terrifying precisely because they are so casual, because those who kill themselves act without any apparent understanding of the consequences of what they're doing — often chatting, smiling, or giggling as they die. In Shyamalan's film, the victims first become momentarily frozen, then turn into zombies, and then frantically and insistently rush to commit suicide, often with music telegraphing the *unusual* nature of the horror we are seeing. With writing which is formulaic and sappy, the film ends in the same problematic way *The Invasion* ended: with an unconvincing *deus ex machina* which brings *The Happening* to a happy close. (Maybe because happy-ending films tend to make more money than unhappy-ending films?) There is even a convenient pregnancy to suggest that life will go on and that the most conventional kind of happiness will ensue. With global warming and other dire environmental problems in real life not at all under control, the ending here seems powerfully out of touch with people's real fears. Even crazier, *The Happening* has a totally mystifying sequence, of severe length, in which an overwrought Betty Buckley playing a kind of demented Mrs. Bates from *Psycho* turns Shyamalan's film into a horror-of-personality film. As a result, *The Happening* becomes schizophrenic, severely in need of integration.

One of the most financially successful Armageddon horror films of all time, *I Am Legend* (which made over $250 million worldwide), was actually the third adaptation of a 1954 novel by Richard Matheson. On screen, Matheson's work had appeared first in the Italian-made *The Last Man on Earth* in 1964 with Vincent Price, and then in the American-made *The Omega Man* in 1971 with Charlton Heston, and finally, under the novel's original title *I Am Legend*, with Will Smith in 2008. It is a testament to Matheson's original material that all three of these films seem quite vital, but none more so than *I Am Legend*, where the sophisticated current state of special effects allowed Matheson's story to be told persuasively and compellingly. Set initially in 2009 as a scientist announces a breakthrough viral cure for cancer (the scientist played by Emma Thompson, uncredited), *I Am Legend* then jumps to 2012 as we discover that her cancer cure has gone horribly wrong. As a result, 5.4 billion people have died worldwide; another 588 million have been transformed into monstrous, muscular mutants; and the 12 million worldwide survivors have largely been eaten by these mutant "darkseekers." *I Am Legend* takes places on Manhattan, where Robert Neville (Will Smith) may be the only surviving human — his mission as a medical researcher to find a cure for the deadly cancer vaccine and reclaim a human identity for the darkseekers. The computer-generated effects communicate a striking, surreal vision of an abandoned Manhattan: streets overgrown by grass and populated by abandoned vehicles. The images of what the world might look like if humans were no longer here, allowing nature to revert to its original state, are quite powerful. Lions and deer run riot through the once sophisticated urban spaces; and the darkseekers and their infected dogs look for food, too, but only at night, allowing the daylight to turn Manhattan into a playground for Neville. It is a testament to Will Smith's magnetism as a movie star and his ability to truly command our eye that he dominates the screen completely with his powerful screen presence; for most of the film, he is the only human character we see. Among his most powerful and moving scenes are those played by Smith between Neville and his dog. When, perhaps inevitably, other human survivors enter the story — Anna and her son — Neville must confront the psychological impact his extended isolation has had on him. At one point, Anna says, "Oh, God," and Neville snaps back, "God didn't do this, Anna. We did." At another point, Neville offers bitter arguments to prove his contention that "There is no God." Anna tries to convince him that there is a God, and that God has a plan. And yet, Neville is an existentialist in the truest sense: he may not believe in God, but like Dr. Rieux in Albert Camus' 1947 novel *The Plague* (which inspires this film as well as the original novel), Neville never shirks from his responsibility to work for the betterment of mankind. He sees his work and service as the only things that can give his life meaning. As one might expect in an Armageddon film, *I Am Legend* develops to a traumatic conclusion in which Neville, Anna, and her son are besieged by the mutants at the moment Neville discovers the cure that can give mankind back its future. The moving ending shows Neville, perhaps even surprising himself, sacrificing his life in such a way that makes the survival of the human race possible. He becomes a Christ figure through a sacrifice that he may not even consider Christian; in the process, his worthy act offers evidence that Anna was right: there may be a plan. The film ends on a spiritual note: "This is his legend. Light up the darkness."

Indeed. As the George W. Bush era comes to its end with the election of the first man to the American presidency with African ancestry, Barack Obama (the same ennobled type as the black, educated protagonist played by Will Smith in *I Am Legend*), global warming and other potential ecological catastrophes loom large in the public mind, particularly with the growing industrialization of China and India, and the context of the diminishing amount of available energy. It will be interesting to see if the horror of Armageddon develops a greater sense of optimism — inspired by the "tipping point" that has convinced many countries, including the United States, to finally address these issues — or develops an even deeper sense of despair — discouraged by the difficulty of finding workable solutions and by the political intractability of worldwide populations focused on conflict and violent confrontation.

Although Barack Obama's mantras of "HOPE" and "YES WE CAN" certainly suggested optimism, at least the first wave of post-election 2009 horror films have projected no similar optimism in our ability to save the planet from atomic or ecological annihilation. On the contrary, high-profile 2009 horror is as fatalistic as ever. For instance, *Knowing*, starring Nicolas Cage, focuses on the major disasters of the last 50 years, including 9/11, before proceeding to show virtually all life on earth incinerated by a solar flare in a special-effects apocalypse. *Terminator Salvation*, with Christian Bale, a revival of *The Terminator* franchise, positions itself in a post-nuclear apocalyptic world set in the year 2018. *2012*, directed by Armageddon-master Roland Emmerich, suggests — per the Mayan calendar — that the world will end in 2012. (And as the film's ad-line queries — invoking traumatic memories of the Indian Ocean tsunami of 2004 and Hurricane Katrina of 2005 — "How would the governments of our planet prepare six billion people for the end of the world? They wouldn't.") The feature film *9*, produced by Tim Burton and directed by Shane Acker from his celebrated short, continues — like 2008's *Wall•E*— to insinuate dark apocalyptic imagery into what is essentially an animated film marketed to children. And the highest-profile "prestige" horror film of 2009, *The Road*, is based on Cormac McCarthy's Pulitzer Prize–winning novel which focuses on the post-apocalyptic despair its author believes is all but inevitable. Despite what these lugubrious films suggest (released post–Obama, if produced pre–Obama), we can nevertheless hope for the diminution in this most expressive horror sub-genre along with the concomitant enlightenment and evolution in the human social sphere this diminution would reflect.

9 — Asian Millennial Horror

The paucity of new ideas in late twentieth-century American horror contributed to the surprising cult success in the United States of recent Asian horror films. Although many commentators refer to this subgenre as "J-horror," this is a bit misnomic, since notable films have come not only from Japan, but from Hong Kong (*The Eye*), South Korea (*Phone* and *A Tale of Two Sisters*), and other Asian countries. Nevertheless, in the subgenre I prefer to call Asian millennial horror, the Japanese films are absolutely central. Always interested in horror, the Japanese cinema pioneered in the fifties and sixties a series of films promulgating the extensive mythology of the monster Godzilla. Whereas the *Godzilla* films drew upon the horror of Armageddon, these more ambiguous Asian millennial horror films draw upon the horror of personality and the horror of the demonic as well.[1]

Unlike recent American horror, these Asian films tend to be less logical in their plots, more slow-moving and atmospheric, and more reliant on silence than sound. Although uncompromising in their disturbing, often gruesome imagery, these films are as infused with sadness as horror. The existence of an afterlife is generally presumed; and while there are living characters who act in psychopathic ways, there are also ghosts and demons. Clearly, many of these films relate to the traditional Japanese ghost story. In fact, highly influencing them is the acclaimed 1962 Masaki Kobayashi–directed art-house horror film *Kwaidan*, particularly the first of its four stories, entitled "The Black Hair"— about a man haunted by the long hair of a wife that he had wronged. Indeed, a recurring, *contemporary* Japanese image is the dead demon-girl (often wet) with long black hair obscuring her face. Whatever complex, cultural references the image of long black hair evokes in Japan are largely lost on American audiences, for whom these films must therefore work significantly differ-

Ringu: In Japanese horror, the hanging black hair derives from traditional Japanese demonic imagery, and the single visible eye derives from classic horror-of-personality film.

Japanese horror film has always been heavily stylized, as in 1962's *Kwaidan*, in which amorphous abstraction dominates the credit sequence as well as the disturbing exterior sets.

ently—and more irrationally. In fact, the Japanese have an amazingly complex taxonomy of ghosts, or *yūrei*, with each ghostly variety having its own name and standard behaviors. The typical *yūrei*, usually dressed in a white burial kimono (and present in the second *Kwaidan* tale, "The Woman of the Snow"), has long black hair because of the Japanese superstitious belief that the hair continues to grow after death. And the typical *yūrei* posture—stiff, with hanging hair, head, and arms—derives in part from the *yūrei* depiction within Kabuki theatre, which used stage technology to sometimes hoist and suspend its bewigged actors.

Clearly, the Japanese horror film has a long tradition that cannot be done justice in a short study. As well, many of these films have never played in the United States, and those that have we invariably see divorced by time and space from their essential moment in the Japanese culture that produced them. Although *Kwaidan* is a significant influence on millennial horror, highlighting *Kwaidan* is a bit arbitrary, because other thematically serious, classic Japanese horror films have doubtless affected the younger generation of filmmakers. Yet at a minimum, I should comment too on the influence of a less-typical Japanese film: *Jigoku* [*Hell*], directed by Nobuo Nakagawa. In opposition to the restrained horror tradition familiar to Western audiences, *Jigoku* (1960) is more graphic and less tasteful,

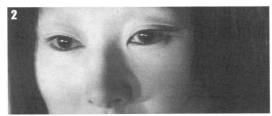

Different "masked" faces as objects of horror in *Kwaidan*: (1) covered with tattoos, and (2) encased in white makeup. The latter is part of the classic *yūrei*, derived from the mask work in Kabuki theatre. Typical *yūrei* can be found in (3) *Kwaidan* (in 1962) and (4) *Ringu* (in 1998).

though stylized. This film's celebrated final sequence —filled with off-putting jump cuts —presents a complex, fantastical representation of hell, showing a debauched doctor literally sawed into pieces; a police officer having his hands cut off; and sinners flayed, eye-gouged, decapitated, boiled in vats of fire-water, and having the flesh and bones ripped from their bodies. One can see each of these two traditions, the classic and the graphic, sometimes synthesized, sometimes not, in these Asian millennial horror films. Perhaps the traditions are most notable in a film like *Audition* that begins largely in one tradition and then veers off wildly into the other.

Certainly, Americans respond to the

In *Cure*, Kiyoshi Kurosawa uses long shots of extended-duration which de-emphasize faces, even in violent scenes. Unlike American horror which uses close-ups and rapid cutting to make us feel emotion, *Cure* invites us to consider the reality of the horror environments. The final image here is so filled with information that the typical viewer fails to see the knife, held by someone obscured by a tree. The knife can be found within the circle overlay [not present in the film itself].

essential integrity of the Asian horror film, which seems genuinely artful and personal—neither a commercial sop to the box office, nor a mindless display of special effects. Asians have always venerated tradition, and many of these films suggest that the dead, improperly treated when alive, are able to return magically, often via the newest technologies—computers, videotapes, cellphones. Are these technologies destroying and perverting the best traditions of the past, or are traditions darkly insinuating themselves into technologies that are themselves being perverted? It is this implicit paradox regarding our ambivalence toward technology and tradition, indeed, toward change—rather than any symbolic meanings specific to, say, Japan or Hong Kong—that Americans are largely responding to.

A good example of an early Asian millennial horror film is *Cure* [*Kyua*], directed by Kiyoshi Kurosawa in 1997. Within the first few minutes, a killer bludgeons a prostitute, then washes off the blood in a shower—a *Psycho* reference. A series of apparently unrelated killings follow; and although the perpetrators admit their crimes, they have no idea why they committed them. Are the killers psychopaths, demons, or part of an oncoming apocalypse? Or is it that the violence "just happened?" Typical to this subgenre, *Cure* moves slowly and uses extended-duration long shots. Because the camera watches from such significant distance and the soundtrack uses only a limited musical track (sounding much like industrial noise), we are kept at an emotional distance from the action. As much an Antonioni-style art film as a horror film, *Cure*'s compositions are formal and controlled. Ultimately, *Cure* suggests that "mesmerism" is the cause of its violence. The power to hypnotize, along with the impulse to murder, transfers from one person to another like a virus—making *Cure* about how we are gradually changing, how we are developing amnesia about our pasts and our moral traditions as contemporary life reprograms us into something dangerous.

Kurosawa's *Charisma* [*Karisuma*] from 1999, is even odder: a horror allegory which is clearly apocalyptic. Ponderous and ambiguous, *Charisma* begins with a hostage-taker who delivers an odd ransom note: "Restore the Rules of the World." But what are these rules that need to be restored? Because the protagonist, a police officer named Yabuike, fails to take the appropriate aggressive action, the hostage is killed. Distraught, Yabuike moves to the country to take stock of his life. His new environment, a forest, seems strangely malevolent: all the trees are dying, but one strange mutation, a tree nicknamed "Charisma," is struggling to live. With "foul-smelling ozone, ultra-violet rays, poison everywhere," it seems that Charisma is producing a toxin which is killing the forest. So what are we to do with this nonconformist tree? Key to this film's allegory is the detail that Charisma has been

In *Charisma*, (1) Yabuike (Kôji Yakusho) walks in a malevolent forest of dying trees, himself an integral part of that dark malevolence, despite his attempts to do good. (2) The potential consequences of Yabuike's efforts are ecological destruction on an atomic scale.

brought from outside Japan and so is alien to Japanese tradition. Or does Charisma belong, simply because it is alive and now there? Yabuike says, "There are forces trying to live, forces trying to kill," but a professor he visits thinks that these forces are really one and the same, that in either direct or indirect ways, all of us must kill in order to live and flourish. The professor asserts that it's impossible to save both the forest and Charisma, that one or the other will be killed and it's naively idealistic to think otherwise. So is it the Darwinian principle that ultimately only the strongest survive that's at the center of these "rules of the world?" If so, are these rules moral? The professor says to Yabuike, "My goal is to restore the rules of the forest, which are probably the rules of the world. For that, you need force. You came to this forest looking for freedom. Freedom's just another disease. A truly healthy human longs to obey." Is obedience central to the Japanese tradition? Would destroying Charisma for *not* conforming be a celebration of fascism? Perhaps Charisma represents racial impurity or the immigrant, or maybe even the foreign influence brought into Japan by new technologies such as the internet, or through international trade within the new global marketplace. When Charisma is burned, we see a mushroom cloud of its poison, which suggests Charisma's meaning relates to atomic technology. Yet the film's final image suggests that Yabuike — for an idealistic principle — has actually initiated a greater apocalypse, destroying the whole forest and perhaps even the region. Director Kurosawa leaves his allegory ambiguous and thus more resonant: must we conform if we wish to live in harmony? Must those in power always decide how much nonconformism they can tolerate before others will suffer too greatly? And a critical question for all countries, post–9/11, and particularly for democracies, is whether freedom must be limited to ensure the propagation of civilization. Can we allow intellectual poison in our midst? And who decides what *is* poison and what isn't? In many ways, *Charisma* is a political horror film whose intriguing ideas put American horror film to shame. And yet, true to genre, by the end of the film, human-on-human violence erupts in terrifying ways: murder by sledge hammer and sword.

Ringu, directed by Hideo Nakata in 1998, is perhaps the most influential Asian horror film, since it led to a wildly successful American remake. Notably at the center of *Ringu* is *family*, as a divorced couple and their child become involved with a videotape that causes the death in seven days of anyone who views it. Fragmentary, technically unsophisticated, often visually inscrutable, but surreal, the videotape includes central images of a young woman combing her long black hair. Tellingly, when those who have seen the video but have not yet died are photographed, they look deformed — their deformities prophetic in depicting their own death throes and similar to the deformities manifested after the bombings of Hiroshima and Nagasaki. Thus *Ringu* suggests that technology — from the atomic

Ringu suggests the existence of encroaching demons by using images which transform from positive to negative.

bomb and television to the VCR and Polaroids — leads to death. Just as more and more become mesmerized in *Cure*, more see the videotape in *Ringu*: two adolescent girls, then the protagonist mother, then her ex-husband, then their child. Will all of them die from this videotape which hosts the mistreated demon child Sadako, the long-haired ghost who is able literally to emerge from the television and kill people? *Ringu* suggests that although we think of contemporary technology as scientific advance, it is actually a conduit to our most primal fears. Although the bonds of the

The *yūrei* in *Ringu* is sometimes photographed so abstractly that she becomes terrifying in her inscrutability.

nuclear family are too weak to allow our protagonist family to reconstitute itself (i.e., the father dies), the mother/child bonds prove to be stronger. The revelation at *Ringu*'s end is that a person can escape the curse by showing someone else the videotape, effectively passing the curse on.

Had *Ringu* been made in fifties America, it would have been a clear metaphor for naming names in the context of blacklisting and scapegoating. But in 1998, its moral meaning is less clear. Certainly it suggests that in today's world, selfishness, rather than selflessness, is rewarded. Is life just an existential game of Old Maid? Or worse: a life-and-death pyramid scheme? In an odd way, *Ringu* reflects the same capitalist ethic inherent in contemporary American TV shows like *Survivor* and *Big Brother*— where those in a social group are required to cooperate according to defined rules in order to survive, but also required to turn on each other, scapegoating at least one person at a time to protect their own interests. Japanese culture, more than American culture, has long had a profound sense of shared responsibility for group cohesion; *Ringu* suggests that that sense has begun to disintegrate. The new global economy requiring all countries to compete contributed to the bursting of the Japanese economic bubble in the early nineties, as well as the changing of the traditional Japanese practice of lifetime employment with one company based on a seniority system rewarding loyalty. Has an amoral, capitalist self-interest now become the supreme value even in Japan, trumping tradition?

The American remake *The Ring*, directed by Gore Verbinski in 2002, carefully follows

Subtle differences between the Japanese *Ringu* and the American remake *The Ring*: In the former (1), the boy gazes upward, innocent, vulnerable, dwarfed by the stairway, but central within the image. In the latter (2), the boy gazes forward, robotic, rigid, alienated from the persons in the other room and almost demonically self-possessed.

When an American teenager (played by Amber Tamblyn) in *The Ring* shrieks in horror, special effects turn her into the expressive Edvard Munch painting *The Scream*.

the original's plot, but with a different sensibility. The mother, here played by A-list actress Naomi Watts, is almost immediately presented as a bad mother, overly interested in her career. And her child is dark-eyed and less innocent — in fact, almost demonic in appearance and as creepy as the haunted videotape. Especially skillful is the way *The Ring* contrives much more plot — especially an electrocution in a bathtub and a horse committing suicide. Yet the ambiguities of the Japanese original are replaced by traditional horror

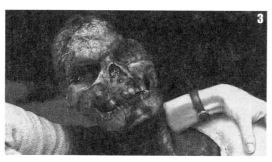

The Ring is filled with dozens of references to other films, including (1) Alfred Hitchcock's *Psycho* (the shower sequence, but here with Naomi Watts); (2) Michelangelo Antonioni's *L'eclisse* (the wordless, final montage); (3) *Psycho* again (the discovery of the mummified Mrs. Bates); and (4) Hitchcock's *Rear Window* (spying on neighbors).

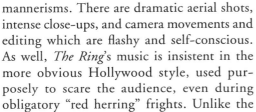

The long blonde hair of *The Ring*'s heroine (Naomi Watts) contrasts with the straight black hair of the *yūrei* (Daveigh Chase).

mannerisms. There are dramatic aerial shots, intense close-ups, and camera movements and editing which are flashy and self-conscious. As well, *The Ring*'s music is insistent in the more obvious Hollywood style, used purposely to scare the audience, even during obligatory "red herring" frights. Unlike the original *Ringu*, *The Ring* speeds along, dazzling and distracting us. As a result, we are rarely allowed the opportunity to be contemplative or genuinely disturbed. Tricked out with near-subliminal images, *The Ring,* if more sophisticated visually, is also decidedly less personal. If *Ringu* is the more honorable work, *The Ring* is definitely more fun. In fact, with its frequent and eclectic postmodern *hommage*, *The Ring* becomes an entertaining trivia game, as much a reflexive movie about other movies, as a horror film. For instance, *The Ring*'s image of Watts on a balcony refers to Antonioni's *L'eclisse*; its image of a dilating eye refers to Gus Van Sant's *Psycho* remake; its image of a man in a wheelchair (though pointedly watching TV) to Jimmy Stewart in Hitchcock's voyeuristic *Rear Window*; a bare

The beautifully abstract images that appear on the forbidden videotape in *The Ring* resemble experimental film images of the fifties and sixties.

tree to the memorable credit sequence of the HBO TV series *Six Feet Under*; hair floating underwater to Shelley Winters' death in *Night of the Hunter*. As well, there are references to *The Fly*, *The Sixth Sense*, the original *Ringu*, and (somewhat gratuitously) the original *Psycho*— both its shower scene and climactic cellar scene. Unlike the original *Ringu*, *The Ring*'s end credits include hundreds of special effects collaborators, an indication of exactly where the film allocated its resources.

This remake was followed by an American sequel, *The Ring Two*, in 2005. Because *The Ring*'s director was unavailable, Hollywood turned to Hideo Nakata, the director of the Japanese original. Although less cohesive than its American predecessor, *The Ring Two* is more mysterious. Its horrific images are more expressive and more ambiguous in meaning: an insect emerging from a faucet; a tree of flames growing along a wall; a pattern scratched in wallpaper by a ghostly girl; water which floats up rather than spills down. *The Ring Two* seems more about maternal anxieties in a post-feminist age. For instance, the little boy insists on calling his mother by her given name, "Rachel"— a detail that unsettled American audiences. Has Rachel been too distant emotionally for her son to think of her as his mom? To others, Rachel seems to be an abusive mother — which aligns her with the abusive mother of the demon child who wants to possess Rachel's son. *The Ring Two* understands that although women know they should be good mothers, they sometimes may want to kill their children, and their desire (like Rachel's) for fulfilling work outside the home is at odds with the maternal instinct. When Rachel almost spits out "I'm not your fucking mommy!" to the demon child, her declaration reflects her internal anger at having to be a mother at all, an ambivalence most women feel guilty expressing. By the end of the film, the demon's possession of Rachel's son paradoxically allows Rachel to prove her maternal love by apparently killing her child. Not surprisingly, fans of the very Americanized *The Ring* were less enthusiastic about this sequel with its more troubling Asian sensibility. Like its predecessor, *The Ring Two* employs many references: a disquieting scene of deer attacking refers to a similar scene of birds attacking in Hitchcock's *The Birds,* as well as to a surreal scene involving deer in David Lynch's *The Straight Story*; a shrieking face (quoted also in *The Ring*) specifically recalls Edvard Munch's painting *The Scream*; the recurring image of the bathtub recalls a variety of horror-of-personality films, especially *The Nanny*; a camera movement into a close-up of someone's ear recalls the opening of *Blue Velvet*; and so forth. Even more exploited in *The Ring Two* is the demon with the long black hair covering her face, especially remarkable because its strangeness as a symbol (meaningless, if you will) to American audiences makes *The Ring Two* notably inscrutable.

Not surprisingly, the success of *The Ring* resulted in many Asian horror films being remade into American versions. The third tale in Takashi Shimizu's cycle of *Ju-on* films (*Ju-on 3* [*The Grudge*] in 2003) was remade for Hollywood by Shimizu himself as *The Grudge* in 2004, just as the fourth tale (*Ju-on 4* [*The Grudge 2*] in 2003) was remade for Hollywood in 2006; Hideo Nakata's *Honogurai Mizu No Soko Kara* [*Dark Water*] in 2002 was remade by Walter Salles as *Dark Water* in 2005; Kiyoshi Kurosawa's *Kairo* [*Pulse*] in 2001 was remade as *Pulse* by Jim Sonzero in 2006; Oxide Pang's *Gin Gwai* [*The Eye*] was remade as *The Eye* by David Moreau and Xavier Palud in 2008. Although these and other American remakes invariably have higher budgets, slicker production values, more special effects, and often sensuous imagery, by no means do they feel as authentic. Rather, they feel like high-quality forgeries engineered by American producers on a postmodern quest for the grail of contemporary horror: huge international profits. And with American studios hiring Asian directors to make English-language horror films, and Asian directors now

In *Ju-on 3: The Grudge*, a demonic child and apocalyptic cats illustrate how these millennial Asian films synthesize a variety of conventional horror elements.

making their Asian-language horror films with cognizance of the western market, the *cultural moment* of Asian millennial horror seems somehow already less present. (For instance, where is artistic integrity when Japanese director Masayuki Ochiai prepares two versions of his film *Shutter* so that some special effects for the Japanese audience can be replaced with different effects for the American audience?) The American remakes, though interesting enough, are increasingly formulaic and not forging new ground. Indeed, one suspects that the most disturbing Asian horror films will not be remade by Hollywood, or if they are, will doubtless lack the genuinely subversive power of the originals.

For instance, *Suicide Club* [*Jisatsu Saakuru*], written and directed by Sion Sono in 2002, is one of the more politically incorrect horror films, amorally unconcerned about whether it might actually promote suicide. It begins with 54 smiling schoolgirls joining hands and throwing themselves onto subway tracks as a train passes. What especially horrifies

is the gulf between the violence of their communal suicides and the girls' oblivious cheerfulness. Why did they kill themselves? Had they been studying too hard, a result of the Japanese culture of discipline? Or are they committing some new form of *seppuku*, the Japanese ritual of honor suicide? (Particularly in the late nineties, when Japan began confronting the social implications of its economic problems, several high-profile business

Three of the ways to kill yourself in *Suicide Club*: (1) cheerfully jump off a building, (2) mutilate yourself until you bleed to death, or (3) hang yourself with friends.

leaders committed *seppuku*. Were these suicides the inspiration for *Suicide Club*?) Mysteriously, we discover that a website has been announcing specific suicides before they've taken place. Another horrifying scene shows over a dozen giggling students, on the spur of the moment, jump off the roof of their school during a recess. "I wanna die." "Do it with me." "I will if you will." The idea of suicide strikes them all as fun; surreally their blood splatters in unison across the school windows. Without any soundtrack music, this scene — one of the most disturbing in all horror film — works precisely because its reality seems so mundane. The students are like lemmings. And then a woman slicing vegetables purposely cuts her fingers off, a comedian stabs himself, a worker stuffs his mouth with pills, as suicide spreads exponentially like a virus or an irresistible genetic impulse, suggesting an apocalypse. *Suicide Club* resembles *Killing Game* [*Jeux de Massacre*], the theatre-of-the-absurd play by Eugène Ionesco in which every character who appears on stage dies. The suicidal impulse is attributed to a variety of sources: is it communicated through the internet, passed via e-mail, transmitted over cellphones? Perhaps it is sent telepathically by "Genesis" — the self-proclaimed "Charles Manson of the information age" and leader of an androgynous pop group that sings longingly of death in lyrics like "I want to die as beautifully as Joan of Arc inside a Bresson film." [In an inscrutable subplot, Genesis tortures and kills young people he keeps imprisoned in tied sacks, which move weirdly in relation to the captives' movements.] Or, as a character proposes, are people killing themselves because of embedded codes on CD box covers and pop posters? Clearly, the technological is being used as a tool to invoke the terror of the primal. The worst possibility is that these self-destructive messages are coming from everywhere, that these new technologies are not good for us, and that the semiological signs now dominating our environments have become more dangerous than even Jean-Luc Godard predicted. In short: is our environment destroying our free will? One child chastises a detective trying to solve the case: "Why couldn't you feel the pain of others as you could your own?" Yet the young people obsessed with whether suicide severs your connection with your self seem already alienated from their authentic feelings and don't really express emotional pain. *Suicide Club* ends by suggesting that perhaps a little girl at the school (representing the youngest generation, for whom technology is a given?) may actually be the leader of the suicide club. Certainly one cannot imagine many contemporary Hollywood horror films similarly filled with ideas.

The Japanese *Suicide Club* was followed the next year (2003) by two fascinating horror films from South Korea: *Oldboy* and *A Tale of Two Sisters*. Directed by Park Chan-wook, *Oldboy* shows its protagonist, Oh Dae-su, drunk in a police station. A family man with a wife and daughter, Oh Dae-su says that his unusual name means "getting through one day at a time"—which is precisely what he is shortly forced to do. After the credits end, with

Like the horror-of-personality film, the Korean *Oldboy* communicates intensity with the close-up of the single eye.

a narrative suddenness Dae-su is shown imprisoned in a private complex that resembles a hotel room. He has already been there three months, an ellipsis which is disturbing because it contradicts our expectations as to how a narrative is supposed to develop. The imprisonment, which has nothing to do with his drunkenness, is sinister: Dae-su (abducted by whom?) has become the subject of a sadistic long-term experiment, his every move watched on a bank of video monitors. Neither he nor we know why he has been put there, only that he won't be released until fifteen years have passed. He is gassed nightly with Valium; and his captor — whom we can occasionally hear, but not see — says: "I'm a sort of scholar ... and my field of study is you." The fifteen years go by slowly, and we share Dae-su's bizarre hallucinations, experience the grinding loneliness of his isolation, and witness his psychological change, his hardening in response to the manipulations of his captivity. The sadistic incarceration, which seems pointless, becomes the cruelest demonstration of the existential meaninglessness of life. To indicate the passing of the years, we are shown a newsreel montage of historical events — including a plane hitting a World Trade Center tower on 9/11. Has our protagonist been an early victim of some new kind of terrorism?

When Oh Dae-su is finally released just as suddenly, life in the "real world" seems to be "life in a bigger prison." But now he is an obsessed man, his imprisonment having turned him into an uncaring monster, eager for revenge. With help from the internet, he tracks down his captor and discovers it is an old high school classmate, Lee Woo-jin. But Dae-su's punishment is not yet over. Not only has Woo-jin killed the wife of Dae-su and potentially every woman Dae-su has ever loved, including his daughter, Woo-jin says he intends to kill every woman Dae-su *will* ever love. In a surprising revelation we discover that Woo-jin long ago committed incest with his sister, and that the young Dae-su unknowingly took an action which led Woo-jin's sister to commit suicide. But the most horrifying revelation is that Woo-jin's revenge, technically, was *not* the imprisonment, but what was planned for afterwards. We discover that during his incarceration Dae-su was brainwashed and hypnotized so that upon his release he would unknowingly fall in love with his own daughter, not dead at all, who has been similarly brainwashed and hypnotized for the last fifteen years. And indeed, Woo-jin's diabolical plan comes to horrifying fruition. The sushi chef Oh Dae-su has fallen in love with is revealed to be his daughter, unrecognized; tragically, Dae-su learns that he has had sex with his daughter and violated the incest taboo. He and Woo-jin are now moral equals. Although "Oh Dae-su" is not exactly "Oe-di-pus," the names are close enough for us to realize that *Oldboy* is a horror reworking of classic Greek

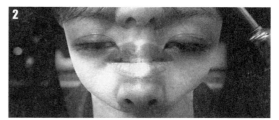

Park Chan-wook's eclectic devices in *Oldboy* encompass (1) composition in depth, (2) surreal superimpositions, (3) split screen, and (4) filmic references (such as to Bergman's *Persona*).

themes of family vengeance and fated tragedy. *Oldboy* ends with Oh Dae-su, like Oedipus, committing an act of self-mutilation as penance for his abomination. Bloodily he cuts off his tongue (as did Oedipus gouge out his eyes). Both horror film and tragedy, *Oldboy* suggests there is a monster within each of us; although fate has the capacity to unleash that monster, our humanity co-exists with the monster in an uneasy, schizophrenic balance. In the course of his ingenious plot, director Park Chan-wook includes expressive imagery, as well as references to a number of notable films, including Brian De Palma's *Obsession* and *Sisters*, and Ingmar Bergman's *Persona*. Notably, *Oldboy*, almost winning the *Palme D'Or* at Cannes, was awarded the *Grand Prix*, quite significant for a horror film.

A Tale of Two Sisters, written and directed by Kim Ji-woon and untypically sensuous for Asian horror film, uses lush, saturated colors in its cinematography, and a lyrical, Western-style score. The story of two girls and a potentially evil stepmother living in a mysterious house evokes a fairy-tale sensibility, totally appropriate for the folktale from which this film was adapted. *A Tale of Two Sisters* is filled with dream images — some presented as almost subliminal shock cuts which evoke early Alain Resnais, others presented as more standard Asian millennial horror, seamlessly integrated so as to create maximum ambiguity. *A Tale of Two Sisters* also includes typical horror devices: scary stairways, magic spells, menstrual blood, mirror images, mysterious ghosts, a haunted house, and so forth. But is the house actually haunted by the sisters' dead mother? The surprise revelation at the end of this film is that one sister, Su-yeon, despite having been consistently shown in the ongoing narrative, has long been dead; and the other sister, Su-mi, is in actuality deranged and has been hallucinating her sister's presence all along. The narrative we have been watching, therefore, is an unreliable one. Or to put it another way: *A Tale of Two Sisters* is really an unacknowledged remake of the underrated American horror film *The Other*, which thirty-

two years earlier presented virtually the same plot and shocking narrative revelation. As in *Oldboy*, *A Tale of Two Sisters* also references Bergman — specifically *Through a Glass Darkly* (originally entitled *The Wallpaper*), about a daughter who goes crazy and hears voices coming from the wallpaper, which she is physically able to enter. In *A Tale of Two Sisters*, also centered on the manifestations of mental illness, wallpaper takes on a similarly

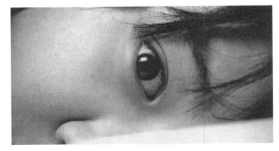

The Korean *A Tale of Two Sisters* is largely a contemporary horror-of-personality film, employing that subgenre's striking iconography, including (1) mirrors, (2) stairways, and (3) the singly photographed eye.

As Asian millennial horror, *A Tale of Two Sisters* (1) employs the traditional *yūrei* imagery of the girl with hanging, black hair; as well as (2) the alienating long shot which obscures faces within a formal composition; and (3) bravura camera placement from an unexpected angle.

Two images in *A Tale of Two Sisters* are especially expressive: (1) an unbalanced composition of one sister next to so much empty space that it suggests the permanent absence of the other sister; and (2) a striking, surreal superimposition that creates melodramatic intensity.

expressive role. *A Tale of Two Sisters* is almost indiscriminate in its filmic borrowings. One provocative example is the film's use of the "bloody sack"—which appeared so notably in Luis Buñuel's *That Obscure Object of Desire* as well as in the Japanese films *Audition* and *Suicide Club*. And notable, too—even if we realize it only retrospectively—is how *A Tale of Two Sisters* early on shows one sister with her long black hair obscuring her face like a *yūrei*, the traditional ghost from so many Japanese horror films. Certainly this image should have alerted us, even in this Korean film, that at least one sister was already dead. By its end, *A Tale of Two Sisters*, like many of these Asian horror films, moves beyond ambiguity into potential obscurity, especially disturbing for the typical American audiences who expect even horror films to be easily apprehensible. (Not surprisingly, Hollywood remade *A Tale of Two Sisters* in 2009 as *The Uninvited*, but in a version markedly less subtle, with the original's ambiguities replaced by generic conventions decidedly familiar.)

The most subversively upsetting of all the Asian horror directors is Takashi Miike. The word "surreal" is often used to describe works which merely traffic in strange imagery, but occasionally, there is a film like Miike's *Visitor Q* [*Bizita Q*], made in 2001, which invokes surrealism in the sense intended by André Breton and the original surrealists: that is, as a work beyond traditional morality that explores the strange, irrational, violent, sexual recesses of the subconscious with the same discipline it explores the conscious. Because *Visitor Q* shows the effect of a stranger's visit on each member of the protagonist's family, the film has an isomorphic relationship to Pasolini's *Teorema*. But *Visitor Q* is also centered on the protagonist's TV show, which is dedicated to showing Japan's most disturbing home videos and is a celebration of voyeurism which answers questions such as "Have you ever done it with your dad?" or "Have you ever hit your mother?" In the course of *Visitor Q*, we see these questions answered affirmatively, and much, much more — particularly in relationship to the dysfunctional sadomasochistic family (or are they actually quite functional?) at the film's center. We see a housewife mom who works as a prostitute and wears a kale facial mask as she is beaten by her son for buying the wrong toothbrush. We see a daughter who sleeps with her dad, who is himself a sadomasochist who invites a stranger to hit him with a rock. And in a key scene, we see the young stranger literally milking the mom's nipples. (And the mom can milk herself to such a degree that her kitchen floor is awash in milk and one must use an umbrella to keep dry.) "Some things are truly strange," says the father as he realizes that witnessing his son being bullied has not made the father mad, just horny. And so the horrific, voyeuristic thrills celebrated by *Visitor Q* become outright mania when the protagonist father videotapes himself raping the corpse of a woman he's killed. *Visitor Q* is clearly an iconoclastic film designed to shock; no one is crazier than anyone else, and everyone participates in violence. Amorally, this film — which seems pro-incest and includes a scene showing the daughter and father suckling at the mother's breasts — suggests that the family that kills and participates in S/M sex together, stays together. *Visitor Q* plays like a surreal horror version of the suburban sitcom *The Adventures of Ozzie and Harriet*.

Although the Asian millennial horror films have much to recommend them, too many of these films are of uneven quality, with individual scenes often more impressive than the whole. Takashi Miike's *Audition* [*Ôdishon*], on the other hand, directed in 1999, is consistently impressive and authentic, a horror masterpiece from beginning to end. What makes *Audition* so notable is its narrative strategy: although most of the film is a subtle, often tender love story about two lonely people tentatively coming together, in its last act particularly, *Audition* veers off unexpectedly in such a disturbing, violent direction that the audience feels assaulted. Rarely has a film had such a visceral impact (and the climax would be less shocking without the more mundane, sometimes sweet scenes that precede it). Central to its narrative strategy, *Audition* develops its story very slowly. Seven years after his wife's death, Shigeharu Aoyama decides to hold an audition to find a new wife (and mother to his teenage son). The pretext for the audition is a movie role; although his charade is morally suspect, Aoyama is so earnest and melancholy that we forgive him this ethical lapse. One friend tells him that "the whole of Japan is lonely." Another friend tells him that "Japan is finished." Are these sentiments connected? Does loneliness finish you off? (The film's conclusion suggests that loneliness does.) Aoyama's son Shigehiko tells his father, somewhat metaphorically, "Black sea bream start as male, then some become female — unisex." Certainly it would be easier if people could be that sexually self-sufficient.

At the audition Aoyama sometimes looks at the women as if they are consumer objects, but he is so earnest that we empathize with him nevertheless. He says, "It's like buying my first car." An accidental coffee stain on an application fatefully chooses the woman for him: Asami Yamazaki. When we first see her, she is dressed totally in white, a color which in Japan is not only for marriage, but for mourning. Talking about a hip injury which forced

The *Audition* sequence in which Aoyama (Ryo Ishibashi) meets Asami (Eihi Shiina) uses formal compositions of the appropriate grace and balance for a burgeoning love story. Yet the first image emphasizes Asami's inscrutability and dark hair, and the insistent angle for the successively closer shots of Asami harken to similar techniques used by Hitchcock in *Psycho*, thus subtextually suggesting horror. Compare with the frame grabs on page 227.

her to abandon a potential ballet career, she seems as sad as Aoyama and thus potentially his soul-mate. Giving up on her dreams "is like accepting death," she says with a Zen resignation, and — as she so often does — directs her gaze downward. Although these two souls seem kindred, Aoyama's friend doesn't like Asami, believing that "something chemical" is wrong with her. Demure and sweet, Asami appears to be without friends or sustaining human connection. Not until forty-five minutes into *Audition* is there its first surreal rupture, though a subtle one. An ominous tree obscures a woman (is it Aoyama's late wife or Asami?); and Asami, on the floor, contemplates a filled cloth sack. These images seem to belong to Aoyama's dream. If there is any strangeness to *Audition* up to this point, it is primarily in the striking compositions of these images: the ominous black telephone in Asami's flat, the bones of the back of Asami's neck, her odd posture as she sits on the floor, her long hair drooping like that of the demons in other Japanese horror films of the period. Later, when we see Asami with the cloth sack a second time, we realize that *this* image may not be Aoyama's dream, but real; then suddenly, the sack moves violently. With an ellipsis, the narrative jumps from this disturbing, mysterious image (or is it just metaphorical?) to return to its love story, almost making us forget the brief rupture as we now watch Aoyama and Asami develop their relationship. In a moving love scene when Asami removes her clothes to reveal childhood burns and scars, she seems achingly vulnerable. When she asks if Aoyama can love only her, he agrees. As there is yet another narrative ellipsis, we presume they make love. But when Aoyama wakes up, Asami is gone.

Even though this image (especially in its original color) is aesthetic and romantic, Asami's face is hidden and her long black hair is emphasized, conventional signs of an evil _yūrei_.

At this point of the narrative, _Audition_ emulates _Vertigo_, as Aoyama searches for his heroine to make her his wife, yet realizing her life contains mystery. Who was responsible for her physical mistreatment as a girl? Aoyama's search leads to disturbing discoveries: at the now inactive ballet studio where she once studied, its director is paralyzed and disfigured, and an ambiguous image suggests he may have branded Asami between her legs with red-hot tongs. And the owner of a bar Asami may have worked at was killed and dismembered: "The police tried to recompose her body.... Three extra fingers and an ear came up. An extra tongue as well.... Isn't it a terrible world?" In Aoyama's vision, we see the severed tongue flapping on the floor in a puddle of blood. In an extraordinary sequence which seems to indicate that Aoyama has been drugged, the narrative again ruptures. While he is unconscious, we see a different version of an earlier scene between him and Asami. Is this new version what really took place? Or is Aoyama re-imagining the earlier scene? Scenes of Aoyama having oral sex with a co-worker and then with his son's girlfriend suggest definitively that we are watching a dream. But then Aoyama comes face-to-face with the mysterious sack from earlier, out of which emerges a near naked demon missing an ear, a tongue, and three fingers. Asami feeds the demon her vomit, and then as the narrative continues to rupture, transcending both time and space, Asami strangles and decapitates, with surgical wire, the ballet director who had tortured her. At this point, the surrealism has absolute integrity, because reality, memory, fantasy, projection, and dream are intermixed beyond our ability to distinguish them.

When Aoyama gains consciousness from his drugged state, for a moment we hold to the hope that _Audition_ has not actually forsaken its love story for such horror. But now, with Aoyama awake, the film descends into more horror than we could have possibly imagined. We learn that Asami has returned to Aoyama's house and killed the family dog (always a bad sign in a horror film). She now wears a leather apron like a geisha dominatrix and tells Aoyama that although his body has been paralyzed, his nerves have not, so that he "can enjoy the pain and suffer incredibly." Director Miike presents the torture scene that follows with documentary precision, leaving nothing to our imagination or off-camera. Asami inserts a huge hypodermic needle into Aoyama's tongue, then slowly inserts a number of long needles into various nerve centers of his body in order to create maximum pain. Through it all, she retains her demure expression, and the torture she inflicts is punctuated by her high-pitched, repeated, sing-song tones — translated in the subtitles as "deeper,

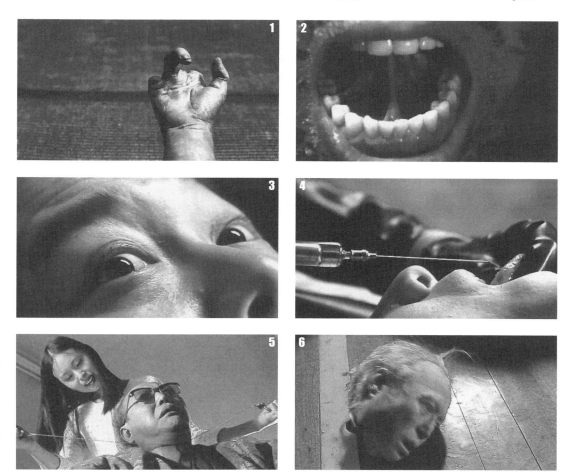

Particularly in the last sections of *Audition*, any generic romantic conventions give way to brutal horror conventions, as the audience is assaulted with close-ups of torture: (1) a mutilated hand, (2) a mouth without its tongue, (3) eyes about to be assaulted with needles, (4) a tongue injected with a hypodermic, (5) a man garroted with surgical wire, and (6) a severed head.

deeper." Asami has presumed that the audition was something Aoyama characteristically conducted to take advantage of young women for sex. "Words create lies. Pain can be trusted," she says. She inserts two needles directly under his eyes. As if all this weren't enough, Asami uses surgical wire to slowly amputate his left foot, which she tosses away with a thud, before turning her attention to his right foot. This torture sequence is so extended and unexpected that as spectators, we feel punished and betrayed. What has happened to our love story? The success of Miike's horror derives from his stunning breach of the inherent contract between artist and audience. We feel almost as if the director has molested *us*; and on no level is what we are seeing entertaining. (Indeed, like the French *Irréversible*, *Audition* is one of those rare films that sends spectators literally running out of the theatre.) Contributing to this horrific effect, too, is the fact that the horror genre — from Fay Wray in *King Kong* to Janet Leigh in *Psycho*—has conventionally victimized females; *Audition* has the courage to show a powerfully strong woman victimizing a passive man.

Also horrifying is our realization that Asami plans to kill Aoyama's son precisely because Aoyama loves him — and not only her, as Aoyama had glibly promised her. Just as Asami is about to attack Aoyama's son, another sudden narrative rupture returns us to the scene where Aoyama and Asami first made love, just before Aoyama fell asleep. We think: is it possible that *Audition*'s torture sequence has all been Aoyama's bad dream? This time, when Aoyama wakes up after having made love, Asami has *not* disappeared and instead, accepts his marriage proposal. "I didn't become the heroine of the movie," she says demurely, "but I became the real heroine." And in a reflexive line, she adds: "It's like a dream." The way the film has jumped backwards is reassuring, because we have been allowed to return to *Audition*-the-love-story, and to attribute the disturbing torture material to the elaborate dream of a nervous groom subconsciously working through his fears of re-marriage.

Hitchcock contended that a good director (emulating the behavioralist Pavlov) should always emotionally manipulate the audience. Director Miike here manipulates his audience more brutally than Hitchcock ever did (even in *Psycho*), because at the moment we finally relax, Miike cuts back to the torture scene, and we realize definitively that the *torture* is indeed the reality, and the recent respite nothing but Aoyama's wishful fantasy. Sadly, life at the millennium is defined by violence, madness, torture, loneliness. As Asami struggles to kill Aoyama's son she falls backwards down the stairs. When her neck palpitates strangely, we hope we may be again veering off into the unreal. But alas, Miike allows us no escape. With Aoyama footless and Asami injured, both are on the floor and apparently dying, in the weirdest update ever of the finale of King Vidor's *Duel in the Sun*. Yet Aoyama and Asami look at each other tenderly and offer affectionate sentiments while the soundtrack's piano offers a simple, expressive love theme. Asami: "I never expected that we would meet again. Sorry to have been childish. It's a hassle living alone. I didn't have anybody to talk with. You are the first one to support me ... warmly wrapping me. Trying to understand me." Aoyama: "It's hard to forget about. But someday you'll feel that life is wonderful. That's life, isn't it?" And the final image — which suggests that all of us start innocent and hopeful, no matter where we end — is of Asami as a little girl, wrapping her feet for ballet. Certainly there has been no other Asian horror film superior to *Audition*; and one suspects no American remake could offer the same subversive message.

At least one final Asian film seems especially worthy of the final discussion in this chapter: *The Host*, directed in Korea in 2006 by Bong Joon-ho and released in the United States in 2007. This film notably moves away from the eccentricities of recent Asian millennial horror and instead refurbishes the classic Japanese monster movie *Godzilla*. Amazingly, it succeeds in a spectacular way. Whereas the monsters in the *Godzilla* movies were clear metaphors for the atomic bomb, the monster in *The Host* is a metaphor for something new: environmental irresponsibility, especially by Americans. *The Host* begins its story on February 9, 2000, at a United States Army base in South Korea where an American military officer orders a Korean worker to dispose of a great volume of toxic chemicals by pouring them down the sink. Although the officer is told they will enter the water supply, he forces the worker to comply. This scene in *The Host* is actually inspired by ongoing tensions between the American military and a growing number of South Koreans, especially following a real incident in 2000, when an American army man was caught dumping at least 20 gallons of toxic formaldehyde into the Han River from Yongsan Garrison, in Seoul. Koreans claimed grave environmental damage and an increase in cancer deaths, which the American military denied. Especially since, thousands of Koreans have been demonstrating against their own government's plan to allow Americans to expand Camp Humphreys, a U.S. base in Pyongtaek. Koreans claim not only that this is a land giveaway to a virtual occupier, but that the American military is continually polluting the Han River with discarded oil and other toxic materials—polluting with impunity because its signed agreement with the Korean government exempts it from having to follow most Korean environmental laws.

When *The Host* jumps ahead two years to a period *after* the terrorist attack of 9/11—a psychological/sociological shift which looms subtextually over the film—a mutated monster created by the chemical dumping emerges from the Han River and starts killing indiscriminately. Unlike *Godzilla*, this monster is fast-moving; and though it can travel on land, it is a kind of giant, amphibial squid. At the center of *The Host* is a loving, if slightly dysfunctional three-generation family of five who cling emotionally to each other, *literally* in one startling scene combining pathos with slapstick as they thrash about the floor in grief as one. Our greatest affection goes to Hyun-seo, the plucky little girl at the film's center; in a shocking scene, the monster grabs her by its tail and drags her into the river. Although we presume Hyun-seo is dead, we discover shortly that she is still alive. Although the family struggles mightily to save her for most of the film, perhaps *The Host*'s key surprise is that she dies anyway in the film's final moments just as she is pulled from the monster's throat. In fact, both she and her grandfather, the family patriarch, become innocent victims of the monster—that is, innocent victims of a terrorist monster created by American policy. And of course the initial American environmental crime was itself abetted by the Korean government.

After 9/11, Americans asked obsessively: "Why do so many people around the world hate us?" And in *The Host*, the monster represents the United States' refusal to sign the Kyoto Accords, the continuing United States presence in South Korea, and even of American arrogance in Iraq—particularly in how our own paranoia regarding terrorism may be leading to world paranoia. For instance, soon after Hyun-seo is snatched, it is revealed that the monster is also a host for a deadly virus that can spread and cause apocalyptic death; as a result, the South Korean government rounds up the hundreds of near-victims of the monster, including our protagonist family. Except: There really isn't a virus. The government is wrong in its assertion, or is lying, or is arrogant. Just as there were no weapons of mass destruction in Iraq, there is no supervirus being spread by the Han River monster. Because of the government's inability to capture the real villain (the monster) or to confront the truth of how the monster got created (United States policies), the government is now pursuing a different target (Korean citizens), imagining or purposely manufacturing imminent danger where no danger exists. The film accuses the Korean government officials of following a poor role model when it acts like the United States, which attacked a country (Iraq) where no imminent threat existed, because the United States was not skillful enough to capture the real monster (Osama bin Laden). As these revelations unfold, it becomes clear that *The Host* is a millennial horror film which was powerfully conceived as suspenseful, comical, moving entertainment with great special effects and a political kick. *The Host* ends with horrible tragedy for its central family, as government hysteria regarding its mishandling of the danger results in civil liberties being trampled and the real monster given free reign to cause even more misery and death. *The Host* climaxes with a nightmarish vision of environmental pollution and chemical agent testing gone horribly wrong, with Korean political demonstrators gassed and unable to stop the madness.

Even as *The Host* performed financially well in the United States for a foreign film and extraordinarily well worldwide (almost $100 million), Americans were oblivious to the real hostilities behind the film. If *The Host*'s monster were to emerge from the Hudson River and literally attack New York City, one wonders if Americans would finally start paying attention to political complaints in other parts of the world. Or would we simply ask, in genuine ignorance and surprise, "Why does this Asian monster hate us?" rather than "How did we create this hatred?"

10—Postmodern Remakes, the Averted Gaze, and Some Glimmerings of the New

While Asian filmmakers were pioneering expressive millennial horror, most American filmmakers—either out of touch with what was culturally frightening or unwilling to go there—were taking refuge in established subjects and mining the horror genre in search of properties, going as far back as 1931's *Dracula*. What resulted was a spate of horror remakes. Because movies were costing so much, Hollywood was unwilling to invest in the untested: surely, it thought, the tried and true would still be valid, especially if dressed up in new clothes. Those new clothes were primarily bigger-and-better stunts and flashier special effects, particularly CGI (computer-generated imagery) driven by ever-evolving animation software. The effect of all these remakes (and tricked-out sequels) was truly postmodern, since now King Kong, Norman Bates, Godzilla, the Mummy, and Japanese demons with long black hair could all inhabit our movie screens within the same contemporary cultural landscape as Freddy and Leatherface. What is shocking is how many of these postmodern

An expressive silhouette in *Bram Stoker's Dracula*.

305

remakes have been critically panned and/or financially unsuccessful (the real Hollywood sin), without diminishing the postmodern onslaught of more remakes (and sequels).

Relatively recent high-profile remakes include *Night of the Living Dead* and *Lord of the Flies* in 1990; *What Ever Happened to Baby Jane?* in 1991; *Bram Stoker's Dracula* in 1992; *Body Snatchers* [*Invasion of the Body Snatchers*] in 1993; *Mary Shelley's Frankenstein* in 1994; *Diabolique* in 1996; *Psycho* and *Godzilla* in 1998; *The Mummy, The Haunting,* and *House on Haunted Hill* in 1999; *Planet of the Apes* in 2001; *Willard* and *The Texas Chainsaw Massacre* in 2003; *Dawn of the Dead* and *The Stepford Wives* in 2004; *War of the Worlds, The Amityville Horror, The Cabinet of Dr. Caligari, House of Wax, The Fog,* and *King Kong* in 2005; *The Hills Have Eyes, When a Stranger Calls, The Omen, Night of the Living Dead 3D, Poseidon* [*The Poseidon Adventure*], and *The Wicker Man* in 2006; *Halloween* and *Invasion* [*Invasion of the Body Snatchers*] in 2007; *Day of the Dead* and *The Day the Earth Stood Still* in 2008; and *My Bloody Valentine 3-D* and *Friday the 13th* in 2009. Even an exceedingly minor 1960 film, *13 Ghosts,* was remade in 2001— in the hope that nostalgic baby-boomers would encourage their teens to see it? The remake was titled *Thir13en Ghosts* upon the dubious supposition that a new graphic spelling could make the material sufficiently relevant. Horror remakes for television included lots of Stephen King: *The Shining* in 1997, *Carrie* in 2002, *'Salem's Lot* in 2004. And of course, the American remakes of the imaginative Asian horror films became a burgeoning market, inaugurated by *The Ring* in 2002 and continuing through *The Eye* in 2008 and beyond. Even an apparently original film like 2004's *Van Helsing,* though not borrowing a familiar title, is a recycling of *Frankenstein, Dracula,* and *The Wolf Man.* Admittedly, some of these remakes have their occasional points of interest — such as the casting of Mia Farrow (from the seminal *Rosemary's Baby*) in *The Omen* remake as Mrs. Baylock, the second nanny of the demonic child. However, few of these remakes deserve much attention, since most are more like amusement park rides than coherent, personal works of art.

Of these remakes, *Bram Stoker's Dracula* and *King Kong* seem at opposite poles. The former, which could fairly have been called *Francis Ford Coppola's Dracula,* because the film feels so personal, totally eschews CGI special effects and instead uses the legacy of German expressionism to create a contemporary sensibility. Conversely, Peter Jackson's impersonal *King Kong,* which one admires grudgingly as a great 90-minute movie that takes over three hours, is dominated by its persuasive effects. Whereas the 1933 *King Kong* showed the terrifying return of the primitive to a Depression-era America whose modern, industrial identity was collapsing, the 2005 remake nostalgically re-introduced an old-fashioned monster

Images from ***The Mummy Returns*** reveal the conservative nature of the contemporary American horror film: (1) A nuclear family (Brendan Fraser, Freddie Boath, and Rachel Weisz) responding to a special effect identifies the film as popcorn horror for the entire family, sure to appeal without offending with any real ideas or content; (2) A screaming black man (Shaun Parkes, for comic relief) expands the film's demographic appeal while contributing to its subtextual racism.

Francis Ford Coppola's version of **Bram Stoker's Dracula** only uses effects possible in the silent-film era his film evokes: (1) a model miniature, (2) expressionistic lighting, (3) sumptuous decor, (4) an optical iris, and (5 and 6) different makeups which suggest physical transformation when joined together by a dissolve.

to a digital America which was counting screen pixels and editing its own movies on home computers. In other words, the remake — though lots of fun — is in no sense about genuine fear.

So why for so long have American directors been retreating from the *now*?

Because to face the *now* would have required exploring a variety of political and emotional realities in a country which largely held it unpatriotic to suggest that it was not perpetually "morning in America." Subversive or controversial ideas are not exactly the mother's milk of contemporary capitalism. To invest a hundred million dollars on a film is risky, because the nation is filled with special-interest groups quick to take offense and organize boycotts, and the world is filled with potential ticket-buyers with a wide range of values and interests. (The *Superman* remake of 2006 revised the superhero's conventional commitment to "truth, justice, and the American way" to the lesser "truth and justice," so as not to offend the international America-haters who might otherwise buy *Superman* tickets.) Besides, for most people, special-effects movies are great amusement, so why veer from that garden path to look at the real landscape, treacherous and scary, just out of view?

Ever since *Star Wars* in 1977, America had begun averting its gaze. Neil Postman, writing in 1985, offered profoundly relevant ideas about the sorry direction of American culture in his book *Amusing Ourselves to Death: Public Discourse in the Age of Show Business*. Postman's argument derives from his analysis of the differences between the futuristic visions of George Orwell, as expressed in *Animal Farm* and *1984*, and of Aldous Huxley, as expressed in *Brave New World* and *Brave New World Revisited*. According to Postman, Huxley was more clearly on target:

> What Orwell feared were those who would ban books. What Huxley feared was that there would be no reason to ban a book for there would be no one who wanted to read one. Orwell feared those who would deprive us of information. Huxley feared those who would give us so much that we would be reduced to passivity and egoism. Orwell feared that the truth would be concealed from us. Huxley feared the truth would be drowned in a sea of irrelevance. Orwell feared we would become a captive culture. Huxley feared we would become a trivial culture, preoccupied with some equivalent of the feelies, the orgy porgy, and the centrifugal bumblepuppy. As Huxley remarked in *Brave New World Revisited*, the civil libertarians and rationalists who are ever on the alert to oppose tyranny "failed to

In a camera movement in *Memento* which contains visual information so subliminal that most spectators miss it, a false memory gives way to a repressed truth: It wasn't Sammy (Stephen Tobolowsky) who killed his wife, but our protagonist Leonard (Guy Pearce).

In a film that is both romantic comedy and futuristic horror, (1) lovers (Kate Winslet and Jim Carrey) pursue the benefits of induced amnesia, as *Eternal Sunshine of the Spotless Mind* explores several visual metaphors for the loss of memory, including (2) out-of-focus imagery, (3) underexposure, and (4) overexposure.

take into account man's almost infinite appetite for distractions." In [Orwell's] *1984*, Huxley added, people are controlled by inflicting pain. In *Brave New World*, they are controlled by inflicting pleasure. In short, Orwell feared that what we hate will ruin us. Huxley feared that what we love will ruin us.[1]

And so even that most subversive American genre, the horror film, moved toward simple amusement because it was easy and unproblematic. And yet, as a subconscious testimony, many of the most successful films implicitly evoked American obliviousness, this refusal to look clearly at contemporary problems, politics, or horror. For instance, in the key film *Memento* (in 2000), the protagonist suffers from an actual mental disorder, unable to retain any memory longer than a few minutes. He tries to remember things by tattooing salient information all over his body; one tattoo, ambiguous, reads "MEMORY IS TREACHERY." By the end of the film we discover that his refusal to face the truth of his past is a strategy he has specifically chosen so he can live in his fool's paradise. *The Sixth Sense* (in 1999) and *The Others* (in 2001) were both about protagonists so oblivious to the realities of the world that they couldn't even recognize that they were already dead. *Vanilla Sky* (in 2001) with Tom Cruise essentially took the same strategy; and *The Bourne Identity* (in 2002) and *The Manchurian Candidate* (in 2004) both dealt with amnesia. In the highly regarded *Eternal Sunshine of the Spotless Mind* (in 2004), the protagonist undergoes a procedure to erase his memories of his girlfriend, to spare him continuing emotional pain. Avoiding emotional pain seems almost a new American right, and such avoidance is disastrous for the horror film. This new "right" explains why Americans were largely hostile to *United 93*, for instance — they didn't want to have to think about 9/11 and wouldn't be made to do so. It also explains why Americans didn't care that George W. Bush didn't allow them to see the coffins of soldiers killed in Iraq, and why Americans decreasingly watch our

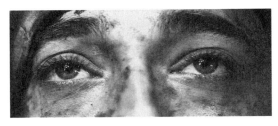

Although *The Jacket* is fairly traditional horror, its Gulf War images suggest the film is about political amnesia — appropriate as social comment on the War in Iraq, still raging when the film was made. Images of Iraq and George H.W. Bush lead inexorably to the unfeeling eyes of the victimized soldier (Adrian Brody).

nightly news or read newspapers, where upsetting truths and images lurk. To counter diminished circulation and ratings, newspapers and TV news have become centers of feel-good "infotainment." This purposive amnesia aids our flight from reality and can be found in many successful horror films, like *Identity* (in 2003) and *The Forgotten* (in 2004). *The Village* (in 2004) requires the heroine to make the suspect moral choice to embrace amnesia in regard to the disturbing truths she learns and — even worse — to conspire to keep her fellow citizens in a permanent state of obliviousness. And tellingly, the cult horror film *The Jacket* (in 2005) put amnesia in the political context of Operation Desert Storm. Despite our best attempts to remain detached and amused, these films — even as they distract us — speak on a subtextual level directly to our subconscious and pronounce indictment. This American obliviousness, especially omnipresent the last ten years and destructive in the artistic realm, is disastrous in the political realm. As Neil Postman pointed out in 1985:

> I don't suppose there has been a story in years that received more continuous attention from television [than the "Iranian Hostage Crisis."] We may assume, then, that Americans know most of what there is to know about this unhappy event. And now, I put these questions to you: Would it be an exaggeration to say that not one American in a hundred knows what language the Iranians speak? Or what the word "Ayatollah" means or implies? Or knows any details of the tenets of Iranian religious beliefs? Or the main outlines of their political history? Or knows who the Shah was, and where he came from? ... Nevertheless, everyone had an opinion about this event, for in America everyone is entitled to an opinion.... It is probably more accurate to call them emotions rather than opinions, which would account for the fact that they change from week to week, as the pollsters tell us.[2]

And it is this intellectual and political obliviousness that is reflected in the most popular American films, even in an era dominated by terrorist fears and Middle East war.

In 2005, at least four highly regarded films offered thoughtful, serious ideas in an attempt to counter the American cinema's dominant sensibility of frivolousness: Ang Lee's *Brokeback Mountain* (about a tragic homosexual love in an unaccepting society), Paul Haggis' *Crash* (about contemporary racism among Americans of all ethnicities), Stephen Gaghan's

Syriana (about the internecine politics of Big Oil and the Middle East), and George Clooney's *Good Night and Good Luck* (about the need to confront political demagoguery). Many commentators suggested that these films indicated the beginning of a new era in the American cinema. Yet it must be noted that these four films domestically brought in about $218 million — not very impressive considering that in the same year, the sixth *Star Wars* film, the first *Narnia Chronicles* film, the fourth *Harry Potter* film, and the *War of the Worlds* remake (all driven by special effects) domestically made over $1.2 *billion*, and internationally over $3 billion. These box-office figures suggest that discussion of an American film renaissance is premature at best. And films released since 2005 — such as the blockbuster sequel *Pirates of the Caribbean: Dead Man's Chest*, which *cost* $225 million to make and brought in over a billion dollars internationally — reveal no sign that this postmodern era of amusement is changing. Indeed, in 2007 the third installment of *Pirates*, despite generally awful reviews, grossed just under a billion dollars; and in 2008 the fourth installment of *Indiana Jones* approached that figure.

Along with their lowbrow tastes, more people than ever have strong, polarizing, uninformed opinions; low percentages of Americans vote or participate regularly in the political process (though one cannot but hope that that will finally change); and even as the world fills with greater political horror and violence, horror films continue to traffic in the expected and we amuse ourselves with *American Idol* and the exploits of "Brangelina."[3] Sadly, Neil Postman (and Aldous Huxley) got it right.

One of the few recent horror films to forage into new territory is the original *Saw*, released in 2004, which seems the first genuinely post–9/11 horror film. (Unfortunately, *Saw*'s many sequels — a horror record of five in five years!— are more mercenary than visionary, offering repetition not elaboration.) Directed by James Wan and written by Leigh Whannell, *Saw* plunges into its action immediately — as two strangers, Dr. Lawrence Gordon and Adam, wake up as prisoners chained in a dark, dirty washroom turned into a torture chamber. Neither man knows how he got there or why, but in order to survive, the men are required to perform gruesome tasks by an unseen sadist. For instance, Dr. Gordon is told that if he doesn't kill Adam by a certain time, Dr. Gordon's family will die. *Saw* asks the question: Could *you* kill an innocent person if your failure to do so would result in your own death or the deaths of those you love? (A prominent 2003 news story may have been a partial inspiration for *Saw*: Brian Douglas Wells, a pizza-delivery man from Erie, Pennsylvania, was apparently told that if he didn't rob a bank, the bomb that was strapped to his neck would be detonated. He attempted to rob the bank, but the bomb killed him anyway.[4])

Saw presents a world of Hobson's choices in which traditional morality feels inadequate because all the choices are repugnant. What to do? Is accepting death the only moral choice when we are otherwise required to take a morally repugnant alternative? *Saw* resonates because so many Hobson's choices were manifest on 9/11. For instance, the United 93 passengers were given two horrifying options: allow the hijackers to *probably* crash the plane at some time uncertain into a chosen target, or potentially crash it themselves. And of course the victims on the upper floors of the burning World Trade Center towers were given similar unbearable options: wait to die in the engulfing flames, or commit suicide by jumping from the building. *Saw*, though filled with violence, is about the emotional horror of being forced to make an impossible choice. In one of *Saw*'s key scenes, Dr. Gordon is forced to listen to violent mayhem over a cellphone, helpless to prevent it, or for that matter, to understand exactly what's happening. The scene evokes the real-life situations

Saw encompasses two sensibilities: (1) the sensibility of horror — with a serial killer in a disquiet-ing mask, and (2) the sensibility of documentary — with images suggestive of detention and wartime torture chambers as photographed with low-end camcorders.

of those who on 9/11 listened on cellphones to loved ones who were trapped and expecting death. Ultimately, Dr. Gordon is willing to saw off his own leg so he can unchain himself to kill the innocent Adam in order to save his own family. Like Lina Wertmüller's *Seven Beauties*, *Saw* is about what we will do in order to survive. And we will do plenty. (For instance, in a particularly grisly flashback, a young woman awakens to discover that a bomb has been locked onto her face and that the only way to prevent its explosion is to cut open an unconscious person who has been made to swallow the key to that lock. The young woman survives, because ultimately — as Abu Ghraib testifies — it is not really that hard to convince someone to torture or abuse another.)

Although *Saw* is technically a horror-of-personality film about the psychopathic "Jig-saw" killer who creates these tests, Jigsaw's identity, though a surprise, is not that relevant to the film's strategy. Indeed, we barely see him. Central to *Saw* is its suggestion that all of us are capable of violence and cruelty toward others, because we believe, on some deep level, that the lives of those in other clans, of those we don't know, are less important than the lives of those in our own clans, of those we do know. Through its metaphorical plot, *Saw* sheds light on Abu Ghraib, the War in Iraq, religious fundamentalism, suicide bombers — indeed, the emotional underpinnings of the fascist sensibility, so relevant to our times.

Saw's final irony is that its psychopath is a cancer survivor who has arranged these sadis-tic trials so that those who survive them will start living their lives larger and with more gratitude. It's notable that Dr. Gordon is an oncologist in the position of offering patients their own difficult choices — take a poisonous treatment with side effects including perma-nent tissue damage and death, or risk dying from the untreated cancer. Yet Dr. Gordon is oblivious to much, even to the human connections in his own life, which is why his wife asks him: "How can you walk through life pretending that you're happy?" And so Dr. Gor-don clearly *needs* to undergo trial and change; who among us might not?

Another horror film which seems genuinely unique is *Donnie Darko*, written and directed by Richard Kelly in 2001, and nominated for a variety of international awards. *Donnie Darko*'s sense of indecipherability both limited its traditional audience and boosted its cult audience. Certainly, the film defies categorization. Donnie, a suburban teenager who sees a therapist and is on medication, may be crazy because he's haunted by a demonic six-foot rabbit with an apocalyptic vision. ("28 days, 6 hours, 42 minutes, 12 seconds... That is when the world will end.") On the other hand, maybe Donnie is sane, the rabbit is real, and the world will end. Or maybe there is a temporary alternate universe that will end — but only if Donnie sacrifices himself, exhibiting a genuinely Christian virtue anti-

A political horror film with surreal, satirical, ambiguous imagery, *Donnie Darko* connects reactionary, right-wing American politics, as represented by President George H. W. Bush, to potential apocalypse. If Donnie (Jake Gyllenhaal) represents a subversive force, what the demonic six-foot rabbit represents is much less clear.

thetical to the hypocritical fundamentalist culture all around him. Psychological, demonic, and apocalyptic horror all intertwine in this political allegory. Oddly for a contemporary horror film, *Donnie Darko* is a period piece — set during the time of the Michael Dukakis/ George H. W. Bush presidential debate of October 1988, more than a decade prior to the film's release. Donnie's parents are rabid Bush fans; and Kitty Farmer, Donnie's gym teacher, wholeheartedly supports Dan Quayle and complains that "No one cares about responsibility, morality, family values." Kitty, who also wants to ban Graham Greene's "The Destructors" as pornography (although she confuses its author with Lorne Greene, the star of *Bonanza*), enjoys wearing her "God is Awesome" T-shirt. Donnie, on the other hand, believes the search for God is absurd, even though the airplane motor that falls from the sky onto his bed may be a spiritual message. Clearly, *Donnie Darko* is looking back, and not with nostalgia, at the early days of fundamentalism's hijacking of American politics through its "family values" agenda. Despite his suburban upbringing, Donnie will have no part of traditional family values: he masturbates without guilt, accuses a right-wing motivational speaker (who is both hypocrite and pedophile) of being "the fucking Antichrist," and consorts with the demonic rabbit, Frank, who encourages Donnie to surreal acts of destruction.

Using wide angle lenses, a lyrical moving camera, and even backwards-motion to help explain its complex ideas and conundrums, *Donnie Darko* is always visually fascinating —

and nowhere more so than in its visual manifestation of "destiny," which looks like a liquid protuberance which extends from your chest to lead you around, like a snake pulling you. *Donnie Darko* is also filled with postmodern references to other films or works of horror: to Stephen King, to *Halloween*, to *Frightmare*, to *The Evil Dead*, to *Pretty Poison*, to the Jimmy Stewart comedy *Harvey*, and to *The Last Temptation of Christ* (which may suggest that we are to see Donnie as a Christ figure). Like Anthony Perkins at the end of *Psycho,* the skillful Jake Gyllenhaal (as Donnie) has a habit of looking up, slightly cross-eyed, from his downturned head. Ultimately, *Donnie Darko* suggests a horrific science-fiction version of an Escher print, a puzzle — like *"Don't Look Now"* — that exists "beyond the fragile geometry of space," but with a strong measure of social satire as a corrective for America's moralistic culture.

11 — Guillermo Del Toro

Even more a political horror film than *Donnie Darko*, the great *Pan's Labyrinth*, written and directed by the Mexican *auteur* Guillermo Del Toro, was released in the United States at the end of 2006. Although Del Toro had attracted a cult following ever since his debut feature *Cronos* in 1993 (even winning some international awards for his work) and attracted huge box office for his work on *Blade II* in 2002, *Pan's Labyrinth* definitively broke through to enormous critical acclaim internationally *and* impressive box office. Indeed, rarely had a horror film been given so many awards, including Academy awards for best art direction, cinematography, and makeup, and nominations for best foreign film, music, and original screenplay; an Independent Spirit award for cinematography and nomination for best feature; BAFTA awards for best foreign film, makeup, and costuming; a Golden Globe nomination for best foreign film; a New York Film Critics award for best cinematography; an L. A. Film Critics award for best production design; a National Society of Film Critics award for best film; and seven Goya awards from Spain. Yet weirdly, there was the erroneous presumption in many reviews, particularly in the United States, that *Pan's Labyrinth* was a *sui generis* masterpiece that was without precedent.

It is at least true that few of Del Toro's films are standard horror in the way we usually understand the genre. And although *Dark Dreams 2.0* is predominantly organized by considerations of genre, it seems appropriate to focus this chapter (and the Cronenberg chapter) on how considerations of authorship conflate with genre. At the moment, Del Toro's horror films have more in common with Spanish cinema of the seventies than contempo-

The children in *Spirit of the Beehive* are mesmerized by horror film, which connects effortlessly to our (and their) most profound fears.

rary American horror, yet one suspects Del Toro's films — particularly *Pan's Labyrinth*— may yet inspire the flowering of a more widespread horror subgenre not uncommon in Spanish cinema: a fantastical horror of the political. Certainly Del Toro's films are both more eclectic — drawing from fairy tale, action-adventure, and comic book sources as much as from horror — and more personal, emerging from the obsessions of their imaginative creator. And there tends to be a difference between Del Toro's films in English, which have a blockbuster sensibility and a harder-driving, American-style narrative, and Del Toro's films in Spanish, which have an art-film sensibility and a political subtext embedded within a slower, more ambiguous narrative.[1]

Although the English films are inferior to the Spanish, they are interesting enough. For instance, *Mimic*, Del Toro's horror-of-Armageddon film from 1997, if routine in many ways, contains sequences, ideas, and monstrous creatures as expressive as any in contemporary horror. The film's opening credits would be impressive by themselves as contemporary gallery art. The huge cockroaches dominating *Mimic*, explained as the result of DNA manipulation gone wrong, are in the service of Del Toro's conscious attempt at a cautionary tale and a contemporary Frankenstein story (though with an autistic boy standing in for *Frankenstein*'s little girl). As a dark joke, *Mimic*'s first victim plunges to his death in front of a sign in the shape of a cross, with printed words that attest, quite erroneously, that "Jesus Saves." And quite amorally, a monster cockroach kills and eats the two characters who are children, plucky and cute, if unfortunately doomed. The mutant bugs, with their brown wings and bowed heads, at times resemble Catholic monks, which gives *Mimic*, set in Holy Trinity Chapel and the New York City subway, an interesting subtext. (Del Toro himself was significantly influenced by his rabidly Catholic grandmother, who at one point, appalled by his Gothic imagination, arranged for his exorcism.) When *Mimic* ends, the heroine has a rosary wrapped around her wrist: a religious icon which appears in several of Del Toro's films. Most important in *Mimic* are the excitement and imagination Del Toro brings to the creation of his monsters. Although the distinction may seem subtle in *Mimic*, which is driven by special effects, Del Toro is interested in these effects not for their own sake, but for their ability to help him create creatures which might stand respectably alongside the most famous creatures of classic literature and mythology. *Mimic*'s insects by no means achieve that distinction, but Del Toro's film was definitely a trial run for the more complicated works Del Toro would produce later.

Another English-language film (again highlighting a rosary) is Del Toro's *Hellboy* in 2004, which draws on sources even more eclectically postmodern: action-adventure; cultural satire; *The Lord of the Rings*; apocalyptic horror; *Doc Savage, Conan*, and *Hulk* comic books; Flash Gordon serials; science fiction; Edgar Allan Poe horror stories; Jules Verne and Robert Louis Stevenson; and maybe even a little of Dante's *Inferno*. Although one might think such contrary inspirations would result in a filmic mess, *Hellboy* is persuasive as a cinematic amusement park ride. The protagonist is the anti-hero Hellboy, a red-skinned, cigar-smoking, superhuman hulk. With his devil horns purposely filed down, Hellboy has rejected his demonic heritage in order to transform into a standard superhero who inhabits the same weird universe as Hitler, Rasputin, creatures from Hell, and American law enforcement. Based on graphic novels by Mike Mignola for Dark Horse comics and obviously intended to inaugurate a film franchise, *Hellboy* is imbued by Del Toro with both sincere sentiment and a fetching madness (such as when in the middle of a fight with a horrific monster, Hellboy momentarily turns away to safeguard a box of cute kittens). In this film, Del Toro's creatures are especially imaginative; it's clear the director embraces commercial Hollywood

In *Hellboy*, Guillermo Del Toro's weird synthetic vision combines serious Catholic imagery with the tongue-in-cheek popular culture of the comic book. Underneath the prosthetics of the adult Hellboy is actor Ron Perlman.

for the opportunity to access adequate financial resources for the creation of his monster mythologies. The fact that *Hellboy* grossed about $100 million dollars worldwide, an indication of a certain popular success beyond Del Toro's enthusiastic cult, allowed the director to release in 2008 *Hellboy II: The Golden Army*, which continues his fantastical mythology.

Although these English-language works have their admirers, Del Toro's Spanish-language works are more artful and allow for the clearer expression of Del Toro's personal obsessions — particularly those relating to politics, children, and the central role of fantasy in our lives. Surprisingly, virtually none of the casual reviews of *Pan's Labyrinth* acknowledged Del Toro's earlier Spanish-language film *The Devil's Backbone*, released in 2001, which is almost a prequel.[2] Like *Pan's Labyrinth*, *The Devil's Backbone* presents a large-eyed child protagonist who is brought to a new home where a fascist presence must be confronted, a confrontation which mysteriously unleashes a rich, disturbing fantasy world. Although Del Toro was born in Mexico, both his key films deal with the Spanish Civil War — a seminal event within Spanish political culture both specifically and symbolically. Del Toro's Mexico had served as asylum for a great number of cultural and political refugees from Francisco Franco's Spain. Even the great Spanish surrealist Luis Buñuel spent much of the forties, fifties, and sixties making Mexican films as an expatriate, many of these films (particularly *Los Olvidados*) seeming wrenched from the Spanish earth of Buñuel's ancestral Calanda home. Clearly, the Mexican and Spanish film industries share profound connections.

If few reviews of *Pan's Labyrinth* acknowledged *The Devil's Backbone*, even fewer acknowledged the critical influence on Del Toro of one of the most seminally important Spanish films of all: *Spirit of the Beehive*, made in 1973, two years before the death of Franco. *Spirit of the Beehive* was directed by the Spaniard Victor Erice, who set the film in his own birth year, 1940, one year after the Spanish Civil War had officially ended, although in a period when Franco was still rounding up and killing scattered Republican rebels in order to instill fear and terror. *Spirit of the Beehive*, as both art film and horror film, employs virtually all the elements Del Toro would later incorporate into his own master works: a fascist context, a large-eyed child protagonist, expressive landscapes, a sense of fable, great ambiguity, imaginative monsters, and a universe of exceptional brutality and fantasy. In fact, many other directors working in Spanish language horror would also incorporate these elements from Erice's masterpiece — such as director Agustín Villaronga, who made the disturbing 1987 *In a Glass Cage* (discussed elsewhere in this book, about pedophilia and fascism), as well as the 2000 *El Mar*, which starts as historical period drama before transforming into unforgettable (and homoerotic) horror about the legacy of Fascism.

Indeed, *Spirit of the Beehive*, the seminal inspiration for these other horror films, begins with the words "*Erase una vez...*" [Once upon a time...], which immediately establishes the fairy-tale, fable-like quality of the narrative being linked to the Spanish fascist era. Although in the film the Spanish Civil War is over, a spooky pallor hangs over the film's nuclear family: the young girl Ana, who is the protagonist, her sister Isabel, and their father and mother, Fernando and Teresa. Teresa understands that "our ability to really feel life has vanished." This is not surprising, because the rigidity and obsessiveness of fascism have broken the country and banished imagination. (Years later, in Del Toro's *Pan's Labyrinth*, Captain Vidal's obsessiveness for order will serve as a similar fascist opposition to imagination and fantasy.) In the animating incident of *Spirit of the Beehive*, the young Ana, unforgettably played by Ana Torrent, watches a roving screening of James Whale's *Frankenstein* starring

Francoist horror films and the films inspired by them highlight an expressive, dark-eyed child whose innocence becomes compromised: Ana Torrent in *Spirit of the Beehive*, Alexander Goodwin in *Mimic*, Fernando Tielve in *The Devil's Backbone*, Ivana Baquero in *Pan's Labyrinth*. What is the legacy of fascism?

In *Spirit of the Beehive*, father and daughter (Fernando Fernán Gomez and Ana Torrent) are drawn to the image of Frankenstein (Boris Karloff), which works as a powerful, if ambiguous political metaphor.

Boris Karloff and becomes haunted by the image of the monster. "Why did he kill her?" asks Ana, wondering why the Frankenstein monster killed a little girl with whom Ana empathized. Like the Frankenstein monster, Ana begins roaming the landscape, but she is looking for the monster, whom she believes to be near. Although little happens in *Spirit of the Beehive*, ominousness is everywhere. For instance, Ana seems always to be coming closer and closer to danger: too close to a deep well, to railroad tracks, to bees, to a fire, to poisonous mushrooms, to a loaded gun. But she doesn't fall in, get run over, get stung, get burned, get poisoned, or get shot. But is Ana coming too close to her father? In presenting the insular world of children, Erice notes that dangers can be real or imagined. But which danger is which?

The most notable strategy of *Spirit of the Beehive* is Erice's adherence to what has been called the "Francoist aesthetic." Although Franco allowed some interesting films to be released in Fascist Spain (perhaps as an escape valve for cultural energy), he was unwilling to tolerate specific political criticism within the Spanish cinema. As a result, the most provocative Spanish films of the period would purposely tell their tales within the aesthetic of great, inscrutable symbolism, which would be harder to censor. In *Spirit of the Beehive*, ellipses and ambiguities dominate the narrative and purposely exclude key story elements, forcing each spectator to mentally construct his or her own uncensorable narrative. As a result, it is impossible to report definitively all the narrative events in *Spirit of the Beehive* or to explicate their meanings. It appears that the ex-lover for whom Teresa still cares, was (or still is?) a member of the Republican Army, which suggests that Teresa's husband Fernando, along with most in their town, have at least recently been supporters of the Nation-

Formal in his visual strategies, director Victor Erice consistently photographs the sisters in *Spirit of the Beehive* in long shots of extended duration, with the camera angle straight-on and the girls' faces often turned away from us.

alists and Franco. Later, in a beautiful reflecting pool, the young Ana sees (or imagines?) the arrival of Frankenstein, only this Frankenstein looks as much like her father Fernando as the actor Boris Karloff, and he reaches out silently, about to kill her. Is Ana's father a murderer, like so many of the Nationalists? Is Frankenstein a metaphor for Franco and repressiveness? Does Frankenstein kill because his knowledge that he is a monster who doesn't fit in creates an irresistible impulse to psychopathologically dominate others? And do the bees in Fernando's beehives represent the Spanish people in this town, doing their jobs in a regimented spirit as demanded? And do those demands only come from some higher source or from their own deeply-held, natural impulses?

Not only does Erice not provide answers, he barely offers clues or draws attention to the questions inherent in his unconsummated symbols. Later, when Teresa's ex-lover returns to a house on the Castilian plain that the Spanish Civil War has largely destroyed, he appears — with his gun — to be a monster, too, though is befriended briefly by Ana. Yet his visit comes to nothing, since he is killed before he can re-establish contact with Teresa (or at least probably before). We see his murder from an alienating distance, and Erice makes no attempt to create excitement or suspense; instead, we see that the geometric patterns of the lightbursts from the gunfire come from four different locations, and we see no shooters. Has the ex-lover been killed by citizens of the town? Might Fernando have been a shooter? Or might the dead man have been betrayed by Teresa, the new Fascist Spain having robbed her of the ability to love him and forced her to conform? With consistency, Erice offers no clear signs to help us distinguish fantasy from reality and instead presents everything with the same integrity: a single surreality. At the end of *Spirit of the Beehive*, the young Ana goes out onto the terrace in the moonlight to utter an incantation to summon the Frankenstein monster, but what this final action means, disquieting enough, is up to us to decipher. At least we know that although there are fantasy monsters, there are also real monsters; unfortunately, some of them are our fathers and our mothers and our neighbors. And that is both a political and personal horror.

Erice's film has been extraordinarily influential, even on director Carlos Saura, arguably the most famous Spanish director. Saura's film *Cría Cuervos* (1976) clearly follows in the footsteps of *Spirit of the Beehive*, again casting the evocative Ana Torrent as a young girl named Ana. *Cría Cuervos* reprises many of Erice's themes, particularly in associating the masculine force in the house, Ana's father, with fascism. The feminine force in *Cría Cuervos*, her mother — already dead by the time the film begins — is associated with the gracious Spain defeated and killed by Franco in the civil war. Saura's film feels subtly demonic, since Ana is able to talk to her dead mother and mix magic potions that she hopes will kill; indeed, the real world and spirit world of *Cría Cuervos* are so similarly lugubrious that we cannot clearly tell what is really happening and what is not. Ironically, *Cría Cuervos*— which begins with Ana's father dying, was shot while Francisco Franco was on his deathbed and Spain was about to be delivered from fascism; as a result, Saura's film becomes a sad and ambiguous meditation on Franco's legacy to a Spain soon to be at a crossroads. And yet the political components of this expressive film were largely subtextual, beyond censorship. Not only again is Torrent astonishing, but so is actress Geraldine Chaplin (Saura's longtime partner and Charlie Chaplin's daughter) in the dual role of Ana's mother and Ana as a young woman. In fact, Geraldine Chaplin's role was so iconic that her appearance in Spanish films thereafter often referred to her performance here.

Within the context of the Francoist aesthetic, particularly as practiced in Erice's and Saura's masterpieces, *The Devil's Backbone*, which Del Toro directed in 2001 (in association with Spanish producer Agustín Almodóvar, brother of director Pedro), takes place in 1939, just before the official end of the civil war. A demonic horror film which veers off in its own idiosyncratic directions, *The Devil's Backbone* begins with a voice-over asking, "What is a ghost? A tragedy doomed to repeat itself... An instant of pain, perhaps. Something dead which still seems to be alive. An emotion suspended in time. Like a blurry photograph. Like an insect trapped in amber." The expressive, mysterious images accompanying the voice-over go by too fast for us to comprehend them. (At the end of *The Devil's Backbone*, the narrative cleverly circles back to replay this imagery, only now with our comprehending it.) Throughout his film, Del Toro's images are stunning and disturbing: a woman with a sculpted, wooden leg; a slimy garden slug; a huge unexploded bomb in a public exterior, looking like a surreal military statue; a Buñuelian chicken; a prized marble made of snot and mud; and so forth.

Like *Pan's Labyrinth*, *The Devil's Backbone* begins with its large-eyed child protagonist brought to a new home: Carlos, who must now live on an impoverished estate for leftists' children orphaned by the civil war, the enterprise run by Carmen, a one-legged woman played by Marisa Paredes. (It is notable that Paredes played a key role in *In a Glass Cage*,

In similarly composed images in *The Devil's Backbone*, Carlos (Fernando Tielve) confronts Santi (Junio Valverde), his ghostly alter-ego.

Guillermo Del Toro's films, especially *The Devil's Backbone*, have an integrity of vision which is especially impressive, considering that various of his images draw upon different traditions: (1) Italian neorealism, (2) German expressionism, (3) the American western (particularly evoking the opening of John Ford's *The Searchers*).

another horror film dealing with the fascist legacy of Spain; and Carmen's stump immediately suggests an *hommage* to the fetishism of the Spanish/Mexican director Luis Buñuel, the implicit mentor to every surrealist filmmaker.) The world of the orphanage is explored through the eyes of Carlos; thus the spectacle of the civil war, with its horrifying violence, is presented not with the bravado of a genre film, but with the terrifying simplicity of a child's vision. Carlos almost immediately sees the ghost of Santi, a dead orphan whose bed Carlos has been given. One of the charms of Del Toro's film is that it wastes no time with the obligatory, tiresome, horror-film scenes of denial and incredulity. Instead it's much more direct: Carlos saw a ghost? Well, yes, of course he did; the characters know it's true, and we do, too. It is refreshing to have the mythological dimension of life affirmed so easily. Before long, in a key scene, Carlos saves another boy, Jaime, from drowning in the yellow water of an indoor, rainwater reservoir. The amber water bubbling up around Jaime (a budding, comic-book artist, perhaps an autobiographical version of Del Toro) creates a visceral reality more disturbing than the supernatural ghost of Santi. As well, the scene strangely evokes the passion in the controversial, otherworldly 1987 *Piss Christ*, a gallery work by Hispanic artist Andres Serrano, which was a photograph of a crucifix, also aglow in amber bubbles, apparently submerged in urine.

The noble Carmen is helped in her humanitarian and political efforts by the even nobler Dr. Casares, who comments on the horror of 1939: "I'm a man of science. But Spain is filled with superstition. Europe is sick with fear now, and fear sickens the soul. And that, in turn, makes us see things." So perhaps it is political turmoil that opens up the world of fantasy and ghosts. And then Dr. Casares talks about a birth deformity called the devil's backbone — a spinal cord which develops on the outside of a fetus — which, according to superstition, is a sign of evil. Dr. Casares shows Carlos the deformed backbone on a fetus which has been preserved in a bottle filled with amber liquid, a strangely transcendent icon which also evokes the Serrano work. Dr. Casares calls the liquid "limbo water" (composed of rum and clovers) and says that people believe the devil's backbone "happens to children who shouldn't be born. 'Nobody's children.' But that's a lie. Poverty and disease. That's all it is." When we see the ghost of Santi, a special effect puts bubbles about him too, just as in the limbo water or in the rainwater. Eventually we learn that Santi was killed by the villain Jacinto, the oldest orphan who in young adulthood has come to so hate his background that he has embraced a personal fascism. As if set on fire by civil war bombing, we even see the ghost of Santi literally smoldering, a victim, like so many innocent children, of political conflict. Also called "the one who sighs," Santi predicts much of the horrifying climax of *The Devil's Backbone*, in which Jacinto, reduced to terrorism, sets off a huge explosion — an image of hell — in order to kill as many people as possible, including the orphans. The fact that Del Toro has earlier shown Jacinto naked and as so erotic that even the freedom-fighter Carmen cannot resist him despite his cruelty and fascism, adds a complex tension to the film. Clearly, *The Devil's Backbone* is also suggesting there is something erotic about fascism itself, about its fetishism for order and its call for obedience. In another memorable scene of political horror, we see a variety of international volunteers who have been fighting for Spanish democracy all executed perfunctorily with gunshots to the head. The spiritual antipode to the fascists is Dr. Casares, who, as both a humanist and a man of science, is connected to the magic and mysteries of life. Surrounded by culture, especially his classical music and his books, it is Dr. Casares who must sacrifice his life to try to vanquish the dumb, erotic Jacinto, who practices such banal evil and casual violence. The paradox for Del Toro is that the children — the most vulnerable potential victims — must themselves resort to violence in order to save their lives and re-establish any sense of humanist values and of a civilized culture. Here, as in *Pan's Labyrinth*, the fascist world and fantastical world ultimately connect as Carlos and Jaime deliver Jacinto to the ghost of Santi for proper punishment.

Oddly, the young actors who played Carlos and Jaime in *The Devil's Backbone*, set in the year 1939, also appear in *Pan's Labyrinth*, Guillermo Del Toro's follow-up film set in 1944. The two actors, older and no longer childly innocent, make cameo appearances as anti-fascists who survived *The Devil's Backbone* only to be executed by Franco's fascists in *Pan's Labyrinth*. Del Toro has spoken eloquently about how *Pan's Labyrinth* was specifically a reaction to the events of 9/11 (2001) and that day's aftermath.[3] And so five years after 9/11, Del Toro released a second film about fascist horror, purposely setting it five years after the first. Whereas *Pan's Labyrinth* takes place after the end of the Spanish Civil War, the violence still continues. On some level, *Pan's Labyrinth*, widely released late in 2006, may have resonated with the public because of its subtextual implications regarding the nature of contemporary evil: Five years after the spectacular success of al-Qaeda's attack on the United States, al-Qaeda had yet to accomplish any subsequent victory of equal magnitude or notable

The Devil's Backbone contrasts the iconography of fascist violence with the iconography of Catholicism. The similar angle in the composition of these two images suggests that Franco's bombs have martyred the Spanish people.

definitiveness. More than three years after President George W. Bush's speech declaring "Mission Accomplished" in Iraq, neither the United States nor any involved party had been able to credibly claim victory; and the now-acknowledged Iraqi civil war was dragging on, with the American invasion and occupation having unleashed Guernica-like violence, ethnic cleansing, and chaos. The problem of the fascist sensibility — ingrained in those who successfully commit horrifying, calculated campaigns of violence, despite the objections of those with enough humanity left to notice — seems absolutely intractable. So what is an innocent to do when faced with the implacability of such horror? *Pan's Labyrinth* gives us another large-eyed child who must confront the evil of the fascist sensibility. The outcome of that confrontation may be ambiguous, but *Pan's Labyrinth*, as cinema, is unambiguously a masterpiece. Indeed, it is one of the few films which has the chance to follow in the footsteps of *Psycho* and *The Birds* and ignite its own, new subgenre of horror: political horror — perfect for a world whose political institutions are spinning wildly out of control. Whether Del Toro continues to make these political horror films, with their fantastical elements, or whether other directors are inspired to elaborate and develop this potential subgenre remains to be seen. But certainly one can imagine a number of potential subjects and titles: *Bones of Darfur, Dirty Bombs on Wall Street, The Constitution Killers, Dead Sea Spirits, The Aborted Unborn at the Great Wall, Ghosts in Gaza, The Right-Wing Born-Again Flying Robots, The Undead of Abu Ghraib...*

The title of Guillermo Del Toro's 2006 film was actually *El Laberinto del Fauno* [The Labyrinth of the Faun], much more appropriate than *Pan's Labyrinth*, its American release title, since the faun depicted is not, strictly speaking, Pan. Del Toro's film begins with a large-eyed little girl, the protagonist Ofelia, arriving with her mother at the estate of Captain Vidal, the rigid fascist who is to be Ofelia's new stepfather. The "stepparent" theme is archetypal in fairy tales, which present stepparents as the embodiment of cruel disregard, if not outright evil. Indeed, *Pan's Labyrinth* is filled with overt visual and narrative references to classics of children's literature, including *The Wizard of Oz, Alice in Wonderland, David Copperfield*, and the fairy tales of Hans Christian Andersen. Although Captain Vidal's world is rigid and oppressive, Ofelia's is fantastical and creative. From the beginning of the film, she imagines herself a fairy-tale princess: Princess Moana, "the daughter of the King of the Underworld." Ofelia's arrival to the fascist world is watched over by a kind of magical praying mantis, and not too long after, Ofelia runs off to explore a woodland labyrinth overseen by a mythological faun who gets younger and younger as the film progresses. In fairy-tale fashion, the faun gives Ofelia tasks to complete before the moon becomes full. Del Toro's virtue is in presenting Ofelia's fairy-tale world and Captain Vidal's fascist world with the same amount of sincerity and credibility: they co-exist. (In fact, at the beginning of *Pan's Labyrinth*, Del Toro follows the point-of-view of the magical insect, a visual trope which immediately gives the fairy-tale world a persuasive reality, because that world is initially unmediated by Ofelia's perspective.) Here, as throughout, Del Toro's camera is constantly meandering, never still, which gives the film an expressive restlessness. The sensuous, glowing cinematography manipulates the color palette and deeply saturates the colors, resulting in stunning images. Even the sound mix is extraordinary, subtle and delicate, rather than loud and bombastic.

As *Pan's Labyrinth* progresses, elements from fairy tales and mythology become increasingly important to Ofelia. There is a Book of Crossroads, upon whose blank pages messages can mysteriously appear. And there are magic stones, a golden key, an insect which turns into a fairy, a special potion, and a mandrake root which animates into a human form.

Pan's Labyrinth is filled with beautiful, memorable images: (1) a stunning texture in the fairytale woods, (2) expressive orbs of light as Ofelia (Ivana Baquero) opens her magic book, (3) an enchanted passageway that has sexual overtones, and (4) the mythological faun of ambiguous meaning (Doug Jones).

(Not since David Cronenberg's *Naked Lunch* have magical insects been more important to a serious film.) In several scenes, Ofelia is costumed like the heroine of *Alice in Wonderland*, which provides a clue as to what *Pan's Labyrinth* is expressing. Although too many contemporary readers remember the two *Alice* books only as whimsy or fantasy, writers as notable as Joyce Carol Oates have valorized these books as the clearest expressions of rebellion against a crazy, adult world by a child who has not yet been co-opted by that world. The fairy-tale world is "curiouser and curiouser," certainly, but Alice ultimately rejects that world and its autocratic Queen of Hearts when Alice grows to her full size and declares, "You're nothing but a pack of cards!"

And so *Pan's Labyrinth*, too, is about its protagonist's discovery of her own stature, her inner strength. Captain Vidal rejects Ofelia's magical world, but even more tellingly, so does Ofelia's mother, who tells her daughter: "Magic does not exist. Not for me, you, or anyone else." But the reason that magic does not exist for the grown-ups is because they are not imaginative enough to see it. Not only does Ofelia reject the fascist Captain Vidal, she often rejects her fairy-tale faun, disobeying several of the faun's commands. Central to the film is Ofelia's rejection of *any* external impulse to exert control over her: she insists on making her own decisions, a key narrative point congruent to Del Toro's contention that his film is about "choice and disobedience," key values in the fight against fascism during the Spanish Civil War, as well as critically needed values today in our post–9/11 world.

Although adults often sentimentalize children's literature, much of it is genuinely gruesome, with sexual subtexts and violence, a fact that Del Toro understands. When Ofelia enters the fantasy world of the labyrinth through a portal in a tree, that passage is shaped to look like Ofelia is passing through a vagina. And part of Ofelia's fairy-tale narrative is juxtaposed with the milking of a cow, which Del Toro purposely photographs to look as

Pan's Labyrinth includes expressive *hommage* to other films, among which are (1) the phallic close-up of a milked cow, from Luis Buñuel's *Los Olvidados* (which also ends tragically with the murder of the child protagonist); and (2) the ruby-colored shoes from Mervyn Le Roy's MGM musical *The Wizard of Oz.*

disturbingly sexual as possible. Captain Vidal's world, although too repressed and rigid to be very sexual, is nevertheless a world of plenty. While the rebels are still fighting for democracy and much of the Spanish populace is going hungry, the fascist leaders and their supporters are living well. At a banquet Captain Vidal hosts, the table laden with food, he ridicules the rebels still fighting for freedom and proclaims that "I want my son to be born in a new, clean Spain. These people hold the mistaken belief that we're all equal. But there's a big difference. The war is over and we won. And if we need to kill every one of these vermin to settle it, then we'll kill them all, and that's that." To characterize political enemies as less than human is typical to the totalitarian mind. (In recent Rwanda, for instance, genocide was committed against the Tutsis, who were widely called "cockroaches.") Notably, a priest attending the banquet essentially reveals the Catholic Church to be fascist collaborator when he says, about the rebels, that "God has already saved their souls. What happens to their bodies hardly matters to Him." Del Toro shows us that the rebels are going hungry, getting sick without medicine, suffering amputations without anesthetic, and being killed by the fascists. Captain Vidal is not only a fascist, but a sociopath; in contrast, Ofelia's real father was a tailor, an Everyman-evoking occupation standard in the fairy-tale literature.

The fairy-tale sequences alternate with the fascist sequences in carefully constructed visual and narrative parallels. Perhaps surprisingly, the horror of the fascist violence is purposely downplayed. For Del Toro, this is appropriate, since so often the casual deaths of civilians, children, and refugees hoping to escape war violence are considered less consequential, at least historically, than the deaths of soldiers in critical battles which determine a war's outcome. The scariest violence *is* the most casual. In this regard, the political violence Del Toro gravitates toward suggests the contemporary violence in Iraq; and certainly the civil war in Spain that he depicts resonates with the civil war in Iraq, which emerged as an unintended consequence of the war to topple Saddam Hussein. As well, parallel to Captain Vidal's callous rejection of human equality is the disparate relative value Americans attribute to American lives lost on 9/11 versus Iraqi civilian lives lost in the War in Iraq. Although Captain Vidal is an outright villain, the mythological faun Ofelia encounters is by no means a hero. For Del Toro, fauns are neither good nor bad, but a representation of nature, which is amoral, containing elements of creation and destruction. The faun instructs Ofelia to trace a chalk outline on her wall to create a magical doorway which will lead her to the most frightening and imaginative creature ever devised by Del Toro: the Pale Man.

The most horrifying creature in *Pan's Labyrinth* is the Pale Man (also played by Doug Jones), a blind monster who understands little except his material world and thirst for violence. The Pale Man is in part a metaphor for Captain Vidal (Sergi López), and by extension, for Franco and political repression.

The Pale Man is a baggy-skinned monster with only half a face who sits at his banquet table while his eyes sit on a platter in front of him. The banquet table not only evokes Captain Vidal's fascist banquet, but the extravagant tea-party in *Alice in Wonderland*.

But Del Toro's sequence is darker than Lewis Carroll's, because Del Toro shows us a huge pile of shoes which evokes concentration camps and genocide. At the Pale Man's banquet, Ofelia eats a grape — an act forbidden by the faun. Will that act seal Ofelia's death? Yet by disobeying, Ofelia has embraced her freedom to act independently according to her own nature. In a horrific, gruesome act, the Pale Man grabs the first of the two fairies who are Ofelia's traveling companions and bites off the head before proceeding to eat the fairy — the image specifically recreating Goya's famous print "Saturn Devouring His Son." As in a nightmare, Ofelia runs for her life from this monster through the long, red-tinged chamber which Del Toro has described as "uterine-shaped." Yes, even monsters like the Pale Man (and Captain Vidal) are *born*: evil is thus the most natural thing in the world.

Perhaps *Pan's Labyrinth*'s primary theme is how in the context of brutality and violence, it is our understanding of the real, sociopolitical world around us that marks the end of childhood. And by *childhood*, Del Toro does not mean the end of innocence, exactly, for children are never really innocent, but the end of fantastical, imaginative horror, which comes to be replaced with the real, plodding horror of the everyday. Evil, ultimately, is banal. By the end of *Pan's Labyrinth*, the narrative ambiguity becomes even greater, in congruence to the style of the Francoist aesthetic (regardless that Del Toro's film was made three decades after the death of Franco). Although Del Toro presents his film's final act of violence in an almost offhand manner, it is emotionally unbearable: Ofelia is shot and killed by her stepfather.

But then we see ruby slippers clicking — a reference to the end of *The Wizard of Oz —*

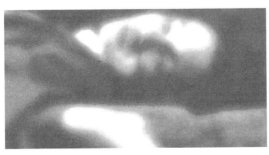

and we see Ofelia come back to life in a different, fantastical world, reunited with her mother and her tailor father, who looks like a mythic god. If Ofelia has become immortal, it is because she has *not* followed the orders from her stepfather or the faun and has instead made her own decisions. We see the faun in this fantastical world, too, which suggests that perhaps he didn't really intend for Ofelia to follow all his orders in any case. Perhaps her real challenge, devious because it was more difficult and remained unstated, was to develop her sense of self and the ability to resist all authority, even the faun's. But before we have the time to consider whether this is a potentially happy ending (which requires that we interpret these final heavenly images as real), Del Toro cuts to Ofelia dead in the woodland labyrinth, shot by her stepfather. So is Ofelia dead or is Ofelia immortal? Perhaps only now do we remember that the film's opening shot showed the dead Ofelia in this exact spot, but with the blood moving backwards *into* her body, time reversing. So maybe if we are patient and wait, Ofelia will come to life again in the real world, too.

Guillermo Del Toro's creative subgenre of the political horror film may well turn out to be important to the overall horror genre. But if it doesn't, it *should*, for there are enough deaths, genocides, wars, diseases, and untold miseries specifically caused by political failures worldwide which deserve creative treatment within the horror genre. And while Del Toro's two Spanish Civil War films rely heavily on special effects, they are so filled with ideas that they seem in opposition to the special effects films of the American cinema, which dazzle but never provoke. Perhaps like the children in horror films who look nerv-

Pan's Labyrinth is one of a few films that ends with the murder of its child protagonist. Or does it? The fairy-tale quality allows the final sequence, where Ofelia (Ivana Baquero) is bathed in golden light, to be interpreted as Catholic resurrection or as delusion that gives way to the grimmest death.

ously to the skies to see what will come next, we can look hopefully for Del Toro to navigate current industry practices to produce more of these political horror films and help take the horror genre which he has called "one of the last of the brave genres of film" to a newer, more relevant place.

A promising sign is certainly provided by *The Orphanage* [*El Orfanato*], a 2007 film directed by Juan Antonio Bayona, but executive produced by Guillermo Del Toro. The orphanage setting of this ghostly horror film suggests connection to Franco's adventures in Spain, where so many children were orphaned by the civil war. It is increasingly clear that the historical period of Franco and his legacy is as relevant to the genre of political horror as is the nineteenth century American West relevant to the genre of the western. Like Del Toro's *The Devil's Backbone* and *Pan's Labyrinth* (and Erice's *Spirit of the Beehive* and Saura's *Cría Cuervos*), the major character of Bayona's film is a large-eyed, haunted-looking child, here named Simón (played by Roger Príncep), who initially knows neither that he is adopted nor that he has HIV. The revelation of these truths, which his mother (played by Bélen Rueda) keeps from him, is devastating and leads to tragic, cosmic consequences. Simón has a variety of invisible friends ... or are they really ghosts? And if they are ghosts, why are they there? On a profound level, *The Orphanage* asks us whether we really take care of our children, and takes us to task for our shortcomings. The film includes several unforgettable shocks — including one of the cinema's most unexpected deaths — but is most notable for being almost old-fashioned in how intricately plotted is its story, especially rare in the horror genre today, whose writers are often too lazy or cynical to attempt complex plotting and instead rely on pure sensation. A Jungian expert within the film attests that "It is in the subconscious that the living co-exist with the dead" — thus intellectually buoying the ghostly connections in *The Orphanage*. Notably, in *hommage* to her seminal position in the Spanish cinema, director Bayona cast Geraldine Chaplin as Aurora, a medium who is able to connect to the past, if traumatically. In its final act, *The Orphanage* shows how the actions of adults bring about the deaths of children and raises the issue of appropriate expiation; in the 2007 context of Iraq and Darfur, is there a much more salient theme for a horror film with a child protagonist to consider? Like *Pan's Labyrinth,* that centrally referenced — among other children's tales—*Alice in Wonderland* and *The Wizard of Oz, The Orphanage* centrally references a children's tale: *Peter Pan*, about a group of children who do not grow up, and about one child, Wendy, who with some melancholy, does. With surprising twists, beautiful cinematography, and consistently remarkable performances, *The Orphanage* is that rare horror film in which every line of dialogue and image (indeed, even the graphics of the credit sequence) are part of a totally coherent whole. Incidentally, one wonders whether there are autobiographical ghosts lurking in this story about orphan Simón Sanchéz written by another Sanchéz, screenwriter Sergio. Certainly, one can only hope that a decade from now, a thriving subgenre of political horror can be traced back to the remarkable Guillermo Del Toro.

12 — David Cronenberg

Although the occasional *Donnie Darko* or *Pan's Labyrinth* surprised with their originality, for several decades horror has by and large been a disappointing, underperforming
genre. Blame should be assigned not only to the ascendancy of postmodern pastiche, but
to the insincerity of directors who are as quick to claim the mantle of "*auteur*" as to allow
the studio executive and test audience to determine exactly what their "personal" visions
should be. You want a happier ending? You've got it. You want more violence or less sex?
Fine. Too many of today's directors make deals rather than films, avoiding personal or controversial material for fear of sabotaging their commercial careers. (Maybe these directors —
as a display of honesty — should put *those* fears in their horror films.) In fact, there is only
one director currently working in horror in the English language who has demonstrated the
same kind of authentic artistic integrity as Europe's Michael Haneke. And that is the courageous David Cronenberg, from Canada, who serves as the horror genre's most senior *auteur*,
creating one thought-provoking, profoundly personal, squirmy film after another. Indeed,
even Cronenberg's first feature in 1975, the low-budget, rarely seen *Shivers* (also known as
They Came from Within and *The Parasite Murders*) is an extraordinary film which resem-

This expressionistic image from *Spider* evokes German silent film and reveals David Cronenberg's
visual mastery: in a rented room, a man's posture suggests a missing head, and hence, mental illness.

330

bles Eugène Ionesco's violent 1970 play *Killing Game* (*Jeux de Massacre*), both with subjects which center on epidemics and narratives which eschew a strong central spine and follow a myriad of characters. Less comic than *Killing Game*, *Shivers* presents an epidemic which is virtually venereal and culminates in a violent and orgiastic *Walpurgisnacht* which is subversive, destructive, and profoundly unsettling. Cronenberg's films, as intellectually rigorous as Haneke's, explore new areas of horror that other directors would shrink from, if indeed they would ever even consider. Apocalyptic examinations of physical and psychological disintegration, Cronenberg's films resonate with contemporary life as it is inexorably evolving. And Cronenberg's key horror films — *Rabid* (1977), *The Brood* (1979), *Scanners* (1981), *Videodrome* (1983), *The Fly* (1986), *Dead Ringers* (1988), *Naked Lunch* (1991), *Crash* (1996), *eXistenZ* (1999), and *Spider* (2002) — represent one of the most sustained records of artistic achievement since Hitchcock, Antonioni, Fellini, and Bergman in their prime.

Exploiting some of the issues raised in Susan Sontag's *Illness as Metaphor*, Cronenberg shows human beings whose bodies are transformed by disease or mutation into a more advanced, if psychologically traumatizing, state. The illness or mutated body becomes an other to be feared, as well as a metaphor for secret desires or social impulses. Ultimately, the body takes a revenge upon the individual, who often becomes alienated from and painfully imprisoned in his or her body. Cronenberg's films also show future apocalypse brought about by technology hailed as evolutionary. Within this context, *Scanners* (1981) is an especially important masterwork — the *Psycho* of eighties-generation horror. *Scanners* inherently reflects the paranoid sensibility of America post–Watergate and skillfully exploits the contemporary fear of the carcinogenic substance. It differs from the atomic anxiety-inspired horror film in that it is not the earth that explodes, but one's head; indeed, one of the strongest images of all contemporary horror can be found in *Scanners*, when business and government executives in an auditorium watch patiently, expectantly, and then with horror, as one scanner makes another scanner's head explode like a bursting balloon. Another powerful image — of a deranged sculptor who can live in a larger-than-life sculpture of his own head (placed on its side and divorced from any body, thus resembling the sculpture *l'Écoute* by Henri de Miller, which sits surreally in front of the *St-Eustache* church in Paris) — evokes the Cronenbergian conception that we are all prisoners of our identities and obsessions. Underpinning this fable of science-gone-mad are archetypal story patterns — the search for a father, and the Cain-and-Abel struggle between a good brother and an evil brother. True to form for the horror-of-Armageddon subgenre, *Scanners* ends bleakly and ambiguously, implying that horror will escalate as we advance to ever greater destructive capabilities.

Three other early Cronenberg films form a kind of trilogy of frightening body mutations. *The Brood*, directed by Cronenberg in 1979, deals with feminist-inspired hostility, especially that of women toward the physical reality of childbirth and the demands of child rearing. *The Brood* argues implicitly for the nonpropagation of the species by showing violent children — born from a sac outside the mother's body — who come to embody all the tensions and hostilities reposited in the nuclear family. Especially disturbing is the image of Samantha Eggar as Nola, bloodily tearing open her own fetal sac with her teeth. Another fascinating horror film, if not Cronenberg's most wholly successful, is *Videodrome* (1982), which predicts a sadomasochistic human future and contemplates our destruction as we lose our humanity and almost literally turn into videocassette recorders. Indeed, the image of a man growing a kind of deformed vaginal slit for a videocassette is especially repellent,

In David Cronenberg's *Scanners*, the exploding of one's head becomes the perfect, horrifying metaphor for contemporary tension.

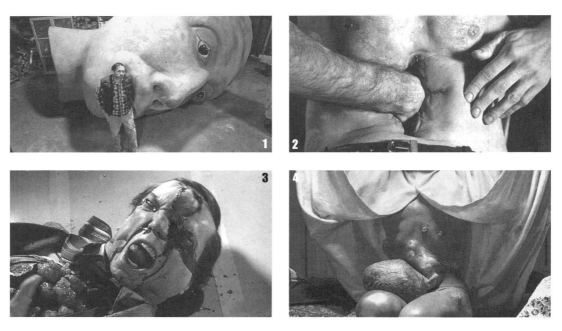

Another powerful Cronenberg metaphor in *Scanners* is the artist (Robert Silverman as Pierce) who can literally live in his own (sculpted) head. In Cronenberg's horror films, the body (1) is always evolving in disturbing ways, as shown by (2) James Woods' "vaginal" slit in *Videodrome*, (3) Les Carlson's violently morphing body in *Videodrome*, and (4) Samantha Eggar's external fetal sac in *The Brood*.

Relationships are easier when we are healthy, attractive, and carefree. *The Fly*, **starring Geena Davis and Jeff Goldblum, asks whether we can still love each other when illness transforms us.**

balancing Cronenberg's earlier image, in *Rabid* (1977), of a woman growing a kind of deformed pineal set of jaws under her arm.

The Fly was a remake in only the most technical sense. Cronenberg completely re-imagined the fifties original into a surprisingly intimate, philosophical treatise on his most recurring obsession: the horror of the human body. For Cronenberg, organic form is neither pure nor aesthetic; he is less interested by Michelangelo's *David* than by the viscera revealed by the Renaissance scalpel. Cronenberg understands that human beings are often alienated not only from their bodies, but from their bodily processes, which take revenge upon the soul. In *The Fly*, Jeff Goldblum plays a contemporary mad scientist — charming, glib, smart — whose experiments accidentally begin to change his body, which gradually takes on characteristics of a fly. Increasingly, he becomes physically repulsive — both to himself and to his girlfriend, played by Geena Davis. What makes *The Fly* especially notable is the way the film works as metaphor for the AIDS epidemic. Released when American society, terrified in the mid-eighties, was calling AIDS a punishment from God and scapegoating gays, *The Fly* was in development at the same time as *An Early Frost*, the TV movie considered the first major AIDS film. In Cronenberg's movie, the scientist's early manifestations of bodily change resemble the skin lesions of Kaposi's sarcoma, the cancer so common in the early stages of AIDS-related immune dysfunction. As these changes transform him into something monstrous-looking that even his girlfriend recoils from, *The Fly* asks a profound question: Do we, as human beings, have enough compassion to embrace the bodily degradations of others, or will our own revulsion turn us into even greater monsters? *The Fly* becomes one of the most suspenseful and *important* horror films, because it attempts to measure, in horrifying, fearful times, the human capacity for empathy and love. Although *The Fly* was so financially successful that Cronenberg could have taken a Hollywood pay-off and directed studio blockbusters for hire, to his credit he chose to continue to explore his own quirky obsessions.

When the twins in *Dead Ringers* are photographed together, whether (1) as children (Jonathan and Nicholas Haley), or (2) as adults (Jeremy Irons) in a *Pietà* pose as murder/suicide victims, the balanced frames exude a restful harmony. But when a twin is photographed singly, as in images 3 and 4, the unbalanced frames suggest an ominous tension.

Cronenberg's *Dead Ringers*, in 1988, goes where other directors would be unwilling to go. Based on the real-life story of twin gynecologists Stewart and Cyril Marcus, who became drug addicts and lost their minds before being found dead in their New York City apartment, *Dead Ringers* allowed Cronenberg to confront his fascination with and concurrent fear of sex, particularly as focused on the physical structures of women's sex organs. When we first see the twins, in the film named Elliot and Beverly, they are little boys who are already co-dependent. (In one of Beverly's dreams, he and Elliot are Siamese twins, literally connected.) Precocious, the boys ask a little girl if she's willing to have sex with the two of them in their bathtub. When grown up, Elliot and Beverly (both played by Jeremy Irons) are respected doctors living lifestyles of the rich and famous. Because they believe they may share a nervous system, they think nothing of sharing their women (although the women rarely realize it). And so they develop a relationship with Claire Niveau (played by Geneviève Bujold), attracted by her trifurcate uterus. Although we don't know exactly why the twins descend into addiction and madness, their descent seems related to their profession, which requires them to have an intimate, clinical relationship with the vaginas of a great number of women.

With *Dead Ringers*, Cronenberg explores his obsession with insertion into the body — specifically, into the vagina. (The film recalls the penetration in *Videodrome*, but without that film's stylized exaggeration and traditional horror excesses.) As Beverly increasingly believes the insides of women are mutant and deformed, he designs a series of grotesquely sculpted "Gynaecological Instruments for Operating on Mutant Women." The artist who forges these instruments displays them as surrealist modern art in a gallery, although Beverly intends them for surgical insertion into women. Or is Beverly lying to himself: are they really intended for the separation of Siamese twins? Either way, they seem instruments of sexual torture. By the end of *Dead Ringers*, Beverly uses the instruments to mutilate his brother ("Separation can be a terrifying thing"); and the dead twins end up naked and decomposing in their luxury apartment, victims of ... what? Perhaps of the processes of sex. The final image is of the brothers in a Pietà pose, suggesting tenderness, sacrifice, and spirituality, but we don't see this image until the physical body has been transcended. Cronenberg is so skillful a director he makes us viscerally feel his revulsions. He anatomizes the fear of sex inherent in Puritan culture as rooted in a sense of the unclean sinfulness of the body, a fear that few artists would be courageous enough to admit to, let alone to explore.

Naked Lunch, directed by Cronenberg in 1991, presents the 1953 New York City world of "beat" writer and bug exterminator Bill Lee (essentially a stand-in for William Burroughs, the author of the imaginative, autobiographical novel of the same name). In this world suffused with surrealism where "Nothing is true; everything is permitted," we see Bill Lee (like Burroughs in real life) killing his wife in a drug-induced haze. True to surrealist principles, Bill Lee realizes he must "Exterminate all rational thought" and is committed to automatic writing, since "To rewrite is to lie." We watch in horror as he mentally spins out of control — along with the narrative, which is increasingly unreliable and associated with Bill Lee's point of view. As he abuses the powder used to kill cockroaches — his drug of choice — he becomes more and more deranged, and the hallucinogenic "Interzone" he inhabits becomes dominated by apocalyptic bugs. Indeed, Burroughs and Cronenberg conjure a bug-infested world where bugs are both talkative and intellectual. Particularly unsettling is the huge bug that speaks out of anus-shaped "lips" on its back. Even Bill Lee's typewriter becomes a huge bug head, with penis-like extensions which drip a seminal fluid when the writing is inspired. Ultimately, *Naked Lunch* suggests a *Repulsion*-like fear of sexuality; in one striking reference, Bill Lee walks down a hallway whose odd walls clearly emulate the hallway of groping hands that terrify the heroine in *Repulsion*. But in *Naked Lunch*, what the hero fears is clearly homosexuality, his own recognized problem with "sexual ambivalence." Indeed, the most horrific image in *Naked Lunch* from Cronenberg, one of the least homophobic directors, is one which depicts male-to-male intercourse as profoundly bestial, not unlike the mating of large, grotesque insects.

Fascinated and repelled by sex of all kinds, Cronenberg made *Crash* in 1996, a film that prompts audiences to watch open-mouthed, in a genuine, stunned shock. Based on the novel by J.G. Ballard, *Crash* unites Cronenberg's repulsion by the body with his obsession with sex. James Spader plays "James Ballard," a director whose erotic interests expand when, during a serious car accident, he becomes sexually aroused at the moment of impact. Subsequently, Ballard is introduced to a cult of sexual renegades who eroticize traffic and car crashes, and fetishize bruises and scars. (Not surprisingly, *Crash* takes place on and near the freeways of Southern California.) At the center of this sexual minority is Vaughan, played by Elias Koteas. Without safety equipment, Vaughan re-creates famous, fatal crashes (such as the ones that killed James Dean and beheaded Jayne Mansfield) for the erotic pleasure of his fellow fetishists. A former designer of computerized traffic systems, Vaughan is particularly fascinated by Gabrielle — whose car crash has turned her into a kind of Prosthetic Woman — because he is interested in "the re-shaping of the human body by modern technology." After Ballard admits this alternative sexuality is satisfying but hard to understand, Vaughan explains: "It's a benevolent psychopathology that beckons toward us ... a lifetime of sexual energy ... mediating the sexuality of those who have died with an inten-

Naked Lunch begins (1), (2), and (3) as a stylishly designed period piece showcasing the early fifties and then transforms into the drugged vision of its protagonist (Peter Weller). The transformation — triggered by (4) a standard typewriter turning into a (5) living bug typewriter — is followed by unforgettable surreal images, including (6) a human-size bug clubgoer and (7) a bug's talking anus.

sity that is impossible in any other form. To experience that! To live with that!" *Crash* engenders our dread, not only because we fear the crashes and their consequences, but because some of its sex scenes approach the explicitness of pornography, appropriate for what Cronenberg is trying to accomplish, but still shocking (especially since *Crash* was released in conventional theatres).

Lest we think these characters are all bohemian oddballs or lowlifes, Holly Hunter plays a fellow sexual pilgrim who is a physician. And since everyone in the film is bisexual, what unites all the sexual acts we see is not some strict equation of gender or number, but the presence of a car. We see sex in a speeding car, while watching car-crash "pornography," in

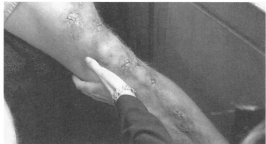

Quite unconventionally, *Crash* eroticizes traffic, bruises, and car accidents. Note how these fetishes are each positioned at the same angle within the frame to indicate their congruence.

a parking garage while surrounded by cars, while going through a car wash, and with prosthetics made necessary by a car crash. Alarmingly, driving recklessly and crashing are presented as foreplay to sex and/or to death, the ultimate orgasm. At the end of the film Ballard causes the crash of his wife, Katharine (with whom he is in an open relationship). As she crawls out of her overturned car and collapses on the grass, alive and intact, we breathe a sigh of relief. But then, horrifically, we realize that they were both hoping she would be seriously hurt for the erotic thrill it would provide. (And the fact that Katharine is only one lesson away from getting her pilot's license is even scarier. Imagine the erotic charge she would get from crashing a plane, something Cronenberg implicitly suggests may be her destiny.) To Cronenberg's credit as a horror director with a profoundly subversive, surreal

The explicit sexuality of *Crash* (with actors Deborah Kara Unger and James Spader) purposely diminishes the boundary between horror and pornography, increasing spectator unease. Note that these erotic bodies are positioned at the same angle as the previous *Crash* fetish images.

vision, he presents the sexuality of *Crash* without personal judgment, but with both morbid fascination and clinical distance.

eXistenZ, made in 1999, is perhaps the Cronenberg masterpiece, an imaginative horror film that transcends convention to become visionary and philosophical. Cronenberg's view of the future seems inspired by Neil Postman's *Amusing Ourselves to Death*—particularly Postman's idea that our culture is insisting on escaping reality by retreating into worlds of pleasure. In *eXistenZ*, Jennifer Jason Leigh plays Allegra Geller, the inventor of a video game called eXistenZ. (Her previous game, ArtGod, gave each player the opportunity to be God, "artist and mechanic.") Consonant with Cronenberg's fear of the body, the eXistenZ game pod, which is unnerving and factory-produced, looks like some fantastical body organ with concavities, protuberances, and nipples, all connected to an umbilical cord. Jude Law plays Ted Pikul, a helpmate to Allegra when they find themselves in the midst of industrial intrigue to control eXistenZ. (Of course, they are also trying to control and understand *existence* as well, since it is difficult to distinguish reality from the fictional virtual reality of the game.) In Cronenberg's vision, virtual reality games require a master bio-port inserted permanently into the spine, not far above the anus. It's almost unfathomable, but undeniably true: *eXistenZ* is a major feature film centrally about the fear of anal penetration. Ted, who has never been bio-ported, admits "I have this phobia about having my body penetrated." The bio-port procedure is like an anal rape. When carried out by a man, the procedure is photographed in a way that clearly suggests gay anal sex. When eXistenZ is about to be loaded into Ted's bio-port, the pod must be lubricated, because new bio-ports are tight until they have been used frequently. Cronenberg shows us a close-up of the bio-

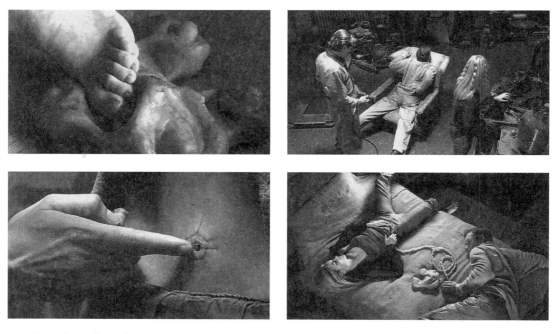

Everything about the virtual reality game "*eXistenZ*" seems sexualized. (1) The game pod is a chimerical sexual organ — useful also for foot fetishism. (2) The bioport procedure — necessary to play the game — resembles an anal rape (Jude Law submits to Willem Dafoe, while Jennifer Jason Leigh watches). (3) Your port can be lubricated and fingered as foreplay to the game. And (4) the pod can be used to connect play-partners umbilically.

port, so we can see that it looks like an anus. And when the penis-like umbilical is inserted, the image takes on an unmistakable homosexual dimension. Ted tells Allegra that it hurts; and when, in close-up, Allegra inserts her fingers into the opening, the image seems pornographic. Later, Ted sticks his tongue into Allegra's bio-port and confesses: "I feel really vulnerable." And when Ted's bio-port gets infected and requires an antibiotic, Allegra tells him, "Of course, we can't play until it's done." (Although "play" refers to the play of eXistenZ, it should be noted that "play" is internet slang for having sex, particularly among gay men.) It's fascinating that in an America so polarized and fearful over homosexuality, Cronenberg is the only director to make a general-audience film that forces spectators to confront their potential fear of anal sex and to look at sexual images they may find repugnant.

Forty minutes into the film, Allegra and Ted enter the virtual reality game, which is started by rubbing the pod's nipples. Or have they already been in a virtual reality game for quite a while, as the film's surprise ending will suggest? With hindsight, we might presume that the insect-sized two-headed dragon we see, a "mutated amphibian, a sign of the times," is an unreal component of the game, rather than a "real" convention of Cronenberg's science-fiction future. Yet if reality and virtual reality are indistinguishable, could one *ever* tell which is which, and would there ultimately be any real ontological difference? Cronenberg is fascinated with the moral and philosophical implications of virtual reality, which becomes a metaphor for the pleasure and fiction that society has become so attuned to that it has lost the ability to understand the moral meaning of reality. As Ted "plays" within the virtual reality game, he says, "I'm feeling disconnected from my real life. I actually think there's a level of psychosis involved here." But when he manages to pause the game and escape the virtual reality, his real life feels unreal, like a game, and the people in his life seem to be characters, too. (Or is Ted's "real" life actually a virtual reality game, too, because he's playing a game within a game?) At one point, the excitement of playing eXistenZ — which is also a metaphor for going to the movies — makes Ted want to kill a character in the game. And so he does, without hesitation or guilt. Later, with great excitement, Allegra kills someone in the game, too. Is this culture of sensation why Americans are increasingly disconnected from the consequences of their actions? And of their political (in)actions, too?

In a key monologue, Ted characterizes eXistenZ: "I don't like it here. I don't know what's going on.... We're both stumbling around together in this unformed world ... whose rules and objectives are largely unknown, seemingly indecipherable or even, possibly nonexistent, always on the verge of being killed by forces that we don't understand." Allegra retorts: "It's a game that everyone's already playing!" Clearly, Allegra is suggesting that on one level, eXistenZ is existence itself: engendering chaos, confusion, and spiritual doubt. Although Allegra and Ted are the heroes of Cronenberg's film, because they are championing eXistenZ, they may actually be the villains, at least in a philosophical sense. Allegra's enemies may be the good guys, because they are working for the "victory of realism" by trying to destroy Allegra and all virtual reality games (and movies, TV, and art?). With formalism destroyed — no more shallow distractions, no more special effects — we would be forced to return to the reality of the world and find meaning and redemption within our own quotidian lives. Is there any more serious, relevant topic for a horror film to consider in these millennial times?

Despite the clues planted throughout, the ending of *eXistenZ* is surprising, suggesting that a virtual reality game began much earlier than we thought and that the people we've been watching are game characters with very different real-life identities. In fact, Jennifer

David Cronenberg punctuates *eXistenZ* with sudden, screaming outbursts by Jude Law and Jennifer Jason Leigh which provide *frissons* of shock.

Jason Leigh, as it turns out, is not playing Allegra Geller, designer of the virtual reality game eXistenZ, but Allegra Geller, an enemy of realism who is playing the role of a virtual reality game designer within a virtual reality game called transCendenZ. (And even more mind-boggling, there may be another level of reality that Cronenberg's film hints at, but leaves unexplored: that Jennifer Jason Leigh may actually be playing a virtual reality game player who is playing an enemy of realism playing the role of a virtual reality game designer in a virtual reality game which is neither eXistenZ nor transCendenZ.) The final scene, violent and dramatic, shows several murders followed by a plaintive cry from someone about to die violently: "Tell me the truth, are we still in the game?" In this culture of game-playing and pleasure, Cronenberg understands that we have lost our moral compass.

Spider, a character study in psychopathology directed by Cronenberg in 2002, is one of the finest films ever made about mental illness, worthy of consideration alongside Ingmar Bergman's *Through a Glass Darkly* and John Cassavettes' *A Woman Under the Influence*. *Spider* starts with credits over a variety of Rorschach-like patterns and textures which vaguely resemble spiders. Ralph Fiennes plays Dennis Kleg, AKA Spider, a middle-aged man released from long-term confinement in an asylum who is now trying to establish a life for himself. From his first appearance, in a stunningly choreographed shot that shows him the last to get off a train, Spider seems crazy: unshaven, disheveled, mumbling, fearful, tentative, lost, troubled. We know immediately that this man is unlikely to achieve any success. In the neighborhood of his childhood, Spider settles into a boarding house inhabited by the similarly troubled, all overseen by the eccentric Mrs. Wilkinson, played by Lynn Redgrave. Even surrounded by others with mental problems, Spider exhibits extreme behaviors which are odd and profoundly disquieting: he wears four shirts, he is scarily secretive, he lays down to embrace the garden dirt, he wraps himself with newspaper to protect himself from the gasworks, he journals obsessively in a language comprehensible only to him. A clear indication of his madness, Spider is sometimes photographed as a dark-shadowed figure out of a German expressionist silent film — totally appropriate considering how little Spider speaks. Cobweb patterns are everywhere — in Spider's lampshade; in his childhood room; in a broken, reconstructed window; in the cat's cradle string game; and particularly in the surreal and vaguely threatening framework of the huge gasworks.

In flashbacks, the adult Spider and the child Spider inhabit the same frame, a strategy which allows Cronenberg to show the adult Spider coming to terms with his past. As we watch the young Spider, we see the demoralizing, vulgar world of his father, an alcoholic who hangs out at the pub flirting with Yvonne, the town tart. Is paternal abuse the

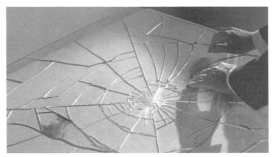

Cronenberg weaves many web patterns like these three into *Spider*— in part symbolizing the psychological self-deceit of the protagonist (played by Ralph Fiennes as an adult and Bradley Hall as a child).

cause of Spider's lifetime mental problems? In striking contrast is Spider's mother, played by Miranda Richardson, who is shown as wonderful and caring. In Cronenberg's slow-moving art film, traditional horror elements don't erupt until the father kills the mother after she interrupts him having sex with Yvonne. To our amazement, the murder is successfully concealed, and Yvonne moves in and becomes Spider's stepmother. Only gradually does it become clear that we are not watching objective flashbacks, but an unreliable narrative which is a manifestation of Spider's ongoing delusional world. Cronenberg's most intriguing narrative strategy is one of the most clever castings since Buñuel cast two different actresses in the same role in alternating scenes in *That Obscure Object of Desire*. How Cronenberg's film works is skillfully tied to the specific moment that each spectator realizes that Miranda Richardson — in a brilliant performance — is playing both Spider's mother *and* the town tart, Yvonne, a casting which

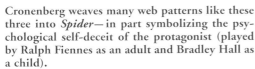

Spider uses the iconic locations of *Psycho* and the horror-of-personality films: (1) the stairway (lit more brightly than Ralph Fiennes' face), and (2) the bathroom. (3) Especially disturbing and untypical to conventional cinema is this image of a naked man, vulnerable in a fetal position.

Startlingly original performances dominate *Spider*, especially by Miranda Richardson, who portrays (1) Spider's mother and (2) the town tart. Although (3) Lynn Redgrave plays Spider's landlady, (4) Richardson takes over that performance as well.

is not immediately perceived or easily apprehensible and which we gradually realize is not just a stunt, but an integrated artistic choice which helps us understand Spider's psychological problems and his past. A spooky child certainly, the young Spider is already crazy and possessed by visions. Indeed, *Spider* presents us virtually *no* clear objective reality; this is made strikingly clear in a present-day sequence in which Miranda Richardson suddenly shows up in yet a third role: a sluttier version of Lynn Redgrave's Mrs. Wilkinson. Perhaps now we realize that Spider obsessively sees his mother in virtually all women — but why? In the terrifying climax, we watch the young Spider calmly kill Yvonne by using a makeshift web of string to turn on the gas. At the moment she dies, Spider's father is suddenly shown as compassionate and human, and the dead Yvonne is "replaced" by Spider's mother, dead in Yvonne's place. Finally, the truth of Spider's past is clear: his father was never the total sinner, his mother was never the total saint, and Yvonne was largely a mental construct of Spider, who — lost in his delusions — tragically killed his mother and psychologically blamed his father. If *Psycho* is about matricide as seen from the outside looking in, *Spider* is about matricide from the inside looking out. And it is terrifying being *inside* Spider. David Cronenberg's masterful film — as much a rigorously insightful medical case study as an ominous, one-of-a-kind horror film — is yet another manifestation of the director's genuinely astonishing talent.

13 — 9/11 and Beyond

In the fifties and sixties, horror film underwent a transformation because our understanding of the world changed profoundly. We no longer trusted our neighbors; we feared new forms of destruction brought about by science and atomic technology; and we understood evil more presently and less metaphorically than ever as a result of World War II and the Holocaust. In contrast, conventional horror films like *Dracula* seemed meager and unimportant. If the horror film today seems largely *not* to have progressed in the last three decades to include major new subgenres of horror, it may be because our fears have not especially changed since the sixties. They may have been ratcheted up in emotional intensity, but they are not fundamentally different. As horrible as 9/11 was, the destruction and death wrought on that day were not as extensive or extreme as that which resulted from the bombings of Hiroshima and Nagasaki in 1945. Of course, the significant difference is that 9/11 happened in the United States; and so perhaps for the first time, Americans were forced to develop a more personal, emotional understanding of the meaning of violence in the world. Interpersonal violence, criminal violence, political violence, and even the cinematic violence in our own movies — all of these on some level would now be viewed through the prism of 9/11.

For the huge majority of Americans, 9/11 — though an unprecedented trauma — was witnessed and experienced via the television screen. Its transmission via this medium (the same medium that presents most of our movies to us) is not incidental to the central emotional position 9/11 now occupies in the minds of so many. In my book *The Suspense Thriller: Films in the Shadow of Alfred Hitchcock*, I discuss in detail the ideas of Altan Löker, the Turkish film theorist who has shown how certain kinds of narratives create suspense and

World Trade Center towers: *after*, from the film *9/11*.

343

anxiety by manipulating us, as spectators, to participate psychologically. According to Löker, we participate by making wishes in regard to the narrative. Our wishes often relate to our desire to contribute to a protagonist's success. (*"Don't open that door!"*) Other times they relate to our desire to experience spectacle. (*"Force the killer to take his mask off, so we can see his face!"*) And these wishes, explains Löker, are rarely bound by moral considerations.

On the morning of September 11th, 2001, those Americans who turned on their televisions saw the north tower of the World Trade Center smoldering and heard the report that perhaps a small plane had crashed into it at 8:45 A.M. At first, neither the newscasters covering the event nor the millions watching it understood the implications of what was being shown. In the next few minutes as the coverage continued, I suspect there were few viewers who were not *hoping* to see video footage of the plane crashing into that north tower. *What does it look like when a small plane crashes into a building?* From a purely voyeuristic perspective, it must be recognized that the spectacle of that would be interesting to see. (Löker cautions us against our tendency to fictionalize or falsely ennoble our reactions.) On some level, when at 9:03 A.M. the second hijacked plane crashed, before our eyes, into the south tower, we were especially horrified, because the plane had apparently come as a response to our own desire for spectacle. It was as if we had gotten our wish, but a wish that had come in an unanticipated package deal, complete with terrifying things we didn't want: For one thing, we now understood that the plane wasn't small, but a conventional airliner. For another, we understood that we—*voyeurs to the wished-for spectacle*—had witnessed, in the moment of that second crash, the terror, physical suffering, and deaths of a great number of human beings. As if to punish us for our voyeurism, at 10:05 A.M., the south tower crashed to the ground, bringing apocalyptic destruction—a destruction beyond our ability to anticipate or imagine. At that moment, I suspect not a single American watching television was able to turn from the screen. Now that we knew what was capable of happening, we watched that north tower with the avid, anxious world, and we waited, in increasing terror... If we had earlier, in our misguided desire, wanted spectacle, we were going to be rewarded in the worst possible way: with the most horrific mass killing and destruction ever witnessed by millions of people around the world at the moment it was happening.

Twenty-three minutes later, at 10:28 A.M., the north tower collapsed as well. Eventually, video footage was found of the first plane hitting the north tower, and we saw that collision, too, and then video after video of those two planes, from a variety of distances

World Trade Center towers: *before*, from the film *9/11.*

and vantage points, hitting their targets again and again. For me, one of the most upsetting video images was from a surveillance camera inside an office building, which shows an oblivious office worker typing at his computer station, while behind him, visible through a window, the first hijacked plane crashes into the north tower. Even after the plane crashes, the worker continues as before. "American Obliviousness" could have been that video's title. And we saw, too, the towers collapsing — from one angle, then another — and the cloud of detritus moving like a monster through the streets as New Yorkers frantically attempted to outrun it.

For days, for weeks, for years, we've been punished psychologically: those images repeatedly replayed, irrevocably burned into our consciousness. One irrevocable horror is that the images from that day are trapped inside us, a permanent part of who we now are. And then later, there were more images of horror: in Afghanistan, in Iraq, in Abu Ghraib, in London, in Madrid, in Israel, in Lebanon... Certainly Osama bin Laden's design of the psychological component of the 9/11 attacks could not have been more skillfully contrived. Not only did the attacks emulate the Hollywood thriller, they surpassed the thriller with a horrific intensity both more visceral and emotional. In other words, Hollywood fantasy was trumped by reality.

And therein lies the true problem with the horror film in the first years of the twenty-first century. With perhaps the exceptions of David Cronenberg, Michael Haneke, and Guillermo Del Toro, we do not have film directors (or writers) with the imagination of Osama bin Laden.

I suspect that new subgenres of horror film may yet appear, tied to not-yet-understood byproducts of the exponential rate of change in our digital age. For instance, that the democratization of knowledge provided by the internet also allows universal access to methods of mass destruction cannot help but undermine our naive faith in democracy — as can the disarming truth that people can democratically vote for what is essentially totalitarian repression and violence. And with the internet comes a loss of privacy that newer generations don't even recognize as troubling, if they even recognize the loss at all. Whereas there is worry for those around the world who are *not* connected via the newest technologies, there is a more sophisticated worry that in the very near future none of us will ever be able to become *disconnected*. And with no Walden Pond, no natural world, there will be little opportunity for reflection or self-knowledge. Sensation and distraction, as in David Cronenberg's *eXistenZ*, will replace the real world, and real human connection will be increasingly rare. At the moment, futurists, sociologists, and the occasional political scientist may alert us to these dangers, but by and large, these fears are as yet too abstract to register emotionally. But it will be these fears (and others, beyond our limited imaginations) which will inhabit the horror subjects that future subgenres will explore. As of yet, our horror directors are not up to this visionary task.

In the meantime, horrific documentary images from the real world proliferate, and our television and computer screens bring us these new, ever-more-terrifying visions of apocalyptic shock and awe *live*, with a ratcheted intensity: in our living rooms, in our bedrooms, into our subconscious.

And the horror film has been unable to keep up.

Appendix I

A Proposed Canon of Modern Horror

I firmly believe in lists. Although most of *Dark Dreams 2.0* has been an attempt to understand how the modern horror film works, my own views undoubtedly determine my taste. Herewith, to make my prejudices explicit, are my candidates for the greatest modern horror films, performances, and directors of the last fifty years. Note how American films dominate the first half of my list, foreign films the second half, a fact which itself provides inherent criticism of the recent American film industry.

GREATEST MODERN HORROR FILMS

Invasion of the Body Snatchers (1956)
Psycho (1960)
Peeping Tom (1960)
The Innocents (1961)
What Ever Happened to Baby Jane? (1962)
The Birds (1963)
The Haunting (1963)
Hush...Hush, Sweet Charlotte (1964)
Repulsion (1965)
The Collector (1965)
Rosemary's Baby (1968)
Night of the Living Dead (1968)
The Hellstrom Chronicle (1971)
"Don't Look Now" (1973)
Eraserhead (1977)
The Last Wave (1977)
Dressed to Kill (1980)
Scanners (1981)
In a Glass Cage (1986)
The Vanishing (1988)

The Seventh Continent (1989)
Henry: Portrait of a Serial Killer (1990)
The Silence of the Lambs (1991)
Naked Lunch (1991)
Benny's Video (1992)
71 Fragments of a Chronology of Chance (1994)
Funny Games (1997)
The Sixth Sense (1999)
eXistenZ (1999)
Requiem for a Dream (2000)
American Psycho (2000)
The Piano Teacher (2001)
Irréversible (2002)
Audition (2002)
Spider (2002)
Elephant (2003)
United 93 (2006)
Children of Men (2006)
Pan's Labyrinth (2006)
Funny Games (2008)

GREATEST MODERN HORROR PERFORMANCES

Anthony Perkins in *Psycho* (1960)
Janet Leigh in *Psycho* (1960)
Deborah Kerr in *The Innocents* (1961)
Bette Davis in *What Ever Happened to Baby Jane?* (1962)
Julie Harris in *The Haunting* (1963)
Bette Davis in *Hush...Hush, Sweet Charlotte* (1964)
Mia Farrow in *Rosemary's Baby* (1968)
Tuesday Weld in *Pretty Poison* (1968)
Elizabeth Montgomery in *The Legend of Lizzie Borden* (1975)
Angie Dickinson in *Dressed to Kill* (1980)
Faye Dunaway in *Mommie, Dearest* (1981)
Kathy Bates in *Misery* (1990)

Anthony Hopkins in *The Silence of the Lambs* (1991)
Jodie Foster in *The Silence of the Lambs* (1991)
Arno Frisch in *Funny Games* (1997)
Haley Joel Osment in *The Sixth Sense* (1999)
Christian Bale in *American Psycho* (2000)
Ellen Burstyn in *Requiem for a Dream* (2000)
Isabelle Huppert in *The Piano Teacher* (2001)
Robin Williams in *One Hour Photo* (2002)
Monica Bellucci in *Irréversible* (2002)
Vincent Cassel in *Irréversible* (2002)
Miranda Richardson in *Spider* (2002)
Ralph Fiennes in *Spider* (2002)
Christian Bale in *The Machinist* (2004)
Judi Dench in *Notes on a Scandal* (2006)

GREATEST MODERN HORROR DIRECTORS

Alfred Hitchcock
Robert Aldrich
Roman Polanski
Brian De Palma

David Cronenberg
Michael Haneke
Guillermo Del Toro

Appendix II

Interviews with Horror Directors: Aldrich, Castle, Harrington, Romero, Friedkin (1977)

While the various horror films delight the genre critic with their sustained conventions and archetypes, those same films represent for their directors the eternal Hollywood dichotomy between artistic aspirations and commerce. Without denying the aesthetic merits or integrated patterns implicit in their films (and occasionally acknowledging them with a surprisingly intellectual understanding), the Hollywood directors generally view their films primarily in terms of box office, financing, story values, casting, and gambits for attracting audiences. This is not surprising, because the financial success of a film is crucial for a Hollywood director who otherwise would have trouble raising the money to make another. Nevertheless, in the first of the five director interviews that follow, Robert Aldrich suddenly veers off from talking about the genesis of his films in order to discuss his personal world view, which holds life as unceasing struggle. Genre films (and especially horror films) have a peculiar relationship to the Hollywood system: they thrive on it; and their conventions are set as much by the mysterious process by which the public proffers its box-office coin in approval, as by the conscious, "artistic" visions of their creators. The following interviews with important horror film directors Robert Aldrich (1918–1983), William Castle (1914–1977), Curtis Harrington (1926–2007), George A. Romero (1940–), and William Friedkin (1935–), all conducted in the early seventies, reveal a fascinating view of the realities of the genre and offer a valuable contrast to the critical and theoretical considerations in *Dark Dreams.*

Alfred Hitchcock, the director most responsible for inspiring contemporary horror directors, appears in the trailer advertising ***Psycho.***

349

ROBERT ALDRICH

The office of Robert Aldrich is located in Los Angeles, one block south of the Melrose Paramount Studio. Masculine and tasteful, Aldrich's office is decorated with ad displays of his films and other curios. "I like Bette Davis and I like Joan Crawford," says a matinee matron in a *New Yorker* cartoon on the wall, "But I don't know if I like Bette Davis and Joan Crawford together!" Emerging from his office, Aldrich is a large, jovial, and instantly likeable man in his mid-fifties who has the most remarkably long and owlish eyebrows. In his inner office, I choose a large black easy chair from which to conduct the interview, and he chooses its matching overstuffed sofa under a huge and hauntingly evocative oil painting of Kim Novak in her leading role in *The Legend of Lylah Clare.*

How did you first get interested in doing What Ever Happened to Baby Jane?

ALDRICH: A lady named Geraldine Hersey had been my English secretary on *Ten Seconds to Hell* and *The Angry Hills.* When I was in Africa doing *Sodom and Gomorrah* I got this long letter from her and an English publication, *What Ever Happened to Baby Jane?*— a hardback. No one had ever heard of its author Henry Farrell. At least I hadn't. I read it and was fascinated. I went through all the problems of trying to find out who owned it and who the author was. Lo and behold, the publication rights were owned in America, the author wasn't an Englishman but rather a Hollywood screenwriter, and the movie rights had already been purchased by another Hollywood screenwriter named Harry Essex. So consequently the price for that material had skyrocketed in terms of the commodity market, but I wanted it very badly. At that time the honeymoon was still on between Joe Levine and myself— because he was very happy with *Sodom and Gomorrah* and had already sold a lot of it to England and made lots of money, so he and I bought it together, and we collectively employed Lukas Heller as the screenwriter. Subsequently I wrote to Bette Davis, whom I had never met.

Did Davis have any initial hesitation about doing the movie?

ALDRICH: In those days it was much more difficult to induce Bette Davis to do a picture, and she had never done a picture of that kind before. Davis was a very proud lady about her talent, and rightfully so. Therefore, I was very apprehensive about her willingness to be in the movie. So I took a lot of time composing a letter that was arrogant, but I thought necessarily so, saying that if this isn't the best screenplay you've ever read, don't do the picture, but if it is, I'd like an appointment and I'll come to New York to see you. About a month went by and then I got a very long, very polite, but very aloof letter from Miss Davis saying that no, it wasn't the best screenplay she had ever read, but that it came close. She'd be delighted to meet with me, but didn't know if she'd want to make the picture or not. So I came to New York two or three weeks after that and met with Davis and her lawyer. They were terribly hospitable and friendly, and Davis asked only professional questions. At the end of the three- or four-hour conversation she said: "Fine, if the economics can be resolved, I'd like to do it." I don't think I talked to Crawford first. I had already done a picture with her, *Autumn Leaves*, and we had a very good relationship, so I had reason to believe I could get her. We had some billing problems, but everyone was eventually satisfied.

Did the two of them have any problems on the set?

ALDRICH: Not on *Baby Jane*. They obviously didn't like each other, but they were totally professional and ladylike. Any comments about one or the other they would reserve for the privacy of their own dressing room when the other one wasn't around. I was very careful and very fair. I had to be objective in terms of getting the best picture. I think it would be unwise to give either of those ladies an edge, but they were totally professional on *Baby Jane*.

It seems that one of your abilities is to cast expertly. Lots of directors engage in the old trick of casting against the grain and then getting applause. In most

Robert Aldrich on the set of *Hush, Hush...Sweet Charlotte*, flanked by actresses Bette Davis and Olivia de Havilland.

of your films you consistently cast with the grain and use the actor's own persona as an integral part of the character.

ALDRICH: Many people don't quite understand this, because they think this kind of casting invades the province of the writer. But since you're in an art or craft that has to do with communication, if the audience — through their evaluation of who the actor is playing the part — can understand the character, you can telescope ten pages of the script because the audience will instantly know who the character is, how he behaves, where he comes from, what his background is, etc. I don't say that the other concept doesn't work, but it doesn't for me. In *Baby Jane*, we thought that if you made a movie about the periphery of Hollywood which had something to do with the ancient Hollywood, and put in two stars who were getting old, people would read into that picture a secret show-biz mythology, almost a nostalgia.

The audience feels that they are privy to real-life secrets about Crawford and Davis.

How close did you work with Lukas Heller, the screenwriter?

ALDRICH: We're very close. We've done lots of pictures together. You always buy the material first and then do your overlay, that is, you write a long position paper on what's wrong with the material and what you want to do with it. Then you come in and the writer reads the overlay and the material, and then you argue — you pretend to discuss — why you think you're right and why he thinks he's right. The final result is usually a combination of both.

How faithful are you to the script? I get a strong impression that your movies come out exactly as the script has been written, that it has all been worked out with extreme care.

ALDRICH: I think that's true because on those pictures we rehearsed: three weeks on *Baby Jane*, two weeks on *Hush...Hush, Sweet Charlotte*. What you see in the film is not necessarily what you see in the script, but it is what you saw at the end of those weeks of rehearsal. In other words, actors — as much as you may dislike them — quite often contribute, especially someone as talented as Davis. "I don't think I'd say that. Wouldn't I say this instead?" etc. Probably she'd say something in between. The script may veer ninety degrees in rehearsal. You also find that it has holes. I can work with Heller because he's English, and English writers don't have the ego problem of American writers. They come prepared to submerge their pride in ownership for the welfare of the project. So they don't mind if at the end of the rehearsal period you say: "This doesn't work, this doesn't structure, go back and in an hour come back with another version." What happens at the end of the rehearsal period is that you get a refined version of what you began with.

Why after Baby Jane *did you decide to make* Hush... Hush, Sweet Charlotte, *which is basically a variation of the first film?*

ALDRICH: I really had a marvelous relation with Davis and she hadn't done anything worthwhile in between. I had made a terrible picture with Henry Farrell called *4 for Texas*, and he had this other book, not yet published, which he brought to me. I sent it to Davis and she liked it. I thought it would be a marvelous vehicle for her. It really didn't disturb me, it would be different enough from *Baby Jane* so I couldn't be characterized as only a horror-film director. *Charlotte* is a bigger kind of movie, and the marketplace was very anxious for that kind of movie. In fact, Crawford was originally in the picture. They were counting on the reteaming of Farrell, Crawford, Davis, Heller, and Aldrich, but hopefully it would be better, because the story was better.

How did you decide on using de Havilland instead of Crawford?

ALDRICH: After Crawford got sick, the insurance company had an option to either cancel the picture or give us a short period of time to recast. Our position was that the whole reason for making the picture was to rejoin Crawford and Davis,

so we couldn't substitute just anybody. The only persons we could all agree on (Davis, Fox, and our company all had cast approval) were de Havilland and Katharine Hepburn. I had a strong feeling, however, that Davis didn't really want Hepburn to do it, and I knew Hepburn would probably never do it, no matter what we offered her. So I went to Switzerland where de Havilland was living. She had some reluctance about doing it, because obviously she was going to finish second to Davis. Unlike *Baby Jane*, *Charlotte* is really a one-vehicle picture, but she accepted.

The other piece of casting that is exceptional is Mary Astor as Jewel. We are constantly aware of how beautiful she used to be, and the image of Astor now old and bloated is mythically and mysteriously sad.

ALDRICH: I have a hunch that was also Davis' idea, and Mary was brilliant. Our problem was convincing her to do it. She had just published a very successful book and had found a whole new life for herself. Both Davis and de Havilland had been under contract at Warners when Mary had been there, and they were very close friends, so they helped to convince her.

In Baby Jane *we finally see that Baby Jane is really not the guilty one. In* Charlotte *we discover that Charlotte is not really crazy. The motif of the character who is in some way a misfit, outside the mainstream of society, and yet who can exhibit more sense and humanity than others, is your theme.*

ALDRICH: Well, I've always thought these people were normal, and the societies outside them weren't. There is a theme I always look for. It comes from *The Big Knife* when Jack Palance says to his agent: "Struggle, Charlie, you may still win a blessing." It has to do with man's intention to try to contain and manipulate his own destiny. It's the struggle that counts. A movie is about what high-school coaches with no talent tell their teams: "This is character-building." And the struggle must change and develop the character. Movies aren't about winning. Football is about winning. Movies are about how people cope with losing or at least try to get a draw in life.

Do you like unhappy endings?

ALDRICH: I don't really. I'd love to do a comedy, but can't get anybody to let me. I'm really a very funny fellow — but no one else thinks so. Most of my pictures have very funny things. I don't look for unhappy endings, but I don't think much of life ends happily. And since I try to make films that are reasonably truthful, chances are they'll end unhappily.

Will you do more in horror?

ALDRICH: I know that I had wanted to do a take-off— not a put-down — of *Dracula.* And I couldn't get anyone interested. But obviously, now it's too late. The French have made it. Brooks has made *Young Frankenstein.* Warhol even made a *Frankenstein* and *Dracula.* But a few years ago I knew that was going to be the next breakthrough.

I can't discuss horror without asking about The Exorcist.

ALDRICH: I thought I had an outside chance to direct that picture — for about fifteen seconds. Before Friedkin was hired, [writer William Peter] Blatty had a terrible argument with Warner Brothers and was thinking of pulling the property away from them. I talked to him about buying the property, but I'm sure he didn't take it seriously because he needed a lot of money and I didn't have a lot of money. Everyone in Holly-

wood was disturbed about *The Sting,* because it won the Academy award over *The Exorcist,* but they shouldn't have been, because if they had any brains they wouldn't take the Academy seriously. The two films are not even in the same league. I do think Friedkin blew the movie in the last three minutes though. I don't think the audience understands the interior relationships and the exchange the devil makes; that is, the life of the child for Father Karras. I have many quarrels with the picture, but that may be envy.

And finally, one last question. What films and film-makers do you think have influenced you?

ALDRICH: I really don't know. I know those are profound questions people rightfully concern themselves with, but ... I know I had a million opportunities. People of our generation spent our youth in the motion-picture theatre. You went to ten movies a week. When I came to California I was very lucky to work with an awful lot of great directors: Milestone, Wellman, Polonsky, Rossen, Chaplin, Renoir, Losey. If you can't learn from great directors when they're directing, who can you learn from? It's like having a front-row seat in a post-postgraduate course in how to become a director.

WILLIAM CASTLE

William Castle has become uniquely identified with horror films over the years. While many disdain or dismiss his work as not a serious contribution to the genre, most should be willing to concede that Castle is a filmmaker who knows how to entertain. Castle has a friendly manner not unlike the quality that comes across in his brief screen appearances. One senses in him an unselfconscious desire to serve the audience and an instinctual grasp of showmanship. About *The Exorcist,* he said: "I went to that five times — twice to see the picture, the other times I watched the audience."

[Interview conducted by Dan R. Scapperotti]

William Castle talks directly to the audience of ***The Tingler.***

There is a sense of "fun" to your fifties horror films. Were you trying to accomplish anything else in these films?

CASTLE: I get calls from all over the United States, in fact I get letters from all over the world, from students who are studying film and have taken these films and are looking for hidden meanings. It's a very strange thing. I definitely feel that possibly in my unconscious I was trying to say something. Many of the films are being taken very seriously today at the universities where they study them. I never expected that they would put under a microscope pictures that I made in the fifties and sixties and look for hidden meanings. Nevertheless, that's what is happening. One of the questions I had from one of the students who called me from one of the universities was: "When you were doing *Strait-Jacket* with Joan Crawford, and she stepped off the train and the smoke enveloped her and just completely fogged her out, was the feeling that you were trying to get that she was going back to the fetus position in her mother's womb? Is that true?" You know, you didn't want to say that actually it was merely that you were trying to make time, and the smoke didn't work. And I think about inner meaning: truly, it is possible that deeply buried within my unconsciousness was the feeling of trying to say something. And I get this from *The Tingler*, where they say: "Was it my cry against war and was it antiestablishment?" Many, many times, possibly without really knowing what I was doing, I hit upon a nerve. I think it's very much the same thing they're seeing in W.C. Fields. "Was he antiestablishment?" Well, W. C. Fields was a character and whether he was "antiestablishment" probably never occurred to him. And it's the same with Laurel and Hardy, the Marx Brothers, and the little horror films I made. They all have something, and the meanings are far more sophisticated today, and are looked for much more deeply. But that's our audience.

How did the success of Psycho *affect* Homicidal*?*

CASTLE: I was accused of aping Hitchcock on *Homicidal. Time* magazine reviewed the film in 1962 and said it was better than *Psycho*. Whether it was or not is up to the audience to decide, not to me. They said it was a more original piece and more exciting. I must say that in those days I was very deeply a Hitchcock lover, as I still am, and I was very deeply influenced by Mr. Hitchcock. I didn't go and deliberately try to copy *Psycho*, because *Homicidal* is altogether a different story, but it had the same shocking ingredients. We both had a gimmick, and I think that was where I tried to beat Hitchcock. His gimmick on *Psycho* was a

great piece of showmanship. I believe the picture lasted for about an hour and fifty minutes, and during that time no one was allowed into the theatre. You had to wait in line if you came in five minutes after the picture started, or a half-hour, or whatever. You were allowed to buy a ticket, but you had to wait outside. Not until the picture was over was the new audience let in.[1] I was surprised, but the contract between the theatres and the distributors stated this, and it was policed. I waited in line in New York for a half-hour. But I thought this was fabulous, that people actually waited out in line as long as two hours to get in. It was an amazing thing, very much like *The Exorcist* more recently.[2] I felt I'd have to do something to top Mr. Hitchcock and have something more provocative as far as a gimmick was concerned, and I think I did it with my "Fright Break." The "Fright Break" was in the last sixty seconds of the film where my voice would be on screen saying: "Ladies and gentlemen, this is William Castle. You are cordially invited, if you're too frightened to see the last sixty seconds, to be my guest and go to the box office and get your full admission price refunded." That in itself was quite a daring statement to make, because there were big houses then with two or three thousand people. And outside we actually refunded money at the last minute at a display we called "The Coward's Corner." Very few people did go out, some just to see if we would indeed pay the admission price, and others would leave their girlfriend or boyfriend in the theatre and collect the one admission. But in a full house it was one percent at most.

In comparison to your earlier horror films, Homicidal *seems to be more sophisticated. Were you striving for something more than just scaring your audience?*

CASTLE: Oh yes. I was growing up at the time. You know, as one grows and does more and more films, one becomes a little more sophisticated. I was trying really to do a shocker on an intellectual plane.

Eugenie Leontovich and Jean Arless give fascinating performances in the film. Did you consider trying to get bigger names?

CASTLE: I didn't have the money. That is the reason I associated myself so closely with my own films. I was the star because I had no choice. I had to have somebody that I could get before the public.

How do you feel about the success of the two Arless personas in the film?

CASTLE: That's very interesting and a whole story in itself. That would make a book. I wanted to use a complete unknown because if any of the audience recognized the character that was playing the two parts, it would spoil it, because they would then know it was either a man or a woman. I got a girl who was completely unknown and I changed her name to Jean Arless. I made up the name Jean because it's ambiguous, you don't know whether it's a boy or a girl. I transformed this girl, who was a very beautiful girl, into a boy. We cut her hair, we had false appliances made for her mouth to change its structure, we changed her nose, and did everything we could to give her face a masculine appearance. She did all the scenes involving the boy first, and, in effect, became the boy offscreen as well as onscreen, and then did a transformation as the girl. She wore a wig over the cut hair, becoming a very feminine, delightful lady. The two parts of her — the two ids — were constantly at war with one another. It took a long time for this girl to get over this double transformation, and for a long time she didn't know what she was. People didn't know. Even to this day when they see the picture on television or in a re-release, they'll ask if it were a girl or boy. At the end of the picture, you'll remember, I had *her* come out and had *him* come out on a split screen, and they bowed to each other and bowed to the audience for a curtain call.

Was that double curtain call your idea?

CASTLE: Yes. And people would argue outside, was it indeed a girl or was it a boy? And I had a lot of fun with that because I never really told what it was.

Strait-Jacket seems to show the influence of What Ever Happened to Baby Jane? *To what extent were you influenced by that film?*

CASTLE: I was influenced by it. I think that Bob Aldrich is a very fine talent. I saw *Baby Jane* and I was amazed at the business it was doing, how good the film was, and at seeing two great super-

stars playing in this shocker. It was just an amazing phenomenon. I saw it three or four times and I said I must do a film with de Havilland or Davis or Crawford. I developed *Strait-Jacket* from an idea of my own. While it was in no way the same story, we used Crawford. The film, I think, did more business than *Baby Jane*. It was one of my most successful films.

In Strait-Jacket *we have what appears to be one of your favorite devices — the hatchet murder. Are you particularly fond of this?*

CASTLE: No. As a matter of fact, where else is it shown in any of my pictures?

In House on Haunted Hill *you have the woman using an axe.*

CASTLE: Oh yes. It's always a good gimmick, you know. For *Strait-Jacket* I got the springboard from Lizzie Borden. From the Lizzie Borden murders I devised a woman and her problem with that axe. I'm not axe-happy.

The career of Joan Crawford was somewhat revitalized by What Ever Happened to Baby Jane? *How was Crawford to work with on* Strait-Jacket?

CASTLE: Oh God, Joan Crawford is one of the great, great stars of any time. She is disciplined, she is dedicated, she is marvelous to work with. She's the best star I've used in any of my pictures, outside of Vincent Price. I resurrected his career too. It was starting on *House on Haunted Hill* and during *The Tingler* that got him going with the American International Pictures. He's never stopped since then. But getting back to Crawford, I did another film with her as soon as I could, a picture that I like and one of my best: *I Saw What You Did*.

Do you feel that crazy people are more horrifying than monsters like Frankenstein?

CASTLE: Not necessarily. It's a different technique. One is horror, the other is shocker. Of course, I have my own definition of horror, and I have my own definition of the thriller. Hitchcock makes thrillers (or shockers). I make both. A horror picture is taking a monster and having the audience scream or be frightened by this monster — *Godzilla, The Creature from the Black Lagoon*. A thriller or a shocker involves an identifiable person that you might be — a girl in jeopardy, or somebody in trouble — that the audience roots for or identifies with. So there is a difference between the thriller or the shocker and the horror piece. I get very frightened of people rather than monsters. I think people are more fun to work with than monsters anyway.

CURTIS HARRINGTON

Curtis Harrington, who began his career as the experimental filmmaker of the notable surreal short *Fragment of Seeking*, lives in the Hollywood Hills in a well-decorated house furnished wisely and in good taste. On the wall is a French movie poster for his film *Games*, which reads *Diable à 3* [*The Devil at 3*]. Harrington himself is a pleasant, friendly person whose films exhibit a certain nostalgic sense of the macabre. He has worked ably in the horror-of-personality genre, and more consistently than any other director.

[Interview conducted by Dale Winogura and Stuart Kaminsky]

Curtis Harrington, in a formal portrait taken in his longtime Los Angeles home on Vine Way.

Do you think you are a typed director, typed as a director of mental anguish?

HARRINGTON: In the eyes of the motion-picture industry, such as it is, I am probably "typed" as a director of horror films and thrillers. The concept "director of mental anguish" is one that I'm afraid most producers in Hollywood wouldn't understand.

What has been the extent of your involvement with your films?

HARRINGTON: *How Awful About Allan* was offered to me by George Edwards and Aaron Spelling. *What's the Matter with Helen?* was a project I was deeply involved in from the time it was just a gleam in Henry Farrell's eye. It was Farrell's original story and screenplay, but it was absolutely a project that I was instrumental in bringing about.

How much of the writing do you do on your films?

HARRINGTON: I contributed conceptually to some of the writing of *What's the Matter with Helen?* I co-wrote the original story of *Games*. The amount of writing I actually do varies tremendously from project to project. My preference is to work very closely with a writer on the development of a film that I want to do, since I do not consider myself to be a first-class writer — especially of dialogue, which I consider to be a special skill.

In Games *and* What's the Matter with Helen? *would you say that you were working within and against genre conventions at the same time?*

HARRINGTON: It's hard for me to think of them in those terms because I'm really more interested in using the genre to express my own interests. In *Games*, for instance, the whole concept goes back to what Henry James wrote, in which underlying it all is the story of the contrast between European decadence and American innocence. These are the elements I like to work with. As far as I'm concerned, I have yet to make a horror film. I would like to make one. Horror films are usually of a more fantastic genre, in the tradition of *Frankenstein* and *Dracula*. Those, to me, are true horror films. What I have made are really psychological mystery stories. Certainly I'm not unaware of the debt that *Games* owes to *Diabolique*. There are elements of horror in those films; I just wouldn't call them horror films. The whole idea of *Games* really came about because of my intense admiration for the work of Josef von Sternberg — *The Blue Angel, The Devil Is a Woman, Shanghai Express, Anatahan, Blonde Venus*. I very much wanted to create a latter-day vehicle for Marlene Dietrich at the time. The only reason why she didn't play it was that the heads of the studio simply would not entertain the thought of her even being in it. I was never even allowed to present the script to her. They felt she was not a star of current enough importance, whereas Simone Signoret was still considered to be much more of a current star.

There is a rich, granular texture to Games *that is very well realized. How was this achieved?*

HARRINGTON: I had the good fortune to work with William Fraker, who is in many ways my favorite of all the cameramen I've worked with. This was his first film. Before this he was an assistant cameraman. Despite my visual orientation, I'm not a director who can tell the cameraman where to put the lights, but I certainly tell him in essence what I want, then he can technically achieve it. The better the cameraman is, the less I have to say to him, and that was certainly the case with Bill Fraker.

There was a diffused quality to the film. Was that done with both diffused filters and lighting?

HARRINGTON: Yes. We chose that as the style. I used that effect again very consciously in *The Killing Kind*. We used a Harrison fog filter on most work of greater or lesser density. In *Games*, it was portraying a kind of enclosed, hothouse world in which these people lived. *The Killing Kind* is my most realistic film; even though it deals with murder and obsessive personality, it really deals with the everyday. There is no exoticism in it whatsoever. There, I was trying to make an overall comment on the whole thing, which is ultimately, in a way, a kind of nightmare. I wanted that slight removal from reality to put you in a more subjective world.

What conscious connections do you find between Games *and* Diabolique?

HARRINGTON: Certain plot devices are the only main connections between the two. I wanted to do a story that would seem like a fantasy about a supernatural visitation that would be revealed as a hoax at the end, which was exactly what *Diabolique* was.

How do you feel about What's the Matter with Helen?

HARRINGTON: To me, the film was a very affectionate re-creation of a period in Los Angeles history, which I have my own tremendous feelings of nostalgia for. I was trying to show lives on the fringe of Hollywood in the thirties, not within the industry. I had tremendous feelings of sympathy for both characters in the story.

You never have all-white, all-black characters in your films. Like Hitchcock, you work for the shades of gray.

HARRINGTON: That to me is very important because I try to make my characters real rather than something that is a matter for the author's convenience. Ambiguity of character and situation is something that intrigues me. I would love to do more Pirandellian themes because they fascinate me.

How do you feel about the similarities in plot structure of the horror-of-personality films, including your own?

HARRINGTON: I do not look for such similarities, so these are the things that are [evident] after the fact. I think you find in the work of a great many artists that, in essence, they tend to say the same thing over and over again. This is not a bad or negative thing. It is up to the critic to attach whatever importance he wants to them. These may be unconscious resonances, and I think it is bad for anyone who works creatively to become aware of all this. I've always felt it was wrong for an artist to be psychoanalyzed. The one or two times that I've failed is when I've worked out something intellectually. I have to have a kind of gut feeling about what I'm doing, and just follow that.

Your sense of nostalgia is strangely inverted. You're affectionate towards it, and yet rather critical of it. It can be comforting to live in the past, but also dangerous and even tragic, as What's the Matter with Helen? *and* The Killing Kind *show.*

HARRINGTON: That was very much in Signoret's character in *Games* also. The whole nostalgia thing was ruthlessly used by her to pull that girl in. In the trunk scene, when she pulls out mementos from the past, she is using nostalgia to create a certain impression. My nostalgia is really for periods in which I didn't live at all. I feel no nostalgia at all for the forties, when I was young.

Did you choose the title for Who Slew Auntie Roo?

HARRINGTON: No, certainly not. The film, while in production, was called *The Gingerbread House.* This was an appropriate title and it was the title I gave the script. *Who Slew Auntie Roo?* was the producers' idea of a commercial title. It is my opinion that it harmed the commercial chances of the film. There is one cut in the film that was imposed by the producer: the abrupt end of the confrontation scene between Auntie Roo and her servant. I also did not approve of the casting of the actor who played the servant. That was also imposed by the producers.

How did the project develop?

HARRINGTON: I was approached by American International to do the film. Also, Shelley Winters, who had worked with me on *What's the Matter with Helen?*, asked for me to direct her in it. It was not a project that I personally wanted particularly to do.

Did you write any of it?

HARRINGTON: I did no actual writing on the film, though I did suggest some of the plot elements — especially the idea of Auntie Roo keeping the mummified body of her dead child, having been unable psychologically to bury her. Gavin Lambert contributed quite a bit of the dialogue. The first draft of the script was laid in the present day, and it was my idea to place it in the early twenties. I have a great fondness for all the imagery and quality of the traditional Victorian Christmas celebration. I tried to put as much as I could of that in the film. It was just a rather thin little fable. I found Shelley Winters' mad behavior vastly amusing. I do feel that I achieved the pathos of the situation at the end. There are an awful lot of moments in it that are purely filmic that I did on the set.

Where did you find the sinister house in which Auntie Roo lives?

HARRINGTON: The house was a real house at Shepperton Studios that ordinarily is used there as the main administration building. The facade of the house was completely revamped for the film by art director George Provis.

Your concern with complex detail is striking, especially in Auntie Roo *and* Helen. *How much attention do you personally pay to art direction?*

HARRINGTON: I give a great deal of attention to art direction and set direction. I am personally concerned with every prop. I give my people a general idea of what I want, then if I don't see what I want, I become even more specific.

How long did it take you to shoot Auntie Roo, *and how much did it cost?*

HARRINGTON: We had a forty-day shooting schedule. I don't know the final cost, but I imagine it to be around $800,000.

You seem to work particularly well with Shelley Winters.

HARRINGTON: We seem to understand each other. She is sometimes a difficult, headstrong actress, but she is also extremely talented. She makes wonderful choices as an actress, and has an unerring sense of dramatic truth. The little displays of temperament are easy to cope with when you know you are getting something worthwhile on the screen.

Are you satisfied with Auntie Roo?

HARRINGTON: I'm not wholly satisfied with any film I've made. I feel that I did just about the best I could do with *Auntie Roo*, however, under the circumstances. When I was younger, I felt that by the brilliance of style alone, a director could transform anything. I don't believe that anymore. You've got to have something to work with. This was brought home to me especially in relation to *Who Slew Auntie Roo?* It had a very weak, incredibly lousy script. Believe me, what I finally shot is an incredible improvement over the original. Even so, it was very difficult to do enough with it to make it work. I was also saddled with a very bad cameraman that I couldn't control. I still think that whatever flaws it had, it turned out astonish-

ingly well, considering that it was a terrible uphill struggle for me all the way.

GEORGE A. ROMERO

When Continental Films dumped *Night of the Living Dead* onto the summer/fall drive-in circuit in 1968 with a typically crass exploitation campaign, who could have expected that this cheap, black-and-white horror film was anything more than what it appeared to be? Director George A.

Romero, in 1968 still an independent filmmaker working out of Pittsburgh, not Hollywood, is chiefly responsible for the film's unexpected intelligence and sophistication.

[Interview conducted by Tony Scott]

Do you have any special interest or fondness for making horror films?

ROMERO: I didn't in the beginning. When we made *Night of the Living Dead*, we made it as our first picture, and our friends in distribution circles told us to make something exploitative because it's safer. So we decided to do a horror film. Now when we did it, we said, we're not going to do just a horror film, we're going to really go out with it and try to make it gutsy. I have a theory that there are so many films that haven't been done, that *have*

been done a hundred times, but haven't been done [properly] yet. One of them for example, is *Tarzan of the Apes*. Because it hasn't been done yet.[3] I'd like to do it exactly the way Burroughs wrote it, and I think it would be a tremendous piece of a Victorian kind of escapism.

How long have you been based in Pittsburgh?

ROMERO: I came out here to go to school at Carnegie Tech to study painting and design and Spanish background. I'm influenced by the Span-

George A. Romero, surrounded by his zombies from *Day of the Dead.*

ish painters. I think that perhaps my approach to the visualization of something comes out of that rather than any influence from any director or cinematographer that I've studied.

I think that may be what gives the film that Romero touch.

ROMERO: I think that anyone who has an eye for composition or the translation of anything to a two-dimensional format is influenced by two-dimensional things that he's seen, not so much by film. No matter how many times you watch a film, you may see any given shot for a matter of, in the aggregate, two or three minutes, whereas you can look at a painting or a graphic that you have in your home, something that you really like, endlessly.

How did you develop the theme of Night of the Living Dead?

ROMERO: I wrote a short story which was in fact an allegory, a statement about society which dealt with a siege by the living dead. It was much less contrived than the film is, from the standpoint that it was purely allegorical. Now a lot of the people that have seen the film are seeing the allegory coming out of the film anyway.

I've heard it called a political film.

ROMERO: That was in my head when directing it, when we were looking for an approach to it, but I don't think it is really reflected in the film.

Did you have any trouble with the cast and crew, getting them to take the film seriously because it was a horror film?

ROMERO: Not really, no. Of course we've always had a pretty good group of people. We have a totally in-house unit. We work with each other well. We know what our intentions are and we don't have any internal strife or anything like that — so we have a pretty good time. You have fun no matter what you're doing. You can be doing *Hamlet* and I think you'll have fun doing it.

Did you have any trouble getting money or backing for the actual production of Night of the Living Dead?

ROMERO: Yes. It was our first time out and Pittsburgh is a very wealthy city, but it's the kind of

money that's in Pittsburgh; it's not gambling money, it's nuts-and-bolts industrial money. It's very difficult. When we first went around, we tried for about three years before we made *Living Dead* to get people to fund some kind of a project, thinking all along that we were going to do a serious piece. In fact, we had a script that I had written that we were trying to promote. We had an entire package put together and we couldn't get any cash here and we tried to get cash in New York. People were interested in the script, but they wanted to buy it, take it away, and make it. We said no, our idea is to make the film. When we told people here in Pittsburgh that we were going to make a feature film that was going to be released, they would say, "Uh huh, oh yeah..." and walk away. That was that. We just couldn't do it. We finally formed another corporation. There were ten of us, and the corporation was called Image Ten. We each put in a little bit of seed money, which was enough to buy our film stock, and we talked to the cast on the basis of deferred payments. The cast agreed and we started to shoot; but of course we were still doing commercial and industrial films. Therefore, *Living Dead* was shot over a period of nine months with great breaks in between to come back and do a pickle commercial or something, which was distressing. After we got some footage in the can where we could screen rushes for people, people started coming around saying, "Hey, that looks like a movie!" and we said, "Well, that's what it is!" And they said, "Oh yeah..." and finally started to put up money.

How would the film have been different if it had been made by AIP in Hollywood?

ROMERO: I think that there probably would have been a scientist in the group, explaining what was going on. I think the ending would have been different. In fact, American International turned the picture down on the basis of it being too unmitigating. They told us that if we would reshoot the ending they would distribute it; that is, have Ben survive.

Do you feel that comedy is appropriate in horror films? Hammer Films very seldom have humor. Does it make it almost camp when it's too serious?

ROMERO: I think it does. Hammer films have excellent production values, they have a tremendous feel for that Gothic aura, they have good people, good actors, but there is something about their films that is just... stiff upper lip, and every damn one is exactly the same. They're all kind of on one line, and you never get off it. There's material in *Living Dead* that gets a kind of nervous laughter. I know Hitchcock has a philosophy: he will always follow a very tense sequence with a little piece of comedy. He does it all the time. If you study his work, it works very well. In *Living Dead* we have a couple of instances like that. Right in the middle of the uptight-thing with the posse, the sheriff is saying some very funny things. I don't think it's counterproductive at all.

Does it bother you when you're in an audience with your own film, and the audience reacts differently than you expected them to?

ROMERO: No. I always find it interesting. I really think that anyone that endeavors to do anything creative is really trying to communicate, and reaching people in any way is a substantial thing. When I was acting, I did a play called *The Connection* [by Jack Gelber] and played a character named Leach. I had to come down center stage and take a needle in the arm and take an overdose and then go into fits with my arm hanging off the proscenium with the needle hanging out of the vein. We did it with nose putty. And every night it was a different reaction. It was really a tremendous thing. We got nervous laughter to that, we got some cringing, we got some people in nausea — and you know you're doing something. That's a gratifying thing. I've seen *Night of the Living Dead* with audiences three or four times. It has, pretty much, a uniform reaction.

A subsequent production is The Crazies.

ROMERO: The original title was *The Mad People*, and I liked the original title better. That film also was originally written as a pure allegory; the basic premise being that everyone in the world is operating at some level of insanity. You know, the old question, what is sane, what is insane? The device that was used in the story was the accidental spill of a biological weapon into the water supply of a little town. In the original version, the romantic leads were to get separated. Nobody knows what's going on. Suddenly the military moves in and — bang! — they're all over the place. They want to contain the virus caused by the seepage into the water supply. The whole time there's a bomber over the town because of the possibility of the virus being carried out; there's the chance that they may have to bomb the town. We were going to end it with the two lovers, after having been separated, running toward each other and just before they reach each other on the screen, the screen was going to go white and the military were going to destroy the town with the bomb. But we didn't do that.

WILLIAM FRIEDKIN

As William Friedkin sat in his eighth-floor suite at the Continental Plaza Hotel in Chicago drinking coffee and fielding questions, he conveyed the impression of a young man confident enough in his craft that pretensions and defenses were not necessary. He began his career in the mailroom at WGN-TV in Chicago. Within two years he was directing live TV, which led to documentary films and eventually an entry into feature-film directing. In his mid-thirties and clad in corduroys and open-neck shirt, Friedkin occasionally adjusted his wire-rimmed glasses as he spoke quite candidly about *The Exorcist*.

[Interview conducted by Bill Crouch]

FRIEDKIN: Strange as it may sound, I tried not to make a film about Satan. *The Exorcist* is more about the mystery of faith, the mystery of goodness. What it is to me is a realistic film about unexplainable things. I personally have no strong conviction about Satan or a personified devil. I have no strong conviction against that either, but I didn't want to make a film that pushed that. There is a very solid underpinning in the film for any other explanation that one may wish to

A young William Friedkin chats on the set of *The Exorcist* with star Ellen Burstyn.

gather, but I take it that not too many people want other explanations.

Were you surprised about the strong reaction the film evoked from many?

FRIEDKIN: On the front pages of newspapers there are pictures and stories about people being led out of the theatre on stretchers, or running out screaming, fainting, vomiting. All over the country I've gotten calls from radio stations asking me how I feel about that. I'm shocked that all that happened. I thought that people might be moved by the film. I never thought they would become hysterical or start screaming or fainting. That was never in my wildest imagination. I can't understand, I don't know what to say about that.

What do you see as the purpose of the prologue or the Iraq scene of the film?

FRIEDKIN: The Iraq scene introduces to you what kind of man Father Merrin is, the man who is called in as an exorcist. It establishes, in a kind of abstract fashion, that Merrin gets a premonition that he is going to have to perform an exorcism. It also establishes the fact that he is not a very well man. That he is a very sick man. And this sick old man, who is given to believe in omens and symbols, is going to be asked to drive a demon out of a little girl. It's a terrific device that was in

the novel. I remember Blatty telling me that at one point his publisher asked him to cut it out of the novel. He did take it out before the book went to publication, and then he missed it because he realized that it sets the tone for the whole thing. It starts the thing out on a kind of strange mysterious level. It's not apparent why you're seeing it, but later when you think about it, it all becomes clear. So I used it to foreshadow things visually that occur later. For example, in my mind, the picks that you see being pushed into the ground foreshadow the crucifix being driven into the girl's vagina. The dirt oozing out in several shots foreshadows the vomiting. And I clearly shot every sound and sequence to foreshadow something that you see or hear later. Another example of this is the blacksmith sequence. The anvil sound is in the exorcism, and the blacksmith who only has one eye, his eye resembles the little girl's eyes when they go up into their sockets.

Are there any aspects of the film which you conceived as having larger symbolic implications?

FRIEDKIN: Well, I should say that I know what things were in my head when I shot the film. I really couldn't tell you what anything means on a more symbolic level. I never got out of high school! But I do know that the prologue was intended as visual metaphor. I tell stories with pictures, and I have these visual metaphors that have meaning to me, but I don't know what they mean to you. They aren't deep, for God's sake. Alejandro Jodorowsky uses very difficult and meaningful psychological and religious symbols in his movies [*The Holy Mountain*, *El Topo*]. I have no training in religion or psychology and I'd be a fool to try to put that sort of thing in. But I do try to put in visual metaphor. In the early days of movies, they used rain when somebody was sad.

What you constantly try to do is use the elements that you can to make a unifying thread. The threads that run through a film that come together at the film's end are what generally stay in people's minds. They generally don't talk about the plot. They talk about what the elements and metaphors mean. Generally a film that moves you has a lot more going for it than what's on the surface.

Could you elaborate on how some of the special effects of The Exorcist *were accomplished?*

FRIEDKIN: I'm not going to give that away. A film works on an audience successfully because of its editing. If any of the people standing in line to see the film were to have stood in the studio watching the filming they would not have been impressed by the way in which we put the material together. I'll tell you two things: One, there are no optical effects, that is, achieved by any special printing process. They were all done live, including the vomit. The second thing I'll tell you is that the levitation was done without wires and involved the use of magnetic fields.

How did you decide on the quality of the voice for the demon?

FRIEDKIN: I have a cassette recording of an actual exorcism performed in Rome. It's in Italian. It involves the exorcism of a fourteen year old boy. I got the tape through the Jesuit Provincial of New York, and on the tape are the sounds produced by this young man supposedly possessed. The exorcism goes on for hours on this tape, and it's those sounds that I emulated for the demon. Because it was never clear to me in the novel, nor was Blatty able to verbalize how the demon *should* sound, I made the decision to use a woman's voice for the demon and not a man. But I wanted a woman's voice that would be sharp, abrasive, and slightly neutral — by that I mean neither male nor female. Certainly not a voice that anyone could say: "Oh, that's just a man's voice." To give you an idea of what a voice sounds like while under the influence of a so-called demonic possession — it generally gets deeper, gravely. If you've ever seen anyone having an epileptic fit, the voice takes on that character. Demonic possession is close to epilepsy, emphysema, the cursing disease, but it is when many supernatural events surround the victim that they know it's none of the above.

Are you completely satisfied with the way The Exorcist *turned out?*

FRIEDKIN: I would always change everything I've done if I had the opportunity. But then I never do. Once I've finished a picture and delivered it to the studio, I make it a very special point that "that's it." Especially if it seems to be working. It's like Barbra Streisand. She's out in the street working with a broken nose. Everybody told her before she started, "Go fix your nose, it'll never work." And she's out there in the street working and she's a hit. So why fix it? There are a lot of technical faults in *The Exorcist* and *The French Connection* that I'm aware of, that for laziness or whatever else, I wasn't able to correct. I now am able to correct them; they'd let me. But I won't do it if it's working for the audience. I just take this attitude and say: "I've made this picture, that's the best I could do at this stage of my ability, and to hell with it." I'll try and fix what I know is wrong with the film on the next film I make.

Can you tell me what fear is and how you try to deal with it in your films?

FRIEDKIN: Yes, I can talk about it anyway. There's a difference between rational and irrational fear. I've tried to explore both in a couple of pictures. *The Birthday Party* happens to be about irrational fear. Irrational fear is a bit more difficult to deal with because it involves paranoia. To simplify it, *The Birthday Party* is about five people in a room, and somebody says something and one person in the room thinks it is funny, the other pays no attention to it at all, somebody else is shocked by what is said, and the [remaining] person is terrified for no apparent reason because what was said has struck some chord in this person that goes so deep he can't even communicate the reason for his fear even to himself. Irrational fear, which we all go through, is deep seated and psychological. It would take years of analysis to get to. Why, for example, when you go to a party and there are 150 people enjoying themselves, do you feel absolutely terrified of social contact? Rational fear, on the other hand, is induced by something called expectancy set, which is the personal feeling that something terrifying is going to happen to you. For example, you're walking down the street at night and you're convinced, not for reasons of paranoia, that someone is following you. So every sound you hear, whether it's a car coming around the corner, or leaves on the street, or a twig breaking under your foot, or footsteps, everything contributes to your fear, and this is because you're expecting to be frightened. The cinema takes advantage of this factor. Alfred Hitchcock takes advantage of the fact that an audience comes into the theatre expecting to be scared. When they are standing in line they are afraid. So he takes them for about an hour and dangles them and lets them do it for themselves until he hits them with something — and at that point, when he hits them, he either fulfills their expectations and fantasy or he lets them down, depending on how skillful is his punch. The same is true for *The Exorcist*. People are afraid while they're standing in line. And for the first hour of the film, while there is little more than exposition and some of that very hard to follow unless you've read the book, people are working themselves into an emotional state that is conducive to becoming terrified. Those are the factors that contribute to fear. Fear is generally something that is behind you, speaking in psychological terms. It's generally something behind you that you cannot see but that you can feel, like a loud sound or someone touching you suddenly. Or it's something behind the door that's about to be opened. Most of the nightmares that you read about someone having involve someone coming up to a closed door behind which there is the unknown. Another factor, in more physical terms, would be a cold chill on the back of the neck, be it a hand or a chill when there is no cold. That's what fear is and does. Not so much the butterflies in your stomach, which come from anxiety, but that feeling on the back of your neck: a chill.

What particular directors do you admire?

FRIEDKIN: Of working directors, I particularly admire Kubrick, and of directors who are no longer active, Raoul Walsh. There are a lot of films I like, but I wouldn't necessarily say that everything that those directors have made I admire. For instance, *Citizen Kane* is the best film I've ever seen, but I don't like most of Welles' other work. I don't even relate the intelligence of *Citizen Kane* to the intelligence of *The Magnificent Ambersons*. I like *Treasure of Sierra Madre*, but not too much else of John Huston's. *All About Eve, Paths of Glory, 8½, White Heat, 2001, L'Avventura*, these are the movies I use a lot, by that I mean, look at and assimilate.

Do you consider yourself an auteur?

FRIEDKIN: No, just a filmmaker.

Appendix III

Filmographies

Compiled by Thomas G. Kohn

The following filmographies attempt to list — in chronological order — the films in the horror subgenres discussed in this book. Note that these filmographies are not comprehensive, which is neither possible nor desirable in a genre which produces so many thousands of films, many of which are of low quality and interest.

The dates provided are usually the year of first release in the United States, as documented in the *New York Times* for films released before 1968, and as documented in online sources such as the Internet Movie Database (IMDb.com) or in regularly updated books such as *Leonard Maltin's Movie & Video Guide* for films released after 1968. Where a significant discrepancy exists between the date of a film's completion and the date of its first U.S. release, both years may be provided. Of course the actual release year in other countries can vary. The dates of any single, pre-release screenings in film festivals have generally been ignored.

These filmographies include the collaborative details of director, screenwriter, producer, musical score, cinematographer, film editor, art director, production designer, set decorator, costume designer, makeup designer, visual effects designer, special effects designer, choreographer, sound designer, primary cast, and significant awards won. In films since about 1970, listed credits for technical artists expanded — especially in special effects, visual effects, and sound — often obscuring the most central contributors. In these cases, the citation here may excise a specific credit in its entirety. Likewise, the listing of cast members is usually limited to eight or fewer names, with some exceptions made for large casts with actors of renown in minor roles. Whenever possible, credits have been obtained from the films themselves. Note also that awards listed include wins only from the most major film organizations and exclude nominations.

The filmographies are organized into the following eight categories:

- Horror of Personality
- Horror of Armageddon
- Japanese Horror of Armageddon
- Horror of the Demonic
- Asian Millennial Horror
- David Cronenberg's Horror
- Postmodern Horror Remakes
- Horror Franchise Sequels

The filmographies for the Horror of Personality, the Horror of Armageddon, and the Horror of the Demonic are loosely defined and include films — listed chronologically — that influenced or were influenced by the particular subgenre.

The filmography for the Japanese Armageddon Horror, particularly, makes no pretense at being exhaustive. These Japanese "monster" movies, almost all for Toho Studios, were often released internationally using a dazzling array of multiple titles and in versions which were dubbed, recut, and often augmented by additional footage with non–Japanese stars — which makes it almost impossible to provide exact information in a compact format. Dates are sometimes the original Japanese release, other times the re-cut American release.

The filmography for Asian Millennial Horror provides a representative sampling only.

The filmography for Horror Franchise Sequels is comprised of those films in a series of at least three which were essentially farmed out to directors other than their original creators, which is why George A. Romero's very personal *Night of* *the Living Dead* series is one of the few "franchises" that will not be found in this category.

Only director David Cronenberg gets a filmography of his own — because although many of his films fit into the horror subgenres described by *Dark Dreams 2.0*, Cronenberg's films ultimately seem to have more in common with each other.

LEGEND

Art: art direction
C: cinematographer
CDn: costume design
Ch: choreography
D: director
Ed: film editor
H: hair design
M: music
Mk: makeup design

P: producer
PDn: production design
S: sound design
Sc: screenwriter, teleplay writer
SDn: set design
SDc: set decorator
SFx: special effects design
T: title design
VFx: visual effects design

HORROR OF PERSONALITY

Meshes of the Afternoon (1943). **D:** Maya Deren, Alexander Hammid. **Sc, Ed:** Maya Deren. **M:** Teiji Ito. **C:** Alexander Hammid. **Cast:** Maya Deren, Alexander Hammid.

Fragment of Seeking (1946). **D:** Curtis Harrington. **C:** Gregory J. Markopoulos. **Cast:** Curtis Harrington.

Diabolique [*Les Diaboliques*] (1955). **D, P:** Henri-Georges Clouzot. **Sc:** Jérôme Geronimi, Henri-Georges Clouzot. Based on novel by Boileau-Narcejac. **M:** Georges Van Parys. **C:** Armand Thirard. **Ed:** Madeleine Gug. **Art:** Léon Barsacq. **S:** William-Robert Sivel. **Cast:** Simone Signoret, Véra Clouzot, Paul Meurisse, Charles Vanel, Jean Brochard, Pierre Larquey, Michel Serrault, Thérèse Dorny. **New York Film Critics** Best Foreign Film. **Edgar Award** Best Foreign Film.

I Bury the Living (1958). **D:** Albert Band. **Sc:** Louis Garfinkle. **P:** Albert Band, Louis Garfinkle. **M:** Gerald Fried. **C:** Frederick Gately. **Ed:** Frank Sullivan. **PDn:** Edward Vorkapich. **SDc:** Gene Redd. **CDn:** Bob Richards. **Mk:** Jack P. Pierce. **VFx:** Slavko Vorkapich. **Cast:** Richard Boone, Theodore Bikel, Peggy Maurer, Robert Osterloh, Herbert Anderson, Howard Smith, Russ Bender, Glen Vernon.

Macabre (1958). **D, P:** William Castle. **Sc:** Robb White. Based on novel by Theo Durrant. **M:** Les Baxter. **C:** Carl E. Guthrie. **Ed:** John F. Schreyer. **Art:** Jack T. Collis, Robert Kinoshita. **Cast:** William Prince, Jim Backus, Ellen Corby, Christine White, Jacqueline Scott, Susan Morrow, Philip Tonge, Jonathan Kidd.

Screaming Mimi (1958). **D:** Gerd Oswald. **Sc:** Robert Blees. Based on novel by Frederic Brown. **P:** Harry Joe Brown, Robert Fellows. **M:** Mischa Bakaleinikoff. **C:** Burnett Guffey. **Ed:** Gene Havlick, Jerome Thoms. **Art:** Cary Odell. **SDn:** Frank A. Tuttle. **Ch:** Lee Scott. **Cast:** Anita Ekberg, Philip Carey, Gypsy Rose Lee, Harry Townes, Linda Cherney, Romney Brent, Alan Gifford, Oliver McGowan.

The Screaming Skull (1958). **D:** Alex Nicol. **Sc, P:** John Kneubuhl. **M:** Ernest Gold. **C:** Floyd Crosley. **Ed:** Betty Jane Lane. **Mk:** Don Roberson. **S:** Al Overton. **Cast:** John Hudson, Peggy Webber, Russ Conway, Tony Johnson, Alex Nicol.

Terror in the Haunted House [*My World Dies Screaming*] (1958). **D:** Harold Daniels. **Sc:** Robert C. Dennis. **P:** William S. Edwards. **M:** Darrell Calker. **C:** Frederick E. West. **Ed:** Tholen Gladden. **Art:** A. Leslie Thomas. **SDc:** Tom Oliphant. **CDn:** Harry Thomas. **Mk:** Harry Thomas. **Cast:** Gerald Mohr, Cathy O'Donnell, William Ching, John Qualen, Barry Bernard.

The Bat (1959). **D:** Crane Wilbur. **Sc:** Crane Wilbur. Based on play by Mary Roberts Rinehart and Avery Hopwood. **P:** C. J. Tevlin. **M:** Louis Forbes. **C:** Joseph Biroc. **Ed:** William Austin. **Art:** David Milton. **SDc:** Rudy Butler. **Mk:** Kiva Hoffman. **Cast:** Vincent Price, Agnes Moorehead, Gavin Gordon, John Sutton, Lenita Lane, Elaine Edwards, Darla Hood, John Bryant.

Horrors of the Black Museum (1959). **D:** Arthur Crabtree. **Sc:** Aben Kandel and Arthur Crabtree. **P:** Herman Cohen. **M:** Gérard Schurmann. **C:** Desmond Dickinson. **Ed:** Geoffrey Muller. **Art:** C. Wilfred Arnold. **Mk:** Jack Craig. **Cast:** Michael Gough, June Cunningham, Graham Curnow, Shirley Anne Field, Geoffrey Keen, Gerald Anderson, John Warwick, Beatrice Varley.

House on Haunted Hill (1959). **D, P:** William Castle. **Sc:** Robb White. **M:** Von Dexter, Richard Loring. **C:** Carl E. Guthrie. **Ed:** Roy Livingston. **Art:** David Milton. **SDc:** Morris Hoffman. **Mk:** Jack Dusick.

H: Jack Dusick. SFx: Herman Townsley. Cast: Vincent Price, Carolyn Craig, Richard Long, Elisha Cook, Carol Ohmart, Alan Marshal, Julie Mitchum.

Mania [***The Flesh and the Fiends***] (1959). D: John Gilling. Sc: John Gilling. Story by Leo Griffiths. P: Robert S. Baker, Monty Berman. M: Stanley Black. C: Monty Berman. Ed: Jack Slade. Art: John Elphick. Mk: Jimmy Evans. Cast: Peter Cushing, June Laverick, Donald Pleasence, George Rose, Renee Houston. Dermot Walsh, Billie Whitelaw.

The Tingler (1959). D, P: William Castle. Sc: Robb White. M: Von Dexter. C: Wilfred M. Cline. Ed: Chester W. Schaeffer. Art: Phil Bennett. SDc: Milton Stumph. Cast: Vincent Price, Judith Evelyn, Darryl Hickman, Patricia Cutts, Pamela Lincoln, Philip Coolidge.

Circus of Horrors (1960). D: Sidney Hayers. Sc: George Baxt. P: Leslie Parkyn, Julian Wintle. M: Muir Mathieson, Franz Reizenstein. C: Douglas Slocombe. Ed: Reginald Mills. Art: Jack Shampan. Mk: Trevor Crole-Rees. Cast: Anton Diffring, Erika Remberg, Yvonne Monlaur, Donald Pleasence, Jane Hylton, Kenneth Griffith, Conrad Phillips, Jack Gwillim.

The Hypnotic Eye (1960). D: George Blair. Sc: Gitta Woodfield, William Read Woodfield. P: Charles B. Bloch. M: Marlin Skiles. C: Archie R. Dalzell. Ed: William Austin. SFx: Milton Olsen. Cast: Jacques Bergerac, Allison Hayes, Marcia Henderson, Merry Anders, Joe Patridge, Guy Prescott, Fred Demara, Jimmy Lydon.

Peeping Tom (1960). D, P: Michael Powell. Sc: Leo Marks. M: Brian Easdale. C: Otto Heller. Ed: Noreen Ackland. Art: Arthur Lawson. Mk: W. T. Partleton. Cast: Carl Boehm, Moira Shearer, Anna Massey, Maxine Audley, Brenda Bruce, Nigel Davenport, Shirley Anne Field, Michael Powell.

Psycho (1960). D, P: Alfred Hitchcock. Sc: Joseph Stefano. Based on novel by Robert Bloch. M: Bernard Herrmann. C: John L. Russell. Ed: George Tomasini. Art: Joseph Hurley & Robert Clatworthy. SDc: George Milo. CDn: Rita Riggs. S: Waldon O. Watson & William Russell. SFx: Clarence Champagne. T: Saul Bass. Cast: Anthony Perkins, Janet Leigh, Vera Miles, John Gavin, Martin Balsam, John McIntire, Simon Oakland, Patricia Hitchcock, Frank Albertson, Lurene Tuttle. **Golden Globes** Best Supporting Actress (Leigh). **Edgar Award** Best Motion Picture.

13 Ghosts (1960). D, P: William Castle. Sc: Robb White. M: Von Dexter. C: Joseph Biroc. Ed: Edwin Bryant. Art: Cary Odell. SDc: Louis Diage. Mk: Ben Lane. Cast: Charles Herbert, Jo Morrow, Rosemary DeCamp, Martin Milner, Donald Woods, Margaret Hamilton, John Van Dreelen.

Anatomy of a Psycho (1961). D, P: Brooke L. Peters. Sc: Jane Mann, "Larry Lee." Cast: Ronnie Burns, Pamela Lincoln, Darrell Howe, Russ Bender, Don Devlin, Robert Stabler.

Homicidal (1961). D, P: William Castle. Sc: Robb White. M: Hugo Friedhofer. C: Burnett Guffey. Ed: Edwin H. Bryant. Art: Cary Odell. SDc: Darrell Silvera. Mk: Ben Lane. Cast: Glenn Corbett, Patricia Breslin, Eugenie Leontovich, Alan Bunce, Richard Rust, James Westerfield, Gilbert Green, Joan Marshall.

Mr. Sardonicus (1961). D, P: William Castle. Sc: Ray Russell. M: Von Dexter. C: Burnett Guffey. Ed: Edwin Bryant. Art: Cary Odell. SDc: James M. Crowe. Mk: Ben Lane. Cast: Oskar Homolka, Ronald Lewis, Audrey Dalton, Guy Rolfe, Vladimir Sokoloff, Erika Peters, Lorna Hanson.

Scream of Fear (1961). D: Seth Holt. Sc, P: Jimmy Sangster. M: Clifton Parker. C: Douglas Slocombe. Ed: Eric Boyd-Perkins, James Needs. PDn: Bernard Robinson. Art: Thomas Goswell. Mk: Basil Newall. Cast: Susan Strasberg, Ronald Lewis, Ann Todd, Christopher Lee, John Serret, Leonard Sachs, Anne Blake, Bernard Browne.

The Cabinet of Caligari (1962). D, P: Roger Kay. Sc: Robert Bloch. M: Gerald Fried. C: John L. Russell. Ed: Archie Marshek. SDn: Howard Bristol. PDn: Serge Krizman. Cast: Glynis Johns, Dan O'Herlihy, Richard Davalos, Lawrence Dobkin, Constance Ford, J. Pat O'Malley, Vicki Trickett, Estelle Winwood.

Trauma (1962). D, Sc: Robert M. Young. P: Joseph Cranston. M: Buddy Collette. C: Jacques R. Marquette. Ed: Harold J. Dennis. Cast: John Conte, Lynn Bari, Lorri Richards, David Garner, Warren J. Kemmerling, William Bissell.

What Ever Happened to Baby Jane? (1962). D, P: Robert Aldrich. Sc: Lukas Heller. Based on novel by Henry Farrell. M: Frank De Vol. C: Ernest Haller. Ed: Michael Luciano. CDn: Norma Koch. Art: William Glasgow. SDc: George Sawley. Mk: Beau Wilson. SFx: Donald Steward. Cast: Bette Davis, Joan Crawford, Victor Buono, Wesley Addy, Julie Allred, Anne Barton, Marjorie Bennett, Bert Freed, Anna Lee, Russ Conway, B. D. Merrill. **Academy Awards** Best Black-and-White Costume Design.

Dementia 13 (1963). D, Sc: Francis Ford Coppola. P: Roger Corman. M: Ronald Stein. C: Charles Hanawalt. Ed: Stuart O'Brien, Mort Tubor. Art: Albert Locatelli. SDc: Eleanor Neil (Coppola). S: Joseph Gross, Liam Saurin. Cast: William Campbell, Luana Anders, Bart Patton, Mary Mitchell, Patrick Magee.

Maniac (1963). D: Michael Carreras. Sc, P: Jimmy Sangster. M: Stanley Black. C: Wilkie Cooper. Ed: Tom Simpson. PDn: Bernard Robinson. Art: Edward Carrick. Mk: Basil Newall, Stella Morris. H: Patricia McDermott. Cast: Kerwin Mathews, Nadia Gray.

The Sadist (1963). D, Sc: James Landis. P: L. Steven Snyder. C: Vilmos Zsigmondv Art: Mark Von Berblineer. Mk: Linda Noonkester. Cast: Arch Hall Jr., Richard Alden, Marilyn Manning, Don Russell, Helen Hovey.

Dead Ringer (1964). D: Paul Henreid. Sc: Albert Beich, Oscar Millard. P: William H. Wright. M: André Previn. C: Ernest Haller. Ed: Folmar Blangsted. Art: Perry Ferguson. SDc: William Stevens. CDn: Don Feld. Mk: Gordon Bau. S: Robert B. Lee. Cast: Bette Davis, Karl Malden, Peter Lawford, Philip Carey, Jean Hagen, George Macready, Estelle Winwood, George Chandler.

Hush...Hush, Sweet Charlotte (1964). D, P: Robert Aldrich. Sc: Henry Farrell, Lukas Heller. Based on novel by Henry Farrell. M: Frank De Vol. C: Joseph F. Biroc. Ed: Michael Luciano. Art: William Glasgow. SDc: Raphael Bretton. CDn: Norma Koch. Cast: Bette

Davis, Olivia de Havilland, Joseph Cotten, Agnes Moorehead, Cecil Kellaway, Victor Buono, Mary Astor, Wesley Addy, William Campbell, Bruce Dern, Frank Ferguson, George Kennedy. **Edgar Award** Best Motion Picture.

Lady in a Cage (1964). **D:** Walter Grauman. **Sc, P:** Luther Davis. **M:** Paul Glass. **C:** Lee Garmes. **Ed:** Leon Barsha. **PDn:** Rudolph Sternad. **Art:** Hal Pereira. **SDc:** Sam Comer. **Mk:** Wally Westmore. **S:** Howard Beals. **Cast:** Olivia de Havilland, James Caan, Jennifer Billingsley, Jeff Corey, Ann Sothern, Rafael Campos, William Swan, Scatman Crothers.

Marnie (1964). **D, P:** Alfred Hitchcock. **Sc:** Jay Presson Allen. Based on novel by Winston Graham. **M:** Bernard Herrmann. **C:** Robert Burks. **Ed:** George Tomasini. **PDn:** Robert Boyle. **SDc:** George Milo. **CDn:** Edith Head, James Linn, Rita Riggs. **Cast:** Tippi Hedren, Sean Connery, Diane Baker, Martin Gabel, Louise Latham, Mariette Hartley, Bruce Dern.

Nightmare (1964). **D:** Freddie Francis. **Sc, P:** Jimmy Sangster. **M:** Don Banks. **C:** John Wilcox. **PDn:** Bernard Robinson. **Art:** Don Mingaye. **Mk:** Roy Ashton. **Cast:** David Knight, Moira Redmond, Jennie Linden, Brenda Bruce, George A. Cooper, Clytie Jessop.

Pyro (1964). **D:** Julio Coll. **Sc:** Luis de los Arcos, Sidney W. Pink. **P:** Richard C. Meyer, Sidney W. Pink. **M:** José Solá. **C:** Manuel Berenguer. **Ed:** Margarita de Ochoa. **Mk:** Carmen Martín. **SFx:** Antonio Molina. **Cast:** Barry Sullivan, Martha Hyer, Sherry Moreland, Soledad Miranda, Luis Prendes, Fernando Hilbeck, Carlos Casaravilla, Marisenka.

Shock Treatment (1964). **D:** Denis Sanders. **Sc:** Sydney Boehm. Based on novel by Winfred Van Atta. **P:** Aaron Rosenberg. **M:** Jerry Goldsmith. **C:** Sam Leavitt. **Ed:** Louis R. Loeffler. **Art:** Jack Martin Smith, Hilyard M. Brown. **SDc:** Walter M. Scott, Paul S. Fox. **CDn:** Moss Mabry. **Mk:** Ben Nye. **SFx:** L. B. Abbott, Emil Kosa Jr. **Cast:** Stuart Whitman, Carol Lynley, Roddy McDowall, Lauren Bacall, Olive Deering, Ossie Davis.

Strait-Jacket (1964). **D, P:** William Castle. **Sc:** Robert Bloch. **M:** Van Alexander. **C:** Arthur Arling. **Ed:** Edwin Bryant. **PDn:** Boris Leven. **SDc:** Frank Tuttle. **Mk:** Ben Lane, Monty Westmore. **SFx:** Richard Albain. **Cast:** Joan Crawford, Diane Baker, Leif Erickson, Howard St. John, John Anthony Hayes, Rochelle Hudson, George Kennedy, Edith Atwater.

The Strangler (1964). **D:** Burt Topper. **Sc:** Bill S. Ballinger. **P:** Samuel Bischoff and David Diamond. **M:** Marlin Skiles. **C:** Jacques R. Marquette. **Ed:** Robert S. Eisen. **Art:** Eugène Lourié, Hal Pereira. **SDc:** Sam Comer, James W. Payne. **Mk:** Wally Westmore. **Cast:** Victor Buono, David McLean, Diane Sayer, Davey Davison, Baynes Barron, Ellen Corby, Michael Ryan, Russ Bender.

Bunny Lake Is Missing (1965). **D, P:** Otto Preminger. **Sc:** John Mortimer & Penelope Mortimer. Based on novel by Evelyn Piper. **M:** Paul Glass. **C:** Denys Coop. **Ed:** Peter Thornton. **PDn:** Don Ashton. **SDc:** Scott Slimon, Elven Webb. **CDn:** Hope Bryce. **Mk:** Neville Smallwood. **S:** Jonathan Bates. **SFx:** Charles Staffell. **T:** Saul Bass. **Cast:** Laurence Olivier,

Carol Lynley, Keir Dullea, Martita Hunt, Anna Massey, Clive Revill, Lucie Mannheim, Finlay Currie.

The Collector (1965). **D:** William Wyler. **Sc:** Stanley Mann, John Kohn. Based on novel by John Fowles. **P:** Jud Kinberg, John Kohn. **M:** Maurice Jarre. **C:** Robert Krasker, Robert Surtees. **Ed:** David Hawkins, Robert Swink. **Art:** John Stoll. **SDc:** Frank Tuttle. **Cast:** Terence Stamp, Samantha Eggar, Mona Washbourne, Maurice Dallimore. **Cannes** Best Actor (Stamp), Best Actress (Eggar). **Golden Globes** Best Actress in Drama (Eggar).

Die! Die! My Darling! [*Fanatic*] (1965). **D:** Silvio Narizzano. **Sc:** Richard Matheson. Based on novel by Anne Blaisdell. **P:** Anthony Hinds. **M:** Wilfred Josephs. **C:** Arthur Ibbetson. **Ed:** John Dunsford. **PDn:** Peter Proud. **Cast:** Tallulah Bankhead, Stefanie Powers, Peter Vaughan, Maurice Kaufmann, Yootha Joyce, Donald Sutherland, Gwendolyn Watts, Robert Dorning.

I Saw What You Did and I Know Who You Are (1965). **D, P:** William Castle. **Sc:** William P. McGivern. Based on novel by Ursula Curtiss. **M:** Van Alexander. **C:** Joseph F. Biroc. **Ed:** Edwin H. Bryant. **PDn:** Alexander Golitzen, Walter M. Simonds. **SDc:** John McCarthy Jr., George Milo. **Mk:** Bud Westmore. **Cast:** Joan Crawford, John Ireland, Leif Erickson, Sarah Lane, Andi Garrett, Sharyl Locke, Patricia Breslin, John Archer, John Crawford, Joyce Meadows.

The Nanny (1965). **D:** Seth Holt. **Sc:** Jimmy Sangster. Based on novel by Evelyn Piper. **P:** Jimmy Sangster. **M:** Richard Rodney Bennett. **C:** Harry Waxman. **Ed:** Tom Simpson. **PDn:** Edward Carrick. **Mk:** Tom Smith. **Cast:** Bette Davis, Wendy Craig, Jill Bennett, James Villiers, William Dix, Pamela Franklin, Jack Watling, Maurice Denham, Angharad Aubrey.

Repulsion (1965). **D:** Roman Polanski. **Sc:** Roman Polanski & Gérard Brach. **P:** Gene Gutowski. **M:** Chico Hamilton. **C:** Gilbert Taylor. **Ed:** Alastair McIntyre. **Art:** Seamus Flannery. **Mk:** Tom Smith. **Cast:** Catherine Deneuve, Ian Hendry, John Fraser, Yvonne Furneaux, Patrick Wymark, Renee Houston, Valerie Taylor, James Villiers.

Who Killed Teddy Bear? (1965). **D:** Joseph Cates. **Sc:** Arnold Drake, story by Arnold Drake and Leon Tokatyan. **P:** Everett Rosenthal. **M:** Charles Calello. **C:** Joseph Brun. **Ed:** Angelo Ross. **Art:** Hank Aldrich. **CDn:** George Sullivan. **Mk:** Enrico Cortese. **T:** Elinor Bunin. **Cast:** Sal Mineo, Juliet Prowse, Jan Murray, Elaine Stritch, Margot Bennett, Dan Travanty (Daniel J. Travanti), Diane Moore, Frank Campanella.

Picture Mommy Dead (1966). **D:** Bert I. Gordon. **Sc:** Robert Sherman. **P:** Robert Aldrich, Bert I. Gordon. **M:** Robert Jackson Drasnin. **C:** Ellsworth Fredericks. **Ed:** John A. Bushelman. **SDc:** Robert R. Benton, Ray Moyer. **CDn:** Leah Rhodes. **SFx:** Charles Spurgeon. **Cast:** Don Ameche, Martha Hyer, Zsa Zsa Gabor, Susan Gordon, Maxwell Reed, Wendell Corey, Signe Hasso, Anna Lee.

Psycho-Circus [*Circus of Fear*] (1966). **D:** John Moxey. **Sc:** Peter Welbeck. Based on novel by Edgar Wallace. **P:** Harry Alan Towers. **M:** Johnny Douglas. **C:** Ernest Steward. **Ed:** John Trumper. **Art:** Frank White. **Mk:** Frank Turner. **Cast:** Christopher Lee, Leo Genn,

Anthony Newlands, Heinz Drache, Eddi Arent, Klaus Kinski, Margaret Lee, Suzy Kendall.

The Psychopath (1966). **D:** Freddie Francis. **Sc:** Robert Bloch. **P:** Max Rosenberg, Milton Subotsky. **M:** Elisabeth Lutyens, Philip Martell. **C:** John Wilcox. **Ed:** Oswald Hafenrichter. **Art:** Bill Constable. **SDc:** John Sumon. **Mk:** Jill Carpenter. **SFx:** Ted Samuels. **Cast:** Patrick Wymark, Margaret Johnston, John Standing, Alexander Knox, Judy Huxtable, Don Borisenko.

Games (1967). **D:** Curtis Harrington. **Sc:** Gene R. Kearney. Story by George Edwards, Curtis Harrington. **P:** George Edwards. **M:** Samuel Matlovsky. **C:** William A. Fraker. **Ed:** Douglas Stewart. **Art:** William D. DeCinces, Alexander Golitzen. **SDc:** John McCarthy Jr., James Redd. **CDn:** Morton Haack. **Mk:** Bud Westmore. **S:** Robert R. Bertrand, Waldon O. Watson. **VFx:** Morton Haack. **Cast:** Simone Signoret, James Caan, Katharine Ross, Don Stroud, Kent Smith, Estelle Winwood, Marjorie Bennett, Ian Wolfe.

In Cold Blood (1967). **D, P:** Richard Brooks. **Sc:** Richard Brooks. Based on book by Truman Capote. **M:** Quincy Jones. **C:** Conrad Hall. **Ed:** Peter Zinner. **Art:** Robert F. Boyle. **SDc:** Jack H. Ahern. **Mk:** Gary Morris. **SFx:** Chuck Gaspar. **Cast:** Robert Blake, Scott Wilson, John Forsythe, Paul Stewart, Gerald S. O'Loughlin, Jeff Corey, John Gallaudet, James Flavin, John Collins, Charles McGraw, Will Geer. **National Board of Review** Best Director.

The Incident (1967). **D:** Larry Peerce. **Sc:** Nicholas E. Baehr. **P:** Edward Meadow, Monroe Sachson. **M:** Terry Knight. **C:** Gerald Hirschfeld. **Ed:** Armond Lebowitz. **PDn:** Manny Gerard. **Art:** Emanuel Gerard. **SDc:** Robert Drumheller. **CDn:** Muriel Gettinger. **Mk:** Herman Buchman. **Cast:** Beau Bridges, Ruby Dee, Jack Gilford, Ed McMahon, Gary Merrill, Donna Mills, Tony Musante, Brock Peters, Thelma Ritter, Martin Sheen, Jan Sterling.

Berserk [*Berserk!*] (1968). **D:** Jim O'Connolly. **Sc:** Herman Cohen, Aben Kandel. **P:** Herman Cohen. **M:** Patrick John Scott. **C:** Desmond Dickinson. **Ed:** Raymond Poulton. **Art:** Maurice Pelling. **CDn:** Jay Hutchinson Scott. **Mk:** George Partleton. **Cast:** Joan Crawford, Ty Hardin, Diana Dors, Michael Gough, Judy Geeson, Robert Hardy, Geoffrey Keen, Sydney Tafler.

The Boston Strangler (1968). **D:** Richard Fleischer. **Sc:** Edward Anhalt. Based on book by Gerold Frank. **P:** Robert Fryer. **M:** Lionel Newman. **C:** Richard H. Kline. **Ed:** Marion Rothman. **S:** Don Bassman, David Dockendorf. **Art:** Jack Martin Smith, Richard Day. **SDc:** Walter M. Scott, Stuart A. Reiss. **Mk:** Dan Striepeke. **Cast:** Tony Curtis, Henry Fonda, George Kennedy, Mike Kellin, Hurd Hatfield, Murray Hamilton, Jeff Corey, Sally Kellerman.

Pretty Poison (1968). **D:** Noel Black. **Sc:** Lorenzo Semple Jr. Based on novel by Stephen Geller. **P:** Marshal Backlar, Joel Black. **M:** Johnny Mandel. **C:** David Quaid. **Ed:** William Ziegler. **Art:** Harold Michelson, Jack Martin Smith. **CDn:** Ann Roth. **S:** David Dockendorf, Dennis Maitland. **SFx:** Billy King, Ralph Winigar. **Cast:** Anthony Perkins, Tuesday Weld, Beverly Garland, John Randolph, Dick O'Neill, Clarice Blackburn, Joseph Bova, Ken Kercheval. **New York Film Critics** Best Screenplay.

Targets (1968). **D, P:** Peter Bogdanovich. **Sc:** Peter Bogdanovich. Story by Polly Platt and Peter Bogdanovich. **M:** Ronald Stein. **C:** Laszlo Kovacs. **PDn:** Polly Platt. **Mk:** Scott Hamilton. **S:** Sam Kopetzky. **Cast:** Tim O'Kelly, Boris Karloff, Arthur Peterson, Monty Landis, Nancy Hsueh, Peter Bogdanovich, Daniel Ades, Stafford Morgan.

Twisted Nerve (1968, 1969 USA). **D:** Roy Boulting. **Sc:** Roy Boulting, Leo Marks. Story by Roger Marshall. **P:** John Boulting and George W. George. **M:** Bernard Herrmann. **C:** Harry Waxman. **Ed:** Martin Charles. **Art:** Albert Witherick. **CDn:** Hazel Graeme and Bridget Sellers. **Cast:** Hayley Mills, Hywel Bennett, Billie Whitelaw, Phyllis Calvert, Frank Finlay, Barry Foster. **BAFTA** Best Supporting Actress (Whitelaw).

Daddy's Gone A-Hunting (1969). **D, P:** Mark Robson. **Sc:** Larry Cohen & Lorenzo Semple Jr. Story by Larry Cohen. **M:** John Williams. **C:** Ernest Laszlo. **Ed:** Dorothy Spencer. **Art:** Stan Johnson, James Sullivan. **SDc:** Charles Thompson. **CDn:** Travilla. **S:** Clarence Peterson. **Cast:** Carol White, Paul Burke, Mala Powers, Scott Hylands, James Sikking, Walter Brooke.

The Mad Room (1969). **D:** Bernard Girard. **Sc:** Bernard Girard & A. Z. Martin. **P:** Norman Maurer. **M:** Dave Grusin. **C:** Harry Stradling Jr. **Ed:** Pat Somerset. **Art:** Sydney Z. Litwack. **SDc:** Sidney Clifford. **CDn:** Moss Mabry. **Cast:** Stella Stevens, Shelley Winters, Skip Ward, Carol Cole, Severn Darden, Beverly Garland, Michael Burns, Barbara Sammeth.

Orgasmo [*Paranoia*] (1969). **D:** Umberto Lenzi. **Sc:** Umberto Lenzi, Ugo Moretti, Marie Claire Solleville. **P:** Salvatore Alabiso. **M:** Piero Umiliani. **C:** Guglielmo Mancori. **Ed:** Enzo Alabiso. **Art:** Giorgio Bertolini. **Cast:** Carroll Baker, Lou Castel, Colette Descombes, Tino Carraro, Lilla Brignone, Franco Pesce, Tina Lattanzi, Jacques Stany.

What Ever Happened to Aunt Alice? (1969). Made for TV. **D:** Lee H. Katzin. **Sc:** Theodore Apstein. Based on novel by Ursula Curtiss. **P:** Robert Aldrich. **M:** Gerald Fried. **C:** Joseph F. Biroc. **Ed:** Frank J. Urioste. **Art:** William Glasgow. **SDc:** John Brown. **CDn:** Renié. **Mk:** William Turner. **Cast:** Geraldine Page, Ruth Gordon, Rosemary Forsyth, Robert Fuller, Mildred Dunnock, Joan Huntington, Peter Brandon, Michael Barbera.

How Awful About Allan (1970). Made for TV. **D:** Curtis Harrington. **Sc:** Henry Farrell. **P:** George Edwards. **M:** Laurence Rosenthal. **C:** Fleet Southcott. **Ed:** Richard Farrell. **Art:** Tracy Bousman. **SDc:** Ken Swartz. **CDn:** Robert Harris Sr., Jerrie Woods. **Mk:** Ted Coodley. **SFx:** Joe Lombardi. **VFx:** John Franco Jr. **Cast:** Anthony Perkins, Julie Harris, Joan Hackett, Kent Smith, Robert H. Harris, Molly Dodd, Billy Bowles, Trent Dolan.

The Honeymoon Killers (1970). **D, Sc:** Leonard Kastle. **P:** Warren Steibel. **C:** Oliver Wood. **Ed:** Richard Brophy, Stan Warnow. **S:** Fred Kamiel. **Cast:** Shirley Stoler, Tony Lo Bianco, Mary Jane Higby, Doris Roberts, Marilyn Chris, Barbara Cason.

Play Misty for Me (1971). **D:** Clint Eastwood. **Sc:** Jo Heims, Dean Riesner. **P:** Robert Daley, Jennings Lang. **M:** Dee Barton. **C:** Bruce Surtees. **Ed:** Carl Pingitore. **Art:** Alexander Golitzen. **SDc:** Ralph Hurst.

CDn: Helen Colvig, Brad Whitney. Cast: Clint Eastwood, Jessica Walter, Donna Mills, John Larch, Jack Ging, Irene Hervey, James McEachin, Clarice Taylor.

See No Evil [*Blind Terror*] (1971). D: Richard Fleischer. Sc: Brian Clemens. P: Leslie Linder, Martin Ransohoff. M: Elmer Bernstein. C: Gerry Fisher. Ed: Thelma Connell. Art: John Hoesli. SDc: Hugh Scaife. CDn: Evelyn Gibbs. Cast: Mia Farrow, Dorothy Alison, Robin Bailey, Diane Grayson, Paul Nicholas, Reg Harding, Lila Kaye, Donald Bisset.

10 Rillington Place (1971). D: Richard Fleischer. Sc: Clive Exton. Based on novel by Ludovic Kennedy. P: Leslie Linder, Martin Ransohoff. M: John Dankworth. C: Denys Coop. Ed: Ernest Walter. Art: Maurice Carter. SDc: Andrew Campbell. Mk: Stuart Freeborn. Cast: Richard Attenborough, Judy Geeson, John Hurt, Pat Heywood, Isobel Black, Phyllis MacMahon, Ray Barron.

What's the Matter with Helen? (1971). D: Curtis Harrington. Sc: Henry Farrell. P: George Edwards. M: David Raksin. C: Lucien Ballard. Ed: William H. Reynolds. Art: Eugène Lourié. SDc: Jerry Wunderlich. CDn: Morton Haack. Cast: Debbie Reynolds, Shelley Winters, Dennis Weaver, Agnes Moorehead, Micheal MacLiammóir.

Who Slew Auntie Roo? [*Whoever Slew Auntie Roo?*] (1971). D: Curtis Harrington. Sc: Robert Blees, Gavin Lambert. Story by Jimmy Sangster. P: Samuel Z. Arkoff, James H. Nicholson, Jimmy Sangster. M: Kenneth V. Jones. C: Desmond Dickinson. Ed: Tristam Cones. Art: George Provis. Cast: Shelley Winters, Mark Lester, Chloe Franks, Ralph Richardson, Lionel Jeffries, Hugh Griffith, Rosalie Crutchley, Pat Heywood.

Frenzy (1972). D, P: Alfred Hitchcock. Sc: Anthony Shaffer. Based on novel by Arthur La Bern. M: Ron Goodwin. C: Gil Taylor. Ed: John Jympson. PDn: Syd Cain. Art: Bob Laing. Mk: Harry Frampton. SFx: Albert Whitlock. Cast: Jon Finch, Alec McCowen, Barry Foster, Billie Whitelaw, Anna Massey, Barbara Leigh-Hunt, Bernard Cribbins, Vivien Merchant, Jean Marsh.

Images (1972). D, Sc: Robert Altman. P: Tommy Thompson. M: John Williams. C: Vilmos Zsigmond. Ed: Graeme Clifford. PDn: Leon Ericksen. Mk: Toni Delaney. SFx: Jerry Johnson. Cast: Susannah York, René Auberjonois, Marcel Bozzuffi, Hugh Millais, Cathryn Harrison, John Morley. Cannes Best Actress (York).

The Killing Kind (1973). D: Curtis Harrington. Sc: Tony Crechales, George Edwards. P: George Edwards. M: Andrew Belling. C: Mario Tosi. Ed: Bryon Crouch. SDc: John Franco Jr. CDn: Tom Rasmussen. Mk: Joe McKinney. Cast: Ann Sothern, John Savage, Ruth Roman, Luana Anders, Cindy Williams, Sue Bernard, Marjorie Eaton, Peter Brocco.

Sisters (1973). D, Sc: Brian De Palma. P: Edward R. Pressman. M: Bernard Herrmann. C: Gregory Sandor. Ed: Paul Hirsch. PDn: Gary Weist. Mk: Jeanne Richmond. Cast: Margot Kidder, Jennifer Salt, Charles Durning, William Finley, Lisle Wilson, Barnard Hughes, Mary Davenport, Dolph Sweet.

Reflections of Murder (1974). Made for TV. D: John Badham. Sc: Carol Sobieski. Based on novel by Boileau-Narcejac. P: Aaron Rosenberg. M: Billy Goldenberg. C: Mario Tosi. Ed: David Rawlins. PDn: Boris Leven. Cast: Tuesday Weld, Joan Hackett, Sam Waterston, Lucille Benson, Michael Lerner, R. G. Armstrong, Ed Bernard, William Turner.

The Texas Chainsaw Massacre (1974). D: Tobe Hooper. Sc: Kim Henkel, Tobe Hooper. P: Tobe Hooper, Lou Peraino. M: Wayne Bell, Tobe Hooper. C: Daniel Pearl. Ed: Larry Carroll, Sallye Richardson. PDn: Robert A. Burns. Art: Robert A. Burns. Mk: W. E. Barnes, Dorothy Pearl. Cast: Marilyn Burns, Allen Danziger, Paul A. Partain, William Vail, Teri McMinn, Edwin Neal.

The Legend of Lizzie Borden (1975). Made for TV. D: Paul Wendkos. Sc: William Bast. P: George LeMaire. M: Billy Goldenberg. C: Robert B. Hauser. Ed: John A. Martinelli. Art: Jack De Shields. SDc: Harry Gordon. CDn: Michael Butler, Guy C. Verhille. Cast: Elizabeth Montgomery, Fionnula Flanagan, Ed Flanders, Katherine Helmond, Don Porter, Fritz Weaver, Bonnie Bartlett, John Beal. Emmy Awards Costume design (Verhille), editing (Martinelli). Edgar Award Best TV Feature/Miniseries.

The Hills Have Eyes (1977). D, Sc: Wes Craven. P: Peter Locke. M: Don Peake. C: Eric Saarinen. Ed: Wes Craven. Art: Robert Burns. CDn: Joanne Jaffe. SFx: Greg Auer, John Frazier. Cast: Susan Lanier, Robert Houston, Martin Speer, Dee Wallace, Russ Grieve, John Steadman, James Whitworth, Virginia Vincent, Michael Berryman, Peter Locke.

Dressed to Kill (1980). D, Sc: Brian De Palma. P: George Litto. M: Pino Donaggio. C: Ralf Bode. Ed: Jerry Greenberg. Art: Gary Weist. SDc: Gary Brink. CDn: Gary Jones, Ann Roth. Cast: Michael Caine, Angie Dickinson, Nancy Allen, Keith Gordon, Dennis Franz, David Margulies.

Mommie Dearest (1981). D: Frank Perry. Sc: Robert Getchell, Tracy Hotchner, Frank Perry, Frank Yablans. Based on book by Christina Crawford. P: Frank Yablans. M: Henry Mancini. C: Paul Lohmann. PDn: Bill Malley. Art: Harold Michelson. SDc: Richard C. Goddard. CDn: Irene Sharaff. SFx: Joseph P. Mercurio, Ken Speed. Cast: Faye Dunaway, Diana Scarwid, Steve Forrest, Howard Da Silva, Mara Hobel, Jocelyn Brando, Priscilla Pointer.

The Times of Harvey Milk (1984). D: Rob Epstein. P: Richard Schmiechen. M: Mark Isham. C: Frances Reid. Ed: Rob Epstein, Deborah Hoffmann. PDn: Michael McNeil. Cast: Harvey Fierstein, Harvey Milk, Anne Kronenberg, Tory Hartmann, Tom Amiano, Jim Elliot, Henry Der, Jeannine Yeomans. Academy Awards Best Documentary Feature. New York Film Critics Best Documentary. Sundance Special Jury Prize Documentary.

Henry: Portrait of a Serial Killer (1986, released 1990). D: John McNaughton. Sc: Richard Fire & John McNaughton. P: Lisa Dedmond, Steven A. Jones, John McNaughton. M: Ken Hale, Steven A. Jones, Robert McNaughton. C: Charlie Lieberman. Ed: Elena Maganini. Art: Rick Paul. CDn: Patricia Hart. SFx: Lee Ditkowski. Cast: Mary Demas, Michael Rooker, Anne Bartoletti, Elizabeth Kaden, Ted Kaden, Denise Sullivan, Anita Ores, Megan Ores.

Landscape Suicide (1986). **D, Sc, P, Ed, C:** James Benning. **Cast:** Rhonda Bell, Elion Sucher.

In a Glass Cage [*Tras El Cristál*] (1987). **D, Sc:** Agustín Villaronga. **P:** Teresa Enrich. **M:** Javier Navarrete. **C:** Jaime Peracaula. **CDn:** Andrés Urdiciaian. **Cast:** Günter Meisner, David Sust, Marisa Paredes, Gisèle Echevarría, Imma Colomer, Josue Guasch, Ricardo Carcelevo.

The Stepfather (1987). **D:** Joseph Ruben. **Sc:** Donald E. Westlake. Story by Carolyn Lefcourt & Brian Garfield and Donald E. Westlake. **P:** Jay Benson. **M:** Patrick Moraz. **C:** John W. Lindley. **Ed:** George Bowers. **PDn:** James William Newport. **Art:** David Willson. **SDc:** Kimberley Richardson. **CDn:** Mina Mittelman. **Cast:** Terry O'Quinn, Jill Schoelen, Shelley Hack, Charles Lanyer, Stephen Shellen, Stephen E. Miller.

The Vanishing [*Spoorloos*] [*L'Homme Qui Voulait Savoir*] (1988). **D:** George Sluizer. **Sc:** George Sluizer. Based on novel by Tim Krabbé. **P:** Anne Lordon, George Sluizer. **M:** Henny Vrienten. **C:** Toni Kuhn. **Ed:** Lin Friedman, George Sluizer. **Art:** Santiago Isidro Pin. **CDn:** Sophie Dussaud. **Mk:** Léone Noël. **Cast:** Bernard-Pierre Donnadieu, Gene Bervoets, Johanna ter Steege, Gwen Eckhaus, Bernadette Le Saché, Tania Latarjet, Lucille Glenn, Roger Souza. **European Film Awards** Best Supporting Actress (ter Steege).

The Seventh Continent [*Der Siebente Kontinent*] (1989). **D:** Michael Haneke. **Sc:** Michael Haneke, Johanna Teicht. **P:** Veit Heiduschka. **C:** Anton Peschke. **Ed:** Marie Homolkova. **PDn:** Rudolf Czettel. **Art:** Rudolf Czettel. **CDn:** Anna Georgiades. **Mk:** Ernst Dummer. **S:** Karl Schlifelner. **Cast:** Dieter Berner, Udo Samel, Leni Tanzer, Silvia Fenz, Robert Dietl, Birgit Doll, Georg Friedrich, Georges Kern, Elisabeth Rath. **Flanders** Best Use of Music in Film. **Locarno** Ernest Artaria Award (Haneke).

Misery (1990). **D:** Rob Reiner. **Sc:** William Goldman. Based on novel by Stephen King. **P:** Rob Reiner, Andrew Scheinman. **M:** Marc Shaiman. **C:** Barry Sonnenfeld. **Ed:** Robert Leighton. **PDn:** Norman Garwood. **Art:** Mark W. Mansbridge. **SDc:** Garrett Lewis. **CDn:** Gloria Gresham. **Cast:** James Caan, Kathy Bates, Richard Farnsworth, Frances Sternhagen, Lauren Bacall, Graham Jarvis. **Academy Awards** Best Actress (Bates). **Golden Globes** Best Actress in Drama (Bates).

The Silence of the Lambs (1991). **D:** Jonathan Demme. **Sc:** Ted Tally. Based on novel by Thomas Harris. **P:** Ron Bozman, Edward Saxon, Kenneth Utt. **M:** Howard Shore. **C:** Tak Fujimoto. **Ed:** Craig McKay. **PDn:** Kristi Zea. **Art:** Tim Galvin. **SDc:** Karen O'Hara. **CDn:** Colleen Atwood. **SFx:** Dwight Benjamin-Creel. **Cast:** Jodie Foster, Anthony Hopkins, Scott Glenn, Anthony Heald, Ted Levine, Diane Baker, Frankie Faison, Kasi Lemmons, Brooke Smith. **Academy Awards** Best Actor (Hopkins), Best Actress (Foster), Best Director, Best Picture, Best Adapted Screenplay. **BAFTA** Best Actor (Hopkins), Best Actress (Foster). **Berlin** Best Director. **Directors Guild of America** Outstanding Directorial Achievement. **Golden Globes** Best Actress in Drama (Foster). **National Board of Review** Best Director, Best Picture, Best Supporting Actor (Hopkins). **New York Film Critics** Best Actor (Hopkins), Best Actress (Foster), Best Director, Best Film. **Writers Guild of America** Best Adapted Screenplay. **Edgar Award** Best Motion Picture.

Benny's Video (1992). **D, Sc:** Michael Haneke. **P:** Veit Heiduschka, Bernard Lang. **C:** Christian Berger. **Ed:** Marie Homolkova. **PDn:** Christoph Kanter. **SDc:** Christian Schuster. **CDn:** Erika Navas. **Mk:** Giacomo Peier. **S:** Karl Schlifelner. **SFx:** Willi Neuner. **Cast:** Arno Frisch, Angela Winkler, Ulrich Mühe, Ingrid Stassner, Stephanie Brehme, Stefan Polasek, Christian Pundy, Max Berner, Hanspeter Müller, Shelley Kästner. **European Film Awards** FIPRESCI Prize (Haneke). **Viennale** Vienna Film Award (Haneke).

Man Bites Dog [*C'est Arrivé Près de Chez Vous*] (1992). **D, P:** Rémy Belvaux, André Bonzel, Benoît Poelvoorde. **Sc:** Rémy Belvaux, André Bonzel, Benoît Poelvoorde, Vincent Tavier. **M:** Jean-Marc Chenut, Laurence Dufrene. **C:** André Bonzel. **Ed:** Rémy Belvaux, Eric Dardill. **Cast:** Benoît Poelvoorde, Jacqueline Poelvoorde-Pappaert, Nelly Pappaert, Hector Pappaert, Jenny Drye, Malou Madou, Willy Vandenbroeck, Rachel Deman, Rémy Belvaux, André Bonzel, Vincent Tavier.

Swoon (1992). **D, Ed:** Tom Kalin. **Sc:** Hilton Als, Tom Kalin. **P:** Christine Vachon. **M:** James Bennett. **C:** Ellen Kuras. **PDn:** Thérèse DePrez. **Art:** Stacey Jones. **CDn:** Jessica Haston. **Mk:** Jim Crawford. **Cast:** Daniel Schlachet, Craig Chester. **Berlin** Caligari (Kalin), Best Feature Film (Kalin).

Kalifornia (1993). **D:** Dominic Sena. **Sc:** Tim Metcalfe. Story by Stephen Levy & Tim Metcalfe. **P:** Steve Golin, Aristides McGarry, Sigurjon Sighvatsson. **M:** Carter Burwell. **C:** Bojan Bazelli. **Ed:** Martin Hunter. **PDn:** Michael White. **Art:** Jeff Mann. **SDc:** Kate J. Sullivan. **CDn:** Kelle Kutsugeras. **SFx:** Jeffrey Knott, Michael Schorr. **Cast:** Brad Pitt, Juliette Lewis, David Duchovny, Michelle Forbes, Kathy Larson, David Milford.

The Vanishing (1993). **D:** George Sluizer. **Sc:** Todd Graff. Based on novel by Tim Krabbé. **P:** Larry Brezner, Paul Schiff. **M:** Jerry Goldsmith. **C:** Peter Suschitzky. **Ed:** Bruce Green. **PDn:** Jeannine C. Oppewall. **Art:** Steve Wolff. **SDc:** Anne Ahrens. **CDn:** Durinda Wood. **SDn:** Richard Yanez. **Cast:** Jeff Bridges, Kiefer Sutherland, Nancy Travis, Sandra Bullock, Park Overall, Maggie Linderman, Lisa Eichhorn, George Hearn.

Clean, Shaven (1994). **D, Sc, P:** Lodge Kerrigan. **M:** Hahn Rowe. **C:** Teodoro Maniaci. **Ed:** Jay Rabinowitz. **PDn:** Tania Ferrier. **Mk:** Rob Benevides. **Cast:** Peter Greene, Megan Owen, Jennifer MacDonald, Molly Castelloe, Robert Albert.

I Can't Sleep [*J'ai Pas Sommeil*] (1994). **D, Sc:** Claire Denis. **P:** Bruno Pésery. **M:** Jean-Louis Murat, John Pattison. **C:** Agnès Godard. **Ed:** Nelly Quettier. **PDn:** Thierry Flamand, Arnaud de Moleron. **CDn:** Claire Fraisse. **S:** Thierry Lebon, Jean-Louis Ughetto. **Cast:** Yekaterina Golubeva, Richard Courcet, Vincent Dupont, Laurent Grévill, Alex Descas, Irina Grjebina, Tolsty, Line Renaud.

71 Fragments of a Chronology of Chance [*71 Fragmente einer Chronologie des Zufalls*] (1994). **D, Sc:** Michael Haneke. **P:** Veit Heiduschka. **C:** Christian Berger. **Ed:** Marie Homolkova. **PDn:** Christoph Kanter. **CDn:** Erika Navas. **S:** Marc Parisotto. **Cast:** Gabriel Cosmin Urdes, Lukas Miko, Otto Grünmandl, Anne Bennent, Udo Samel, Branko Samarovski, Claudia Martini, Georg Friedrich, Klaus Händl.

***La Cérémonie* [*The Ceremony*]** (1995). **D:** Claude Chabrol. **Sc:** Claude Chabrol, Caroline Eliacheff. Based on novel by Ruth Rendell. **P:** Marin Karmitz. **M:** Matthieu Chabrol. **C:** Bernard Zitzermann. **Ed:** Monique Fardoulis. **PDn:** Daniel Mercier. **Art:** Daniel Mercier. **CDn:** Corinne Jorry. **S:** Jean-Bernard Thomasson, Claude Villand. **SFx:** Dominique Colladant, Jean-Pierre Moricourt. **Cast:** Isabelle Huppert, Sandrine Bonnaire, Jean-Pierre Cassel, Jacqueline Bisset, Virginie Ledoyen, Valentin Merlet, Julien Rochefort, Dominique Frot. **César** Best Actress (Huppert). **Los Angeles Film Critics** Best Foreign Film. **National Society of Film Critics** Best Foreign Film. **Venice** Volpi Cup Best Actress (Bonnaire and Huppert, tied).

Dolores Claiborne (1995). **D:** Taylor Hackford. **Sc:** Tony Gilroy. Based on novel by Stephen King. **P:** Taylor Hackford, Charles Mulvehill. **M:** Danny Elfman. **C:** Gabriel Beristain. **Ed:** Mark Warner. **PDn:** Bruno Rubeo. **Art:** Dan Yarhi. **SDc:** Steve Shewchuk. **CDn:** Shay Cunliffe. **Mk:** Luigi Rocchetti, Micheline Trépanier. **H:** Réjean Goderre, Aldo Signoretti. **Cast:** Kathy Bates, Jennifer Jason Leigh, Judy Parfitt, Christopher Plummer, David Strathairn, Eric Bogosian, John C. Reilly, Ellen Muth. **Tokyo** Best Supporting Actress (Muth).

Frisk (1995). **D:** Todd Verow. **Sc:** Jim Dwyer, George LaVoo, Todd Verow. Based on novel by Dennis Cooper. **P:** Jon Gerrans, Marcus Hu. **M:** Lee Ranaldo. **C:** Greg Watkins. **Ed:** Todd Verow. **PDn:** Jennifer Graber. **Art:** Deborah A. Hohenberg. **Mk:** Stéphan Dupuis, Jason Rail. **S:** Mark Jan Wlodarkiewicz. **Cast:** Michael Gunther, Craig Chester, Michael Stock, Raoul O'Connell, Jaie Laplante, Parker Posey, James Lyons, Alexis Arquette.

Nixon (1995). **D:** Oliver Stone. **Sc:** Stephen J. Rivele & Christopher Wilkinson & Oliver Stone. **P:** Oliver Stone, Clayton Townsend, Andrew G. Vajna. **M:** John Williams. **C:** Robert Richardson. **Ed:** Brian Berdan, Hank Corwin. **PDn:** Victor Kempster. **Art:** Richard F. Mays, Donald Woodruff, Margery Zweizig. **SDc:** Merideth Boswell. **CDn:** Richard Hornung. **SFx:** F. Lee Stone. **Cast:** Anthony Hopkins, Joan Allen, Powers Boothe, Ed Harris, Bob Hoskins, E.G. Marshall, David Hyde Pierce, Paul Sorvino, Mary Steenburgen, J.T. Walsh, James Woods. **Los Angeles Film Critics** Best Supporting Actress (Allen). **National Society of Film Critics** Best Supporting Actress (Allen).

***Seven* [*Se7en*]** (1995). **D:** David Fincher. **Sc:** Andrew Kevin Walker. **P:** Phyllis Carlyle, Arnold Kopelson. **M:** Howard Shore. **C:** Darius Khondji. **Ed:** Richard Francis-Bruce. **PDn:** Arthur Max. **Art:** Gary Wissner. **SDc:** Clay A. Griffith. **CDn:** Michael Kaplan. **Cast:** Brad Pitt, Morgan Freeman, Gwyneth Paltrow, Kevin Spacey, R. Lee Ermey, Andy Walker, Daniel Zacapa, John Cassini. **National Board of Review** Best Supporting Actor (Spacey). **New York Film Critics** Best Supporting Actor (Spacey).

Scream (1996). **D:** Wes Craven. **Sc:** Kevin Williamson. **P:** Cathy Konrad, Cary Woods. **M:** Marco Beltrami. **C:** Mark Irwin. **Ed:** Patrick Lussier. **PDn:** Bruce Alan Miller. **Art:** David Lubin. **SDc:** Michele Poulik. **CDn:** Cynthia Bergstrom. **SDn:** Nanci Noblett. **SFx:** Frank Ceglia. **Cast:** David Arquette, Neve Campbell, Courteney Cox, Skeet Ulrich, Rose McGowan, Matthew Lillard, Jamie Kennedy, W. Earl Brown, Drew Barrymore.

Funny Games (1997). **D, Sc:** Michael Haneke. **P:** Veit Heiduschka. **C:** Jürgen Jürges. **Ed:** Andreas Prochaska. **PDn:** Christoph Kanter. **CDn:** Lisy Christl. **Mk:** Waldemar Pokromski. **S:** Walter Amann. **Cast:** Susanne Lothar, Ulrich Mühe, Arno Frisch, Frank Giering, Stefan Clapczynski, Doris Kunstmann, Christoph Bantzer, Wolfgang Glück.

***Henry: Portrait of a Serial Killer, Part* 2** (1998). **D, Sc:** Chuck Parello. **P:** Waleed B. Ali, Chuck Parello. **M:** Robert McNaughton. **C:** Michael Kohnhorst. **Ed:** Tom Keefe. **PDn:** Rick Paul. **Art:** Angela Howard. **CDn:** Patricia Hart. **Mk:** Art Anthony. **SFx:** Don Parsons. **Cast:** Penelope Milford, Neil Giuntoli, Mike Houlihan, James Otis, Rich Baker, Rich Komenich, Kate Walsh, Carri Levinson.

Fight Club (1999). **D:** David Fincher. **Sc:** Jim Uhls. Based on novel by Chuck Palahniuk. **P:** Ross Grayson Bell, Cean Chaffin, Art Linson. **C:** Jeff Cronenweth. **Ed:** James Haygood. **PDn:** Alex McDowell. **Art:** Chris Gorak. **SDc:** Jay R. Hart. **CDn:** Michael Kaplan. **Mk:** Julie Pearce. **H:** Frida Aradottir. **S:** Ren Klyce. **SFx:** Derrick Crane. **Cast:** Edward Norton, Brad Pitt, Helena Bonham Carter, Meat Loaf Aday, Zach Grenier, Richmond Arquette, David Andrews, George Maguire.

American Psycho (2000). **D:** Mary Harron. **Sc:** Mary Harron &Guinevere Turner. Based on novel by Bret Easton Ellis. **P:** Christian Halsey Solomon, Chris Hanley, Edward R. Pressman. **M:** John Cale. **C:** Andrzej Sekula. **Ed:** Andrew Marcus. **PDn:** Gideon Ponte. **Art:** Andrew Stearn. **SDc:** Jeanne Develle. **CDn:** Isis Mussenden. **Mk:** Sandra Wheatle. **H:** Lucy Orton. **S:** Ben Cheah, Paul Urmson. **SFx:** Conrad V. Brink Jr., John MacGillivray. **Cast:** Christian Bale, Justin Theroux, Josh Lucas, Bill Sage, Chloë Sevigny, Reese Witherspoon, Samantha Mathis, Matt Ross, Jared Leto, Willem Dafoe, Guinevere Turner.

Chasing Sleep (2000). **D, Sc:** Michael Walker. **P:** Thomas Bidegain, Olivier Glaas. **C:** Jim Denault. **Ed:** David Leonard. **PDn:** Dan Ouellette. **Art:** Laura Ballinger. **SDc:** T. Dominic Cochran. **CDn:** Kathryn Nixon. **S:** Paul P. Soucek. **SFx:** Robert Standee. **Cast:** Jeff Daniels, Emily Bergl, Gil Bellows, Zach Grenier, Julian McMahon, Ben Shenkman, Molly Price, Patrick Moug.

Memento (2000, 2001 USA). **D:** Christopher Nolan. **Sc:** Christopher Nolan. Story by Jonathan Nolan. **P:** Jennifer Todd, Suzanne Todd. **M:** David Julyan. **C:** Wally Pfister. **Ed:** Dody Dorn. **PDn:** Patti Podesta. **SDc:** Danielle Berman. **CDn:** Cindy Evans. **Mk:** Scott Eddo. **H:** Larry Waggoner. **SFx:** Andrew Sebok. **Cast:** Guy Pearce, Carrie-Anne Moss, Joe Pantoliano, Mark Boone Junior, Russ Fega, Jorja Fox, Stephen Tobolowsky, Harriet Sansom Harris. **Broadcast Film Critics** Best Screenplay. **Independent Spirit** Best Director, Best Feature, Best Screenplay, Best Supporting Female (Moss). **Los Angeles Film Critics** Best

Screenplay. **Sundance** Waldo Salt Screenwriting Award. **Edgar Award** Best Motion Picture.

Requiem for a Dream (2000). **D:** Darren Aronofsky. **Sc:** Hubert Selby Jr., Darren Aronofsky. Based on novel by Hubert Selby Jr. **P:** Eric Watson, Palmer West. **M:** Clint Mansell. **C:** Matthew Libatique. **Ed:** Jay Rabinowitz. **PDn:** James Chinlund. **Art:** Judy Rhee. **SDc:** Ondine Karady. **CDn:** Carolyn Griffell, Laura Jean Shannon. **Cast:** Ellen Burstyn, Jared Leto, Jennifer Connelly, Marlon Wayans, Christopher McDonald, Louise Lasser, Marcia Jean Kurtz, Janet Sarno. **Independent Spirit** Best Cinematography, Best Female Lead (Burstyn).

Scary Movie (2000). **D:** Keenen Ivory Wayans. **Sc:** Shawn Wayans & Marlon Wayans & Buddy Johnson & Phil Beauman and Jason Friedberg & Aaron Seltzer. **P:** Eric L. Gold, Lee R. Mayes. **M:** David Kitay. **C:** Francis Kenny. **Ed:** Mark Helfrich. **PDn:** Robb Wilson King. **Art:** Lawrence F. Pevec. **SDc:** Louise Roper. **CDn:** Darryle Johnson. **Cast:** Anna Faris, Shawn Wayans, Marlon Wayans, Jon Abrahams, Shannon Elizabeth, Cheri Oteri, Lochlyn Munro, Regina Hall.

What Lies Beneath (2000). **D:** Robert Zemeckis. **Sc:** Clark Gregg. Story by Sarah Kernochan and Clark Gregg. **P:** Jack Rapke, Steve Starkey, Robert Zemeckis. **M:** Alan Silvestri. **C:** Don Burgess. **Ed:** Arthur Schmidt. **PDn:** Rick Carter, Jim Teegarden. **SDc:** Karen O'Hara. **CDn:** Susie DeSanto, Bernie Pollack. **Mk:** Deborah La Mia Denaver. **H:** Janice Alexander. **S:** Randy Thom. **Cast:** Harrison Ford, Michelle Pfeiffer, Diana Scarwid, Joe Morton, James Remar, Miranda Otto, Amber Valletta, Katharine Towne.

Ed Gein [*In the Light of the Moon*] (2001). **D:** Chuck Parello. **Sc:** Stephen Johnston. **P:** Mark Boot, Bill Cross, Hamish McAlpine, Michael Muscal. **M:** Robert McNaughton. **C:** Vanja Cernjul. **Ed:** Elena Maganini. **PDn:** Mark Harper. **SDc:** Christopher Larsen. **CDn:** Niklas J. Palm. **SFx:** John Criswell. **Cast:** Steve Railsback, Carrie Snodgrass, Carol Mansell, Ryan Thomas Brockington, Austin James Peck.

Hannibal (2001). **D:** Ridley Scott. **Sc:** David Mamet, Steven Zaillian. Based on novel by Thomas Harris. **P:** Dino De Laurentiis, Martha De Laurentiis, Ridley Scott. **M:** Hans Zimmer. **C:** John Mathieson. **Ed:** Pietro Scalia, Daniele Sordoni. **PDn:** Norris Spencer. **Art:** David Crank, Marco Trentini. **SDc:** Crispian Sallis, Cynthia Sleiter. **CDn:** Janty Yates. **Cast:** Anthony Hopkins, Julianne Moore, Giancarlo Giannini, Gary Oldman, Ray Liotta, Frankie R. Faison, Francesca Neri, Zeljko Ivanek.

The Piano Teacher [*La Pianiste*] (2001). **D:** Michael Haneke. **Sc:** Michael Haneke. Based on novel by Elfriede Jelinek. **P:** Veit Heiduschka. **M:** Francis Haines. **C:** Christian Berger. **Ed:** Nadine Muse, Monika Willi. **PDn:** Christoph Kanter. **SDc:** Hans Wagner. **CDn:** Annette Beaufays. **S:** Guillaume Sciama. **SFx:** László Kovács, Hans Wagner. **VFx:** Geoffrey Kleindorfer. **Cast:** Isabelle Huppert, Annie Girardot, Benoît Magimel, Susanne Lothar, Udo Samel, Anna Sigalevitch. **Cannes** Best Actor (Magimel), Best Actress (Huppert), Grand Prix (*La Pianiste*). **César** Best Supporting Actress (Girardot).

The Child I Never Was [*Ein Leben lang kurze Hosen tragen*] (2002). **D, Sc:** Kai S. Pieck. Based on book by Paul Moor. **P:** Andrea Hanke, Bettina Scheueren. **M:** Kurt Dahlke, Rainer J. G. Uhl. **C:** Egon Werdin. **Ed:** Ingo Ehrlich. **PDn:** Bertram Strauß. **CDn:** Anne Jendritzko. **Cast:** Tobias Schenke, Sebastian Urzendowsky, Ulrike Bliefert, Walter Gontermann, Jürgen Christoph Kamcke, Sebastian Rüger, Stephan Szasz, Roland Riebeling.

Dahmer (2002). **D, Sc:** David Jacobson. **P:** Larry Rattner. **M:** Christina Agamanolis, Marianna Bernoski, Willow Williamson. **C:** Chris Manley. **Ed:** Bipasha Shom. **PDn:** Eric Larson. **Art:** Kelley Wright. **CDn:** Dana Hart, Katie Moore. **Mk:** Michele Tyminski. **S:** Gary Gelfand, Mark Linden. **Cast:** Jeremy Renner, Bruce Davison, Artel Kayàru, Matt Newton, Dion Basco, Kate Williamson.

In My Skin [*Dans Ma Peau*] (2002). **D, Sc:** Marina de Van. **P:** Laurence Farenc. **M:** Esbjorn Svensson. **C:** Pierre Barougier. **Ed:** Mike Fromentin. **PDn:** Baptiste Glaymann. **Art:** Baptiste Glaymann. **CDn:** Marielle Robaut. **Mk:** Dominique Colladant. **S:** Jérôme Aghion, Jérôme Wiciak. **SFx:** Dominique Colladant. **Cast:** Marina de Van, Laurent Lucas, Léa Drucker, Thibault de Montalembert, Dominique Reymond, Bernard Alane.

Irréversible (2002). **D, Sc, Ed:** Gaspar Noé. **P:** Christophe Rossignon. **M:** Thomas Bangalter. **C:** Benoît Debie, Gaspar Noé. **PDn:** Alain Juteau. **CDn:** Laure Culkovic. **SFx:** Rodolphe Chabrier. **Cast:** Monica Bellucci, Vincent Cassel, Albert Dupontel, Jo Prestia, Philippe Nahon, Stéphane Drouot.

One Hour Photo (2002). **D, Sc:** Mark Romanek. **P:** Pamela Koffler, Christine Vachon, Stan Wlodkowski. **M:** Reinhold Heil, Johnny Klimek. **C:** Jeff Cronenweth. **Ed:** Jeffrey Ford. **PDn:** Tom Foden. **Art:** Michael Manson. **SDc:** Tessa Posnansky. **CDn:** Arianne Phillips. **SDn:** Glenn Rivers, Carl Stensel. **S:** Brian Emrich. **Cast:** Robin Williams, Connie Nielsen, Michael Vartan, Dylan Smith, Erin Daniels, Paul Hansen Kim, Lee Garlington, Gary Cole.

Ted Bundy (2002). **D:** Matthew Bright. **Sc:** Stephen Johnston and Matthew Bright. **P:** Hamish McAlpine, Michael Muscal. **M:** Kennard Ramsey. **C:** Sonja Rom. **Ed:** Paul Heiman. **PDn:** Chris Anthony Miller. **SDc:** Beth Wooke. **CDn:** Elena Baranova, Kristin Persson. **S:** John Brasher. **Cast:** Michael Reilly Burke, Boti Ann Bliss, Tricia Dickson, Meadow Sisto.

Elephant (2003). **D, Sc, Ed:** Gus Van Sant. **P:** Dany Wolf. **C:** Harris Savides. **Art:** Benjamin Hayden. **S:** Leslie Shatz. **SFx:** Jor Van Kline. **VFx:** Collin Fowler. **Cast:** John Robinson, Alex Frost, Elias McConnell, Eric Deulen, Nathan Tyson, Carrie Finklea, Kristen Hicks, Alicia Miles, Timothy Bottoms. **Cannes** Palme d'Or (*Elephant*), Best Director (Van Sant). **New York Film Critics** Best Cinematographer.

Gacy (2003). **D:** Clive Saunders. **Sc:** David Birke, Clive Saunders. **P:** Larry Rattner, Tim Swain. **M:** Mark Fontana, Erik Godal. **C:** Kristian Bernier. **Ed:** Jeff Orgill, Chryss Terry. **PDn:** Benjamin Edelberg, Eric Larson. **Art:** Ian Phillips. **SDc:** Nanci Bennett. **CDn:** Oneita Parker. **Mk:** Karrieann Heisner. **S:** Tony Rorretto. **Cast:** Mark Holton, Adam Baldwin, Tom Waldman, Charlie Weber, Allison Lange, Edith Jefferson, Joleen Lutz, Scott Allen Henry.

High Tension [*Haute Tension*] (2003). **D:** Alexandre Aja. **Sc:** Alexandre Aja, Grégory Levasseur. **P:** Alexandre Arcady, Robert Benmussa. **M:** François Eudes. Matthew Bellamy song "New Born." **C:** Maxime Alexandre. **Ed:** Baxter, Al Rundle, Sophie Vermersch. **PDn:** Renald Cotte Verdy, Tony Egry. **Art:** Grégory Levasseur. **SDc:** Gabriela Nechita. **Mk:** Gabi Cretan, Giannetto De Rossi. **Cast:** Cécile De France, Maïwenn Le Besco, Philippe Nahon, Franck Khalfoun, Andrei Finti, Oana Pellea, Marco Claudiu Pascu, Jean-Claude de Goros, Bogdan Uritescu, Gabriel Spahiu.

Identity (2003). **D:** James Mangold. **Sc:** Michael Cooney. **P:** Cathy Konrad. **M:** Alan Silvestri. **C:** Phedon Papamichael. **Ed:** David Brenner. **PDn:** Mark Friedberg. **Art:** Jess Gonchor. **SDc:** Cindy Carr. **CDn:** Arianne Phillips. **Cast:** John Cusack, Ray Liotta, Amanda Peet, John Hawkes, Alfred Molina, Clea DuVall, John C. McGinley, William Lee Scott, Pruitt Taylor Vince.

Monster (2003). **D, Sc:** Patty Jenkins. **P:** Mark Damon, Donald Kushner, Clark Peterson, Charlize Theron, Brad Wyman. **M:** Bt. **C:** Steven Bernstein. **Ed:** Arthur Coburn, Jane Kurson. **PDn:** Edward T. McAvoy. **Art:** Orvis Rigsby. **SDc:** Shawn R. McFall. **CDn:** Rhona Meyers. **S:** Zack Davis, Geoffrey G. Rubay. **Cast:** Charlize Theron, Christina Ricci, Bruce Dern, Lee Tergesen, Annie Corley, Pruitt Taylor Vince, Marco St. John, Marc Macaulay. **Academy Awards** Best Actress (Theron). **Berlin** Best Actress (Theron). **Broadcast Film Critics** Best Actress (Theron). **Golden Globes** Best Actress in Drama (Theron). **Independent Spirit** Best Female Lead (Theron), Best First Feature. **National Board of Review** Breakthrough Performance by Actress (Theron). **National Society of Film Critics** Best Actress (Theron). **Screen Actors Guild** Outstanding Female Lead (Theron).

Twentynine Palms (2003). **D, Sc:** Bruno Dumont. **P:** Rachid Bouchareb, Jean Bréhat. **C:** Georges Lechaptois. **Ed:** Dominique Petrot. **CDn:** Yasmine Abraham. **Mk:** Elizabeth Sloan Freel. **S:** Philippe Lecoeur. **Cast:** Yekaterina Golubeva, David Wissak.

The Machinist (2004). **D:** Brad Anderson. **Sc:** Scott Kosar. **P:** Julio Fernández. **M:** Roque Baños. **C:** Xavi Giménez, Charlie Jiminez. **Ed:** Luis De La Madrid. **Art:** Alain Bainée. **SDc:** Patricia Gil. **CDn:** Patricia Monné, Maribel Pérez. **Mk:** Alma Casal. **H:** Satur Merino. **S:** Fabiola Ordoyo. **SFx:** Esther Villar. **VFx:** Jaume Vilaseca. **Cast:** Christian Bale, Jennifer Jason Leigh, Aitana Sánchez-Gijón, John Sharian, Michael Ironside, Larry Gilliard, Reg E. Cathey, Anna Massey.

Saw (2004). **D:** James Wan. **Sc:** Leigh Whannell. Story by James Wan and Leigh Whannell. **P:** Mark Burg, Gregg Hoffman, Oren Koules. **M:** Charlie Clouser. **C:** David A. Armstrong. **Ed:** Kevin Greutert. **PDn:** Julie Berghoff. **Art:** Nanet Harty. **CDn:** Jennifer Soulages. **SFx:** Tom Bellissimo. **VFx:** Josh Comen, Marlo Pabon. **Cast:** Leigh Whannell, Cary Elwes, Danny Glover, Ken Leung, Dina Meyer, Mike Butters, Paul Gutrecht, Michael Emerson.

BTK Killer (2005). **D, Sc:** Ulli Lommel. **P:** Ulli Lommel, Nola Roeper. **M:** Robert J. Walsh. **C:** Bianco Pacelli. **Ed:** Xgin. **PDn:** Patricia Devereaux. **Mk:** Boston Dawna Chaet. **VFx:** John Kunicki. **Cast:** Gerard Griesbaum, Eric Gerleman, Victoria Ullmann, Shyla Fernandes, Ivy Elfstrom, Michael Barbour, Nola Roeper, Erin Young.

Green River Killer (2005). **D, Sc:** Ulli Lommel. **P:** Ulli Lommel, Nola Roeper. **M:** Robert J. Walsh. **C:** Bianco Pacelli. **Ed:** Xgin. **PDn:** Patricia Devereaux. **CDn:** Jimmy Williams. **Mk:** Boston Dawna Chaet. **VFx:** John Kunicki. **Cast:** George Kiseleff, Jacquelyn Horrell, Georgina Donovan, Shannon Leade, Naidra Dawn Thomson, Shawn G. Smith, Martin Lockhurst, Nola Roeper.

Hostel (2005). **D, Sc:** Eli Roth. **P:** Chris Briggs, Mike Fleiss, Eli Roth. **M:** Nathan Barr. **C:** Milan Chadima. **Ed:** George Folsey Jr. **Pd, CDn:** Franco-Giacomo Carbone. **Art:** David Baxa. **SDc:** Karel Vanásek. **CDn:** Franco-Giacomo Carbone. **Mk:** Rini Lemanova. **Cast:** Jay Hernandez, Derek Richardson, Eythor Gudjonsson, Barbara Nedeljakova, Jan Vlasák, Jana Kaderabkova, Jennifer Lim, Takashi Miike.

The Jacket (2005). **D:** John Maybury. **Sc:** Massy Tadjedin. Story by Tom Bleecker and Marc Rocco. **P:** George Clooney, Peter Guber, Steven Soderbergh. **M:** Brian Eno. **C:** Peter Deming. **Ed:** Emma E. Hickox. **PDn:** Alan MacDonald. **Art:** Isabelle Guay, Jean-Pierre Paquet, Caireen Todd. **SDc:** Liz Griffiths. **CDn:** Douglas Hall. **SDn:** Brent Lambert. **Cast:** Adrien Brody, Keira Knightley, Kris Kristofferson, Jennifer Jason Leigh, Kelly Lynch, Brad Renfro, Daniel Craig, Mackenzie Phillips.

Dexter (2006 to 2009, ongoing). TV Series. **D:** Michael Cuesta; others. **Sc:** James Manos Jr (pilot); Clyde Phillips; others. Based on novel by Jeff Lindsay. **P:** Dennis Bishop (p); Drew Z. Greenberg, Robert Lloyd Lewis; others. **Executive P:** James Manos Jr. **M:** Daniel Licht. **C:** Terry Stacey (p); Romeo Tirone. **Ed:** Elena Maganini. **PDn:** Michael Corenblith (p); Brandy Alexander. **Art:** Richard Fojo. **SDc:** Marthe Pineau (p); Debra Combs. **CDn:** Marina Draghici (p); Jill Ohanneson. **Mk:** Tara Day (p); Keith Hall. **Cast:** Michael C. Hall, Julie Benz, Jennifer Carpenter, Erik King, Lauren Velez, David Zayas, James Remar. **Emmy Awards** Outstanding Main Title Design (Anderson, Bodnar, Daniels, Davis) Outstanding Single Camera Picture Editing for a Drama Series (Maganini).

Notes on a Scandal (2006). **D:** Richard Eyre. **Sc:** Patrick Marber. Based on novel by Zoe Heller. **P:** Robert Fox, Andrew Macdonald, Allon Reich, Scott Rudin. **M:** Philip Glass. **C:** Chris Menges. **Ed:** John Bloom, Antonia Van Drimmelen. **PDn:** Tim Hatley. **Art:** Grant Armstrong, Mark Raggett. **CDn:** Tim Hatley. **Mk:** Lisa Westcott. **Cast:** Judi Dench, Cate Blanchett, Bill Nighy, Andrew Simpson, Phil Davis, Michael Maloney, Juno Temple, Max Lewis. **British Independent Film Awards** Best Actress (Dench), Best Screenplay. **Berlin** Teddy Audience Award (Eyre).

Perfume: The Story of a Murderer (2006). **D:** Tom Tykwer. **Sc:** Andrew Birkin, Bernd Eichinger, Tom Tykwer. Based on novel by Patrick Süskind. **P:** Bernd Eichinger. **M:** Reinhold Heil, Johnny Klimek, Tom Tykwer. **C:** Frank Griebe. **Ed:** Alexander Berner. **PDn:** Uli Hanisch. **CDn:** Pierre-Yves Gayraud. **S:** Stefan Busch, Frank Kruse. **Cast:** Ben Whishaw, David

Calder, Birgit Minichmayr, Sian Thomas, Dustin Hoffman, Rachel Hurd-Wood, Alan Rickman, John Hurt (voice only).

Inside [*À l'Intèrieur*] (2007). **D:** Alexandre Bustillo, Julien Maury. **Sc:** Alexandre Bustillo. **P:** Vérane Frédiani. **P:** Franck Ribière. **M:** François Eudes. **C:** Laurent Barès. **Ed:** Baxter. **SDc:** Marc Thiébault. **CDn:** Martine Rapin. **S:** Jacques Sans. **SFx:** Jacques-Olivier Molon. **VFx:** Jessica Guglielmi, Rodolphe Guglielmi, Bourdonnay Judikael. **Cast:** Béatrice Dalle, Alysson Paradis, Nathalie Roussel, François-Régis Marchasson, Jean-Baptiste Tabourin.

Sweeney Todd: The Demon Barber of Fleet Street (2007). **D:** Tim Burton. **Sc:** John Logan. Based on play by Stephen Sondheim and Hugh Wheeler; Christopher Bond. **P:** John Logan, Laurie MacDonald, Walter Parkes, Richard D. Zanuck. **M:** Stephen Sondheim. **C:** Dariusz Wolski. **Ed:** Chris Lebenzon. **PDn:** Dante Ferretti. **Art:** Gary Freeman, David Warren. **SDc:** Francesca Lo Schiavo. **CDn:** Colleen Atwood. **S:** Steve Boeddeker. **Cast:** Johnny Depp, Helena Bonham Carter, Alan Rickman, Timothy Spall, Sacha Baron Cohen, Jamie Campbell Bower, Laura Michelle Kelly, Jayne Wisener, Edward Sanders. **Academy Awards** Art Direction (Ferretti, Lo Schiavo). **American Cinema Editors** Best Edited Feature Film — Comedy or Musical (Lebenzon). **Golden Globes** Best Motion Picture — Musical or Comedy, Best Performance by an Actor in a Motion Picture — Musical or Comedy (Depp).

Funny Games (2008 USA). **D, Sc:** Michael Haneke. **P:** Christian Baute, Chris Coen, Hamish McAlpine, Andro Steinborn. **C:** Darius Khondji. **PDn:** Kevin Thompson. **Art:** Hinju Kim. **SDc:** Rebecca Meis DeMarco. **CDn:** David C. Robinson. **Cast:** Naomi Watts, Tim Roth, Michael Pitt, Brady Corbet, Devon Gearhart, Boyd Gaines, Siobhan Fallon Hogan, Robert LuPone, Susanne C. Hanke, Linda Moran.

Savage Grace (USA 2008). **D:** Tom Kalin. **P:** Christine Vachon, Pamela Koffler, Iker Monfort, Katie Roumel. **Sc:** Howard A. Rodman. Based on book by Natalie Robins and Steven M. L. Aronson. **C:** Juanmi Azpiroz. **M:** Fernando Velázquez. **Ed:** Enara Goicoetxea, Tom Kalin, John F. Lyons. **PDn:** Victor Molero. **Art:** Deborah Chambers. **Sdc:** Juan Carlos Bravo, Isabelle Domingo, Victor Pavia. **Cdn:** Gabriela Salaverri. **Cast:** Julianne Moore, Stephen Dillane, Eddie Redmayne, Elena Anaya, Unax Ugalde, Hugh Dancy, Anne Reid.

HORROR OF ARMAGEDDON

Nazi Concentration Camps [*Official Allied Forces Film Record of Nazi Death Camps*] (1945). **D:** George Stevens.

The Thing from Another World [*The Thing*] (1951). **D:** Christian Nyby. **Sc:** Charles Lederer. Story by John W. Campbell Jr. **P:** Howard Hawks, Edward Lasker. **M:** Dimitri Tiomkin. **C:** Russell Harlan. **Ed:** Roland Gross. **Art:** Albert S. D'agostino, John J. Hughes. **SDc:** Darrell Silvera, William Stevens. **Mk:** Lee Greenway. **H:** Larry Germain. **S:** Phil Brigandi, Clem Portman. **SFx:** Linwood Dunn, Donald Steward. **Cast:** Margaret Sheridan, Kenneth Tobey, Robert Cornthwaite, Douglas Spencer, James Young, Dewey Martin, Robert Nichols, William Self, Eduard Franz, Sally Creighton, James Arness.

The Day the Earth Stood Still (1951). **D:** Robert Wise. **Sc:** Edmund H. North. Story by Harry Bates. **P:** Julian Blaustein. **M:** Bernard Herrmann. **C:** Leo Tover. **Ed:** William Reynolds. **Art:** Addison Hehr, Lyle Wheeler. **SDc:** Claude Carpenter, Thomas Little. **CDn:** Perkins Bailey, Travilla. **Mk:** Ben Nye. **S:** Harry M. Leonard, Arthur L. Kirbach. **SFx:** Fred Sersen. **Cast:** Michael Rennie, Patricia Neal, Hugh Marlowe, Sam Jaffe, Billy Gray, Frances Bavier, Lock Martin, H. V. Kaltenborn. **Golden Globes** Best Film Promoting International Understanding.

Five (1951). **D, Sc, P, PDn:** Arch Oboler. **M:** Henry Russell. **C:** Sid Lubow, Ed Spiegel, Louis Clyde Stoumen, Arthur Swerdloff. **Ed:** John Hoffman, Sid Lubow, Ed Spiegel, Louis Clyde Stoumen, Arthur Swerdloff. **S:** William Jenkins Locy. **Cast:** William Phipps, Susan Douglas, James Anderson, Charles Lampkin, Earl Lee.

Them! (1954). **D:** Gordon Douglas. **Sc:** Russell Hughes, Ted Sherdeman. Story by George Worthing Yates. **P:** David Weisbart. **M:** Bronislau Kaper. **C:** Sid Hickox. **Ed:** Thomas Reilly. **Art:** Stanley Fleischer. **SDc:** G. W. Berntsen. **Mk:** Gordon Bau. **S:** Francis J. Scheid. **SFx:** Ralph Ayres. **VFx:** Dick Smith. **Cast:** James Whitmore, Edmund Gwenn, Joan Weldon, James Arness, Onslow Stevens, Sean McClory. **Motion Picture Sound Editors** Best Feature Sound Editing.

Invasion of the Body Snatchers (1956). **D:** Don Siegel. **Sc:** Daniel Mainwaring. Story by Jack Finney. **P:** Walter Wanger. **M:** Carmen Dragon. **C:** Ellsworth Fredericks. **Ed:** Robert S. Eisen. **PDn:** Ted Haworth. **SDc:** Joseph Kish. **Mk:** Emile LaVigne. **H:** Mary Westmoreland. **S:** Ralph Butler. **SFx:** Milt Rice. **Cast:** Kevin McCarthy, Dana Wynter, Larry Gates, King Donovan, Carolyn Jones, Jean Willes.

Beginning of the End (1957). **D, P:** Bert I. Gordon. **Sc:** Fred Freiberger, Lester Gorn. **M:** Albert Glasser. **C:** Jack A. Marta. **Ed:** Aaron Stell. **Art:** Walter E. Keller. **SDc:** George Milo. **Mk:** Steve Drumm. **S:** Dick Tyler Sr. **SFx:** Bert I. Gordon, Flora M. Gordon. **Cast:** Peter Graves, Peggie Castle, Morris Ankrum, Than Wyenn, Thomas Browne Henry, Richard Benedict.

The Black Scorpion (1957). **D:** Edward Ludwig. **Sc:** Robert Blees, David Duncan. Story by Paul Yawitz. **P:** Jack Dietz, Frank Melford. **M:** Paul Sawtell. **C:** Lionel Lindon. **Ed:** Richard L. Van Enger. **Art:** Edward Fitzgerald. **S:** Rafael Ruiz Esparza. **SFx:** Willis H. O'Brien, Pete Peterson. **Cast:** Richard Denning, Mara Corday, Carlos Rivas, Mario Navarro, Carlos Múzquiz, Pascual García Peña.

It! The Terror from Beyond Space (1958). **D:** Edward L. Cahn. **Sc:** Jerome Bixby. **P:** Robert E. Kent, Edward Small. **M:** Paul Sawtell, Bert Shefter. **C:** Kenneth Peach. **Ed:** Grant Whytock. **Art:** William Glasgow. **SDc:** Herman N. Schoenbrun. **CDn:** Jack Masters. **Mk:** Layne Britton. **S:** Al Overton. **SFx:** Paul Blaisdell. **Cast:** Marshall Thompson, Shawn Smith, Kim Spalding, Ann Doran, Dabbs Greer, Paul Langton, Ray Corrigan.

Hiroshima, Mon Amour (1959). **D:** Alain Resnais. **Sc:** Marguerite Duras. **P:** Anatole Dauman, Samy Halfon. **M:** Georges Delerue, Giovanni Fusco. **C:** Sacha Vierny, Takahashi Michio. **Ed:** Henri Colpi, Jasmine Chasney. **PDn:** Esaka, Mayo, Pétri. **CDn:** Gérard Collery. **Mk:** A. Marcus, R. Toioda. **H:** Eliane Marcus. **Cast:** Emmanuelle Riva, Eiji Okada, Stella Dassas, Pierre Barbaud, Bernard Fresson. **BAFTA** UN Award (Resnais). **New York Film Critics** Best Foreign Film.

The Killer Shrews (1959). **D:** Ray Kellogg. **Sc:** Jay Simms. **P:** Ken Curtis. **M:** Harry Bluestone, Emil Cadkin. **C:** Wilfrid M. Cline. **Ed:** Aaron Stell. **SDc:** Louise Caldwell. **Mk:** Corinne Daniel. **S:** Earl Snyder. **Cast:** James Best, Ingrid Goude, Ken Curtis, Gordon McLendon, Baruch Lumet.

On the Beach (1959). **D, P:** Stanley Kramer. **Sc:** John Paxton. Based on novel by Nevil Shute. **M:** Ernest Gold. **C:** Daniel Fapp, Giuseppe Rotunno. **Ed:** Frederic Knudtson. **PDn:** Rudolph Sternad. **Art:** Fernando Carrere. **SFx:** Lee Zavitz. **Cast:** Gregory Peck, Ava Gardner, Fred Astaire, Anthony Perkins, Donna Anderson, John Tate. **BAFTA** UN Award (Kramer). **Golden Globes** Best Score (Gold).

The World, the Flesh, and the Devil (1959). **D:** Ranald MacDougall. **Sc:** Ranald MacDougall. Based on novel by M. P. Shiel and story by Ferdinand Reyher. **P:** George Englund. **M:** Miklós Rózsa. **C:** Harold J. Marzorati. **Ed:** Harold F. Kress. **Art:** Paul Groesse, William A. Horning. **SDc:** F. Keogh Gleason, Henry Grace. **CDn:** Kitty Mager. **Mk:** William Tuttle. **SFx:** Lee LeBlanc. **Cast:** Harry Belafonte, Inger Stevens, Mel Ferrer.

The Time Machine (1960). **D, P:** George Pal. **Sc:** David Duncan. Based on novel by H. G. Wells. **M:** Russell Garcia. **C:** Paul C. Vogel. **Ed:** George Tomasini. **Art:** George Davis, William Ferrari. **SDc:** Keogh Gleason, Henry Grace. **Mk:** William Tuttle. **H:** Sydney Guilaroff. **SFx:** Wah Chang, Gene Warren, Tim Baar [Barr]. **Cast:** Rod Taylor, Alan Young, Yvette Mimieux, Sebastian Cabot, Tom Helmore, Whit Bissell, Doris Lloyd. **Academy Awards** Best Effects, Special Effects (Warren, Baar).

Village of the Damned (1960). **D:** Wolf Rilla. **Sc:** Stirling Silliphant, Wolf Rilla, George Barclay. Based on novel by John Wyndham. **P:** Ronald Kinnoch. **M:** Ron Goodwin. **C:** Geoffrey Faithfull. **Ed:** Gordon Hales. **Art:** Ivan King. **Mk:** Éric Aylott. **H:** Joan Johnstone. **SFx:** Tom Howard. **Cast:** George Sanders, Barbara Shelley, Martin Stephens, Michael Gwynn, Laurence Naismith, Richard Warner.

"Anger" [*La Colère*] in *The 7 Capital Sins* [*Les Sept Péchés Capitaux*] [*The Seven Deadly Sins*] (1962). **D:** Sylvain Dhomme. **Sc:** Eugène Ionesco. **M:** Michel Legrand. **C:** Jean Rabier. **Ed:** Jacques Gaillard. **PDn:** Max Douy. **S:** Jean Labussière. **Cast:** Danièle Barraud, Marie-José Nat, Perrette Pradier, Dominique Paturel, Jean-Marc Tennberg.

La Jetée (1962). **D, Sc:** Chris Marker. **P:** Anatole Dauman. **C:** Jean Chiabaut, Chris Marker. **Ed:** Jean Ravel. **S:** Antoine Bonfanti. **M:** Trevor Duncan. **Cast:** Jean Négroni, Hélène Chatelain, Davos Hanich, Jacques Ledoux, André Heinrich, Jacques Branchu, Pierre Joffroy, Étienne Becker. **Prix Jean Vigo** (Marker).

Panic in Year Zero! (1962). **D:** Ray Milland. **Sc:** John Morton, Jay Simms. Based on stories by Ward Moore. **P:** Arnold Houghland, Lou Rusoff. **M:** Les Baxter. **C:** Gilbert Warrenton. **Ed:** William Austin. **PDn:** Daniel Haller. **SDc:** Harry Reif. **Mk:** Ted Coodley. **SFx:** Larry Butler, Pat Dinga. **Cast:** Ray Milland, Jean Hagen, Frankie Avalon, Mary Mitchel, Joan Freeman, Richard Bakalyan.

The Birds (1963). **D, P:** Alfred Hitchcock. **Sc:** Evan Hunter. Story by Daphne Du Maurier. **C:** Robert Burks. **Ed:** George Tomasini. **PDn:** Robert Boyle. **SDc:** George Milo. **CDn:** Edith Head. **Mk:** Howard Smit. **H:** Virginia Darcy. **SFx:** Lawrence A. Hampton. **VFx:** Scott Dougherty. **Cast:** Rod Taylor, Jessica Tandy, Suzanne Pleshette, Tippi Hedren, Veronica Cartwright, Ethel Griffies, Charles McGraw, Ruth McDevitt.

Children of the Damned (1963). **D:** Anton M. Leader. **Sc:** John Briley. **P:** Ben Arbeid. **M:** Ron Goodwin. **C:** Davis Boulton. **Ed:** Ernest Walter. **Art:** Elliot Scott. **SFx:** Tom Howard. **Cast:** Ian Hendry, Alan Badel, Barbara Ferris, Alfred Burke, Sheila Allen, Ralph Michael, Patrick Wymark, Martin Miller.

The Damned [*These Are the Damned*] (1963). **D:** Joseph Losey. **Sc:** Evan Jones. Story by H. L. Lawrence. **P:** Anthony Hinds. **M:** James Bernard. **C:** Arthur Grant. **Ed:** Reginald Mills. **PDn:** Bernard Robinson. **Art:** Don Mingaye. **CDn:** Molly Arbuthnot. **Mk:** Roy Ashton. **H:** Frieda Steiger. **Cast:** Macdonald Carey, Shirley Anne Field, Oliver Reed, Alexander Knox, Walter Gotell, Viveca Lindfors, Kit Williams, Rachel Clay.

Day of the Triffids (1963). **D:** Steve Sekely. **Sc:** Philip Yordan. Based on novel by John Wyndham. **P:** George Pitcher. **M:** Johnny Douglas, Ron Goodwin. **C:** Ted Moore. **Art:** Cedric Dawe. **Mk:** Paul Rabiger. **H:** Eileen Warwick. **SFx:** Wally Veevers. **Cast:** Howard Keel, Nicole Maurey, Janette Scott, Kieron Moore, Mervyn Johns, Ewan Roberts.

Ladybug Ladybug (1963). **D, P:** Frank Perry. **Sc:** Eleanor Perry. Story by Lois Dickert. **M:** Bob Cobert. **C:** Leonard Hirschfield. **Ed:** Armond Lebowitz. **Art:** Albert Brenner. **CDn:** Anna Hill Johnstone. **S:** Stanley Kasper. **Cast:** Jane Connell, William Daniels, James Frawley, Richard Hamilton, Kathryn Hays, Jane Hoffman, Elena Karam, Judith Lowry, Estelle Parsons, Alice Playten.

Lord of the Flies (1963). **D:** Peter Brook. **Sc:** Peter Brook. Based on novel by William Golding. **P:** Lewis M. Allen. **M:** Raymond Leppard. **C:** Gerald Feil, Tom Hollyman. **Ed:** Peter Brook, Gerald Feil, Jean-Claude Lubtchansky. **Mk:** Lydia Rodriguez. **Cast:** James Aubrey, Tom Chapin, Hugh Edwards, Roger Elwin, Tom Gaman, Roger Allen, David Brunjes, Peter Davy.

Dr. Strangelove, or: How I Learned to Stop Worrying and Love the Bomb (1964). **D, P:** Stanley Kubrick. **Sc:** Stanley Kubrick, Terry Southern & Peter George. Based on novel by Peter George. **M:** Laurie Johnson. **C:** Gilbert Taylor. **Ed:** Anthony Harvey. **PDn:**

Ken Adam. **Art:** Peter Murton. **Mk:** Stewart Freeborn. **H:** Barbara Ritchie. **S:** John Cox. **SFx:** Willy Veevers. **VFx:** Vic Margutti. **Cast:** Peter Sellers, George C. Scott, Sterling Hayden, Keenan Wynn, Slim Pickens, Peter Bull, James Earl Jones, Tracy Reed, Jack Creley. **BAFTA** Best British Art Direction (B/W) (Ken Adam), Best British Film, Best Film, UN Award. **New York Film Critics** Best Director. **Writers Guild of America** Best Written Comedy (Kubrick & Southern & George).

Fail-Safe (1964). **D:** Sidney Lumet. **Sc:** Walter Bernstein. Based on novel by Eugene Burdick & Harvey Wheeler. **P:** Max E. Youngstein. **C:** Gerald Hirschfeld. **Ed:** Ralph Rosenblum. **Art:** Albert Brenner. **SDc:** J. C. Delaney. **CDn:** Anna Hill Johnstone. **Mk:** Harry Buchman. **S:** Jack Fitzstephens. **Cast:** Dan O'Herlihy, Walter Matthau, Frank Overton, Ed Binns, Fritz Weaver, Henry Fonda, Larry Hagman, William Hansen.

The Last Man on Earth (1964). **D:** Ubaldo B. Ragona (Italian prints), Sidney Salkow (non–Italian prints). **Sc:** William F. Leicester, Logan Swanson, Furio M. Monetti, Ubaldo B. Ragona. Based on novel by Richard Matheson. **P:** Robert L. Lippert. **M:** Paul Sawtell, Bert Shefter. **C:** Franco Delli Colli. **Ed:** Gene Ruggiero, Franca Silvi. **PDn:** Giorgio Giovannini. **SDc:** Brunello Serena Ulloa. **CDn:** Lilly Menichelli. **Mk:** Piero Mecacci. **Cast:** Vincent Price, Franca Bettoia, Emma Danieli, Giacomo Rossi-Stuart.

The Bedford Incident (1965). **D:** James B. Harris. **Sc:** James Poe. Based on novel by Mark Rascovitch. **P:** James B. Harris, Richard Widmark. **M:** Gérard Schurmann. **C:** Gilbert Taylor. **Ed:** John Jympson. **Art:** Arthur Lawson. **Mk:** Eric Allwright. **Cast:** Richard Widmark, Sidney Poitier, James MacArthur, Martin Balsam, Wally Cox, Eric Portman, Michael Kane, Colin Maitland.

The War Game (1965). Made for BBC TV. **D, Sc, P:** Peter Watkins. **C:** Peter Bartlett, Peter Suschitzky. **Ed:** Michael Bradsell. **CDn:** Vanessa Clarke. **Mk:** Lilias Munro. **Cast:** Michael Aspel, Peter Graham. **Academy Awards** Best Documentary Feature. **BAFTA** Best Short Film, UN Award. **Venice** Special Prize (Watkins).

The Deadly Bees (1967). **D:** Freddie Francis. **Sc:** Robert Bloch, Anthony Marriott. Based on novel by H. F. Heard. **P:** Max Rosenberg, Milton Subotsky. **M:** Wilfred Josephs. **C:** John Wilcox. **Ed:** Oswald Hafenrichter. **Art:** Bill Constable. **SDc:** Andrew Low. **Mk:** Jill Carpenter. **H:** Bobbie Smith. **SFx:** Michael Collins. **VFx:** John Mackie. **Cast:** Suzanna Leigh, Guy Doleman, Frank Finlay, Michael Ripper, Katy Wild, Catherine Finn.

Night of the Living Dead (1968). **D, C:** George A. Romero. **Sc:** John A. Russo, George A. Romero. **P:** Russell W. Streiner, Karl Hardman. **Ed:** George A. Romero, John A. Russo. **H:** Bruce Capristo. **SFx:** Regis Survinski, Tony Pantanello. **Cast:** Duane Jones, Judith O'Dea, Karl Hardman, Marilyn Eastman, Keith Wayne, Judith Ridley.

Planet of the Apes (1968). **D:** Franklin J. Schaffner. **Sc:** Michael Wilson, Rod Serling. Based on novel by Pierre Boulle. **P:** Arthur P. Jacobs. **M:** Jerry Goldsmith. **C:** Leon Shamroy. **Ed:** Hugh S. Fowler. **Art:** William Creber, Jack Martin Smith. **SDc:** Norman Rockett, Walter M. Scott. **CDn:** Morton Haack. **Mk:** John

Chambers. **S:** David Dockendorf, Herman Lewis. **SFx:** L. B. Abbott, Art Cruickshank, Emil Kosa Jr. **Cast:** Charlton Heston, Roddy McDowall, Kim Hunter, Maurice Evans, James Whitmore, James Daly, Linda Harrison, Robert Gunner.

Eye of the Cat (1969). **D:** David Lowell Rich. **Sc:** Joseph Stefano. **P:** Philip Hazelton, Bernard Schwartz, Leslie Stevens. **M:** Lalo Schifrin. **C:** Ellsworth Fredericks, Russell Metty. **Ed:** J. Terry Williams. **Art:** William D. DeCinces, Alexander Golitzen. **SDc:** John Austin, John McCarthy. **CDn:** Edith Head. **Mk:** Bud Westmore. **H:** Larry Germain. **S:** Waldon O. Watson, Frank H. Wilkinson. **Cast:** Michael Sarrazin, Gayle Hunnicutt, Eleanor Parker.

They Shoot Horses, Don't They? (1969). **D:** Sydney Pollack. **Sc:** James Poe, Robert E. Thompson. Based on novel by Horace McCoy. **P:** Robert Chartoff, Irwin Winkler. **C:** Philip H. Lathrop. **Ed:** Fredric Steinkamp. **PDn:** Harry Horner. **SDc:** Frank McKelvey. **CDn:** Donfeld. **Mk:** Frank McCoy. **H:** Sidney Guilaroff. **S:** Tom Overton. **Cast:** Jane Fonda, Michael Sarrazin, Susannah York, Gig Young, Red Buttons, Bonnie Bedelia, Michael Conrad, Bruce Dern. **Academy Awards** Best Supporting Actor (Young). **BAFTA** Best Supporting Actress (York). **Golden Globes** Best Supporting Actor (Young). **National Board of Review** Best Picture. **New York Film Critics** Best Actress (Fonda).

Airport (1970). **D:** George Seaton. **Sc:** George Seaton. Based on novel by Arthur Hailey. **P:** Ross Hunter. **M:** Alfred Newman. **C:** Ernest Laszlo. **Ed:** Stuart Gilmore. **Art:** E. Preston Ames, Alexander Golitzen. **SDc:** Mickey S. Michaels, Jack D. Moore. **CDn:** Edith Head. **Mk:** Bud Westmore. **H:** Larry Germain. **S:** David H. Moriarty, Ronald Pierce, Waldon O. Watson. **Cast:** Burt Lancaster, Dean Martin, Jean Seberg, Jacqueline Bisset, George Kennedy, Helen Hayes, Van Heflin, Maureen Stapleton. **Academy Awards** Best Supporting Actress (Hayes). **Golden Globes** Best Supporting Actress (Stapleton). **Motion Picture Sound Editors** Best Sound Editing — Dialogue.

The Hellstrom Chronicle (1971). **D:** Walon Green. **Sc:** David Seltzer. **P:** David Wolper, Walon Green. **M:** Lalo Schifrin. **C:** Helmuth Barth, Walon Green, Vilis Lapenieks. **Ed:** John Soh. **Cast:** Lawrence Pressman. **Academy Awards** Best Documentary Feature. **BAFTA** Flaherty Documentary Award.

The Omega Man (1971). **D:** Boris Sagal. **Sc:** John William Corrington & Joyce H. Corrington. Based on novel by Richard Matheson. **P:** Walter Seltzer. **M:** Ron Grainer. **C:** Russell Metty. **Ed:** William H. Ziegler. **Art:** Walter M. Simonds. **SDc:** William L. Kuehl. **Mk:** Gordon Bau. **H:** Jean Burt Reilly. **S:** Bob Martin. **Cast:** Charlton Heston, Anthony Zerbe, Rosalind Cash, Paul Koslo, Eric Laneuville.

Willard (1971). **D:** Daniel Mann. **Sc:** Gilbert Ralston (AKA Steven Gilbert). Based on his novel. **P:** Mort Briskin, Bing Crosby. **M:** Alex North. **C:** Robert B. Hauser. **Ed:** Warren Low. **Art:** Howard Hollander. **SDc:** Ralph S. Hurst. **CDn:** Dorothy Barkley, Eric Seelig. **Mk:** Gustaf Norin. **S:** Harold Lewis. **SFx:** Bud Davis. **Cast:** Bruce Davison, Elsa Lanchester, Ernest Borgnine, Sondra Locke, Michael Dante, Jody Gilbert.

Ben (1972). **D:** Phil Karlson. **Sc:** Gilbert Ralston (AKA Steven Gilbert). **P:** Mort Briskin, Bing Crosby. **M:** Walter Scharf. **C:** Russell Metty. **Ed:** Henry Gerstad. **Art:** Rolland M. Brooks. **SDc:** Antony Mondello. **CDn:** Ray Harp, Mina Mittelman. **Mk:** Jack H. Young. **H:** Hazel Washington. **Cast:** Lee Montgomery, Joseph Campanella, Arthur O'Connell, Rosemary Murphy, Meredith Baxter, Kaz Garas, Paul Carr, Richard Van Vleet. **Golden Globes** Best Original Song "Ben" (Scharf, Don Black).

Frogs (1972). **D:** George McCowan. **Sc:** Robert Blees, Robert Hutchison. **P:** George Edwards, Peter Thomas. **M:** Les Baxter. **C:** Mario Tosi. **Ed:** Fred R. Feitshans Jr. **CDn:** Phyllis Garr. **Mk:** Tom Burman. **H:** Jean Austin. **Cast:** Ray Milland, Sam Elliott, Joan Van Ark, Adam Roarke, Judy Pace, Lynn Borden, Mae Mercer, David Gilliam.

Night of the Lepus (1972). **D:** William F. Claxton. **Sc:** Don Holliday, Gene R. Kearney. Based on novel by Russell Braddon. **P:** A. C. Lyles. **M:** Jimmie Haskell. **C:** Ted Voightlander. **Ed:** John McSweeney Jr. **PDn:** Stan Jolley. **SDc:** William F. Calvert. **Mk:** Wes Dawn. **H:** Alma Johnson. **S:** Jerry Jost, Hal Watkins. **Cast:** Stuart Whitman, Janet Leigh, Rory Calhoun, DeForest Kelley, Paul Fix, Melanie Fullerton.

The Pied Piper (1972). **D:** Jacques Demy. **Sc:** Jacques Demy, Andrew Birkin, Mark Peploe. **P:** Sanford Lieberson, David Puttnam. **M:** Donovan. **C:** Peter Suschitzky. **Ed:** John Trumper. **PDn:** Assheton Gorton. **Art:** George Djurkovic. **CDn:** Evangeline Harrison. **Mk:** Bob Lawrence. **SFx:** John Stears. **Cast:** Jack Wild, Donovan, Michael Hordern, John Hurt, Cathryn Harrison, Donald Pleasence, Roger Hammond, Roy Kinnear.

The Poseidon Adventure (1972). **D:** Ronald Neame. **Sc:** Wendell Mayes, Stirling Silliphant. Based on novel by Paul Gallico. **P:** Irwin Allen. **M:** Joel Hirschhorn, Al Kasha, John Williams. **C:** Harold E. Stine. **Ed:** Harold F. Kress. **PDn:** William J. Creber. **SDc:** Raphael Bretton. **CDn:** Paul Zastupnevich. **SFx:** L. B. Abbott. **Cast:** Gene Hackman, Ernest Borgnine, Red Buttons, Carol Lynley, Roddy McDowall, Stella Stevens, Shelley Winters, Jack Albertson. **Academy Awards** Best Original Song "The Morning After" (Kasha, Hirschhorn). **BAFTA** Best Actor (Hackman). **Golden Globes** Best Supporting Actress in a Drama (Winters). **Motion Picture Sound Editors** Best Sound Editing—Dialogue.

Airport 75 (1974). **D:** Jack Smight. **Sc:** Don Ingalls. **P:** William Frye. **M:** John Cacavas. **C:** Philip Lathrop. **Ed:** J. Terry Williams. **Art:** George C. Webb. **SDc:** Mickey S. Michaels. **CDn:** Edith Head. **SFx:** Ben McMahan. **Cast:** Charlton Heston, Karen Black, George Kennedy, Gloria Swanson, Efrem Zimbalist Jr., Susan Clark, Helen Reddy, Linda Blair.

Earthquake (1974). **D, P:** Mark Robson. **Sc:** George Fox, Mario Puzo. **M:** John Williams. **C:** Philip Lathrop. **Ed:** Dorothy Spencer. **PDn:** Alexander Golitzen. **Art:** E. Preston Ames. **SDc:** Frank R. McKelvy. **CDn:** Burton Miller. **S:** Melvin M. Metcalfe Sr., Ronald Pierce. **SFx:** Frank Brendel. **VFx:** Ross Hoffmann. **Cast:** Charlton Heston, Ava Gardner, George Kennedy, Lorne Greene, Geneviève Bujold, Richard Roundtree, Marjoe Gortner, Barry Sullivan. **Academy Awards** Best Sound.

Juggernaut (1974). **D:** Richard Lester. **Sc:** Richard DeKoker, Alan Plater. **P:** Richard DeKoker. **M:** Ken Thorne. **C:** Gerry Fisher. **Ed:** Antony Gibbs. **PDn:** Terence Marsh. **Art:** Alan Tomkins. **CDn:** Evangeline Harrison. **Mk:** Wally Schneiderman. **H:** Mike Jones. **SFx:** John Richardson. **Cast:** Richard Harris, Omar Sharif, David Hemmings, Anthony Hopkins, Shirley Knight, Ian Holm, Clifton James, Roy Kinnear.

The Killer Bees (1974). Made for TV. **D:** Curtis Harrington. **Sc:** John William Corrington, Joyce Hooper Corrington. **P:** Ron Bernstein, Howard Rosenman. **M:** David Shire. **C:** Jack Woolf. **Ed:** Robert A. Daniels, John W. Holmes. **PDn:** Joel Schumacher. **SDc:** Chuck Pierce**Mk:** Paul Stanhope. **H:** Jean Austin. **SFx:** Henry Millar. **VFx:** Frank Van der Veer. **Cast:** Edward Albert, Kate Jackson, Gloria Swanson, Roger Davis, Don McGovern, Craig Stevens, John S. Ragin, Liam Dunn.

Phase IV (1974). **D:** Saul Bass. **Sc:** Mayo Simon. **P:** Paul B. Radin. **M:** Brian Gascoigne. **C:** Dick Bush. **Ed:** Willy Kemplen. **Art:** John Barry. **CDn:** Verena Coleman. **Mk:** Freddie Williamson. **H:** Betty Glasow. **SFx:** John Richardson. **Cast:** Michael Murphy, Nigel Davenport, Lynne Frederick, Alan Gifford, Robert Henderson, Helen Horton.

Rhinoceros (1974). **D:** Tom O'Horgan. **Sc:** Julian Barry. Based on play by Eugène Ionesco. **P:** Ely Landau. **M:** Galt MacDermot. **C:** James Crabe. **Ed:** Bud Smith. **PDn:** Jack Martin Smith. **SDc:** Norman Rockett, Darrell Silvera. **CDn:** Noel Taylor. **Mk:** Jack Petty. **H:** Dee Dee Petty. **SFx:** Robert Dawson. **Cast:** Zero Mostel, Gene Wilder, Karen Black, Joe Silver, Robert Weil, Marilyn Chris, Percy Rodriguez, Robert Fields.

The Towering Inferno (1974). **D:** John Guillermin. **Sc:** Stirling Silliphant. Based on novels by Richard Martin Stern and Thomas N. Scortia & Frank M. Robinson. **P:** Irwin Allen. **D of action sequences:** Irwin Allen. **M:** John Williams. **C:** Fred Koenekamp, Joseph Biroc (action sequences). **Ed:** Harold F. Kress, Carl Kress. **PDn:** William Creber. **Art:** Ward Preston. **SDc:** Raphael Bretton. **CDn:** Paul Zastupnevich. **SFx:** L. B. Abbott. **VFx:** Douglas Trumbull. **Cast:** Steve McQueen, Paul Newman, William Holden, Faye Dunaway, Fred Astaire, Susan Blakely, Richard Chamberlain, Jennifer Jones, O. J. Simpson, Robert Vaughn, Robert Wagner, Susan Flannery, Dabney Coleman. **Academy Awards** Best Cinematography (Koenekamp, Biroc), Best Film Editing. Best Original Song "We May Never Love Like This Again" (Kasha, Hirschhorn). **BAFTA** Anthony Asquith Award for Film Music, Best Supporting Actor (Astaire). **Golden Globes** Best Supporting Actor (Astaire), Most Promising Female Newcomer (Flannery). **Motion Picture Sound Editors** Best Sound Editing—Dialogue.

Bug (1975). **D:** Jeannot Szwarc. **Sc:** William Castle, Thomas Page. Based on novel by Thomas Page. **P:** William Castle. **M:** Charles Fox. **C:** Michel Hugo. **Ed:** Allan Jacobs. **Art:** Jack Martin Smith. **SDc:** Reg Allen. **Mk:** Tom Miller Jr. **H:** Judy Alexander. **SFx:** Phil Cory. **Cast:** Bradford Dillman, Joanna Miles, Richard Gilliland, Jamie Smith Jackson, Alan Fudge, Jesse Vint, Patty McCormack, Brendan Dillon.

The Hindenburg (1975). D, P: Robert Wise. Sc: Nelson Gidding. Based on novel by Michael M. Mooney and story by Richard A. Levinson and William Link. M: David Shire. C: Robert Surtees. Ed: Donn Cambern. PDn: Edward C. Carfagno. SDc: Frank McKelvy. CDn: Dorothy Jeakins. S: Leonard Peterson, Don Sharpless. VFx: Albert Whitlock. Cast: George C. Scott, Anne Bancroft, William Atherton, Roy Thinnes, Gig Young, Burgess Meredith, Charles Durning, Richard A. Dysart.

Jaws (1975). D: Steven Spielberg. Sc: Peter Benchley, Carl Gottlieb. Based on novel by Peter Benchley. P: David Brown, Richard D. Zanuck. M: John Williams. C: Bill Butler. Ed: Verna Fields. PDn: Joseph Alves Jr. SDc: John M. Dwyer. S: John R. Carter, Robert Hoyt. Cast: Roy Scheider, Robert Shaw, Richard Dreyfuss, Lorraine Gary, Murray Hamilton, Carl Gottlieb. **Academy Awards** Best Editing, Best Original Score, Best Sound. **American Cinema Editors** Best Edited Feature. **BAFTA** Anthony Asquith Award for Film Music. **Golden Globes** Best Original Score.

Picnic at Hanging Rock (1975). D: Peter Weir. Sc: Cliff Green. Based on novel by Joan Lindsay. P: Hal McElroy, Jim McElroy. M: Bruce Smeaton. C: Russell Boyd. Ed: Max Lemon. Art: David Copping. CDn: Judy Dorsman. Mk: Jose Perez. Cast: Rachel Roberts, Dominic Guard, Helen Morse, Jacki Weaver, Anne Lambert, Margaret Nelson, Vivean Gray.

The Last Wave (1977). D: Peter Weir. Sc: Peter Weir & Tony Morphett & Petru Popescu. P: Hal McElroy, James McElroy. M: Charles Wain. C: Russell Boyd. Ed: Max Lemon. PDn: Goran Warff. Art: Neil Angwin. SDc: Bill Malcolm. CDn: Annie Bleakley. Mk: Jose Perez. H: Jose Perez. S: Don Connolly, Greg Bell, Phil Judd. SFx: Monty Fieguth, Bob Hilditch. Cast: Richard Chamberlain, Olivia Hamnett, Gulpilil, Frederick Parslow, Vivean Gray, Nandjiwarra Amagula, Walter Amagula, Roy Bara. **Australian Film Institute** Best Cinematography, Best Sound.

Dawn of the Dead [George A. Romero's Dawn of the Dead] (1978). D, Sc, Ed: George A. Romero. P: Dario Argento, Richard P. Rubinstein. M: The Goblins, Agostino Marangolo, Massimo Morante, Fabio Pignatelli, George A. Romero (director's cut), Claudio Simonetti. C: Michael Gornick. SDc: Josie Caruso, Barbara Lifsher. CDn: Josie Caruso. S: Tony Buba. SFx: Tom Savini, Gary Zeller. VFx: Arthur J. Canestro. Cast: David Emge, Ken Foree, Scott H. Reiniger, Gaylen Ross, David Crawford, David Early, Richard France, Howard Smith.

The Swarm (1978). D, P: Irwin Allen. Sc: Stirling Silliphant. Based on novel by Arthur Herzog. M: Jerry Goldsmith. C: Fred J. Koenekamp. Ed: Harold F. Kress. PDn: Stan Jolley. SDc: Stuart Reiss. CDn: Paul Zastupnevich. Mk: Tony Lloyd. H: Ruby Ford. SDn: Harold Fuhrman, Alfred M. Kemper. SFx: L. B. Abbott, Howard Jensen. Cast: Michael Caine, Katharine Ross, Richard Widmark, Richard Chamberlain, Olivia de Havilland, Ben Johnson, Lee Grant, Jose Ferrer, Patty Duke Astin, Slim Pickens, Bradford Dillman, Fred MacMurray, Henry Fonda, Alejandro Rey.

Alien (1979). D: Ridley Scott. Sc: Dan O'Bannon. Story by Dan O'Bannon and Ronald Shusett. P: Gordon Carroll, David Giler, Walter Hill. M: Jerry Goldsmith. C: Derek Vanlint. Ed: Terry Rawlings. PDn: Michael Seymour. Art: Les Dilley, Roger Christian. SDc: Ian Whittaker. CDn: John Mollo. Mk: Tommy Manderson. SFx: Nick Allder, H. R. Giger, Brian Johnson, Carlo Rambaldi. Cast: Tom Skerritt, Sigourney Weaver, Veronica Cartwright, Harry Dean Stanton, John Hurt, Ian Holm, Yaphet Kotto. **Academy Awards** Best Visual Effects. **BAFTA** Best Production Design, Best Soundtrack (Derrick Leather, Jim Shields, Bill Rowe).

The Atomic Café (1982). D, P: Jayne Loader, Kevin Rafferty, Pierce Rafferty. Ed: Jayne Loader, Kevin Rafferty. S: Marge Crimmins. Cast: Lloyd Bentsen, Owen Brewster, Frank Gallop, Lyndon B. Johnson, Nikita Khrushchev, Paul Tibbets.

The Day After (1983). Made for TV. D: Nicholas Meyer. Sc: Edward Hume. P: Robert A. Papazian Jr. M: David Raksin. C: Gayne Rescher. Ed: William Paul Dornisch, Robert Florio. PDn: Peter Wooley. SDc: Mary Ann Good. Mk: Michael Westmore. H: Dorothie J. Long. VFx: Chris Regan. Cast: Jason Robards, JoBeth Williams, Steven Guttenberg, John Cullum, John Lithgow, Bibi Besch, Lori Lethin, Amy Madigan. **Emmy Awards** Outstanding Film Sound Editing — Limited Series or Special, Outstanding Individual Achievement — Special Visual Effects.

Special Bulletin (1983). Made for TV. D: Ed Zwick. Sc, P: Marshall Herskovitz & Ed Zwick. Story by Marshall Herskovitz. Ed: Arden Rynew. PDn: Robb Wilson King. Cast: Rosalind Cash, David Clennon, Ed Flanders, Michael Madsen, George Morfogen, David Rasche, Lane Smith, Kathryn Walker. **Emmy Awards** Outstanding Drama Special, Outstanding Technical Direction, Outstanding Video Tape Editing — Limited Series or Special, Outstanding Writing — Limited Series or Special.

Testament (1983). D: Lynne Littman. Sc: John Sacret Young. Story by Carol Amen. P: Jonathan Bernstein, Lynne Littman. M: James Horner. C: Steven Poster. Ed: Suzanne Pettit. PDn: David Nichols. Art: Linda Pearl. SDc: Waldemar Kalinowski. CDn: Julie Weiss. Cast: Jane Alexander, William Devane, Ross Harris, Roxana Zal, Lukas Haas, Philip Anglim, Lilia Skala.

WarGames (1983). D: John Badham. Sc: Lawrence Lasker, Walter F. Parkes. P: Harold Schneider. M: Arthur B. Rubinstein. C: William A. Fraker. Ed: Tom Rolf. PDn: Angelo P. Graham. Art: James J. Murakami. SDc: Jerry Wunderlich. CDn: Barry F. Delaney. SFx: Joe Digaetano. Cast: Matthew Broderick, Dabney Coleman, John Wood, Ally Sheedy, Barry Corbin, Kent Williams. **American Cinema Editors** Best Edited Feature Film. **BAFTA** Best Sound.

Countdown to Looking Glass (1984). D: Fred Barzyk. Sc: Albert Ruben. P: David R. Loxton. C: Miklós Lente. Ed: Bernie Clayton, Peter C. Frank, Leah Siegel. Art: Ted Watkins. SDc: Barry Kemp, Christine MacLean. CDn: Kathy Vieira. Mk: Shonagh Jabour. H: Ivan Lynch. Cast: Scott Glenn, Michael Murphy, Helen Shaver, Patrick Watson, Nancy Dickerson, Eric Sevareid.

Day of the Dead [George A. Romero's Day of

the Dead] (1985). **D, Sc, Ed:** George A. Romero. **P:** Dario Argento, Richard P. Rubinstein. **M:** The Goblins, Agostino Marangolo, Massimo Morante, Fabio Pignatelli, George A. Romero (director's cut), Claudio Simonetti. **C:** Michael Gornick. **SDc:** Josie Caruso, Barbara Lifsher. **CDn:** Josie Caruso. **S:** Tony Buba. **SFx:** Tom Savini, Gary Zeller. **VFx:** Arthur J. Canestro. **Cast:** David Emge, Ken Foree, Scott H. Reiniger, Gaylen Ross, David Crawford, David Early, Richard France, Howard Smith. **Golden Screen (Germany)** Golden Screen.

The Mosquito Coast (1986). **D:** Peter Weir. **Sc:** Paul Schrader. Based on novel by Paul Theroux. **P:** Jerome Hellman. **M:** Maurice Jarre. **C:** John Seale. **Ed:** Thom Noble. **PDn:** John Stoddart. **Art:** John Wingrove. **SDc:** John Anderson. **CDn:** Gary Jones. **Cast:** Harrison Ford, Helen Mirren, River Phoenix, Conrad Roberts, Andre Gregory, Martha Plimpton, Dick O'Neill, Jason Alexander, Butterfly McQueen.

The Sacrifice [*Offret*] (1986). **D, Sc:** Andrei Tarkovsky. **P:** Anna-Lena Wibom. **C:** Sven Nykvist. **Ed:** Michal Leszczylowski, Andrei Tarkovsky. **PDn:** Anna Asp. **CDn:** Inger Pehrsson. **SFx:** Lars Höglund, Lars Palmquist. **Cast:** Erland Josephson, Susan Fleetwood, Tommy Kjellqvist, Allan Edwall, Gudún S. Gísladóttir, Sven Wollter, Valérie Mairesse, Filippa Franzén. **BAFTA** Best Foreign Language Film (Wibom, Tarkovsky). **Cannes** Best Artistic Contribution (Nykvist); FIPRESCI, Grand Prize of the Jury, Prize of the Ecumenical Jury (Tarkovsky).

Predator (1987). **D:** John McTiernan. **Sc:** Jim Thomas & John Thomas. **P:** John Davis, Lawrence Gordon, Joel Silver. **M:** Alan Silvestri. **C:** Donald McAlpine. **Ed:** Mark Helfrich, John F. Link. **PDn:** John Vallone. **SDc:** Enrique Estévez. **CDn:** Marilyn Vance-Straker. **SFx:** Laurencio Cordero, Al Di Sarro. **Cast:** Arnold Schwarzenegger, Carl Weathers, Elpidia Carrillo, Bill Duke, Jesse Ventura, R. G. Armstrong, Kevin Peter Hall. **Motion Picture Sound Editors** Best Editing of Sound Effects (Richard Shorr).

Arachnophobia (1990). **D:** Frank Marshall. **Sc:** Don Jakoby, Wesley Strick. Story by Don Jakoby & Al Williams. **P:** Richard Vane. **M:** Trevor Jones. **C:** Mikael Salomon. **Ed:** Michael Kahn. **PDn:** James Bissell. **Art:** Christopher Burian-Mohr. **SDc:** Jackie Carr. **CDn:** Jennifer L. Parsons. **SDn:** Carl J. Stensel. **SFx:** Matt Sweeney, Chris Walas. **VFx:** Alison Savitch, David Sosalla. **Cast:** Jeff Daniels, Harley Jane, John Goodman, Julian Sands, Stuart Pankin, Brian McNamara, Mark L. Taylor, Henry Jones.

Tremors (1990). **D:** Ron Underwood. **Sc:** S. S. Wilson & Brent Maddock. Story by S. S. Wilson & Brent Maddock & Ron Underwood. **P:** Brent Maddock, S. S. Wilson. **M:** Ernest Troost. **C:** Alexander Gruszynski. **Ed:** O. Nicholas Brown. **PDn:** Ivo Cristante. **Art:** Don Maskovich. **SDc:** Debra Combs. **CDn:** Abigail Murray. **S:** Oscar Mitt. **VFx:** Lise Romanoff, Robert Skotak. **Cast:** Kevin Bacon, Fred Ward, Finn Carter, Michael Gross, Reba McEntire, Bobby Jacoby.

Poison (1991). **D, Sc:** Todd Haynes. Based on novels by Jean Genet. **P:** Christine Vachon. **M:** James Bennett. **C:** Maryse Alberti, Barry Ellsworth. **Ed:** James Lyons, Todd Haynes. **PDn:** Sarah Stollman. **Art:** Chas

Plummer. **CDn:** Jessica Haston. **Mk:** Angela Johnson, Scott Sliger. **H:** Angela Johnson. **Cast:** Edith Meeks (Hero); Larry Maxwell, Susan Gayle Norman (Horror); Scott Renderer, James Lyons, Tony Pemberton, Andrew Harpending, John Leguizamo (as Damien Garcia) (Homo). **Berlin** Best Feature Film (Haynes). **Sundance** Grand Jury Prize, Dramatic (Haynes).

Jurassic Park (1993). **D:** Steven Spielberg. **Sc:** Michael Crichton, David Koepp. Based on novel by Michael Crichton. **P:** Kathleen Kennedy, Gerald R. Molen. **M:** John Williams. **C:** Dean Cundey. **Ed:** Michael Kahn. **PDn:** Rick Carter. **Art:** John Bell, Jim Teegarden. **SDc:** Jackie Carr. **Mk:** Christina Smith. **H:** Lynda Gurasich. **S:** Gary Rydstrom. **Cast:** Sam Neill, Laura Dern, Jeff Goldblum, Richard Attenborough. **Academy Awards** Best Sound Effects Editing, Best Visual Effects, Best Sound. **BAFTA** Best Special Effects. **Motion Picture Sound Editors** Best Editing of Sound Effects.

The Birds II: Land's End (1994). Made for TV. **D:** "Alan Smithee." **Sc:** Ken Wheat & Jim Wheat and Robert Eisele. **P:** Ted Kurdyla. **M:** Ron Ramin. **C:** Bruce Surtees. **Mk:** Jeff Goodwin, Rodney Petreikis. **SFx:** Kevin Brennan, Vincent Montefusco. **VFx:** David Emerson. **Cast:** Brad Johnson, Chelsea Field, James Naughton, Jan Rubes, Tippi Hedren, Stephanie Milford.

Safe (1995). **D, Sc:** Todd Haynes. **P:** Christine Vachon, Lauren Zalaznick. **M:** Brendan Dolan, Ed Tomney. **C:** Alex Nepomniaschy. **Ed:** James Lyons. **PDn:** David Bomba. **Art:** Anthony R. Stabley. **SDc:** Mary E. Gullickson. **CDn:** Nancy Steiner. **Mk:** David Syner. **Cast:** Julianne Moore, Peter Friedman, Xander Berkeley, Susan Norman, Kate McGregor Stewart, Mary Carver.

Independence Day (1996). **D:** Roland Emmerich. **Sc:** Dean Devlin & Roland Emmerich. **P:** Dean Devlin. **M:** David Arnold. **C:** Karl Walter Lindenlaub. **Ed:** David Brenner. **PDn:** Oliver Scholl, Patrick Tatopoulos. **Art:** Jim Teegarden. **SDc:** Jim Erickson. **CDn:** Joseph Porro. **H:** Aaron F. Quarles, Joy Zapata. **S:** John Paul Fasal, Jonathan Miller. **VFx:** Volker Engel, Douglas Smith, Clay Pinney, Joe Viskocil. **Cast:** Will Smith, Bill Pullman, Jeff Goldblum, Mary McDonnell, Judd Hirsch, Robert Loggia, Randy Quaid, Margaret Colin, Vivica A. Fox, James Rebhorn, Harvey Fierstein. **Academy Awards** Best Visual Effects.

Mars Attacks! (1996). **D:** Tim Burton. **Sc:** Jonathan Gems. **P:** Tim Burton, Larry Franco. **M:** Danny Elfman. **C:** Peter Suschitzky. **Ed:** Chris Lebenzon. **PDn:** Wynn Thomas. **Art:** John Dexter. **SDc:** Nancy Haigh. **CDn:** Colleen Atwood. **Mk:** Valli O'Reilly, Julie Steffes. **H:** Candace Neal. **SDn:** Richard Berger, Ron Mendell. **S:** Randy Thom. **VFx:** Tim McLaughlin. **Cast:** Jack Nicholson, Glenn Close, Annette Bening, Pierce Brosnan, Danny DeVito, Martin Short, Sarah Jessica Parker, Michael J. Fox, Rod Steiger.

Tornado! (1996). **D:** Noel Nosseck. **Sc:** John Logan. **P:** Artie Mandelberg, Stacy Mandelberg, Randy Sutter. **M:** Garry Schyman. **C:** Paul Maibaum. **Ed:** David Codron, Robert Florio. **PDn:** Seven Nielsen. **SDc:** Tad Smalley. **CDn:** Robert Moore. **H:** Catherine Conrad. **Mk:** David Syner. **Cast:** Bruce Campbell, Shannon

Sturges, Ernie Hudson, L. Q. Jones, Bo Eason, Charles Homet.

Twister (1996). **D:** Jan de Bont. **Sc:** Michael Crichton & Anne-Marie Martin. **P:** Ian Bryce, Michael Crichton, Kathleen Kennedy. **M:** Mark Mancina. **C:** Jack N. Green. **Ed:** Michael Kahn. **PDn:** Joseph Nemec III. **SDc:** Ron Reiss. **CDn:** Ellen Mirojnick. **SDn:** Patrick Sullivan. **Cast:** Helen Hunt, Bill Paxton, Cary Elwes, Jami Gertz, Philip Seymour Hoffman, Lois Smith.

Anaconda (1997). **D:** Luis Llosa. **Sc:** Hans Bauer and Jim Cash & Jack Epps Jr. **P:** Verna Harrah, Carole Little, Leonard Rabinowitz. **M:** Randy Edelman. **C:** Bill Butler. **Ed:** Michael R. Miller. **PDn:** Kirk M. Petruccelli. **Art:** Barry Chusid. **SDc:** Daniel L. May. **CDn:** Kathy Monderine. **SDn:** Barbara Mesney. **SFx:** Chuck Gaspar. **VFx:** Bill Ball, Janek Sirrs. **Cast:** Jennifer Lopez, Ice Cube, Jon Voight, Eric Stoltz, Jonathan Hyde, Owen Wilson.

Dante's Peak (1997). **D:** Roger Donaldson. **Sc:** Leslie Bohem. **P:** Gale Anne Hurd, Joseph M. Singer. **M:** John Frizzell. **C:** Andrzej Bartkowiak. **Ed:** Conrad Buff, Tina Hirsch, Howard Smith. **PDn:** Dennis Washington. **Art:** Francis J. Pezza, Thomas T. Taylor. **SDc:** Marvin March. **CDn:** Isis Mussenden. **S:** Michael M. Geisler, Geoffrey Rubay. **Cast:** Pierce Brosnan, Linda Hamilton, Charles Hallahan, Jamie Renée Smith, Jeremy Foley, Elizabeth Hoffman, Grant Heslov.

The Lost World (1997). **D:** Steven Spielberg. **Sc:** David Koepp. Based on novel by Michael Crichton. **P:** Gerald R. Molen, Colin Wilson. **M:** John Williams. **C:** Janusz Kaminski. **Ed:** Michael Kahn. **PDn:** Rick Carter. **SDc:** Gary Fettis. **S:** Gary Rydstrom. **VFx:** George Hull, Mark "Crash" McCreery. **Cast:** Jeff Goldblum, Julianne Moore, Pete Postlethwaite, Richard Attenborough, Vince Vaughn, Arliss Howard, Vanessa Lee Chester, Peter Stormare.

Mimic (1997). **D:** Guillermo Del Toro. **Sc:** Matthew Robbins & Guillermo Del Toro. Based on story by Donald A. Wollheim. **P:** Ole Bornedal, B. J. Rack, Bob Weinstein. **M:** Marco Beltrami. **C:** Dan Laustsen. **Ed:** Peter Devaney Flanagan, Patrick Lussier. **PDn:** Carol Spier. **Art:** Tamara Deverell. **SDc:** Elinor Rose Galbraith. **CDn:** Marie-Sylvie Deveau. **Mk:** Donald Mowat. **SDn:** Michael Madden. **S:** Steve Boeddeker, Randy Thom. **SFx:** Stephen R. Blandino, Thomas Rasada, Kenneth Van Order. **Cast:** Mira Sorvino, Jeremy Northam, Alexander Goodwin, Giancarlo Giannini, Charles S. Dutton, Josh Brolin, Alix Koromzay, F. Murray Abraham.

Volcano (1997). **D:** Mick Jackson. **Sc:** Jerome Armstrong, Billy Ray. **P:** Andrew Z. Davis, Neal H. Moritz. **M:** Alan Silvestri. **C:** Theo van de Sande. **Ed:** Don Brochu, Michael Tronick. **PDn:** Jackson DeGovia. **SDc:** K. C. Fox. **CDn:** Kirsten Everberg. **Mk:** Michael Mills, Elaine L. Offers. **H:** Bonnie Walker, Ellen Powell. **S:** Christopher Boyes. **Cast:** Tommy Lee Jones, Anne Heche, Gaby Hoffmann, Don Cheadle, Jacqueline Kim, Keith David, John Corbett, Michael Rispoli.

King Cobra (1999). **D, Sc:** David Hillenbrand, Scott Hillenbrand. **P:** David Hillenbrand, Scott Hillenbrand, Guy Stodel. **M:** David Berrel (David Hillenbrand). **C:** Philip D. Schwartz. **Ed:** Guy W. Cearley.

PDn: Jack Cloud. **SDc:** Laura Evans. **CDn:** Hana Rausalova. **S:** David Kitchens. **SFx:** Charles Chiodo, Edward Chiodo, Stephen Chiodo. **VFx:** Jeff Matakovich. **Cast:** Pat Morita, Scott Brandon (Scott Hillenbrand), Kasey Fallo, Hoyt Axton, Joseph Ruskin, Courtney Gains, Erik Estrada.

The Perfect Storm (2000). **D:** Wolfgang Petersen. **Sc:** Bill Wittliff. Based on novel by Sebastian Junger. **P:** Gail Katz, Wolfgang Petersen, Paula Weinstein. **M:** James Horner. **C:** John Seale. **Ed:** Richard Francis-Bruce. **PDn:** William Sandell. **Art:** Chas Butcher, Bruce Crone. **SDc:** Ernie Bishop. **CDn:** Erica Edell Phillips. **Mk:** Susan Cabral-Ebert, Donald Mowat. **Cast:** George Clooney, Mark Wahlberg, Diane Lane, John C. Reilly, William Fichtner, Bob Gunton, Karen Allen, Mary Elizabeth Mastrantonio.

Spiders (2000). **D:** Gary Jones. **Sc:** Stephen David Brooks and Jace Anderson & Adam Gierasch. Story by Boaz Davidson. **P:** Boaz Davidson, Danny Lerner. **M:** Bill Wandel. **C:** Jack Cooperman. **Ed:** Christopher Holmes. **PDn:** Maria Terry. **Art:** Michael Costello. **CDn:** Emma Trenchard. **VFx:** Scott Coulter. **Cast:** Lana Parrilla, Josh Green, Oliver Macready, Nick Swarts, Mark Phelan, David Carpenter.

Survivor (2000 through 2009, ongoing). TV series. Borneo (first season) 2000; The Australian Outback (second season) 2001; Africa (third season) 2001-2002; Marquesas (fourth season) 2002; Thailand (fifth season) 2002; The Amazon (sixth season) 2003; Pearl Islands (seventh season) 2003; All-Stars (eighth season) 2004; Vanuatu — Islands of Fire (ninth season) 2004; Palau (tenth season) 2005; Guatemala — The Maya Empire (eleventh season) 2005; Panama — Exile Island (twelfth season) 2006; Cook Islands (thirteenth season) 2006; Fiji (fourteenth season) 2007; China (fifteenth season) 2007; Micronesia — Fans vs. Favorites (sixteenth season) 2008; Gabon — Earth's Last Eden (seventeenth season) 2008. **P:** Mark Burnett. **PDn:** Wendell Johnson, Kelly Van Patter. **Host:** Jeff Probst.

Arachnid (2001). **D:** Jack Sholder. **Sc:** Mark Sevi. **P:** Julio Fernández, Brian Yuzna. **M:** Francesc Gener. **C:** Carlos González. **Ed:** Jaume Vilalta. **PDn:** Llorenç Miquel. **Art:** Enrique Echeverría. **Mk:** Susana Sánchez. **SFx:** Steve Johnson. **VFx:** Jaume Vilaseca. **Cast:** Chris Potter, Alex Reid, José Sancho, Neus Asensi, Ravil Isyanov, Watts Rockeford Allen.

Fear Factor (2001 through 2006, six seasons). TV series. **D:** J. Rupert Thompson. **P:** Rich Brown, Michael J. Glazer, Tom Herschko, Scott Larsen. **M:** Russ Landau. **C:** Vincent Contarino, Victor Nelli Jr., Matt Sohn, Monty Woodard. **SFx:** Michael Kay, Lee McConnell. **Host:** Joe Rogan.

Spiders 2: Breeding Ground (2001). **D:** Sam Firstenberg. **Sc:** Stephen Brooks. Story by Boaz Davidson. **P:** Boaz Davidson, Danny Lerner, David Varod. **M:** Serge Colbert. **C:** Peter Belcher, Plamen Somov. **Ed:** Irit Raz. **PDn:** Carlos Da Silva. **Art:** Johnny Breedt. **SDc:** Valentina Mladenova. **CDn:** Sonya Despotova. **Mk:** Ivon Ivanova. **H:** Rositsa Tsanovska. **VFx:** Ajoy Mani. **Cast:** Stephanie Niznik, Greg Cromer, Daniel Quinn, Richard Moll, Harel Noff, Yuri Savchev.

Cabin Fever (2002). **D:** Eli Roth. **Sc:** Eli Roth, Randy Pearlstein. Story by Eli Roth. **P:** Evan Astrowsky,

Sam Froelich, Lauren Moews, Eli Roth. **M:** Angelo Badalamenti, Nathan Barr. **C:** Scott Kevan. **Ed:** Ryan Folsey. **PDn:** Franco-Giacomo Carbone. **CDn:** Paloma Candelaria. **Cast:** Rider Strong, Jordan Ladd, James DeBello, Cerina Vincent, Joey Kern, Robert Harris.

Eight Legged Freaks (2002). **D:** Ellory Elkayem. **Sc:** Jesse Alexander & Ellory Elkayem. Story by Ellory Elkayem & Randy Kornfield. **P:** Bruce Berman, Dean Devlin. **M:** John Ottman. **C:** John S. Bartley. **Ed:** David Siegel. **PDn:** Charles Breen. **Art:** Charles Butcher. **SDc:** Marcia Calosio. **CDn:** Alix Friedberg. **H:** Scott W. Farley. **SDn:** Matthew Bekoff, Beverli Eagan. **VFx:** Xye. **Cast:** David Arquette, Kari Wuhrer, Scott Terra, Scarlett Johansson, Doug E. Doug, Rick Overton.

11'09"01, September 11 [*September 11*] (2002). **D:** Youssef Chahine (Egypt); Amos Gitaï (Israel); Alejandro González Iñárritu (Mexico); Shohei Imamura (Japan); Claude Lelouch (France); Ken Loach (United Kingdom); Samira Makhmalbaf (Iran); Mira Nair (India); Idrissa Ouedraogo (Burkina Faso); Sean Penn (USA); Danis Tanovic (Bosnia-Herzegovina). **Sc:** Youssef Chahine; Amos Gitai, Marie-Jose Sanselme; Alejandro González Iñárritu; Daisuke Tengan; Claude Lelouch, Pierre Uytterhoeven; Paul Laverty, Ken Loach, Vladimir Vega; Samira Makhmalbaf; Sabrina Dhawan; Idrissa Ouedraogo; Sean Penn; Danis Tanovic. **C:** Mohsen Nasr; Yoav Kosh; stock footage; Masakazu Oka; Pierre-William Glenn; Jorge Müller Silva, Nigel Willoughby; Ebrahim Ghafori; Declan Quinn; Luc Drion; Samuel Bayer; Mustafa Mustafic. **Ed:** Rashida Abdel Salam; Kobi Netanel; Kim Bica, Robert Duffy; Hajime Okayasu; Stéphane Mazalaigue; Jonathan Morris; Mohsen Makhmalbaf; Allyson C. Johnson; Julia Gregory; Jay Lash Cassidy; Monique Rysselinck; Sherif Ezzat. **Cast:** Nour El-Sherif, Ahmed Haroun; Keren Mor, Liron Levo, Tomer Russo; Jake Bern; Tomorowo Taguchi, Kumiko Aso, Akira Emoto, Mitsuko Baisho, Tetsuro Tamba, Ken Ogata; Emmanuelle Laborit, Jérôme Horry; Vladimir Vega, George W. Bush, Henry Kissinger, Augusto Pinochet, Salvador Allende; Maryam Karimi; Tanvi Azmi, Kapil Bawa, Taleb Adlah, George R. Sheffey; Lionel Zizréel Guire, René Aimé Bassinga, Lionel Gaël Folikoue, Rodrigue André Idani, Alex Martial Traoré; Ernest Borgnine; Dzana Pinjo, Aleksandar Seksan, Tatjana Sojic. **Venice** FIPRESCI Prize Best Short Film (Ken Loach), UNESCO Award (all directors).

9/11 (2002). Made for TV. **D:** Gédéon Naudet, Jules Naudet, James Hanlon. **Sc:** Tom Forman, Greg Kandra. **P:** Richard Barber, Paul Larossa, Michael Maloy, Bruce Spiegel, Mead Stone. **M:** Richard Fiocca, Michael S. Patterson. **C:** James Hanlon, Gédéon Naudet, Jules Naudet. **Ed:** Richard Barber, Michael Maloy, Jason Schmidt, Bruce Spiegel, Mead Stone. **S:** John Hassler. **Cast:** Tony Benatatos, Jamal Braithwaite, Joseph Casaliggi, James Hanlon, Gédéon Naudet, Jules Naudet, Joseph Pfeifer, Tom Spinard, Dennis Tardio, George W. Bush, Mychal Judge. **Emmy Awards** Outstanding Nonfiction Special, Outstanding Sound Mixing for Nonfiction.

Signs (2002). **D, Sc:** M. Night Shyamalan. **P:** Frank Marshall, Sam Mercer, M. Night Shyamalan. **M:** James Newton Howard. **C:** Tak Fujimoto. **Ed:** Barbara Tulliver. **PDn:** Larry Fulton. **Art:** Keith P. Cunningham. **SDc:** Douglas Mowat. **CDn:** Ann Roth. **Mk:** Bernadette Mazur. **H:** Francesca Paris. **S:** Richard King. **Cast:** Mel Gibson, Joaquin Phoenix, Rory Culkin, Abigail Breslin, Cherry Jones, M. Night Shyamalan, Patricia Kalember, Ted Sutton.

Time of the Wolf [*Le Temps du Loup*] (2002). **D, Sc:** Michael Haneke. **P:** Veit Heiduschka, Margaret Ménégoz. **C:** Jürgen Jürges. **Ed:** Nadine Muse, Monika Willi. **PDn:** Christoph Kanter. **Art:** James David Goldmark. **CDn:** Lisy Christl. **Cast:** Isabelle Huppert, Béatrice Dalle, Patrice Chéreau, Rona Hartner, Maurice Bénichou, Olivier Gourmet, Brigitte Roüan, Lucas Biscombe.

28 Days Later... [*28 Days Later*] (2002, 2003 USA). **D:** Danny Boyle. **Sc:** Alex Garland. **P:** Andrew Macdonald. **M:** John Murphy. **C:** Anthony Dod Mantle. **Ed:** Chris Gill. **PDn:** Mark Tildesley. **Art:** Rob Gorwood (Rod Gorwood), Patrick Rolfe. **SDc:** Fanny Taylor. **CDn:** Rachael Fleming. **Mk:** Sallie Jaye. **S:** Glenn Freemantle. **Cast:** Cillian Murphy, Naomie Harris, Christopher Eccleston, Megan Burns, Brendan Gleeson.

Arachnia (2003). **D, Sc:** Brett Piper. **P:** Peter Beckwith, David Giancola. **M:** Sutherland Andrew. **C:** Cheryl Friberg, Chuck Harding. **PDn:** Cheryl Friberg. **Art:** Ben Coello. **S:** Toby Fitch. **SFx:** Brett Piper. **Cast:** Rob Monkiewicz, Irene Joseph, David Bunce, Bevin McGraw, Alexxus Young, James Aspden.

Open Water (2003, released 2004). **D, Sc:** Chris Kentis. **P:** Laura Lau. **M:** Graeme Revell. **C:** Chris Kentis, Laura Lau. **Ed:** Chris Kentis. **S:** Glenn T. Morgan, Tom Ozanich. **VFx:** Haven Cousins. **Cast:** Blanchard Ryan, Daniel Travis, Saul Stein, Estelle Lau, Michael E. Williamson, Cristina Zenarro.

Category 6: Day of Destruction (2004). Made for TV. **D:** Dick Lowry. **Sc:** Matt Dorff. **P:** Leslie Belzberg, Randy Sutter. **M:** Jeff Rona, Joseph Stanley Williams. **C:** Neil Roach. **PDn:** Sheila Haley. **Art:** Doug Byggdin. **CDn:** Abram Waterhouse. **Mk:** Joyce Wold. **S:** Scott C. Kolden. **SFx:** Jim Fisher. **VFx:** Tim Pyle. **Cast:** Nancy McKeon, Randy Quaid, Thomas Gibson, Chandra West, Dianne Wiest, Brian Dennehy.

Control Room (2004). **D:** Jehane Noujaim. **Sc:** Julia Bacha, Jehane Noujaim. **P:** Alan Oxman, Bent-Jorgen Perlmutt, Hani Salama, Rosadel Varela. **M:** Thomas DeRenzo, Hani Salama. **C:** Jehane Noujaim. **Cast:** Samir Khader, Josh Rushing, Hassan Ibrahim, Deema Khatib, Tom Mintier, David Shuster.

The Day After Tomorrow (2004). **D:** Roland Emmerich. **Sc:** Roland Emmerich, Jeffrey Nachmanoff. Story by Roland Emmerich. **P:** Roland Emmerich, Mark Gordon. **M:** Harald Kloser, Thomas Wanker. **C:** Ueli Steiger. **Ed:** David Brenner. **Art:** Michele Laliberte. **PDn:** Barry Chusid. **SDc:** Victor J. Zolfo. **CDn:** Renée April. **SFx:** Neil Corbould, Louis Craig, John Palmer. **Cast:** Dennis Quaid, Jake Gyllenhaal, Emmy Rossum, Dash Mihok, Jay O. Sanders, Sela Ward, Austin Nichols, Arjay Smith, Ian Holm. **BAFTA** Best Special Visual Effects (Rob Legato, Pete Travers, Matthew Gratzner, R. Bruce Steinheimer).

Fahrenheit 9/11 (2004). **D, Sc:** Michael Moore. **P:**

Jim Czarnecki, Kathleen Glynn, Michael Moore. **M:** Jeff Gibbs, Bob Golden. **C:** Andrew Black, Mike Desjarlais. **Ed:** Kurt Engfehr, T. Woody Richman, Christopher Seward. **Art:** Dina Varano. **Cast:** George W. Bush, Jeb Bush, James Baker III, Al Gore, Condoleezza Rice, Donald Rumsfeld, Saddam Hussein, George Bush, Osama bin Laden, Larry King, Michael Moore, Richard Clarke, Dick Cheney, Paul Wolfowitz, Ken Lay, John Ashcroft, Britney Spears, Lila Lipscomb, Tony Blair. **Broadcast Film Critics** Best Documentary Feature. **Cannes** Palme d'Or (Fahrenheit 9/11). **New York Film Critics** Best Nonfiction Film. **International Documentary Association** Best Feature (Moore, Glynn, Czarnecki).

The Forgotten (2004). **D:** Joseph Ruben. **Sc:** Gerald Di Pego. **P:** Bruce Cohen, Dan Jinks, Joe Roth. **M:** James Horner. **C:** Anastas N. Michos. **Ed:** Richard Francis-Bruce. **PDn:** Bill Groom. **Art:** Paul D. Kelly. **SDc:** Susan Bode. **CDn:** Cindy Evans. **SFx:** Kevin Gillen. **Cast:** Julianne Moore, Christopher Kovaleski, Matthew Pleszewicz, Anthony Edwards, Jessica Hecht, Linus Roache, Gary Sinise, Dominic West.

The Manchurian Candidate (2004). **D:** Jonathan Demme. **Sc:** Daniel Pyne and Dean Georgaris. Based on novel by Richard Condon, original screenplay by George Axelrod. **P:** Jonathan Demme, Ilona Herzberg, Scott Rudin, Tina Sinatra. **M:** Rachel Portman. **C:** Tak Fujimoto. **Ed:** Carol Littleton, Craig McKay. **PDn:** Kristi Zea. **Art:** Teresa Carriker-Thayer. **SDc:** Leslie E. Rollins. **CDn:** Albert Wolsky. **SDn:** Blake Leyh. **SFx:** Conrad F. Brink. **Cast:** Jeffrey Wright, Denzel Washington, Liev Schreiber, Bill Irwin, Al Franken, Jon Voight, Meryl Streep, Roger Corman.

Shaun of the Dead (2004). **D:** Edgar Wright. **Sc:** Simon Pegg, Edgar Wright. **P:** Nira Park. **M:** Dan Mudford, Pete Woodhead. **C:** David M. Dunlap. **Ed:** Chris Dickens. **PDn:** Marcus Rowland. **Art:** Karen Wakefield. **SDc:** Liz Griffiths. **SFx:** Paul Dunn, Scott McIntyre. **VFx:** Hal Couzens, Jeremy Hattingh. **Cast:** Simon Pegg, Kate Ashfield, Nick Frost, Lucy Davis, Dylan Moran, Nicola Cunningham.

10.5 (2004). Made for TV. **D:** John Lafia. **Sc:** Christopher Canaan and John Lafia & Ronnie Christensen. **P:** Gary Pearl, Lisa Richardson. **M:** Lee Holdridge. **C:** David Foreman. **Ed:** Don Brochu, Michael N. Knue. **PDn:** David Fischer. **Art:** David McLean, Walter Ockley. **SDc:** Mark Lane. **CDn:** Gregory Mah. **Mk:** Margaret Solomon. **H:** Janet MacDonald. **S:** Kris Fenske. **SFx:** David Barkes. **Cast:** Beau Bridges, Kim Delaney, Fred Ward, Dulé Hill, David Cubitt, Kaley Cuoco, Rebecca Jenkins.

The Village (2004). **D, Sc:** M. Night Shyamalan. **P:** Sam Mercer, Scott Rudin, M. Night Shyamalan. **M:** James Newton Howard. **C:** Roger Deakins. **Ed:** Christopher Tellefsen. **PDn:** Tom Foden. **Art:** Tim Beach, Chris Shriver. **SDc:** Larry Dias. **CDn:** Ann Roth. **Cast:** Bryce Dallas Howard, Joaquin Phoenix, Adrien Brody, William Hurt, Sigourney Weaver, Brendan Gleeson, Cherry Jones, Celia Weston.

Land of the Dead [*George A. Romero's Land of the Dead*] (2005). **D, Sc:** George A. Romero. **P:** Mark Canton, Bernie Goldmann, Peter Grunwald. **M:** Reinhold Heil, Johnny Klimek. **C:** Miroslaw Baszak. **Ed:**

Michael Doherty. **PDn:** Arv Grewal. **Art:** Douglas Slater. **SDc:** Marlene Puritt. **CDn:** Alex Kavanagh. **Mk:** Marysue Herron, Greg Nicotero. **H:** Mimi Stables, Regan Noble. **SDn:** Rudy Braun, David G. Fremlin. **Cast:** Simon Baker, John Leguizamo, Dennis Hopper, Asia Argento, Robert Joy, Eugene Clark.

Locusts (2005). Made for TV. **D:** David Jackson. **Sc:** Doug Prochilo. **P:** Christopher Morgan and many others. **M:** Joseph LoDuca. **C:** Derick V. Underschultz. **Ed:** Louis F. Cioffi. **PDn:** Chester Kaczenski. **Art:** Barry Gelber. **SDc:** Matthew Sullivan. **CDn:** Peggy Stamper. **Mk:** Susan Spaid. **H:** Donna Spahn. **SFx:** David K. Nami. **VFx:** Craig Weiss. **Cast:** Lucy Lawless, John Heard, Dylan Neal, Greg Alan Williams, Mike Farrell, Natalia Nogulich.

Supervolcano (2005). Made for TV. **D:** Tony Mitchell. **Sc:** Edward Canfor-Dumas. **P:** Ailsa Orr. **M:** Ty Unwin. **C:** Derek Rogers. **Ed:** Mark Gravil. **PDn:** Paul Joyal. **Art:** Doris Deutschmann. **CDn:** Maria Livingstone. **Mk:** Bev Wright. **H:** James Dean Patten. **S:** John Boyle. **Cast:** Michael Riley, Gary Lewis, Shaun Johnston, Adrian Holmes, Jennifer Copping, Rebecca Jenkins.

War of the Worlds (2005). **D:** Steven Spielberg. **Sc:** Josh Friedman, David Koepp. Based on novel by H. G. Wells. **P:** Kathleen Kennedy, Colin Wilson. **M:** John Williams. **C:** Janusz Kaminski. **Ed:** Michael Kahn. **PDn:** Rick Carter. **SDc:** Anne Kuljian. **SDn:** Joanna Johnston. **H:** Katharine Kremp, David Larson. **VFx:** Christian Alzmann. **Cast:** Tom Cruise, Dakota Fanning, Justin Chatwin, Miranda Otto, Tim Robbins, Rick Gonzalez. **Broadcast Film Critics** Best Young Actress (Fanning).

Apocalypto (2006). **D:** Mel Gibson. **Sc:** Mel Gibson, Farhad Safinia. **P:** Bruce Davey, Mel Gibson. **M:** James Horner. **C:** Dean Semler. **Ed:** Kevin Stitt, John Wright. **PDn:** Tom Sanders. **Art:** Roberto Bonelli. **CDn:** Mayes C. Rubeo. **Mk:** Aldo Signoretti, Vittorio Sodano. **H:** Aldo Signoretti. **SDn:** Carlos Benassini, Erick Monroy. **Cast:** Rudy Youngblood, Dalia Hernandez, Jonathan Brewer, Morris Birdyellowhead, Carlos Emilio Baez, Ramirez Amilcar, Israel Contreras, Israel Rios.

Children of Men (2006). **D:** Alfonso Cuarón. **Sc:** Alfonso Cuarón & Timothy J. Sexton and David Arata and Mark Fergus & Hawk Ostby. Based on the novel by P. D. James. **P:** Marc Abraham, Eric Newman, Hilary Shor, Iain Smith, Tony Smith. **M:** John Tavener. **C:** Emmanuel Lubezki. **Ed:** Alfonso Cuarón, Alex Rodríguez. **PDn:** Jim Clay, Geoffrey Kirkland. **Art:** Ray Chan, Paul Inglis, Mike Stallion. **SDc:** Jennifer Williams. **CDn:** Jany Temime. **Mk:** Graham Johnston, Neill Gorton. **H:** Graham Johnston. **S:** Richard Beggs. **Cast:** Clive Owen, Michael Caine, Julianne Moore, Chiwetel Ejiofor, Claire-Hope Ashitey, Peter Mullan, Danny Huston. **American Society of Cinematographers** Outstanding Achievement in Cinematography in Theatrical Releases. **BAFTA** Best Cinematography, Best Production Design. **Los Angeles Film Critics Association** Best Cinematography. **National Society of Film Critics** Best Cinematography. **Venice Film Festival** Outstanding Technical Contribution (Lubezki), Laterna Magica Prize (Cuarón).

Death of a President (2006). **D:** Gabriel Range. **Sc:** Simon Finch, Gabriel Range. **P:** Simon Finch, Ed Guiney, Gabriel Range. **M:** Richard Harvey. **C:** Graham Smith. **Ed:** Brand Thumim. **PDn:** Gary Baugh. **Cast:** Hend Ayoub, Brian Boland, Becky Ann Baker, Michael Reilly Burke, M. Neko Parham, Malik Bader, George W. Bush, Dick Cheney.

Disaster Zone: Volcano in New York (2006). Made for TV. **D:** Robert Lee. **Sc:** Sarah Watson. **P:** Harvey Kahn, Robert Lee. **C:** Adam Sliwinski. **Ed:** Bethany Handfield. **PDn:** Michael Nemirsky. **SDc:** George Neuman. **CDn:** Andrea Desroches. **VFx:** Mark Rasmussen. **Cast:** Costas Mandylor, Alexandra Paul, Michael Ironside, Michael Boisvert, Eric Breker, Ron Selmour, Pascale Hutton, Zak Santiago.

Fatal Contact: Bird Flu in America (2006). Made for TV. **D:** Richard Pearce. **Sc:** Ron McGee. **P:** Dennis A. Brown. **Art:** Nigel Evans, John Harding. **Mk:** Paul Pattison. **VFx:** Zeljko Barcan, Gordon Oscar. **Cast:** Scott Cohen, Ann Cusack, Kayte Ferguson, Latham Gaines, Brad Hills, Stacy Keach, Joely Richardson, David Ramsey.

Flight 93 (2006). **D:** Peter Markle. **Sc:** Nevin Schreiner. **P:** Clara George. **M:** Velton Ray Bunch. **C:** Mark Irwin. **Ed:** Scott Boyd. **PDn:** Eric Fraser. **Art:** Kendelle Elliott. **CDn:** Lorraine Carson. **Mk:**Connie Parker. **VFx:** Gary Gutierrez. **Cast:** Jeffrey Nordling, Brennan Elliott, Kendall Cross, Ty Olsson, Monnae Michaell, Colin Glazer, April Amber Telek, Marilyn Norry, Tom Butler. **Emmy Awards** Outstanding Sound Editing for a Miniseries, Movie or a Special.

The Great San Francisco Earthquake (2006). Made for TV. **D, Sc:** Philip Smith. **M:** Duncan Glasson. **C:** Lawrence Gardner, Jonathan Partridge. **Ed:** Jake Martin. **PDn:** Joanna Macha. **CDn:** Malgorzata Gwiazdecka. **VFx:** Rosanna Jon. **Cast:** Maxwell Caulfield, Orlando Wells, Robert Jezek, Ian Duncan, Tara Summers, Eric Loren, Angus MacInnes, Robert Carroll.

An Inconvenient Truth (2006). **D:** Davis Guggenheim. **Sc:** Uncredited. Based on book by Al Gore. **P:** Laurie David, Lawrence Bender, Scott Z. Burns. **M:** Michael Brook. "I Need to Wake Up" Melissa Etheridge. **C:** Bob Richman, Davis Guggenheim. **Ed:** Jay Cassidy, Dan Swietlik. **PDn:** John Calkins. **S:** Paul Trautman. **Cast:** Al Gore. **Academy Awards** Best Original Song (Etheridge), Best Documentary Feature (Guggenheim). **American Cinema Editors** Best Edited Documentary Film (Cassidy, Swietlik). **Broadcast Film Critics** Best Documentary Feature. **Los Angeles Film Critics** Best Documentary/Non-Fiction Film. **National Board of Review** Best Documentary. **National Society of Film Critics** Best Non-Fiction Film.

Jericho (2006 to 2008). TV Series. **D:** Stephen Chbosky, Josh Schaer, Jonathan E. Steinberg. **P:** Dan Shotz, Karim Zreik, Jonathan E. Steinberg, Stephen Chbosky, Josh Schaer, and others. **M:** David Lawrence. **C:** David Connell, Rick Bota, Rick Maguire. **Ed:** Patrick McMahon, Conrad Smart, and others. **PDn:** Brandy Alexander, Bernard Hides, and others. **Art:** Gregory Van Horn, Janet Lakeman, and others. **SDc:** Linda Cooper, Shirley Starks. **CDn:** Nicole Gorsuch. **Mk:** Bob Scribner. **Cast:** Skeet Ulrich, Lennie James, Ashley Scott, Kenneth Mitchell, Brad Beyer, April

Parker-Jones, Alicia Coppola, Pamela Reed, Bob Stephenson, Gerald McRaney, Clare Carey, Richard Speight Jr.

Magma: Volcanic Disaster (2006). **D:** Ian Gilmore. **P:** Jeff Beach, Phillip J. Roth, T. J. Sakasegawa. **M:** Nathan Furst. **Ed:** John Quinn. **PDn:** Kes Bonnet. **S:** Mandell Winter. **VFx:** Stanimir Angelov, Tinko Dimov, Aleksandar Yochkolovski. **Cast:** Xander Berkeley, Amy Jo Johnson, Michael Durrell.

The Path to 9/11 (2006). Made for TV. **D:** David L. Cunningham. **Sc:** Cyrus Nowrasteh. **P:** Penelope L. Foster, Cyrus Nowrasteh, Hans Proppe, Mark Winemaker. **M:** John Cameron. **C:** Joel Ransom. **Ed:** Mitchell Danton, Bryan M. Horne, Geoffrey Rowland, Eric A. Sears. **PDn:** John Dondertman. **Art:** Greg Chown. **SDc:** Patricia Larman. **CDn:** Eydi Caines-Floyd. **Mk:** Amanda Terry. **SDn:** Dwight Hendrickson. **SFx:** Tomas Hartl. **VFx:** Anthony Paterson. **Cast:** Harvey Keitel, Stephen Root, Donnie Wahlberg, Barclay Hope, Patricia Heaton, Shaun Toub, Amy Madigan, Nabil Elouhabi, Dan Lauria, Michael Murphy.

Right at Your Door (2006). **D, Sc:** Chris Gorak. **P:** Jonah Smith, Palmer West. **M:** tomandandy. **C:** Tom Richmond. **Ed:** Jeffrey M. Werner. **PDn:** Ramsey Avery. **Art:** Patricio M. Farrell. **SDc:** Stephanie DeSantis. **CDn:** Rebecca Bentjen. **Mk:** Galaxy. **SFx:** Pete Novitch. **VFx:** Joe Bauer. Titles: Andy Roberts. **Cast:** Mary McCormack, Rory Cochrane, Tony Perez, Scotty Noyd Jr.

Snakes on a Plane (2006). **D:** David R. Ellis. **Sc:** John Heffernan, Sebastian Gutierrez. Story by David Dalessandro, John Heffernan. **P:** Craig Berenson, Don Granger, Gary Levinsohn. **M:** Trevor Rabin. **C:** Adam Greenberg. **Ed:** Howard E. Smith. **PDn:** Jaymes Hinkle. **Art:** John Alvarez. **SDc:** Erin Gould, Mary-Lou Storey. **CDn:** Karen L. Matthews. **SDn:** Bryan Sutton, Milena Zdravkovic. **VFx:** Mike Fischer. **Cast:** Samuel L. Jackson, Julianna Margulies, Nathan Phillips, Rachel Blanchard, Flex Alexander, Kenan Thompson, Keith "Blackman" Dallas, Lin Shaye, Bobby Cannavale.

10.5: Apocalypse (2006). Made for TV. **D, Sc:** John Lafia. **M:** Henning Lohner. **C:** David Foreman. **Art:** Michele Laliberte. **Mk:** Jocelyne Bellemare, Cécile Rigault. **SDn:** Brent Lambert. **S:** Christian Rivest. **SFx:** Denis Lavigne, Joe Viskocil. **VFx:** Vincent Fortin, Dennis McHugh, Jihyun Nam. **Cast:** Kim Delaney, Beau Bridges, Frank Langella, Melissa Sue Anderson, Dean Cain, Oliver Hudson, Carly Pope.

Tsunami: The Aftermath (2006). Made for TV. TV miniseries. **D:** Bharat Nalluri. **Sc:** Abi Morgan. **P:** Finola Dwyer. **M:** Alex Heffes. **C:** John de Borman. **Ed:** Barney Pilling. **PDn:** Richard Bridgland. **Art:** Lek Chaiyan Chunsuttiwat, Sloane U'ren. **SDn:** Peter Walpole. **CDn:** Claire Anderson. **Mk, H:** Daniel Phillips, Natalie Reid. **Cast:** Tim Roth, Chiwetel Ejiofor, Sophie Okonedo, Hugh Bonneville, Gina McKee, Samrit Machielsen, Grirggiat Punpiputt, Toni Collette.

United 93 (2006). **D, Sc:** Paul Greengrass. **P:** Tim Bevan, Eric Fellner, Lloyd Levin. **M:** John Powell. **C:** Barry Ackroyd. **Ed:** Clare Douglas, Richard Pearson, Christopher Rouse. **PDn:** Dominic Watkins. **Cast:** Lewis Alsamari, JJ Johnson, Gary Commock, Trish Gates, Polly Adams, Cheyenne Jackson, Opal Alladin, Starla Benford, Nancy McDoniel, Christian Clemenson, David Alan Basche, Jamie Harding, Tobin Miller, Gregg Henry, Ben Sliney. **BAFTA** Best Editing (Douglas, Rouse, Pearson), Direction (Greengrass). **Los Angeles Film Critics** Best Director (Greengrass). **National Society of Film Critics** Best Director (Greengrass). **New York Film Critics** Best Picture.

When the Levees Broke: A Requiem in Four Acts (2006). Made for TV. **D:** Spike Lee. **P:** Spike Lee, Sam Pollard. **M:** Terence Blanchard. **C:** Cliff Charles. **Ed:** Barry Alexander Brown, Geeta Gandbhir, Nancy Novack, Samuel D. Pollard. **VFx:** J. John Corbett. **Emmy Awards** Exceptional Merit in Nonfiction Filmmaking (Pollard, Lee, Nevins, Glover), Outstanding Directing for Nonfiction Programming (Lee), Outstanding Picture Editing for Nonfiction Programming (Pollard, Gandbhir, Novack).

World Trade Center (2006). **D:** Oliver Stone. **Sc:** Andrea Berloff. **P:** Moritz Borman, Debra Hill. Michael Shamberg, Stacey Sher, Oliver Stone. **M:** Craig Armstrong. **C:** Seamus McGarvey. **Ed:** David Brenner, Julie Monroe. **Art:** Richard L. Johnson. **SDc:** Beth A. Rubino. **CDn:** Michael Dennison. **SDn:** Gregory S. Hooper, Randall D. Wilkins. **Cast:** Maria Bello, Nicolas Cage, Stephen Dorff, Maggie Gyllenhaal, Michael Pena, Nicholas Turturro, Stoney Westmoreland. **National Board of Review** Freedom of Expression Award.

Diary of the Dead (2007). **D, Sc:** George A. Romero. **P:** Sam Englebardt, Peter Grunwald, Ara Katz, Art Spigel. **M:** Norman Orenstein. **C:** Adam Swica. **Ed:** Michael Doherty. **PDn:** Rupert Lazarus. **Art:** Jon P. Goulding. **SDc:** Justin Craig. **CDn:** Alex Kavanagh. **Cast:** Michelle Morgan, Joshua Close, Shawn Roberts, Amy Ciupak Lalonde, Joe Dinicol, Scott Wentworth.

I Am Legend (2007). **D:** Francis Lawrence. **Sc:** Mark Protosevich and Akiva Goldsman. Based on novel by Richard Matheson, original script by John William Corrington & Joyce Corrington. **P:** Akiva Goldsman, David Heyman, James Lassiter, Neal Moritz. **M:** James Newton Howard. **C:** Andrew Lesnie. **Ed:** Wayne Wahrman. **PDn:** Naomi Shohan. **Art:** Howard Cummings, Bill Skinner, Patricia Woodbridge. **SDc:** George Detitta. **CDn:** Michael Kaplan. **S:** Jeremy Peirson. **Cast:** Will Smith, Alice Braga, Charlie Tahan, Salli Richardson, Willow Smith, Dash Mihok.

The Mist (2007). **D:** Frank Darabont. **Sc:** Frank Darabont. Based on novel by Stephen King. **P:** Frank Darabont, Liz Glotzer. **M:** Mark Isham. **C:** Ronn Schmidt. **Ed:** Hunter M. Via. **PDn:** Gregory Melton. **Art:** Alex Hajdu. **SDc:** Raymond Pumilia. **CDn:** Giovanna Ottobre-Melton. **Cast:** Thomas Jane, Marcia Gay Harden, Laurie Holden, Andre Braugher, Toby Jones, Nathan Gamble, Frances Sternhagen.

White Light/Black Rain: The Destruction of Hiroshima and Nagasaki (2007). **D, Sc, P:** Steven Okazaki. **C:** Masafumi Kawasaki. **S:** Yuki Fukuda. **Cast:** Harold Agnew, Dr. Shuntaro Hida, Kiyoko Imori, Morris Jeppson, Lawrence Johnston, Pan Yeon Kim.

Blindness (2008). **D:** Fernando Meirelles. **Sc:** Don McKellar. Based on novel by José Saramago. **P:** Andrea Barata Ribeiro, Niv Fichman, Sonoko Sakai. **M:** Uakti (Marco Antônio Guimarães). **C:** César Charlone. **Ed:** Daniel Rezende. **PDn:** Matthew Davies, Tulé Peak.

Art: Joshu de Cartier. **SDc:** Erica Milo. **CDn:** Renée April. **H:** Janie MacKay. **Mk:** Anna Van Steen. **VFx:** Andre Waller. **Cast:** Julianne Moore, Mark Ruffalo, Alice Braga, Yusuke Iseya, Yoshino Kimura, Don McKellar, Danny Glover, Gael García Bernal.

Cloverfield (2008). **D:** Matt Reeves. **Sc:** Drew Goddard. **P:** J.J. Abrams, Bryan Burk. **C:** Michael Bonvillain. **Ed:** Kevin Stitt. **PDn:** Martin Whist. **Art:** Doug J. Meerdink. **SDc:** Robert Greenfield. **CDn:** Ellen Mirojnick. **Cast:** Lizzy Caplan, Jessica Lucas, T.J. Miller, Michael Stahl-David, Mike Vogel, Odette Yustman, Anjul Nigam, Margot Farley.

The Happening (2008). **D, Sc:** M. Night Shyamalan. **P:** Barry Mendel, Sam Mercer, M. Night Shyamalan. **M:** James Newton Howard. **C:** Tak Fujimoto. **Ed:** Conrad Buff IV. **PDn:** Jeannine Claudia Oppewall. **Art:** Anthony Dunne. **SDc:** Jay Hart. **CDn:** Betsy Heimann. **Cast:** Mark Wahlberg, Zooey Deschanel, John Leguizamo, Ashlyn Sanchez, Betty Buckley.

Wall•E (2008). **D:** Andrew Stanton. **Sc:** Andrew Stanton, Jim Reardon. **P:** John Lasseter, Jim Morris. **M:** Thomas Newman. **Ed:** Stephen Schaffer. **Pdn:** Ralph Eggleston. **Cast:** Voices of Ben Burtt, Elissa Knight, Fred Willard, John Ratzenberger, Kathy Najimy, Sigourney Weaver. **Academy Awards** Best Animated Feature (Stanton). **BAFTA** Best Animated Film (Stanton). **Golden Globes** Best Animated Feature.

Knowing (2009). **D:** Alex Proyas. **P:** Alex Proyas, Steve Tisch, Todd Black, Jason Blumenthal. **Sc:** Ryne Douglas Pearson, Juliet Snowden, Stiles White. **C:** Simon Duggan. **M:** Marco Beltrami. **Ed:** Richard Learoyd. **PDn:** Steven Jones-Evans. **Art:** Sam Lennox. **Sdc:** Nicki Gardiner. **Cdn:** Terry Ryan. **Cast:** Nicolas Cage, Chandler Canterbury, Rose Byrne, D. G. Maloney, Lara Robinson, Adrienne Pickering, Nadia Townsend, Ben Mendelsohn.

Terminator Salvation (2009). **D:** McG. **M:** Danny Elfman. **C:** Shane Hurlbut. **Ed:** Conrad Buff. **Pdn:** Martin Laing. **Sdc:** Victor J. Zolfo. **Cdn:** Michael Wilkinson. **Cast:** Christian Bale, Bryce Dallas Howard, Helena Bonham Carter, Jane Alexander.

2012 (2009). **D:** Roland Emmerich. **Sc:** Roland Emmerich, Harald Kloser. **P:** Roland Emmerich, Harald Kloser, Larry J. Franco. **M:** Harald Kloser. **C:** Dean Semler. **Ed:** David Brenner, Peter S. Elliot. **Pdn:** Barry Chusid. **Art:** Don Macauley. **Sdc:** Elikzabeth Wilcox. **Cdn:** Shay Cunliffe. **Cast:** John Cusack, Amanda Peet, Thandie Newton, Woody Harrelson, Oliver Platt, Danny Glover, Chiewetel Ejiofor, Patrick Bauchau.

9 (2009). **D:** Shane Acker. **Sc:** Shane Acker, Pamela Pettler. **P:** Tim Burton and others. **Ed:** Nick Kenway. **Pdn:** Robert St. Pierre, Fred Warter. **Art:** Christopher Vacher. **Cast:** Voices of Elijah Wood, John C. Reilly, Jennifer Connelly, Crispin Glover, Martin Landau, Christopher Plummer.

The Road (2009). **D:** John Hillcoat. **Sc:** Joe Penhall. Based on novel by Cormac McCarthy. **P:** Paula Mae Schwartz, Steve Schwartz, Nick Wechsler. **M:** Nick Cave, Warren Ellis. **C:** Javier Aguirresarobe. **Ed:** Jon Gregory. **Pdn:** Chris Kennedy. **Art:** Gershon Ginsburg. **Sdc:** Robert Greenfield. **Cdn:** Margot Wilson. **Cast:** Viggo Mortensen, Kodi Smith-McPhee, Charlize Theron, Guy Pearce, Robert Duvall.

JAPANESE HORROR OF ARMAGEDDON

***Godzilla, King of the Monsters!* [*Kaijû no Gojira*]** (1956). **D:** Inoshirô Honda. **Sc:** Inoshirô Honda, Takeo Murata. **P:** Edward B. Barison, Richard Kay, Harry Rybnick, Tomoyuki Tanaka. **M:** Akira Ifukube. **C:** Masao Tamai. **Ed:** Terry O. Morse. **PDn:** Satoshi Chuko. **Art:** Satoshi Chuko, Takeo Kita. **SDc:** George Rohr. **S:** Hisashi Shimonaga, Art Smith. **SFx:** Kuichiro Kishida, Hiroshi Mukoyama, Eiji Tsuburaya, Akira Watanabe. **Cast:** Raymond Burr, Takashi Shimura, Akira Takarada, Momoko Kôchi, Akihiko Hirata, Frank Iwanaga.

***Rodan* [*Sora no Daikaijû Radon*]** (1956). **D:** Inoshirô Honda. **Sc:** Takeshi Kimura, Takeo Murata. **P:** Tomoyuki Tanaka. **M:** Akira Ifukube. **C:** Isamu Ashida. **Ed:** Robert S. Eisen, Koichi Iwashita. **PDn:** Tatsuo Kita. **S:** Masanobu Miyazaki. **SFx:** Eiji Tsuburaya, Akira Watanabe. **VFx:** Hiroshi Mukoyama. **Cast:** Kenji Sawara, Yumi Shirakawa, Akihiko Hirata, Akio Kobori, Yasuko Nakata, Minosuke Yamada.

***Warning from Space* [*Uchûjin Tokyo ni Arawaru*]** (1956/1963). **D:** Koji Shima. **Sc:** Hideo Oguni. Based on novel by Gentaro Nakajima. **P:** Masaichi Nagata. **M:** Seitaro Omori. **C:** Kimio Watanabe. **Ed:** Toyo Suzuki. **Art:** Shigeo Mano. **SFx:** Kenmei Yuasa. **Cast:** Keizo Kawasaki, Toyomi Karita, Bin Yagasawa, Shozo Nanbu, Bontaro Miake, Mieko Nagai.

***The Mysterians* [*Chikyu Boeigun*]** (1957). **D:** Inoshirô Honda. **Sc:** Takeshi Kimura. Story by Shigeru Kayama, Jojiro Okami. **P:** Tomoyuki Tanaka. **M:** Akira Ifukube. **C:** Hajime Koizumi. **Ed:** Koichi Iwashita. **PDn:** Teruaki Abe. **SFx:** Eiji Tsuburaya, Akira Watanabe. **Cast:** Kenji Sahara, Yumi Shirakawa, Momoko Kôchi, Akihiko Hirata, Takashi Shimura, Susumu Fujita.

***Mothra* [*Mosura*]** (1961). **D:** Inoshirô Honda. **Sc:** Shinichi Sekizawa. Based on novel by Takehiko Fukunaga. **P:** Tomoyuki Tanaka. **C:** Hajime Koizumi. **Ed:** Kazuji Taira. **PDn:** Teruaki Abe, Takeo Kita. **SFx:** Eiji Tsuburaya, Akira Watanabe. **Cast:** Frankie Sakai, Hiroshi Koizumi, Kyôko Kagawa, Ken Uehara, Emi Ito, Yûmi Ito, Jerry Ito, Takashi Shimura.

***King Kong vs. Godzilla* [*Kingukongu tai Gojira*]** (1962). **D:** Inoshirô Honda. **Sc:** Shinichi Sekizawa. **P:** Tomoyuki Tanaka. **M:** Akira Ifukube. **C:** Hajime Koizumi. **Ed:** Reiko Kaneko. **PDn:** Teruaki Abe, Takeo Kita. **SFx:** Eiji Tsuburaya, Akira Watanabe. **VFx:** Teisho Arikawa. **Cast:** Tadao Takashima, Kenji Sahara, Yu Fujiki, Ichirô Arishima, Jun Tazaki, Akihiko Hirata.

***Dagora, the Space Monster* [*Uchu Daikaijû Dogora*]** (1964). **D:** Inoshirô Honda. **Sc:** Shinichi Sekizawa. Story by Jojiro Okami. **P:** Yasuyoshi Tajitsu. **M:** Akira Ifukube. **C:** Hajime Koizumi. **Ed:** Ryohei Fujii. **PDn:** Takeo Kita. **S:** Hisashi Shimonaga. **SFx:** Kuichiro Kishida. **Cast:** Yosuke Natsuki, Yôko Fujiyama, Hiroshi Koizumi, Nobuo Nakamura, Dan Yuma, Akiko Wakabayashi.

***Ghidrah, the Three-Headed Monster* [*San Daikaijû: Chikyu Saidai no Kessen*]** (1964). **D:** Inoshirô Honda. **Sc:** Shinichi Sekizawa. **P:** Tomoyuki Tanaka. **M:** Akira Ifukube. **C:** Hajime Koizumi. **Ed:** Ryohei Fujii. **PDn:** Takeo Kita. **Art:** Takeo Kita. **S:** Hisashi Shimonaga. **SFx:** Akira Watanabe. **VFx:** Hiroshi Mukoyama. **Cast:** Yosuke Natsuki, Yuriko Hoshi, Hiroshi Koizumi, Akiko Wakabayashi, Emi Ito, Yûmi Ito, Takashi Shimura, Akihiko Hirata.

***Godzilla vs. Mothra* [*Mosura tai Gojira*] [*Godzilla vs. the Thing*]** (1964). **D:** Inoshirô Honda. **Sc:** Shinichi Sekizawa. **P:** Tomoyuki Tanaka. **M:** Akira Ifukube. **C:** Hajime Koizumi. **Ed:** Ryohei Fujii. **PDn:** Takeo Kita. **S:** Hisashi Shimonaga. **SFx:** Akira Watanabe. **VFx:** Teisho Arikawa. **Cast:** Akira Takarada, Yuriko Hoshi, Hiroshi Koizumi, Yu Fujiki, Emi Ito, Yûmi Ito, Kenji Sahara.

***Frankenstein Conquers the World* [*Furankenshutain tai Chitei Kaijû Baragon*]** (1965). **D:** Inoshirô Honda. **P:** Tomoyuki Tanaka. **M:** Akira Ifukube. **C:** Hajime Koizumi. **Ed:** Ryohei Fujii. **PDn:** Takeo Kita. **Art:** Takeo Kita. **Mk:** Riki Konna. **S:** Hisashi Shimonaga. **SFx:** Akira Watanabe. **Cast:** Tadao Takashima, Nick Adams, Kumi Mizuno, Yoshio Tsuchiya, Koji Furuhata, Jun Tazaki, Takashi Shimura.

***Monster Zero* [*Kaijû Daisenso*] [*Godzilla vs. Monster Zero*]** (1965). **D:** Inoshirô Honda. **Sc:** Shinichi Sekizawa. **P:** Tomoyuki Tanaka. **M:** Akira Ifukube. **C:** Hajime Koizumi. **Ed:** Ryohei Fujii. **PDn:** Takeo Kita. **S:** Sadamasa Nishimoto. **SFx:** Akira Watanabe. **VFx:** Sadao Iizuda, Hiroshi Mukoyama. **Cast:** Nick Adams, Akira Takarada, Jun Tazaki, Akira Kubo, Kumi Mizuno, Keiko Sawai, Yoshio Tsuchiya.

***King Kong Escapes* [*Kingukongu no Gyakushu*]** (1967). **D:** Inoshirô Honda. **Sc:** Kaoru Mabuchi. **P:** Tomoyuki Tanaka. **M:** Akira Ifukube. **C:** Hajime Koizumi. **Ed:** Ryohei Fujii. **PDn:** Takeo Kita. **S:** Sadamasa Nishimoto. **SFx:** Yasuyuki Inoue, Eiji Tsuburaya. **VFx:** Hiroshi Mukoyama. **Cast:** Rhodes Reason, Mie Hama, Linda Miller, Akira Takarada, Eisei Amamoto.

***Destroy All Monsters* [*Kaijû Sôshingeki*] [*All Monsters Attack*]** (1968). **D:** Inoshirô Honda. **Sc:** Inoshirô Honda, Kaoru Mabuchi. **P:** Tomoyuki Tanaka. **M:** Akira Ifukube. **C:** Taiichi Kankura. **Ed:** Ryohei Fujii. **PDn:** Takeo Kita. **S:** Sadamasa Nishimoto, Hisashi Shimonaga. **SFx:** Yasuyuki Inoue, Akira Watanabe. **VFx:** Hiroshi Mukoyama. **Cast:** Akira Kubo, Jun Tazaki, Yukiko Kobayashi, Yoshio Tsuchiya, Kyôko Ai, Andrew Hughes.

***Godzilla's Revenge* [*Gojira-Minira-Gabara: Oru Kaijû Daishingeki*] [*Attack All Monsters*]** (1969). **D:** Inoshirô Honda. **Sc:** Shinichi Sekizawa. **P:** Tomoyuki Tanaka. **M:** Kunio Miyauchi. **C:** Sokei Tomioka. **Ed:** Masahisa Himi. **PDn:** Takeo Kita. **SFx:** Sokei Tomioka, Eiji Tsuburaya, Akira Watanabe. **VFx:** Sadao Iizuda, Yukio Manoda. **Cast:** Tomonori Yazaki, Eisei Amamoto, Sachio Sakai, Kazuo Suzuki, Kenji Sahara, Machiko Naka.

***Yog — Monster from Space* [*Kessen! Nankai no Daikaijû*]** (1970). **D:** Inoshirô Honda. **Sc:** Ei Ogawa. **P:** Fumio Tanaka, Tomoyuki Tanaka. **M:** Akira Ifukube. **C:** Taiichi Kankura. **Ed:** Masahisa Himi. **PDn:** Takeo Kita. **S:** Sadamasa Nishimoto. **SFx:** Teisho Arikawa. **VFx:** Yoichi Manoda. **Cast:** Akira Kubo, Atsuko Takahashi, Yukiko Kobayashi, Kenji Sahara, Yoshio Tsuchiya, Yu Fujiki.

Godzilla vs. Hedorah, the Smog Monster [*Gojira tai Hedorâ*] (1971). **D:** Yoshimitsu Banno. **Sc:** Yoshimitsu Banno, Kaoru Mabuchi. **P:** Tomoyuki Tanaka. **M:** Riichiro Manabe. **C:** Yoichi Manoda. **Ed:** Yoshitami Kuroiwa. **PDn:** Yasuyuki Inoue. **SFx:** Teruyoshi Nakano. **VFx:** Yoichi Manoda. **Cast:** Akira Yamauchi, Toshie Kimura, Hiroyuki Kawase, Keiko Mari, Toshio Shiba, Yukihiko Gondo.

Godzilla vs. Gigan [*Chikyû Kogeki Meirei: Gojira tai Gaigan*] [*War of the Monsters*] (1972). **D:** Jun Fukuda. **Sc:** Shinichi Sekizawa. Story by Takeshi Kimura. **P:** Tomoyuki Tanaka. **C:** Kiyoshi Hasegawa. **Ed:** Yoshio Tamura. **PDn:** Yoshifumi Honda. **S:** Fumio Yanoguchi. **SFx:** Yasuyuki Inoue. **VFx:** Yoshiyuki Tokumasa. **Cast:** Hiroshi Ishikawa, Yuriko Hishimi, Minoru Takashima, Tomoko Umeda, Toshiaki Nishizawa, Zan Fujita, Gen Shimizu.

Godzilla vs. Megalon [*Gojira tai Megaro*] (1973). **D:** Jun Fukuda. **Sc:** Jun Fukuda. Story by Takeshi Kimura. **P:** Tomoyuki Tanaka. **M:** Riichiro Manabe. **C:** Yuzuru Aizawa. **Ed:** Michiko Ikeda. **PDn:** Yoshifumi Honda. **S:** Teishiro Hayashi. **SFx:** Teruyoshi Nakano. **VFx:** Sokei Tomioka. **Cast:** Katsuhiko Sasaki, Hiroyuki Kawase, Yutaka Hayashi, Robert Dunham, Kotaro Tomita, Wolf Otsuki, Gen Nakajima.

Tidal Wave [*Nippon Chinbotsu*] [*Japan Sinks*] (1973, 1975 USA version). **D:** Shirô Moritani. **Sc:** Shinobu Hashimoto; Andrew Meyer (English dialogue). Based on novel by Sakyo Komatsu. **P:** Tomoyuki Tanaka. **M:** Masaru Satô. **C:** Daisaku Kimura, Hiroshi

Murai; Eric Saarinen (US version). **Ed:** Michiko Ikeda. **PDn:** Yoshirô Muraki. **SFx:** Teruyoshi Nakano. **Cast:** Lorne Greene, Keiju Kobayashi, Rhonda Leigh Hopkins, Hiroshi Fujioka, Tetsuro Tamba, Ayumi Ishida, Shogo Shimada, John Fujioka.

Godzilla vs. Mechagodzilla [*Gojira tai Mekagojira*] (1974). **D:** Jun Fukuda. **Sc:** Jun Fukuda, Hiroyasu Yamamura. Story by Masami Fukushima, Shinichi Sekizawa. **P:** Tomoyuki Tanaka. **M:** Masaru Satô. **C:** Yuzuru Aizawa. **Ed:** Michiko Ikeda. **PDn:** Kazuo Satsuya. **S:** Fumio Yanoguchi. **SFx:** Teruyoshi Nakano. **VFx:** Sokei Tomioka, Takeshi Yamamoto. **Cast:** Masaaki Daimon, Kazuya Aoyama, Akihiko Hirata, Hiroshi Koizumi, Reiko Tajima, Hiromi Matsushita.

Godzilla [*Gojira*] (1984). **D:** Koji Hashimoto. **Sc:** Hidekazu Nagahara. Story by Tomoyuki Tanaka. **P:** Norio Hayashi, Kiyomi Kanazawa. **M:** Reijiro Koroku. **C:** Kazutami Hara. **Ed:** Yoshitami Kuroiwa. **Pd, Art:** Akira Sakuragi. **SDc:** Akio Tashiro. **CDn:** Kenji Kawasaki. **Mk:** Fumiko Umezawa. **SFx:** Yasuyuki Inoue, Teruyoshi Nakano. **Cast:** Ken Tanaka, Yasuko Sawaguchi, Yosuke Natsuki, Keiju Kobayashi, Shin Takuma, Eitarô Ozawa.

Godzilla 2000 [*Gojira ni-sen Nireniamu*] (1999). **D:** Takao Okawara. **Sc:** Hiroshi Kashiwabara & Wataru Mimura. **P:** Shogo Tomiyama. **M:** Takayuki Hattori. **C:** Katsuhiro Kato. **Ed:** Yoshiyuki Okuhara. **PDn:** Takeshi Shimizu. **S:** Teiichi Saitô. **SFx:** Kenji Suzuki. **VFx:** Toshihiro Ogawa. **Cast:** Takehiro Murata, Hiroshi Abe, Naomi Nishida, Mayu Suzuki, Shirô Sano, Takeshi Ôbayashi.

HORROR OF THE DEMONIC

Day of Wrath [*Vredens Dag*] (1943, 1948 USA). **D:** Carl Theodor Dreyer. **Sc:** Carl Theodor Dreyer, Poul Knudsen, Mogens Skot-Hansen. Based on novel by Hans Wiers-Jenssens. **P:** Carl Theodor Dreyer, Tage Nielsen. **M:** Poul Schierbeck. **C:** Karl Andersson. **Ed:** Anne Marie Petersen, Edith Schlüssel. **Art:** Erik Aaes. **CDn:** Karl Sandt Jensen, Olga Thomsen. **S:** Erik Rasmussen. **Cast:** Thorkild Roose, Lisbeth Movin, Sigrid Neiiendam, Preben Lerdorff, Anna Svierkier, Albert Høeberg, Olaf Ussing.

I Walked with a Zombie (1943). **D:** Jacques Tourneur. **Sc:** Curt Siodmak and Ardel Wray. Based on story by Inez Wallace. **P:** Val Lewton. **M:** Roy Webb. **Ed:** J. Roy Hunt. **Ed:** Mark Robson. **Art:** Albert S. D'agostino, Walter E. Keller. **SDc:** Al Fields, Darrell Silvera. **Mk:** Maurice Seiderman. **Cast:** James Ellison, Frances Dee, Tom Conway, Edith Barrett, James Bell, Christine Gordon.

The Seventh Victim (1943). **D:** Mark Robson. **Sc:** DeWitt Bodeen, Charles O'Neal. **P:** Val Lewton. **M:** Roy Webb. **C:** Nicholas Musuraca. **Ed:** John Lockert. **Art:** Albert S. D'agostino, Walter E. Keller. **SDc:** Harley Miller, Darrell Silvera. **CDn:** Renié. **Cast:** Tom Conway, Jean Brooks, Isabel Jewell, Kim Hunter, Evelyn Brent, Erford Gage, Ben Bard, Hugh Beaumont.

The Devil's Wanton [*Fängelse*] [*Prison*] (1949).

D, Sc: Ingmar Bergman. **P:** Lorens Marmstedt. **M:** Erland von Koch. **C:** Göran Strindberg. **Ed:** Lennart Wallén. **PDn:** P. A. Lundgren. **Mk:** Inga Lindeström. **S:** Olle Jacobsson. **Cast:** Doris Svedlund, Birger Malmsten, Eva Henning, Hasse Ekman, Stig Olin, Irma Christenson.

The Bad Seed (1956). **D, P:** Mervyn LeRoy. **Sc:** John Lee Mahin. Based on novel by William March and play by Maxwell Anderson. **M:** Alex North. **C:** Hal Rosson. **Ed:** Warren Low. **Art:** John Beckman. **SDc:** Ralph Hurst. **CDn:** Moss Mabry. **S:** Stanley Jones. **Cast:** Nancy Kelly, Patty McCormack, Henry Jones, Eileen Heckart, Evelyn Varden, William Hopper, Paul Fix, Jesse White. **Golden Globes** Best Supporting Actress (Heckart).

Black Sunday [*La Maschera del Demonio*] (1960). **D, C:** Mario Bava. **Sc:** Ennio De Concini, Mario Serandrei. George Higgins, English dialogue. Based on story by Nikolai Gogol. **P:** Massimo De Rita, Lou Rusoff. **M:** Roberto Nicolosi, Les Baxter. **Ed:** Mario Serandrei. **CDn:** Tina Loriedo Grani. **SDn:** Giorgio Giovannini. **S:** Robert Sherwood. **Cast:** Barbara Steele, John Richardson, Andrea Checchi, Ivo Garrani, Arturo Dominici, Enrico Olivieri.

Horror Hotel [*The City of the Dead*] (1960). **D:** John Moxey. **Sc:** George Baxt. Story by Milton Subotsky. **P:** Max Rosenberg, Milton Subotsky, Donald Taylor. **M:** Douglas Gamley, Ken Jones. **C:** Desmond Dickinson. **Ed:** John Pomeroy. **Art:** John Blezard. **Mk:** George Claff. **H:** Barbara Barnard. **SFx:** Cliff Richardson. **Cast:** Patricia Jessel, Dennis Lotis, Christopher Lee, Tom Naylor, Betta St. John, Venetia Stevenson.

The Innocents (1961). **D. P:** Jack Clayton. **Sc:** William Archibald and Truman Capote, John Mortimer. Based on novella by Henry James. **M:** Georges Auric. **C:** Freddie Francis. **Ed:** James Clark. **Art:** Wilfred Shingleton. **CDn:** Motley. **Mk:** Harold Fletcher. **H:** Gordon Bond. **Cast:** Deborah Kerr, Peter Wyngarde, Megs Jenkins, Michael Redgrave, Martin Stephens, Pamela Franklin, Clytie Jessop, Isla Cameron. **National Board of Review** Best Director. **Edgar Award** Best Motion Picture.

Burn, Witch, Burn [*Night of the Eagle*] (1962). **D:** Sidney Hayers. **Sc:** Charles Beaumont & Richard Matheson and George Baxt. Based on novel by Fritz Leiber. **P:** Samuel Z. Arkoff, Albert Fennell. **M:** William Alwyn. **C:** Reginald Wyer. **Ed:** Ralph Sheldon. **Art:** Jack Shampan. **Mk:** David Bracknell. **H:** Sophie Devinem, Iris Tilley. **S:** Ted Mason, Alastair McIntyre. **Cast:** Peter Wyngarde, Janet Blair, Margaret Johnston, Anthony Nicholls, Colin Gordon, Kathleen Byron.

"Morella" in *Tales of Terror* (1962). **D, P:** Roger Corman. **Sc:** Richard Matheson. Story by Edgar Allan Poe. **M:** Les Baxter. **C:** Floyd Crosby. **Ed:** Anthony Carras. **PDn:** Bartlett A. Carré, Daniel Haller. **SDc:** Harry Reif. **Mk:** Lou LaCava. **H:** Ray Forman. **S:** Jack Woods. **SFx:** Pat Dinga. **VFx:** Ray Mercer. **Cast:** Vincent Price, Maggie Pierce, Leona Gage, Edmund Cobb.

Witchcraft [*The Devil's Hand*] (1962). **D:** William J. Hole Jr. **Sc:** Jo Heims. **P:** Alvin K. Bubis. **M:** Allyn Ferguson, Michael Terr. **C:** Meredith M. Nicholson. **Ed:** Howard Epstein. **Mk:** Jack P. Pierce. **S:** Philip Mitchell. **Cast:** Linda Christian, Robert Alda, Neil Hamilton, Ariadna Welter, Gene Craft, Jeanne Carmen.

Diary of a Madman (1963). **D:** Reginald Le Borg. **Sc:** Robert E. Kent. Story by Guy de Maupassant. **P:** Robert E. Kent, Edward Small. **M:** Richard LaSalle. **C:** Ellis W. Carter. **Ed:** Grant Whytock. **Art:** Daniel Haller. **SDc:** Victor A. Gangelin. **CDn:** Marjorie Corso. **Mk:** Ted Coodley. **H:** Carmen Dirigo. **S:** Ralph Butler. **SFx:** Norman Breedlove. **Cast:** Vincent Price, Nancy Kovack, Chris Warfield, Elaine Devry, Ian Wolfe, Stephen Roberts.

The Haunted Palace (1963). **D, P:** Roger Corman. **Sc:** Charles Beaumont. Story by H. P. Lovecraft. **M:** Ronald Stein. **C:** Floyd Crosby. **Ed:** Ronald Sinclair. **Art:** Daniel Haller. **Mk:** Ted Coodley. **H:** Lorraine Roberson. **S:** John L. Bury. **Cast:** Vincent Price, Debra Paget, Frank Maxwell, Lon Chaney Jr., Leo Gordon, Elisha Cook Jr.

The Haunting (1963). **D, P:** Robert Wise. **Sc:** Nelson Gidding. Based on novel by Shirley Jackson. **M:** Humphrey Searle. **C:** Davis Boulton. **Ed:** Ernest Walter. **PDn:** Elliot Scott. **SDc:** John Jarvis. **CDn:** Mary Quant. **Mk:** Tom Smith. **H:** Joan Johnstone. **SFx:** Tom Howard. **Cast:** Julie Harris, Claire Bloom, Richard Johnson, Russ Tamblyn, Fay Compton, Rosalie Crutchley.

Dark Shadows (1966 through 1971). TV series. **D:** Lela Swift and others. **Sc:** Art Wallace, Dan Curtis, and others. **P:** Robert Costello (738 episodes, 1966–1969); also Peter Miner, Lela Swift, Sy Tomashoff. **M:** Bob Cobert. **PDn:** John Dapper, Sy Tomashoff. **CDn:** Mary McKinley, Ramsey Mostoller, Hazel Roy. **Mk:** Dennis Eger, Vincent Loscalzo, Dick Smith. **H:** Irene Hamalin, Jack LeGoms, Edith Tilles. **Cast:** Jonathan Frid, Grayson Hall, Nancy Barrett, Joan Bennett, Alexandra Isles, Louis Edmonds, Kathryn Leigh Scott, David Selby, Joel Crothers, Kate Jackson.

The Devil's Own [*The Witches*] (1966, 1967 USA). **D:** Cyril Frankel. **Sc:** Nigel Kneale. Based on novel by Peter Curtis. **P:** Anthony Nelson Keys. **M:** Richard Rodney Bennett. **C:** Arthur Grant. **Ed:** James Needs. **PDn:** Bernard Robinson. **Art:** Don Mingaye. **Mk:** George Partleton. **H:** Frieda Steiger. **S:** Roy Hyde. **Cast:** Joan Fontaine, Kay Walsh, Alec McCowen, Ann Bell, Ingrid Brett, John Collin, Michele Dotrice, Gwen Ffrangcon-Davies.

Eye of the Devil (1967). **D:** J. Lee Thompson. **Sc:** Robin Estridge, Dennis Murphy. Based on novel by Philip Loraine. **P:** John Calley, Martin Ransohoff. **M:** Gary McFarland. **C:** Erwin Hillier. **Ed:** Ernest Walter. **Art:** Elliot Scott. **CDn:** John Furness, Julie Harris. **Cast:** Deborah Kerr, David Niven, Donald Pleasence, Edward Mulhare, Flora Robson, Emlyn Williams, Sharon Tate, David Hemmings.

The Devil's Bride [*The Devil Rides Out*] (1968). **D:** Terence Fisher. **Sc:** Richard Matheson. Based on novel by Dennis Wheatley. **P:** Anthony Nelson Keys. **M:** James Bernard. **C:** Arthur Grant. **Ed:** Spencer Reeve. **PDn:** Bernard Robinson. **Mk:** Eddie Knight. **H:** Patricia McDermott. **SFx:** Michael Staiver-Hutchins. **Cast:** Christopher Lee, Charles Gray, Niké Arrighi, Leon Greene, Patrick Mower, Gwen Ffrangcon-Davies, Sarah Lawson, Paul Eddington.

"Never Bet the Devil Your Head, or Toby Dammit" in *Spirits of the Dead* (1968). **D:** Federico Fellini. **Sc:** Federico Fellini & Bernardino Zapponi. Story by Edgar Allan Poe. **P:** Raymond Eger, Alberto Grimaldi. **M:** Nino Rota. **C:** Giuseppe Rotunno. **Ed:** Ruggiero Mastroianni. **PDn:** Piero Tosi. **Art:** Fabrizio Clerici. **CDn:** Piero Tosi. **VFx:** Joseph Natanson. **Cast:** Terence Stamp, Salvo Randone, David Bresson, Peter Dane, Monica Pardo, Anne Tonietti.

Rosemary's Baby (1968). **D, Sc:** Roman Polanski. Based on novel by Ira Levin. **P:** William Castle. **M:** Christopher Komeda. **C:** William Fraker. **Ed:** Sam O'Steen, Bob Wyman. **PDn:** Richard Sylbert. **Art:** Joel Schiller. **SDc:** Robert Nelson. **CDn:** Anthea Sylbert. **Mk:** Allan Snyder. **H:** Sydney Guilaroff, Vidal Sassoon, Sherry Wilson. **VFx:** Farciot Edouart. **Cast:** Mia Farrow, John Cassavetes, Ruth Gordon, Sidney Blackmer, Maurice Evans, Ralph Bellamy, Angela Dorian, Patsy Kelly, Charles Grodin. **Academy Awards** Best Supporting Actress (Gordon). **David di Donatello Awards** Best Foreign Actress (Farrow). **Golden Globes** Best Supporting Actress (Gordon). **Photoplay Awards** Gold Medal.

Witchfinder General [*The Conqueror Worm*] (1968). **D:** Michael Reeves. **Sc:** Tom Baker, Michael Reeves. Based on novel by Ronald Bassett. **P:** Louis M.

Heyward, Arnold Miller, Philip Waddilove. **M:** Paul Ferris, Kendall Schmidt. **C:** John Coquillon. **Ed:** Howard Lanning. **Art:** Jim Morahan. **Mk:** Dore Hamilton. **H:** Henry Montsash. **SFx:** Roger Dicken. **Cast:** Vincent Price, Ian Ogilvy, Rupert Davies, Hilary Dwyer, Robert Russell, Nicky Henson, Tony Selby.

Crowhaven Farm (1970). Made for TV. **D, P:** Walter Grauman. **Sc:** John McGreevey. **M:** Robert Drasnin. **C:** Fleet Southcott. **Ed:** Aaron Stell. **Art:** Tracy Bousman. **SDc:** Ken Swartz. **CDn:** Robert Harris Sr., Shannon Litton. **Mk:** Ted Coodley. **H:** Bette Iverson. **Cast:** Hope Lange, Paul Burke, Lloyd Bochner, John Carradine, Milton Selzer, Patricia Barry, Virginia Gregg, William Smith.

The Blood on Satan's Claw (1970). **D:** Piers Haggard. **Sc:** Robert Wynne-Simmons. **P:** Peter L. Andrews, Malcolm B. Heyworth. **M:** Marc Wilkinson. **C:** Dick Bush. **Ed:** Richard Best. **PDn:** Arnold Chapkis. **Mk:** Eddie Knight. **H:** Olga Angelinetta. **Cast:** Patrick Wymark, Linda Hayden, Barry Andrews, Avice Landone, Simon Williams, Tamara Ustinov.

Equinox (1970). **D:** Jack Woods. **Sc:** Jack Woods. Story by Mark Thomas McGee. **P:** Jack H. Harris. **C:** Mike Hoover. **Ed:** John Joyce. **Mk:** Robynne Hoover. **S:** Glen Glenn, Bradley Lane. **SFx:** Dave Allen, Dennis Muren. **Cast:** Edward Connell, Barbara Hewitt, Frank Boers Jr., Robin Christopher, Jack Woods, James Phillips.

Hexen bis aufs Blut gequält [***Brenn, Hexe, Brenn***] [***Witches Tortured Till They Bleed***] [***Burn, Witch, Burn***] [***Mark of the Devil***] [***Hexen***] (1970). **D:** Michael Armstrong. **Sc:** Sergio Casstner, Percy Parker. **P:** Adrian Hoven. **M:** Michael Holm. **C:** Ernst W. Kalinke. **Ed:** Siegrun Jäger. **Art:** Max Mellin. **CDn:** Barbara Grupp. **Mk:** Alena Hejdankoba, Gunther Kulier. **S:** Hans-Dieter Schwarz. **Cast:** Herbert Lom, Udo Kier, Olivera Vuco, Reggie Nalder, Herbert Fux, Johannes Buzalski.

The Brotherhood of Satan (1971). **D:** Bernard McEveety. **Sc:** L. Q. Jones, William Welch. Story by Sean MacGregor. **P:** L. Q. Jones, Alvy Moore. **M:** Jaime Mendoza-Nava. **C:** John Arthur Morrill. **Ed:** Marvin Walowitz. **PDn:** Ray Boyle. **SFx:** Steve Karkus. **Cast:** Strother Martin, L. Q. Jones, Charles Bateman, Ahna Capri, Charles Robinson, Alvy Moore.

Macbeth [***The Tragedy of Macbeth***] (1971). **D:** Roman Polanski. **Sc:** Roman Polanski, Kenneth Tynan. Based on play by William Shakespeare. **P:** Andrew Braunsberg. **M:** The Third Ear Band. **C:** Gil Taylor. **Ed:** Alastair McIntyre. **PDn:** Wilfrid Shingleton. **Art:** Fred Carter. **SDc:** Bryan Graves. **CDn:** Anthony Mendleson. **Mk:** Tom Smith. **H:** Biddy Chrystal. **SFx:** Ted Samuels. **Cast:** Jon Finch, Francesca Annis, Martin Shaw, Terence Bayler, John Stride, Nicholas Selby, Stephan Chase. **BAFTA** Best Costume Design. **National Board of Review** Best Picture.

The Mephisto Waltz (1971). **D:** Paul Wendkos. **Sc:** Ben Maddow. Based on novel by Fred Mustard Stewart. **P:** Quinn Martin. **M:** Jerry Goldsmith. **C:** William W. Spencer. **Ed:** Richard Brockway. **Art:** Richard Y. Haman. **SDc:** Raphael Bretton, Walter M. Scott. **CDn:** Moss Mabry. **Mk:** John Chambers, Daniel C. Striepeke. **H:** Pat Abbott. **S:** John A. Bonner. **SFx:** Greg C.

Jensen. **Cast:** Alan Alda, Jacqueline Bisset, Barbara Parkins, Brad Dillman, William Windom, Kathleen Widdoes, Pamelyn Ferdin, Curt Jurgens.

Night of Dark Shadows (1971). **D, P:** Dan Curtis. **Sc:** Sam Hall. Story by Sam Hall, Dan Curtis. **M:** Robert Cobert. **C:** Richard Shore. **Ed:** Charles Goldsmith. **PDn:** Trevor Williams. **CDn:** Domingo Rodriguez. **Mk:** Reginald Tackley. **S:** John H. Bolz. **Cast:** David Selby, Grayson Hall, Kate Jackson, Lara Parker, John Karlen, Nancy Barrett, James Storm.

Simon, King of the Witches (1971). **D:** Bruce Kessler. **Sc:** Robert Phippeny. **P:** Joe Solomon. **M:** Stu Phillips. **C:** David L. Butler. **Ed:** Renn Reynolds. **Art:** Dale Hennesy. **SDc:** Robert De Vestel. **Mk:** Maurice Stein. **SFx:** Roger George. **Cast:** Allyson Ames, Sharon Berryhill, Jerry Brooke, Norman Burton, Angus Duncan, Michael C. Ford.

Child's Play (1972). **D:** Sidney Lumet. **Sc:** Leon Prochnik. Based on play by Robert Marasco. **P:** David Merrick. **M:** Michael Small. **C:** Enrique Bravo, Gerald Hirschfeld. **Ed:** Joanne Burke, Edward Warschilka. **PDn:** Philip Rosenberg. **Cast:** James Mason, Robert Preston, Beau Bridges, Ron Weyand, Charles White, David Rounds.

The Nightcomers (1972). **D:** Michael Winner. **Sc:** Michael Hastings. Based on novella by Henry James. **P:** Elliott Kastner, Michael Winner. **M:** Jerry Fielding. **C:** Robert Paynter. **Ed:** Freddie Wilson, Arnold Crust Jr. **Art:** Herbert Westbrook. **Mk:** Richard Mills. **H:** Stephanie Kaye. **Cast:** Marlon Brando, Stephanie Beacham, Thora Hird, Harry Andrews, Verna Harvey, Christopher Ellis, Anna Palk.

The Other (1972). **D, P:** Robert Mulligan. **Sc:** Tom Tryon. Based on his novel. **M:** Jerry Goldsmith. **C:** Robert L. Surtees. **Ed:** Folmar Blangsted, O. Nicholas Brown. **PDn:** Albert Brenner. **SDc:** Ruby Levitt. **CDn:** Joanne Haas, Tommy Welsh. **Mk:** Joe DiBella. **H:** Dorothy White. **S:** Don J. Bassman, Jack Solomon. **Cast:** Uta Hagen, Diana Muldaur, Chris Udvarnoky, Martin Udvarnoky, Norma Connolly, Victor French.

The Possession of Joel Delaney (1972). **D:** Waris Hussein. **Sc:** Grimes Grice, Matt Robinson. Based on novel by Ramona Stewart. **P:** Martin Poll. **M:** Joe Raposo. **C:** Lou Barlia, Arthur J. Ornitz. **Ed:** John Victor-Smith. **PDn:** Peter Murton. **Art:** Philip Rosenberg. **SDc:** Edward Stewart. **CDn:** Frank L. Thompson. **Mk:** Saul Meth. **H:** Ian Forest, Lee Trent. **Cast:** Shirley MacLaine, Perry King, Lisa Kohane, David Elliott, Miriam Colon, Barbara Trentham, Lovelady Powell, Edmundo Rivera Álvarez.

The Devil's Daughter (1973). **D:** Jeannot Szwarc. **Sc:** Colin Higgins. **P:** Edward K. Milkis, Thomas L. Miller. **M:** Laurence Rosenthal. **C:** J. J. Jones. **Ed:** Rita Roland. **Art:** William L. Campbell. **Cast:** Shelley Winters, Belinda Montgomery, Robert Foxworth, Jonathan Frid, Martha Scott, Joseph Cotten, Barbara Sammeth, Diane Ladd.

"Don't Look Now" (1973). **D:** Nicolas Roeg. **Sc:** Allan Scott, Chris Bryant. Story by Daphne Du Maurier. **P:** Peter Katz. **M:** Pino Donnagio. **C:** Anthony Richmond. **Ed:** Graeme Clifford. **Art:** Giovanni Soccol. **CDn:** Marit Lieberson, Andrea Galer. **Mk:** Giancarlo Del Brocco. **H:** Maria Luisa Garbini, Barry Richardson. **Cast:** Julie Christie, Donald Sutherland, Hilary Mason, Clelia Matania, Massimo Serato, Renato Scarpa, Adelina Poerio. **BAFTA** Best Cinematography.

The Exorcist (1973). **D:** William Friedkin. **Sc:** William Peter Blatty. Based on his novel. **P:** William Peter Blatty. **M:** Jack Nitzsche. **C:** Owen Roizman, Billy Williams. **Ed:** Norman Gay, Evan Lottman, Bud Smith. **PDn:** Bill Malley. **SDc:** Jerry Wunderlich. **CDn:** Joe Fretwell. **Mk:** Dick Smith. **H:** Bill Farley. **S:** Chris Newman. **SFx:** Marcel Vercoutere. **VFx:** Marv Ystrom. **Cast:** Ellen Burstyn, Max von Sydow, Jason Miller, Lee J. Cobb, Kitty Winn, Jack MacGowran, Linda Blair. **Academy Awards** Best Sound, Best Adapted Screenplay. **Golden Globes** Best Director, Best Motion Picture Drama, Best Screenplay, Best Supporting Actress (Blair). **Motion Picture Sound Editors** Best Editing of Dialogue, Best Editing of Sound Effects.

The Pyx (1973). **D:** Harvey Hart. **Sc:** Robert Schlitt. Based on novel by John Buell. **P:** Julian Roffman. **M:** Harry Freedman. **C:** René Verzier. **Ed:** Ron Wisman. **S:** Richard Lightstone. **SFx:** Jacques Godbout. **Cast:** Karen Black, Christopher Plummer, Donald Pilon, Jean-Louis Roux, Yvette Brind'amour, Jacques Godin.

Spirit of the Beehive [***El Espíritu de la Colmena***] (1973). **D:** Víctor Erice. **Sc:** Víctor Erice, Ángel Fernández Santos, Francisco J. Querejeta. **P:** Elías Querejeta. **M:** Luis de Pablo. **C:** Luis Cuadrado. **Ed:** Pablo González del Amo. **Art:** Jaime Chávarri. **SDc:** Adolfo Cofiño. **CDn:** Peris. **Mk:** Ramón de Diego. **S:** Luis Rodríguez. **VFx:** Pablo Núñez. **Cast:** Fernando Fernán Gómez, Teresa Gimpera, Ana Torrent, Isabel Tellería, Juan Margallo, José Villasante.

Abby (1974). **D:** William Girdler. **Sc:** Gordon Cornell Layne. Story by William Girdler. **P:** William Girdler, Mike Henry, Gordon Cornell Layne. **M:** Robert O. Ragland. **C:** William L. Asman. **Ed:** Henry Asman, Corky Ehlers. **PDn:** J. Patrick Kelly III. **S:** John Asman. **SFx:** Samuel E. Price. **Cast:** William Marshall, Terry Carter, Austin Stoker, Carol Speed, Juanita Moore.

It's Alive! (1974). **D, Sc, P:** Larry Cohen. **M:** Bernard Herrmann. **C:** Fenton Hamilton. **Ed:** Peter Honess. **Mk:** Rick Baker. **Cast:** John P. Ryan, Sharon Farrell, James Dixon, William Wellman Jr., Shamus Locke, Andrew Duggan, Guy Stockwell, Daniel Holzman.

The Stranger Within (1974). **D:** Lee Philips. **Sc:** Richard Matheson. **P:** Neil T. Maffeo. **M:** Charles Fox. **C:** Michael D. Margulies. **Ed:** Samuel E. Beetley. **Art:** Hilyard Brown. **SDc:** James Cane. **CDn:** Patricia Norris. **Mk:** Karl Herlinger. **H:** Patricia Miller. **Cast:** Barbara Eden, George Grizzard, Joyce Van Patten, David Doyle, Nehemiah Persoff.

Beyond the Door (1975). **D:** Oliver Hellman, Robert Barrett. **Sc:** Oliver Hellman, Robert Barrett, Aldo Crudo, Sonia Molteni. **P:** Ovidio G. Assonitis, Edward L. Montoro. **M:** Franco Micalizzi, Riz Ortolani. **C:** Roberto D'ettorre Piazzoli. **Ed:** A. J. Curi. **Art:** Piero Filippone. **H:** Giancarlo De Leonardis. **S:** Roberto Arcangeli. **SFx:** Donn Davison, Wally Gentleman. **Cast:** Juliet Mills, Gabriele Lavia, Richard Johnson, Nino Segurini, Elizabeth Turner, Barbara Fiorini.

The Devil's Rain (1975). **D:** Robert Fuest. **Sc:** James Ashton, Gabe Essoe, Gerald Hopman. **P:** James V. Cullen, Michael S. Glick. **M:** Al De Lory. **C:** Alex Phillips Jr. **Ed:** Michael Kahn. **PDn:** Nikita Knatz. **Art:** José Rodríguez Granada. **SDc:** Carlos Carnjean. **Mk:** Ellis Burman Jr. **S:** Gene Eliot. **Cast:** Ernest Borgnine, Tom Skerritt, Joan Prather, Eddie Albert, William Shatner, Ida Lupino, Woody Chambliss, Keenan Wynn, John Travolta.

Race with the Devil (1975). **D:** Jack Starrett. **Sc:** Wes Bishop, Lee Frost. **P:** Wes Bishop. **M:** Leonard Rosenman. **C:** Robert C. Jessup. **Ed:** Allan Jacobs, John F. Link. **CDn:** Nancy McArdle. **Mk:** Dorothy J. Pearl. **SFx:** Richard O. Helmer. **Cast:** Peter Fonda, Warren Oates, Loretta Swit, Lara Parker, R. G. Armstrong.

The Reincarnation of Peter Proud (1975). **D:** J. Lee Thompson. **Sc:** Max Ehrlich. **P:** Frank P. Rosenberg. **M:** Jerry Goldsmith. **C:** Victor J. Kemper. **PDn:** Jack Martin Smith. **SDc:** Robert De Vestel, Barbara Krieger. **Mk:** Jack H. Young. **H:** Virginia Jones. **Cast:** Michael Sarrazin, Jennifer O'Neill, Margot Kidder, Cornelia Sharpe, Paul Hecht, Tony Stephano.

Trilogy of Terror (1975). Made for TV. **D, P:** Dan Curtis. **Sc:** William F. Nolan, Richard Matheson. Story by Matheson. **M:** Bob Cobert. **C:** Paul Lohmann. **Ed:** Les Green. **Art:** Jan Scott. **SFx:** Erik von Buelow. **Cast:** Karen Black, Robert Burton, John Karlen, George Gaynes, Jim Storm, Gregory Harrison, Kathryn Reynolds, Tracy Curtis.

Burnt Offerings (1976). **D, P:** Dan Curtis. **Sc:** Dan Curtis, William F. Nolan. Based on novel by Robert Marasco. **M:** Bob Cobert. **C:** Jacques Marquette. **Ed:** Dennis Virkler. **PDn:** Eugène Lourié. **SDc:** Solomon Brewer. **CDn:** Ann Roth. **Mk:** Al Fleming. **H:** Abraham Meech-Burkestone, Peggy Shannon. **SFx:** Clifford Wenger. **Cast:** Karen Black, Oliver Reed, Burgess Meredith, Eileen Heckart, Lee H. Montgomery, Dub Taylor, Bette Davis.

Carrie (1976). **D:** Brian De Palma. **Sc:** Lawrence D. Cohen. Based on novel by Stephen King. **P:** Brian De Palma, Paul Monash. **M:** Pino Donaggio. **C:** Mario Tosi. **Ed:** Paul Hirsch. **Art:** Jack Fisk, William Kenney. **SDc:** Robert Gould. **CDn:** Rosanna Norton. **Mk:** Wesley Dawn. **H:** Adele Taylor. **SFx:** Gregory M. Auer, Kenneth Pepiot. **Cast:** Sissy Spacek, Piper Laurie, Amy Irving, William Katt, Betty Buckley, Nancy Allen, John Travolta, P. J. Soles. **National Society of Film Critics** Best Actress (Spacek).

Cría Cuervos (1976). **D, Sc:** Carlos Saura. **P:** Elías Querejeta, Carlos Saura. **M:** Frederic Mompou. **C:** Teodoro Escamilla. **Ed:** Pablo González del Amo. **PDn:** Rafael Palmero. **CDn:** Maiki Marín. **H:** Conchita Cano. **Mk:** Romana González. **S:** Bernardo Mens, Miguel Polo. **Cast:** Geraldine Chaplin, Mónica Randall, Florinda Chico, Ana Torrent, Héctor Alterio, Germán Cobos, Mirta Miller.

The Devil Within Her (1976). **D:** Peter Sasdy. **Sc:** Stanley Price. Story by Nato De Angeles. **P:** Norma Corney. **M:** Ron Grainer. **C:** Kenneth Talbot. **Ed:** Keith Palmer. **Art:** Roy Stannard. **Mk:** Eddie Knight. **H:** Stephanie Kaye. **SFx:** Bert Luxford. **Cast:** Joan Collins, Eileen Atkins, Ralph Bates, Donald Pleasence, Caroline Munro, Hilary Mason.

Look What's Happened to Rosemary's Baby (1976). Made for TV. **D:** Sam O'Steen. Sc, **P:** Anthony Wilson. **M:** Charles Bernstein. **C:** John A. Alonzo. **Ed:** Bob Wyman. **Art:** Les Gobruegge. **Cast:** Stephen McHattie, Patty Duke Astin, Broderick Crawford, Ruth Gordon, Lloyd Haynes, David Huffman, Tina Louise, George Maharis, Ray Milland.

Night Child (1976). **D:** Massimo Dallamano. **Sc:** Massimo Dallamano, Franco Marotta, Laura Toscano. **P:** Fulvio Lucisano, William Reich. **M:** Stelvio Cipriani. **C:** Franco Dellicolli. **Ed:** Antonio Siciliano. **PDn:** Luciano Puccini. **Mk:** Dante Trani. **H:** Rosa Luciani. **Cast:** Richard Johnson, Joanna Cassidy, Evelyne Stewart, Nicoletta Elmi, Edmund Purdom.

The Omen (1976). **D:** Richard Donner. **Sc:** David Seltzer. **P:** Harvey Bernhard. **M:** Jerry Goldsmith. **C:** Gilbert Taylor. **Ed:** Stuart Baird. **Art:** Carmen Dillon. **Mk:** Stuart Freeborn. **H:** Pat McDermott. **SFx:** John Richardson. **Cast:** Gregory Peck, Lee Remick, David Warner, Billie Whitelaw, Harvey Stephens. **Academy Awards** Best Original Score. **British Society of Cinematographers** Best Cinematography.

The Premonition (1976). **D:** Robert Allen Schnitzer. **Sc:** Anthony Mahon, Robert Allen Schnitzer. **P:** M. Wayne Fuller. **M:** Henry Mollicone, Pril Smiley. **C:** Victor Milt. **Ed:** Sidney Katz. **PDn:** John Lawless. **Mk:** Rita Ogden. **SFx:** Ken Newman. **Cast:** Sharon Farrell, Edward Bell, Danielle Brisebois, Ellen Barber, Richard Lynch, Jeff Corey.

To the Devil a Daughter (1976). **D:** Peter Sykes. **Sc:** Christopher Wicking. Based on novel by Dennis Wheatley. **P:** Roy Skeggs. **M:** Paul Glass. **C:** David Watkin. **Ed:** John Trumper. **Art:** Don Picton. **Mk:** Eric Allwright, George Blackler. **H:** Jeanette Freeman. **S:** Dennis Whitlock. **SFx:** Les Bowie. **Cast:** Richard Widmark, Christopher Lee, Honor Blackman, Denholm Elliott, Michael Goodliffe, Nastassja Kinski.

Eraserhead (1977). **D, Sc, P, M, Ed, Pd, Art:** David Lynch. **C:** Herbert Cardwell, Frederick Elmes. **S:** David Lynch, Alan Splet. **SFx:** Frederick Elmes, David Lynch. **Cast:** John Nance, Charlotte Stewart, Allen Joseph, Jeanne Bates, Judith Anna Roberts, Laurel Near, V. Phipps-Wilson, Jack Fisk.

Suspiria (1977). **D:** Dario Argento. **Sc:** Dario Argento and Daria Nicolodi. Based on novel by Thomas De Quincey. **P:** Claudio Argento. **M:** Dario Argento, The Goblins. **C:** Luciano Tovoli. **Ed:** Franco Fraticelli. **PDn:** Giuseppe Bassan. **CDn:** Pierangelo Cicoletti. **H:** Maria Teresa Corridoni. **Mk:** Pierantonio Mecacci. **SFx:** Germano Natali. **Cast:** Jessica Harper, Udo Kier, Alida Valli, Joan Bennett, Renato Scarpa, Stefania Casini, Flavio Bucci, Miguel Bosé.

Halloween (1978). **D, M:** John Carpenter. **Sc:** John Carpenter, Debra Hill. **P:** Debra Hill. **C:** Dean Cundey. **Ed:** Charles Bornstein, Tommy Wallace. **PDn:** Tommy Wallace. **SDc:** Craig Stearns. **Mk:** Erica Ulland. **Cast:** Donald Pleasence, Jamie Lee Curtis, Nancy Loomis, P. J. Soles, Charles Cyphers, Kyle Richards, Brian Andrews.

The Amityville Horror (1979). **D:** Stuart Rosenberg. **Sc:** Sandor Stern. Based on novel by Jay Anson. **P:** Elliot Geisinger, Ronald Saland. **M:** Lalo Schifrin. **C:** Fred J. Koenekamp. **Ed:** Robert Brown Jr. **Art:** Kim Swados. **SDc:** Robert Benton. **Mk:** Stephen Abrums. **H:** Christine Lee. **SFx:** Delwyn Rheaume. **VFx:** William Cruse. **Cast:** James Brolin, Margot Kidder, Rod Steiger, Don Stroud, Murray Hamilton.

Friday the 13th (1980). **D, P:** Sean S. Cunningham. **Sc:** Victor Miller. **M:** Harry Manfredini. **C:** Barry Abrams. **Ed:** Bill Freda. **PDn:** Virginia Field. **Art:** Virginia Field. **Mk:** Tom Savini. **Cast:** Betsy Palmer, Adrienne King, Harry Crosby, Laurie Bartham, Jeannine Taylor, Kevin Bacon, Mark Nelson, Robbi Morgan.

The Shining (1980). **D, P:** Stanley Kubrick. **Sc:** Stanley Kubrick, Diane Johnson. Based on novel by Stephen King. **C:** John Alcott. **M:** Wendy Carlos, Rachel Elkind. **Ed:** Ray Lovejoy. **PDn:** Roy Walker. **Art:** Les Tomkins. **Cdn:** Milena Canonero. **Cast:** Jack Nicholson, Shelley Duvall, Danny Lloyd, Scatman Crothers, Barry Nelson, Philip Stone, Joe Turkel.

Ghost Story (1981). **D:** John Irvin. **Sc:** Lawrence D. Cohen. Based on novel by Peter Straub. **P:** Burt Weissbourd. **M:** Philippe Sarde. **C:** Jack Cardiff. **Ed:** Tom Rolf. **PDn:** Norman Newberry. **CDn:** May Routh. **SFx:** Henry Millar Jr. **VFx:** Albert Whitlock. **Cast:** Fred Astaire, Melvyn Douglas, Douglas Fairbanks Jr., John Houseman, Craig Wasson, Patricia Neal, Alice Krige, Jacqueline Brookes.

Cat People (1982). **D:** Paul Schrader. **Sc:** Alan Ormsby. Story by DeWitt Bodeen. **P:** Charles W. Fries. **M:** Giorgio Moroder. **C:** John Bailey. **Ed:** Jacqueline Cambas, Jere Huggins, Ned Humphreys, Bud S. Smith. **PDn:** Ferdinando Scarfiotti. **Art:** Edward Richardson. **SDc:** Bruce Weintraub. **CDn:** Daniel Paredes. **Cast:** Nastassja Kinski, Malcolm McDowell, John Heard, Annette O'Toole, Ruby Dee, Ed Begley Jr., Scott Paulin, Frankie Faison.

Poltergeist (1982). **D:** Tobe Hooper. **Sc:** Steven Spielberg & Michael Grais & Mark Victor. Story by Steven Spielberg. **P:** Frank Marshall, Steven Spielberg. **M:** Jerry Goldsmith. **C:** Matthew F. Leonetti. **Ed:** Michael Kahn. **PDn:** James H. Spencer. **SDc:** Cheryal Kearney. **Mk:** Dottie Pearl. **H:** Toni Walker. **SFx:** Craig Reardon, Mike Wood. **Cast:** Craig T. Nelson, JoBeth Williams, Beatrice Straight, Dominique Dunne, Oliver Robins, Heather O'Rourke, Michael McManus, Virginia Kiser. **BAFTA** Best Special Visual Effects (Richard Edlund).

Christine (1983). **D:** John Carpenter. **Sc:** Bill Phillips. Based on novel by Stephen King. **P:** Richard Kobritz. **M:** John Carpenter, Alan Howarth, George Thorogood. **C:** Donald M. Morgan. **Ed:** Marion Rothman. **PDn:** Daniel Lomino. **SDc:** Cloudia. **CDn:** Darryl Levine. **Mk:** Bob Dawn. **H:** Frankie Bergman. **Cast:** Keith Gordon, John Stockwell, Alexandra Paul, Robert Prosky, Harry Dean Stanton, Christine Belford, Roberts Blossom, William Ostrander.

Cujo (1983). **D:** Lewis Teague. **Sc:** Don Carlos Dunaway, Lauren Currier. Based on novel by Stephen King. **P:** Daniel H. Blatt, Robert Singer. **M:** Charles Bernstein. **C:** Jan De Bont. **Ed:** Neil Travis. **PDn:** Guy Comtois. **SDc:** John Bergman. **CDn:** Jack Buehler. **Mk:** Robin Neal. **H:** Julie Purcell. **Cast:** Dee Wallace, Danny Pintauro, Daniel Hugh-Kelly, Christopher Stone, Ed Lauter, Kaiulani Lee, Billy Jacoby.

The Fourth Man [*De Vierde Man*] (1983, 1984

USA). **D:** Paul Verhoeven. **Sc:** Gerard Soeteman. Based on novel by Gerard Reve. **P:** Rob Houwer. **M:** Loek Dikker. **C:** Jan de Bont. **Ed:** Ine Schenkkan. **Art:** Roland De Groot. **CDn:** Elly Claus. **Mk:** Kathy Kühne. **H:** Kathy Kühne. **Cast:** Jeroen Krabbé, Renée Soutendijk, Thom Hoffman, Dolf de Vries, Geert de Jong, Hans Veerman.

Something Wicked This Way Comes (1983). **D:** Jack Clayton. **Sc:** Ray Bradbury. Based on his novel. **P:** Peter Vincent Douglas. **M:** James Horner. **C:** Stephen H. Burum. **Ed:** Barry Mark Gordon, Argyle Nelson. **PDn:** Richard MacDonald. **Art:** Richard James Lawrence, John B. Mansbridge. **SDc:** Rick Simpson. **CDn:** Ruth Myers. **Cast:** Jason Robards, Jonathan Pryce, Diane Ladd, Royal Dano, Vidal Peterson, Shawn Carson, Mary Grace Canfield, Richard Davalos.

Children of the Corn (1984). **D:** Fritz Kiersch. **Sc:** George Goldsmith. Based on novel by Stephen King. **P:** Donald P. Borchers, Terence Kirby. **M:** Jonathan Elias. **C:** Raoul Lomas. **Ed:** Harry Keramidas. **PDn:** Craig Stearns. **SDc:** Cricket Rowland. **CDn:** Barbara Scott. **VFx:** Max W. Anderson. **Cast:** Peter Horton, Linda Hamilton, R. G. Armstrong, John Franklin, Courtney Gains, Robby Kiger, AnneMarie McEvoy, Julie Maddalena.

Firestarter (1984). **D:** Mark L. Lester. **Sc:** Stanley Mann. Based on novel by Stephen King. **P:** Frank Capra Jr. **M:** Tangerine Dream. **C:** Giuseppe Ruzzolini. **Ed:** David Rawlins, Ronald Sanders. **SFx:** Jeff Jarvis, Michael Wood. **VFx:** William Cruse. **Cast:** David Keith, Drew Barrymore, Freddie Jones, Heather Locklear, Martin Sheen, George C. Scott, Art Carney, Louise Fletcher.

Gremlins (1984). **D:** Joe Dante. **Sc:** Chris Columbus. **P:** Michael Finnell. **M:** Jerry Goldsmith. **C:** John Hora. **Ed:** Tina Hirsch. **PDn:** James H. Spencer. **SDc:** Jackie Carr. **Mk:** Greg LaCava. **H:** Cheri Ruff. **SFx:** Bob MacDonald Jr., Robert MacDonald. **VFx:** Rocco Gioffre. **Cast:** Hoyt Axton, John Louie, Keye Luke, Don Steele, Susan Burgess, Scott Brady, Arnie Moore, Corey Feldman.

A Nightmare on Elm Street (1984). **D, Sc:** Wes Craven. **P:** Robert Shaye. **M:** Charles Bernstein. **C:** Jacques Haitkin. **Ed:** Pat McMahon, Rick Shaine. **PDn:** Greg Fonseca. **SDc:** Anne Huntley. **CDn:** Dana Lyman. **Mk:** Kathy Logan, David Miller. **H:** RaMona. **SFx:** Jim Doyle. **Cast:** John Saxon, Ronee Blakley, Heather Langenkamp, Amanda Wyss, Nick Corri, Johnny Depp, Charles Fleischer, Robert Englund.

Angel Heart (1987). **D, Sc:** Alan Parker. **Sc:** Alan Parker. Based on novel by William Hjortsberg. **P:** Elliott Kastner, Alan Marshall. **M:** Trevor Jones. **C:** Michael Seresin. **Ed:** Gerry Hambling. **PDn:** Brian Morris. **Art:** Armin Ganz, Kristi Zea. **CDn:** Aude Bronson-Howard. **Mk:** David Forrest. **H:** Victor De Nicola. **SFx:** J. C. Brotherhood. **Cast:** Mickey Rourke, Robert De Niro, Lisa Bonet, Charlotte Rampling, Stocker Fontelieu, Brownie McGhee, Michael Higgins.

Hellraiser (1987). **D:** Clive Barker. **Sc:** Clive Barker. Based on his novel. **P:** Christopher Figg. **M:** Christopher Young. **C:** Robin Vidgeon. **Ed:** Richard Marden. **PDn:** Mike Buchanan. **Art:** Jocelyn James. **CDn:** Joanna Johnston. **Mk:** Bob Keen, Geoff Portass.

Cast: Andrew Robinson, Clare Higgins, Ashley Laurence, Sean Chapman, Oliver Smith, Robert Hines.

Child's Play (1988). **D:** Tom Holland. **Sc:** Don Mancini and John Lafia and Tom Holland. Story by Don Mancini. **P:** David Kirschner. **M:** Joe Renzetti. **C:** Bill Butler. **Ed:** Edward Warschilka & Roy E. Peterson. **PDn:** Daniel A. Lomino. **SDc:** Cloudia. **CDn:** April Ferry. **Mk:** Michael A. Hancock. **H:** Marina Pedraza. **S:** John Riordan. **SFx:** Richard O. Helmer. **VFx:** Peter Donen. **Cast:** Catherine Hicks, Chris Sarandon, Alex Vincent, Brad Dourif, Dinah Manoff, Tommy Swerdlow.

Jacob's Ladder (1990). **D:** Adrian Lyne. **Sc:** Bruce Joel Rubin. **P:** Alan Marshall. **M:** Maurice Jarre. **C:** Jeffrey Kimball. **Ed:** Tom Rolf. **PDn:** Brian Morris. **Art:** Jeremy Conway, Wray Steven Graham. **SDc:** Kathleen Dolan. **CDn:** Ellen Mirojnick. **Mk:** Richard Dean. **H:** Lyndell Ouiyou. **SFx:** Conrad Brink, Gordon J. Smith. **VFx:** Jay McClennen. **Cast:** Tim Robbins, Elizabeth Peña, Matt Craven, Pruitt Taylor Vince, Jason Alexander, Patricia Kalember, Eriq La Salle, Danny Aiello, Ving Rhames, Brian Tarantina, S. Epatha Merkerson.

Beloved (1998). **D:** Jonathan Demme. **Sc:** Akosua Busia, Richard LaGravenese, Adam Brooks. Based on novel by Toni Morrison. **P:** Jonathan Demme, Kate Forte, Gary Goetzman, Edward Saxon, Oprah Winfrey. **M:** Rachel Portman. **C:** Tak Fujimoto. **Ed:** Andy Keir, Carol Littleton. **PDn:** Kristi Zea. **Art:** Tim Galvin. **SDc:** Karen O'Hara. **CDn:** Colleen Atwood. **Cast:** Oprah Winfrey, Danny Glover, Thandie Newton, Kimberly Elise, Beah Richards, Lisa Gay Hamilton, Albert Hall, Irma P. Hall, Jason Robards.

End of Days (1998). **D, C:** Peter Hyams. **Sc:** Andrew W. Marlowe. **P:** Armyan Bernstein, Bill Borden. **Ed:** Jeff Gullo, Steven Kemper. **PDn:** Richard Holland. **Art:** Charles Daboub Jr. **SDc:** Gary Fettis. **CDn:** Bobbie Mannix. **Cast:** Arnold Schwarzenegger, Gabriel Byrne, Robin Tunney, Kevin Pollak, Cch Pounder, Udo Kier, Rod Steiger.

What Dreams May Come (1998). **D:** Vincent Ward. **Sc:** Ron Bass. Based on novel by Richard Matheson. **P:** Barnet Bain, Stephen Simon. **M:** Michael Kamen. **C:** Eduardo Serra. **Ed:** David Brenner, Maysie Hoy. **PDn:** Eugenio Zanetti. **Art:** Jim Dultz, Joshua Rosen, Tomas Voth, Christian Wintter. **SDc:** Cindy Carr. **CDn:** Yvonne Blake. **SFx:** David Crawford, Rod M. Janusch. **Cast:** Robin Williams, Cuba Gooding Jr., Annabella Sciorra, Max von Sydow, Jessica Brooks Grant, Josh Paddock, Rosalind Chao, Werner Herzog.

The Blair Witch Project (1999). **D, Sc, Ed:** Daniel Myrick, Eduardo Sanchez. **P:** Robin Cowie, Gregg Hale. **M:** Tony Cora. **C:** Neal Fredericks. **PDn:** Ben Rock. **Art:** Ricardo R. Moreno, Eduardo Sanchez. **Cast:** Heather Donahue, Joshua Leonard, Michael Williams, Bob Griffin, Jim King, Sandra Sanchez, Ed Swanson, Patricia DeCou. **Independent Spirit** Best First Feature — Under $500,000.

The Ninth Gate (1999). **D, P:** Roman Polanski. **Sc:** John Brownjohn & Enrique Urbizu and Roman Polanski. Based on novel by Arturo Pérez-Reverte. **M:** Wojciech Kilar. **C:** Darius Khondji. **Ed:** Hervé de Luze. **PDn:** Dean Tavoularis. **Art:** Gerard Viard. **SDc:**

Philippe Turlure. **CDn:** Anthony Powell. **SFx:** Gilbert Pieri. **Cast:** Johnny Depp, Frank Langella, Lena Olin, Emmanuelle Seigner, Barbara Jefford, Jack Taylor, Jose Lopez Rodero, Allen Garfield. **European Film Awards** Outstanding European Achievement in World Cinema (Polanski).

The Rage: Carrie II (1999). **D:** Katt Shea. **Sc:** Rafael Moreu. **P:** Paul Monash. **M:** Danny B. Harvey. **C:** Donald M. Morgan. **Ed:** Richard Nord. **PDn:** Peter Jamison. **Art:** Geoffrey S. Grimsman, Dan Morski. **SDc:** Linda Spheeris. **CDn:** Theoni V. Aldredge. **Mk:** John R. Bayless, Barney Burman. **S:** Alan Rankin. **SFx:** Ron Bolanowski, Thomas R. Burman. **VFx:** Erika Walczak. **Cast:** Emily Bergl, Jason London, Amy Irving, J. Smith-Cameron, Dylan Bruno.

The Sixth Sense (1999). **D, Sc:** M. Night Shyamalan. **P:** Kathleen Kennedy, Frank Marshall, Barry Mendel. **M:** James Newton Howard. **C:** Tak Fujimoto. **Ed:** Andrew Mondshein. **PDn:** Larry Fulton. **Art:** Philip Messina. **SDc:** Douglas Mowat. **CDn:** Joanna Johnston. **Cast:** Bruce Willis, Haley Joel Osment, Toni Collette, Olivia Williams, Mischa Barton, Donnie Wahlberg, M. Night Shyamalan, Angelica Torn, Greg Wood.

Stigmata (1999). **D:** Rupert Wainwright. **Sc:** Tom Lazarus, Rick Ramage. Story by Tom Lazarus. **P:** Frank Mancuso Jr. **M:** Elia Cmiral, Billy Corgan. **C:** Jeffrey L. Kimball. **Ed:** Michael J. Duthie, Michael R. Miller. **PDn:** Waldemar Kalinowski. **Art:** Anthony R. Stabley. **SDc:** Florence Fellman, Marco Niro. **CDn:** Louise Frogley. **Cast:** Patricia Arquette, Gabriel Byrne, Jonathan Pryce, Nia Long, Dick Latessa.

Left Behind (2000). **D:** Vic Sarin. **Sc:** Alan McElroy and Paul Lalonde and Joe Goodman. Based on novel by Tim LaHaye & Jerry B. Jenkins. **P:** Joe Goodman, Paul Lalonde, Peter Lalonde, Ralph Winter. **M:** James Covell. **C:** George Jiri Tirl. **Ed:** Michael Pacek. **PDn:** Arthur W. Herriott. **Art:** Jim Phillips. **SDc:** Susan Young. **CDn:** Sharon McDonell. **SFx:** Michael Gagnon. **Cast:** Kirk Cameron, Brad Johnson, Gordon Currie, Janaya Stephens, Clarence Gilyard Jr., Colin Fox.

El Mar (2000). **D:** Agustín Villaronga. **P:** Isona Passola. **Sc:** Agustín Villaronga, Biel Mesquida, Antoni Aloy. Based on novel by Blai Bonet. **C:** Jaume Peracaula. **M:** Javier Navarrete. **Ed:** Raúl Román. **Pdn, Art:** Francesc Candini. **Cdn:** Mercè Paloma. **Cast:** Roger Casamajor, Bruno Bergonzini, Antònia Torrens, Hernán González, Juli Mira, Simón Andreu, Ángela Molina, David Lozano.

The Devil's Backbone [*El Espinazo del Diablo*] (2001). **D:** Guillermo Del Toro. **Sc:** Guillermo Del Toro and Antonio Trashorras & David Muñoz. **P:** Pedro Almodóvar, Guillermo Del Toro. **M:** Javier Navarrete. **C:** Guillermo Navarro. **Ed:** Luis de la Madrid. **Art:** César Macarrón. **SDc:** Pablo Perona Navarro, María del Pilar Revuelta. **CDn:** José Vico. **H:** Fermín Galán. **Mk:** Jorge Hernández. **S:** Miguel Rejas. **SFx:** Reyes Abades, Carmen Aguirre, Alfonso Nieto. **Cast:** Eduardo Noriega, Marisa Paredes, Federico Luppi, Fernando Tielve, Íñigo Garcés, Irene Visedo, José Manuel Lorenzo, Junio Valverde.

Donnie Darko (2001). **D, Sc:** Richard Kelly. **P:** Adam Fields, Nancy Juvonen, Sean McKittrick. **M:** Michael Andrews. **C:** Steven Poster. **Ed:** Sam Bauer, Eric Strand. **PDn:** Alexander Hammond. **SDc:** Jennie Harris. **CDn:** April Ferry. **Cast:** Jake Gyllenhaal, Holmes Osborne, Maggie Gyllenhaal, Daveigh Chase, Mary McDonnell, James Duval, Arthur Taxier, Patrick Swayze, Noah Wyle, Drew Barrymore, Katharine Ross.

The Others (2001). **D, Sc, M:** Alejandro Amenábar. **P:** Fernando Bovaira, José Luis Cuerda, Sunmin Park. **C:** Javier Aguirresarobe. **Ed:** Nacho Ruiz Capillas. **PDn, Art:** Benjamín Fernández. **SDc:** Emilio Ardura, Elli Griff. **CDn:** Sonia Grande. **Cast:** Nicole Kidman, Fionnula Flanagan, Christopher Eccleston, Alakina Mann, James Bentley, Eric Sykes, Elaine Cassidy, Renée Asherson.

Left Behind II: Tribulation Force (2002). **D:** Bill Corcoran. **Sc:** John Patus and Paul Lalonde. Based on novel by Tim LaHaye & Jerry B. Jenkins. **P:** Peter Lalonde, Nicholas D. Tabarrok. **M:** Gary Koftinoff. **C:** Michael Storey. **Ed:** Michael Doherty. **PDn:** Harold Thrasher. **Art:** Dean A. O'Dell. **SDc:** Jerri Thrasher. **CDn:** Sharon McDonell. **Mk:** Vann E. Gouweleeuw. **Cast:** Kirk Cameron, Brad Johnson, Gordon Currie, Janaya Stephens, Clarence Gilyard Jr., Lubomir Mykytiuk, David Macniven.

Birth (2004). **D:** Jonathan Glazer. **Sc:** Jean-Claude Carrière & Milo Addica & Jonathan Glazer. **P:** Lizie Gower, Nick Morris, Jean-Louis Piel. **M:** Alexandre Desplat. **C:** Harris Savides. **Ed:** Sam Sneade, Claus Wehlisch. **PDn:** Kevin Thompson. **Art:** Jonathan Arkin. **SDc:** Ford Wheeler. **CDn:** John A. Dunn. **SFx:** John M. Ottesen, Ronald Ottesen. **Cast:** Nicole Kidman, Cameron Bright, Danny Huston, Lauren Bacall, Alison Elliott, Arliss Howard, Michael Desautels, Anne Heche.

Godsend (2004). **D:** Nick Hamm. **Sc:** Mark Bomback. **P:** Marc Butan, Sean O'Keefe, Cathy Schulman,**m:** Brian Tyler. **C:** Kramer Morgenthau. **Ed:** Niven Howie, Steve Mirkovich. **PDn:** Doug Kraner. **Art:** Arvinder Grewal, Nicolas Lepage, Jarik Van Sluijs. **SDc:** Nigel Hutchins, Susan Ogu. **CDn:** Suzanne McCabe. **Cast:** Greg Kinnear, Rebecca Romijn-Stamos, Robert De Niro, Cameron Bright, Merwin Mondesir, Sava Drayton.

Hellboy (2004). **D:** Guillermo Del Toro. **Sc:** Guillermo Del Toro. Story by Guillermo Del Toro and Peter Briggs. Based on comic books by Mike Mignola. **P:** Lawrence Gordon, Mike Richardson, Lloyd Levin. **M:** Marco Beltrami. **C:** Guillermo Navarro. **Ed:** Peter Amundson. **PDn:** Stephen Scott. **Art:** Marco Bittner Rosser, Peter Francis, James Hambidge. **SDc:** Hilton Rosemarin. **CDn:** Wendy Partridge. **Mk:** Matt Rose. Sound: Steve Boeddeker. **Cast:** Ron Perlman, Selma Blair, Jeffrey Tambor, Karel Roden, Rupert Evans, Doug Jones, Brian Steele, John Hurt.

The Passion of the Christ (2004). **D:** Mel Gibson. **Sc:** Benedict Fitzgerald, Mel Gibson. **P:** Mel Gibson, Bruce Davey, Stephen McEveety. **M:** John Debney. **C:** Caleb Deschanel. **Ed:** John Wright. **PDn:** Francesco Frigeri. **SDc:** Carlo Gervasi. **Mk:** Keith Vanderlaan. **CDn:** Maurizio Millenotti. **Cast:** James Caviezel, Monica Bellucci, Claudia Gerini, Maia Morgenstern, Sergio Rubini, Rosalinda Celentano, Hristo Jivkov, Mattia

Sbragia, Luca De Dominicis. **Motion Picture Sound Editors** Best Editing of Music.

Resident Evil: Apocalypse (2004). **D:** Alexander Witt. **Sc:** Paul W. S. Anderson. **P:** Paul W. S. Anderson, Jeremy Bolt, Don Carmody. **M:** Jeff Danna. **C:** Derek Rogers, Christian Sebaldt. **Ed:** Eddie Hamilton. **PDn:** Paul Denham Austerberry. **Art:** Nigel Churcher. **SDc:** Steven Essam. **CDn:** Mary McLeod. **Cast:** Milla Jovovich, Sienna Guillory, Oded Fehr, Thomas Kretschmann, Sophie Vavasseur, Raz Adoti, Jared Harris.

Constantine (2005). **D:** Francis Lawrence. **Sc:** Kevin Brodbin, Frank Cappello. Story by Kevin Brodbin. Based on comic book by Jamie Delano & Garth Ennis. **P:** Lauren Shuler Donner, Akiva Goldsman, and others. **M:** Klaus Badelt, Brian Tyler. **C:** Philippe Rousselot. **Ed:** Wayne Wahrman. **PDn:** Naomi Shohan. **Art:** David Lazan. **SDc:** Douglas A. Mowat. **CDn:** Louise Frogley. **Mk:** Jim Charmatz. **H:** Susan Germaine, Candace Neal. **SDn:** Steven Schwartz, Stan Tropp. **S:** Charles Maynes, Jeremy Peirson. **SFx:** Jason Matthews, Joey Orosco. **Cast:** Keanu Reeves, Rachel Weisz, Shia LaBeouf, Djimon Hounsou, Max Baker, Tilda Swinton.

The Exorcism of Emily Rose (2005). **D:** Scott Derrickson. **Sc:** Paul Harris Boardman & Scott Derrickson. **P:** Paul Harris Boardman, Beau Flynn, Gary Lucchesi, Tom Rosenberg, Tripp Vinson. **M:** Christopher Young. **C:** Tom Stern. **Ed:** Jeff Betancourt. **PDn:** David Brisbin. **Art:** Sandi Tanaka. **SDc:** Lesley Beale. **CDn:** Tish Monaghan. **Mk:** Gitte Axen, Mindy Hall. **SDn:** Chris Beach. **S:** Paul N. J. Ottosson. **SFx:** Bill Orr, Keith VanderLaan. **VFx:** Keith VanderLaan, J. M. Logan, Michael Shelton. **Cast:** Laura Linney, Tom Wilkinson, Campbell Scott, Jennifer Carpenter, Colm Feore, Duncan Fraser, Mary Beth Hurt, Henry Czerny, Shohreh Aghdashloo.

Hide and Seek (2005). **D:** John Polson. **Sc:** Ari Schlossberg. **P:** Barry Josephson. **M:** John Ottman. **C:** Dariusz Wolski. **Ed:** Jeffrey Ford. **PDn:** Steven J. Jordan. **Art:** Emily Beck, Dennis Bradford. **SDc:** Judy Gurr, Beth Kushnick. **CDn:** Aude Bronson-Howard. **Mk:** John Caglione Jr., Ilona Herman. **H:** Milton Buras, Ilona Herman. **S:** Erik Aadahl. **SFx:** Steven Kirshoff. **Cast:** Robert De Niro, Dakota Fanning, Famke Janssen, Elisabeth Shue, Amy Irving, Dylan Baker, Melissa Leo.

Left Behind: World at War (2005). **D:** Craig R. Baxley. **Sc:** Paul Lalonde, Peter Lalonde, André van Heerden. Based on novel by Tim LaHaye & Jerry B. Jenkins. **P:** Peter Lalonde, Nicholas Tabarrok, André van Heerden. **M:** Gary Chang. **C:** David Connell. **Ed:** Sonny Baskin. **PDn:** Rupert Lazarus. **Art:** Jon P. Goulding. **SDc:** Brendan Smith. **CDn:** Sharon McDonell. **SDn:** Anthony A. Ianni. **S:** Steve Marian. **SFx:** John LaForet. **VFx:** Stevie Ramone. **Cast:** Louis Gossett Jr., Kirk Cameron, Brad Johnson, Gordon Currie, Janaya Stephens, Arnold Pinnock, Jessica Steen, Laura Catalano.

Lemming (2005). **D:** Dominik Moll. **Sc:** Gilles Marchand, Dominik Moll. **P:** Michel Saint-Jean. **M:** David Sinclair Whitaker. **C:** Jean-Marc Fabre. **Ed:** Mike Fromentin. **PDn:** Michel Barthélémy. **Art:** Pierre Duboisberranger. **CDn:** Virginie Montel, Isabelle Pannetier. **Cast:** Laurent Lucas, Charlotte Gainsbourg, Charlotte Rampling, André Dussollier.

Revelations (2005). TV Miniseries. **D:** Lesli Linka Glatter, David Semel, Lili Fini Zanuck. Teleplay by Mark Kruger, David Seltzer. **P:** Jessika Borsiczky, David Roessell. **M:** Joseph Vitarelli. **C:** Joel Ransom, Brian J. Reynolds. **Ed:** Juan Carlos Garza, Jill Savitt, Sondra Watanabe, Lynne Willingham. **PDn:** Douglas Higgins, Philip Toolin. **SFx:** Jeremy Hays, Brendon O'Dell. **VFx:** Aaron Greenberg, Eric J. Robertson, Greg Russell. **Cast:** Bill Pullman, Natascha McElhone, Michael Massee, Mark Rendall, Martin Starr, Chelsey Coyle, Brittney Coyle.

Pan's Labyrinth [**El Laberinto del Fauno**] (2006). **D:** Guillermo Del Toro. **Sc:** Guillermo Del Toro. **P:** Álvaro Augustín, Alfonso Cuarón, Bertha Navarro, Guillermo Del Toro, Frida Torresblanco. **M:** Javier Navarrete. **C:** Guillermo Navarro. **Ed:** Bernat Vilaplana. **PDn:** Eugenio Caballero. **CDn:** Lala Huete, Rocío Redondo. **Mk:** David Martí, José Quetglás, Arjen Tuiten. **SDn:** Pilar Revuelta. **S:** Martín Hernández, Roland N. Thai. **Cast:** Sergi López, Maribel Verdú, Ivana Baquero, Alex Angulo, Ariadna Gil, Doug Jones, Eusebio Lazaro, Paco Vidal, Federico Luppi. **Academy Awards** Best Achievement in Art Direction (Caballero, Revuelta), Best Achievement in Cinematography, Best Achievement in Makeup (Martí, Ribé). **Art Directors Guild** Excellence in Production Design Award Feature Film — Fantasy Film (Caballero, Liste, Zaragoza, Castro). **BAFTA Awards** Best Costume Design (Huete), Best Film not in the English Language (Cuarón, Navarro, Torresblanco, Del Toro), Best Make Up & Hair (Quetglás, Sánchez. **Costume Designers Guild** Excellence in Costume Design for Film — Fantasy (Huete). **Goya Awards** Best Cinematography (Navarro), Best Editing (Vilaplana), Best Makeup and Hairstyles (Quetglás, Sánchez), Best New Actress (Baquero), Best Screenplay — Original (Del Toro), Best Sound (Polo, Hernández), Best Special Effects (David, Abades, Burrell, Irastorza, Ruiz). **Independent Spirit Awards** Best Cinematography (Navarro). **Los Angeles Film Critics Association Awards** Best Production Design (Caballero). **Motion Picture Sound Editors** Best Sound Editing for Sound Effects and Foley in a Foreign Film (Hernández, Diaz, Thai, Blanco, Quevedo, Zamorano, Blanco). **New York Film Critics Circle Awards** Best Cinematographer (Navarro).

The Orphanage [**El Orfanato**] (2007). **D:** Juan Antonio Bayona. **Sc:** Sergio G. Sánchez. **P:** Álvaro Augustín, Joaquín Padro, Mar Targarona. **ExP:** Guillermo del Toro. **M:** Fernando Velázquez. **C:** Óscar Faura. **Ed:** Elena Ruiz. **PDn:** Josep Rosell. **Art:** Iñigo Navarro. **SDc:** Iñigo Navarro. **CDn:** Maria Reyes. **H:** Itziar Arrieta. **Mk:** Lola López, David Martí, Montse Ribé. **SDn:** Paula de la Fuente, Blanca Francoli. **S:** Oriol Tarragó. **SFx:** Lluís Castells. **VFx:** Jesús Luque. **Cast:** Belén Rueda, Fernando Cayo, Roger Príncep, Mabel Rivera, Montserrat Carulla, Geraldine Chaplin. **Motion Picture Sound Editors** Best Sound Effects, Foley, Dialogue & Adr in a Foreign Feature Film (Tarragó, others).

Hellboy II: The Golden Army (2008). **D:** Guillermo del Toro. **Sc:** Guillermo del Toro. Story by Guillermo del Toro & Mike Mignola. **P:** Lawrence Gordon, Lloyd Levin, Mike Richardson, Joe Roth. **M:** Danny Elfman. **C:** Guillermo Navarro. **Ed:** Bernat Vilaplana. **PDn:** Stephen Scott. **Art:** Anthony Caron-Delion, John Frankish, Paul Laugier, Mark Swain, Judit Varga. **SDc:** Elli Griff. **CDn:** Sammy Sheldon. **Mk:** Mike Elizalde. **S:** Martín Hernández, Roland N. Thai. **Cast:** Ron Perlman, Selma Blair, Doug Jones, John Alexander, James Dodd, Luke Goss, Anna Walton, Jeffrey Tambor, John Hurt.

ASIAN MILLENNIAL HORROR

Ringu: Kanzen-Ban (1995). Made for TV. **D:** Chisui Takigawa. **Sc:** Joji Iida, Soshigaya Taizo. Based on novel by Kôji Suzuki. **Cast:** Katsunori Takahashi, Yoshio Harada, Ayane Miura, Mai Tachihara, Maha Hamada, Tomorowo Taguchi, Akiko Hinagata, Takayuki Godai.

Cure [***Kyua***] (1997). **D, Sc:** Kiyoshi Kurosawa. Based on his novel. **P:** Tetsuya Ikeda, Satoshi Kanno, Atsuyuki Shimoda, Tsutomu Tsuchikawa. **M:** Gary Ashiya. **C:** Tokusho Kikumura. **Ed:** Kan Suzuki. **PDn:** Tomoyuki Maruo. **Mk:** Yuuichi Matsui. **S:** Hiromichi Kori. **Cast:** Kôji Yakusho, Masato Hagiwara, Tsuyoshi Ujiki, Anna Nakagawa, Yoriko Douguchi, Yukijiro Hotaru, Denden, Ren Osugi.

Ringu (1998). **D:** Hideo Nakata. **Sc:** Hiroshi Takahashi. Based on novel by Kôji Suzuki. **P:** Takashige Ichise, Shinya Kawai, Takenori Sento. **M:** Kenji Kawai. **C:** Junichirô Hayashi. **PDn:** Iwao Saito. **Mk:** Yoshiichi Matsui, Takuya Wada. **S:** Yoshiya Obara. **SFx:** Hajime Matsumoto. **VFx:** Hajime Matsumoto. **Cast:** Nanako Matsushima, Asakawa, Miki Nakatani, Hiroyuki Sanada, Yuko Takeuchi, Hitomi Sato, Yoichi Numata, Yutaka Matsushige.

Audition [***Ôdishon***] (1999). **D:** Takashi Miike. **Sc:** Daisuke Tengan. Based on novel by Ryu Murakami. **P:** Satoshi Fukushima, Akemi Suyama. **M:** Kôji Endô. **C:** Hideo Yamamoto. **Ed:** Yasushi Shimamura. **PDn:** Tatsuo Ozeki. **CDn:** Tomoe Kumagai. **Mk:** Yuuichi Matsui. **Cast:** Ryo Ishibashi, Eihi Shiina, Tetsu Sawaki, Jun Kunimura, Renji Ishibashi, Miyuki Matsuda, Toshie Negishi, Ren Osugi.

Charisma [***Karisuma***] (1999). **D, Sc:** Kiyoshi Kurosawa. **P:** Satoshi Kanno, Atsuyuki Shimoda. **M:** Gary Ashiya. **C:** Junichirô Hayashi. **Ed:** Junichi Kikuchi. **Art:** Tomoyuki Maruo. **S:** Makio Iya. **Cast:** Kôji Yakusho, Hiroyuki Ikeuchi, Ren Osugi, Yoriko Douguchi, Jun Fubuki, Akira Otaka, Yutaka Matsushige, Sachiko Meguro.

Ringu II (1999). **D:** Hideo Nakata. **Sc:** Hideo Nakata, Hiroshi Takahashi. **P:** Taka Ichise, Makoto Ishihara. **M:** Kenji Kawai. **C:** Hideo Yamamoto. **Ed:** Nobuyuki Takahashi. **Mk:** Yuuichi Matsui. **Cast:** Miki Nakatani, Hitomi Sato, Kyôko Fukada, Fumiyo Kohinata, Kenjiro Ishimaru, Yûrei Yanagi, Rikiya Otaka, Yoichi Numata.

Ju-on [***The Curse***] (2000). **D, Sc:** Takashi Shimizu. **P:** Takashige Ichise, Kazuo Katô, Masaaki Takashima. **M:** Gary Ashiya, Shiro Sato. **C:** Nobuhito Kisuki. **S:** Mitsuo Tokita. **SFx:** Hajime Matsumoto. **VFx:** Hiroyuki Tashiro. **Cast:** Yûrei Yanagi, Chiaki Kuriyama, Hitomi Miwa, Asumi Miwa, Yoriko Dôguchi, Tarô Suwa, Yuue, Takako Fuji.

Ju-on 2 [***The Curse 2***] (2000). **D, Sc:** Takashi

Shimizu. **P:** Takashige Ichise, Kazuo Katô, Masaaki Takashima. **M:** Gary Ashiya. **C:** Nobuhito Kisuki. **S:** Mitsuo Tokita. **VFx:** Hiroyuki Tashiro. **Cast:** Yuuko Daike, Makoto Ashikawa, Kahori Fujii, Mayuko Saitô, Yûrei Yanagi, Tomohiro Kaku, Takako Fuji.

Ringu 0: Bâsudei [***Ringu 0: Birthday***] (2000). **D:** Norio Tsuruta. **Sc:** Hiroshi Takahashi. Story by Kôji Suzuki. **P:** Takashige Ichise. **M:** Shinichiro Ogata. **Cast:** Yukie Nakama, Seiichi Tanabe, Kumiko Aso, Yoshiko Tanaka, Ryûji Mizukami, Takeshi Wakamatsu, Kaoru Okunuki, Daisuke Ban.

Pulse [***Kairo***] (2001). **D, Sc:** Kiyoshi Kurosawa. **P:** Hiroshi Yamamoto. **M:** Takefumi Haketa, Takeshi Haketa. **C:** Junichirô Hayashi. **PDn:** Tomoyuki Maruo. **S:** Makio Ika. **VFx:** Shûji Asano, Masaru Tateishi. **Cast:** Haruhiko Katô, Kumiko Aso, Koyuki, Kurume Arisaka, Masatoshi Matsuo, Shinji Takeda, Jun Fubuki, Shun Sugata.

Visitor Q [***Bizita Q***] (2001). **D:** Takashi Miike. **Sc:** Itaru Era. **P:** Reiko Arakawa, Seiichiro Kobayashi, Susumu Nakajima. **M:** Kôji Endô. **C:** Hideo Yamamoto. **Ed:** Yasushi Shimamura. **PDn:** Yutaka Uki. **S:** Yoshiya Obara. **Cast:** Kenichi Endo, Shungiku Uchida, Kazushi Watanabe, Shôko Nakahara, Fujiko, Jun Mutô.

The Eye [***Gin Gwai***] [***Jian Gui***] (2002). **D:** Oxide Pang, Danny Pang. **Sc:** Jo Jo Yuet-chun Hui, Oxide Pang, Danny Pang. **P:** Peter Ho-Sun Chan, Lawrence Cheng. **M:** Orange Music. **C:** Decha Srimantra. **Ed:** Oxide Pang, Danny Pang. **Art:** Simon So. **CDn:** Jittima Kongsri, Stephanie Wong. **S:** Oxide Pang. **VFx:** Jack Ho. **Cast:** Lee Sin-je, Lawrence Chou, Chutcha Rujinanon, Yut Lai So, Candy Lo, Yin Ping Ko, Pierre Png, Edmund Chen.

Honogurai Mizu No Soko Kara [***Dark Water***] (2002). **D:** Hideo Nakata. **Sc:** Hideo Nakata, Takashige Ichise, Yoshihiro Nakamura. Based on novel by Kôji Suzuki. **P:** Takashige Ichise. **M:** Kenji Kawai, Shikao Suga. **C:** Junichirô Hayashi. **Ed:** Nobuyuki Takahashi. **PDn:** Katsumi Nakazawa. **S:** Masayuki Iwakura. **Cast:** Hitomi Kuroki, Rio Kanno, Mirei Oguchi, Asami Mizukawa, Fumiyo Kohinata, Yu Tokui, Isao Yatsu, Shigemitsu Ogi.

Phone [***Pon***] (2002). **D:** Byeong-ki Ahn. **M:** Sang-ho Lee. **C:** Yong-shik Mun. **Cast:** Ji-won Ha, Yu-mi Kim, Woo-jae Choi, Ji-yeon Choi, Seo-woo Eun.

The Ring [American remake] (2002). **D:** Gore Verbinski. **Sc:** Ehren Kruger. Based on novel by Koji Suzuki. **P:** Laurie MacDonald, Walter F. Parkes. **M:** Hans Zimmer. **C:** Bojan Bazelli. **Ed:** Craig Wood. **PDn:** Tom Duffield. **Art:** Patrick M. Sullivan Jr. **SDc:** Rosemary Brandenburg. **CDn:** Julie Weiss. **Cast:** Naomi Watts, Martin Henderson, David Dorfman,

Brian Cox, Jane Alexander, Lindsay Frost, Amber Tamblyn, Rachael Bella.

Suicide Club [*Jisatsu Saakuru*] (2002). **D, Sc:** Sion Sono. **P:** Masaya Kawamata, Toshikazu Tomita, Seiji Yoshida. **M:** Tomoki Hasegawa. **C:** Kazuto Sato. **Ed:** Akihiro Onaga. **Cast:** Ryo Ishibashi, Akaji Maro, Masatoshi Nagase, Saya Hagiwara, Hideo Sako, Takashi Nomura, Tamao Satô, Mai Hosho.

Bright Future [*Akarui Mirai*] (2003). **D, Sc:** Kiyoshi Kurosawa. **P:** Takashi Asai. **M:** Pacific 231. **C:** Takahide Shibanushi. **Ed:** Kiyoshi Kurosawa. **PDn:** Yasuaki Harada. **CDn:** Michiko Kitamura. **S:** Hiromichi Kori. **Cast:** Jô Odagiri, Tadanobu Asano, Tatsuya Fuji, Takashi Sasano, Marumi Shiraishi.

Gozu [*Gokudô Kyôfu Dai-Gekijô*] (2003). **D:** Takashi Miike. **Sc:** Sakichi Satô. **P:** Kana Koido, Harumi Sone. **M:** Kôji Endô. **C:** Kazunari Tanaka. **Ed:** Yasushi Shimamura. **PDn:** Akira Ishige. **SDc:** Akira Sakamoto. **S:** Hitoshi Tsurumaki. **Cast:** Hideki Sone, Shô Aikawa, Kimika Yoshino, Shôhei Hino, Keiko Tomita, Harumi Sone, Renji Ishibashi.

Ju-on 3 [*The Grudge*] (2003). **D, Sc:** Takashi Shimizu. **P:** Taka Ichise. **M:** Shiro Sato. **C:** Tokusho Kikumura. **Ed:** Nobuyuki Takahashi. **PDn:** Toshiharu Tokiwa. **S:** Komatsu Masato. **Cast:** Megumi Okina, Misaki Ito, Misa Uehara, Yui Ichikawa, Kanji Tsuda, Kayoko Shibata, Yukako Kukuri, Shuri Matsuda.

Ju-on 4 [*The Grudge 2*] (2003). **D, Sc:** Takashi Shimizu. **P:** Taka Ichise. **M:** Shiro Sato. **C:** Tokusho Kikumura. **Ed:** Nobuyuki Takahashi. **PDn:** Toshiharu Tokiwa. **S:** Masato Komatsu. **VFx:** Hajime Matsumoto. **Cast:** Noriko Sakai, Chiharu Nîyama, Kei Horie, Yui Ichikawa, Shingo Katsurayama.

Oldboy (2003). **D:** Chan-wook Park. **Sc:** Jo-yun Hwang, Chun-hyeong Lim, Joon-hyung Lim, Chan-wook Park. **Story by** Garon Tsuchiya, Nobuaki Minegishi. **P:** Seung-yong Lim. **C:** Jeong-hun Jeong. **Ed:** Sang-beom Kim. **Art:** Seong-hie Ryu. **CDn:** Sankyung Cho. **S:** Seung-cheol Lee. **Cast:** Min-sik Choi, Ji-tae Yu, Hye-jeong Kang, Dae-han Ji, Dal-su Oh, Byeong-ok Kim, Seung-shin Lee, Jin-seo Yun. **British Independent Film Awards** Best Foreign Film. **Cannes** Grand Prix.

A Tale of Two Sisters [*Janghwa, Hongryeon*] (2003). **D, Sc:** Ji-woon Kim. **M:** Byung-woo Lee. **C:** Mo-gae Lee. **Ed:** Hyeon-mi Lee. **Art:** Geun-hyeon Jo. **Cast:** Kap-su Kim, Jung-ah Yum, Su-jeong Lim, Geun-yeong Mun.

The Grudge [American remake] (2004). **D:** Takashi Shimizu. **Sc:** Stephen Susco. Based on screenplay by Takashi Shimizu. **P:** Doug Davison, Taka Ichise, Roy Lee, Robert G. Tapert. **M:** Christopher Young. **C:** Lukas Ettlin, Hideo Yamamoto. **Ed:** Jeff Betancourt. **PDn:** Iwao Saito. **S:** Paul N. J. Ottosson. **CDn:** Shawn Holly Cookson. **Cast:** Sarah Michelle Gellar, Jason Behr, William Mapother, Clea DuVall, KaDee Strickland, Grace Zabriskie, Bill Pullman, Rosa Blasi.

Dark Water [American remake] (2005). **D:** Walter Salles. **Sc:** Rafael Yglesias. Based on novel by Kôji Suzuki. **P:** Doug Davison, Roy Lee, Bill Mechanic, Diana Pokorny. **M:** Angelo Badalamenti. **C:** Affonso Beato. **Ed:** Daniel Rezende. **PDn:** Thérèse DePrez. **Art:** Nicholas Lundy, Andrew M. Stearn. **SDc:** Nick Evans, Clive Thomasson. **CDn:** Michael Wilkinson. **S:** Frank Gaeta. **SFx:** Kaz Kobielski, Mark Rice. **VFx:** Mark O. Forker, John P. Mesa, William Mesa. **Cast:** Jennifer Connelly, John C. Reilly, Tim Roth, Dougray Scott, Pete Postlethwaite, Camryn Manheim, Ariel Gade, Perla Haney-Jardine.

The Ring Two [American remake] (2005). **D:** Hideo Nakata. **Sc:** Ehren Kruger. Based on novel by Kôji Suzuki. **P:** Laurie MacDonald, Walter F. Parkes. **M:** Henning Lohner. **C:** Gabriel Beristain. **Ed:** Michael N. Knue. **PDn:** James D. Bissell. **Art:** Christa Munro. **SDc:** Lauri Gaffin. **CDn:** Wendy Chuck. **Cast:** Naomi Watts, Simon Baker, David Dorfman, Elizabeth Perkins, Gary Cole, Sissy Spacek, Ryan Merriman, Emily VanCamp.

The Grudge 2 [American remake] (2006). **D:** Takashi Shimizu. **Sc:** Stephen Susco. Based on screenplay by Takashi Shimizu. **P:** Taka Ichise, Sam Raimi, Rob Tapert. **M:** Christopher Young. **C:** Katsumi Yanagijima. **Ed:** Jeff Betancourt. **PDn:** Iwao Saito. **Art:** Tomoko Kotakemori. **SDc:** Tatsuo Ozeki. **CDn:** Kristin M. Burke, Miyuki Taniguchi. **S:** Paul N.J. Ottosson. **SFx:** Jidekazu Kishiura. **Cast:** Amber Tamblyn, Arielle Kebbel, Jennifer Beals, Edison Chen, Sarah Michelle Gellar, Misako Uno, Takako Fuji.

The Host [*Gwoemul*] (2006). **D:** Joon-ho Bong. **Sc:** Chul-hyun Baek, Joon-ho Bong, Jun-won Ha. **P:** Yong-bae Choi, Neung-yeon Joh. **M:** Byung-woo Lee. **C:** Hyung-ku Kim. **Ed:** Sun-min Kim. **PDn:** Seonghie Ryu. **SDn:** Coll Anderson, Sean Garnhart. **Cast:** Kang-ho Song, Hie-bong Byeon, Hae-il Park, Du-na Bae, Ah-sung Ko.

Pulse [American remake] (2006). **D:** Jim Sonzero. **Sc:** Ray Wright. Based on original screenplay by Kiyoshi Kurosawa. **P:** Michael Leahy, Joel Soisson. **M:** Elia Cmiral. **C:** Mark Plummer. **Ed:** Marc Jakubowicz, Robert K. Lambert, Bob Mori, Kirk M. Morri. **PDn:** Ermanno Di Febo-Orsini, Gary B. Matteson. **Art:** Sorin Popescu. **SDc:** Adrian Curelea. **H:** Michael Davis. **VFx:** Jared Sandrew, Stephen Wilson. **Cast:** Kristen Bell, Ian Somerhalder, Christina Milian, Rick Gonzalez, Jonathan Tucker, Samm Levine, Octavia L. Spencer, Jeremy Guskin.

The Eye (2008). **D:** David Moreau, Xavier Palud. **Sc:** Sebastian Gutierrez. Based on screenplay by Jo Jo Yuet-chun Hui and Oxide Pang and Danny Pang. **P:** Don Granger, Paula Wagner. **M:** Marco Beltrami. **C:** Jeffrey Jur. **Ed:** Patrick Lussier. **PDn:** James Spencer. **Art:** Naython Vane. **SDc:** Joseph Litsch. **CDn:** Michael Dennison. **Cast:** Jessica Alba, Alessandro Nivola, Parker Posey, Rade Serbedzija, Fernanda Romero, Rachel Ticotin, Obba Babatundé, Danny Mora.

DAVID CRONENBERG'S HORROR

Shivers [***They Came from Within***] [***The Parasite Murders***] (1975, 1976 USA). **D, Sc:** David Cronenberg. **P:** Ivan Reitman. **C:** Robert Saad. **Ed:** Patrick Dodd. **Art:** Erla Gliserman. **Mk:** Joe Blasco, Suzanne Riou-Garand. **S:** Danny Goldberg. **Cast:** Paul Hampton, Joe Silver, Lynn Lowry, Allan Migicovsky, Susan Petrie, Barbara Steele, Ronald Mlodzik, Barry Baldaro.

Rabid (1977). **D, Sc:** David Cronenberg. **P:** John Dunning. **C:** René Verzier. **Ed:** Jean LaFleur. **Art:** Claude Marchand. **Mk:** Joe Blasco. **SFx:** Al Griswold. **Cast:** Marilyn Chambers, Frank Moore, Joe Silver, Howard Ryshpan, Patricia Gage, Susan Roman, Roger Periard, Lynne Deragon.

The Brood (1979). **D, Sc:** David Cronenberg. **P:** Claude Héroux. **M:** Howard Shore. **C:** Mark Irwin. **Ed:** Alan Collins. **Art:** Carol Spier. **Mk:** Shonagh Jabour. **H:** James Brown. **SFx:** Allan Kotter. **Cast:** Oliver Reed, Samantha Eggar, Art Hindle, Henry Beckman, Nuala Fitzgerald, Cindy Hinds, Susan Hogan, Gary McKeehan.

Scanners (1981). **D, Sc:** David Cronenberg. **P:** Claude Heroux. **M:** Howard Shore. **C:** Mark Irwin. **Ed:** Ronald Sanders. **Art:** Carol Spier. **CDn:** Delphine White. **H:** Constant Natale. **SDn:** Alfred. **S:** Don Cohen. **SFx:** Gary Zeller, Dennis Pike. **Cast:** Jennifer O'Neill, Stephen Lack, Patrick McGoohan, Lawrence Dane, Michael Ironside, Robert Silverman, Lee Broker, Mavor Moore.

The Dead Zone (1983). **D:** David Cronenberg. **Sc:** Jeffrey Boam. Based on novel by Stephen King. **P:** Debra Hill. **M:** Michael Kamen. **C:** Mark Irwin. **Ed:** Ronald Sanders. **PDn:** Carol Spier. **Art:** Barbara Dunphy. **SDc:** Tom Coulter. **CDn:** Olga Dimitrov. **Cast:** Christopher Walken, Brooke Adams, Tom Skerritt, Herbert Lom, Anthony Zerbe, Colleen Dewhurst, Martin Sheen, Nicholas Campbell.

Videodrome (1983). **D, Sc:** David Cronenberg. **P:** Claude Héroux. **M:** Howard Shore. **C:** Mark Irwin. **Ed:** Ronald Sanders. **Art:** Carol Spier. **SDc:** Angelo Stea. **CDn:** Delphine White. **Mk:** Rick Baker. **H:** Booth L. Thomas, Constant Natale. **SFx:** Frank Carere. **VFx:** Michael Lennick. **Cast:** James Woods, Sonja Smits, Deborah Harry, Peter Dvorsky, Les Carlson, Jack Creley, Lynne Gorman, Julie Khaner.

The Fly (1986). **D:** David Cronenberg. **Sc:** David Cronenberg, Charles Edward Pogue. Story by George Langelaan. **P:** Stuart Cornfeld. **M:** Howard Shore. **C:** Mark Irwin. **Ed:** Ronald Sanders. **PDn:** Carol Spier. **Art:** Rolf Harvey. **SDc:** Elinor Rose Galbraith. **CDn:** Denise Cronenberg. **Mk:** Chris Walas, Stéphan Dupuis, Shonagh Jabour. **H:** Ivan Lynch. **SDn:** James McAteer. **SFx:** Louis Craig, Ted Ross, Chris Walas, Clark Johnson. **VFx:** Lesley Mallgrave, Hoyt Yeatman. **Cast:** Jeff Goldblum, Geena Davis, John Getz, Joy Boushel, Les Carlson, George Chuvalo, Michael Copeman, David Cronenberg. **Academy Awards** Best Makeup (Walas, Dupuis).

Dead Ringers (1988). **D:** David Cronenberg. **Sc:** David Cronenberg, Norman Snider. Based on novel by Bari Wood, Jack Geasland. **P:** Marc Boyman, David Cronenberg. **M:** Howard Shore. **C:** Peter Suschitzky. **Ed:** Ronald Sanders. **PDn:** Carol Spier. **Art:** James McAteer. **SDc:** Elinor Rose Galbraith. **CDn:** Denise Cronenberg. **Mk:** Eva Coudouloux, Shonagh Jabour. **H:** Ivan Lynch. **SFx:** Gordon Smith. **Cast:** Jeremy Irons, Genevieve Bujold, Heidi Von Palleske, Barbara Gordon, Shirley Douglas, Stephen Lack, Nick Nichols, Lynne Cormack. **Los Angeles Film Critics** Best Director, Best Supporting Actress (Bujold). **New York Film Critics** Best Actor (Irons).

Naked Lunch (1991). **D:** David Cronenberg. **Sc:** David Cronenberg. Based on novel by William S. Burroughs. **P:** Jeremy Thomas. **M:** Ornette Coleman, Howard Shore. **C:** Peter Suschitzky. **Ed:** Ronald Sanders. **PDn:** Carol Spier. **Art:** James McAteer. **SDc:** Elinor Rose Galbraith. **CDn:** Denise Cronenberg. **Mk:** Christine Hart. **H:** Rhoda Ancill, Veronica Ciandre, Carmen MacDonald, Lucy Orton. **Cast:** Peter Weller, Judy Davis, Ian Holm, Julian Sands, Roy Scheider, Monique Mercure, Nicholas Campbell, Michael Zelniker. **National Society of Film Critics** Best Director, Best Screenplay. **New York Film Critics** Best Screenplay, Best Supporting Actress (Davis).

Crash (1996 UK, 1994 USA). **D, P:** David Cronenberg. **Sc:** David Cronenberg. Based on novel by J. G. Ballard. **M:** Howard Shore. **C:** Peter Suschitzky. **Ed:** Ronald Sanders. **PDn:** Carol Spier. **Art:** Tamara Deverell. **SDc:** Elinor Rose Galbraith. **CDn:** Denise Cronenberg. **Mk:** Shonagh Jabour. **H:** Mary-Lou Green-Benvenuti. **Cast:** James Spader, Holly Hunter, Elias Koteas, Deborah Kara Unger, Rosanna Arquette, Peter MacNeill, Yolande Julian, David Cronenberg.

eXistenZ (1999). **D, Sc:** David Cronenberg. **P:** Robert Lantos, Andras Hamori, David Cronenberg. **M:** Howard Shore. **C:** Peter Suschitzky. **Ed:** Ronald Sanders. **PDn:** Carol Spier. **Art:** Tamara Deverell. **SDc:** Elinor Rose Galbraith. **CDn:** Denise Cronenberg. **Mk:** Stéphan Dupuis. **H:** Mary Lou Green, Réjean Goderre. **SFx, VFx:** Jim Isaac. **Cast:** Jennifer Jason Leigh, Jude Law, Ian Holm, Don McKellar, Callum Keith Rennie, Sarah Polley, Robert A. Silverman, Christopher Eccleston, Willem Dafoe.

Spider (2002). **D:** David Cronenberg. **Sc:** Patrick McGrath. Based on his novel. **P:** Catherine Bailey, David Cronenberg, Samuel Hadida. **M:** Howard Shore. **C:** Peter Suschitzky. **Ed:** Ronald Sanders. **PDn:** Andrew Sanders. **Art:** Arvinder Grewal, Lucy Richardson. **SDc:** Marina Morris. **CDn:** Denise Cronenberg. **Mk:** Stéphan L. Dupuis. **H:** Mary Lou Green-Benvenuti. **Cast:** Ralph Fiennes, Miranda Richardson, Gabriel Byrne, Lynn Redgrave, John Neville, Bradley Hall, Gary Reineke, Philip Craig. **Directors Guild of Canada** Outstanding Direction, Outstanding Sound Editing — Long Form, Outstanding Feature Film.

POSTMODERN HORROR REMAKES

Invasion of the Body Snatchers (1978). **D:** Philip Kaufman. **Sc:** W.D. Richter. Based on novel by Jack Finney. **P:** Robert H. Solo. **M:** Denny Zeitlin. **C:** Michael Chapman. **Ed:** Douglas Stewart. **PDn:** Charles Rosen. **SDc:** Doug von Koss. **CDn:** Agnes Anne Rogers. **SFx:** Russ Hessey, Dell Rheaume. **Cast:** Donald Sutherland, Brooke Adams, Jeff Goldblum, Veronica Cartwright, Leonard Nimoy, Art Hindle, Lelia Goldoni, Kevin McCarthy, Don Siegel.

The Thing [*John Carpenter's The Thing*] (1982). **D:** John Carpenter. **Sc:** Bill Lancaster. Story by John W. Campbell Jr. **P:** David Foster, Lawrence Turman. **M:** Ennio Morricone. **C:** Dean Cundey. **Ed:** Todd Ramsay. **PDn:** John L. Lloyd. **Art:** Henry Larrecq. **SDc:** John Dwyer. **Cast:** Kurt Russell, A. Wilford Brimley, T. K. Carter, David Clennon, Keith David, Richard Dysart, Charles Hallahan, Peter Maloney.

Lord of the Flies (1990). **D:** Harry Hook. **Sc:** Sara Schiff. Based on novel by William Golding. **P:** Lewis M. Allen, Ross Milloy. **M:** Philippe Sarde. **C:** Martin Fuhrer. **Ed:** Harry Hook. **PDn:** Jamie Leonard. **CDn:** Doreen Watkinson. **Cast:** Balthazar Getty, Chris Furrh, Danuel Pipoly, Badgett Dale, Andrew Taft, Edward Taft, Gary Rule, Terry Wells.

Night of the Living Dead (1990). **D:** Tom Savini. **Sc:** George A. Romero. Based on screenplay by John A. Russo, George A. Romero. **P:** John A. Russo. **M:** Paul McCollough. **C:** Frank Prinzi. **Ed:** Tom Dubensky. **PDn:** Cletus Anderson. **Art:** James C. Feng. **SDc:** Brian J. Stonestreet. **CDn:** Barbara Anderson. **SFx:** Matt Vogel. **Cast:** Tony Todd, Patricia Tallman, Tom Towles, McKee Anderson, William Butler, Katie Finneran, Bill Mosley, Heather Mazur.

The Addams Family (1991). **D:** Barry Sonnenfeld. **Sc:** Caroline Thompson & Larry Wilson. **P:** Scott Rudin. **M:** Marc Shaiman. **C:** Owen Roizman. **Ed:** Dede Allen, Jim Miller. **PDn:** Richard MacDonald. **Art:** Margie Stone McShirley. **SDc:** John Sweeney. **CDn:** Ruth Myers. **Mk:** Fern Buchner. **S:** Cecelia Hall. **SFx:** Tony Gardner, David Miller, Tom Williamson. **Cast:** Anjelica Huston, Raul Julia, Christopher Lloyd, Elizabeth Wilson, Christina Ricci, Judith Malina, Dan Hedaya, Paul Benedict, Dana Ivey.

What Ever Happened to Baby Jane? (1991). Made for TV. **D:** David Greene. **Sc:** Brian Taggert. Based on novel by Henry Farrell. **P:** Barry Bernardi. **M:** Peter Manning Robinson. **Ed:** Paul Dixon. **Cast:** Vanessa Redgrave, Lynn Redgrave, Bruce A. Young, Amy Steel, John Scott Clough, John Glover, Samantha Jordan, Erinn Canavan, Michael Flynn.

Bram Stoker's Dracula (1992). **D:** Francis Ford Coppola. **Sc:** James V. Hart. Based on novel by Bram Stoker. **P:** Francis Ford Coppola, Fred Fuchs, Charles Mulvehill. **M:** Wojciech Kilar. **C:** Michael Ballhaus. **Ed:** Anne Goursaud, Glen Scantlebury, Nicholas C. Smith. **PDn:** Thomas Sanders. **Art:** Andrew Precht. **SDc:** Garrett Lewis. **CDn:** Eiko Ishioka. **Mk:** Greg Cannom, Michèle Burke, Matthew W. Mungle. **Cast:** Gary Oldman, Winona Ryder, Anthony Hopkins, Keanu Reeves, Richard E. Grant, Cary Elwes, Bill Campbell, Sadie Frost, Tom Waits. **Academy Awards** Best Costume Design, Best Sound Effects Editing, Best Makeup.

Body Snatchers (1993). **D:** Abel Ferrara. **Sc:** Stuart Gordon & Dennis Paoli and Nicholas St. John. Based on novel by Jack Finney and story by Raymond Cistheri and Larry Cohen. **P:** Robert H. Solo. **M:** Joe Delia. **C:** Bojan Bazelli. **Ed:** Anthony Redman. **PDn:** Peter Jamison. **Art:** John Huke. **SDc:** Linda Spheeris. **CDn:** Margaret Mohr. **S:** Robert L. Sephton. **SFx:** Ken Brilliant, Phil Cory. **VFx:** Jim Danforth. **Cast:** Gabrielle Anwar, Terry Kinney, Billy Wirth, Christine Elise, R. Lee Ermey, G. Elvis Phillips, Forest Whitaker, Meg Tilly.

Mary Shelley's Frankenstein [*Frankenstein*] (1994). **D:** Kenneth Branagh. **Sc:** Steph Lady, Frank Darabont. Based on novel by Mary Shelley. **P:** Francis Ford Coppola, James V. Hart, John Veitch. **M:** Patrick Doyle. **C:** Roger Pratt. **Ed:** Andrew Marcus. **PDn:** Tim Harvey. **Art:** Desmond Crowe, John Fenner. **CDn:** James Acheson. **Cast:** Robert De Niro, Kenneth Branagh, Tom Hulce, Helena Bonham Carter, Aidan Quinn, Ian Holm, Richard Briers, John Cleese.

Diabolique (1996). **D:** Jeremiah Chechik. **Sc:** Don Roos. Based on novel by Boileau-Narcejac and screenplay by Henri-Georges Clouzot. **P:** James G. Robinson, Marvin Worth. **M:** Randy Edelman. **C:** Peter James. **Ed:** Carol Littleton. **PDn:** Leslie Dilley. **Art:** Dennis Bradford. **SDc:** Michael Seirton. **CDn:** Michael Kaplan, L'wren Scott. **Cast:** Sharon Stone, Isabelle Adjani, Chazz Palminteri, Kathy Bates, Spalding Gray, Shirley Knight, Allen Garfield.

The Shining (1997). Made for TV. **D:** Mick Garris. **Sc:** Stephen King. Based on his novel. **P:** Mark Carliner. **M:** Nicholas Pike. **C:** Shelly Johnson. **Ed:** Patrick McMahon. **PDn:** Craig Stearns. **Art:** Randy Moore. **SDc:** Ellen Totleben. **CDn:** Warden Neil. **SFx:** Lou Carlucci, Patrick M. Gerrety. **VFx:** Boyd Shermis. **Cast:** Steven Weber, Rebecca De Mornay, Courtland Mead, Melvin Van Peebles, Pat Hingle, Elliott Gould, Stephen King, Sam Raimi. **Emmy Awards** Outstanding Makeup, Sound Editing.

Godzilla (1998). **D:** Roland Emmerich. **Sc:** Dean Devlin & Roland Emmerich. Story by Ted Elliott & Terry Rossio and Dean Devlin & Roland Emmerich. **P:** Dean Devlin, Kelly Van Horn, Peter Winther. **M:** David Arnold, Michael Lloyd. **C:** Ueli Steiger. **Ed:** Peter Amundson, David Siegel. **PDn:** Oliver Scholl. **Art:** Oana Bogdan, Robert Woodruff. **SDc:** Victor Zolfo. **CDn:** Joseph A. Porro. **Cast:** Matthew Broderick, Jean Reno, Maria Pitillo, Hank Azaria, Kevin Dunn, Michael Lerner, Harry Shearer, Arabella Field.

Psycho (1998). **D:** Gus Van Sant. **Sc:** Joseph Stefano. Based on novel by Robert Bloch. **P:** Brian Grazer, Gus Van Sant. **M:** Rob Zombie. **C:** Christopher Doyle. **Ed:** Amy E. Duddleston. **PDn:** Tom Foden. **Art:** Carlos Barbosa. **SDc:** Rosemary Brandenburg. **CDn:** Beatrix Aruna Pasztor. **H:** Lana Heying. **Cast:** Vince Vaughn, Anne Heche, Julianne Moore, Viggo Mortensen, William H. Macy, Philip Baker Hall, Chad Everett, James LeGros.

The Haunting (1999). **D:** Jan de Bont. **Sc:** David Self. Based on novel by Shirley Jackson. **P:** Susan Arnold, Donna Arkoff Roth, Colin Wilson. **M:** Jerry Goldsmith. **C:** Karl Walter Lindenlaub. **Ed:** Michael Kahn. **PDn:** Eugenio Zanetti. **Art:** Martin Laing, Jonathan Lee, Troy Sizemore. **SDc:** Cindy Carr. **CDn:** Ellen Mirojnick. **Cast:** Lili Taylor, Liam Neeson, Catherine Zeta-Jones, Owen Wilson, Bruce Dern, Marian Seldes, Todd Field, Virginia Madsen.

House on Haunted Hill (1999). **D:** William Malone. **Sc:** Dick Beebe. Story by Robb White. **P:** Gilbert Adler, Joel Silver, Robert Zemeckis. **M:** Don Davis. **C:** Rick Bota. **Ed:** Anthony Adler. **PDn:** David F. Klassen. **Art:** Richard F. Mays. **SDc:** Lauri Gaffin. **CDn:** Ha Nguyen. **Cast:** Geoffrey Rush, Famke Janssen, Taye Diggs, Peter Gallagher, Chris Kattan, Ali Larter, Bridgette Wilson, Peter Graves.

The Mummy (1999). **D, Sc:** Stephen Sommers. **P:** Sean Daniel, James Jacks. **M:** Jerry Goldsmith. **C:** Adrian Biddle. **Ed:** Bob Ducsay. **PDn:** Allan Cameron. **Art:** Giles Masters, Tony Reading, Clifford Robinson, Peter Russell. **SDc:** Peter Howitt. **CDn:** John Bloomfield. **Cast:** Brendan Fraser, Rachel Weisz, John Hannah, Arnold Vosloo, Kevin J. O'Connor, Oded Fehr, Jonathan Hyde, Erick Avari, Tuc Watkins.

Planet of the Apes (2001). **D:** Tim Burton. **Sc:** William Broyles Jr., Lawrence Konner, Mark Rosenthal. Based on novel by Pierre Boulle. **P:** Richard D. Zanuck. **M:** Danny Elfman. **C:** Philippe Rousselot. **Ed:** Chris Lebenzon, Joel Negron. **PDn:** Rick Heinrichs. **Art:** Sean Haworth, Philip Toolin. **SDc:** Rosemary Brandenburg, Peter Young. **CDn:** Colleen Atwood, Donna O'Neal. **Cast:** Mark Wahlberg, Tim Roth, Helena Bonham Carter, Michael Clarke Duncan, Paul Giamatti, Estella Warren, Cary-Hiroyuki Tagawa, David Warner.

Thir13en Ghosts [*Thirteen Ghosts*] (2001). **D:** Steve Beck. **Sc:** Neal Marshall Stevens, Richard D'ovidio. Based on screenplay by Robb White. **P:** Gilbert Adler, Joel Silver, Robert Zemeckis. **M:** John Frizzell. **C:** Gale Tattersall. **Ed:** Derek G. Brechin, Omar Daher, Edward A. Warschilka. **PDn:** Sean Hargreaves. **Art:** Tim Beach, Don Macaulay. **SDc:** Dominique Fauquet-Lemaitre. **CDn:** Jenni Gullett. **Cast:** Tony Shalhoub, Embeth Davidtz, Matthew Lillard, Shannon Elizabeth, Alec Roberts, JR Bourne, Rah Digga, F. Murray Abraham.

Carrie (2002). Made for TV. **D:** David Carson. **Sc:** Bryan Fuller. Based on novel by Stephen King. **P:** David Carson, Stephen Geaghan. **M:** Laura Karpman. **C:** Victor Goss. **Ed:** Anthony A. Lewis, Jeremy Presner. **PDn:** Stephen Geaghan. **Art:** Susan Parker. **CDn:** Candace Cruikshank. **SFx:** Randy Shymkiw. **VFx:** Martin Halle, Gordon Oscar. **Cast:** Angela Bettis, Patricia Clarkson, Rena Sofer, Kandyse McClure, Emilie de Ravin, Tobias Mehler.

The Texas Chainsaw Massacre (2003). **D:** Marcus Nispel. **Sc:** Scott Kosar. Based on screenplay by Kim Henkel, Tobe Hooper. **P:** Michael Bay, Mike Fleiss. **M:** Steve Jablonsky. **C:** Daniel Pearl. **Ed:** Glen Scantlebury. **PDn:** Greg Blair. **Art:** Scott Gallagher. **SDc:** Randy Smith Huke. **CDn:** Bobbie Mannix. **S:** Scott Martin Gershin. **SFx:** Rocky Gehr. **Cast:** Jessica

Biel, Jonathan Tucker, Erica Leerhsen, Mike Vogel, Eric Balfour, Andrew Bryniarski, R. Lee Ermey, David Dorfman.

Willard (2003). **D:** Glen Morgan. **Sc:** Glen Morgan. Based on novel by Gilbert Ralston, Aka Stephen Gilbert. **P:** Glen Morgan, James Wong. **M:** Shirley Walker. **C:** Robert McLachlan. **Ed:** James Coblentz. **PDn:** Mark S. Freeborn. **Art:** Catherine Ircha. **SDc:** Mark Lane. **CDn:** Gregory Mah. **Mk:** Rachel Griffin, Cheri Montesanto-Medcalf, Bill Terezakis. **SDn:** Tony Wohlgemuth. **S:** Jon Title. **Cast:** Crispin Glover, R. Lee Ermey, Laura Elena Harring, Jackie Burroughs, Kimberly Patton, William S. Taylor, Edward Horn, Gus Lynch. **Canadian Society of Cinematographers** Best Feature Cinematography.

Dawn of the Dead (2004). **D:** Zack Snyder. **Sc:** James Gunn. Based on screenplay by George A. Romero. **P:** Marc Abraham, Eric Newman, Richard P. Rubinstein. **M:** Tyler Bates. **C:** Matthew F. Leonetti. **Ed:** Niven Howie. **PDn:** Andrew Neskoromny. **Art:** Arvinder Grewal. **SDc:** Steve Shewchuk. **CDn:** Denise Cronenberg. **H:** Carol Hartwick, Diana Ladyshewski, JoAnn MacNeil. **SDn:** Kim Karon, Mayumi Konishi. **SFx:** Laird McMurray. **Cast:** Sarah Polley, Ving Rhames, Jake Weber, Mekhi Phifer, Ty Burrell, Michael Kelly, Kevin Zegers, Michael Barry.

'Salem's Lot (2004). Made for TV. **D:** Mikael Salomon. **Sc:** Peter Filardi. Based on novel by Stephen King. **P:** Brett Popplewell. **M:** Patrick Cassidy, Lisa Gerrard, Christopher Gordon. **C:** Ben Nott. **Ed:** Robert A. Ferretti. **Art:** Michael Plummer. **Mk, H:** Helen Magelaki. **SDn:** Michael Bell. **SFx:** Clint Ingram, Ali Pearce. **VFx:** David Vána. **Cast:** Rob Lowe, Andre Braugher, Donald Sutherland, Samantha Mathis, Robert Mammone, Daniel Byrd, Rutger Hauer, James Cromwell. **Australian Cinematographers Society** Cinematographer of the Year (Nott).

The Stepford Wives (2004). **D:** Frank Oz. **Sc:** Paul Rudnick. Based on novel by Ira Levin. **P:** Donald De Line, Gabriel Grunfeld, Scott Rudin, Edgar J. Scherick. **M:** David Arnold. **C:** Rob Hahn. **Ed:** Jay Rabinowitz. **PDn:** Jackson De Govia. **Art:** Kent Matheson, Peter Rogness. **SDc:** Debra Schutt. **CDn:** Ann Roth. **Cast:** Nicole Kidman, Matthew Broderick, Bette Midler, Glenn Close, Christopher Walken, Roger Bart, David Marshall Grant, Jon Lovitz, Meredith Vieira, Lorri Bagley.

Van Helsing (2004). **D, Sc:** Stephen Sommers. **P:** Bob Ducsay, Stephen Sommers. **M:** Alan Silvestri. **C:** Allen Daviau. **Ed:** Ray Bushey III, Bob Ducsay, Kelly Matsumoto, Jim May. **PDn:** Allan Cameron. **SDc:** Cindy Carr, Anna Pinnock. **CDn:** Gabriella Pescucci, Carlo Poggioli. **Cast:** Hugh Jackman, Kate Beckinsale, Richard Roxburgh, David Wenham, Shuler Hensley, Elena Anaya, Will Kemp, Kevin J. O'Connor, Robbie Coltrane.

The Amityville Horror (2005). **D:** Andrew Douglas. **Sc:** Scott Kosar. Based on novel by Jay Anson. **P:** Michael Bay, Andrew Form, Brad Fuller. **M:** Steve Jablonsky. **C:** Peter Lyons Collister. **Ed:** Roger Barton, Christian Wagner. **PDn:** Jennifer Williams. **Art:** Marco Rubeo. **SDc:** Daniel B. Clancy. **CDn:** David C. Robinson. **H:** Dominic Mango. **SDn:** Kevin Cross, Kerry

Sanders. **SFx:** David J. Barker, John D. Milinac. **Cast:** Ryan Reynolds, Melissa George, Jesse James, Jimmy Bennett, Chloë Grace Moretz, Rachel Nichols, Philip Baker Hall, Isabel Conner.

The Cabinet of Dr. Caligari (2005). **D, Sc, Ed:** David Lee Fisher. **P:** Paula Elins, Leonard McLeod. **M:** Eban Schletter. **C:** Christopher Duddy. **PDn:** Kim Richey. **Art:** Michael J. Bertolina. **CDn:** Paula Elins. **VFx:** Josiah Holmes Howison. **Cast:** Judson Pearce Morgan, Daamen J. Krall, Doug Jones, Lauren Birkell, Neil Hopkins, William Gregory Lee.

The Fog (2005). **D:** Rupert Wainwright. **Sc:** Cooper Layne. **P:** John Carpenter, David Foster, Debra Hill. **M:** Graeme Revell. **C:** Nathan Hope. **Ed:** Dennis Virkler. **PDn:** Michael Diner, Graeme Murray. **Art:** Michael Diner, Catherine Schroer. **SDc:** Rose Marie McSherry. **CDn:** Monique Prudhomme. **Mk:** Toby Lindala, Connie Parker. **H:** Sanna Seppanen. **VFx:** Alp Altiner, Jess Bryden, Atsushi Imamura, Josh Mossotti. **Cast:** Tom Welling, Maggie Grace, Selma Blair, DeRay Davis, Kenneth Welsh, Adrian Hough, Sara Botsford, Cole Heppell.

House of Wax (2005). **D:** Jaume Collet-Serra. **Sc:** Chad Hayes, Carey W. Hayes. Story by Charles Belden. **P:** Susan Levin, Joel Silver, Robert Zemeckis. **M:** John Ottman. **C:** Marc Spicer, Stephen Windon. **Ed:** Joel Negron. **PDn:** Graham "Grace" Walker. **Art:** Brian Edmonds, Nicholas McCallum. **SDc:** Beverley Dunn. **CDn:** Alex Alvarez, Graham Purcell. **Mk:** Rosalina Da Silva, David Grasso, Anita Morgan, Andy Schoneberg, Kevin Wasner. **H:** Anita Morgan, Shane Thomas. **VFx:** Mark Chataway, Dale Duguid. **Cast:** Elisha Cuthbert, Chad Michael Murray, Brian Van Holt, Paris Hilton, Jared Padalecki, Jon Abrahams, Robert Richard, Dragitsa Debert.

King Kong (2005). **D:** Peter Jackson. **Sc:** Fran Walsh, Philippa Boyens, Peter Jackson. Story by Merian C. Cooper, Edgar Wallace. **P:** Jan Blenkin, Carolynne Cunningham, Peter Jackson, Fran Walsh. **M:** James Newton Howard. **C:** Andrew Lesnie. **Ed:** Jamie Selkirk. **PDn:** Grant Major. **Art:** Simon Bright, Dan Hennah. **SDc:** Dan Hennah. **CDn:** Terry Ryan. **Mk, H:** Peter Swords-King. **SFx:** Greg Broadmore, Stephen Crowe. **VFx:** Joe Letteri, Brian Van't Hul, Christian Rivers, Richard Taylor. **Cast:** Naomi Watts, Jack Black, Adrien Brody, Thomas Kretschmann, Colin Hanks, Andy Serkis, Evan Parke, Jamie Bell, Peter Jackson, Frank Darabont. **Academy Awards** Best Sound, Best Sound Editing, Best Visual Effects. **BAFTA** Best Special Visual Effects. **National Board of Review** Special Achievement, Special Effects.

The Hills Have Eyes (2006). **D:** Alexandre Aja. **Sc:** Alexandre Aja, Grégory Levasseur. **P:** Wes Craven, Peter Locke, Marianne Maddalena. **M:** tomandandy. **C:** Maxime Alexandre. **Ed:** Baxter. **PDn:** Joseph C. Nemec III. **Art:** Tamara Marini. **SDn:** Alessandra Querzola. **CDn:** Danny Glicker. **Mk:** Scott Patton. **SFx:** Franco Ragusa. **VFx:** Jamison Scott Goei. **Cast:** Maxime Giffard, Michael Bailey Smith, Tom Bower, Ted Levine, Kathleen Quinlan, Dan Byrd, Emilie de Ravin, Aaron Stanford.

Night of the Living Dead 3D (2006). **D:** Jeff Broadstreet. **Sc:** Robert Valding. Based on screenplay by George A. Romero, John A. Russo. **P:** Jeff Broadstreet. **M:** Jason Brandt. **C:** Andrew Parke. **Ed:** Robert Valding. **PDn:** Chris Davis. **Art:** Josh Ritcher. **SDc:** Yvonne von Wallenberg. **CDn:** Lisa Norcia. **S:** Kurt Thum. **VFx:** Adam Lima. **Cast:** Brianna Brown, Joshua DesRoches, Sid Haig, Greg Travis, Johanna Black, Adam Chambers.

The Omen (2006). **D:** John Moore. **Sc:** Dan McDermott. **P:** John Moore, Glenn Williamson. **M:** Marco Beltrami. **C:** Jonathan Sela. **PDn:** Patrick Lumb. **Art:** Katerina Kopicová, Martin Kurel. **CDn:** George L. Little. **Mk:** Fiona Connon, Matthew W. Mungle. **H:** Stephen Rose, Stephen Rose. **SFx:** Martin Oberlander, Ian Wingrove. **Cast:** Liev Schreiber, Julia Stiles, Mia Farrow, David Thewlis, Michael Gambon, Amy Huck, Pete Postlethwaite, Seamus Davey-Fitzpatrick.

Poseidon (2006). **D:** Wolfgang Petersen. **Sc:** Mark Protosevich. Based on novel by Paul Gallico. **P:** Mike Fleiss, Akiva Goldsman, Duncan Henderson. **M:** Klaus Badelt. **C:** John Seale. **Ed:** Peter Honess. **PDn:** William Sandell. **Art:** Kevin Ishioka, Mike Mansbridge. **SDc:** Robert Gould. **CDn:** Erica Edell Phillips. **S:** Peter Michael Sullivan. **SFx:** H. Barclay Aaris. **Cast:** Kurt Russell, Josh Lucas, Richard Dreyfuss, Jacinda Barrett, Emmy Rossum, Kevin Dillon, Freddy Rodríguez, Andre Braugher.

When a Stranger Calls (2006). **D:** Simon West. **Sc:** Jake Wade Wall. **P:** John Davis, Wyck Godfrey, Ken Lemberger. **M:** James Dooley. **C:** Peter Menzies Jr. **Ed:** Jeff Betancourt. **PDn:** Jon Gary Steele. **Art:** Gerald Sullivan. **CDn:** Marie-Sylvie Deveau. **Mk:** Kimberly Meyer, Kristina Vogel, Gigi Williams. **H:** Vickie Mynes. **SDn:** Patrick M. Sullivan Jr. **VFx:** Mitchell S. Drain, Nathan McGuinness. **Cast:** Camilla Belle, Tommy Flanagan, Katie Cassidy, Tessa Thompson, Brian Geraghty, Clark Gregg.

The Wicker Man (2006). **D:** Neil LaBute. **Sc:** Neil LaBute. Based on screenplay by Anthony Shaffer. **P:** Nicolas Cage, Randall Emmett, Norman Golightly, Avi Lerner, Joanne Sellar. **M:** Angelo Badalamenti. **C:** Paul Sarossy. **Ed:** Joel Plotch. **PDn:** Phillip Barker. **Art:** Michael Diner. **SDc:** Shannon Murphy. **CDn:** Lynette Meyer. **Mk:** Francesca von Zimmermann. **S:** Ronald Eng. **VFx:** Mark Freund, Jordan Markov, Stefan Tchakarov. **Cast:** Nicolas Cage, Ellen Burstyn, Kate Beahan, Frances Conroy, Molly Parker, Leelee Sobieski, Diane Delano, Michael Wiseman.

Halloween (2007). **D, Sc:** Rob Zombie. Based on screenplay by John Carpenter and Debra Hill. **P:** Malek Akkad, Andy Gould, Rob Zombie. **M:** Tyler Bates. **C:** Phil Parmet. **Ed:** Glenn Garland. **PDn:** Anthony Tremblay. **Art:** T.K. Kirkpatrick. **SDc:** Lori Mazuer, Stephanie Ziemer. **CDn:** Mary McLeod. **H:** Renee Ferruggia, Vickie Mynes. **Mk:** Luis García. **Cast:** Malcolm McDowell, Brad Dourif, Tyler Mane, Daeg Faerch, Sheri Moon Zombie, William Forsythe, Richard Lynch, Udo Kier, Clint Howard, Bill Moseley.

The Invasion (2007). **D:** Oliver Hirschbiegel, James McTeigue (additional director) (uncredited). **Sc:** Dave Kajganich. Based on novel by Jack Finney. **P:** . **P:** Joel Silver. **M:** John Ottman. **C:** Rainer Klausmann. **Ed:** Hans Funck, Joel Negron. **PDn:** Jack Fisk. **Art:** Caty Maxey, James Truesdale. **SDc:** Leslie Frankenheimer, Maria Nay. **CDn:** Jacqueline West. **SDn:** Bryan Watkins. **Cast:** Nicole Kidman, Daniel Craig, Jeremy Northam, Jackson Bond, Jeffrey Wright, Veronica Cartwright, Josef Sommer, Celia Weston, Roger Rees.

Day of the Dead (2008). **D:** Steve Miner. **Sc:** Jeffrey Reddick. Based on screenplay by George A. Romero. **P:** Boaz Davidson, James Glenn Dudelson, Randall Emmett, George Furla, M. Dal Walton III. **M:** Tyler Bates. **C:** Patrick Cady. **Ed:** Nathan Easterling. **PDn:** Carlos Da Silva. **Art:** Sonya Savova. **SDc:** Rosen Stefanov. **CDn:** Gina Hendrix. **Cast:** Mena Suvari, Nick Cannon, Michael Welch, AnnaLynne McCord, Stark Sands, Matt Rippy, Pat Kilbane, Taylor Hoover, Ving Rhames.

The Day the Earth Stood Still (2008). **D:** Scott Derrickson. **Sc:** David Scarpa. Based on screenplay by Edmund H. North. **P:** Paul Harris Boardman, Gregory Goodman, Erwin Stoff. **M:** Tyler Bates. **C:** David

Tattersall. **Ed:** Wayne Wahrman. **Pdn:** David Brisbin. **Art:** Don Macaulay. **Sdc:** Elizabeth Wilcox. **Cdn:** Tish Monaghan. **Cast:** Keanu Reeves, Jennifer Connely, Kathy Bates, Jon Hamm, Jaden Smith, John Cleese.

My Bloody Valentine 3-D (2009). **D:** Patrick Lussier. **Sc:** Todd Farmer and Zane Smith. Based on screenplay by John Beaird. **P:** Jack L. Murray. **M:** Michael Wandmacher. **C:** Brian Pearson. **Ed:** Cynthia Ludwig, Patrick Lussier. **Pdn:** Zack Grobler. **Sdc:** Maurin L. Scarlata. **Cdn:** Leeann Redaka. **Cast:** Jensen Ackles, Jaime King, Kerr Smith, Betsy Rue.

Friday the 13th (2009). **D:** Marcus Nispel. **Sc:** Damian Shannon, Mark Swift. **P:** Michael Bay. **M:** Steve Jablonsky. **C:** Daniel Pearl. **Ed:** Ken Blackwell. **Pdn:** Jeremy Conway. **Art:** John Frick. **Sdc:** Randy Huke. **Cdn:** Marian Ceo. **Cast:** Jared Padalecki, Danielle Panabaker, Travis Van Winkle, Derek Mears.

Horror Franchise Sequels

Sequels to *Psycho* (1960)

Psycho II (1983). **D:** Richard Franklin. **Sc:** Tom Holland. **P:** Hilton A. Green. **M:** Jerry Goldsmith. **C:** Dean Cundey. **Ed:** Andrew London. **PDn:** John W. Corso. **SDc:** Jennifer Polito. **CDn:** Peter V. Saldutti, Marla Denise Schlom. **SDn:** Martha Johnston. **S:** Andrew London. **SFx:** Greg C. Jensen. **VFx:** Albert Whitlock. **Cast:** Anthony Perkins, Vera Miles, Meg Tilly, Robert Loggia, Dennis Franz, Hugh Gillin, Robert Alan Browne.

Psycho III (1986). **D:** Anthony Perkins. **Sc:** Charles Edward Pogue. **P:** Hilton A. Green. **C:** Bruce Surtees. **Ed:** David E. Blewitt. **PDn:** Henry Bumstead. **SDc:** Mickey S. Michaels. **CDn:** Peter V. Saldutti, Marla Denise Schlom. **Mk:** Mark Reedall, Michael Westmore. **H:** Vivian McAteer. **SFx:** Louis R. Cooper, Danny Lester, Karl G. Miller. **VFx:** Syd Dutton, Bill Taylor. **Cast:** Anthony Perkins, Diana Scarwid, Jeff Fahey, Roberta Maxwell, Hugh Gillin, Robert Alan Browne.

Psycho IV (1990). **D:** Mick Garris. **Sc:** Joseph Stefano. **P:** Les Mayfield, George Zaloom. **M:** Graeme Revell. **C:** Rodney Charters. **Ed:** Charles Bornstein. **PDn:** Michael Hanan. **Art:** Mark Zuelzke. **SDc:** Doug Mowat. **CDn:** Marla Denise Schlom, Mary Ellen Winston. **Mk:** Janeen Davis. **H:** Gary Walker. **SDn:** Tricia Eckoff, Mark Garner. **SFx:** Rick Jones. **Cast:** Anthony Perkins, Henry Thomas, Olivia Hussey, Cch Pounder, Warren Frost, Donna Mitchell.

Sequels to *Planet of the Apes* (1968)

Beneath the Planet of the Apes (1970). **D:** Ted Post. **Sc:** Paul Dehn. Story by Paul Dehn, Mort Abrahams. **P:** Arthur P. Jacobs. **M:** Leonard Rosenman. **C:** Milton Krasner. **Ed:** Marion Rothman. **Art:** William Creber, Jack Martin Smith. **SDc:** Walter M. Scott, Sven Wickman. **CDn:** Morton Haack. **Mk:** John Chambers. **S:** Stephen Bass, David Dockendorf. **SFx:** L. B. Abbott, Art Cruickshank. **Cast:** James Franciscus, Kim Hunter, Maurice Evans, Linda Harrison, Paul Richards, Victor Buono, James Gregory, Jeff Corey.

Escape from the Planet of the Apes (1971). **D:** Don Taylor. **Sc:** Paul Dehn. **P:** Arthur P. Jacobs. **M:** Jerry Goldsmith. **C:** Joseph Biroc. **Ed:** Marion Rothman. **Art:** William Creber, Jack Martin Smith. **SDc:** Stuart A. Reiss, Walter M. Scott. **Mk:** John Chambers. **H:** Mary Babcock. **S:** Theodore Soderberg, Dean Vernon. **SFx:** L. B. Abbott, Howard A. Anderson. **Cast:** Roddy McDowall, Kim Hunter, Bradford Dillman, Natalie Trundy, Eric Braeden, William Windom, Sal Mineo, Albert Salmi.

Conquest of the Planet of the Apes (1972). **D:** J. Lee Thompson. **Sc:** Paul Dehn. **P:** Arthur P. Jacobs. **M:** Tom Scott. **C:** Bruce Surtees. **Ed:** Marjorie Fowler, Alan Jaggs. **PDn:** Philip M. Jefferies. **Art:** Philip Jefferies. **SDc:** Norman Rockett. **Mk:** John Chambers. **S:** Don Bassman, Herman Lewis. **SFx:** L. B. Abbott. **Cast:** Roddy McDowall, Don Murray, Natalie Trundy, Hari Rhodes, Severn Darden, Lou Wagner, John Randolph, Asa Maynor.

Battle for the Planet of the Apes (1973). **D:** J. Lee Thompson. **Sc:** John William Corrington & Joyce Hooper Corrington. Story by Paul Dehn. **P:** Arthur P. Jacobs. **M:** Leonard Rosenman. **C:** Richard H. Kline. **Ed:** John C. Horger, Alan L. Jaggs. **Art:** Dale Hennessey. **SDc:** Robert De Vestel. **Mk:** John Chambers. **S:** Don Bassman, Herman Lewis. **SFx:** L. B. Abbott, Gerald Endler. **Cast:** Roddy McDowall, Claude Akins, Natalie Trundy, Severn Darden, Lew Ayres, Paul Williams, France Nuyen, John Huston.

Sequels to *The Exorcist* (1973)

Exorcist II: The Heretic (1977). **D:** John Boorman. **Sc:** William Goodhart. **P:** John Boorman, Richard Lederer. **M:** Ennio Morricone. **C:** William A. Fraker. **Ed:** Tom Priestley. **PDn:** Richard MacDonald. **Art:** Jack T. Collis. **SDc:** John Austin. **CDn:** Robert De Mora. **Mk:** Gary Liddiard, Dick Smith. **H:** Lynda Gurasich. **VFx:** Albert Whitlock. **Cast:** Linda Blair, Richard Burton, Louise Fletcher, Max von Sydow, Kitty Winn, Paul Henreid, James Earl Jones, Ned Beatty.

The Exorcist III (1990). **D, Sc:** William Peter Blatty. Based on his novel. **P:** Carter De Haven. **M:** Barry Devorzon. **C:** Gerry Fisher. **Ed:** Peter Lee Thompson, Todd Ramsay. **PDn:** Leslie Dilley. **Art:** Henry Shaffer. **Mk:** Greg Cannom. **H:** Cydney Cornell, Mike Smithson. **SDn:** Tim Eckel. **Cast:** George C. Scott, Ed Flanders, Brad Dourif, Jason Miller, Nicol Williamson, Scott Wilson, Nancy Fish, George Dicenzo.

Exorcist: The Beginning (2004). **D:** Renny Harlin. **Sc:** Alexi Hawley. Story by William Wisher, Caleb Carr. **P:** Will Raee, James G. Robinson. **M:** Trevor Rabin. **C:** Vittorio Storaro. **Ed:** Mark Goldblatt, Todd E. Miller. **PDn:** Stefano Maria Ortolani. **Art:** Eugenio Ulissi. **SDc:** Carlo Gervasi. **CDn:** Luke Reichle, Marco Scotti. **H:** Marlene Stoller, Gioncarlo De Leonardis. **S:** Harry Cohen, Ann Scibelli. **SFx:** Danilo Bollettini. **Cast:** Stellan Skarsgård, Izabella Scorupco, James D'arcy, Remy Sweeney, Julian Wadham, Andrew French, Ralph Brown, Ben Cross.

Dominion: Prequel to the Exorcist (2005). **D:** Paul Schrader. **Sc:** William Wisher, Caleb Carr. **P:** James G. Robinson. **M:** Angelo Badalamenti, Trevor Rabin. **C:** Vittorio Storaro. **Ed:** Tim Silano. **PDn:** John Graysmark. **Art:** Andy Nicholson, Marco Trentini. **CDn:** Luke Reichle. **Mk:** Jake Garber, Fabrizio Sforza. **SFx:** Danilo Bollettini. **Cast:** Stellan Skarsgård, Gabriel Mann, Clara Bellar, Billy Crawford, Ralph Brown, Israel Aduramo, Andrew French, Antonie Kamerling.

Sequels to *The Texas Chainsaw Massacre* (1974)

The Texas Chainsaw Massacre 2 (1986). **D:** Tobe Hooper. **Sc:** L. M. Kit Carson. Based on characters by Kim Henkel, Tobe Hooper. **P:** Menahem Golan, Yoram Globus. **M:** Tobe Hooper, Jerry Lambert. **C:** Richard Kooris. **Ed:** Alain Jakubowicz. **PDn:** Cary White. **SDc:** Michael Peal. **CDn:** Carin Hooper. **Cast:** Dennis Hopper, Caroline Williams, Jim Siedow, Bill Moseley, Bill Johnson, Ken Evert.

Leatherface: The Texas Chainsaw Massacre 3 (1990). **D:** Jeff Burr. **Sc:** David Schow. Based on characters by Kim Henkel, Tobe Hooper. **P:** Robert Engelman. **M:** Jim Manzie, Patrick Regan. **C:** James L. Carter. **PDn:** Mick Strawn. **Cast:** Kate Hodge, Ken Foree, R. A. Mihailoff, Viggo Mortensen, William Butler, Joe Unger.

The Return of the Texas Chainsaw Massacre (1994). **D:** Kim Henkel. **Sc:** Kim Henkel. Based on characters by Kim Henkel, Tobe Hooper. **P:** Kim Henkel, Robert Kuhn. **M:** Wayne Bell, Robert Jacks. **C:** Levie Isaacks. **Ed:** Sandra Adair. **PDn:** Deborah Pastor. **Art:** Ann Yzuel. **CDn:** Kari Perkins. **SFx:** Andy Cockrum, J. M. Logan. **Cast:** Renee Zellweger, Matthew McConaughey, Robert Jacks, Tonie Perenski, Joe Stevens, Lisa Marie Newmyer, John Harrison, Tyler Cone.

The Texas Chainsaw Massacre: The Beginning (2006). **D:** Jonathan Liebesman. **Sc:** Sheldon Turner. Story by Sheldon Turner, David J. Schow. **P:** Michael Bay, Mike Fleiss, Andrew Form, Brad Fuller, Bradley Fuller, Kim Henkel, Tobe Hooper. **M:** Steve Jablonsky. **C:** Lukas Ettlin. **Ed:** Jonathan Chibnall, Jim May.

PDn: Marco Rubeo. **Art:** John Frick. **SDc:** Randy Huke. **CDn:** Marian Ceo. **Mk:** Scott Patton. **VFx:** Holly Gregory Horter. **Cast:** Jordana Brewster, Taylor Handley, Diora Baird, Matt Bomer, Lee Tergesen, R. Lee Ermey.

Sequels to *Jaws* (1975)

Jaws 2 (1978). **D:** Jeannot Szwarc. **Sc:** Carl Gottlieb, Howard Sackler. Based on characters by Peter Benchley. **P:** David Brown, Richard D. Zanuck. **M:** John Williams. **C:** Michael Butler. **Ed:** Steve Potter, Arthur Schmidt, Neil Travis. **PDn:** Joe Alves. **Art:** W. Stewart Campbell, Gene Johnson. **SDc:** Philip Abramson. **CDn:** Bill Jobe. **H:** Phil Leto. **S:** Jim Alexander. **SFx:** Roy Arbogast, Robert A. Mattey, Kevin Pike. **Cast:** Roy Scheider, Lorraine Gary, Murray Hamilton, Joseph Mascolo, Ann Dusenberry.

Jaws 3-D (1983). **D:** Joe Alves. **Sc:** Carl Gottlieb, Michael Kane, Richard Matheson. Based on novel by Peter Benchley, story by Guerdon Trueblood. **P:** Rupert Hitzig. **M:** Alan Parker. **C:** Chris Cordon, James A. Contner. **Ed:** Corky Ehlers, Randy Roberts. **PDn:** Woods Mackintosh. **Art:** Paul Eads, Chris Horner. **CDn:** Dresden Urquhart. **Mk:** Kathryn Bihr. **H:** David Forrest. **S:** Sandy Berman. **VFx:** Austin McKinney, Robert Skotak. **Cast:** Dennis Quaid, Bess Armstrong, Simon MacCorkindale, Louis Gossett Jr., John Putch, Lea Thompson.

Jaws: The Revenge (1987). **D, P:** Joseph Sargent. **Sc:** Michael De Guzman. **M:** Michael Small. **C:** John McPherson. **Ed:** Michael Brown. **PDn:** John J. Lloyd. **Art:** Don Woodruff. **SDc:** John M. Dwyer, Hal Gausman. **Mk:** Tony Lloyd, Dan Striepeke. **SDn:** Steve Schwartz. **Cast:** Lorraine Gary, Lance Guest, Mario Van Peebles, Michael Caine, Karen Young, Judith Barsi, Lynn Whitfield, Mitchell Anderson.

Sequels to *The Omen* (1976)

Damien: Omen II (1978). **D:** Don Taylor. **Sc:** Stanley Mann, Michael Hodges. Story by Harvey Bernhard. **P:** Harvey Bernhard. **M:** Jerry Goldsmith. **C:** Bill Butler, Gil Taylor. **Ed:** Robert Brown Jr. **PDn:** Fred Harpman, Philip M. Jefferies. **Mk:** Robert Dawn, Lillian Toth. **H:** Lillian Toth. **SFx:** Ira Anderson Jr. **VFx:** Stanley Cortez, Chuck Taylor. **Cast:** William Holden, Lee Grant, Jonathan Scott-Taylor, Robert Foxworth, Nicholas Pryor, Lew Ayres, Sylvia Sidney, Lance Henriksen. **Motion Picture Sound Editors** Best Editing of Dialogue, Best Editing of Sound Effects.

The Final Conflict: Omen III (1981). **D:** Graham Baker. **Sc:** Andrew Birkin. **P:** Harvey Bernhard. **M:** Jerry Goldsmith. **C:** Phil Meheux, Robert Paynter. **Ed:** Alan Strachan. **PDn:** Herbert Westbrook. **Art:** Martin Atkinson. **SDc:** Tessa Davies. **Mk:** Freddie Williamson. **H:** Betty Glasow. **SFx:** Ian Wingrove. **Cast:** Sam Neill, Rossano Brazzi, Don Gordon, Lisa Harrow, Barnaby Holm, Mason Adams, Robert Arden.

Omen IV: The Awakening (1991). **D:** Jorge Montesi, Dominique Othenin-Girard. **Sc:** Brian Taggert. Story by Harvey Bernhard & Brian Taggert. **P:** Harvey Bernhard. **M:** Jonathan Sheffer. **C:** Martin Fuhrer. **Ed:** Bruce Giesbrecht, Frank Irvine. **PDn:** Richard Wilcox.

Art: Lawrence F. Pevec. SDc: Marti Wright. CDn: Susan De Laval. Mk: Charles Porlier, Tibor Farkas. H: Roy Sidick. SFx: Gary Paller, Steve Davis. Cast: Faye Grant, Michael Woods, Michael Lerner, Madison Mason, Ann Hearn, Jim Byrnes, Don S. Davis, Asia Vieira.

Sequels to *Halloween* (1978)

Halloween II (1981). D: Rick Rosenthal. Sc, P: John Carpenter, Debra Hill. M: John Carpenter, Alan Howarth. C: Dean Cundey. Ed: Mark Goldblatt, Skip Schoolnik. PDn: J. Michael Riva. SDc: Peg Cummings. Mk: Michael Germain. H: Frankie Bergman. SFx: Lawrence J. Cavanaugh, Frank "Paco" Munoz. Cast: Jamie Lee Curtis, Donald Pleasence, Charles Cyphers, Jeffrey Kramer, Lance Guest.

Halloween III: Season of the Witch (1982). D, Sc: Tommy Lee Wallace. P: John Carpenter, Debra Hill. M: John Carpenter, Alan Howarth. C: Dean Cundey. Ed: Millie Moore. PDn: Peter Jamison. SDc: Linda Spheeris. Mk: Tom Burman, Ron Walters. H: Frankie Bergman. SFx: Jon G. Belyeu. VFx: Charles Moore. Cast: Tom Atkins, Stacy Nelkin, Dan O'Herlihy, Michael Currie, Ralph Strait.

Halloween 4: The Return of Michael Myers (1988). D: Dwight H. Little. Sc: Alan B. McElroy. Story by Dhani Lipsius, Larry Rattner, Benjamin Ruffner, Alan B. McElroy. P: Paul Freeman. M: Alan Howarth. C: Peter Lyons Collister. Ed: Curtiss Clayton. Art: Roger S. Crandall. SDc: Nickle Lauritzen. CDn: Rosalie Wallace. Mk: Susan Reyes. H: Diane Memmott. SFx: John Buechler. Cast: Donald Pleasence, Ellie Cornell, Danielle Harris, Beau Starr, George P. Wilbur, Kathleen Kinmont, Michael Pataki.

Halloween 5: Michael Myers' Revenge (1989). D: Dominique Othenin-Girard. Sc: Shem Bitterman, Michael Jacobs, Dominique Othenin-Girard. P: Ramsey Thomas. M: Alan Howarth. C: Robert Draper. Ed: Jerry Brady, Charles Tetoni. PDn: Brenton Swift. Art: Richard Honigman. SDc: Chava Danielson, Steven Lee. CDn: Simon Tuke. Mk: Mony Mansano, Scott Oshita. H: Mony Mansano. SDn: Kim Hix. Cast: Donald Pleasence, Ellie Cornell, Matthew Walker, Danielle Harris, Wendy Kaplan, Beau Starr.

Halloween 6: The Curse of Michael Myers (1995). D: Joe Chappelle. Sc: Daniel Farrands. P: Paul Freeman. M: Alan Howarth, Paul Rabjohns. C: Billy Dickson. Ed: Randy Bricker. PDn: Bryan Ryman. Art: T. K. Kirkpatrick. CDn: Ann Gray Lambert. S: Mark Hopkins McNabb. Cast: Donald Pleasence, Paul Stephen Rudd, Marianne Hagan, Mitchell Ryan, Kim Darby, Bradford English, Keith Bogart, Mariah O'Brien.

Halloween H20: 20 Years Later (1998). D: Steve Miner. Sc: Robert Zappia, Matt Greenberg. Story by Robert Zappia. P: Paul Freeman. M: John Ottman. C: Daryn Okada. Ed: Patrick Lussier. PDn: John Willett. Art: Dawn Snyder. SDc: Beau Petersen. CDn: Deborah Everton. Mk: Tania McComas. H: Voni Hinkle. SDn: Thomas Reta, Dawn Swiderski. S: Steve Boeddeker. SFx: John Hartigan. Cast: Jamie Lee Curtis, Josh Hartnett, Adam Arkin, Michelle Williams, LL Cool J, Janet Leigh.

Halloween: Resurrection (2002). D: Rick Rosenthal. Sc: Larry Brand, Sean Hood. Story by Larry Brand. P: Paul Freeman, Michael Leahy. M: Danny Lux. C: David Geddes. Ed: Robert A. Ferretti. PDn: Troy Hansen. Art: David McLean. SDc: Johanna Mazur. CDn: Brad Gough. Mk: Gary J. Tunnicliffe, Diana Davison, Leslie Graham, Lisa Mitchell. SFx: Kim Mortensen. Cast: Jamie Lee Curtis, Brad Loree, Busta Rhymes, Bianca Kajlich, Sean Patrick Thomas, Daisy McCrackin, Katee Sackoff, Luke Kirby.

Sequels to *Alien* (1979)

Aliens [*Alien 2*] (1986). D: James Cameron. Sc: James Cameron. Story by James Cameron, David Giler, Walter Hill. Based on characters created by Dan O'Bannon, Ronald Shusett. P: Gale Anne Hurd. M: James Horner. C: Adrian Biddle. Ed: Ray Lovejoy. PDn: Peter Lamont. SDc: Crispian Sallis. CDn: Emma Porteous. Mk: Peter Robb-King. H: Elaine Bowerbank. VFx: Peter Russell. Cast: Sigourney Weaver, Carrie Henn, Michael Biehn, Lance Henriksen, Paul Reiser, Bill Paxton. **Academy Awards** Best Sound Effects Editing, Best Visual Effects. **BAFTA** Best Special Visual Effects. **Motion Picture Sound Editors** Best Sound Editing in a Foreign Feature.

Alien³ [*Alien 3*] (1992). D: David Fincher. Sc: David Giler, Walter Hill, Larry Ferguson. Story by Vincent Ward. Based on characters by Dan O'Bannon, Ronald Shusett. P: Gordon Carroll, David Giler, Walter Hill. M: Elliot Goldenthal. C: Alex Thomson. Ed: Terry Rawlings. PDn: Norman Reynolds. Art: James Morahan. SDc: Belinda Edwards. CDn: David Perry, Bob Ringwood. H: Colin Jamison. S: Harry E. Snodgrass. SFx: George Gibbs. Cast: Sigourney Weaver, Charles S. Dutton, Charles Dance, Paul McGann, Brian Glover. **Motion Picture Sound Editors** Best Editing of Adr.

Alien: Resurrection [*Alien 4*] (1997). D: Jean-Pierre Jeunet. Sc: Joss Whedon. Based on characters by Dan O'Bannon, Ronald Shusett. P: Bill Badalato, Gordon Carroll, David Giler, Walter Hill. M: John Frizzell. C: Darius Khondji. Ed: Hervé Schneid. PDn: Nigel Phelps. Art: Andrew Neskoromny. SDc: John M. Dwyer. CDn: Bob Ringwood. Mk: Naomi Donne, Barry R. Koper. H: Alan D'angerio. S: Leslie Shatz, Paul Urmson. Cast: Sigourney Weaver, Winona Ryder, Dominique Pinon, Ron Perlman, Kim Flowers, Dan Hedaya.

Alien vs. Predator (2004). D: Paul W. S. Anderson. Sc: Paul W. S. Anderson, Dan O'Bannon, Ronald Shusett. Based on characters by Dan O'Bannon, Ronald Shusett, Jim Thomas, John Thomas. P: Gordon Carroll, John Davis, David Giler, Walter Hill. M: Harald Kloser. C: David Johnson. Ed: Alexander Berner. PDn: Richard Bridgland. SDc: Peter Walpole. CDn: Magali Guidasci. Mk, H: Lesley Lamont-Fisher. Cast: Sanaa Lathan, Raoul Bova, Lance Henriksen, Ewen Bremner, Colin Salmon, Tommy Flanagan.

AVPR: Aliens vs Predator — Requiem (2007). D: Colin Strause, Greg Strause. Sc: Shane Salerno. P: John Davis, David Giler, Walter Hill. M: Brian Tyler. C: Daniel C. Pearl. Ed: Dan Zimmerman. PDn: Andrew

Neskoromny. **Art:** Helen Jarvis. **SDc:** Shane "Perro" Viaeu. **CDn:** Angus Strathie. **Cast:** Steven Pasquale, Reiko Aylesworth, John Ortiz, Johnny Lewis, Ariel Gade, Kristen Hager, Sam Trammell, Robert Joy.

Sequels to *The Amityville Horror* (1979)

Amityville II: The Possession (1982). **D:** Damiani Damiani. **Sc:** Tommy Lee Wallace. Based on novel by Hans Holzer. **P:** Dino De Laurentiis, Stephen R. Greenwald, Ira N. Smith. **M:** Lalo Schifrin. **C:** Franco Di Giacomo. **Ed:** Sam O'Steen. **PDn:** Pier Luigi Basile. **Art:** Ray Recht. **SDc:** George DeTitta Jr. **CDn:** William Kellard. **Mk:** Joe Cuervo. **H:** Werner Sherer. **SFx:** John Caglione Jr., Glen Robinson. **Cast:** James Olson, Burt Young, Rutanya Alda, Jack Magner, Andrew Prine, Diane Franklin, Moses Gunn, Ted Ross.

Amityville 3-D (1983). **D:** Richard Fleischer. **Sc:** William Wales. **P:** Stephen F. Kesten. **M:** Howard Blake. **C:** Fred Schuler. **Ed:** Frank J. Urioste. **Art:** Giorgio Postiglione, Justin Scoppa Jr. **SDc:** Justin Scoppa Jr. **CDn:** Clifford Capone. **Mk:** John Caglione Jr., Vincent Callaghan. **H:** Anthony Cortino. **S:** John Fundus, Peter Ilardi. **Cast:** Tony Roberts, Tess Harper, Robert Joy, Candy Clark, John Beal, John Harkins.

Amityville: The Evil Escapes (1989). **D:** Sandor Stern. **Sc:** Sandor Stern. Based on novel by John G. Jones. **P:** Kenneth Atchity, Barry Bernardi. **M:** Rick Conrad. **C:** Tom Richmond. **Ed:** Skip Schoolnik. **PDn:** Kandy Stern. **Mk:** Bob Arrollo. **SFx:** Richard Stutsman. **Cast:** Patty Duke, Jane Wyatt, Fredric Lehne, Lou Hancock, Norman Lloyd, Robert Alan Browne, Gloria Cromwell, Peggy McCay.

The Amityville Curse (1990). **D:** Tom Berry. **Sc:** Michael Krueger & Norvell Rose. Based on novel by Hans Holzer. **P:** Franco Battista. **M:** Milan Kymlicka. **C:** Rodney Gibbons. **Ed:** Franco Battista. **PDn:** Richard Tassé. **CDn:** Trixi Fortier. **Mk:** R. S. Cole, Patrick Shearn. **H:** Roxy d'Alonzio. **SFx:** Ryal Cosgrove. **Cast:** Kim Coates, Dawna Wightman, Helen Hughes, David Stein, Anthony Dean Rubes, Cassandra Gava.

It's About Time [*Amityville 1992: It's About Time*] (1992). **D:** Tony Randel. **Sc:** Christopher DeFaria, Antonio Toro. Based on novel by John G. Jones. **P:** Christopher DeFaria. **M:** Daniel Licht. **C:** Christopher Taylor. **Ed:** Rick Finney. **PDn:** Kim Hix. **SDc:** Natalie Pope. **CDn:** Randall Thropp. **Mk, H:** Susan Reiner. **S:** Joseph Zappala. **VFx:** Peter Kuran. **Cast:** Stephen Macht, Shawn Weatherly, Megan Ward, Damon Martin, Jonathan Penner, Nita Talbot.

Amityville: A New Generation (1993). **D:** John Murlowski. **Sc:** Christopher DeFaria & Antonio M. Toro. **P:** Christopher DeFaria. **M:** Daniel Licht. **C:** Wally Pfister. **Ed:** Rick Finney. **PDn:** Sherman Williams. **Art:** Kurt Meisenbach. **SDc:** Michael Stone. **CDn:** Yvette Correa. **Mk:** Elizabeth Barczewska, Michele Bloom. **S:** Joseph Zappala. **SFx:** Ed Martinez. **VFx:** Joshua Culp. **Cast:** Ross Partridge, Julia Nickson-Soul, Lala, David Naughton, Barbara Howard, Jack R. Orend, Richard Roundtree, Terry O'Quinn.

Amityville: Dollhouse (1996). **D:** Steve White. **Sc:** Joshua Michael Stern. **P:** Zane W. Levitt, Steve White, Mark Yellen. **M:** Ray Colcord. **C:** Tom Callaway. **Ed:**

Kert Vandermeulen. **PDn:** Jerry Fleming. **SDc:** Sarah Brooks Alcorn. **CDn:** Nanette M. Acosta. **Mk:** Constance Hall. **H:** Constance Hall. **SFx:** Larry Roberts. **Cast:** Robin Thomas, Starr Adreeff, Allen Cutler, Rachel Duncan, Jarrett Lennon, Clayton Murray.

Sequels to *Friday the 13th* (1980)

Friday the 13th Part 2 (1981). **D, P:** Steve Miner. **Sc:** Ron Kurz. **M:** Harry Manfredini. **C:** Peter Stein. **Ed:** Susan E. Cunningham. **PDn:** Virginia Field. **CDn:** Ellen Lutter. **Mk:** Carl Fullerton. **H:** Cecilia Verardi. **SFx:** Steve Kirshoff. **Cast:** Amy Steel, John Furey, Adrienne King, Kirsten Baker, Stu Charno, Warrington Gillette.

Friday the 13th Part 3: 3D (1982). **D:** Steve Miner. **Sc:** Martin Kitrosser, Carol Watson. **P:** Frank Mancuso Jr. **M:** Harry Manfredini, Michael Zager. **C:** Gerald Feil. **Ed:** George Hively. **PDn:** Robb Wilson King. **SDc:** Dee Suddleson. **H:** Shannon Ely. **SFx:** Martin Becker. **Cast:** Dana Kimmell, Paul Kratka, Richard Brooker, Nick Savage, Rachel Howard, David Katims.

Friday the 13th: The Final Chapter (1984). **D:** Joseph Zito. **Sc:** Barney Cohen. **P:** Frank Mancuso Jr. **M:** Harry Manfredini. **C:** João Fernandes. **Ed:** Joel Goodman. **PDn:** Shelton H. Bishop. **Art:** Joe Hoffman. **SFx:** Tom Savini. **Cast:** Kimberly Beck, E. Erich Anderson, Corey Feldman, Barbara Howard, Peter Barton, Joan Freeman, Crispin Glover.

Friday the 13th: A New Beginning (1985). **D:** Danny Steinmann. **Sc:** Martin Kitrosser, David Cohen, Danny Steinmann. Story by Martin Kitrosser, David Cohen. **P:** Timothy Silver. **M:** Harry Manfredini. **C:** Stephen L. Posey. **Ed:** Bruce Green. **PDn:** Robert Howland. **Mk:** Martin Becker. **SFx:** Frankie Inez. **Cast:** John Shepard, Melanie Kinnaman, Shavar Ross, Richard Young, Carol Lacatell, Corey Parker, Corey Feldman.

Friday the 13th Part VI: Jason Lives (1986). **D, Sc:** Tom McLoughlin. **P:** Don Behrns. **M:** Harry Manfredini. **C:** Jon Kranhouse. **Ed:** Bruce Green. **PDn:** Joseph T. Garrity. **Art:** Pat Tagliaferro. **Mk:** Brian Wade. **Cast:** Thom Mathews, Jennifer Cooke, David Kagen, Kerry Noonan, Renée Jones, Tom Fridley.

Friday the 13th Part VII: The New Blood (1988). **D:** John Carl Buechler. **Sc:** Manuel Fidello, Daryl Haney. **P:** Iain Paterson. **M:** Harry Manfredini, Fred Mollin. **C:** Paul Elliott. **Ed:** Maureen O'Connell, Martin Jay Sadoff, Barry Zetlin. **PDn:** Richard Lawrence. **CDn:** Jacqueline Johnson. **VFx:** Lou Carlucci. **Cast:** Kane Hodder, Lar Park-Lincoln, Kevin Blair, Terry Kiser, Susan Blu, Susan Jennifer Sullivan.

Friday the 13th Part VIII: Jason Takes Manhattan (1989). **D, Sc:** Rob Hedden. **P:** Randolph Cheveldave. **M:** Fred Mollin. **C:** Bryan England. **Ed:** Steve Mirkovich. **PDn:** David Fischer. **SDc:** Linda Vipond. **CDn:** Carla Hetland. **Mk:** Jamie Brown, Laurie Finstad. **Cast:** Todd Shaffer, Tiffany Paulsen, Timothy Burr Mirkovich, Kane Hodder, Jensen Daggett, Peter Mark Richman.

Jason Goes to Hell: The Final Friday (1993). **D:** Adam Marcus. **Sc:** Dean Lorey, Jay Huguely. Story by Jay Huguely, Adam Marcus. **P:** Sean S. Cunningham. **M:** Harry Manfredini. **C:** Bill Dill. **Ed:** David Handman. **PDn:** Whitney Brooke Wheeler. **SDc:** Natalie Pope. **CDn:** Julie Rae Engelsman. **Mk:** Kimberly Greene. **VFx:** Al Magliochetti. **Cast:** Kane Hodder, John D. LeMay, Kari Keegan, Steven Williams, Steven Culp, Erin Gray, Richard Gant.

Jason X [*Friday the 13th Part X*] (2001). **D:** Jim Isaac. **Sc:** Todd Farmer. **P:** Noel Cunningham. **M:** Harry Manfredini. **C:** Derick V. Underschultz. **Ed:** David Handman. **PDn:** John Dondertman. **Art:** James Oswald. **SDc:** Clive Thomasson. **CDn:** Maxyne Baker. **Mk:** Stéphan Dupuis, Irene Kent. **H:** Paul R. J. Elliot. **S:** Wally Weaver. **Cast:** Kane Hodder, Lexa Doig, Chuck Campbell, Lisa Ryder, Peter Mensah, Melyssa Ade.

Freddy vs. Jason (2003). **D:** Ronny Yu. **Sc:** Damian Shannon & Mark Swift. **P:** Sean S. Cunningham. **M:** Graeme Revell. **C:** Fred Murphy. **Ed:** Mark Stevens. **PDn:** John Willett. **Art:** Ross Dempster. **SDc:** Rose Marie McSherry. **CDn:** Gregory Mah. **SFx:** Wayne Beauchamp, Connor McCullagh. **Cast:** Robert Englund, Ken Kirzinger, Monica Keena, Jason Ritter, Kelly Rowland, Christopher George Marquette.

Sequels to *Poltergeist* (1982)

Poltergeist II: The Other Side (1986). **D:** Brian Gibson. **Sc:** Michael Grais, Mark Victor. **P:** Michael Grais, Mark Victor. **M:** Jerry Goldsmith. **C:** Andrew Laszlo. **Ed:** Thom Noble, Bud S. Smith. **PDn:** Ted Haworth. **SDc:** George R. Nelson. **Mk:** Adam Hill, Ben Nye Jr. **H:** Lynda Gurasich. **SDn:** Roy Barnes, Greg Papalia. **S:** Craig Harris. **SFx:** Brian Tipton. **Cast:** Jo-Beth Williams, Craig T. Nelson, Heather O'Rourke, Oliver Robins, Zelda Rubinstein, Will Sampson, Julian Beck, Geraldine Fitzgerald.

Poltergeist III: The Final Chapter (1988). **D:** Gary Sherman. **Sc:** Gary Sherman, Brian Taggert. **P:** Barry Bernardi. **M:** Joe Renzetti. **C:** Alex Nepomniaschy. **Ed:** Ross Albert. **PDn:** Paul Eads. **Art:** W. Steven Graham. **SDc:** Linda Lee Sutton. **CDn:** Tom McKinley. **S:** Oscar Mitt. **SFx:** Calvin Joe Acord. **VFx:** Gary Sherman. **Cast:** Tom Skerritt, Nancy Allen, Heather O'Rourke, Zelda Rubinstein, Lara Flynn Boyle.

Sequels to *Children of the Corn* (1984)

Children of the Corn II: The Final Sacrifice (1993). **D:** David F. Price. **Sc:** A L Katz & Gilbert Adler. Based on story by Stephen King. **P:** David G. Stanley, Scott A. Stone. **M:** Daniel Licht. **C:** Levie Isaacks. **Ed:** Barry Zetlin. **Art:** Tim Eckel. **SDc:** Natalie K. Pope. **CDn:** Giovanna Ottobre-Melton. **Mk:** Steve Painter. **SFx:** Ray Bivins. **Cast:** Terence Knox, Paul Scherrer, Ryan Bollman, Ned Romero, Christie Clark, Rosalind Allen, Ed Grady, Wallace Merck.

Children of the Corn III (1995). **D:** James D.R. Hickox. **Sc:** Dode B. Levenson. Based on story by Stephen King. **P:** Gary DePew, Brad Southwick. **M:** Daniel Licht. **C:** Gerry Lively. **Ed:** Chris Peppe. **PDn:** Blair A. Martin. **SDc:** Susanna Vertal. **CDn:** Mark Bridges. **VFx:** Dan Winthrop. **Cast:** Daniel Cerny, Ron Melendez, Jim Metzler, Nancy Lee Grahn, Jon Clair, Mari Morrow, Michael Ensign, Duke Stroud.

Children of the Corn IV: The Gathering (1996).

D: Greg Spence. **Sc:** Stephen Berger and Greg Spence. Based on story by Stephen King. **P:** Gary DePew. **M:** David C. Williams. **Ed:** Christopher Cibelli. **PDn:** Adele Plauche. **Art:** Carla Curry. **Mk:** Abiiba S. Howell. **Cast:** Naomi Watts, Jamie Renée Smith, Karen Black, Mark Salling, Brent Jennings, Toni Marsh, Lewis Flanagan III, Brandon Kleyla.

Children of the Corn V: Fields of Terror (1998). **D, Sc:** Ethan Wiley. Based on story by Stephen King. **P:** Jeff Geoffray, Walter Josten. **M:** Paul Rabjohns. **C:** David Lewis. **Ed:** Peter Devaney Flanagan. **PDn:** Deborah Raymond, Dorian Vernacchio. **SDc:** Neil O'Sullivan. **CDn:** Malou Magnusson. **Cast:** Stacy Galina, Alexis Arquette, Eva Mendez, Greg Vaughan, Angela Jones, Ahmet Zappa, Fred Williamson, Dave Buzzotta.

Children of the Corn 666: Isaac's Return (1999). **D:** Kari Skogland. **Sc:** Tim Sulka & John Franklin. Based on story by Stephen King. **P:** Bill Berry, Jeff Geoffray, Walter Josten. **M:** Terry Michael Huud. **C:** Richard Clabaugh. **Ed:** Peter Devaney Flanagan, Troy Takaki. **PDn:** Stuart Blatt. **SDc:** Melissa Hibbard. **CDn:** Niklas J. Palm. **Cast:** Natalie Ramsey, John Franklin, Paul Popowich, Nancy Allen, Stacy Keach, Alix Koromzay, John Patrick White, Sydney Bennett.

Children of the Corn: Revelation (2001). **D:** Guy Magar. **Sc:** S.J. Smith. Based on story by Stephen King. **P:** Michael Leahy, Joel Soisson. **M:** Steve Edwards. **C:** Danny Nowak. **Ed:** Kirk Morri. **PDn:** Troy Hansen. **SDc:** Johanna Mazur. **CDn:** Brad Gough. **Cast:** Claudette Mink, Kyle Cassie, Michael Ironside, Troy Yorke, Michael Rogers, Taylor Hobbs, Jeffrey Ballard, Sean Smith.

Sequels to *A Nightmare on Elm Street* (1984)

A Nightmare on Elm Street 2: Freddy's Revenge (1985). **D:** Jack Sholder. **Sc:** David Chaskin. **P:** Robert Shaye. **M:** Christopher Young. **C:** Jacques Haitkin, Christopher Tufty. **Ed:** Bob Brady, Arline Garson. **CDn:** Gail Viola. **H:** Robin L. Neal. **VFx:** Paul Boyington. **Cast:** Mark Patton, Kim Myers, Robert Rusler, Clu Gulager, Hope Lange, Robert Englund.

A Nightmare on Elm Street 3: Dream Warriors (1987). **D:** Chuck Russell. **Sc:** Wes Craven, Frank Darabont, Chuck Russell, Bruce Wagner. Story by Bruce Wagner. **P:** Robert Shaye. **M:** Angelo Badalamenti. **C:** Roy H. Wagner. **Ed:** Terry Stokes, Chuck Weiss. **Art:** C. J. Strawn, Mick Strawn. **SDc:** James R. Barrows. **CDn:** Camile Schroeder. **H:** H. Wayne Coker. **S:** David Lewis Yewdall. **VFx:** Jeff Matakovich, Hoyt Yeatman. **Cast:** Heather Langenkamp, Craig Wasson, Patricia Arquette, Robert Englund, Larry Fishburne, John Saxon, Priscilla Pointer, Brooke Bundy, Dick Cavett, Zsa Zsa Gabor.

A Nightmare on Elm Street 4: The Dream Master (1988). **D:** Renny Harlin. **Sc:** Brian Helgeland, Scott Pierce, Ken Wheat. Story by William Kotzwinkle, Brian Helgeland. **P:** Robert Shaye, Rachel Talalay. **M:** John Easdale, Craig Safan. **C:** Steven Fierberg, Christopher Tufty. **Ed:** Michael N. Knue, Jack Tucker, Chuck Weiss. **PDn:** C. J. Strawn, Mick Strawn. **Art:** Thomas A. O'Conor. **CDn:** Audrey M. Bansmer. **Mk:** R. Christopher Biggs, Kevin Yagher. **H:** Alicia M. Tripi. **VFx:** Paul Hettler. **Cast:** Tuesday Knight, Ken Sagoes, Rodney Eastman, Lisa Wilcox, Andras Jones, Robert Englund.

A Nightmare on Elm Street 5: The Dream Child (1989). **D:** Stephen Hopkins. **Sc:** Leslie Bohem. Story by John Skipp, Craig Spector, Leslie Bohem. **P:** Rupert Harvey, Robert Shaye. **M:** Jay Ferguson. **C:** Peter Levy. **Ed:** Brent A. Schoenfeld, Chuck Weiss. **PDn:** C. J. Strawn. **Art:** Timothy Gray. **SDc:** John P. Jockinsen. **CDn:** Sara Markowitz. **Mk:** Kathryn Miles Kelly. **H:** Lynne K. Eagan. **SDn:** Thomas A. O'Conor. **VFx:** Jeff Matakovich, Alan Munro. **Cast:** Robert Englund, Lisa Wilcox, Erika Anderson, Valorie Armstrong, Michael Ashton, Beatrice Boepple.

Nightmare on Elm Street 6: The Final Nightmare (1991). **D:** Rachel Talalay. **Sc:** Michael De Luca. Story by Rachel Talalay. **P:** Robert Shaye, Aron Warner. **M:** Brian May. **C:** Declan Quinn. **Ed:** Janice Hampton. **PDn:** C. J. Strawn. **Art:** James R. Barrows. **SDc:** Rebecca Carriaga. **CDn:** Nanrose Buchman. **Cast:** Robert Englund, Lisa Zane, Shon Greenblatt, Lezlie Deane, Ricky Dean Logan, Yaphet Kotto, Roseanne, Tom Arnold, Elinor Donahue, Johnny Depp, Alice Cooper.

Wes Craven's New Nightmare [***Nightmare on Elm Street VII: New Nightmare***] (1994). **D, Sc:** Wes Craven. **P:** Marianne Maddalena. **M:** J. Peter Robinson. **C:** Mark Irwin. **Ed:** Patrick Lussier. **PDn:** Cynthia Charette. **Art:** Diane McKinnon, Troy Sizemore. **SDc:** Ruby Guidara. **CDn:** Mary Jane Fort. **H:** Camille Henderson. **SDn:** Stephen Alesch. **S:** Paul B. Clay. **SFx:** Lou Carlucci, Vincent Montefusco. **VFx:** John Coats, William Mesa. **Cast:** Heather Langenkamp, Robert Englund, Miko Hughes, Wes Craven, John Saxon, Robert Shaye.

Freddy vs. Jason (2003). **D:** Ronny Yu. **Sc:** Damian Shannon, Mark Swift. **P:** Sean S. Cunningham. **M:** Graeme Revell. **C:** Fred Murphy. **Ed:** Mark Stevens. **PDn:** John Willett. **Art:** Ross Dempster. **SDc:** Rose Marie McSherry. **CDn:** Gregory Mah. **SFx:** Wayne Beauchamp, Connor McCullagh. **Cast:** Robert Englund, Ken Kirzinger, Monica Keena, Jason Ritter, Kelly Rowland, Christopher George Marquette.

Sequels to *Hellraiser* (1987)

Hellbound: Hellraiser II (1988). **D:** Tony Randel. **Sc:** Peter Atkins. Story by Clive Barker. **P:** Christopher Figg. **M:** Christopher Young. **C:** Robin Vidgeon. **Ed:** Richard Marden. **PDn:** Michael Buchanan. **Art:** Andy Harris. **CDn:** Jane Wildgoose. **Mk:** Aileen Seaton. **H:** Heather Jones. **SFx:** Bob Keen, Graham Longhurst. **VFx:** Cliff Culley. **Cast:** Clare Higgins, Ashley Laurence, Kenneth Cranham, Imogen Boorman, Sean Chapman, William Hope, Doug Bradley.

Hellraiser III: Hell on Earth (1992). **D:** Anthony Hickox. **Sc:** Peter Atkins. Story by Peter Atkins & Tony Randel. **P:** Christopher Figg, Lawrence Mortorff. **M:** Randy Miller. **C:** Gerry Lively. **Ed:** Christopher Cibelli, James D. R. Hickox. **PDn:** Steve Hardie. **Art:** Tim Eckel. **CDn:** Leonard Pollack. **S:** Tim Gedemer. **SFx:** Ray Bivins, Bob Keen. **VFx:** Steve Wright. **Cast:** Kevin Bernhardt, Lawrence Mortorff, Terry Farrell, Ken Carpenter, Sharon Hill, Paula Marshall.

Hellraiser: Bloodline [***Hellraiser IV***] (1996). **D:** "Alan Smithee." **P:** Nancy Rae Stone. **M:** Daniel Licht. **C:** Gerry Lively. **Ed:** Randolph K. Bricker, Rod Dean, Jim Prior. **PDn:** Ivo Cristante. **CDn:** Dayna Cussler, Eileen Kennedy. **Mk:** Gary J. Tunnicliffe, Kevin Yagher. **SFx:** John Hartigan. **VFx:** Rick Kerrigan, Alberto Menache. **Cast:** Bruce Ramsay, Valentina Vargas, Doug Bradley, Charlotte Chatton, Adam Scott, Kim Myers.

Hellraiser: Inferno [***Hellraiser V***] (2000). **D:** Scott Derrickson. **Sc:** Paul Harris Boardman, Scott Derrickson. **M:** Walter Werzowa. **C:** Nathan Hope. **Ed:** Kirk M. Morri. **PDn:** Deborah Raymond. **Art:** Andrew Max Cahn. **CDn:** Julia Schklair. **Mk:** Wendi Lynn Allison. **H:** Solina Tabrizi. **SFx:** Gary J. Tunnicliffe. **VFx:** Jamison Scott Goei. **Cast:** Craig Sheffer, Nicholas Turturro, James Remar, Doug Bradley, Nicholas Sadler, Noelle Evans.

Hellraiser: Hellseeker [***Hellraiser VI***] (2002). **D:** Rick Bota. **Sc:** Carl Dupre, Tim Day. **P:** Michael Leahy, Ron Schmidt. **M:** Stephen Edwards. **C:** John Drake. **Ed:** Anthony Adler, Lisa Mozden. **PDn:** Troy Hansen. **Art:** David McLean. **SDc:** Matthew Versteeg. **CDn:** Brad Gough. **Mk:** Gary J. Tunnicliffe. **VFx:** Jamison Scott Goei, Kevin VanHook. **Cast:** Dean Winters, Ashley Laurence, Charles Stead, Rachel Hayward, Sarah-Jane Redmond, Jody Thompson.

Hellraiser: Deader [***Hellraiser VII***] (2005). **D:** Rick Bota. **Sc:** Neal Marshall Stevens, Tim Day. **P:** David S. Greathouse, Ron Schmidt. **M:** Henning Lohner. **Mk:** Gary J. Tunnicliffe. **S:** Steven Avila, Kurt Thum. **VFx:** Jamison Scott Goei. **Cast:** Doug Bradley, Kari Wuhrer.

Hellraiser: Hellworld (2005). **D:** Rick Bota. **Sc:** Carl Dupre. Based on story by Joel Soisson. **P:** Ron Schmidt. **M:** Lars Anderson. **C:** Gabriel Kosuth. **Mk:** Daniela Busoiu. **H:** Letitia Ghenea. **S:** Kurt Thum. **SFx:** Kevin Carter, Ionel Popa. **VFx:** Jamison Scott Goei, Paul Runyan. **Cast:** Stelian Urian, Katheryn Winnick, Anna Tolputt, Khary Payton, Henry Cavill, Christopher Jacot, Doug Bradley.

Sequels to *Predator* (1987)

Predator 2 (1990). **D:** Stephen Hopkins. **Sc:** Jim Thomas, John Thomas. **P:** John Davis, Lawrence Gordon, Joel Silver. **M:** Alan Silvestri. **C:** Peter Levy. **Ed:** Mark Goldblatt, Bert Lovitt. **PDn:** Lawrence G. Paull. **Art:** Geoff Hubbard. **SDc:** Rick Simpson. **CDn:** Marilyn Vance-Straker. **Mk:** Scott H. Eddo. **H:** Paul Abascal. **Cast:** Kevin Peter Hall, Danny Glover, Gary Busey, Ruben Blades, Maria Conchita Alonso, Bill Paxton, Robert Davi, Adam Baldwin. **Australian Cinematographers Society** Cinematographer of the Year (Levy).

Alien vs. Predator (2004). **D:** Paul W. S. Anderson. **Sc:** Paul W. S. Anderson, Dan O'Bannon, Ronald Shusett. **P:** Gordon Carroll, John Davis, David Giler, Walter Hill. **M:** Harald Kloser. **C:** David Johnson. **Ed:** Alexander Berner. **PDn:** Richard Bridgland. **SDc:** Peter Walpole. **CDn:** Magali Guidasci. **Mk, H:** Lesley Lamont-Fisher. **Cast:** Sanaa Lathan, Raoul Bova, Lance Henriksen, Ewen Bremner, Colin Salmon, Tommy Flanagan.

AVPR: Aliens vs Predator — Requiem (2007). **D:**

Colin Strause, Greg Strause. **Sc:** Shane Salerno. **P:** John Davis, David Giler, Walter Hill. **M:** Brian Tyler. **C:** Daniel C. Pearl. **Ed:** Dan Zimmerman. **PDn:** Andrew Neskoromny. **Art:** Helen Jarvis. **SDc:** Shane "Perro" Viaeu. **CDn:** Angus Strathie. **Cast:** Steven Pasquale, Reiko Aylesworth, John Ortiz, Johnny Lewis, Ariel Gade, Kristen Hager, Sam Trammell, Robert Joy.

Sequels to *Child's Play* (1988)

Child's Play 2 (1990). **D:** John Lafia. **Sc:** Don Mancini. **P:** David Kirschner. **M:** Graeme Revell. **C:** Stefan Czapsky. **Ed:** Edward Warschilka. **PDn:** Ivo Cristante. **Art:** Donald Maskovich. **SDc:** Debra Combs. **CDn:** Pamela Skaist. **Mk:** Deborah Larsen. **H:** Scott Williams. **SFx:** Mike Reedy. **VFx:** Michael Douglas Middleton. **Cast:** Alex Vincent, Jenny Agutter, Gerrit Graham, Christine Elise, Brad Dourif, Grace Zabriskie, Peter Haskell.

Child's Play 3 (1991). **D:** Jack Bender. **Sc:** Don Mancini. **P:** Robert Latham Brown. **M:** John D'Andrea, Cory Lerios. **C:** John R. Leonetti. **Ed:** Scott Wallace, Edward A. Warschilka Jr. **PDn:** Richard Sawyer. **SDc:** Ethel Robins Richards. **Mk:** Scott Oshita. **SDn:** Sean Haworth. **S:** James Bolt. **SFx:** Mark Rappaport. **VFx:** Thomas Boland. **Cast:** Justin Whalin, Perrey Reeves, Jeremy Sylvers, Travis Fine, Dean Jacobson, Brad Dourif, Peter Haskell, Dakin Matthews.

Bride of Chucky [*Child's Play 4*] (1998). **D:** Ronny Yu. **Sc:** Don Mancini. **P:** Grace Gilroy, David Kirschner. **M:** Graeme Revell. **C:** Peter Pau. **Ed:** Randolph K. Bricker, David Wu. **PDn:** Alicia Keywan. **Art:** James McAteer. **SDc:** Mike Harris, Carol Lavoie. **CDn:** Lynne MacKay. **H:** Judi Cooper-Sealy. **SDn:** Gordon White. **S:** Brian Williams. **SFx:** Arthur Langevin. **Cast:** Jennifer Tilly, Brad Dourif, Katherine Heigl, Nick Stabile, Alexis Arquette, Gordon Michael Woolvett, John Ritter, Lawrence Dane.

Seed of Chucky [*Child's Play 5*] (2004). **D, Sc:** Don Mancini. **P:** David Kirschner, Corey Sienega. **M:** Pino Donaggio. **C:** Vernon Layton. **Ed:** Chris Dickens. **H:** Sian Richards. **VFx:** Graham Cristie, Frank Lawas. **Cast:** Jennifer Tilly, Brad Dourif, Billy Boyd, Redman, John Waters.

Sequels to *Tremors* (1990)

Tremors II: Aftershocks (1996). **D:** S. S. Wilson. **Sc:** Brent Maddock & S. S. Wilson. **P:** Christopher DeFaria, Nancy Roberts. **M:** Jay Ferguson. **C:** Virgil L. Harper. **Ed:** Bob Ducsay. **PDn:** Ivo Cristante. **Art:** Ken Larson. **SDc:** Michele Poulik. **CDn:** Rudy Dillon. **Mk:** Loretta James-Demasi. **H:** Camille Henderson. **S:** Joseph Zappala. **SFx:** Peter Chesney. **VFx:** Jim Aupperle. **Cast:** Fred Ward, Christopher Gartin, Helen Shaver, Michael Gross, Marcelo Tubert, Marco Hernandez.

Tremors 3: Back to Perfection (2001). **D:** Brent Maddock. **Sc:** John Whelpley. Story by S. S. Wilson & Brent Maddock & Nancy Roberts. **P:** Nancy Roberts, S. S. Wilson. **M:** Kevin Kiner. **C:** Virgil L. Harper. **Art:** Alberto Gonzalez-Reyna. **SDc:** Amanda Moss Serino. **CDn:** Debbie Shine. **SFx:** Larry Fioritto, Sean Kennedy. **VFx:** Linda Drake, Glen David Miller. **Cast:**

Michael Gross, Shawn Christian, Susan Chuang, Charlotte Stewart, Tony Genaro, Barry Livingston.

Tremors 4: The Legend Begins (2004). **D:** S. S. Wilson. **Sc:** Scott Buck. Story by S. S. Wilson & Brent Maddock & Nancy Roberts. **P:** Nancy Roberts. **M:** Jay Ferguson. **C:** Virgil L. Harper. **Ed:** Harry B. Miller III. **Art:** Bruton Jones. **SDc:** Amanda Moss Serino. **CDn:** Jennifer L. Parsons. **H:** Brooks Stenstrom. **Cast:** Michael Gross, Sara Botsford, Billy Drago, Brent Roam, August Schellenberg.

Sequels to *Scream* (1996)

Scream 2 (1997). **D:** Wes Craven. **Sc:** Kevin Williamson. **P:** Cathy Konrad, Marianne Maddalena. **M:** Marco Beltrami. **C:** Peter Deming. **Ed:** Patrick Lussier. **PDn:** Bob Ziembicki. **Art:** Ted Berner. **SDc:** Bob Kensinger. **CDn:** Kathleen Detoro. **SDn:** Martin Roy Mervel. **SFx:** Tom Chesney, Robert DeVine. **Cast:** David Arquette, Neve Campbell, Courteney Cox, Sarah Michelle Gellar, Jamie Kennedy, Laurie Metcalf, Jerry O'Connell.

Scream 3 (2000). **D:** Wes Craven. **Sc:** Ehren Kruger. Based on characters by Kevin Williamson. **P:** Cathy Konrad, Marianne Maddalena, Kevin Williamson. **M:** Marco Beltrami. **C:** Peter Deming. **Ed:** Patrick Lussier. **PDn:** Bruce Alan Miller. **Art:** Thomas Fichter. **SDc:** Gene Serdena. **CDn:** Abigail Murray. **SDn:** Sloane U'ren. **S:** Todd Toon. **Cast:** David Arquette, Neve Campbell, Courteney Cox Arquette, Patrick Dempsey, Parker Posey, Scott Foley, Emily Mortimer.

Sequels to *The Mummy* (1999)

The Mummy Returns [*The Mummy 2*] (2001). **D, Sc:** Stephen Sommers. **P:** Sean Daniel, James Jacks. **M:** Alan Silvestri. **C:** Adrian Biddle. **Ed:** Ray Bushey III, Bob Ducsay, Kelly Matsumoto. **PDn:** Allan Cameron. **SDc:** Peter Young. **CDn:** John Bloomfield. **Cast:** Brendan Fraser, Rachel Weisz, John Hannah, Arnold Vosloo, Oded Fehr, The Rock.

The Scorpion King [*The Mummy III*] [*The Mummy 3*] (2002). **D:** Chuck Russell. **Sc:** Stephen Sommers, William Osborne, David Hayter. Story by Stephen Sommers, Jonathan Hales. **P:** Sean Daniel, James Jacks, Kevin Misher, Stephen Sommers. **M:** John Debney. **C:** John R. Leonetti. **Ed:** Greg Parsons, Michael Tronick. **PDn:** Ed Verreaux. **Art:** Doug J. Meerdink, Greg Papalia. **SDc:** Kate J. Sullivan. John Bloomfield. **Cast:** The Rock, Steven Brand, Michael Clarke Duncan, Kelly Hu, Bernard Hill, Grant Heslov.

The Mummy: Tomb of the Dragon Emperor (2008). **D:** Rob Cohen. **Sc:** Alfred Gough & Miles Millar. Based on screenplays by John L. Balderston, Stephen Sommers. **P:** Sean Daniel, Bob Ducsay, James Jacks, Stephen Sommers. **M:** Randy Edelman. **C:** Simon Duggan. **Ed:** Kelly Matsumoto, Joel Negron. **PDn:** Nigel Phelps. **Art:** David Gaucher, Isabelle Guay, Nicolas Lepage, Jean-Pierre Paquet. **SDc:** Anne Kuljian, Philippe Lord. **CDn:** Sanja Milkovic Hays. **S:** Bruce Stambler. **Cast:** Brendan Fraser, Jet Li, Maria Bello, John Hannah, Luke Ford.

Sequels to *Scary Movie* (2000)

Scary Movie 2 (2001). **D:** Keenen Ivory Wayans. **Sc:** Shawn Wayans, Marlon Wayans, Alyson Fouse, Greg Grabianski, Dave Polsky, Michael Anthony Snowden, Craig Wayans. **P:** Eric L. Gold. **M:** Rossano Galante, Mark McGrath. **C:** Steven Bernstein. **PDn:** Cynthia Charette. **Art:** Cat Smith. **SDc:** Robert Kensinger. **CDn:** Valari Adams, Mary Jane Fort. **Cast:** Anna Faris, Marlon Wayans, James DeBello, Shawn Wayans, David Cross, Regina Hall, Chris Masterson, Tim Curry.

Scary Movie 3 (2003). **D:** David Zucker. **Sc:** Craig Mazin, Pat Proft. **P:** Robert K. Weiss. **M:** James L. Venable. **C:** Mark Irwin. **Ed:** Malcolm Campbell, Jon Poll. **PDn:** William Elliott. **Art:** William Heslup. **SDc:** Rose Marie McSherry. **CDn:** Carol Ramsey. **Cast:** Pamela Anderson, Jenny McCarthy, Marny Eng, Charlie Sheen, Simon Rex, Jianna Ballard, Jeremy Piven, Anna Faris.

Scary Movie 4 (2006). **D:** David Zucker. **Sc:** Craig Mazin, Jim Abrahams, Pat Proft. **P:** Craig Mazin, Robert K. Weiss. **M:** James L. Venable. **C:** Thomas E. Ackerman. **Ed:** Craig Herring, Tom Lewis. **PDn:** Holger Gross. **Art:** William Heslup. **CDn:** Carol Ramsey. **SDn:** Chris Beach, Milena Zdravkovic. **S:** Jeremy Peirson. **Cast:** Anna Faris, Regina Hall, Craig Bierko, Anthony Anderson, Chingy, Dr. Phillip C. McGraw, Carmen Electra, Chris Elliott, Cloris Leachman, James Earl Jones, Leslie Nielsen, Charlie Sheen, Shaquille O'Neal, Mike Tyson.

Sequels to *Saw* (2004)

Saw II (2005). **D:** Darren Lynn Bousman. **Sc:** Leigh Whannell and Darren Lynn Bousman. **P:** Mark Burg, Gregg Hoffman, Oren Koules. **M:** Charlie Clouser. **C:** David A. Armstrong. **Ed:** Kevin Greutert. **PDn:** David Hackl. **Art:** Michele Brady. **SDc:** Liesl Deslauriers. **CDn:** Alex Kavanagh. **SFx:** Tim Good. **Cast:** Tobin Bell, Shawnee Smith, Donnie Wahlberg, Dina Meyer, Lyriq Bent.

Saw III (2006). **D:** Darren Lynn Bousman. **Sc:** Leigh Whannell. **P:** Mark Burg, Gregg Hoffman, Oren Koules. **M:** Charlie Clouser. **C:** David A. Armstrong. **Ed:** Kevin Greutert. **PDn:** David Hackl. **Art:** Anthony A. Ianni. **SDc:** Liesl Deslauriers. **CDn:** Alex Kavanagh. **SDn:** Dwight Hendrickson. **S:** Mark Gingras. **Cast:** Tobin Bell, Shawnee Smith, Donnie Wahlberg, Dina Meyer, Leigh Whannell, Lyriq Bent, Angus Macfadyen.

Saw IV (2007). **D:** Darren Lynn Bousman. **Sc:** Patrick Melton & Marcus Dunstan. **P:** Mark Burg, Gregg Hoffman, Oren Koules. **M:** Charlie Clouser. **C:** David A. Armstrong. **Ed:** Kevin Greutert, Brett Sullivan. **PDn:** David Hackl. **Art:** Anthony A. Ianni. **SDc:** Liesl Deslauriers. **CDn:** Alex Kavanagh. **Cast:** Tobin Bell, Shawnee Smith, Donnie Wahlberg, Lyriq Bent, Angus Macfadyen, Scott Patterson, Betsy Russell, Costas Mandylor.

Saw V (2008). **D:** David Hackl. **Sc:** Patrick Melton & Marcus Dunstan. **P:** Mark Burg, Oren Koules. **C:** David A. Armstrong. **Ed:** Kevin Greutert. **SDc:** Liesl Deslauriers. **CDn:** Alex Kavanagh. **Mk:** Colin Penman. **SFx:** Jeff Skochko. **VFx:** Jon Campfens. **Cast:** Tobin Bell, Shawnee Smith, Scott Patterson, Julie Benz, Betsy Russell, Costas Mandylor.

Saw VI (2009). **D:** Kevin Greutert. **Sc:** Marcus Dunstan, Patrick Melton. **P:** Mark Burg, Oren Koules. **C:** David A. Armstrong. **Ed:** Andrew Coutts. **PDn:** Anthony A. Ianni. **Art:** Elis Lam. **CDn:** Alex Kavanagh. **Mk:** Colin Penman. **VFx:** Jan Campfens. **Cast:** Shawnee Smith, Tobin Bell, Costas Mandylor, Betsy Russell, Tanedra Howard, James Van Patten.

Notes

Chapter 1

1. It is interesting to note that although Hitchcock also pioneered in the second subgenre of horror — the horror of Armageddon — when he made *The Birds* in 1963, this subgenre of outside forces taking over the world with no pseudoscientific, religious, or psychological explanation acceptable did not really thrive until roughly the late sixties and early seventies (*Willard*, *Ben*, *Frogs*, *Night of the Lepus*, etc.) — the same period as these later matter-of-fact horror-of-personality films.

Chapter 2

1. Eugène Ionesco, "The Playwright's Role," *London Observer*, June 29, 1958.

2. J. L. Styan, *The Dark Comedy* (Cambridge, England, Cambridge University Press, 1962), p. 232.

3. From the perspective of 2009, this thirty-year-old reference to Spielberg as a newcomer seems especially amusing, given the director's total domination of the American cinema for three decades. Has Spielberg — director of *Close Encounters of the Third Kind*, *Raiders of the Lost Ark*, *E. T.: The Extraterrestrial*, *The Color Purple*, *Schindler's List*, and *Saving Private Ryan* — ever since needed to be identified, for clarity's sake, as the director of *The Sugarland Express*? And certainly this *Jaws* discussion is somewhat predictive of Spielberg's later horror blockbuster *Jurassic Park*, which raises so many similar issues.

4. Strictly speaking, as delivered, Quint's monologue regarding the sinking of *The Indianapolis* on July 30, 1945, includes several historical errors.

Chapter 3

1. Note that throughout this chapter when I discuss witchcraft and its popular depiction in the cinema, I am not referring to the Wicca religion, which still remains generally misunderstood.

Chapter 5

1. Robin Wood, "Return of the Repressed," *Film Comment*, July-August 1978; "Gods and Monsters," *Film Comment*, September-October 1978.

2. When I viewed *Dressed to Kill* late in 1980 at the Little Art Theatre in Yellow Springs, Ohio, a group of fifteen or so demonstrators were protesting the film. They carried placards announcing their opposition to rape and their conviction that the pornographic/erotic aspects of the film would lead to an increase in violence against women in Yellow Springs itself. None of these protestors had seen the film, although they had been alerted to the film by local feminist leaders, who had been monitoring other organized protests around the country. Violence in this liberal and small community did not evidently increase following the screening, although a spirited dialogue centering on women's issues and freedom of expression was promoted in the local newspaper as well as among villagers.

3. Film teachers can — because of their knowledge of the filmmaking process — easily become inured to the emotional/visceral response a film can provoke. I have since refrained from using *The Hills Have Eyes* in the classroom, although I must note that Michael Haneke's *The Seventh Continent* and *Funny Games* and Gaspar Noé's *Irréversible* have instigated similarly powerful emotional responses.

4. In recognition of *Mommie Dearest* and *The Times of Harvey Milk*, one could make a credible argument for a subgenre that could be called horror biography. Another striking example would be Oliver Stone's controversial *Nixon*, in which some scenes create empathy for American President Richard M. Nixon, even as other scenes clearly suggest he is a psychopathic misfit, fatally unable to relate to others normally. Anthony Hopkins' portrait of Nixon as a three-dimensional monster is as memorable as Anthony Perkins' Norman Bates or Boris Karloff's Frankenstein. (It is also worth noting that in 2008, Gus Van Sant effectively remade *The Times of Harvey Milk* as a great *fiction* film starring Sean Penn as Milk and Josh Brolin as that monster Dan White, scrupulously following the structure of the documentary film, yet surprisingly (if laudably), de-emphasizing the horror and focusing on the hope.

5. In fact, my follow-up to the original edition of *Dark Dreams* is *The Suspense Thriller: Films in the*

Shadow of Alfred Hitchcock, originally published by McFarland in 1986. Although I've spent years researching the differences between horror films and thrillers, it seems increasingly clear to me that the horror-of-personality subgenre — because of its lack of a mystical/fantastical element — can just as easily be discussed in the context of the contemporary thriller. The generic vocabulary would include reference to the Poe crime triangle of detective, victim, villain; the archetype of moral confrontation; the psychotraumatic influence of a past crime on the present; and so on. For more information, see *The Suspense Thriller*, particularly chapters 1, 4, and 9.

6. The effeminacy of Buffalo Bill was widely criticized by gay activists, who found the association of serial killers with homosexuality offensive. Given the paucity of mainstream gay roles in Hollywood, the activists' ire was understandable, though the publicity associated with the basically homosexual orientation of the real-life Jeffrey Dahmer seems to have undercut the reality that most serial killers have been heterosexual. Although director Jonathan Demme denied that Buffalo Bill was meant to be homosexual, Demme, perhaps surprisingly, agreed with the activists by noting that while he himself has gay friends, he has not tended to present gay characters in his films — something he tried to correct in his subsequent film, *Philadelphia*, a serious drama about AIDS. Yet the entirety of the horror genre, and particularly the horror of personality, has tended to associate the murderous impulse with some sexual "otherness." In these films, violence to the body derives from Eros — although the specific nature of that dangerous erotic impulse has generally been left ambiguous and undefined. Still, most of Hitchcock's villains (such as Norman Bates in *Psycho* or Uncle Charlie in *Shadow of a Doubt*, invariably among the director's most interesting characters) have always seemed subtextually homosexual. And there is transvestism in Brian De Palma's *Dressed to Kill*; and lesbian overtones in *What's the Matter with Helen?*, *What Ever Happened to Baby Jane?*, and *Hush...Hush, Sweet Charlotte*. So *The Silence of the Lambs* seems hardly unique in its (mis)representation of gender-identity issues — which suggests, of course, that gender issues scare a great many Americans, including Hollywood writers and directors.

7. Haneke seems obsessed with the killing of animals: the goldfish in *The Seventh Continent*, the pig here, the dog in *Funny Games*, the rooster in his 2006 thriller *Caché*.

8. Not surprisingly, when Michael Jackson died unexpectedly on June 25, 2009, under mysterious controversial circumstances, his death became an international news story for weeks in America, radically diminishing the coverage of more critically important events, including the increasing casualties and violence in the war in Afghanistan; the popular uprising in Iran, violently suppressed by its Supreme Leader, against the fraudulent Iranian election results; and President Obama's ongoing attempts to finally achieve universal health coverage for all Americans. In essence, Jackson became the "waxy, yellow buildup" on the linoleum kitchen floor in *Mary Hartman, Mary Hart-man* that distracted Mary from everything that was really important.

9. On April 20, 1999, at Columbine High School in Littleton, Colorado, two suburban students, Dylan Klebold and Eric Harris, went on a violent rampage with rifles, assault weapons, and explosives, killing 12 classmates and a teacher before turning their weapons on themselves.

10. As perhaps it was for Seung-hui Cho, who on April 16, 2007, killed 32 people (shooting over 60 altogether) on the college campus of Virginia Tech, breaking the previous "record" for mass murder. Subsequently released were Cho's video ravings, including images of Cho posturing with his weapons — visual material which clearly evoked Hollywood movies and action-adventure movie posters.

11. On September 16, 2001, the avant-garde composer Karlheinz Stockhausen got into trouble for suggesting much the same thing. In a press conference in which he had been discussing a composition about Lucifer as the "cosmic spirit of rebellion, of anarchy [who] uses his high degree of intelligence to destroy creation," Stockhausen was asked about the terrorist events of 9/11 and replied: "Well, what happened there is, of course — now all of you must adjust your brains — the biggest work of art there has ever been. The fact that spirits achieve with one act something which we in music could never dream of, that people practice ten years madly, fanatically, for a 'concert.' And then die. And that is the greatest work of art that exists for the whole cosmos. Just imagine what happened there. There are people who are so concentrated on this single performance, and then five thousand people are driven to Resurrection. In one moment."

Chapter 6

1. Coppola's sequel, true to the gangster conventions, countered the rise of Michael Corleone in Part I with his moral fall in Part II, and the fall of Don Corleone in Part I with the Don's rise in Part II. Not only does Coppola's sequel thus complete the original, it adds layers of rich texture and shows how the immigrant experience and ambiguous morality of American capitalism are central to the gangster genre and to America itself. Conversely, *Friday the 13th Part VIII* is simply an attempt to wring every last dollar out of a franchise which had long ago turned into a consumable product, created on the assembly line. And not even a superior original can guarantee notable sequels. For instance, although *Psycho II, III,* and *IV* contain a few interesting elements, especially the melancholy presence of actors Anthony Perkins and Vera Miles decades older, these sequels are nevertheless almost totally forgettable.

Chapter 7

1. Strictly speaking, although there were five *Exorcist* films altogether, the fourth installment — the pol-

itics of its production turbulent — was taken away from director Paul Shrader shortly before the film's scheduled release for being too cerebral. The studio asked director Renny Harlin to make the film more violent by shooting additional footage and re-editing. Harlin's version was released as *Exorcist: The Beginning* in 2004; when it failed to perform to expectations, Shrader managed to get his version of the fourth installment, *Dominion: Prequel to the Exorcist*, released in 2005, also to disappointing results.

2. It's notable that although the French cinema of the same period pioneered many notable horror-of-personality films, it has produced virtually no demonic films. Might France's strong separation of church and state, its absence of a Puritan legacy, and its profound belief in secular humanism be responsible for the lack of French demonic films?

3. Quoted in an advertisement for *The Fourth Man* in the *New York Native*, July 2–15, 1984, Section 2, page 8.

4. *Eraserhead* has been less influential in the American film industry than in Europe, where many intellectual, experimental filmmakers have been hugely inspired by Lynch's surrealism to make their own odd films that at least skirt the horror genre. A typical example is the 2004 Belgian film *Nuit Noir* [*Black Night*], by Olivier Smolders, which presents a protagonist who is in essence a handsome eraserhead. Slow and ominous, additionally evoking Kafka and the Tintin comic books by Belgian artist Hergé, *Nuit Noir* takes place in the surreality of a future earth in which there is sunlight only once a day for fifteen seconds. Like Lynch's work, *Nuit Noir* includes a complex soundtrack, surreal images, doublings, existential transformations, and ambiguity that cannot be explained away. Another example is the ambiguous 2003 French film *Dancing* [*Ballroom*], directed by Patrick Mario Bernard and Pierre Trividic (who also wrote and starred), and Xavier Brillat. *Dancing's* first image moves into a tight close-up of grass à la Lynch's *Blue Velvet* and then shows us an insect close-up. A sexually explicit tale of gay lovers who are also artists, *Dancing* includes psychological transformations, portentous silences, and a refusal to traffic in traditional dramatic action.

5. Charles Krauthammer, "Gibson's Blood Libel," *The Washington Post*, March 5, 2004.

6. In retrospect, Gibson's denials that he or his film were anti–Semitic seemed especially unconvincing when on July 28, 2006, he was arrested for drunk driving and launched into an anti–Semitic tirade, asking if the arresting officers were Jewish and asserting that Jews were responsible for all the wars in the world.

7. Bob Pardi, March 6, 2004, letter to author.

8. Garry Wills, "God in the Hands of Angry Sinners," *New York Review of Books*, Volume 51, Number 6, April 8, 2004.

9. The DVD of *Godsend* contains interminable alternate endings. Even worse is the filmmakers' commentary, including their confusion about which film to steal from to find the best ending — should they more imitate *The Omen* or *The Bad Seed*? Their pretentious, casual talk reveals that they fail to under-

stand how their lack of conviction shows that as artists they have little to say and no point of view. This DVD commentary should serve as cautionary tale for all Hollywood filmmakers that it is generally better to let a film speak for itself. And yet similarly, the DVD version of *Hide and Seek* proudly claims that it "Includes 4 Alternate Endings!" Producers don't realize that a claim of this kind is really a misguided selling point, more sign of artistic incoherence rather than added value.

Chapter 8

1. *Signs* was not the first recent film to do so. Two successful films in 1996 both presented hostile aliens: *Independence Day* (directed by Roland Emmerich, starring Bill Pullman and Mary McDonnell as the President and First Lady), and *Mars Attacks!* (directed by Tim Burton, starring Jack Nicholson and Glenn Close as the President and First Lady). The former was horrific science-fiction, the latter a black comedy in which the aliens were goofy and sadistic. Both films included sequences in which iconic American monuments, like the White House, are destroyed by aliens. After the terrorists destroyed the World Trade Center towers, many politicians and administrators insisted these attacks had been totally unexpected and unimaginable. How so, unimaginable? Hadn't these officials been going to the movies for the last twenty-five years? The American cinema had been exporting films chock-full of exactly the kind of explosions that the 9/11 terrorists brought home to America. Of course, whereas in the American cinema, explosions are without real consequence, in life, explosions have consequences which are devastating and earth-changing.

2. Leonard Pitts, Jr., "It's Not Too Soon to Be Reminded of That Terrible Morning in September," *Dayton Daily News*, May 7, 2006.

Chapter 9

1. A problem in discussing Asian directors is that although the Asian "family name" generally precedes the "given name," longstanding translation practices (even by Asian studios) have reversed this order. Although this Westernizing protocol has extended to translated credits on the screen, this protocol — culturally insensitive — is no longer always followed. For a critic, it is impossible to take a consistent stance and still communicate with clarity to a Western audience. For instance, a passing reference to "Kurosawa Akira" would confuse those who have only known the director as "Akira Kurosawa." Crazily, DVDs and their packaging may sometimes refer to a director using both naming conventions. And for a non–Asian-language speaker, it is perilous to presume definitively which convention is being used. Throughout my text, I've tended to use the Westernizing protocol for Japanese directors, whose cinema has been studied widely

in the West for over half a century, but the Asian pro-tocol for Korean directors, whose horror films have been of more recent interest. Yet note that the credits in the Appendix III filmographies, usually based on studio publicity or onscreen translations, may use a convention which contradicts my textual choice.

Chapter 10

1. Neil Postman, *Amusing Ourselves to Death: Public Discourse in the Age of Show Business*, New York: Viking Penguin, 1985, pp. vii–viii.

2. Postman, p. 107.

3. Brad Pitt and Angelina Jolie, for those who have been on Mars since 2006.

4. In July 2007, the FBI posthumously named the "victim" (Brian Douglas Wells) as a co-conspirator, suggesting that he had in fact been in on the planning of the robbery, though probably without realizing that the bomb was real.

Chapter 11

1. Tellingly, Del Toro's first feature, *Cronos*, which uses both Spanish and English dialogue, thus combining each of these tendencies, attracted both an art-house and a popular audience. Drawing upon Poe and Lovecraft, *Cronos* is a disguised vampire film which consciously replaces the majority of the over familiar vampire film conventions with Del Toro's own inventions and obsessions: insects, timepieces, independent children, and family melodrama. With its emphasis on special-effects makeup, *Cronos* emerges from Del Toro's early work as a makeup artist creating designs for other directors.

2. The twenty-first century has seen newspapers continuing their process of eviscerating "serious" movie coverage, axing local reviewers in favor of the syndicated. As these reviews become increasingly "consumer oriented" (which invariably means dumbed-down), they become puerile and perfunctory, reduced to assigning a letter grade, describing the plot, and offering an opinion, often sarcastic. On the other hand, the internet blogosphere and the plethora of on-line film-related sites offer reviews and analyses which are often genuinely insightful, if lost in the internet noise. So for film culture, these developments provide both bad and good news.

3. Generally, a director's commentary track on a DVD release is a pretty lame affair. Del Toro's commentary on the DVD of *Pan's Labyrinth* is actually extraordinary, revealing both the intellect and conceptual artistry of this very literate director. Many of the perceptions in the following discussion, particularly those that shed light on Del Toro's intentions, derive from material there.

Appendix II

1. Through the sixties, all movies, except for the occasional reserved seat blockbuster like *The Sound of Music*, still tended to be projected continuously, without a break to clear the audience or clean the theatre. As a result, patrons would come in whenever they wanted — often midway through — and then stay until that point in the film where they had come in. This was particularly true when there was a double feature and people would come in at the end of the "B" film.

2. As of the date of this edition of *Dark Dreams 2.0*, most major cities have multiplexes of 16–20 screens; a popular film in its opening weeks is exhibited on as many screens as possible — sometimes over a dozen in every city — to take advantage of massive publicity. When *The Exorcist* came out, before the era of the multiplex, the producers took the additional step of initially releasing the film to only one theatre screen in each major city, and *not* opening widely across the country at the same time — thus ensuring enormous patron anticipation, as well as long lines which became a key component of the film's publicity machine.

3. At least it hadn't as of 1973, when this interview was conducted. In 1984, a very credible version called *Greystoke: The Legend of Tarzan, Lord of the Apes* was directed by Hugh Hudson which was much more faithful to the original novel's Victorian spirit.

Bibliography

The following works influenced the writing of this volume and should prove useful to the reader interested in the cinema in general and the horror film in particular.

Abastado, Claude. *Eugene Ionesco*. Paris: Bordas, 1971.

Blatty, William Peter. *The Exorcist*. New York: Bantam Books, 1971.

Bloch, Robert. *Psycho*. New York: Bantam Books, 1959.

Butler, Ivan. *Horror in the Cinema*. New York: A.S. Barnes, 1967.

Clarens, Carlos. *Horror Movies*. London: Secker and Warburg, 1968.

Cowie, Peter, editor. *A Concise History of the Cinema*. New York: A.S. Barnes, 1971.

De Quincy, Thomas. "On Murder Considered as One of the Fine Arts." Originally published in 1827, republished in a variety of editions.

Derry, Charles. *The Suspense Thriller: Films in the Shadow of Alfred Hitchcock*. Jefferson, North Carolina: McFarland, 1988, republished 2001.

Esslin, Martin. *Theatre of the Absurd*. Garden City: Anchor Books, 1961.

Frye, Northrop. *Anatomy of Criticism: Four Essays*. Princeton: Princeton University Press, 1957.

Halliwell, Leslie. *The Filmgoer's Companion*. New York: New American Library, 1969.

Huss, Roy Gerard, and T. J. Ross, editors. *Focus on the Horror Film*. Englewood Cliffs, New Jersey: Prentice-Hall, 1972.

Ionesco, Eugène. *Jeux de Massacre*. Paris: Gallimard, 1970.

_____. *Plays, Volumes I–VII*, translated by Donald Watson. London: John Calder.

_____. "The Playwright's Role." *London Observer*. June 29, 1958.

Kaminsky, Stuart M., with Jeffrey H. Mahan. *American Television Genres*. Chicago: Nelson-Hall, 1985.

Knight, Arthur. *The Liveliest Art*. New York: Curtis Books, 1974.

Kracauer, Siegfried. *From Caligari to Hitler*. Princeton: Princeton University Press, 1947.

Krauthammer, Charles. "Gibson's Blood Libel," *The Washington Post*. March 5, 2004.

LaValley, Albert J., editor. *Focus on Hitchcock*. Englewood Cliffs: New Jersey: Prentice-Hall, 1972.

MacCann, Richard Dyer, editor. *Film: A Montage of Theories*. New York: Dutton, 1966.

Maltin, Leonard, editor. *TV Movies*. New York: New American Library, 1969 (and revised virtually every year since, with slightly different titles, such as *Leonard Maltin's Movie & Video Guide* or *Leonard Maltin's 2007 Movie Guide*).

Michael, Paul. *American Movies Reference Book: The Sound Era*. London: Prentice-Hall, 1969.

Perkins, V. F. *Film as Film*. Middlesex, England: Penguin Books, 1972.

Pitts, Leonard, Jr. "It's Not Too Soon to Be Reminded of That Terrible Morning in September," *Dayton Daily News*. May 7, 2006.

Postman, Neil. *Amusing Ourselves to Death: Public Discourse in the Age of Show Business*. New York: Viking Penguin, 1985.

Quigley, Martin, Jr., and Richard Gertner. *Films in America*. New York: Golden Press, 1970.

Sarris, Andrew. *The American Cinema*. New York: Dutton, 1968.

Styan, J. L. *The Dark Comedy*. Cambridge: Cambridge University Press, 1962.

Taylor, John Russell. *Cinema Eye, Cinema Ear*. New York: Hill and Wang, 1964.

Waller, Gregory A., editor. *American Horrors: Essays on the Modern American Horror Film*. Urbana and Chicago: University of Illinois Press, 1987.

Wills, Garry. "God in the Hands of Angry Sinners," *New York Review of Books*. Volume 51, Number 6, April 8, 2004.

Wood, Robin. "Gods and Monsters," *Film Comment*. September-October 1978.

_____. *Hitchcock's Films*. New York: A. S. Barnes, 1965.

_____. *Hollywood from Vietnam to Reagan*. New York: Columbia University Press, 1986.

_____. "Return of the Repressed," *Film Comment*. July-August 1978.

Index

*Numbers in **bold italics** indicate pages with photographs.*

415